INDIA DEVELOPMENT REPORT
2012–13

INDIA DEVELOPMENT REPORT 2012–13

edited by
S. Mahendra Dev

OXFORD
UNIVERSITY PRESS

Oxford University Press is a department of the University of Oxford.
It furthers the University's objective of excellence in research, scholarship,
and education by publishing worldwide. Oxford is a registered trademark of
Oxford University Press in the UK and in certain other countries

Published in India by
Oxford University Press
YMCA Library Building, 1 Jai Singh Road, New Delhi 110001, India

© Oxford University Press and Indira Gandhi Institute of Development Research 2013

The moral rights of the author have been asserted

First Edition published in 2013

All rights reserved. No part of this publication may be reproduced, stored in
a retrieval system, or transmitted, in any form or by any means, without the
prior permission in writing of Oxford University Press, or as expressly permitted
by law, by licence, or under terms agreed with the appropriate reprographics
rights organization. Enquiries concerning reproduction outside the scope of the
above should be sent to the Rights Department, Oxford University Press,
at the address above

You must not circulate this work in any other form
and you must impose this same condition on any acquirer

ISBN-13: 978-0-19-809201-8
ISBN-10: 0-19-809201-6

Typeset in 10.5/12.7 Minion Pro
by Excellent Laser Typesetters, Pitampura, Delhi 110 034
Printed in India at Rakmo Press Pvt. Ltd., New Delhi 110 020

Preface

The trend rate of GDP growth in the last twenty-year period in India was more than 6 per cent per annum. The growth rate was 9.3 per cent per annum in 2005–6 to 2007–8, preceding the global financial crisis. The economy recovered quickly after the 2008–9 crisis period. After having achieved 8.4 per cent growth in 2009–10 and 2010–11, the GDP growth declined to 6.5 per cent in 2011–12 and is expected to be around the same in 2012–13 due to the US and Euro Zone crisis and domestic policy uncertainties. Investment rates also declined. There are many macroeconomic challenges such as high inflation, high current account deficit, depreciation of rupee, high fiscal deficit, decline in exports, and so on that confront the country. In spite of short-run problems, our medium-term prospects of achieving more than 8 per cent GDP growth are still high.

There have been some improvements in inclusive growth since the mid-2000s. Agricultural growth was around 3.3 per cent per annum during Eleventh Plan period. Poverty declined by 1.5 per cent per annum between 2004–5 and 2009–10. It is the fastest decline of poverty compared to earlier periods. The poverty of socially disadvantaged sections declined in recent years. Provisional estimates of 2011–12 (68th Round of NSS) also reveal significant growth in the average monthly per capita expenditure in both rural and urban areas. Real wages of agricultural labourers have improved. However, there are concerns about high inequalities, slow social sector development, and high malnutrition among children. There are severe governance problems too.

India has achieved much in the last two decades of the reform period. However, a lot remains to be done for achieving all the goals of higher growth and inclusive development. Naturally, the question arises: What next?

The *India Development Report* (*IDR*) series provides an independent assessment of the Indian economy including contemporary problems, issues, and policies. The Twelfth Five Year Plan aspires for 'Faster, More Inclusive and Sustainable Growth'. Keeping this objective in view, the *IDR 2012–13* (seventh in the series) examines the post-reform performance and the policies needed to achieve India's economic, social, and environmental goals in the next decade and beyond. I am happy to note that Indira Gandhi Institute of Development Research (IGIDR) is celebrating its silver jubilee this year. Therefore, *IDR 2012–13* has special significance for IGIDR as it is a Silver Jubilee report. A whole range of issues facing India's development are covered in the *Report*. These include macroeconomic developments, economic growth, inflation, fiscal policy, agriculture, industry and trade, financial sector, energy, environment, urban sector, migration, poverty, inequality, human development, elementary education, and corruption.

The publication of this *Report* has provided us an opportunity to present the research of IGIDR scholars to a wider audience. While most of the papers are written by IGIDR faculty and students, a few scholars from other institutes have also contributed papers. The views expressed in this volume are those of the individual authors.

I am grateful to Srijit Mishra and C. Veeramani for coordinating the publication of the *Report* and for their contribution to the overview chapter. The papers were initially presented in a workshop organized at IGIDR. I am thankful to discussants

K.L. Krishna, Vikas Chitre, Gopal Kadekodi, S.L. Shetty, Kanaka Sabhapathy, and Romar Correa for their useful comments. All the papers were revised based on their comments. Thanks are also due to the contributors of this volume and the Economic and Political Weekly Research Foundation (EPWRF) for providing the statistical appendices. I thank Jaysree and Mahesh Mohan for coordinating the production of the chapters and the Oxford University Press team for the editorial support in bringing out the *Report*.

S. MAHENDRA DEV
Director, Indira Gandhi Institute of Development Research

Contents

List of Tables	xii
List of Figures	xvi
List of Boxes	xix
List of Statistical Profile	xx
List of Abbreviations	xxiii
List of Contributors	xxvi

1. Overview—India's Experience with Reforms: What Next? ... 1
S. Mahendra Dev, Srijit Mishra, and C. Veeramani

Macroeconomic Performance 4
Sectoral Issues 6
Poverty, Inequality, and Human Development 10
Other Emerging Issues 12
What Next? 14
References 14

2. Macroeconomic Overview: The Growth Story ... 16
Manoj Panda

Introduction 16
National Income Growth 17
Other Macroeconomic Developments 23
Growth Prospect—An Assessment 28
References 31

3. Propagation Mechanisms in Inflation: Governance as Key ... 32
Ashima Goyal

Introduction 32
Size and Persistence 33

Propagation Mechanisms: Food Prices, Wages, Exchange Rates, and Aggregate Prices 35
Price Setting Behaviour 36
Demand and Supply Shocks 37
Governance Failures, Chronic Cost Shocks 39
Growth and Inflation Tradeoffs and the Output Sacrifice 41
Policy 43
Long-term Structural and Fiscal Reforms 44
Conclusion 45
References 45

4. **Fiscal Deficits, Credibility, and Inflation Persistence: Lessons from Thatcher and Volcker Disinflations** 47

   Pankaj Kumar, Pratik Mitra, and *Naveen Srinivasan*

   Introduction 47
   Establishing Anti-inflationary Credibility: Lessons from Thatcher and Volcker Disinflations 48
   Empirically Evaluating the Link Between Policy Regime Credibility and Inflation Persistence 51
   Lessons and Conclusions 55
   References 58

5. **Is Fiscal Policy in India Pro-cyclical?** 59

   R. Krishnan and *Rajendra R. Vaidya*

   Introduction 59
   Fiscal Cyclicality—Conceptual, Theoretical, and Methodological Issues 60
   Empirical Results 61
   Conclusion 77
   References 77

6. **Performance and Key Policy Issues of Indian Agriculture** 79

   S. Mahendra Dev and *Vijay Laxmi Pandey*

   Introduction 79
   Performance of Agriculture 79
   Key Policy Issues 85
   Other issues 90
   Summing Up 91
   References 92

7. **Sectoral Linkages, Multipliers, and the Role of Agriculture** 95

   G. Mythili and *Nitin Harak*

   Introduction 95
   Scope of the Study 96
   Objectives 96
   Sectoral Composition and Growth Rate 96
   An Overview of Sectoral Linkages 97
   Theoretical and Analytical Aspects of SAM 99
   Analysis and Results 101
   Summary and Policy Implications 105
   References 115

8. **Services-led Growth, Employment, Skill, and Job Quality: A Study of Manufacturing and Service Sectors in Urban India** — 116

   K.V. Ramaswamy and *Tushar Agrawal*

   Context and Focus   116
   Employment Growth and Structure   117
   Structure of Urban Workforce, Worker Status, and Job Quality   120
   Wage Inequality, Education, and Social Security   124
   Conclusions   128
   References   131

9. **The 'Miracle' Still Waiting to Happen: Performance of India's Manufactured Exports in Comparison to China** — 132

   C. Veeramani

   Introduction   132
   Relative Contribution of the Manufacturing Sector to GDP and Exports   133
   Relative Factor Endowments   138
   Pattern of Export Specialization   140
   Global Production Networks and Vertical Specialization   143
   Geographical Direction of Exports   146
   Concluding Remarks and the Way Forward   147
   References   149

10. **Borrowing by Indian Firms** — 151

    Renuka Sane and *Susan Thomas*

    The Issues   151
    Evidence of Financing from Funding Sources   153
    Evidence From the Structure of Liabilities   154
    Cross-sectional Heterogeneity by Firm Age   155
    The Corporate Bond Market   155
    Foreign Financing   156
    Conclusions   158
    References   158

11. **Sustainability of Biomass Energy in India: The Case of Biodiesel Production from Tree-borne Oils** — 159

    Vinod Kumar Sharma

    Introduction   159
    Bioenergy Case Studies in East Asia   161
    Indian Study on Biodiesel   161
    Conclusions   164
    References   166

12. **Access to Modern Energy Services: The Road Not Taken** — 167

    B. Sudhakara Reddy

    Modern Energy—Planned Scarcity   167
    Household Energy Use in India—The Wood, the Bad, and the Ugly   168

Access to Energy Services—The Targets 169
Collective Self-reliance—A New Business Model 173
The Implementation—What Can 'They Do' and What Can 'I' Do? 176
Beyond the Rehearsals 179
References 180

13. Provision of Civic and Environmental Services in the Urban Centres of India: Present Trends and the Way Forward   181

Sudhakar Yedla

Introduction 181
Water Supply 182
Sanitation 188
Solid Waste Management 189
Initiatives Facilitating/Augmenting the Provision of Service in Urban Areas 193
The Way Forward 196
References 198

14. On the Internal Mobility of Indians: Knowledge Gaps and Emerging Concerns   200

S. Chandrasekhar and *Ajay Sharma*

Introduction 200
Defining Mobility and the Extent of Mobility 201
To Migrate or to Commute 204
Emerging Concerns and Knowledge Gaps 207
References 208

15. Poverty in India and Its Decompositions: A Critical Appraisal of the New Method   209

Durgesh C. Pathak and *Srijit Mishra*

Introduction 209
The New Method: Some Issues 209
Measures and Concepts 210
Recent Estimates and Patterns 211
Concluding Remarks 222
References 222

16. Indian Inequality: Patterns and Changes, 1993–2010   224

Sripad Motiram and *Vamsi Vakulabharanam*

Introduction 224
Analysis and Results 225
Discussion and Conclusions 231
References 231

17. Promoting Human Development in India: Scope for Distributive Options   233

M.H. Suryanarayana and *Ankush Agrawal*

Introduction 233
Domestic Goalposts 234
Data Sources 235

Estimates and Findings   236
Sum up   244
References   246

18. Challenges for Right to Education in India: 247

Preet Rustagi

Policy Framework and Programmes for School Education—Broad Contours   248
Achievements and Remaining Challenges over the SSA Period   249
Remaining Issues and Constraints   256
Concluding Remarks   261
References   265

19. Prosecuting Corruption in India: Evidence from Karnataka   266

P.G. Babu, Vikas Kumar, and *Poonam Mehra*

Introduction   266
Background   268
Data and Analysis   269
The Way Ahead   282
References   284

A Statistical Profile of India's Development   287

Tables

1.1	GDP Growth Rates by Sectors: 2003–4 to 2012–13	2
1.2	Average Monthly Per Capita Expenditure (URP) in Rs, at 2004–5 Prices	3
1.3	Employment Share of Major Sectors (%), UPSS	4
1.4	Growth of Employment (% per annum), UPSS	4
1.5	Employment Elasticity with Respect to GDP	5
2.1	Growth in Real GDP	17
2.2	Index Number of Area and Yield	20
2.3	Growth in Industrial GDP by Sub-sectors	21
2.4	Industrial Production by Use-based Classification: Average Growth Rates, Coefficient of Variation, and Weights	22
2.5	Savings and Capital Formation (As % of GDP at Current Market Prices)	23
2.6	Receipts and Disbursements of Consolidated General Government	25
2.7	Fiscal Parameters of Central Government (As per cent of GDP)	25
2.8	Balance of Payments	26
2.9	Major Foreign Trade Parameters	27
3.1	Growth, Inflation, and Policy Rates	40
3.2	Monetary and Fiscal Policy and Outcomes in High Inflation and Other Years (Average Annual Rates)	43
4.1	Maximum Likelihood Estimates	52
5.1	Components of Expenditures of the Central Government	62
5.2	Concordant Index and Correlations of Cycles (Classical Cycle)	66
5.3	Concordant Index and Correlations of Cycles (Growth Cycle)	70
5.4	Regression Estimates after Correcting for First Order Autocorrelation	76
6.1	Trend Growth Rate of Agriculture Sector and Overall Economy (at 2004–5 prices)	80
6.2	Trend Growth Rate in the Value of Output	81
6.3	Growth Rate of Area, Production, and Yield of Major Crops	81
6.4	Total Factor Productivity (TFP) in Agriculture and Non-agriculture	82
6.5	Annual Growth Rate in TFP and Share of TFP Growth in Output Growth	83

6.6	State-wise Growth in Labour Productivity (2004–5 Prices)	84
6.7	State-wise Instability in NSDP from Agriculture at 2004–5 Prices	86
6.8	Crop Group's Share in Value of Output at 2004–5 Prices	88
7.1	Sectoral Value Added Composition and the Growth Rate	96
7.2	Schematic Social Accounting Matrix	100
7.3	Sectoral Output Multipliers	102
7.4	Full Income Multipliers	102
7.5	Total Output and Income Multipliers	103
7.6	3×3 Sectoral Output, Factor, and Household Income Multipliers	104
7.7	Circular Flow Multiplier	105
A7.1	Multiplier Decomposition	107
A7.2	Detailed Classification of the Sectors	108
A7.3a	Social Accounting Matrix, 1997–8	109
A7.3b	Social Accounting Matrix, 2003–4	111
A7.3c	Social Accounting Matrix, 2006–7	113
8.1	Structure of GDP and Growth Rate (%): 1999–2000 and 2009–10	118
8.2	Employment Growth Rates (%) by Sector in India: 1993–4 to 2009–10	119
8.3	Employment Growth Rates (%) by Sector in Urban India: 1993–4 to 2009–10	119
8.4	Structure of Urban Employment by Sector	119
8.5	Distribution of Absolute Employment Change by Sector (in million, 2009 over 1999)	120
8.6	Age-specific Distribution (%) by Worker Status and Gender in Manufacturing and Services: 1999–2000 and 2009–10	122
8.7	Distribution of Workers (%) of Each Status by Location of Workplace: Manufacturing and Services	123
8.8	Distribution of Workers (%) by Enterprise Size: Manufacturing and Services	124
8.9	Wage Inequality among Regular Workers in Urban India: 1999–2009	125
8.10	Distribution of Male and Female Workers by Level of Education	127
8.11	Access to Social Security Benefit: Industry Distribution 2004–5 and 2009–10	129
8.12	Workers with Job Contracts for More Than Three Years: Industry Distribution 2004–5 and 2009–10	129
A8	Concordance between Location Codes in NSS surveys	130
9.1	Sectoral Composition of GDP	135
9.2	Sectoral Composition of Employment	135
9.3	Average Annual Growth Rates of Exports, Values in US$	136
9.4	Relative Endowments	138
9.5	Educational Attainment	139
9.6	Composition of Exports	141
9.7	World Market Shares	142
9.8	Export Composition according to Factor Intensity Classification	143
9.9	Share of Parts and Components in Manufacturing Trade	144
9.10	Vertical Specialization in Manufacturing across Selected Asian Countries (import content of exports), VS indices	145
9.11	Share of High-income OECD Countries in Exports from India and China	147
10.1	Sources of Funds Aggregated for All Non-financial Firms	154
10.2	Structure of Liabilities of Indian Non-financial Firms	154
10.3	Variation across Age	155
10.4	Corporate Bond Trades	156
11.1	Global Feed Stocks for Biodiesel Production	160

12.1	Household Energy Consumption (1950–2010)	168
12.2	End Uses and Rationale for Using Various Energy Carriers	169
12.3	Energy Accessibility for Cooking (2010)	170
12.4	Electricity Accessibility	171
12.5	Village and Household Electrification Rates among Various States (2010)	172
12.6	Energy Affordability among Different Income Groups (2010)	173
12.7	Average Budget Share of All Household Energy	173
12.8	Rural-Urban Disparities in Electricity Use and Service Provision	174
12.9	Cost Estimates of Providing Cooking Services for Households	175
12.10	Cost Estimates for Providing Electricity Connections	176
13.1	Share of Urban Population in India (1951–2011)	182
13.2	Sectoral Share of Water Demand in India, 2010–50	183
13.3	Per Capita Water Availability in India, 1951–50	183
13.4	State-wise Water Supply in Class I Cities in India, 2008	184
13.5	Prime Source of Drinking Water in Rural and Urban Areas in India (distribution per 100 HH), 2008–9	186
13.6	Projected Funds Requirement for the Eleventh Five Year Plan	195
13.7	Projected Capital and Revenue Expenditure for the Twelfth Five Year Plan	196
13.8	Some of the PPP Initiatives (Indicative) Implemented in Indian Cities for the Provision of Services	197
14.1	Size of Migrant Population	202
14.2	Estimated Size of the Non-agricultural Workforce Based on Sector of Residence and Place of Work (all-India)	203
14.3	Distribution of Internal Migrants by Last Usual Place of Residence for Each Component of Rural-Urban Migration Streams	205
14.4	Migration Rates from Different NSSO Rounds	206
14.5	Return Migration Rate	206
15.1	Incidence, Depth, and Severity of Poverty and Inequality across States in India, 2004–5 and 2009–10	214
15.2	Sectoral Decomposition of Change in Poverty Between 2004–5 and 2009–10	216
15.3	Growth-Inequality Decomposition of Change in Poverty at the All-India Level	216
15.4	Incidence, Depth, and Severity of Poverty and Inequality across Sub-groups in India (2004–5 and 2009–10)	219
16.1	Inequality (Gini) for Major States	226
16.2	Theil Decomposition Analysis	231
17.1	Domestic Goalposts for the Human Development Index	235
17.2	Key Indicators: States and All-India	237
17.3	Estimates of Sub-indices by Dimension, with and without Adjustment for Inequality: International Goalposts	238
17.4	Estimates of Global HDI and IHDI across States	239
17.5	Estimates of Sub-indices by Dimension, with and without Adjustment for Inequality: Domestic Goalposts	244
17.6	Estimates of HDI and IHDI across States: Domestic Goalposts	245
17.7	Correlation Between Ranks Based on Different Pairs of HDI and its Sub-indices (Domestic Goalposts)	245
18.1	Effective Literacy Rates in India	250

18.2	Effective Literacy Rates by Social Group, and Muslims—Rural /Urban	250
18.3	Mean Year of Schooling	251
18.4	Current Attendance by Age and Social Group	253
18.5	Percentage of Schools Established between 2002–3 to 2008–9	253
18.6	Some Education-related Statistics	253
18.7	Distance of School	253
18.8	School Facilities Over the Years	254
18.9	Number of Schools Requiring Infrastructure Facilities in 2009–10 (in lakh)	254
18.10	Distribution of Districts in 2011 by Literacy Rates	255
18.11	Listing of Districts with Below 50 Literacy Rates	255
18.12	Gender Parity Index in Enrolment	256
18.13	Age-wise Percentage of Never Enrolled Persons in Rural-Urban Areas	256
18.14	Proportion of Students Currently Attending by Age and Income Groups	257
18.15	Major Reasons for Discontinuance/Dropping out	257
18.16	Number of Institutions by Management	258
18.17	Proportion of Students Availing Free Education	259
18.18	Proportion of Students Getting Educational Incentives	259
18.19	Average Annual Expenditure Per Student Per Year by Level of Education	260
A18.1	Percentage of Children Currently Attending an Educational Institute by State, Sector (2007–8)	263
19.1	Tenures of Chief Ministers and Lokayuktas (25 July 1995–26 March 2011)	271
19.2	Cases Resulting in Conviction	274

Figures

2.1	Annual Growth in Real GDP in India	18
2.2	Share of Agriculture, Industry, and Services (in %)	18
2.3	Average Growth Rate in Crop Agriculture	19
2.4	Average Growth of Various Service Sectors, 2000–11	22
2.5	Annual Growth Rates in Demand Components	24
2.6	Per Capita GSDP 2004–5 and Average Growth Rates 2004–8 and 2008–12	29
3.1a	Inflation in WPI and CPI	33
3.1b	Inflation in the Components of WPI (Three Month Moving Averages)	33
3.1c	Inflation in CPI (food) and WPI (Non-food Manufacturing)	34
3.1d	Domestic and International Fuel Inflation and Changes in the Rupee Value (Appreciation)	34
3.2	The Contribution of Demand and Supply Shocks to Inflation	38
3.3	Indian and International Oil Prices	41
3.4	Aggregate Demand and Supply	42
3.5	Real Wages Per Worker Year	43
4.1	US and UK Long-term Interest Rate	49
4.2	Inflation Persistence and Month-on-Month Variation in Long Interest Rate	53
4.3	Inflation Persistence and Primary Deficit to GDP Ratio	54
5.1	Total Expenditure of the Central Government	63
5.2	Total Expenditure of Administrative Departments	64
5.3	Total Expenditure of Departmental Commercial Undertakings	64
5.4	Total Expenditure of the Central Government (Rolling Correlations)	67
5.5	Total Expenditure of Administrative Departments (Rolling Correlations)	67
5.6	Subsidies of Administrative Departments (Rolling Correlations)	68
5.7	Total Grants of Administrative Departments (Rolling Correlations)	68
5.8	Total Grants to States and UTs (Rolling Correlations)	69
5.9	Total Grants to Local Bodies and Others (Rolling Correlations)	69
5.10	Total Grants to Local Bodies (Rolling Correlations)	70
5.11	Total Grants to Others (Rolling Correlations)	71

5.12	Total Expenditure of Departmental Commercial Undertakings (Rolling Correlations)	71
5.13	Total Expenditure of the Central Government (Recursive Correlations)	72
5.14	Total Expenditure of Administrative Departments (Recursive Correlations)	72
5.15	Subsidies of Administrative Departments (Recursive Correlations)	73
5.16	Total Grants of Administrative Departments (Recursive Correlations)	73
5.17	Total Grants to States and UTs (Recursive Correlations)	74
5.18	Total Grants to Local Bodies and Others (Recursive Correlations)	74
5.19	Total Grants to Local Bodies (Recursive Correlations)	75
5.20	Total Grants to Others (Recursive Correlations)	75
5.21	Total Expenditure of Departmental Commercial Undertakings (Recursive Correlations)	76
6.1	Growth in the Agriculture Sector	80
6.2	State-wise Growth in Agricultural GDP at 2004–5	83
6.3	Labour Productivity in 2009–10 at Constant Prices (2004–5)	84
6.4	Land Productivity in the Year 2006–7	85
6.5	Average Annual Growth in Land Productivity	86
6.6	Investment in Agriculture	89
7.1	Value added Annual Growth Rate from 1997–8 to 2006–7	97
8.1	Average Daily Real Wage (in Rs) by Deciles in Manufacturing and Services	125
8.2	Difference in Log Real Wage between 1999 and 2009 by Deciles: Manufacturing versus Services	126
8.3	Difference in Log Real Wage between 1999 and 2009 by Percentiles: Manufacturing versus Services	126
8.4	Returns to Education by Industry: 2009–10	128
9.1	Average Annual Growth Rates across Sectors, India, 1970–2010	134
9.2	Average Annual Growth Rates across Sectors, China, 1970–2010	134
9.3	Share of Manufacturing in Total Merchandise Exports	136
9.4	World Market Shares of Exports, India	137
9.5	World Market Shares of Exports, China	137
11.1	Biodiesel Demand in India at Various Blending Rates	161
12.1	Household Energy Transition	170
12.2	Electricity Access (1951–2001) (Village and Household level)	171
12.3	Primary Physical Resources and Actors Mapping	177
12.4	Financial Resources and Actors Mapping	177
13.1	Water Supply and Sanitation Coverage by Region, 2000	182
13.2	Number of Class I Cities in Different States having Different Levels of Water Supply, 2008	185
13.3	Number of Class II Cities in Different States having Different Levels of Water Supply, 2008	185
13.4	Households Access to Safe Drinking Water, 2008–9 (Tap/Hand pump/Tube well) in India	186
13.5	Per Capita Water Supply in Metropolitan Cities, 2005	187
13.6	Share of Domestic and Non-domestic Use of Water Supplied in Metropolitan Cities	187
13.7	Water Supply Duration and Frequency in Metropolitan Cities, 2005	188
13.8	Sewage Generation and Treatment Capacity in Different States, 2010	189
13.9	Sewage Generation and Treatment Capacity in Different Metropolitan Cities, 2010	190
13.10	Municipal Solid Waste Generation in Different States of India, 2009–10	191
13.11	Waste Generation Rates in Metropolitan Cities, 2010–11	191

13.12	Per capita Waste Generation in Metropolitan Cities, 2010	192
13.13	A Multi-pronged Approach to the Provision of Basic Civic and Environmental Services in Urban Areas	193
13.14	Details of JNNURM Projects Completed in Different States and for Different Sectors	195
15.1	Change in Poverty Shares (2004–5 to 2009–10)	212
15.2a	Growth Incidence Curve for Rural India (2004–5 and 2009–10)	217
15.2b	Growth Incidence Curve for Urban India (2004–5 and 2009–10)	217
16.1a	Rural Inequality for 2004–5 and 2009–10 (Major States)	226
16.1b	Urban Inequality for 2004–5 and 2009–10 (Major States)	227
16.1c	Inequality for 2004–5 and 2009–10 (Major States)	228
16.2a	Growth and Inequality in Rural India	228
16.2b	Growth and Inequality in Urban India	229
17.1	HDI across Indian States (International Goalposts)	240
17.2	IHDI across Indian States (International Goalposts)	241
17.3	Loss in HDI due to Inequalities	242
17.4	HDI and Its Dimensions: Indian States (International Goalposts)	242
17.5	Distribution of HDI and Its Dimensions: Countries (International Goalposts)	243
17.6	Profiles of HDI, IHDI, and Their Dimensions: Indian States (Domestic Goalposts)	243
18.1	Number of Illiterates in India (in millions)	251
18.2	Education Status of 5–29 Year Age Group in India	252
18.3	Age-specific Attendance Ratio by Age Group	252
18.4	Declining Gender Gap in Literacy Rates over Four Decades (from 1981 to 2011)	255
19.1	Number of Cases Initiated in Different Years	270
19.2	Ratio of Trap to Raid Cases Initiated in Different Years	271
19.3	Trap and Raid Cases Initiated under Different Lokayuktas	272
19.4	Cases Initiated under Different Chief Ministers	272
19.5	Trap and Raid Cases Initiated Per Year under Different Lokayuktas	273
19.6	Cases against Officials of Highest Cadres under Different Lokayuktas	274
19.7	Cases against Officials of Highest Cadres under Different Chief Ministers	275
19.8	Ratio of Trap to Raid Cases Initiated under Different Lokayuktas	275
19.9	Departmental Spread of Corruption	276
19.10	Share of Different Tiers of Bureaucracy in Corruption	277
19.11a	Geographical Spread of Corruption	278
19.11b	Number of Cases per Million Population	279
19.12	The Life Cycle of Cases	279
19.13	Rate of Processing of Cases (in %) at Different Stages	280
19.14	Average Age of Pending Cases (in years) at Different Stages of Prosecution	281
19.15	Distribution of Convictions by Designation of Officials	281

Boxes

3.1	Causality between Consumer and Wholesale Prices	36
3.2	Price Setting Behaviour Deduced from an Estimated Aggregate Supply	37
4.1	Statement on Economic Policy	50
6.1	Story of Gujarat and Punjab Agriculture	91
12.1	Village Electrification Programmes	171
12.2	Options for Modern Energy Supply	174
14.1	Definition of Key Terms Related to Migration	201
18.1	Achievements over the SSA Period	250

A Statistical Profile of India's Development

A1	**NATIONAL INCOME**		
	A1.1	Key National Accounts Aggregates—2004–5 Series (at Constant Prices)	289
	A1.2	Key National Accounts Aggregates—2004–5 Series (at Current Prices)	293
	A1.3	Gross and Net Domestic Savings By Type of Institutions (at Current Prices)	294
	A1.4	Gross Capital Formation by Type of Institutions at 2004–5 Prices	298
	A1.5	Gross Capital Formation by Type of Institutions at Current Prices	300
	A1.6	Net Capital Stock by Type of Institutions and Capital–Output Ratios	304
	A1.7	Rank of States in Descending Order of Per Capita State Domestic Product in Real Terms	308
A2	**PRODUCTION**		311
	A2.1	Production Trends in Major Agricultural Crops	311
	A2.2	Trends in Yields of Major Crops	314
	A2.3	Horticulture and Livestock Production	316
	A2.4	Value of Output from Agriculture, Horticulture, and Livestock	318
	A2.5	Structural Changes in Indian Industry and Decadal Growth	322
	A2.6	Index of Industrial Production with Major Groups and Sub-groups	323
	A2.7	Index of Industrial Production with Major Groups and Sub-groups Full Fiscal Year Averages Based on 2004–5=100	325
A3	**BUDGETARY TRANSACTIONS**		327
	A3.1	Budgetary Position of Government of India	327
	A3.2	Consolidated Budgetary Position of State Governments at a Glance	330
A4	**MONEY AND BANKING**		332
	A 4.1	Money Stock Measures	332
	A4.2	Selected Indicators of Scheduled Commercial Bank Operations (Year-end Outstandings)	336
	A4.3	Trends in Statewise Bank Deposits and Credit and Credit–Deposit Ratios	338
	A4.4	Distribution of Outstanding Credit of Scheduled Commercial Banks According to Occupation	342

A STATISTICAL PROFILE OF INDIA'S DEVELOPMENT

A5	**CAPITAL MARKET**	344
	A5.1 Resources Mobilization from the Primary Market	344
	A5.2 Trends in Resource Mobilization by Mutual Funds (Sector-wise)	346
	A5.3 Trends in Resource Mobilization by Mutual Funds	348
	A5.4 Trends in FII Investments	350
	A5.5 Business Growth of Capital Market Segment of National Stock Exchange	352
	A5.6 Settlement Statistics of Capital Market Segment of NSE of India	354
	A5.7 Business Growth of Futures and Options Market Segment, National Stock Exchange	355
	A5.8 Business Growth on the WDM Segment: NSE	356
	A5.9 Business Growth and Settlement of Capital Market Segments, Bombay Stock Exchange	357
	A5.10 Working of Clearing Corporation of India Limited (CCIL)	358
A6	**PRICES**	359
	A6.1 Wholesale Price Index: Point-to-Point and Average Annual Changes	359
	A6.2 Cost of Living Indices	362
	A6.3 Cost of Living Index	364
A7	**BALANCE OF PAYMENTS**	366
	A7.1 Foreign Exchange Reserves (End Period)	366
	A7.2 Balance of Payments 1990-1 to 2010-11	368
	A7.3 Invisibles in India's Balance of Payments—by Category: Receipts & Payments	376
A8	**EXCHANGE RATE**	378
	A8.1 Exchange Rate for the Indian Rupee vis-à-vis Some Select Currencies (Indian Rupee per Currency)	378
	A8.2 Indices of Real Effective Exchange Rate (REER) and Nominal Effective Exchange Rate (NEER) of the Indian Rupee	382
A9	**FOREIGN TRADE**	
	A9.1 India's Foreign Trade	383
	A9.2 Changing Scenerio in Foreign Trade	384
	A9.3 Foreign Trade with Major Trading Partners	388
A10	**FOREIGN INVESTMENT AND NRI DEPOSITS**	392
	A10.1 Foreign Investment Inflows	392
	A10.2 NRI Deposits—Outstandings	393
	A10.3 FDI Inflows: Year-wise, Route-wise, Sector-wise Break-up, and Country-wise Break up	394
A11	**POPULATION**	395
	A11.1 State-wise Population 1951–2001	395
	A11.2 State-wise Rural and Urban Population of India: 1951–2001	397
	A11.3 State-wise Sex Ratio (females per 1000 males)	400
	A11.4 State-wise Literacy Rate: 1951 to 2001	402
	A11.5 State-wise Infant Mortality Rate: 1961, 1981, 1991, 2001, and 2010	404
	A11.6 Number of Child Population in the Age Group 0–6 Years by Sex	406
A12.	**SOCIAL SECTOR**	408
	A12.1 Human Development Index for India by State 1981, 1991, and 2001	408
	A12.2 Number & Per Cent of Population below Poverty Line and Poverty Line (in Rs)	410
	A12.3 Poverty Line and Number of Poor in Rural and Urban Areas across States, 1993–4, 2004–5, and 2009–10, New Method	414

A12.4	Head Count Ratio and Share of Poor for Rural and Urban Areas across States, 1993–4 to 2009–10, New Method	416
A12.5	Education Statistics	418
A12.6	Indian Health Statistics	419
A13	**EMPLOYMENT**	**420**
A13.1	Total Population, Workers, and Non–workers as Per Population Censuses	420
A13.2	Number of Persons Employed per 1000 Persons according to Usual Status and Current Weekly Status Approaches	421
A13.3	Per 1000 Distribution of the Usually Employed by Status of Employment for All, i.e., Principal and Subsidiary Status Workers	422
A13.4	Unemployment Rate (Number of Persons Unemployed Per 1000 Persons in the Labour Force)	423
A13.5	State–wise Sectoral Distribution of Usual (Principal + Subsidiary) Status Workers: 1983 to 2009–10	425
A14	**HOUSEHOLD INDEBTEDNESS**	**427**
A14.1	Household Indebtedness in India: A Profile	427
A15	**ECONOMIC CENSUS**	**430**
A15.1	Trends in Employment in Agricultural (Excluding Crop Production and Plantation) and Non–agricultural Enterprises 1980–2005	430
A15.2	Trends in Number of Agricultural (Excluding Crop Production and Plantation) and Non–agricultural Enterprises	433
A16	**INTERNATIONAL COMPARISON**	**436**
A16.1	Human Development Characteristics of Some Selected Countries	436

Abbreviations

APMC	Agriculture Produce Marketing Regulation Act
AS	Aggregate Supply
BDFs	Biomass derived fuels
CAD	Current account deficit
CBI	Central Bureau of Investigation
CDP	City development plan
CDS	Credit default swap
CPCB	Central Pollution Control Board
CPHEEO	Central Public Health and Environmental Engineering Organization
CPI	Consumer price index
CPIAL	Consumer price index for agricultural labourers
CPII	Consumer price inflation
CPIIW	Consumer price index for industrial workers
CRR	cash reserve ratio
CV	Coefficient of variation
CVC	Chief Vigilance Commissioner
CW	casual wage
CWSN	Children with special needs
DGCI&S	Director General of Commercial Intelligence and Statistics
DPEP	District Primary Education Programme
EAS	East Asia Summit
ECB	External Commercial Borrowing
ECTF	Energy Cooperation Task Force
EE	Energy empowerment
EGS	Education guarantee scheme
EM	Emerging Market
ER	Exchange Rate
ERIA	Economic Research Institute for ASEAN and East Asia
ESI	Export similarity index
FD	Fiscal Deficit
FDI	Foreign direct investment
FII	Foreign institutional investment

FRBM	Fiscal Responsibility and Budget Management
FYP	Five Year Plan
GCFA	Gross capital formation in agriculture and allied sectors
GDCF	gross domestic capital formation
GDP	gross domestic product
GFC	Global financial crisis
GHG	Green house gas
GIC	Growth incidence curve
GNI	Gross national income
GoI	Government of India
GSDP	Gross State Domestic Product
GST	Goods and service tax
HDI	Human development index
HVC	High value chain
ICDS	Integrated Child Development Services
IEA	International Energy Agency
IFC	International Finance Corporation
IHDI	Inequality-adjusted Human Development Index
IIED	Institute for Environment and Development
IIP	Index of industrial production
I-O	Input-output
IPCC	Intergovernmental Panel on Climate Change
ITC	International Trade Centre
IWMP	Integrated Watershed Management Programme
JNNURM	Jawaharlal Nehru National Urban Renewal Mission
KGBV	Katurba Gandhi Balika Vidyalaya
LPI	Logistic Performance Index
MGNREGA	Mahatma Gandhi National Rural Employment Guarantee Act
MGNREGS	Mahatma Gandhi National Rural Employment Guarantee Scheme
MIPB	Manufacturing Industry Promotion Board
MoEF	Ministry of Environment and Forests
MoSPI	Ministry of Statistics and Programme Implementation
MoUD	Ministry of Urban Development
MoWR	Ministry of Water Resources
MPCE	Monthly per capita expenditure
MS	Mahila Samkhya
MSP	Minimum support price
MSW	Municipal solid waste
MTFS	Medium-Term Financial Strategy
NACP	National AIDS Control Programme
NAPCC	National Action Plan on Climate Change
NBF	National Biodiesel Mission
NCF	National Curriculum Framework
NFSM	National Food Security Mission
NIES	Newly Industrialized Economies
NIMZ	National Manufacturing and Investment Zones
NIUA	National Institute of Urban Affairs
NKE	New Keynesian
NMP	National Manufacturing Policy
NPEGEL	National Programme for Education of Girls at Elementary Level
NSDP	Net state domestic produce
NSS	National Sample Survey

NSSO	National Sample Survey Organisation
OB	Operation Blackboard
OBC	Other Backward Caste
PFCE	Private final consumption expenditure
PPP	Purchasing power parity
PTR	Pupil teacher ratio
QR	Quantitative restrictions
RBI	Reserve Bank of India
RDF	Reduce derived fuel
RKVY	Rashtriya Krishi Vikas Yojana
RMSA	Rashtriya Madhyamik Shiksha Abhiyan
RNFS	Rural non-farm sector
RSBY	Rashtriya Swasthya Bima Yojana
RTE	Right to Education
RTI	Right to Information
RW	regular wage
SAM	Social Accounting Matrix
SC	Scheduled Caste
SDP	State domestic product
SE	Self-employment
SEO	Seasoned equity offering
SET	Sustainable energy technology
SITC	Standard International Trade Classification
SME	Small and medium enterprise
SSA	Sarva Shiksha Abhiyan
SSR	Small scale reservation
ST	Scheduled Tribe
STP	Sewage treatment plant
SWM	Solid waste management
TBOs	Tree borne oils
TFP	Total factor productivity
TFPG	total factor productivity growth
UEE	Universal elementary education
UFW	Unaccounted for water
ULB	Urban local bodies
UNFCC	United Nations Framework Convention on Climate Change
UPSS	Usual Principal Status and Subsidiary Status
WPI	Wholesale price index
WPII	Wholesale price inflation
WTE	Waste to energy

Contributors

S. Mahendra Dev	Director (Vice Chancellor), Indira Gandhi Institute of Development Research, Mumbai
Srijit Mishra	Associate Professor, Indira Gandhi Institute of Development Research, Mumbai
C. Veeramani	Associate Professor, Indira Gandhi Institute of Development Research, Mumbai
Manoj Panda	Professor, Indira Gandhi Institute of Development Research, Mumbai
Ashima Goyal	Professor, Indira Gandhi Institute of Development Research, Mumbai
Pankaj Kumar	PhD Scholar, Indira Gandhi Institute of Development Research, Mumbai
Pratik Mitra	PhD Scholar, Indira Gandhi Institute of Development Research, Mumbai
Naveen Srinivasan	Associate Professor, Indira Gandhi Institute of Development Research, Mumbai
R. Krishnan	Associate Professor, Indira Gandhi Institute of Development Research, Mumbai
Rajendra R. Vaidya	Professor, Indira Gandhi Institute of Development Research, Mumbai
Vijay Laxmi Pandey	Associate Professor, Indira Gandhi Institute of Development Research, Mumbai
G. Mythili	Professor, Indira Gandhi Institute of Development Research, Mumbai
Nitin Harak	PhD Scholar, Indira Gandhi Institute of Development Research, Mumbai
K.V. Ramaswamy	Professor, Indira Gandhi Institute of Development Research, Mumbai
Tushar Agrawal	PhD Scholar, Indira Gandhi Institute of Development Research, Mumbai
Renuka Sane	Research Economist, Indira Gandhi Institute of Development Research, Mumbai
Susan Thomas	Assistant Professor, Indira Gandhi Institute of Development Research, Mumbai
Vinod Kumar Sharma	Professor, Indira Gandhi Institute of Development Research, Mumbai
B. Sudhakara Reddy	Professor, Indira Gandhi Institute of Development Research, Mumbai
Sudhakar Yedla	Associate Professor, Indira Gandhi Institute of Development Research, Mumbai
S. Chandrasekhar	Associate Professor, Indira Gandhi Institute of Development Research, Mumbai
Ajay Sharma	PhD Student, Indira Gandhi Institute of Development Research, Mumbai

Durgesh C. Pathak	Assistant Professor, Birla Institute of Technology and Science, Pilani
Sripad Motiram	Associate Professor, Indira Gandhi Institute of Development Research, Mumbai
Vamsi Vakulabharanam	Associate Professor, University of Hyderabad
M.H. Suryanarayana	Professor, Indira Gandhi Institute of Development Research, Mumbai
Ankush Agrawal	Assistant Professor, Institute of Economic Growth, Delhi
Preet Rustagi	Professor, Institue for Human Development, New Delhi
P.G. Babu	Professor, Indira Gandhi Institute of Development Research, Mumbai
Vikas Kumar	Assistant Professor, Azim Premji University, Bengaluru
Poonam Mehra	Assistant Professor, National Institute of Securities Markets, Mumbai

1

Overview—India's Experience with Reforms
What Next?

S. Mahendra Dev, Srijit Mishra, and C. Veeramani

India has achieved much in the last two decades of the reform period. The country is now a $1.8 trillion economy, the fourth largest in the world. However, a lot remains to be done for achieving all the economic, social, and environmental goals of the nation. In the post-reform period, India has done well in some indicators such as economic growth, exports, balance of payments, resilience to external shocks, service sector growth, significant accumulation of foreign exchange, information technology (IT) and the stock market, and improvements in telecommunications.[1]

What are the recent trends in Gross Domestic Product (GDP) growth? The trend rate of GDP growth in the last 20-year period has been more than 6 per cent per annum. The growth rate was nearly 9 per cent per annum during 2003–4 to 2007–8 and 9.3 per cent per annum during 2005–8. All the three sectors (agriculture, industry, and services) contributed to growth. The acceleration in growth was more due to the performance of manufacturing and agriculture during this period. For example, the manufacturing sector showed a growth rate of 14.3 per cent and 10.3 per cent respectively in 2006–7 and 2007–8 (Table 1.1).

For about five years, starting from 2003–4, one observes a structural break regarding investments in the country. Savings and investments increased significantly in the period 2004–5 to 2007–8. During the 1990s, savings and investments hovered in the range of 21–24 per cent of GDP. The domestic savings rate rose from 23.7 per cent in 2000–1, to 32.2 per cent in 2004–5, and to 36.4 per cent in 2007–8. Similarly, the investment rate increased from 24.3 to 32.7 per cent and to 37.7 per cent during the same period.

The pre-global financial crisis period was characterized by high GDP growth of more than 9 per cent per annum, low inflation, low fiscal deficit, and higher trade and capital flows. In other words, all the macroeconomic fundamentals were in good shape and the economy was buoyant.

The global financial crisis that originated in the US in 2008 transmitted to other countries. India is more globally integrated now as compared to 1991 when reforms started. Due to a slowdown in external and domestic demand, GDP growth in India declined from 9.3 per cent in 2007–8 to 6.7 per cent in 2008–9. To address the negative fallout of the global slowdown on the Indian economy, the government responded by adopting policy measures such as fiscal stimulus and an easy monetary policy. It may be noted that India's counter-cyclical fiscal stimulus began much before the dramatic deterioration of the global financial markets. In fact, it started in February 2008, six months before the start of the crisis. This included the payout of a part of the

---

[1] For an assessment of Indian economy during the reform period, see Acharya and Mohan (2010); Ahluwalia and Little (2012). On understanding reforms, see Tendulkar and Bhavani (2007).

Table 1.1 GDP Growth Rates by Sectors: 2003–4 to 2012–13 (% per annum)

Annual Rates	2003–4	2004–5	2005–6	2006–7	2007–8	2008–9 P	2009–10 QE	2010–11 Rev	2011–12 Proj.	2012–13 Proj.
Agriculture & allied activities	10.0	0.0	5.1	4.2	5.8	0.1	1.0	7.0	2.8	0.5
Manufacturing	6.6	8.7	10.1	14.3	10.3	4.3	9.7	7.6	2.5	4.5
Industry	7.4	10.3	9.7	12.2	9.7	4.4	8.4	7.2	3.4	5.3
Services	8.5	9.1	10.9	10.1	10.3	10.0	10.5	9.3	8.9	8.9
Non-agriculture	8.1	9.5	10.5	10.8	10.1	8.1	9.8	8.6	7.1	7.7
GDP (factor cost)	8.5	7.5	9.5	9.6	9.3	6.7	8.4	8.4	6.5	6.7

Source: Reports of the Economic Advisory Council to the Prime Minister, July 2008, October 2009, and August 2012, New Delhi.

arrears to government employees, following the Sixth Pay Commission report and the debt relief (farm loan waiver) package to alleviate the debt burden of distressed farmers. The vote on account budget has not announced further fiscal stimulus but increased expenditure on the Mahatma Gandhi National Rural Employment Guarantee Scheme (MGNREGS).

The Indian economy recovered quickly after the 2008–9 crisis period. GDP growth rate increased significantly from 6.7 per cent in 2008–9 to 8.4 per cent in 2009–10 in spite of a drought. Despite global integration, GDP growth in India largely depends on the domestic economy (on domestic consumption). It gives some resilience to external factors although one does not subscribe to the decoupling theory. Monetary policy, fiscal policy, export policies, and some of the structural advantages, including a calibrated approach to capital convertibility etc. helped in the quick recovery and resilience. The manufacturing sector's growth rate was 9.7 per cent in 2009–10 as compared to 4.4 per cent in 2007–8. GDP growth rate was 8.4 per cent in 2010–11 with a growth of 7 per cent and 7.6 per cent respectively in the agriculture and manufacturing sectors.

Global factors like the Euro zone debt crisis and the rise in oil prices affected the Indian economy in 2011–12 and 2012–13. High interest rates due to the increase in inflation also reduced the investment rate and GDP growth declined from 8.4 per cent in 2010–11 to 6.5 per cent in 2011–12. The manufacturing sector recorded only a 2.5 per cent growth rate in 2011–12 (Table 1.1). According to the projections of the Prime Minister's Economic Advisory Council, GDP growth is expected to be around 6.7 per cent in 2012–13 while the Reserve Bank of India indicates that the growth will be around 6.5 per cent in the same year.[2] Agriculture growth will be affected due to drought in some parts of the country. Growth in the manufacturing sector is expected to rise in 2012–13 as compared to that in 2011–12.

Currently, particularly in the short run, India has many macroeconomic challenges:

- Nearly 7 per cent overall inflation and 10 per cent food inflation in July 2012.
- Current account deficit of 4.2 per cent in 2011–12.
- Depreciation of the rupee of about 19 per cent in nominal terms between June 2011 and June 2012.
- Fiscal deficit of nearly 6 per cent for central government (including off-budget liabilities) and 8.2 per cent for the centre and states together in 2011–12.
- Decline in gross domestic capital formation (GDCF) from 38 per cent in 2007–08 to 35.5 per cent in 2011–12. If we look at GDCF without valuables (like gold), the decline is large from 37 per cent to 32.7 per cent or 4.3 percentage points of GDP (EAC 2012).
- Decline in exports in the first quarter (April–July) of 2012 to $75.2 billion compared to $76.5 billion in first quarter of 2011—a decline of 1.7 per cent.
- The index of industrial production was 0.8 per cent during April–May 2012 as compared to 5.7 per cent during April–May 2011.

Both global and domestic factors have been responsible for a decline in economic growth in 2011–12 and 2012–13. For example, high interest rates are partly responsible for the decline in the growth in investment. Uncertainty in policies due to coalition governments is also responsible for the reduction in investment rates. However, as pointed out by Subbarao (2012), India in 2012 is different from that of 1991 as the country is more resilient now. In spite of short-run problems, our medium-term prospects of achieving more than 8 per cent GDP growth are still high.

What is the progress in achieving inclusive growth? India has done well on many indicators of progress in the post-reform period. However, exclusion has continued in terms

---

[2] Credit rating agencies and international organizations put the growth rate at around 5.5 to 6.0 per cent in 2012–13.

of low agriculture growth, low-quality employment growth, low human development, rural–urban divides, gender and social inequalities, and regional disparities. Social exclusion is taking place in terms of regions, social and marginal groups, women, minorities, and children.[3] The Eleventh Five Year Plan and the Approach Paper of the Twelfth Five Year Plan also highlight these exclusions and argue for more inclusive growth.

There have been some improvements in agricultural growth and poverty reduction since the mid-2000s. Agriculture growth was around 3.3 per cent per annum during the Eleventh Plan period. This was due to increase in investments in agriculture and other policies.

If we use the methodology of the Tendulkar Committee, poverty declined by 1.5 percentage points per annum between 2004–5 and 2009–10. It is the fastest decline compared to the earlier periods 1993–4 to 2004–5 and 1983–4 to 1993–4. Provisional estimates for 2011–12 (68th National Sample Survey Round) also reveal significant growth in average monthly per capita expenditure (MPCE). Average MPCE grew at an annual rate of 3.7 per cent in rural areas and 4 per cent in urban areas (Table 1.2). This growth is much higher than earlier periods. Both higher GDP growth and public interventions in schemes like NREGS could be responsible for the rise in average MPCE and faster decline in poverty in both rural and urban areas. Real wages of agricultural labourers also increased significantly partly due to MGNREGS.

Table 1.2 Average Monthly Per Capita Expenditure (URP) in Rs, at 2004–5 Prices

NSS Round/Year	Rural	Urban	Ratio of Urban to Rural
61st Round 2004–5	558.78	1052.36	1.88
68th Round 2011–12	707.24	1359.75	1.92
Growth rate per annum 2011–12 over 2004–5 (%)	3.7	4.2	—

Note: URP: Uniform Reference Period of 30 days.
Source: Computed based on press release 1 August 2012, NSSO, Ministry of Statistics and Programme Implementation.

However, inequalities have increased in the post-reform period in consumption across social groups and states although there is a debate on rising inequalities.[4] For example, the 2009–10 consumption data shows that poverty declined faster among Scheduled Tribes than it did among others. Although there have been achievements in the social sector during the reform period, the progress has been very slow. India has had success in growth but there is extreme failure in progress in social indicators (Drèze and Sen 2011).[5] For example, malnutrition among children is stubborn at 45 per cent in spite of high GDP growth in the post-1991 period. It is known that we are not only behind China but the progress is slower than in Bangladesh and some other South Asian countries. There are severe governance problems.[6]

There is a perception among many people that we should have some flagship social protection programmes like MGNREGS and others to achieve inclusive growth. No doubt these programmes are important for protecting the poor. But, inclusive growth is much broader than this and productive inclusion in terms of quality employment should be the focus of the Twelfth Plan. Jobless growth is a concern but on the other hand we should not have growthless jobs.[7] In other words, generating employment per se without growth should not be the policy prescription. We should generate productive jobs. The government should have a strategy and framework to achieve this objective.

We examine here the changes in employment across sectors and growth and elasticity of employment. Employment shares of major sectors provided in Table 1.3 reveal that: (a) There has been a decline in the share of agriculture over time but still 51 per cent of the total workers were in this sector in 2009–10; (b) There has hardly been any increase in the share of the manufacturing sector since 1987–8; (c) The share of the construction sector increased significantly from 1.84 per cent in 1972–3 to 9.60 per cent in 2009–10; and (d) The share of the tertiary sector rose from about 15 per cent in 1972–3 to 26.7 per cent in 2009–10. In spite of these changes, there is a mismatch between the share of employment and the share of GDP. For example, the share of agriculture in GDP is only 14 per cent but its employment share is very high at 51 per cent. The share of the tertiary sector in GDP is nearly 60 per cent but its employment share is only 27 per cent. Similarly, the manufacturing sector which provides productive jobs has not improved its share in employment.

The employment growth declined from 2.44 per cent during 1972–83 to 1.50 per cent during 1999–2010 (Table 1.4). This decline occurred in agriculture, manufacturing, and the tertiary sector while growth increased in the construction and secondary sectors.

---

[3] For more on this, see Dev (2008).
[4] Bhagwati and Panagariya (2012) argue that economic reforms have led to improvements in inclusive growth and the social groups have benefited.

[5] See Nagaraj (2012) on growth, inequality, and social development in India. On the relationship between economic growth and social development, see Rangarajan (2009).
[6] On governance issues, see Jalan (2005).
[7] For more on this, see Dev (2012).

Table 1.3 Employment Share of Major Sectors (%), UPSS

	1972–3	1977–8	1983	1987–8	1993–4	1999–2000	2004–5	2009–10
Agriculture & allied activities	73.92	70.98	68.59	64.87	63.98	60.32	56.30	51.30
Manufacturing	8.87	10.16	10.66	12.22	10.63	11.01	12.27	11.50
Construction	1.84	1.75	2.24	3.76	3.24	4.41	5.69	9.60
Secondary sector	11.30	12.55	13.78	17.04	14.96	16.24	18.78	22.02
Tertiary sector	14.78	16.47	17.63	18.09	21.07	23.43	24.92	26.67
Total	100.0	100.0	100.0	100.0	100.0	100.0	100.0	100.0

Note: UPSS: Usual Principal Status and Subsidiary Status.
Source: Derived from Papola and Sahu (2012).

Table 1.4 Growth of Employment (% per annum), UPSS

	1972–3 to 1983	1983 to 1993–4	1993–4 to 2004–5	1999–2000 to 2009–10
Agriculture & allied activities	1.70	1.35	0.67	–0.13
Manufacturing	4.28	2.00	3.17	1.95
Construction	4.43	5.67	7.19	9.72
Secondary sector	4.43	2.82	3.97	4.64
Tertiary sector	4.21	3.77	3.41	2.83
Total	2.44	2.02	1.84	1.50

Note: UPSS: Usual Principal Status and Subsidiary Status.
Source: Derived from Papola and Sahu (2012).

The elasticity of employment with respect to GDP also reveals trends similar to those of growth rates in employment (Table 1.5). The overall employment elasticity was 0.52 during 1972–83 but it fell by more than half to 0.20 during 1999–2010. The elasticity declined for the agriculture, manufacturing, and tertiary sectors. It was high for the construction and secondary sectors. The tertiary sector is not absorbing employment although its GDP growth is 9 to 10 per cent. Increase in labour intensity in the manufacturing sector is essential for an increase in productive jobs.

The previous *India Development Report 2011* (*IDR*) examined the experience of the Indian economy during the two decades of structural reforms. The Twelfth Five Year Plan aspires for 'Faster, More Inclusive and Sustainable Growth'. Keeping in view the objective of the Twelfth Plan, the present *India Development Report 2012–13* examines the post-reform performance and the policies needed in the next decade and beyond to achieve economic, social, and environmental goals as discussed below.

MACROECONOMIC PERFORMANCE

We have seen above that India's growth has declined to around 6.5 per cent. How has the economy been performing? What should be done to revive GDP growth? How can inflation be controlled? Is fiscal policy pro- or counter-cyclical in India? These are the questions addressed in this section.

Growth Story

Manoj Panda (Chapter 2) reviews major macroeconomic developments in India in recent years from a medium-term perspective. His chapter discusses growth in national income by broad sectors and deals with developments in selected macroeconomic policies. It also makes an assessment of the growth process. The most important feature of the India growth story is that it is mostly driven by the steady expansion of the services sector during the last three decades. It grew by 9–10 per cent during the Tenth and Eleventh Five Year Plan periods. Agricultural growth has generally been low at about 3 per cent per annum on a decadal basis except during the 1980s when the average growth stood at above 4 per cent. The performance of industry has been moderate since the 1970s, growing at a rate close to that of GDP growth. The strong performance of the services sector could be attributed to several factors: elastic household demand, intermediate demand by production activities, emerging comparative advantage in

Table 1.5 Employment Elasticity with Respect to GDP

	1972–3 to 1983	1983 to 1993–4	1993–4 to 2004–5	1999–2000 to 2009–10
Agriculture & allied activities	0.46	0.49	0.26	−0.05
Manufacturing	0.78	0.41	0.47	0.25
Construction	1.44	1.16	0.94	1.06
Secondary sector	0.87	0.53	0.59	0.60
Tertiary sector	0.77	0.57	0.43	0.30
Total	0.52	0.41	0.29	0.20

Note: UPSS: Usual Principal Status and Subsidiary Status.

Source: Derived from Papola and Sahu (2012).

skilled labour, exploitation of potential in the export market, and technological change.

An analysis across the states shows that in some states such as Bihar, Madhya Pradesh, Assam, Rajasthan, and Jammu and Kashmir, the Gross State Domestic Product (GSDP) performed better during the post-crisis period. Interestingly, these states also happen to be in the bottom half in per capita GSDP rankings. Two other states of Odisha and, to a lesser extent, Uttar Pradesh, have recorded reasonable growth rates in recent years. This is a welcome change in the development process of the country because of the concentration of a high incidence of poverty in these states. According to the Director General of Commercial Intelligence and Statistics (DGCI&S) data for 2010–11, about two-thirds of India's exports originated from the five states of Gujarat, Maharashtra, Tamil Nadu, Karnataka, and Andhra Pradesh. These states, whose production structure is relatively more export-oriented, have invariably been adversely affected due to the crisis.

According to Panda, several measures are needed to revive growth such as: (a) Rationalization and restructuring of government current expenditure including reduction in oil subsidies; (b) Raising the volume of tax revenue; (c) Taking advantage of the demographic dividend; (d) Reforms in factor markets like labour market reforms; and (e) Attention to land acquisition issues. Lastly, it is argued that the growth process must be broad based so that benefits of growth are widespread.

Inflation

After an initial jump, the post-reform period saw inflation fall to unprecedented lows. The resurgence of inflation since 2007 has been associated with sharp food and oil price inflation. Food and oil prices are relative prices, but as Ashima Goyal (Chapter 3) suggests, propagation mechanisms allow these to affect aggregate prices. Governance failures broadly defined as dysfunctional systems that create poor incentives, or narrowly defined as inappropriate government policies are responsible for many of these propagation mechanisms. Firm price-setting, response to cost shocks, and the relationship between wages, prices, and the exchange rate are also important dimensions of the inflationary process.

Goyal analyses these understudied issues. Recent high and persistent consumer price inflation may have been due to multiple supply shocks, so inflation may come down as the commodity cycle turns. Half of the Indian firms reset their prices in any period, and a little more than half are forward-looking in their price setting. Cost shocks have a larger impact on price compared to demand proxied by changes in money supply. Price inertia reduces the size of the monetary tightening that is required. A sharp rise in interest and exchange rates exerts a negative impact for highly leveraged firms.

Food prices and exchange rate affect aggregate prices considerably—requiring a prompt policy response, using a mixture of supply-side, tax, trade, and exchange rate policies. Multiple supply shocks are estimated to have caused inflation, but since they did not become persistent, second round price effects did not set in. So output remained below potential. First round effects have to be allowed for asymmetric price adjustments. Supply shocks took the form of upward shifts of aggregate supply elasticity in the sense that costs did not rise with output. Thus, as Goyal opines, poor governance contributed to chronic costs creeping at all levels of output.

Pankaj Kumar, Pratik Mitra, and Naveen Srinivasan (Chapter 4) [hereafter referred to as Kumar et al.] also examine the issues relating to inflation. Since the global financial turmoil of 2008, the Indian economy has grappled with high and persistent inflation. To deal with the inflationary pressure, the Reserve Bank cumulatively raised the cash reserve ratio (CRR) by 100 basis points and the policy rate (the repo rate) 13 times by 375 basis points between January 2010 and October 2011. Despite these policy actions, the inflation rate continues to remain persistently high. What explains the current inflation predicament?

In this regard Kumar et al. believe that the experience of the Thatcher government in the UK and the Volcker regime in the US in the early 1980s are full of lessons about our own, less drastic predicament with inflation. They suggest that large contemporary government deficits unaccompanied by concrete prospects for future government surpluses promote realistic doubts about whether monetary restraint must be abandoned sooner or later to help finance the deficit. It is insufficient to announce and maintain restrictive monetary policies.

Kumar et al. argue that agents will also look at fiscal policy in their attempt to determine whether the 'reform' can be sustained. If fiscal policy is incompatible with the 'reform' in monetary policy, agents will attach positive probability to the event that the reform will be abandoned in the future. The result will be an increase in inflationary expectations. Hence the 'unpleasant' policy lesson that the budget deficit must also be cut back to make a monetarist inflation-control programme work. In sum, a prudent anti-inflation policy includes containing the deficit to an amount that can be comfortably financed without printing money. They are of the view that today's debate about inflation largely misses this point, and therefore, fails to contend with the greatest danger of inflation that we face.

Fiscal Policy

Fiscal policy is crucial for influencing changes in several macro variables. R. Krishnan and Rajendra R. Vaidya (Chapter 5) empirically verify the generalization in literature that fiscal policy is pro-cyclical in developing economies and counter-cyclical in developed economies. They do this by analysing the fiscal behaviour, exclusively, of India over the period 1950–2008. Counter-cyclical fiscal policies intend to smooth business cycle fluctuations and reduce the adverse welfare consequences arising out of such fluctuations. A few studies conducted exclusively on India recorded episodes of pro-cyclical behaviour, based on which questions on the government's ability to smooth out cyclical swings had arisen. If this conclusion is validated in a more detailed study then it could be argued that fiscal policy may have fallen far short of the potential it has to stabilize output. Theoretical literature identifies various reasons ranging from credit constraints, lack of strong institutions, social pulls, political pressures, and corruption, for the presence of pro-cyclicality.

Without trying to empirically verify any competing hypotheses, Krishnan and Vaidya address the pro-cyclicality issue in general. Using data from the 'Economic and Functional Classification' of the budget over the period 1950–1 to 2008–9 they use various components of government expenditure as a measure of fiscal policy. They define a cycle using the Bry-Boschan idea that is quite popular in business cycle literature and then quantify pro-cyclicality by measuring the degree of synchronization of the two cycles. The results show that fiscal policy has been generally a-cyclical over the period of study, with most of the major expenditure components showing a-cyclicality. The exception to this finding is that the expenditure component of total grants, especially grants to states and grants to others, exhibits pro-cyclical behaviour. This evidence shows that the fiscal policy has not been blatantly pro-cyclical as has been the case with many developing countries. On the whole, this finding suggests that we still lack a fiscal policy design that encourages a counter-cyclical policy. Graduating from an a-cyclical fiscal stance to a counter-cyclical stance is an important challenge that the Indian economy will have to face in the coming decades.

SECTORAL ISSUES

In this section, we examine sectoral issues. These cover agriculture, industry and trade, finance, energy, and urban sectors.

Agriculture

Agriculture remains a very crucial sector for inclusive and sustainable growth of the Indian economy as it employs 51 per cent of the total workforce, and 46 per cent of the total geographical area. Though the share of agriculture and allied sectors in GDP has declined steadily from 38.8 per cent in 1980–1 to 14.2 per cent in 2010–1, the fact that approximately 41.8 per cent of the rural population lived below the poverty line in 2004–5 emphasizes the need for high growth in the agriculture sector. S. Mahendra Dev and Vijay Laxmi Pandey (Chapter 6) examine the performance and key policy issues in Indian agriculture.

The overall performance of agriculture and its allied sectors was not up to the mark during 2000–1 to 2010–11, considering the fact that much emphasis was laid on this sector from 2005 onwards. The trend suggests that the growth rate of this sector was only 2.79 per cent during this period. However, Indian agriculture has been showing signs of revival since the mid-2000s due to different initiatives taken by the government. However, there are still significant spatial and temporal differences in the performance of agriculture in different states. The states which were doing very well before the reforms are showing signs of stagnation or deceleration in the post-reform period, especially Haryana, Punjab, Tamil Nadu, and Andhra Pradesh. However, Gujarat recorded a remarkable growth rate in the 2000s which may be partly attributable to the development of good infrastructure.

For achieving more inclusive, faster, and sustainable growth along with 4 per cent growth in the agriculture sector during the Twelfth Five Year Plan, there is a need to give more emphasis on issues related to land and water management, rainfed agriculture, agricultural markets, new and improved technologies, and investment in agriculture. Therefore, what is required is developing land lease markets and widespread plans for developing degraded land, adopting integrated farming systems, adopting best practices, and rationalizing input subsidies. Nevertheless, to revitalize rainfed agriculture, a comprehensive programme is required at the local level with active participation of all the stakeholders. For efficient and equitable management of water, water user's associations should be formed in line with participatory irrigation management. The strategies so far have concentrated on rice and wheat in irrigated areas. Future growth will need to rely on a dual strategy of diversification into non-cereal high-value crops like pulses, fruits, vegetables, milk, and meat and focusing on rainfed areas, small farmers, and the eastern regions which have tremendous untapped potential.

An analysis of sectoral linkages provides valuable insights into policies to decide on priority sectors for injecting stimulation. G. Mythili and Nitin Harak (Chapter 7) examines these linkages using the Social Accounting Matrix (SAM) multiplier analysis. SAM multipliers give both direct and indirect linkages and this study computes SAM multipliers for three periods—1997–8, 2003–4, and 2006–7. The results show that agriculture is the most influential sector in generating output and income in the other sectors and in household income. A unit of exogenous expenditure in the industry and services sectors respectively generated a paltry 0.25 and 0.30 in the agriculture sector, whereas a unit injection in the agriculture sector generated a significant 0.77 and 0.79 respectively in the industry and services sectors for 2006–7. This implies that the slowdown of agriculture is going to affect the overall growth in the long run despite the declining share of agriculture in total GDP. That service sector growth could not influence household income to the same extent that agriculture did is consistent with earlier findings that employment growth in the services sector is far behind the sector's own growth and studies have questioned the sustainability of service sector growth per se.

A temporal comparison of the multipliers reveals a declining trend in most of the multipliers; income multipliers decline sharply when we move from 2003–4 to 2006–7. Declining multipliers over time indicate that the economy, particularly agriculture, could not take full advantage of the service sector boom to enjoy spillover benefits. Hence the policy should focus on ways to increase the efficiency of the agriculture and industry sectors by appropriate use of services, including IT. Strengthening rural infrastructure, credit delivery, expansion of irrigation, and phasing out of misdirected subsidies are some of the measures for improving agriculture growth directly. Among the industry sub-sectors, agro-processing is emerging as the most significant one for output multipliers, GDP multipliers, and income multipliers. Addressing the constraints in this sector would not only help in the expansion of the sector to meet increasing demand, but will also strengthen the forward linkages of agriculture. The scope of this empirical exercise is limited. Mythili and Harak indicate that due to the limitations of SAM, the results should be treated at most as indicative.

Industry and Trade

A process of reorientation of India's industrial policy framework began during the 1980s, which gained further momentum during the 1990s. The reforms were aimed at removing several barriers to entry imparted by the controlled regime. The policy changes included the dismantlement of the industrial licensing system, dereservation of industries for the public sector, relaxing of restrictions on industrial investment and expansion, disinvestment of government equity in public sector enterprises, and opening up of industries for foreign direct investment (FDI). The quantitative restrictions on importing capital goods and intermediates were completely removed in 1992, although the ban on importing consumer goods continued, with some exceptions, until the late 1990s.

It was held that industrial and trade reforms would stimulate a more competitive environment leading to higher efficiency and growth in the industrial sector. India's industrial value added grew at a rate of about 6 per cent per annum during the 1980s and 1990s and at a rate of 8.5 per cent during 2000–10.[8] Clearly, this performance is better as compared to India's past record but pales in comparison with the performance recorded by the East Asian Newly Industrialized Economies (NIEs) and China (Weiss 2011).[9]

It is well known that China followed the conventional pattern of growth shifting labour from agriculture to labour-intensive manufacturing. By contrast, India seems to be skipping the intermediate stage of industrialization and directly moving to the final stage of services-led growth. During the last two decades (1990–2010), the share of manufacturing in India's GDP has remained low in the range of 14–17 per cent as against 30–33 per cent in China. International comparisons suggest that manufacturing's actual

---

[8] Industry includes mining, manufacturing, electricity, gas, water, and construction.

[9] India's average industrial growth rate during 1970–80 was 4.4 per cent.

share of GDP in India is lower than what is predicted while the opposite is the case in China (ADB 2007). Further, in contrast to employment-intensive growth in China, India's manufacturing growth followed a relatively capital-intensive path. Lack of dynamism in labour-intensive manufacturing has considerably slowed down the process of transferring the large pool of India's surplus labour from agriculture into the well paying modern sectors. Thus, Indian growth has not been effective in reducing poverty on the scale that was possible in China and in other industrialized countries in East Asia.

In this context, the chapter by K.V. Ramaswamy and Tushar Agrawal (Chapter 8) analyses the growth and structure of employment using the National Sample Surveys (NSS) carried out in 1999–2000 and 2009–10. The analysis throws light on the future role of manufacturing and services as providers of employment to large numbers joining the labour force. They do not find any acceleration in service sector employment growth relative to manufacturing in urban areas. The good news is that young males have increased their share of regular employment both in manufacturing and services. However, compared to manufacturing, the services sector exhibits a greater degree of duality in terms of the incidence of informality and wage inequality. Further, the services sector is relatively more skill demanding and hence the higher skilled workers in the services sector have experienced greater increases in their real wages. The skill composition of the workforce is markedly different between the two sectors with services clearly skill biased. Social security conditions are not found to be relatively much superior in services. The results strongly suggest that the services sector is an unlikely destination for the millions of low-skilled job-seekers. India needs to focus on the manufacturing sector to provide large-scale employment.

Drawing upon the experience of China's export success in manufacturing, C. Veeramani (Chapter 9) provides some explanations for the lacklustre performance of this sector in India. The chapter highlights certain idiosyncrasies pertaining to the pattern of specialization, structure of trade, and the nature of inward foreign direct investment in Indian manufacturing. In contrast to China, the pattern of India's industrial specialization is disproportionately biased towards capital and skill-intensive industries. While India's import substitution policy regime created a bias in favour of capital and skill-intensive manufacturing, the reforms since 1991 have not been comprehensive enough to remove this bias. Though the post-1991 policy changes have gone a long way towards product market liberalization by easing entry barriers, factor markets (labour and land) are still plagued by severe distortions and policy-induced rigidities. Arguably, government interventions in factor markets have had the unintended consequence of creating a bias in the incentive structure against labour-intensive manufacturing. Trade liberalization by itself does not guarantee specialization in line with a country's comparative advantage if other policies militate against the efficient pattern of resource allocation.

Veeramani notes that a high level of vertical specialization-based trade, which occurs when countries specialize in particular stages of a good's production sequence rather than in the entire good, has been an important factor in driving Chinese export growth. China, through specialization in labour-intensive processes and product lines, has successfully integrated its manufacturing sector with the global production networks. Inward FDI has been instrumental in integrating China's manufacturing with global vertical production chains. A bulk of FDI flows to China's manufacturing sector has been export promoting in nature, which represents international fragmentation of the production process by multinationals. In contrast, due to its idiosyncratic specialization, India has been locked out of the vertically integrated global supply chains in manufacturing industries. Inward FDI into India is primarily market seeking rather than export promoting. Vertical specialization has been discouraged in India on account of restrictive labour laws, inefficient infrastructure, a burdensome regulatory environment, an inefficient land acquisition process, and poor trade facilitation.

Financial Sector

A well-functioning financial sector is essential for growth and macroeconomic stability. India has undertaken some important financial reforms since 1991 with a view to reducing 'financial repression' and for promoting financial development which results in more efficient allocation of funds and connections between savers and investors. Wide-ranging policy changes have been undertaken in the areas of banking, equity market, and the foreign exchange market (Mohan 2005; Reddy 2002). Along with liberalization, a number of measures have also been undertaken to develop a regulatory mechanism that will ensure the safety and solvency of the financial sector in the deregulated environment. During the post-reform period, there have been noticeable improvements in competitiveness, efficiency, and productivity of the Indian financial system (Mohan 2005).

However, the Committee on Financial Sector Reforms (formed in 2009), headed by Raghuram Rajan, makes a strong case for a new generation of financial sector reforms. The report submitted by the committee notes that 'the financial sector is not able to meet the scale or sophistication of the needs of large corporate India, as well as of public infrastructure, and does not penetrate deeply enough to meet the needs of small and medium-sized enterprises in much of the country'(p. 1).[10]

Substantial success has been achieved in building India's equity market during the last two decades while the debt market remains one of the least developed financial markets in the country. Renuka Sane and Susan Thomas (Chapter 10) discuss some issues related to 'borrowing of Indian firms'. Borrowing takes place based on future prospects of firms, and is not just based on collateral. Big firms borrow from the bond market, while banks lend to borrowers who are unable to access the bond market. A substantial scale of debt capital comes into the country from abroad, as foreign investment in rupee denominated debt. The chapter analyses Indian evidence for large companies and finds substantial failures on all three fronts (bond market, bank finance, and foreign investment). Borrowing by Indian firms takes place in a difficult institutional environment, with a poorly functioning financial system. This has far-reaching consequences for the economy, including areas such as competition policy and infrastructure investment.

Energy Sector Issues

Managing India's energy situation is a critical challenge for sustaining the process of economic growth. It is important to reduce the energy intensity of GDP while simultaneously taking steps to increase energy supply from both conventional and non-conventional sources. Achieving these objectives requires important reforms in the area of energy pricing, regulation, and incentives.[11] Reforms in these areas should be carried out in a phased manner while at the same time minimizing the adverse impacts on vulnerable groups.

Vinod Kumar Sharma, in his contribution (Chapter 11), argues that biomass energy offers a sustainable alternative compared to other forms of energy and highlights the importance of promoting biodiesel production from tree-borne oils. The Indian biodiesel industry is still in its early stages as compared to the ethanol industry. However, the demand for diesel is about five times higher than that for petrol, and thus more attention is required on increased biodiesel production. Promotion of biomass energy, if implemented judiciously, would result in substantial economic and social gains through reduction in imports of fossil fuels, generation of large-scale employment, energy security through renewable energy forms, and reduction in the overall environmental impacts of energy generation. Utilization of waste lands for biofuel plantations would augment the land resources and would not have any adverse effect on arable land used for food crops. Also, since no edible oils are used as feedstock for biodiesel production, the debate on 'food versus fuel' may not be of much relevance for India.

Sharma also reports the findings from a field survey of biofuel plantations and biodiesel producers from three sites in Andhra Pradesh. The case study found a visible increase in employment and income of individuals employed in jatropha and other oil tree plantations. However, the companies involved in biodiesel production reported shortage of supply of oil tree seeds and, to sustain production, they are using various other feedstocks such as animal fat and waste oils. This defeats the basic purpose of the national biofuel policy (biodiesel production using jatropha and other tree oils) and the problem needs to be tackled on an urgent basis.

To achieve its objective of sustainable and equitable development, India needs to substantially expand the supply of modern affordable energy services to all its citizens while at the same time maintaining an environmental and social balance. The chapter by B. Sudhakara Reddy (Chapter 12) highlights that the policies should aim at improving accessibility and affordability of modern energy services to the poor. In India, even as recently as 2010, only 65 per cent of the households had electricity connections and 70 per cent had no access to gaseous fuels for cooking. As many as 37 per cent of the total primary energy used by the household sector comes from non-commercial fuels such as fuel wood and dung. Despite growing attention to energy access, investment in energy services in India remains low.

Reddy's paper develops a framework for improving the availability, accessibility, and affordability of modern energy services. The framework envisages that social entrepreneurs at the grassroots facilitate large-scale diffusion of sustainable energy technologies.[12] The government should encourage local entrepreneurs on energy service delivery. It should also try to cooperate with local authorities, local bodies in charge of energy development, the private sector (in particular small and medium-sized enterprises), local micro-finance institutions, and civil society organizations. Access to modern energy services can thus be provided through a micro-enterprise energy service delivery system with the government providing the necessary infrastructure. This can

---

[10] The *Report of the Committee on Financial Sector Reforms* is available at: http://planningcommission.gov.in/reports/genrep/report_fr.htm. Last accessed on 6 August 2012.

[11] See Ahluwalia (2011) for a discussion on the importance of rationalizing the prices of various energy items (electricity, diesel, LPG, kerosene, and coal) and of adopting non-price measures to improve energy efficiency.

[12] The technologies that can be considered are gaseous fuels (LPG and biogas) for cooking, and electricity (centralized and decentralized) for lighting. They are relatively easy to deploy leading to a 'win-win-win' situation (where the entrepreneur gets profits, consumers get modern energy services, and society gets a clean environment).

result in reliable, high-quality, sustainable, and continuous access to modern energy carriers.

Urban Sector Issues

Continuation of high economic growth implies that the urban percentage of India's population is expected to increase significantly during the coming decades. According to the 2011 Census, about 31 per cent of India's population lives in urban areas. The urban percentage of India's population is expected to reach about 40 per cent by 2030, implying an increase in the urban population from about 377 million today to around 600 million. Opportunities in urban areas for employment, education, etc. have been pull factors attracting a large number of migrants from rural to urban areas, which results in urban sprawls and increasing number of slums.

The existing urban infrastructure is quite inadequate to face the challenges posed by the rising population in cities. The Jawaharlal Nehru National Urban Renewal Mission (JNNURM) is a central government programme for transferring resources from the centre to the states on the condition that the states and the municipalities undertake specific reforms in urban governance and finances. The programme aims to improve the coverage and supply of urban infrastructure, tackle the problem of urban slums through resettlement and other measures, and provide basic services to the urban poor. To date, however, the programme has produced mixed results. There have been difficulties in the proper implementation of the programme due to the lack of implementation capacity at the city level and due to a reluctance on the part of the states to undertake reforms.

In this context, the chapter by Sudhakar Yedla (Chapter 13) presents an overview of the coverage of basic civic and environmental services in Indian cities. His analysis covers services such as water supply, sanitation, and solid waste management. While assessing the coverage and quality of these civic services, the chapter attempts to identify the gaps between the present situation and global standards, assesses various initiatives employed for their improvements, and finally suggests a way forward for achieving better civic and environmental services in the urban centres in the country. The chapter argues that water and sewage tariffs are an important means of augmenting the financial capabilities of the cities in the country. It is important to enforce a differentiated and equitable fee for solid waste collection. This will not only strengthen the financial position of the city administration but also will induce the citizens to generate lesser waste.

The process of 'exclusionary' urbanization is said to take place when there is forced or market-driven deprivation of a section of urban residents from basic urban amenities such as clean water, affordable housing, sanitation, sewage facilities, as well as legal citizenship in the cities and large urban settlements. The chapter by S. Chandrasekhar and Ajay Sharma (Chapter 14) reports a number of indicators supporting the argument that urbanization in India is exclusionary. In a scenario where cities are unwelcoming of migrants and there is an anaemic employment growth in the agricultural and non-farm sectors, an alternative, albeit effective, livelihood strategy is commuting daily from rural to urban areas for work. Another aspect of mobility is migration, which is of various types—temporary, permanent, return, and short-term. The chapter focuses on the different forms of mobility and provides their estimates based on data from official sources.

Chandrasekhar and Sharma also identify key knowledge gaps. First, we need to understand how the sources of income of rural households in India have changed over time. We need to be able to quantify the importance of remittances by migrants and the economic contributions of commuting workers as a source of income. Second, we need to understand why estimates of various types of migration flows, in particular short migration flows, captured by official data are at variance with localized studies. It is important to identify and plug the source of this disconnect. Third, we do not fully understand the extent to which rural–urban migration contributes to the phenomenon of urbanization of poverty. And finally, given the concern over exclusionary urbanization we need to understand the legal and structural impediments to migration.

POVERTY, INEQUALITY, AND HUMAN DEVELOPMENT

This section examines performance and issues relating to poverty, inequality, and human development. According to some scholars, alleviation of absolute poverty is more important than reduction in inequality for a developing country like India.[13] This view refers to the work of Simon Kuznets who says that with economic growth inequality increases initially and declines over time (the famous 'inverted U' curve hypothesis). Many others say that inequalities matter and reduction in inequalities is important for higher growth, reduction in poverty, higher human development, and reduction in macro vulnerabilities.[14]

---

[13] For example, see Tendulkar (2010) for such a view.
[14] For a view on why inequalities matter for reduction in macro vulnerabilities, see Seth (2012). Also see Nagaraj (2012) on inequalities in India.

Poverty and Inequality

Durgesh C. Pathak and Srijit Mishra (Chapter 15) dwell on two aspects. First, they critically discuss the new method of measuring poverty that was suggested in the *Report of the Expert Group to Review the Methodology for Estimation of Poverty* (Government of India 2009). In doing so, they raise some concerns implicit in the report. One concern is the need to go beyond calories to have an understanding of nutritional requirements, which could not be adequately addressed in the new method. Another concern is the need to incorporate expenditure on health, education, and sanitation, as these are not being adequately provided by the state, which also raises serious apprehensions on whether India is a welfare state. Yet another concern is the need to come up with multi-dimensional measures of poverty, which has not been done in the report. Despite these and some other concerns, the chapter contends that the approach followed in the report is out of pragmatic considerations that would give some reasonable comparisons across sub-groups and over time. Nevertheless, it purports that some additional information could have been put in the public domain to take the debate beyond the poverty line.

The second aspect dealt by Pathak and Mishra is using the new poverty lines to compute its incidence, depth, severity, and inequality across states and some other sub-groups as also sectoral and growth-inequality decompositions at the aggregate all-India level for 2004–5 and 2009–10. Among the old hotspots of BMORU (undivided Bihar, undivided Madhya Pradesh, Odisha, Rajasthan, and undivided Uttar Pradesh), Rajasthan and Uttarakhand have moved out and Assam has come in. Madhya Pradesh and Odisha show considerable reductions, but it is the increase of incidence in Bihar (which otherwise seems to have done well during this period) that raises curious eyebrows. The seven major states (Chhattisgarh, Assam, Bihar, Madhya Pradesh, Odisha, Uttar Pradesh, and Jharkhand) with high incidences are referred to as CABMOUJ (pronounced *kab mouj*, which in Hindi means 'when to relax'). There seems to be an increase in urbanization of poverty. Four Northeastern states and two smaller union territories have also shown some reversals in poverty reductions. An analysis across caste, occupations, religion, land size, and gender shows the usual expected patterns, but of concern is greater vulnerability of children (0–14 years age group) and increasing poverty levels in the higher education groups. Appropriate planning and implementation will require complementing this information with quantitative and qualitative information at the district and sub-district levels.

Taking us away from the domain of absolute deprivation to relative deprivations, Sripad Motiram and Vamsi Vakulabharanam (Chapter 16) examine the changes and patterns of inequality in India since the 1990s using NSS data on consumption expenditure. In this process, they update and build upon their contribution to the previous issue of the *IDR 2011*. They look at both inter-personal (vertical) inequality and inter-group (horizontal) inequality, that is, among sub-groups of the population. In terms of inter-personal inequality, they find a rising trend in inequality since the 1990s at the rural, urban, and all-India levels. However, in the most recent period (from 2004–5 to 2009–10), the changes are less pronounced—rural inequality has reduced whereas urban inequality and inequality at the all-India level have increased slightly.

Motiram and Vakulabharanam also attempt to get a disaggregated perspective by looking at the performance of individual states in the period 2004–5 to 2009–10. During this period, many states saw a decline in rural inequality; on the contrary many states also saw an increase in urban inequality, and the all-India picture is mixed, with some states witnessing an increase and the others witnessing a decrease. Based on this disaggregated perspective, they suggest that growth is associated with increases in inequality, that is, states that are witnessing higher growth rates in real consumption expenditure are also the ones witnessing higher rates of increase (or lower rates of reduction) in inequality.

Moving to horizontal inequality, Motiram and Vakulabharanam use a decomposition of a Theil index and consider the social group (caste), sector (rural-urban), and state. They observe the following: Social group inequality has reduced during recent times (2004–5 to 2009–10) and is even lower than what it was in 1993–4. Sectoral inequality has also reduced during recent times but continues to remain higher than what it was in 1993–4. It is a matter of serious concern that inter-state inequalities have been steadily increasing between 1993–4 and 2009–10. A related work by Vakulabharanam (2010) also points to widening inter-class inequalities. Overall, their findings suggest that inter-personal inequality, regional inequality (both sectoral and inter-state inequalities), and class-based inequalities could pose challenges for the future.

Human Development

M.H. Suryanarayana and Ankush Agrawal (Chapter 17) seek to quantify the loss in human development due to inequalities in the different dimensions of human development across states in India. This is done using the methodology to estimate a new index called the Inequality-adjusted Human Development Index (IHDI) proposed in the *Human Development Report 2010* (UNDP 2010). With appropriate revisions in the goalposts with reference to the Indian context, inequality-adjustment parameters are estimated using information from different NSS rounds and the life tables on relevant variables.

Suryanarayana and Agrawal provide useful policy insights for a strategy seeking to promote human development by a distributive policy option that is addressing inequalities across dimensions in different states in the country. They show substantial loss in human development due to inequalities in different dimensions across states. The potential loss due to inequalities is the highest in education among the three dimensions. The fact that the inequalities in the education dimension are the highest is in consonance with the findings in the global context. It calls for a focus specifically on areas and social groups that continue to face constraints in accessing education. Similarly, the inequalities are staggering in the case of health. In both education and health, not only is the attainment of the people low but the extent of inequality, too, is high. Given the spectacular growth that the country has witnessed in the last decade, policies promoting economic growth need to be integrated with distributional dimensions of education and health.

The issues of concern for education as a whole are currently one of access, equity, inclusion, and quality. Keeping this in the background Preet Rustagi (Chapter 18) focuses on elementary schooling since it forms the base of the educational edifice. Efforts to ensure universal elementary education have recorded gains amidst many gaps and challenges. The Right of Children to Free and Compulsory Education Act (RTE), 2009, which provides for education to all six to 14-year-olds as an entitlement calls for a serious consideration of where we stand today in the context of elementary education that shows persistence of inequalities across locations, social groups, and between gender.

The requirements for meeting RTE goals are laid down in a roadmap. Even if the requisite financial and physical allocations are made, Rustagi rightly raises concern on whether the norms and standards can be met leading to quality education outcomes. For instance, the mechanics of training teachers may occur and generate a number of trained teaching personnel, but ensuring that this results in quality education and improving learner achievements calls for a different input need which is dynamic and creative. Similarly, involving mechanisms for motivation and incentivization as well as governance to improve the effectiveness of provisioning and delivery are critical for enhancing the quality of education. Equally important are issues such as the value of children as labour versus affordability of education. Or, for that matter the relational dynamics between different agents like students, parents, teachers, officials, and the management. Focus on governance, teacher training, pedagogy, and cohesive understanding among different agents regarding educational quality is essential.

Another important aspect of human development is public health, which was last discussed in the *India Development Report 2004–5* (Mishra 2005). The three broad issues addressed there are still relevant. First, India faces the dual burden of communicable and non-communicable diseases and the latter also affect the poor adversely. Second, being a state subject, there are wide variations across states in the public provisioning of health services and as a result the poorer states are hard-pressed. Third, India is among the few countries with only two-sevenths of the expenditure being publicly funded on health in 2010; the remaining being largely out-of-pocket expenditure with an increasing reliance on unregulated private caregivers that mushroom on supplier-induced demand.

Access to, utilization, and quality of care particularly for the poor and the sick remain important concerns. Given these, it is laudable that the *High Level Expert Group Report on Universal Health Coverage for India* takes a people-centric view towards 'Ensuring equitable access for all Indian citizens, resident in any part of the country, regardless of income level, social status, gender, caste or religion, to affordable, accountable, appropriate health services of assured quality (promotive, preventive, curative and rehabilitative) as well as public health services addressing the wider determinants of health delivered to individuals and populations, with the government being the guarantor and enabler, although not necessarily the only provider, of health and related services' (Planning Commission 2011: 3). The report suggests substantive reforms in six critical areas—health financing and financial protection, health service norms, human resources for health, community participation and citizen engagement, access to medicines, vaccines and technology, and management and institutional reforms. What is more, many of these concerns have been articulated by members of the Expert Group and their collaborators in a series of scientifically peer-reviewed articles that also culminated in a call for universal healthcare (Reddy et al. 2011).

OTHER EMERGING ISSUES

In this section, we deal with two other emerging issues—corruption and climate change.

Corruption

Corruption is increasingly being challenged as unacceptable. The Asia Pacific Human Development Report of 2008 focuses on this (UNDP 2008). Public debate in India is also divided between those who demand a powerful national institution to prosecute corruption and those who want to continue with the existing decentralized system, albeit after reforms. The best case for a national anti-corruption ombudsman (lokpal) is to show that the existing ombudsmen (lokayuktas) in the states are performing satisfactorily. And even otherwise an assessment of their performance should inform the design of the proposed national institution. However, there has been no systematic effort by either the Parliament or civil society to evaluate the experience of the existing anti-corruption agencies in the states. P.G. Babu, Vikas Kumar, and Poonam Mehra (Chapter 19) examine the role of a provincial ombudsman in Karnataka between 1995 and 2011. Their analysis shows that tackling corruption requires a fundamental restructuring of both the core administrative functions of the government, which account for more than 80 per cent of cases of corruption, and the criminal legal system, which accounts for almost the entire delay in prosecution of corruption. It also shows that at present the design of anti-corruption ombudsmen leaves a lot to the personality of the lokayukta and presents an incentive structure that does not support a sustained drive against corruption.

Climate Change

Climate change is a global environmental problem which has been receiving increasing attention at national and international levels. Climate change is already having an impact on the lives of the people, particularly the poor. This is evident in a number of ways. Consistent warming trends and more frequent and intense extreme weather events such as droughts, cyclones, floods, and hailstorms have been observed across many countries of the world.

Who is responsible for green house gas (GHG) emissions? If we see the cumulative emissions (during 1900–2005) which are responsible for current rise in global temperatures, the US accounts for 30 per cent followed by EU with 25 per cent. India accounts for less than 2 per cent of the total cumulated emissions. In 2005, out of the total GHG emissions, North America accounted for 18 per cent followed by China (16 per cent) and EU (12 per cent). India's share was 4 per cent (GoI 2012). If we compare per capita emissions in 2008, US had 18 CO_2 tonnes while China and India respectively had 5.30 CO_2 tonnes and 1.52 CO_2 tonnes (GoI 2012). These figures indicate that mainly developed countries contributed to global GHG emissions. In other words, unsustainable consumption patterns of the rich industrialized nations have led to accumulation of GHGs.

However, India should be concerned about climate change because of its adverse impact on the country. A vast majority of the population depends on climatic sensitive sectors like agriculture, forestry, and fishery for livelihood in the country. The adverse impact of climate change in the form of declining rainfall and rising temperatures and thus increased severity of droughts and flooding, would threaten food security and livelihood in the economy. For example, rise in temperatures will affect wheat yields.

India has prepared a document the 'National Action Plan on Climate Change' (NAPCC). It provides a direction for changes at the national level in policy, planning, and public–private partnerships and lays out a global vision for modifying longer time trends for sustainable development. Successful adaptation coupled with mitigation holds the key to food security and livelihoods for the twenty-first century in India.

For the first time, a new chapter on 'Sustainable Development and Climate Change' has been added to the recent Economic Survey 2011–12 of the Government of India. This chapter throws light on the impact of climate change on India, the current state of global negotiations, and India's voluntary actions. Apart from adopting the National Action Plan on Climate Change, India has announced 'a domestic goal of reducing the emission intensity of its GDP by 20–25 per cent of the 2005 level by 2020' (GoI 2012: 291–2). States have also been asked to prepare state-level action plans on climate change. India has to undertake many adaptation and mitigation policies in order to tackle the climate change problem. There are also synergies between adaptation and mitigation policies.[15]

Global cooperation is important for solving climate change related problems. The issue of climate change is an important agenda at the national and global levels. The Rio summit in 1992 linked development and poverty to the environment. Internationally, setting up of the United Nations Framework Convention on Climate Change (UNFCCC) in 1992 was a landmark for putting in place institutions and processes for effective action by different countries of the world. The main objective of the FCCC (convention) is to stabilize GHGs and prevent global warming and other climate changes.

The convention prepared the ground for international action, which led to the adoption of the Kyoto Protocol in 1997. According to the Kyoto Protocol, a target is set for developed countries (individually or jointly) to reduce overall emissions by an average of 5 per cent below 1990 levels in the first commitment period (2008–12). All major countries except the US have ratified the Kyoto Protocol. Many developed countries are going to miss the first commitment period targets by the end of 2012.

The Durban climate change conference (Conference of Parties, Cop 17) was held in November–December 2011. This is an important step in climate change negotiations.

---

[15] See Dev (2011) for adaptation and mitigation policies in agriculture in the context of the Asia–Pacific region.

A significant outcome of the Durban conference was establishing a second commitment period for the Kyoto Protocol which will begin on 1 January 2013 and end either in December 2017 or December 2010. In Durban, the world recognized India's spirited defence of the developing countries in ensuring that the objectives of social and economic development will not be compromised (GoI 2012).

Rio+20 United Nations Conference on sustainable development was held in Rio in June 2012. The focus of the conference was on a 'green economy'. The Rio+20 summit is a disappointment as far as negotiations on climate change are concerned. There was no progress in the negotiations in the commitments made by developed countries. Now it is also doubtful whether the developed countries will deliver the committed funds because of the global financial crisis. However, India and other developing countries should keep on putting pressure on the developed countries to honour their commitments, keeping in view their historical responsibilities.

WHAT NEXT?

After big bang reforms in the early 1990s, India followed a gradual approach in policymaking during the reform period. Now, second generation reforms have to be undertaken. There is a need to have measures in order to have a medium-term sustained growth of 8 to 9 per cent in the next two decades. High growth is also necessary for inclusive growth. We should move towards achieving 'faster, more inclusive and sustainable growth'. A lot of progress has been made in all the sectors in the post-reform period. But, among others, there are five disappointments which are inter-related: (1) Slow infrastructure development; (2) Failure in increasing the labour-intensive manufacturing sector; (3) Not taking advantage of demographic dividend by enhancing vocational training and skills; (4) Slow social sector development and; (5) Governance failures. These need the attention of policymaking.

REFERENCES

Acharya, Shankar and Rakesh Mohan (2010), *India's Economy: Performance and Challenge, Essays in Honour of Montek Singh Ahluwalia*. New Delhi: Oxford University Press.

Ahluwalia, Isher and I.M.D. Little (eds) (2012), *India's Economic Reforms and Development: Essays for Manmohan Singh*. Second edition. New Delhi: Oxford University Press.

Ahluwalia, Montek (2011), 'Prospects and Policy Challenges in the Twelfth Plan', *Economic and Political Weekly*, 46(21): 88–105.

Asian Development Bank (ADB) (2007), *Asian Development Outlook*. Manila: ADB.

Bhagwati, Jagdish and Arvind Panagariya [eds] (2012), *India's Reforms: How They Produced Inclusive Growth, Studies in Indian Economic Policies*. New Delhi: Oxford University Press.

Dev, S. Mahendra (2008), *Inclusive Growth in India, Agriculture, Poverty and Human Development*. New Delhi: Oxford University Press.

———. (2011), 'Climate Change, Rural Livelihoods and Agriculture (with a focus on food security) in Asia–Pacific Region', Working Paper No. 2011-14. Mumbai: Indira Gandhi Institute of Development Research (IGIDR).

———. (2012), 'Inclusive Growth: Focus on Productive Jobs', *Economic Times*, 8 June.

Drèze, Jean and Amartya Sen (2011), 'Putting Growth in its Place: It has to be but a means to development, not an end in itself', *Outlook* magazine, 14 November 2011. Available at: http://www.outlookindia.com/article.aspx?278843, last accessed on 16 August 2012.

Economic Advisory Council [EAC] (2012), *Economic Outlook, 2012/13*. New Delhi: EAC to the Prime Minister, Government of India.

Government of India [GoI] (2009), *Report of the Expert Group to Review the Methodology for Estimation of Poverty*. New Delhi: Planning Commission, (Chairperson: Late Suresh D. Tendulkar).

———. (2012), *Economic Survey 2011–2*. New Delhi: Ministry of Finance.

Jalan, Bimal (2005), *The Future of India: Politics, Economics and Governance*. New York and New Delhi: Viking and Penguin.

Mishra, Srijit (2005), 'Public Health Scenario in India', in Kirit Parikh and R. Radhakrishna (eds), *India Development Report 2004–05*. New Delhi: Oxford University Press, pp. 62–83.

Mohan, Rakesh (2005), 'Financial Sector Reforms in India: Policies and Performance Analysis', *Economic and Political Weekly*, 40(12): 1106–21.

Nagaraj, R. [ed.] (2012), *Growth, Inequality and Social Development in India: Is Inclusive Growth Possible?* UK: United Nations Research Institute for Social Development, Palgrave Macmillan.

Papola, T.S. and P.P. Sahu (2012), 'Growth and Structure of Employment', ISID Occasional Paper Series, 2010/01, New Delhi.

Planning Commission (2011), *High Level Expert Group Report on Universal Health Coverage for India*. New Delhi: Public Health Foundation of India.

Rangarajan, C. (2009), *Monetary Policy, Financial Stability and Other Essays*. New Delhi: Academic Foundation.

Reddy, Y.V. (2002), 'Dimensions of Financial Development, Market Reforms, and Integration: The Indian Experience', in Montek S. Ahluwalia, Y.V. Reddy, and S.S. Tarapore (eds), *Macroeconomics and Monetary Policy: Issues for a Reforming Economy*. New Delhi: Oxford University Press, pp. 282–306.

Reddy, K.S., V. Patel, P. Jha, V.K. Paul, A.K. Shiva Kumar, and L. Dandona (2011), 'Towards Achievement of Universal Health Care in India by 2020: A Call to Action', *The Lancet*, 377 (9767): 760–8.

Seth, Anuradha (2012), 'From Crisis to Resilience: Why Inequality Matters', *The Hindu*, 8 August, Chennai.

Subbarao, D. (2012), 'India, Macro economic Situation: Assessment and Prospects', Lecture delivered at Indian Merchant Chambers, 19 June, Mumbai.

Tendulkar, S.D. (2010), 'Inequality and equity during rapid growth process', in S. Acharya and Rakesh Mohan (eds), *India's Economy: Performance and Challenges*. New Delhi: Oxford University Press, pp. 82–99.

Tendulkar, S.D. and A. Bhavani (2007), *Understanding Reforms: Post 1991 India*. New Delhi: Oxford University Press.

United Nations Development Programme [UNDP] (2008), *Tackling Corruption, Transforming Lives: Accelerating Human Development in Asia and the Pacific*. Delhi: Macmillan.

———. (2010), *Human Development Report 2010—The Real Wealth of Nations: Pathways to Human Development*. Basingstoke and New York: Palgrave Macmillan.

Vakulabharanam, Vamsi (2010), 'Does Class Matter? Class Structure and Worsening Inequality in India', *Economic and Political Weekly*, 45(29): 67–76.

Weiss, John (2011), *The Economics of Industrial Development*. UK: Routledge.

2

Macroeconomic Overview
The Growth Story

*Manoj Panda**

INTRODUCTION

Macroeconomic developments in India during the last two decades reveal several strengths and weaknesses of the economy. The India growth story is now well-known and is no more disputed. Gross domestic product (GDP) grew by about 6 per cent on a long-term basis during the last two decades. The best phase in growth was witnessed during 2003–8 when the annual average growth stood at about 8.5 per cent. India has been among the fastest growing economies in the world during the last decade. Savings and investment rates have risen close to those noticed in the fast-growing East Asian economies. The Indian economy has been closely integrated with the global economy after the reforms as is evident from the rising share of trade and capital flows in relation to the size of the economy. Substantial foreign investment flows reflect the strong fundamentals of the economy as perceived by global investors. On the weaknesses side, the growth trajectory, particularly that of the industrial sector, has been uneven. Fiscal and trade deficits have remained high in recent years reflecting somewhat fragile macroeconomic stability. There has also been a feeling of disquiet among several sections of the population because of rising economic disparities and slow progress in poverty reduction.

The growth witnessed in the post-reform era has helped India's per capita income to cross the $1,000 mark a few years ago to graduate to lower middle-income status by international comparisons. It is now recognized that going by the total size India is steadily progressing on the path to becoming a major economy in the world. India occupies the ninth position by size in global ranking at $1.7 trillion in nominal terms and the fourth position at $4.2 trillion in purchasing power parity (PPP) terms. It is, however, important to remember that India still has a long way to go to meet the world average living standard. Compared to the global average, its per capita income is way below at one-seventh in nominal dollar terms and one-third in PPP terms. India continues to face challenges of mass poverty, high illiteracy, and lack of basic healthcare for a large section of its population. An important implication of the inclusion of India in the lower middle-income category in global ranking is that most of the poor in the world now live in middle-income countries instead of in low-income countries. With China's impressive record on the poverty reduction front, about a third of the world's poor now live in India.

The global financial crisis did have its effect on the Indian economy as was reflected in reduced growth in 2008–9.

---

* The author is grateful to the team of discussants and other participants at a seminar organized at IGIDR and in particular to K.L. Krishna for very useful written comments. He would also like to thank Sai Manohar for help in preparing several tables and figures, and to C. Ravi and Venkata Narayan for useful discussions.

The economy revived partially in the next two years, but dropped again in 2011–12. The government is currently attempting to revive business sentiments to induce private investors to raise activity levels. Against this backdrop, this chapter reviews the major macroeconomic developments in India in recent years from a medium-term perspective.[1] The next section discusses growth in national income by broad sectors. The section that follows deals with developments in the sphere of selected macroeconomic policies. The last section makes an assessment of the Indian growth process.

NATIONAL INCOME GROWTH

Table 2.1 shows the average annual growth in India's real GDP by three broad sectors—agriculture, industry, and services as well as the total for various decades since the 1950s. Triggered by an expansionary fiscal policy and limited reforms, the Indian economy moved to a higher growth path of 5.6 per cent during the 1980s from an average rate of 3–4 per cent per annum during the three decades prior to 1980. Although there was a high growth phase with annual growth rates ranging between 6.4 and 8.1 per cent during 1994–7, GDP growth on an *average basis* during the first decade after the initiation of economic reforms was only slightly higher than those during the 1980s.[2] A breakthrough occurred in the decade 2002–12, when annual GDP growth averaged above 7.5 per cent. On a medium-term basis, the best performance in national income growth was witnessed during 2003–4 to 2007–8 when it averaged 8.7 per cent and was rated as the second highest in the world, next only to that of China.

A major feature of the growth process during the last three decades is that fluctuations have narrowed down considerably (Figure 2.1). The year-to-year variations in GDP were very large till the 1970s ranging between -5 to +10 per cent. It is important to note that the annual growth rate has not been negative since 1980–1 and has in fact exceeded 4 per cent since 1992–3, clearly reflecting a new growth path of the economy. This has largely been due to the underlying changing structure of the economy away from agriculture to non-agriculture as is now discussed.

Table 2.1 Growth in Real GDP (% per annum)

Period	Agriculture	Industry	Services	GDP
1950s	2.7	5.6	3.9	3.6
1960s	2.5	6.3	4.8	4.0
1970s	1.3	3.6	4.4	2.9
1980s	4.4	5.9	6.5	5.6
1990s	3.2	5.7	7.3	5.8
2000s	2.5	7.7	8.6	7.2
X Plan (2002–7)	2.4	9.2	8.8	7.6
XI Plan (2007–12)	3.3	6.7	9.9	7.9

Source: Central Statistical Organization.

The most important feature of the pattern of India's growth story is that it is mostly driven by the steady expansion of the services sector during the last three decades. It grew by 9–10 per cent during the Tenth and Eleventh Five Year Plan periods (Table 2.1). Agricultural growth was generally low at about 3 per cent per annum on a decadal basis except during the 1980s when the average growth stood above 4 per cent. The performance of industry has been moderate since the 1970s, growing at a rate close to that of GDP.

Composition

The sectoral composition of the Indian economy has changed considerably with a steady fall in the share of agriculture and rise in the share of the services sector. The share of agriculture in GDP fell drastically from about 55 per cent in 1950–1 to 14 per cent in 2011–12 (Figure 2.2). The share of industry (including construction), which was only about 14 per cent in the early 1950s, rose to 27 per cent in 1990–1, but has remained invariant since then. The composition of GDP has been continuously moving in favour of services, which now account for 59 per cent of GDP.

There has been an interesting debate on whether or not the Indian experience on the compositional shift in GDP is typical of international experience. The Kuznets–Chenery hypothesis on the pattern of growth has been that as the share of agriculture in GDP falls, the share of manufacturing picks up rapidly and that of services moderately till a country reaches a fairly high level of development, and after that a compositional shift takes place from manufacturing to services. The Indian experience seems to contradict this view. However, experience across countries since the 1970s indicates that the share of services has been rising faster than that anticipated by Kuznets or Chenery. For example, Virmani (2004) and Gordon and Gupta (2004) point out that the Indian experience is nearly in line with current international experience. In a more elaborate analysis, Kochhar et al. (2006) find that correcting for per capita income and

---

[1] This chapter is basically confined to growth-related issues and does not deal with developments in several critical areas such as poverty, inequality, and inflation since other chapters in this volume deal with them at length. It, of course, recognizes that these issues cannot be neglected in an assessment of the growth prospects of the economy.

[2] While the magnitude of the decadal average growth during the 1990s was similar to that during the 1980s, many observers have argued that the growth process during the 1990s was more sustainable than the one in the 1980s.

18 INDIA DEVELOPMENT REPORT

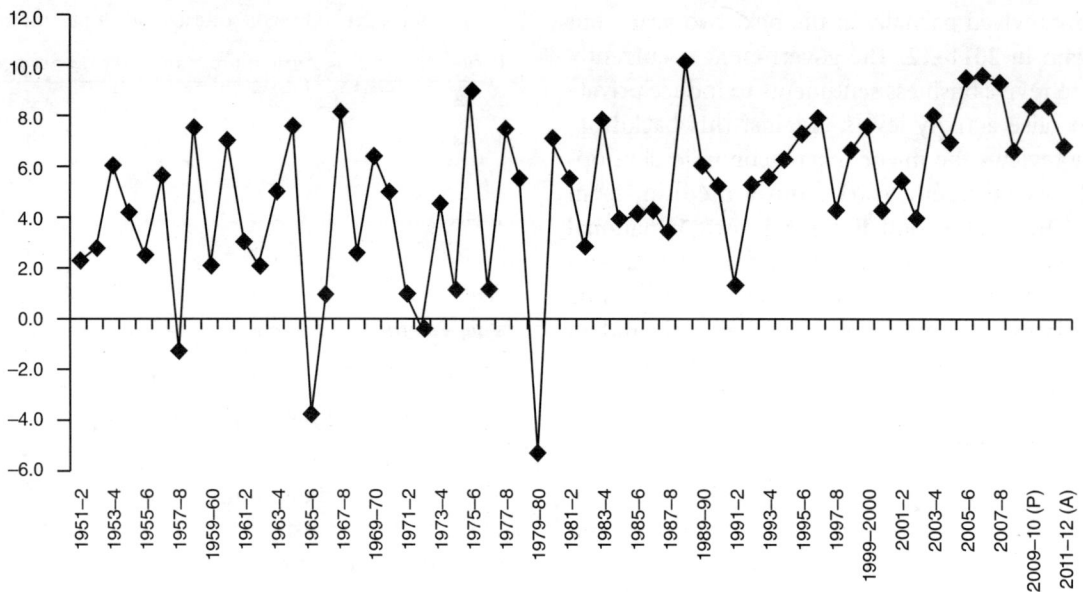

Figure 2.1 Annual Growth in Real GDP in India

Source: Central Statistical Organization.

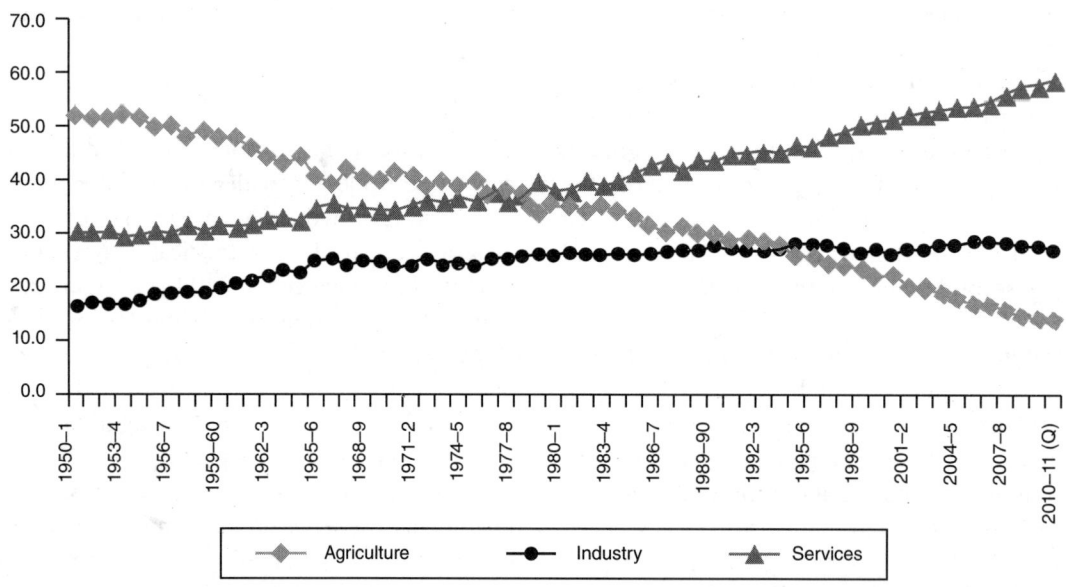

Figure 2.2 Share of Agriculture, Industry, and Services (in %)

Source: Central Statistical Organization.

size, India was not an outlier in manufacturing in 1981 but it was 3.6 percentage points below the norm in services in that year. However, they observe that the Indian industrial sector has performed poorly since the 1980s compared to other similar countries 'ironically when reforms were removing the shackles on manufacturing'. In the post-1980s period, service sector growth has been considerably high going by the global norm.

The performance of the industry and services sectors in India in creating jobs in line with international experience has been very disappointing. Papola and Sahu (2012) point out that elasticity of employment with respect to GDP was 0.56 during 1972–3 to 1983, but it fell by more than half to 0.20 during 1999–2000 to 2009–10. The services sector which is the main driver of growth in particular was not absorbing the rapidly growing proportion of the workforce.[3] A majority of the country's population continues to substantially depend on agriculture for their livelihood despite the rapid decline in the sector's share in GDP. As a result, the ratio of value added per worker in non-agriculture to that in agriculture rose from 4.5 in 1993–4 to 6.1 in 2009–10. Reducing this disparity will primarily depend on the ability of the non-agriculture sectors to absorb low skill labour from agriculture in the long run. In the medium run, however, higher agricultural growth will help reduce this disparity as well as correct the imbalances reflected in excess demand and the resulting relative price rise for agricultural produce.

Agriculture

The index number of food grain production has increased by about 2 per cent per annum since 1990 while the non-food grain component increased by 2.3 and 3.2 per cent during the 1990s and 2000s respectively (Figure 2.3). The increase in output can mostly be attributed to rise in yield per hectare rather than in the expansion of area, though there has been a shift in area from food grains to non-food grain crops (Table 2.2).

The relative shift in the cropping pattern is largely driven by changing demand patterns. Gross production of food grains increased from 176 million tonnes (MT) in 1990–1 to 241 MT in 2010–11. The corresponding growth rate of about 1.6 per cent per year was just about the population growth rate during this period. Per capita net availability of food grains has been fluctuating around 440 grams per day, despite a huge buildup of stocks, indicating a saturation point.

While the food grain growth potential will be limited due to an inelastic demand factor, growth potential in the non-food grains segment is large due to the high income elasticity of demand. Given the diversity in climatic conditions, India can produce a wide variety of high value and employment-intensive horticulture crops. Protein foods such as milk and meat are another area with good growth potential due to favourable demand patterns. Accounting for about a quarter of GDP in agriculture and the allied sector, livestock has recently emerged as an important sub-sector within it to supplement crop incomes and provide safeguards against large year-to-year fluctuations in farmers' incomes. The income generated in this sector gets more equitably distributed between and within households since livestock production activities are skewed in favour of small farmers and the women workforce in India.

Despite the falling share of agriculture in the national income, the role of agriculture in the Indian growth process continues to be significant for several reasons: improvement in the livelihood of a majority of the labour force, provision of food security to the increasing population, and meeting raw material demands of agro-based manufacturing.

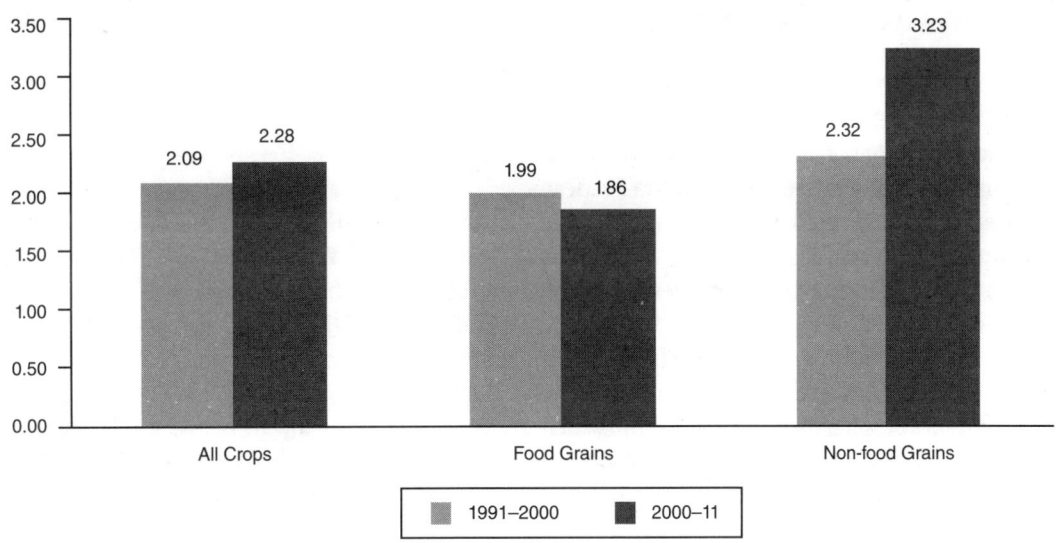

Figure 2.3 Average Growth Rate in Crop Agriculture

Source: Central Statistical Organization.

---

[3] It is interesting to note that, as per Bosworth and Collins (2007), the service sector in China accounted for 33 per cent of GDP and 31 per cent of the labour force in 2004.

Table 2.2 Index Number of Area and Yield
(Triennium ending 1981–2 =100.0)

Year	Area			Yield		
	Food Grains	Non-food Grains	All Crops	Food Grains	Non-food Grains	All Crops
1990–1	100.7	120.0	105.2	137.8	128.0	133.8
1995–6	97.3	132.6	105.4	145.6	137.0	141.8
2000–1	95.4	127.4	102.0	153.8	133.5	143.1
2001–2	95.5	127.6	102.9	164.8	138.9	153.4
2002–3	89.7	115.6	95.7	143.2	126.3	135.7
2003–4	97.3	125.4	103.8	165.3	151.2	159.2
2004–5	94.6	137.5	104.5	156.5	147.6	152.5
2005–6	95.8	140.9	106.2	176.7	163.5	180.6
2006–7	97.5	143.0	108.0	180.4	169.9	185.8
2007–8	97.7	144.7	108.6	191.1	170.9	190.5
2008–9	96.8	148.7	108.8	196.1	150.0	178.4
2009–10	95.6	143.4	106.7	184.7	157.8	179.4
2010–11	99.1	150.1	110.9	197.4	170.7	194.1

Source: Ministry of Finance (various issues).

Admittedly, agriculture growth rate will be lower than that of industry or services. But, the need to raise it from the current level cannot be denied given the various forms of stress emanating from this sector. Attaining a higher growth rate would require action on several fronts.

Both private and public capital formation in agriculture has shown increasing trends in recent years. Despite this increase in investment, agricultural growth has stagnated due to low profit margins relative to other activities. It is not viewed as a remunerative activity. The stagnation is best reflected in two recent facts: (a) about 40 per cent of the farmers would like to step out of agriculture given a choice, and (b) farmers in some districts of coastal Andhra Pradesh decided that observing a 'crop holiday' for the kharif season in 2011 best served their interests. Agriculture in many parts of the country is facing rising costs of land development, high paid out wage bills and other input costs, inadequate availability of credit, depletion in the water table in areas dependent on groundwater, and an obsolete tenancy system.

More focused attention is needed on several fronts such as irrigation, power supply, credit, technology, and land development. An analysis carried out by Chand (2010) shows that public and private investment played an important role in inducing more than half of the agricultural growth, while the rest was due to other factors such as fertilizer use, technology, terms of trade, and crop diversification. In a time series analysis, important emerging factors often get neglected. Growth of agriculture and the allied sector will require stronger linkages with agro-processing sectors and adoption of post-harvest technologies such as cold storage, refrigerated transportation, quality control, and certification to ensure food safety measures. Developing a competitive market value chain that could ensure a fair deal for the farmers will help them shift attention to commercial agricultural growth targeting domestic as well as exports markets. Institutional reforms are needed to provide a better deal to tenants even as property rights of landowners are safeguarded. Lastly, there is a need to better understand the behaviour of farmers by influential sections such as academicians and the media.[4]

Industry

Annual growth in the industrial sector has fluctuated widely varying between 2.5 and 12 per cent during the last decade (Table 2.3). The best phase was 2004–5 to 2007–8 when industrial GDP growth was above 9.5 per cent for four successive years. After a downturn to about 4.5 per cent in 2008–9, it peaked up to 7–8 per cent during the next two years, but fell again to below 4 per cent during 2011–12. The manufacturing sector, which accounts for close to 60 per cent of the industrial value added, has been the prime driver of industrial GDP growth. The construction sector, which contributes about a quarter of industrial GDP, grew at an average rate of 9 per cent during the period 2000–11

---

[4] For example, on the experience of Bt. Cotton in India, Herring and Rao (2012: 51) conclude: 'The Bt failure literature requires some explanation not only for its prominence, but also because it clashes so egregiously with farmer behavior.'

Table 2.3 Growth in Industrial GDP by Sub-sectors

Year	Mining & Quarrying	Manufacturing	Electricity, Gas, & Water Supply	Construction	Industry Total
1990–1	10.5	4.8	6.7	11.8	7.3
1995–6	5.9	15.5	6.8	6.0	11.3
2000–1	2.3	7.3	2.2	6.1	6.0
2001–2	1.9	2.3	1.8	4.0	2.6
2002–3	8.4	6.9	4.7	8.3	7.2
2003–4	2.7	6.3	4.6	12.4	7.3
2004–5	7.9	7.4	7.9	16.3	9.8
2005–6	1.3	10.1	7.1	12.8	9.7
2006–7	7.5	14.3	9.3	10.3	12.2
2007–8	3.7	10.3	8.3	10.8	9.7
2008–9 (R)	2.1	4.3	4.6	5.3	4.4
2009–10 (P)	6.3	9.7	6.3	7.0	8.4
2010–11 (Q)	5.0	7.6	3.0	8.0	7.2
2011–12 (A)	−2.2	3.9	8.3	4.8	3.9
Averages					
1990–9	4.9	5.8	7.3	5.6	5.7
2000–11	3.9	7.5	5.7	8.9	7.4

Source: Central Statistical Organization.

compared to 5.5 per cent in the previous decade. The mining and quarrying sector has been growing at an average rate of 4–5 per cent during the last two decades. The decline in average growth of 'electricity, gas and water' has been a matter of concern and industrialists have been complaining of supply bottlenecks on this count, particularly during the summer months when demand peaks up.

Table 2.4 gives summary statistics for the manufacturing sector in terms of average growth rate, coefficient of variation (CV), and weight by use-based classification. The capital goods and consumer durables sectors recorded the highest growth rate at 13 per cent per year during 1994–5 and 2011–12. The variability in annual growth rates was large for both the sectors. They together accounted for only about 17 per cent of the industrial output weight and so their contribution to overall manufacturing growth remained low. For high total manufacturing growth, attention must shift to basic goods, intermediates, and consumer non-durables which have registered average growth rates of 5–7 per cent only. Variability in annual growth as reflected by CV declined for all the sectors during 2003–12 over 1994–2003, except for consumer non-durables.

Services

Figure 2.4 depicts average growth rates for various service-related sectors during 2000–11. Communication continued to be the fastest growing component within the services sector with an average growth rate of about 25 per cent per annum followed by banking and insurance at about 11 per cent. A point to note here is that communication accounted for less than 1 per cent of GDP in 2000–1, but its contribution had risen to 4 per cent by 2011–12 in real terms. However, its share in GDP in nominal terms increased very little from 1.6 to 1.8 per cent during the same period as a result of falling relative prices. Gains to consumers accrued not only from high volume growth but also from a steep price fall due to removal of monopolies and introduction of fast technological changes.

Other segments of the services sector have been growing at 6–11 per cent on an annual average basis. The banking and insurance sector recorded strong growth at 11 per cent during 2000s. Trade, real estate, and business services (which include information technology) performed well with an average growth of 8–9 per cent during 2000–11. The strong performance of the services sector could be attributed to several factors: elastic household demand, intermediate demand by production activities, emerging comparative advantage in skilled labour, exploitation of potential in the export market, and technological changes.

Storage and public administration are two segments in the services sector where growth is relatively low. While downsizing the public administration has been a deliberate policy objective, developing storage facilities has recently

Table 2.4 Industrial Production by Use-based Classification: Average Growth Rates, Coefficient of Variation, and Weights

Year	Basic Goods	Capital Goods	Intermediate Goods	Consumer Durables	Consumer Non-durables
Average 1994–2003	5.39	6.68	7.31	10.44	6.52
Average 2003–12	6.06	19.30	6.47	17.03	6.07
Average 1994–2012	5.72	12.99	6.89	13.74	6.29
CV 1994–2003	0.550	0.718	0.651	0.811	0.541
CV 2003–12	0.343	0.640	0.531	0.483	0.865
CV 1994–2012	0.451	0.870	0.605	0.653	0.711
Weight 1993–4	35.57	9.26	26.51	5.37	23.30
Weight 2004–5	45.68	8.83	15.69	8.46	21.35

Source: Ministry of Finance (various issues).

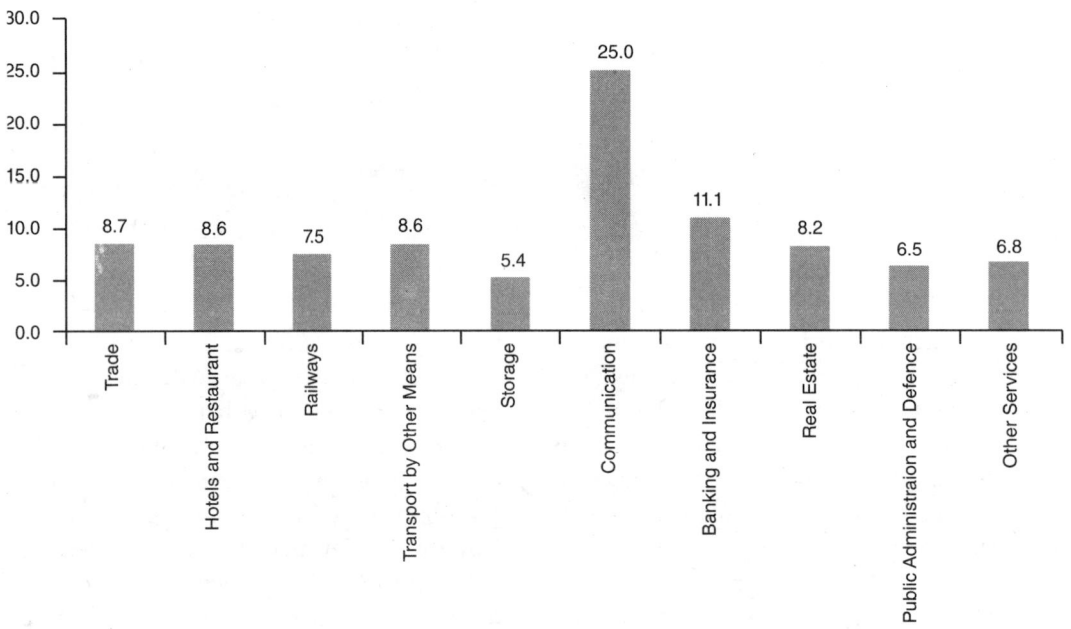

Figure 2.4 Average Growth of Various Service Sectors, 2000–11

Source: Central Statistical Organization.

become a policy priority. A country-wide network of storage facilities will complement road connectivity in integrating rural areas with a dynamic urban economy.

Factor Productivity

Several studies have attempted to analyse sources of growth using the growth accounting framework.[5] A general consensus that seems to have emerged is that there has been a significant rise in total factor productivity (TFP) in the Indian economy. According to Bosworth et al. (2007), TFP grew by 2 per cent per annum during 1980–2004 compared to a mere 0.2 per cent per annum during 1960–80. They estimate that the TFP rise contributed as much as 1.8 percentage points (75 per cent) of the 2.4 percentage points increase in the growth rate during 1980–2004 over 1960–80; agriculture, industry, and services accounted for 0.5, 0.3, and 1 percentage points, respectively, to the total TFP contribution. Thus, according to these studies, while the quantum of capital and labour used in the production process plays an important role in maintaining growth at the old rates, it is TFP that mostly accounts for the rise in growth rate.

---

[5] See, for example, Rodrik and Subramamanian (2005), Bosworth et al. (2007), and Goldar and Mitra (2010).

OTHER MACROECONOMIC DEVELOPMENTS

Savings and Investments

The gross domestic savings rate in India remained between 20 and 25 per cent of GDP for about a decade and a half since the late 1980s, but there has been a significant jump in recent years. It crossed 32 per cent in 2004–5, reached a peak of 36.8 per cent in 2007–8, and varied between 32 and 34 per cent during 2008–10 (Table 2.5). It may be noted that all sources of savings—household, private corporate, and public sector—contributed to this rise of about 10 percentage points of GDP. Public sector savings,[6] which were negative during 1998–2003, again turned positive after 2002–3, though this was highly volatile and significantly contributed to the variation in aggregate savings.

The behaviour of the rate of capital formation closely follows that of the domestic savings rate. It remained higher by 2–3 percentage points than the domestic savings rate reflecting the extent of reliance on foreign savings or net capital flows that go to finance the current account deficit.[7] The increase in total investment by about 10 percentage points since 2004–5 has been primarily due to private corporate investment (Chaudhuri 2010). The investment rate was affected by the global slowdown in 2008–9 by about 4 percentage points of GDP in 2008–9, but partially recovered in the following two years. As Figure 2.5 shows, it was the investment component in final demand rather than the consumption component that absorbed most of the real demand shock in India during the global crisis. Growth in real fixed investment dropped to as low as 3.5 per cent in 2008–9 as against 16 per cent in the previous year and remained low at 6–8 till 2011–12. This might be a critical factor constraining the revival of the economy in the medium term unless there is a compensating rise in productivity.

This jump in the savings rate in the 2000s helped India place itself among the high savings nations category that includes East Asian countries. The key role of investment

Table 2.5 Savings and Capital Formation (As % of GDP at Current Market Prices)

Year	Gross Domestic Savings				Gross Fixed Capital Formation				
	Household Sector	Private Corporate Sector	Public Sector	Total Savings	Public Sector	Private Sector	Total	Errors and Omissions	Adjusted Total
1995–6	16.2	4.8	2.6	23.6	8.6	17.5	26.1	−0.8	25.3
1996–7	15.8	4.4	2.2	22.4	7.8	14.3	22.1	1.6	23.7
1997–8	18.1	4.2	1.9	24.2	7.4	17.1	24.5	1.1	25.6
1998–9	19.5	3.8	−0.2	23.2	7.3	16.3	23.5	0.7	24.2
1999–2000	21.8	4.3	−0.5	25.7	7.7	18.5	27	−0.2	26.8
2000–1	21.4	3.7	−1.3	23.8	7.2	16.4	24.2	0.1	24.4
2001–2	23.2	3.3	−1.6	24.9	7.2	17.8	25.7	−1.3	24.3
2002–3	22.3	3.9	−0.3	25.9	6.5	18	25	−0.2	24.8
2003–4	23.2	4.6	1.3	29.0	6.6	18.7	26.2	0.7	26.9
2004–5	23.6	6.6	2.3	32.4	7.4	23.8	32.5	0.4	32.8
2005–6	23.5	7.5	2.4	33.4	7.9	25.2	34.3	0.4	34.7
2006–7	23.2	7.9	3.6	34.6	8.3	26.4	35.9	−0.2	35.7
2007–8	22.4	9.4	5.0	36.8	8.9	28.1	38	0.1	38.1
2008–9	23.6	7.4	1.0	32.0	9.4	24.8	35.5	−1.2	34.3
2009–10	25.4	8.2	0.2	33.8	9.2	25.2	36.1	0.5	36.6
2010–11Q	22.8	7.9	1.7	32.3	8.8	24.9	35.8	−0.7	35.1

Note: Q: Quick estimates; GDCF total includes (a) errors and omissions, and (b) valuables (introduced in the new series).

Source: Ministry of Finance (various issues).

---

[6] Public sector or government savings refers to revenue less current expenditure of the consolidated government; revenue includes surpluses of public enterprises passed on to the government.

[7] The Indian economy generated current account surplus for three years starting 2002–3.

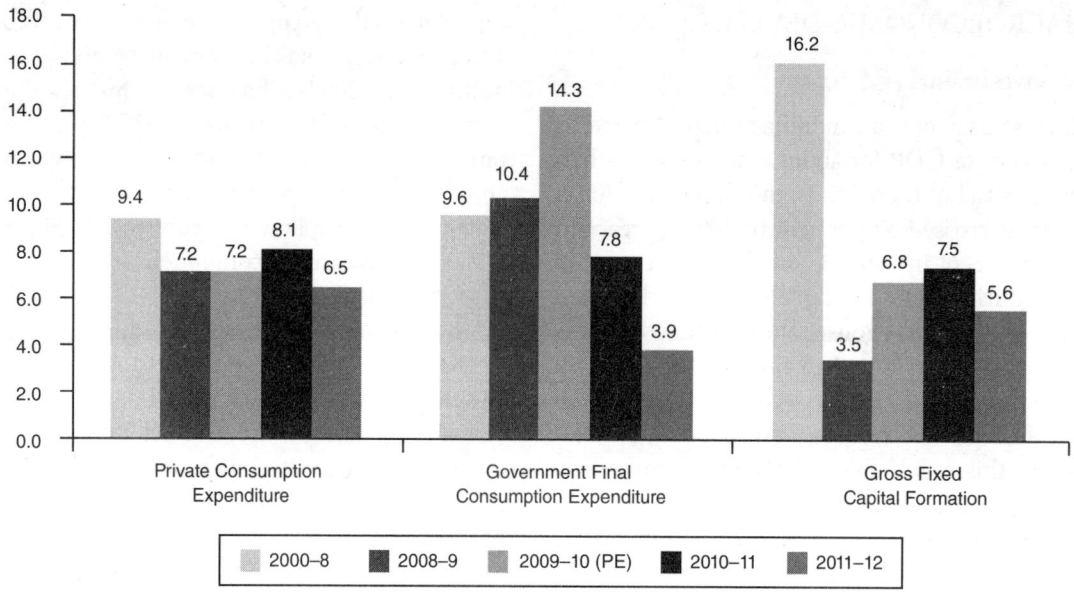

Figure 2.5 Annual Growth Rates in Demand Components
Source: Ministry of Finance (various issues).

in the GDP acceleration process is well known and has recently been reiterated by Basu and Maertens (2007) and Basu (2008). Given an incremental capital output ratio between 4 and 4.5, a capital formation rate of above 35 per cent of GDP will be required to realize the long-term growth potential of the economy at 8–9 per cent per annum. One might draw attention here to an alternative view. Robertson (2010) argues that capital has contributed relatively less to India's growth than it did to the East Asian economies due to the acceleration in productivity growth in India. Admitting that the increases in the investment rate have played an important role so far, he argues that 'a policy focus on further increases in investment would be misguided' leading to 'funding of projects with poor rates of return' (p. 120). More importantly, 'this may be at the expense of consumption for basic needs and spending on useful social projects' (p. 120).

Fiscal Developments

The expansionary fiscal policy followed by the government to combat the global crisis led to a faster increase in government expenditure compared to GDP growth. The total expenditure of the central and state governments in India rose to 29.2 per cent of GDP in 2010–11 from 25.8 per cent in 2006–7 (Table 2.6). The central government accounts for slightly more than half of the combined central and state government expenditures and the states together the rest. At the time of the global crisis, central government expenditure was already on an expansionary path in 2007–8 when it increased by 1.7 per cent of GDP over the previous year (Table 2.7). After the crisis, the centre reduced central excise duties by about 25 per cent in mid-2008–9 to raise effective demand in the economy. This rate cut as well as reduced GDP growth led combined government tax receipts to fall to 15.2 per cent of GDP in 2009–10 from 17.6 per cent in 2007–8.

As a result of these developments, the gross fiscal deficit of the centre and the states rose from a more comfortable level of 4.1 per cent of GDP in 2007–8 to as high as 9.4 per cent of GDP in 2009–10. This order of fiscal imbalance was similar to what had prevailed during the 1991 crisis. Fiscal deficit has continued to be high at about 8 per cent of GDP since 2008–9, causing great concern among policy-makers. There is also the danger that the continued high level of fiscal imbalance may get precipitated in an external balance of payments crisis in an open macro-economy environment.

The combined revenue deficit of the governments, which nearly got eliminated in 2007–8, has increased since then mostly on account of the central government's revenue receipts and revenue expenditure mismatch. One significant recent development has been disciplined budgetary management by state governments in checking the revenue deficit in response to legislative commitments in the Fiscal Responsibility and Budget Management (FRBM) Act. In fact, the states together succeeded in generating revenue surplus in 2006–7 and 2007–8 as indicated by the lower revenue deficit of the consolidated general government (Table 2.6) compared to that of the central government

Table 2.6 Receipts and Disbursements of Consolidated General Government (As % of GDP)

		1990–1	2000–1	2006–7	2007–8	2008–9	2009–10	2010–11 (RE)	2011–12 (BE)
I	Total receipts (A+B)	26.8	28.7	26.2	26.7	28.6	28.6	28.9	27.0
	A. Revenue receipts (1+2)	18.6	18.1	20.4	21.3	19.8	18.7	20.9	19.4
	1. Tax receipts	15.4	14.6	16.9	17.6	16.5	15.2	16.1	16.3
	2. Non-tax receipts	3.2	3.5	3.6	3.7	3.4	3.5	4.8	3.1
	of which interest receipts	1.1	0.9	0.5	0.5	0.4	0.4	0.3	0.3
	B. Capital receipts	8.2	10.5	5.8	5.4	8.7	9.8	8.0	7.6
	1. Disinvestment proceeds	0.0	0.1	0.1	0.9	0.0	0.4	0.3	0.5
	2. Recovery of loans and advances	0.6	0.5	0.0	0.1	0.2	0.2	0.1	0.1
II	Total Disbursements (a+b+c)	28.8	28.5	25.8	26.4	28.4	28.7	29.2	26.8
	a. Revenue	22.8	24.8	21.7	21.5	24.1	24.5	24.7	22.7
	b. Capital	3.9	2.9	3.7	4.5	3.9	3.8	3.9	3.8
	c. Loans and advances	2.0	0.9	0.4	0.4	0.4	0.4	0.6	0.4
III	Revenue deficit	4.2	6.6	1.3	0.2	4.3	5.7	3.8	3.3
IV	Gross fiscal deficit	9.4	9.6	5.4	4.1	8.4	9.4	7.9	6.9

Source: Ministry of Finance (various issues).

Table 2.7 Fiscal Parameters of Central Government (As % of GDP)

		1990–1	2000–1	2006–7	2007–8	2008–9	2009–10	2010–11	2011–12 (RE)	2012–13 (BE)
A	Total expenditure (1+2)	18.49	15.49	13.59	15.29	15.83	15.64	15.60	14.80	14.81
	1. Revenue expenditure	12.91	13.22	11.99	11.92	14.22	13.92	13.56	13.04	12.77
	(a) Interest payments	3.77	4.72	3.50	3.43	3.44	3.25	3.05	3.09	3.18
	2. Capital expenditure	5.58	2.27	1.60	2.37	1.61	1.72	2.04	1.76	2.03
B	Revenue receipts									
	(a) Gross tax revenue (a1 + a2)	10.10	8.97	11.03	11.90	10.84	9.53	10.33	10.12	10.70
	a1. Direct tax	1.90	3.30	5.40	6.30	6.00	5.80	5.81	5.62	5.66
	a2. Indirect tax	8.20	5.67	5.63	5.60	4.84	3.73	4.52	4.50	5.04
	(b) Centre net tax revenue	7.54	6.50	8.18	8.81	7.94	6.97	7.43	7.21	7.66
	(c) Non-tax revenue	2.10	2.66	1.94	2.05	1.74	1.78	2.85	1.40	1.63
	3. Centre net revenue Receipt (b)+(c)	9.65	9.16	10.12	10.87	9.68	8.74	10.27	8.61	9.29
C	Capital receipts	6.85	6.38	3.36	3.43	6.16	6.90	5.33	6.19	5.51
D	Revenue deficit (1–3)	3.26	4.05	1.87	1.05	4.54	5.18	3.29	4.43	3.48
E	Gross fiscal deficit	7.84	5.65	3.32	2.55	6.04	6.39	4.87	5.86	5.10
F	Gross primary deficit	4.06	0.93	–0.18	–0.88	2.59	3.14	1.82	2.76	1.92

Source: Ministry of Finance (various issues).

(Table 2.7). A revenue surplus meant that state governments borrowed to meet capital or investment expenditure that helped in expanding the income generation capacity of the economy. Major steps need to be taken by the centre to urgently contain its revenue expenditure.

Foreign Trade

India could not take advantage of the considerable expansion in world trade during the 1970s and 1980s and its share in world exports in fact had come down from 0.6 per cent in

1970 to 0.4 per cent in 1980 due to the export pessimism outlook by policymakers. The foreign trade regime went through extraordinary changes during the economic reforms process in the 1990s and played a pivotal role in steering the new economic policy. Changes in trade volume and capital flows were the major driving forces in bringing about structural changes during the last two decades in the Indian economy.

The success on the trade front is best judged by the fact that exports expanded by 13-fold from US $19 billion in 1990–1 to $250 billion in 2010–11 and imports too by a similar order from $28 billion to $381 billion during these years (Table 2.8). Invisible transactions rose by about 20 times during the same period. These significant achievements also get reflected in relation to the growing size of the economy. Foreign trade transactions (exports and imports together), which accounted for 14.6 per cent of GDP in 1990–1, rose to 22.5 per cent by 2000–1, and 36.5 per cent in 2010–11 (Table 2.9). Adding invisible transactions of another 17.8 per cent, the total current account transactions currently form about 55 per cent of GDP. High trade deficit levels of above 7 per cent of GDP have been a matter of policy concern, though net invisible receipts have helped keep the current account balance under 3 per cent of GDP.

Foreign investments, which were virtually negligible in the early 1990s, rose to $50 billion in 2009–10 in net terms but dropped to $40 billion in 2010–11. Inflows on account of foreign investments were $289 billion and outflows $249 billion in 2010–11. Of these, foreign direct investment (FDI) was small with inflows of $33 billion and outflows of $7 billion in 2010–11. But, portfolio investments were fairly large with inflows of $253 billion and outflows of $221 billion in the same year. Receipts and payments of loans stood at $108 and $79 billion respectively in 2010–11. India has not succeeded in attracting large FDI inflows. A larger volume of FDI could play a stable role in promoting exports, market diversification, and technology transfer.

Another significant development worth noting has been overseas investment by Indian companies in sectors such as iron and steel, information technology, pharmaceuticals, and petroleum. Such investments, at times taking the form of controlling shares in some of the well-known global companies, have opened up new business opportunities as well as challenges for Indian entrepreneurs.

India's performance on the trade front may also be judged in relation to the volume of world trade. Indian exports and imports accounted for 0.5 and 0.7 per cent of global trade in 1990; but they accounted for 1.5 and 2.2 per cent of world trade in 2010, respectively. Yet, India continues to be a small player in world merchandise trade transactions. In exports of services, it played a larger role at the global-level ranking between second in computer and information services and twelfth in travel services in 2010.

Foreign exchange reserves, which had reached $309 billion by the end of 2007–8, dropped to $252 billion by

Table 2.8 Balance of Payments (US Dollar Billion)

		1990–1	2000–1	2005–6	2006–7	2007–8	2008–9	2009–10	2010–11 (PR)	2011–12 (P)
1	Exports	18.5	45.5	105.2	128.9	166.2	189.0	182.4	250.5	150.9
2	Imports	27.9	57.9	157.1	190.7	257.6	308.5	300.6	381.1	236.6
3	Trade balance	–9.4	–12.5	–51.9	–61.8	–91.5	–119.5	–118.2	–130.6	–85.7
4	Invisibles									
	a) Receipts	7.5	32.3	89.7	114.6	148.9	167.8	163.4	198.2	105.9
	b) Payments	7.7	22.5	47.7	62.3	73.1	76.2	83.4	113.6	53.0
	c) Net invisibles	–0.2	9.8	42.0	52.2	75.7	91.6	80.0	84.6	52.9
5	Current account	–9.7	–2.7	–9.9	–9.6	–15.7	–27.9	–38.2	–45.9	–32.8
6	Capital account (A to D)	7.2	8.5	25.0	46.2	107.9	7.8	51.6	59.0	38.5
	A) Net foreign investment	0.1	5.9	15.5	14.8	43.3	8.3	50.4	39.7	13.6
	B) Net external assistance	2.2	0.4	1.7	1.8	2.1	2.4	2.9	4.9	0.7
	C) Net commercial borrowing	3.3	4.9	6.2	22.7	38.5	5.9	9.6	23.5	16.5
	D) Others	1.6	–2.6	1.5	6.9	23.9	–8.8	–11.2	–9.1	–9.1
7	Overall balance (5+6)	–2.5	5.9	15.1	36.6	92.2	–20.1	13.4	13.1	5.7
8	Monetary movements	2.5	–5.9	–15.1	–36.6	–92.2	20.1	–13.4	–13.1	–5.7
9	Reserves (increase –/ decrease +)	1.3	–5.8	–15.1	–36.6	–92.2	20.1	–13.4	–13.1	–5.7

Source: Ministry of Finance (various issues).

Table 2.9 Major Foreign Trade Parameters (as per cent of GDP)

	1990–1	2000–1	2005–6	2006–7	2007–8	2008–9	2009–10	2010–11 (RE)
Export	5.8	9.9	13.0	13.6	13.4	15.6	13.2	14.5
Import	8.8	12.6	19.4	20.1	20.8	25.4	21.8	22.0
Trade balance	−3.0	−2.7	−6.4	−6.5	−7.4	−9.8	−8.6	−7.5
Invisible receipts	2.4	7.0	11.1	12.1	12.0	13.8	11.8	11.4
Invisible payments	2.4	4.9	5.9	6.6	5.9	6.3	6.0	6.4
Net invisibles	−0.1	2.1	5.2	5.5	6.1	7.5	5.8	5.0
Current receipts	8.0	16.9	24.0	25.6	25.4	29.3	25.0	25.9
Current account balance	−3.0	−0.6	−1.2	−1.0	−1.3	−2.3	−2.8	−2.6
Foreign investment	0.0	1.5	2.6	3.1	5.0	2.0	4.7	3.2
Debt–GDP ratio	28.7	22.5	16.7	17.5	18.0	20.5	18.0	17.3
Debt–Service ratio	35.3	16.6	10.1	4.7	4.8	4.4	5.5	4.2
Import cover of reserves (in months)	2.5	8.8	11.6	12.5	14.4	9.8	11.1	9.6

Source: Reserve Bank of India.

the following year due to the global crisis, recovered to the pre-crisis level towards the end of 2011, but fell again later. The reserves are currently adequate to provide imports a cover of about eight months while they provided a cover of about a year during 2005–8. This fall in reserves relative to imports in a scenario of rising world oil prices limits the Reserve Bank of India's (RBI's) options to intervene in the exchange market. India's external debt-GDP ratio at less than 20 per cent in recent years and debt service ratio in single digits seem comfortable.

Effects of the Global Crisis

A closer integration of India in the global market meant that Indian economy could no longer remain immune to major global economic developments. Policymakers who advocated that India might not be affected by the global economic crisis in 2008 quickly abandoned the 'decoupled' hypothesis as the crisis spread to several countries. Gains of coupling obviously went with associated costs as measured by reduced GDP growth.

There were several channels through which the crisis affected India. First, net foreign investment came down sharply by $35 billion in 2008–9 when many foreign investors reallocated their portfolios away from India to meet their domestic cash needs. It rebounded quickly in 2009–10 but fell again in the following year. It is worth noting that net portfolio investment turned negative and stood at $-14 billion in 2008–9 in the wake of the global crisis, causing concerns for policymakers. Stock market prices, which are closely correlated with the foreign institutional investment (FII) flows, fell sharply in 2008. The overall stock price index continued to be way below the pre-crisis level even after four years. Business sentiments have not recovered, fearing spread of contagion first in West Asia and later in the Euro zone where the crisis deepened during 2011–12.

A second channel through which the global crisis affected India was through reduction in exports growth. Exports were growing at 20–25 per cent prior to the crisis, but dropped to 13 per cent in 2008–9 and had an absolute fall by 3 per cent in 2009–10. Service exports in particular dropped by 9.4 per cent in 2009–10, though they bounced back in the following year. Contraction of exports demand affected aggregate demand and GDP growth in the economy.

Third, contraction of trade and capital flows in turn affected the exchange rate. Nominal exchange rate depreciated sharply from Rs 40.3 per dollar in 2007–8 to Rs 46 in 2008–9, and to Rs 47.4 in 2009–10, but appreciated to Rs 45.6 in 2010–11. The onset of the crisis in the Euro region again put pressure on the exchange rate with the rupee depreciating to above Rs 55 to a dollar in mid-2012. Real effective exchange rate (36-currency index) computed by the RBI also shows similar direction-wise movements.

The Union Government and RBI adopted several fiscal and monetary policy measures in response to the crisis. The government adopted an expansionary fiscal policy and reduced central excise duties by about 25 per cent to raise effective demand. Using a computable general equilibrium model, Ganesh-Kumar and Panda (2009) estimate that the total adverse effect of the global crisis on Indian GDP was potentially about 5 per cent and the government possibly neutralized about half of it through various fiscal measures.

One silver lining in this context is the diversification of the direction of trade which helped India to moderate the impact of the global crisis. The share of Asian and ASEAN countries in India's total trade rose from about a third to more than half while that of Europe and America fell considerably during the last decade. The US, which was India's top trading partner in 2007–8, now occupies the third position with UAE and China occupying the top two positions. Similarly, Indonesia, Korea, Iran, and Nigeria have entered as new major partners replacing Italy, Malaysia, France, and Australia. The success in diversification reflects the ability of Indian traders to make use of comparative advantages across countries in a changing world.

Regional Growth Pattern

In a large country such as India, the regional growth pattern is important for judging the well-being of the population. Figure 2.6 depicts the major states arranged by their per capita income in 2004–5 and the average growth rate in gross state domestic product (GSDP) attained by them during 2004–5 to 2007–8 and from 2008–9 to 2011–12. It is evident that GSDP growth dropped in most of the states after the global crisis. There are, however, some states such as Bihar, Madhya Pradesh, Assam, Rajasthan, and Jammu and Kashmir where GSDP performed better during the post-crisis period. Interestingly, these states also happen to be in the bottom half in per capita GSDP rankings. Two other states of Odisha and, to a lesser extent, Uttar Pradesh recorded reasonable growth rates in recent years. This is a welcome change in the development process of the country because of the concentration of a high incidence of poverty in these states.[8]

According to the DGCI&S data[9] for 2010–11, about two-thirds of India's exports originated from the five states of Gujarat, Maharashtra, Tamil Nadu, Karnataka, and Andhra Pradesh. These states whose production structure is relatively more export oriented have invariably been adversely affected.[10]

GROWTH PROSPECT—AN ASSESSMENT

The Indian economy has undisputedly moved to a higher growth path during the last three decades. The break point from the earlier 'Hindu rate' could be placed in the late 1970s to the early 1990s depending on whether one takes a purely statistical approach or looks for policy changes underlying the process to explain the break.[11] Limited reforms and an expansionary fiscal policy helped the economy to achieve an average growth rate of 5.5 per cent in the 1980s, but its sustainability was doubtful. Lack of resilience was evident when a macroeconomic crisis occurred in the wake of the Gulf War and the oil price rise in 1990 and 1991. The policies of the 1980s were associated with high levels of domestic and foreign debt leading to fiscal and balance of payments crisis.

Economic reforms initiated in 1991 were wide-ranging, involving abolition of the industrial licensing system, liberalizing trade, and unfreezing the exchange rate among others. The resilience of the economy as it developed in the post-reform period gets reflected in successfully meeting several challenges such as the East Asian crisis in the late-1990s, the Gulf War in early 2000, and severe drought in 2002. As discussed earlier, in the wake of the global economic crisis, economic growth in India slowed down considerably in 2008–9 and recovered partly in the next two years. World trade, which fell by about a quarter in 2009, has not yet recovered to the pre-crisis level of $16 trillion. With new signs of a deepening Euro zone crisis, the global economic scenario does not seem promising at present.[12] Yet, India continues to perform reasonably well in comparison to most other nations.

India looks forward to a considerably higher level of living in the next few decades. The average level of living prevailing in 1950–1 had doubled in 39 years (by 1989–90), but redoubled in the next 17 years (by 2006–7) due to higher growth. If India wants to raise its per capita income close to current world average levels, it will require a sustained increase in per capita level of living of above 5 per cent per annum (that is, a real GDP growth of at least 7 per cent per annum) for about three decades.

Attaining above 8 per cent growth consecutively for five years between 2003 and 2007 by the Indian economy attracted world-wide attention and many observers believed that India, like China, was riding on the high road of growth. The post-reform experience shows that India's growth path, unlike that of China, is going to be considerably uneven. Some analysts believe that the high growth story has come to an end and an average growth rate of 5–6 per cent might be more of a rule and see this as the 'new Hindu rate' of growth. Many others, however, are more optimistic and argue that conditions are ripe to maintain an average growth rate of 7–8 per cent as experienced in the last decade. The government has, in fact, targeted an even higher growth rate

---

[8] See the chapters on poverty in this volume for more details.

[9] See, Ministry of Finance (2011–12: 171). State of origin of exports data are as reported to customs without any validation check and hence should be taken as indicative.

[10] Kumar and Subramanian (2012) also found that the more globalized states took a bigger hit during 2008 and 2009.

[11] See, DeLong (2003), Virmani (2004), Rodrik and Subramanyan (2005), Balakrishnan and Parameswaran (2007), Basu (2008), and Panagariya (2008) among others.

[12] See, for example, IMF's *World Economic Outlook*, April 2012.

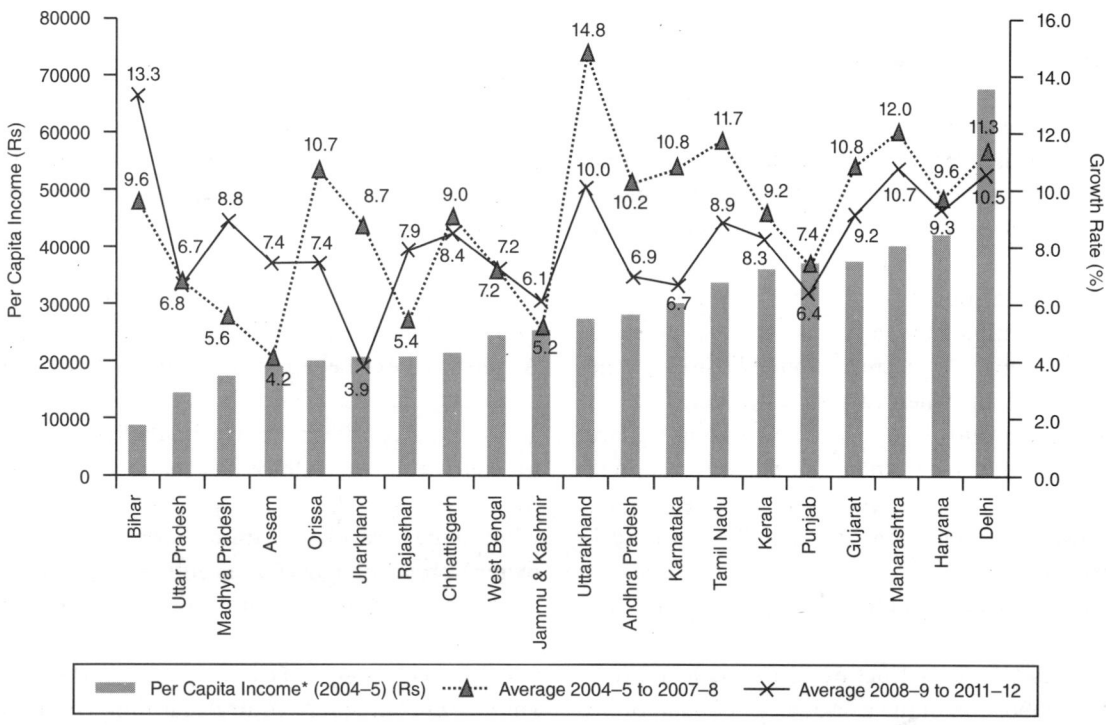

Figure 2.6 Per Capita GSDP 2004–5 and Average Growth Rates 2004–8 and 2008–12

Note: Data for 2011–12 were not available for Gujarat, Rajasthan, Madhya Pradesh, and Maharashtra.
Source: Central Statistical Organisation.

of 9 per cent during the Eleventh Plan and in the Twelfth Five Year Plan (approach paper). If the realized growth rate will be at the lower end of this spectrum during the 2010s, India's global positioning by GDP criteria might be delayed by a decade or so. Given that current global recessionary conditions might continue till 2013, it would be difficult to achieve a 9 per cent growth rate during the Twelfth Plan period of 2012–17. An average growth rate of 8 per cent could be in the feasible range with bold but mature policy responses.

In the absence of the revival of the manufacturing sector, a higher GDP growth rate cannot be achieved. Given that the nature of the Indian manufacturing sector has been 'idiosyncratic' (Kochhar et al. 2006), it is necessary to create an enabling environment for private investors to cope with business and financial risks in an unprotected environment and meet challenges of global competitiveness. Panagariya (2008) makes a persuasive case that large private firms will not enter into labour-intensive manufacturing without labour market reforms leading to a flexible exit policy. Policy initiatives must also be strengthened to close both physical and human infrastructure gaps, particularly in the backward regions. The Twelfth Five Year Plan approach paper recognizes the need for a new policy paradigm for the manufacturing sector so that manufacturing contributes to a quarter of GDP by 2025.

A number of structural factors have contributed to a higher growth rate in the last decade. The rise in the gross capital formation rate from 25 per cent of GDP to 38 per cent during 2002–8 played an important role in raising GDP growth during this period. As discussed earlier, it dropped by about 3 percentage points after the global crisis, mirroring a similar fall in domestic savings rate which was primarily due to a fall in government savings. Raising government savings will be a critical element in restoring savings and investment levels in the economy. This in turn will depend on: (a) rationalization and restructuring of government current expenditure, and (b) raising the volume of tax revenue. Non-merit goods subsidies such as those on oil or power once introduced are difficult to reduce or remove in a democratic setup. Yet, the need for a broad agreement among the major political parties on prioritizing the subsidies and limiting them to essentials such as food, drinking water, health, and education cannot be overemphasized for maintaining macroeconomic stability. Proper monitoring of the several welfare programmes, particularly the centrally sponsored schemes, is another area that can raise efficiency of the programmes and reduce expenditure.

India is often seen as having a soft government in so far as its tax mobilization efforts are concerned as the tax-GDP ratio has remained below 18 per cent. Going by international standards, there is certainly scope to raise this by a couple of percentage points to provide fiscal support to infrastructure and social sector programmes. Other steps include implementation of the goods and service tax (GST), reducing tax evasions, and expanding the tax base. Finally, the rights and entitlement approach by citizens for several public services must be accompanied by the willingness of society to pay for the services, particularly by those capable of doing so. An entitlement mindset without adequate and stable sources of funding is not viable in the long run. It cripples the government fiscal position in the future leading to a macroeconomic crisis, and the burden of adjustment, when carried out, often falls on the lower income groups in terms of downsizing welfare programmes. The entitlement attitude is evident even among rich households and the corporate sector. An emerging economy must develop growth-oriented social, political, and business norms.

Another factor that may contribute in pushing the long-term growth rate upwards is the so-called demographic dividend. The current age structure of the population is such that the proportion of the working age population to the total population is expected to increase in the coming decades. If the available labour force can be engaged in productive activities without a decline in productivity, it could be a source of additional growth. Creating appropriate employment opportunities for the fast-growing labour force with skill development that matches emerging demand patterns of a growing economy is a major challenge for deriving demographic dividends. Two points may be made in this connection. First, a faster and more stable expansion of labour-intensive industrial sectors, such as agro-processing, could be vital in absorbing the growing labour force since the labour absorption capacity of the services sector has been modest. Second, the working age population also happens to be the major saving class in an economy and the demographic dividend could potentially have a positive feedback effect on household saving rates.[13]

While reforms in the product market have been extensive, the factor markets have remained virtually untouched. Factor market reforms would be essential to fully realize the gains from economic reforms. Labour laws applicable to organized industry in India are too restrictive for the exit of non-viable industries and stand in the way of reallocating factors to take advantage of new technology and changing market conditions. Some of the labour laws meant to protect the interests of the working class in effect protect only a small segment of labourers already employed in the organized sector and go against the interests of the working class as a whole. It is necessary to develop a regulatory framework that permits closure of non-viable units within a reasonable timeframe so that unemployed resources can be re-employed in other productive uses. As Krishna (2012) points out, restrictive labour laws 'have not only reduced employment prospects in organized manufacturing but also constrained its growth by adversely affecting investment and productivity'.

Similarly, the land market is another area that needs immediate attention. Problems with the century-old Land Acquisition Act have recently attracted attention due to constraints faced by industry and a new land acquisition act is under consideration by the Parliament. A thin land market within agriculture has also been a constraint for the sector's growth. Developing a proper lease market will require a regulatory framework that protects a land-owner's property rights but incentivizes the introduction of technology and investment by ensuring tenancy certainty in the medium run. A proper tenancy registration system will also help tenants to claim benefits in the event of crop failures. Encouraging a contract farming system could help in developing linkages with agro-processing units. Similarly, opening up of the retail market to foreign players could help in developing supply chain and market linkages. The regulatory mechanism must ensure that both small and big players have access to the market on fair terms.

Lastly, the growth process must be broad-based so that benefits of growth are widespread. When the benefits accrue to a small group and large sections are left behind, social stability becomes the casualty and the growth process itself comes to a halt. Admittedly, some rise in inequality cannot be avoided in the early stages of development as is evident from the global experience.[14] But unchecked inequality could cause social problems such as those currently noticed in large parts of the tribal belt in the country. The fact that the Scheduled Tribe (ST) and Scheduled Caste (SC) groups have the highest incidence of absolute poverty means that there is a need to reorient welfare programmes towards the STs and SCs. But, ironically, many states are not utilizing even the mandated budgetary provisions under ST and SC sub-plans. The state must be an active agent in providing certain basic needs to all its citizens, particularly to those away from the mainstream. Without a new social contract towards this end, the growth process itself might be jeopardized. Developing a broad consensus for balancing the distributional objective with the growth objective requires innovative state craft.

---

[13] A point recognized by Basu (2008).

[14] See Panagariya (2008) and Weisskopf (2011) for two different views regarding policy focus on inequality.

REFERENCES

Balakrishnan, Pulapre and M. Parameswaran (2007), 'Understanding Economic Growth in India: A Pre-requisite', *Economic and Political Weekly*, 42(27–28): 2915–22.

Basu, Kaushik (2008), 'The Enigma of India's Arrival: A Review of Arvind Virmani's Propelling India: From Socialist Stagnation to Global Power', *Journal of Economic Literature* 46(2): 396–406.

Basu, Kaushik and Annemie Maertens (2007), 'The Pattern and Causes of Economic Growth in India', *Oxford Review of Economic Policy*, 23(2): 143–67.

Bosworth, Barry and Susan Collins (2007), 'Accounting for Growth: Comparing China and India', National Bureau of Economic Research, Working Paper No. 12943, Cambridge, MA.

Bosworth, Barry, Susan Collins, and Arvind Virmani (2007), 'Sources of Growth in the Indian Economy', National Bureau of Economic Research Working Paper No. 12901, Cambridge, MA.

Chand, Ramesh (2010), 'Achieving 4 per cent Growth on Agriculture during the Eleventh Five Year Plan: Feasibility and Constraints', in Pulin Nayak, Biswanath Goldar, and Pradeep Agrawal (eds), *India's Economy and Growth: Essays in Honour of V.K.R.V. Rao*. New Delhi: Sage Publications India Pvt. Ltd., pp. 69–86.

Chaudhuri, Saumitra (2010), 'How Realistic and Sustainable is India's Aspiration to Clock 10 per cent Growth?', India Policy Forum. New Delhi: NCAER.

DeLong, J. Bradford (2003), 'India since Independence: An Analytic Growth Narrative', in Dani Rodrik (ed.), *In Search of Prosperity: Analytic Narratives on Economic Growth*. Princeton and Oxford: Princeton University Press.

Ganesh-Kumar, A. and Manoj Panda (2009), 'Global Economic Shocks and Indian Policy Response: An Analysis Using a CGE Model', in Kirit S. Parikh (ed.), *Macro-Modelling for the Eleventh Five Year Plan of India*. New Delhi: Planning Commission, Government of India and Academic Foundation, pp. 119–90.

Goldar, Biswanath and Arup Mitra (2010), 'Productivity Increase and Changing Sectoral Composition: Contribution to Economic Growth in India', in Pulin Nayak, Biswanath Goldar, and Pradeep Agrawal (eds), *India's Economy and Growth: Essays in Honour of V.K.R.V. Rao*. New Delhi: Sage Publications India Pvt. Ltd., pp. 35–68.

Gordon, James and Poonam Gupta (2004), 'Understanding India's Services Revolution', IMF Working Paper No. WP/04/171. Washington DC: International Monetary Fund.

Herring, Ronald J. and N. Chandrasekhara Rao (2012), 'On the "Failure of Bt Cotton"—Analysing a Decade of Experience', *Economic and Political Weekly*, 47(18): 45–53.

International Monetary Fund (2012), 'World Economic Outlook April 2012: Growth Resuming, Dangers Remain', International Monetary Fund, Washington, DC.

Kochhar, Kalpana, Utsava Kumar, Raghuram Rajan, Arvind Subramanian, and Ioannis Tokatlidis (2006), 'India's Pattern of Development: What Happened, What Follows', Working Paper 12023. Cambridge, MA: National Bureau of Economic Research.

Krishna, K.L. (2012), '"Idiosyncratic" Industrial Development in India: Employment Implications', Dr Gorakh Nath Singh Memorial Lecture. Patna: A.N. Sinha Institute of Social Studies.

Kumar, Utsav and Arvind Subramanian (2012), 'Growth in Indian States in the First Decade of 21st Century: Four Facts', *Economic and Political Weekly* 47(3): 48–57.

Ministry of Finance (various issues), *Economic Survey*. New Delhi: Government of India.

——— (2012), *Economic Survey 2011–12*. New Delhi: Government of India.

Panagariya, Arvind (2008), *India: The Emerging Giant*. New York: Oxford University Press.

Papola, T.S. and P.P. Sahu (2012), 'Growth and Structure of Employment', ISID Occasional Paper Series, 2010/01, New Delhi.

Planning Commission (2011), *Faster, Sustainable and More Inclusive Growth: An Approach to the 12th Five Year Plan*. New Delhi: Government of India.

Robertson, Peter E. (2010), 'Investment Led Growth in India: Fact or Mythology?', *Economic and Political Weekly*, 45(40): 120–4.

Rodrik, Dani and Arvind Subramanian (2005), 'From "Hindu Growth" to Productivity Surge: The Mystery of the Indian Growth Transition', *IMF Staff Papers*, 52(2): 193–228.

Virmani, Arvind (2004), 'India's Economic Growth: From Socialist Rate of Growth to Bharatiya Rate of Growth', Working Paper No. 122. New Delhi: Indian Council for Research on International Economic Relations.

Weisskoff, Thomas (2011), 'Why Worry about Inequality in the Booming Indian Economy?', *Economic and Political Weekly*, 46(47): 41–51.

3

Propagation Mechanisms in Inflation
Governance as Key

Ashima Goyal*

INTRODUCTION

After an initial jump, the post-reform period saw inflation fall to unprecedented lows. The resurgence of inflation since 2007 has been associated with sharp food and oil price inflation. Food and oil prices are relative prices, but propagation mechanisms allow these to affect aggregate prices. Governance failures, broadly defined as dysfunctional systems that create poor incentives or narrowly defined as inappropriate government policies, are responsible for many of these propagation mechanisms.[1] Firm price-setting, the response to cost shocks, and the relationship between wages, prices, and the exchange rate are important dimensions of the inflationary process. In an open economy border prices impact domestic prices. Policies are inappropriate also to the extent that they are not based on these relationships.

This chapter analyses these understudied issues, including the contribution of demand and supply shocks to inflation, the policy response, and the growth inflation tradeoff. Recent high and persistent consumer price inflation may have been due to multiple supply shocks, so inflation may come down as the commodity cycle turns. Estimations of aggregate supply show the average price increase to be 10 per cent and the decrease only 5 per cent—so 5 per cent inflation is required to accommodate a relative price increase. This is an example of a propagation mechanism. Half of the Indian firms reset their prices in any period, and a little more than half are forward-looking in their price setting. Cost shocks have a larger impact on price compared to demand proxied by changes in money supply. Price inertia reduces the size of the monetary tightening that is required. A sharp rise in interest and exchange rates is a negative for highly leveraged firms.

Some relative prices such as food prices and the exchange rate have a greater impact on aggregate prices—requiring a prompt policy response, using a mixture of supply-side, tax, trade, and exchange rate policies. Multiple supply shocks are estimated to have caused inflation, but since they did not become persistent, second round price effects did not set in. So output remained below potential. Since prices rise more easily than they fall, a first round price increase following a supply shock had to be allowed. Supply shocks took the form of upward shifts of the elastic aggregate supply—they did not reduce a fixed capacity. Thus average costs rose, not the marginal costs that rise with output. Poor governance contributed to chronic costs creeping in at all levels of output.

---

* I would like to thank V.S. Chitre, Romar Correa, Kanagasabapathy, K.L. Krishna, and S.L. Shetty for very useful comments, Reshma Aguiar for secretarial support, and Sanchit Arora for research assistance.

[1] International agencies define governance broadly as accountability, stability, effectiveness, rule of law, and regulation. The World Bank has focused on these issues.

With such a structure, policy-induced demand tightening can anchor inflationary expectations and prevent a wage-price spiral that shifts up costs, but at a large sacrifice of output. This sacrifice in growth was large during past supply shocks and policy contraction generally exceeded the fall in output. Monetary and fiscal policies tend to expand and contract together. There was a large negative demand impulse over 2010–12, but the impact constrained growth more than inflation. Credit has grown at less than GDP ever since the global financial crisis.

The best policies are those that reduce average production costs. If propagation mechanisms can be reformed so that demand can support an elastic aggregate supply, sacrificing growth as well as inflation can fall. The analysis provides a new understanding of how supply constraints affect the economy.

SIZE AND PERSISTENCE

Inflation based on the Indian consumer price index (CPI) and wholesale price index (WPI) (Figure 3.1a) shows sustained divergence over 2008–10. CPI was high and persistent, while WPI and its components such as fuel and manufactured products were more volatile (Figure 3.1b). The divergence can be explained by the larger share of food (48.5 per cent) in CPI and of fuel (15 per cent) in WPI. Just as food prices rose, fuel prices crashed in July 2008. That, along with the slowdown following the monetary tightening of the summer, and the global financial crisis (GFC) that set in from the autumn, explain the negative WPI inflation in early 2009. But continuing high food prices and a quick recovery in oil prices led to the sharp resurgence of WPI inflation in early 2010 although demand, as reflected in the

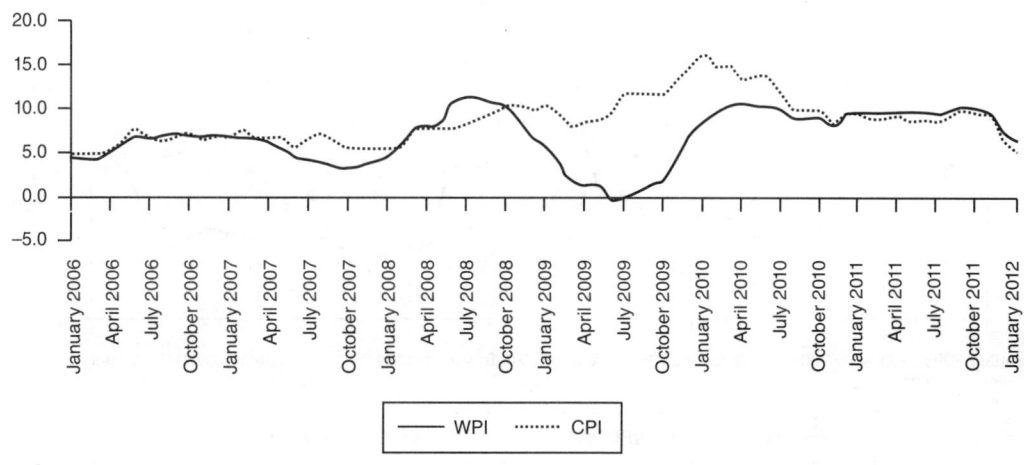

Figure 3.1a Inflation in WPI and CPI

Source: Reserve Bank of India, http://www.rbi.org.in; and Office of the Economic Advisor, http://eaindustry.nic.in. Last accessed in March 2012.

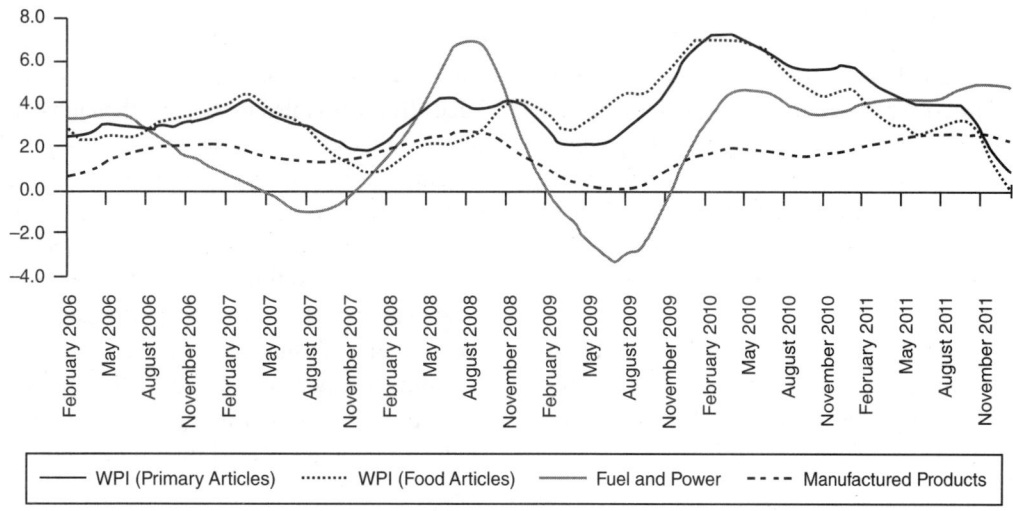

Figure 3.1b Inflation in the Components of WPI (Three Month Moving Averages)

Source: Office of the Economic Advisor, http://eaindustry.nic.in/. Last accessed in March 2012.

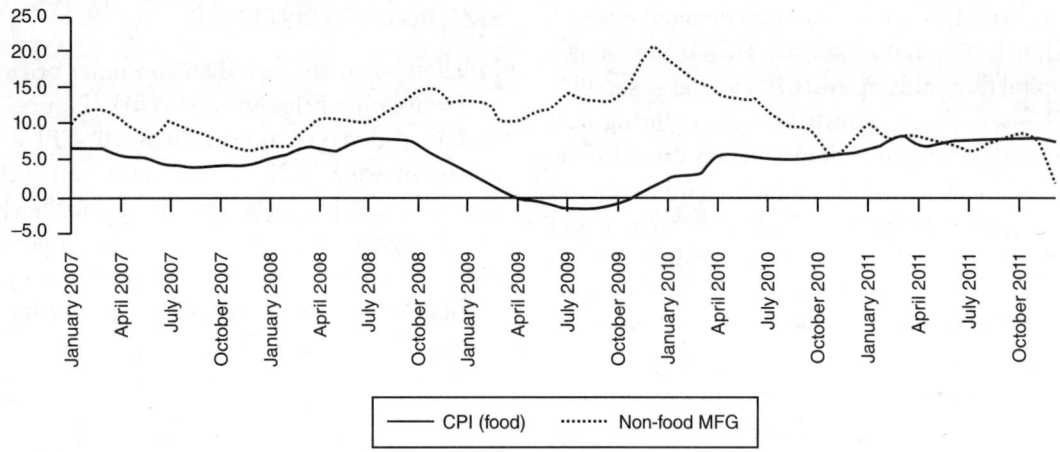

Figure 3.1c Inflation in CPI (Food) and WPI (Non-food Manufacturing)
Source: Labour Bureau, http://labourbureau.nic.in. Last accessed in March 2012.

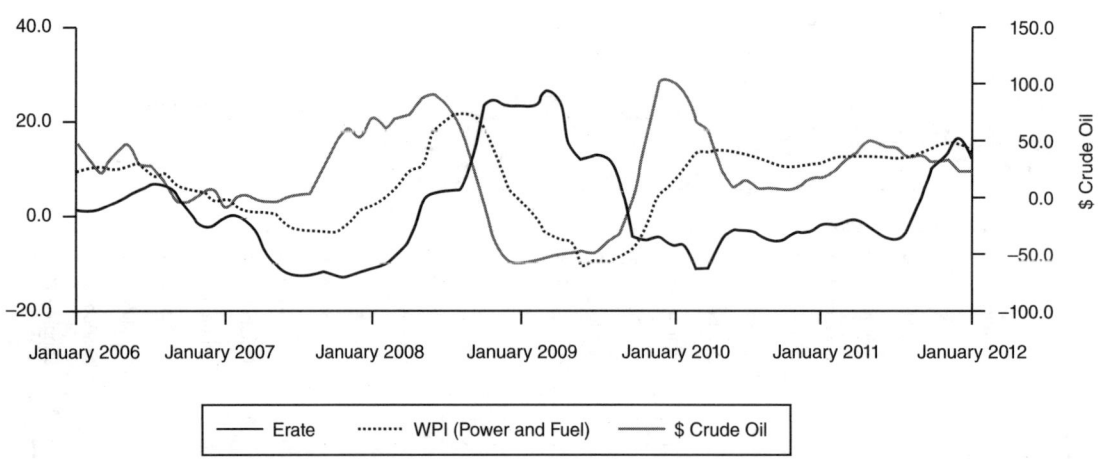

Figure 3.1d Domestic and International Fuel Inflation and Changes in the Rupee Value (Appreciation)
Source: Reserve Bank of India http://www.rbi.org.in, and www.eia.doe.gov. Last accessed in March 2012.

credit uptake,[2] remained low. Figure 3.1b, which shows the momentum or three-month moving average of inflation in WPI components, suggests that WPI manufacturing follows fluctuations in food and fuel. Figure 3.1c, which graphs WPI non-food manufacturing, the Reserve Bank of India's (RBI's) measure of core or demand driven inflation with CPI food inflation, also shows the persistence of the latter pulling up the former.

The large exchange rate depreciation in 2008–9 (Figure 3.1d) may have contributed to the momentum in food prices, since the border prices of food affect the minimum support price, and food articles are now traded goods (Goyal 2010). There was also more pass-through of international oil price changes to domestic prices, since many categories of the latter are now market determined. Only diesel, kerosene, and gas prices continue to be administered. When depreciation in the rupee and dollar crude prices rise together, as they did in 2008–9 and 2011, WPI manufacturing rises. Deeper analysis has brought out the causality between these components of inflation (Box 3.1).

Commodity price driven inflation is not normally persistent. But food inflation remained at above double digits for a longer period than it ever had in the past. This may have been a coincidence since international food prices peaked in 2007 and agricultural growth in the poor rainfall years of 2008–9 and 2009–10 was only 0.1 and 1 per cent, respectively. But it may also indicate structural

---

[2] Indian policy also used effective counter-cyclical prudential regulations to damp bubbles in real estate, even as the creation of excess international liquidity was driving up asset and commodity prices.

inadequacies in the agricultural supply response required as dietary patterns changed with rising per capita incomes (Gokarn 2011). Restrictions on movement and marketing of agricultural goods were an example of poor governance vitiating price signals and the supply response.

Food inflation did soften following the good harvest of 2010–11, although it remained high in protein items and was volatile in vegetables. But time series tests[3] also do not show persistence, so it is possible that Indian inflation can come down to the early 2000 levels. There is normally a commodity cycle: many years of soft prices follow sustained high prices as supply expands. There are signs of this happening in oil prices, so higher demand from China and India is not altering the commodity cycle.

PROPAGATION MECHANISMS: FOOD PRICES, WAGES, EXCHANGE RATES, AND AGGREGATE PRICES

Mainstream economists are unwilling to accept that a relative price change can affect aggregate prices. So the initial rise in high food price inflation in India in 2007 was dismissed as a passing relative price adjustment even when it had persisted for two to three years. To argue that relative prices cannot affect inflation assumes perfectly clearing markets and flexible prices and wages. Then a fall in one price balances a rise in another with no effect on the aggregate price level.

But there are a number of propagation mechanisms that allow relative prices to affect the aggregate price level. First, relative price shocks can raise the price level if price increases exceed price decreases. Aggregate price depends on the distribution of relative price changes—the level rises when the distribution is skewed to the right. Tripathi and Goyal (2011) provide evidence that price increase exceeds decrease in India and show that distribution-based measures of supply shocks perform better than traditional measures such as prices of energy and food. Real world markets do not work in a textbook frictionless fashion. Administered prices also prevent a fall in prices—this is part of governance failure.

Second, some relative prices, among them food prices and the exchange rate, have more of an impact on aggregate prices. Given the large share of food in a typical consumption basket food prices are critical for Indian inflation. Sustained high food inflation has a second round impact on wages and therefore the general level of prices.[4] Since both prices and wages rise more easily than they fall, a rise in a key price can raise wages and therefore, other prices, becoming inflation (Box 3.1).

Third, CPII pulled up the WPII partly through a new propagation mechanism. It demonstrated poor governance since the second round effect of policies was not understood. India's large rural population had kept unskilled wages at subsistence levels. But the Mahatma Gandhi National Rural Employment Guarantee Act (MGNREGA) employment insurance schemes raised subsistence wages above productivity. States competed with each other in raising minimum wages since the centre was footing the bill.[5] For the first time, minimum wages were actually implemented. This is a good thing. But the demand for all types of agricultural produce rose, and productivity did not rise in step. MGNREGA's record in creating assets is poor as is that in infrastructure improvements. Persistent inflation, even with growth below potential can be explained if a trend rise in wages exceeds that in agricultural productivity (Goyal 2010). Supply chain inefficiencies meant that the high prices that consumers were paying were not reaching farmers and motivating a supply response.

The exchange rate affects inflation since international food inflation now influences domestic. Moreover, India imports many intermediate goods, including oil, so currency depreciation adds to general costs and prices. Since imported costs enter the price level, a higher real wage requires a more appreciated real exchange rate. Rising real wages require a more appreciated real exchange rate. But if a policy of nominal depreciation is followed to encourage exports (for example, if inflows are inadequate to finance a current account deficit), a painful and prolonged rise in nominal wages and prices, can occur. A rise in one pushes up the other to form the fourth propagation mechanism (Goyal 2010). Since the exchange rate affects the political economy of food prices and wages, its contribution to inflation is broader than that just from goods or commodity price pass-through.

Sri Lanka and Bangladesh avoided much exchange rate depreciation during the global crisis. They were the only South Asian countries whose CPI inflation dropped to low single digits by 2009. A strategic nominal depreciation can also abort the pass-through of a temporary rise in foreign prices—such as an oil price shock. In India, after

---

[3] Bicchal et al. (2013) in a careful study of different measures of core inflation find persistence-based measures to be among the worst performers as measures of the core. The trend HP filter, heavily influenced by end points of the data, is one of the best.

[4] Ministry of Finance (2012: chapter 4, p. 78) studies wage adjustment in textiles. While wages generally adjust with a lag, there was sharp over-correction in the peak food inflation years of 2007 and 2008.

[5] Regressing state wage and average state wage inflation in recent years on macroeconomic variables gave positive and highly significant values for WPI (food) inflation and exchange rate depreciation.

> **Box 3.1** Causality between Consumer and Wholesale Prices
>
> Consumer prices are a weighted average of the prices of domestic and imported consumption goods, and producer prices feed into final consumer prices, so wholesale price inflation (WPII) should cause consumer price inflation (CPII). But if average wages respond to food prices, costs rise. If producer prices are set as a mark-up on wage costs, the mark-up depends on demand pressures, and wages depend on consumer prices, then domestic price inflation is a function of consumer prices through this aggregate supply (AS) link. So causality should run from CPII, for which food is the dominant component, to WPII. There is stronger evidence that CPII and food price inflation Granger causes wholesale price inflation (in the sense that past values of the first explain the second) when controls are used for other macroeconomic variables affecting the indices. That exchange rate depreciation Granger causes CPI food inflation also supports the identity. There is evidence of longer-term convergence between domestic and international prices in the major food grains. Moreover, there should exist a long-term equilibrium relationship between consumer and wholesale price inflation and the exchange rate, and also through the AS function. The two long-run (cointegrating) relationships are found to hold. They are:
>
> $$WPI_{t-1} - 1.127CPI_{t-1} - 1.045IIP_{t-1} - 1.003OIL_{t-1} - 0.838ER_{t-1}$$
>
> $$CPI_{t-1} - 1.501WPI_{t-1} - 0.029ER_{t-1}$$
>
> The first, which is AS, implies that WPI rises with CPI, IIP, oil prices, and the exchange rate. The second, which is identity, implies that CPI is the sum of WPI and the exchange rate. In estimating the adjustment to equilibrium for the CPI equation only the second CPI identity was significant, while for WPI the co-integrating equation derived from the AS equation was significant. So adjustment equations are written for only the CPI and WPI variables in matrix form below, with t-values in brackets.
>
> $$\begin{bmatrix} \Delta CPI_t \\ \Delta WPI_t \\ \Delta IIP_t \\ \Delta OIL_t \\ \Delta ER_t \end{bmatrix} = \begin{bmatrix} -0.044(3.354) & -0.004(-0.686) \\ 0.015(-1.019) & -0.39(3.395) \\ \vdots & \vdots \end{bmatrix} \begin{bmatrix} CPI_{t-1} - 1.50WPI_{t-1} - 0.029ER_{t-1} \\ (NA)\ (-6.549)\ (-2.362) \\ -1.13CPI_{t-1} + WPI_{t-1} - 1.045IIP_{t-1} - 1.003OIL_{t-1} - 0.838ER_{t-1} \\ (-6.815)\ (NA)\ (-2.823)\ (-7.029)\ (-4.963) \end{bmatrix} +$$
>
> $$\begin{bmatrix} -0.220(-2.118) \\ 0.211(2.589) \\ \vdots \end{bmatrix} + \begin{bmatrix} 0.379 & 0.349 & 0.022 & 0.002 & 0.014 \\ (3.79) & (-4.15) & (2.268) & (0.372) & (0.712) \\ 0.319 & 0.069 & 0.023 & 0.031 & 0.014 \\ (6.074) & (4.790) & (1.759) & (2.793) & (1.587) \\ \vdots & \vdots & \vdots & \vdots & \vdots \end{bmatrix} \begin{bmatrix} \Delta CPI_t \\ \Delta WPI_t \\ \Delta IIP_t \\ \Delta OIL_t \\ \Delta ER_t \end{bmatrix} + \begin{bmatrix} u_{1t} \\ u_{2t} \\ u_{3t} \\ u_{4t} \\ u_{5t} \end{bmatrix}$$
>
> Differential shocks on the two series, together with slow, long, and short-run convergence explain their recent sustained divergence. While OIL is not significant in the short run for CPI adjustment (ΔCPI), for ΔWPI, OIL, ER (exchange rate), and IIP (index of industrial production) came out to be strongly significant. Food price inflation is also co-integrated with manufacturing inflation.
>
> Output is found to be below capacity. There is no evidence of a structural break in the time series on inflation, and there is no substantial change in the relationships in sub-periods. Reform seems to have barely touched the deeper structural factors affecting the Indian inflationary process. In Goyal's (2008) estimates of NKE aggregate demand and supply curves for India also, lagged CPI inflation affects WPI inflation. Expected future CPI values significantly affect CPI inflation, but WPI inflation is backward-looking.
>
> *Source*: Goyal and Tripathi (2011).

the depreciation immediately following the crisis in 2008 inflows were allowed to determine the exchange rate. They resumed soon and were about equal to the current account deficit (CAD), so intervention in FX markets was negligible. The depreciation reversed. But at strategic periods when inflation showed signs of softening, there were outflows due to global issues such as the Euro debt crisis—and therefore, unrelated to the domestic cycle. Periodic depreciation prevented the softening of inflation. Expectations of high inflation firmed up. The nation's exchange rate policy was unable to smooth shocks in another failure in terms of the second definition of governance. Another set of propagation mechanisms includes many policies that give short-term benefits but raise hidden or indirect costs thus creating cost-push inflation. This set comes under the first definition of poor governance, and is analysed later in more detail.

To understand cost-push inflation, the price setting process and the way firms pass on costs should be studied. The next section presents some results from such an exercise.

PRICE SETTING BEHAVIOUR

Indian monetary policy has largely focused on the relationship between money supply and prices with the economy assumed to be near full capacity. But under cost shocks, firms' price setting is important for inflation. There is a large body literature on estimations of aggregate supply following the modern New Keynesian (NKE) approach, but little work in the Indian context. The estimations reported in this section were done at three levels of aggregation: aggregate data for AS, disaggregated price indices to derive the estimate of skewness as a measure of supply shocks, and disaggregated industry level data for price setting at this level. The key results were similar.

When a firm experiences a shock to its desired relative price, it resets the price only when the change is large enough to cover the costs of the process of change. That is, firms respond to large shocks and not to small shocks. These asymmetric relative price changes can be a measure of aggregate supply shocks. Tripathi and Goyal (2011) find that the distribution based measures of supply shocks are significant in estimations of aggregate supply.

Average price increase over time is greater than average price decrease. While price increase is around 10 per cent, price decrease is less than 5 per cent. Changes in the price level are positively related to skewness of relative price changes. Therefore an aggregate inflation of about 5 per cent is required to accommodate relative price changes. The estimated Indian Phillips curve shows that half of the Indian firms reset their prices in any period, and a little more than half are forward-looking in their price setting (Box 3.2).

In a disaggregated study of the effects of oil shocks on firm pricing, Tripathi (2012) found the coefficients on money supply growth while positive were generally much smaller than on cost variables. There was evidence of forward-looking behaviour.

Using time series methods, it is possible to estimate the relative impact of demand and supply shocks on inflation, and test whether long-run aggregate supply is elastic or inelastic. One or the other restriction has to be imposed to estimate the shocks from price and output time series.

DEMAND AND SUPPLY SHOCKS

If the restriction of elastic long-run supply (or supply does not affect output in the long run) is imposed, then supply

---

Box 3.2 Price Setting Behaviour Deduced from an Estimated Aggregate Supply

A hybrid Philips curve (Gali 2008) includes backward (the lagged inflation term) and forward (π_{t+1}) looking behaviour. Apart from these terms, current inflation is a function of current marginal cost. The coefficients are functions of three model parameters: θ, which measures the degree of price stickiness; ω, measures the degree of backwardness in price settings, and the discount factor β:

$$\pi_t = \alpha_f E_t\{\pi_{t+1}\} + \gamma mc_t + \alpha_b \pi_{t-1} + e_t$$

where:

$$\phi = \theta + \omega[1-\theta(1-\beta)]$$
$$\alpha_f = \beta\theta\phi^{-1}$$
$$\alpha_b = \omega\phi^{-1}$$
$$\gamma = (1-\omega)(1-\phi)(1-\beta\theta)\phi^{-1}$$

The estimated version of the hybrid Philips curve is:

$$\pi_t = 0.69 E_t\{\pi_{t+1}\} + 0.27 mc_t + 0.28 \pi_{t-1} + e_t$$

The parameter θ is estimated to be about 0.516, that is, about half of the Indian firms reset their prices in any period. The parameter ω is estimated to be about 0.34, that is, 34 per cent of the price setting industries are backward-looking. The parameter β came out to be 0.96.

PC was also estimated with the variable *AsymX*, a measure of supply shocks derived from asymmetric price adjustment. In the NKE approach, when a price is varied, it is set as a function of the expected future marginal cost. A proportionate relationship is assumed between the output gap and marginal cost. A cost shock, then, is anything that disturbs this relationship. Such deviations can occur due to mark-up shocks as costs of intermediate inputs rise:

$$\pi_t = 0.77 E_t\{\pi_{t+1}\} + 0.021 mc_t + 0.25 \pi_{t-1} + 0.023 AsymX_t + e_t$$

The coefficient of *AsymX* is small but is significant. Including the asymmetry measure leads the coefficient on marginal cost to fall substantially. The slope or marginal cost coefficient in the previous regression was higher because it was capturing part of the shift in curve due to supply shocks.

Source: Tripathi and Goyal (2011).

shocks should account for the major part of measured inflation and demand shocks should have a sustained impact on output levels.

If the restriction of in elastic long-run aggregate supply (or demand does not affect output in the long run) is imposed, then supply shocks should have little sustained impact on measured inflation, and only supply shocks should affect long-run output levels. These predictions serve as tests on Indian longer-run aggregate supply.

On successively imposing these identifications in a two-equation structural model, a high elasticity of long-run supply could not be ruled out because supply shocks had a large impact on inflation and demand shocks had a large and persistent effect on output levels.

The long-run restriction allows inflation to be decomposed into that due to short-run structural demand and supply shocks. Figure 3.2 reports these for 2010 and 2011 (Goyal and Arora 2012). The inflation figure is the annualized month on month rise in WPI. The output series used were the index of industrial production (IIP). Figure 3.2 shows the dominance of supply shocks in causing inflation, while demand shocks were largely negative.[6] The large positive supply shocks over the end of 2010 to early 2011 can be explained by low agricultural growth, and the new plateau oil prices reached after the Arab spring (see Figure 3.1d). The sharp exchange rate depreciation following the escalating Euro debt crisis was probably responsible for the peak in supply shocks towards the end of 2011.

There were multiple supply shocks, but they were not sustained, suggesting that a wage price spiral, or second round pass-through had not set in. A good measure of potential output, under frequent supply shock conditions is when such pass-through occurs so supply shocks are sustained at above 5 per cent. Since prices rise more than they fall, first round cost shocks must be passed through, so positive manufacturing or core inflation alone does not imply that the output is above potential. And falling growth in a slowdown does not imply that the potential growth has fallen.[7]

The identification procedure does not impose any short-run restrictions; elastic long-run supply is consistent with short-run supply bottlenecks that raise inflation. These could either be due to a steep short-run AS or to an upward shift of an elastic AS. Recent episodes suggest that short-run supply is also not inelastic.

The sharp monetary tightening raising short rates above 9 per cent in the summer of 2008 precipitated a collapse in industrial output even before the September fall of Lehman. The tightening came after a period of high growth. The economy was feared to be overheating and inflation, following the international spike in fuel and food, was high. A demand shock, with a near vertical supply curve should affect inflation more than output. But the reverse happened. WPI did not fall until November when Indian fuel prices fell, but CPI remained high. The rapid recovery also indicated a reduction in demand rather than a more

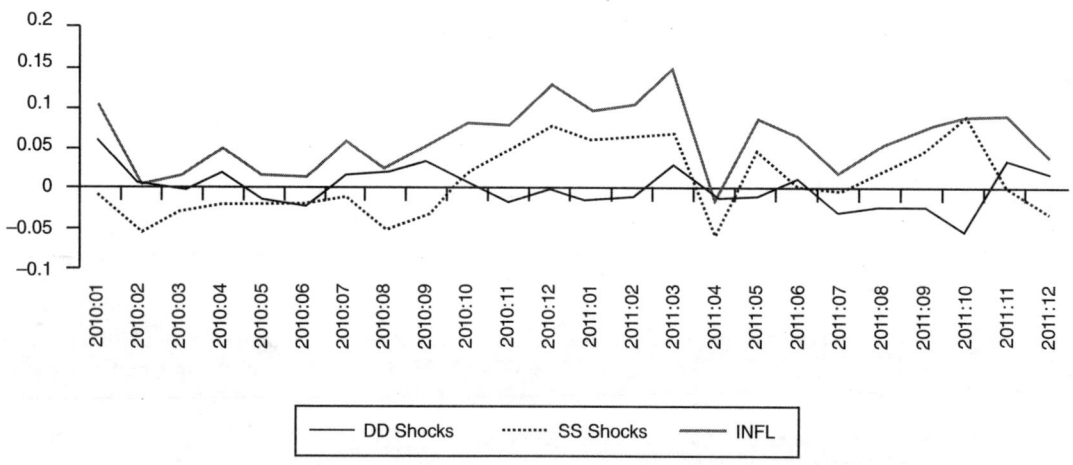

Figure 3.2 The Contribution of Demand and Supply Shocks to Inflation

Source: Goyal and Arora (2012).

---

[6] This was the period in which the IMF (2011) classified the Indian economy as overheating with large excess demand. But growth fell steeply in the second half of 2011 as monetary tightening continued.

[7] Time series filter (such as the HP filter) based estimates of potential output are regarded as incorrect since such filters tend to be heavily influenced by the end point.

intractable destruction of capacity. Although IIP began to slow from April 2011, the repo rate was raised from 6.75 in May to a peak 8.5 in October of that year. Manufacturing fell from 7.2 in Q1 of 2011–12 to –0.3 in the last quarter of 2011–12. But WPI inflation at the end of 2011 was at 9 per cent. The rise in policy rates affected output again, not inflation. If prices and wages are sticky, it will be output that adjusts first after a monetary shock. Labour availability contributes to a flat supply curve—the NSSO 66th Round showed double digit unemployment among the skilled in 2009–10. Short-term training institutes adapting skills to requirements mushroomed. Higher growth during catch-up periods implies that unemployable labour becomes employable. Structural unemployment reduces in a reversal of the process whereby cyclical unemployment becomes structural as the unemployed lose skills after a long out-of-work period. Then a demand stimulus alone cannot reduce unemployment. In a growing economy remedial training becomes available to upskill available labour.

There is other evidence. The low coefficients on the output gap and IIP suggest a flat AS—a rise in industrial output does not have much impact on prices (Box 3.1). The demand variable is insignificant in short-run adjustment indicating elastic AS. Including supply shocks reduced the coefficient of marginal cost (Box 3.2) again showing the Indian aggregate supply curve to be flat, but subject to shifts. These results suggest that the aggregate Indian supply curve, when estimated including a proper measure of supply shocks, is flat. There is, however, an important role for supply shocks, which takes the form of shifts of the supply curve. A similar structure of AS is theoretically derived for an open EM with a dualistic labour market in Goyal (2011a).

The estimated supply shocks are therefore due to shifts in the supply curve. The interest elasticity of aggregate demand is rising as retail and housing loans rise. But the still large informal sector reduces it. Poor governance is a factor that shifts up the supply curve at all levels of output, not just at the margin.

GOVERNANCE FAILURES, CHRONIC COST SHOCKS

While commodity price shocks and the propagation mechanisms they trigger, are a major source of the multiple supply shocks identified in the previous section, governance failures also impart an upward bias to prices, forming a fifth set of propagation mechanisms. Poor public service delivery raises costs. Large consumption subsidies and tax breaks reduce government spending on essential infrastructure, creating bottlenecks that raise costs. Potential expansion in capacity is lost. Taxes in themselves create distortions—direct taxes reduce effort, and indirect taxes raise prices and costs.

Wastage and ineffective expenditure add to these costs. Large government borrowings raise financing costs for private investment.

Many populist policies give short-term benefits but raise hidden or indirect costs. This holds even for policies that prevent prices from rising. Examples are price caps that freeze key prices and user charges. These distort relative prices and therefore, the allocation of resources. Both producers and consumers get wrong signals. Distortions in fertilizer and diesel prices have destroyed the environment and created serious health costs. Subsidized diesel has created a black market in adulterated petrol. Free electricity and over-irrigation have harmed the water table, and soil fertility—again raising costs of production.

If user charges are not raised when costs of production are going up, the quality of the service is normally reduced. This partly explains the poor quality of many public services which creates indirect costs.

Moreover, since administered prices become a political decision, it is difficult to change them. Thus despite steep cost escalations passenger fares have not been raised in the Indian Railways since 2003. Freight rates have been raised, since this is an indirect charge that a voter does not perceive. So a voter pays less for train travel but more for every piece of goods consumed as transport costs rise. Indirect costs are even higher—Indian rail lost freight to subsidized environmentally polluting diesel trucks with much higher social costs.

While some administered prices are frozen, others where there are active lobbies, are raised too much. The minimum support price (MSP) given to farmers tends to impart an upward bias in food prices. The distance from international prices is used to force a rise in domestic prices. One reason for low inflation over 2003–7 was low global food prices—so Indian MSPs were not raised. In 2007 as the gap between domestic and international food grain prices rose sharply, farmers' lobbies secured steep rises over the next few years.

Farmers benefit from stable prices—a sharp price rise induces oversupply in the next season and reduces farm income. Raising producer prices steeply yet attempting to protect the consumer through the public distribution system is a source of corruption, apart from the distortions in movement of food grains and monopoly marketing channels created to ease government procurement. All of these disrupt supply chains and raise costs. Crime is encouraged as low-price food grains meant for the poor are diverted to where prices are higher.

World commodity prices rise and fall sharply. In India since they are administered they do not rise as sharply, but they also never fall—so over time the cumulative rise can be more. Figure 3.3 shows that Indian fuel prices are less volatile than international prices, but unlike for the latter,

Table 3.1 Growth, Inflation, and Policy Rates

	2008–9: Q1–Q4				2009–10: Q1–Q4				2010–11: Q1–Q4				2011–12: Q1–Q4			
	Q1	Q2	Q3	Q4	Q1	Q2	Q3	Q4	Q1	Q2	Q3	Q4	Q1	Q2	Q3	Q4
Growth (Y-o-Y) (%) (constant 2004–5 prices)																
GDP at factor cost	7.9	7.7	5.8	5.9	6.3	8.6	7.3	9.4	8.5	7.6	8.2	9.2	8.0	6.7	6.1	5.3
Manufacturing	7.0	6.6	2.6	1.3	2.0	6.1	11.4	15.2	9.1	6.1	7.8	7.3	7.3	2.9	0.6	-0.3
GFCF/GDP*	33.0	34.8	31.5	32.7	30.4	31.9	30.9	34.5	32.2	34.0	32.3	31.4	33.9	33.4	30.3	30.9
Inflation (Y-o-Y) (%)																
WPI	9.6	12.5	8.6	3.2	0.5	-0.1	5.0	10.2	11.0	9.3	8.9	9.3	9.4	9.7	8.9	7.0
CPI-IW	7.8	9.0	10.2	9.5	8.9	11.6	13.2	15.1	13.6	10.5	9.3	9.0	8.9	9.2	8.4	7.2
Policy Rate																
Overnight (call) money	6.8	9.5	7.8	4.2	3.2	3.2	3.2	3.3	4.2	5.4	6.6	6.8	7	7.8	8.6	8.9

Note: * This row represents the ratio and not growth rate.

Source: CSO press release and Reserve Bank of India.

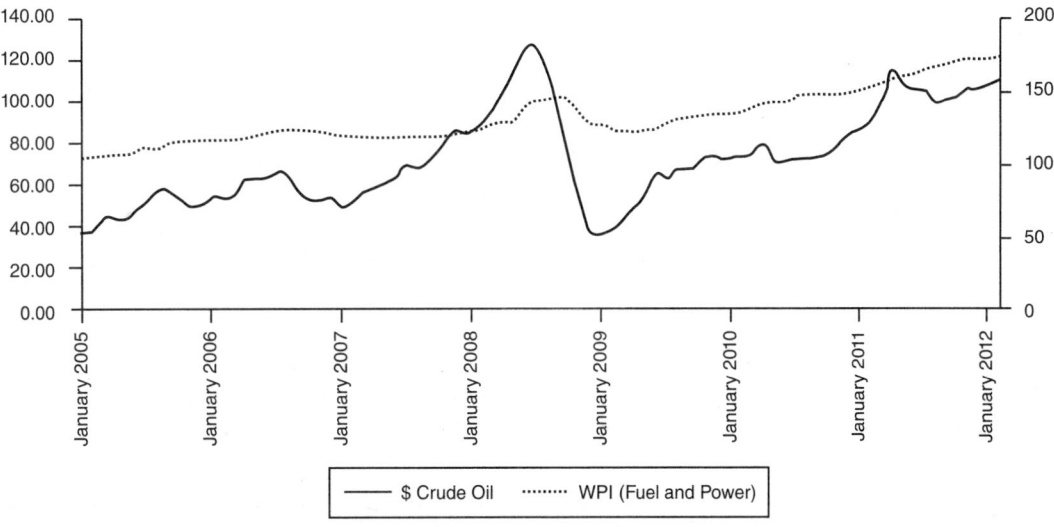

Figure 3.3 Indian and International Oil Prices
Source: Reserve Bank of India http://www.rbi.org.in, and www.eia.doe.gov. Last accessed in March 2012.

the trend is upwards. Inflation was higher[8] over time. Such a system of price setting can convert a temporary supply shock into a persistent shock. In recent periods domestic prices also fluctuated as exchange rate fluctuations raised non-administered components (Figure 3.1d).

This structure of AS-AD has implications for the tradeoff between growth and inflation and the output sacrifice.

GROWTH AND INFLATION TRADEOFFS AND THE OUTPUT SACRIFICE

The standard Phillips curve suggests that higher wages induce more effort, raising output and inflation—so higher output can be attained at the cost of higher inflation. There is a potential short-run tradeoff between output and inflation. But if the behaviour is forward-looking, the inflation becomes anticipated. Since expected real wages fall there is no output increase but inflation rises. There is no long-run tradeoff—a macroeconomic stimulus only raises inflation without affecting real output. If expectations affect current behaviour, there is no short-run tradeoff either. One school has gone further in saying that the distortions that inflation creates reduce growth. That logic suggests macroeconomic stimuli would only raise inflation, and latter would lower growth. The inflation threshold where such negative effects kick in is estimated at about 10 per cent in EMs (Jha and Dang 2012). RBI (2011: Box 11.4, p. 32) put this threshold at about 5 per cent for the Indian economy. The *Economic Survey 2010–11* points out that real exchange rate appreciation as wages rise may require a higher rate of inflation in EMs—so a higher growth requires higher inflation exceeding world inflation. It should be possible, however, to accommodate the factors making for higher inflation within the threshold of 5 per cent, which still exceeds world inflation.

The NKE school models pricing power together with forward-looking behaviour (Box 3.2). If current or future demand is causing inflation, raising interest rates such that excess demand falls to zero for all time can lower inflation with no cost in terms of output. A short-run tradeoff between inflation and output variability arises only if there are cost shocks. Since supply shocks have been frequent in India it is useful to analyse the tradeoff in that context.

If the AD-AS structure is as derived in the previous section with AS elastic but subject to upward shocks, policies that shift AD alone without reducing costs or shifting AS downwards involve a large output sacrifice (Figure 3.4), without much impact on inflation. But without policies that shift down AS, a large output sacrifice may become necessary to moderate sticky inflation expectations and the rise in wages that itself shifts up the AS curve.[9] If policy is able to abort the propagation mechanisms pushing up the AS curve, output and employment sacrifice from supply shocks can be reduced even as inflation is kept within bounds.

The social impact of the sacrifice is high since a slowdown reduces employment and wages more in the informal sector.

---

[8] Over 1975–6 to 2011–12 average annual international crude inflation works out to 8.9 per cent, while Indian FPLL WPI inflated at 9.5 pa per annum.

[9] Basu (2011) shows how policymakers' inflation forecasts tend to be underestimated since they attempt to anchor expectations. But more than just words are required for statements to be credible.

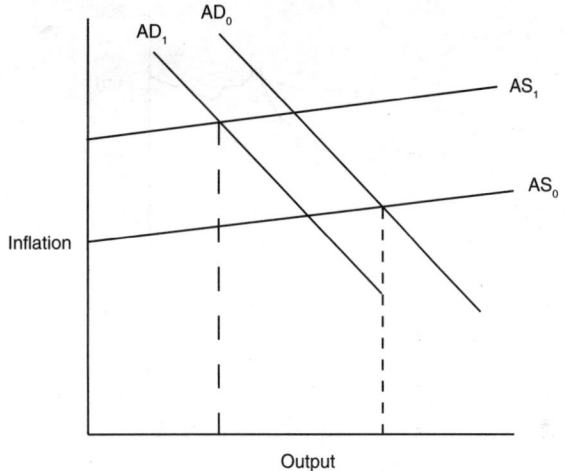

Figure 3.4 Aggregate Demand and Supply
Source: Goyal (2010).

Figure 3.5, based on ASI data, shows that in the downturn following peak interest rates after the East Asian crisis, manufacturing real wages did not fall—these were indexed to inflation. But non-manufacturing real wages which may not have been so indexed fell.[10] India's large informal labour probably bore the brunt of the slowdown as lower employment reduced their pricing power.

But informal wages are also now being partially indexed through MGNREGA, so employment growth will fall but sticky real wages will keep up cost pressures. In 2011 MGNREGA wages were indexed to CPI agricultural wages, and in 2012 they exceeded state minimum wages in 21 states. They set a floor to wages in many informal sector activities, and reduced indexation lags.

Policy-induced Demand Shocks and Output Sacrifice

The official understanding of monetary policy in India is that a huge monetary overhang built up due to financing of large fiscal deficits created excess demand that had to be sharply reduced during periods of high inflation. But every period of double-digit inflation in India was associated with a supply shock. It is possible to check for the size of contraction in demand and in factors affecting demand (relative to GDP) during these periods. Excessive contraction would be a failure of governance in the sense of inappropriate macroeconomic policies.

Table 3.2 shows the 'monetary' and 'fiscal' shocks and the sum of the two in the 'policy' variable. These shocks identify policy-induced demand shock, and also show if monetary and fiscal policies acted in concert or at cross purposes. The bold figures show the monetary and fiscal response to periods of inflation above 8 per cent, which were all periods of an adverse supply shock. Table 3.2 gives the average annual rates over inflationary and non-inflationary years.

The monetary policy shock is calculated as the change in reserve money growth before 2002 and the change in the repo rate after 2002. The fiscal policy shock is the change in the sum of central government revenue and capital expenditure each as a percentage of GDP.[11] That is, period t gives the total of the two fiscal policy variables and the monetary policy variable each minus their respective values in period t-1. A negative value implies that policy contraction exceeded that in GDP. Policy amplified supply shocks since the contractionary impulse exceeded the fall in output. It was negative in years when the GDP growth rate fell due to a supply shock. The only shock period in which policy was counter-cyclical was 2008–9 when the GFC constituted a large negative external demand shock. Monetary policy was also not pro-cyclical over 1995–2008, as it generally was in other periods. Also monetary policy and fiscal expenditure tend to expand and to contract together.

The 'credit' variable does a similar calculation for broad money M3, bank credit to the commercial sector, and total bank credit, the sum divided by three. Credit also contracted in periods of policy tightening, and it has grown at less than the GDP rate ever since the GFC. Finally the 'demand' shock measures changes in domestic absorption relative to GDP. It is the sum of changes in private final consumption expenditure (PFCE), government expenditure (G), and gross domestic capital formation (GDCF), each as a percentage of GDP.

In general, Table 3.2 shows that each shock, plus the policy response, imparted a considerable negative impulse to aggregate demand, even as the supply shock pushed up costs. Demand remained positive through the first oil shock years but fell steeply in 1975–6. It was consistently negative through the 1980s, which were the years of the largest fiscal deficits and RBI accommodation! Since Table 3.2 measures final demand categories, perhaps large government transfers were siphoned away, perhaps abroad, without reaching beneficiaries and creating demand.

---

[10] ASI puts items like servicing watches in non-manufacturing. These wages seem to be more responsive to demand conditions. As Kanagasabapathy pointed out, their rise in the preceding high growth period exceeded the trend, implying non-manufacturing wage growth exceeded trend growth in wages.

[11] Changes in spending are a better measure of the fiscal impulse than fiscal deficit. The latter should increase during an economic slowdown as revenues fall to function as an automatic non-discretionary stabilizer. Krishnan and Vaidya (2013, this volume) explore the cyclical properties of government consumption.

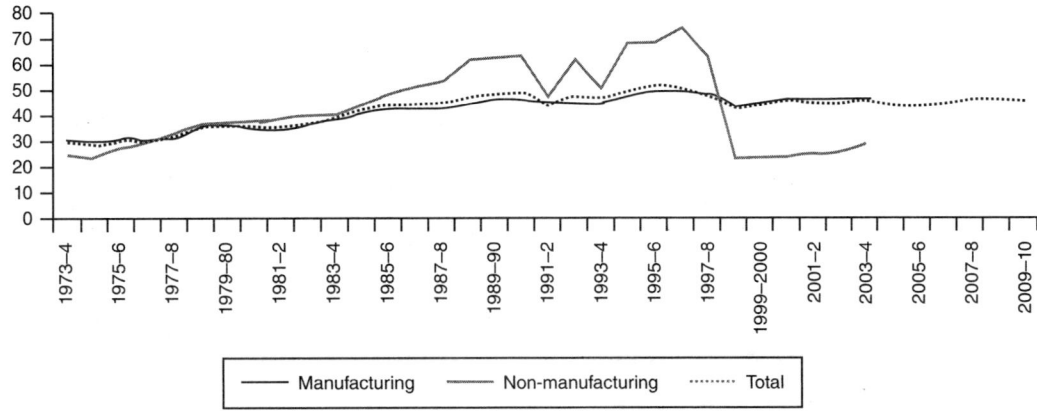

Figure 3.5 Real Wages Per Worker Year [CPI(IW)] (in '000s)
Source: Annual Survey of Industries (ASI) and http://mospi.nic.in. Last accessed in March 2012.

Table 3.2 Monetary and Fiscal Policy and Outcomes in High Inflation and Other Years (Average Annual Rates)

Years	Monetary Shock	Fiscal Shock	Policy Shock	Credit Shock	Demand Shock	Real GDP Growth	WPI Inflation
1972–5	−0.4	−0.4	−0.8	−0.6	0.4	1.8	8.5
1975–9	0.7	1	1.8	0.8	0.3	5.8	1.6
1979–81	0.4	−0.6	−0.3	−1.3	−3.1	1	7.7
1981–90	0.3	0.4	0.7	0.1	−0.6	5.6	8
1990–2	−0.4	−0.9	−1.3	−0.6	−1.3	4	1.4
1992–4	1.3	0.1	1.4	1.7	0.3	5.7	8.4
1994–5	0.6	−0.6	0.1	−0.9	1.8	6.4	2.6
1995–2008	0.1	−0.1	0	0.1	0.6	7	5.2
2008–9	0.5 (−1.1)	1.4	1.9 (0.3)	−0.7	−0.7	6.7	8.1
2009–10	0.0	0.2	0.2	−1.2	1.3	8.4	3.8
2010–12	−1.8 (−0.5)	−0.5	−2.3 (−1)	−0.8	−2.4	7.7	9.4

Source: Reserve Bank of India, http://www.rbi.org.in and CSO press releases.

Notes: From 2001 the rise in the repo rate rather than fall in reserve money is used as the measure of monetary tightening. The terms in brackets shows policy shocks using change in reserve money. Figures in bold indicate the years in which inflation was in double digits; WPI—Wholesale Price Index; GDP—Gross Domestic Product.

Policy shocks were no longer negative after the mid-1990s, and demand shocks remained positive. But they became highly negative in 2011–12, as policy contracted severely.

Rates of inflation and the output sacrifice were lower under recent shocks, although policy reactions remained as severe, suggesting greater resilience and diversity with a larger share of the private sector. Policy needs to play a stabilizing role, with more nuanced and smaller forward-looking adjustments.

POLICY

Monetary–Fiscal Coordination

Price adjustment is asymmetric, that is prices rise more easily than they fall. So monetary tightening in response to cost shock will impact output more than prices. It follows that policy may allow the price level effect of a temporary price shock without tightening. The first round pass through of a cost shock such as higher oil prices into manufacturing prices, for example, should not be regarded as core inflation.

But if key relative prices that trigger propagation mechanisms are involved, policy must react quickly. Typically, monetary tightening has occurred as second round effects set in. The supply shock itself is extended because of delayed administrative pass-through. Instead, early but mild tightening, to at least the neutral interest rate, together with supply-side measures, could anchor inflationary expectations without a sharp reduction in demand. Short-term supply-side measures include fiscal moves such as reduction in excise and tariffs, freer movement of food, and imports. A nominal exchange rate appreciation can abort pass-through for a temporary oil price shock.

The idea that policy should tighten severely if inflation is above a threshold is flawed because strict inflation targeting is never optimal (Goyal 2011a), some weight must be given to output, and the tightening moderated when growth slows.

Size and Speed of Monetary Tightening

The size of required tightening may be low if the share of lagged and administered prices is large. Since the cumulative effect of past steps will continue to slow the economy, tightening cycles must not be prolonged. If, however, price setting is forward-looking, but prices once set are sticky, a quick policy response to inflation can abort a price rise. The policy rate change itself can be moderate since firms will internalize a future rise in rates on the changed policy path.

Estimated real and nominal price rigidities imply that a sharp policy response to a rise in expected future excess demand can prevent the 66 per cent of forward-looking firms from raising prices. Since the higher prices persist for about a year, policy that anchored inflation expectations would reduce the persistence of inflation. This is without any cost to output since inflation is reduced by reducing future, not current, output gaps.

However, 34 per cent of the firms continue to be backward-looking, so there is some price inertia and lagged effects of policy rate changes. A reduced but continuing share of administered prices aggravates this. So policy response to supply shocks should be moderate—to anchor inflationary expectations to prevent second round pass-through yet allow lagged adjustment to play out.

High interest rates tax the most dynamic interest elastic component of the economy such as investment which reduces capacity. When nominal interest rates are high firms prefer to earn higher returns on their surplus cash, rather than invest it. It is difficult to destroy the pricing power of cash-rich firms through interest rate hikes. Since mark-ups tend to be counter-cyclical, prices are sticky downwards. What gets destroyed is capacity utilization and expansion. Even if real interest rates are low, they normally coincide with supply shocks when costs rise for both firms and consumers. Sharp spikes in interest rates must also be avoided since they affect the repaying ability of indebted firms, and reduce the loan quality of banks.

Strategic capital controls and signalling can also affect exchange rates separately from interest rate policy. In Indian conditions the exchange rate may have a broader reach compared to the interest rate—it affects costs in the informal sector and headline as well as core inflation. Even so, large spikes in the exchange rate must also be avoided, since they affect firms who have borrowed abroad, as well as exporters, adversely.

LONG-TERM STRUCTURAL AND FISCAL REFORMS

A rise in productivity will allow higher wages to be consistent with a more depreciated and competitive real exchange rate required to reduce CAD, thus closing one propagation mechanism. A rise in agricultural productivity, especially, will reduce pressures for rising wages and domestic second round inflation, thus reducing real exchange rate appreciation from higher domestic inflation differentials. China has similar population levels. A sharp rise in agricultural productivity preceded its industrial transition. Given past failures, a new approach that strengthens local institutions and creates new options for farmers is required. Multi-brand FDI in retail is one such option but will take long to fructify. Domestic changes to improve inter-state connectivity and competition in agricultural marketing could be faster, and would make FDI more effective when and if it did come in. Even if the government needs to procure more it must do so in competitive markets without artificial divisions.

Since MGNREGA is a source of wage indexation and inflation propagation, it must be focused on creating assets through conditional allocations. Officials implement a clear target given to them. With asset creation as the objective, employment will be created as a by-product.

Agricultural production and distribution are now on the concurrent list. The centre can legislate on the movement of goods and on creating a national market. It could push through a new bill using new political alignments. But even without that, two or more states can pass a resolution on goods movement under Article 252 of the Constitution. States can be motivated by making key allocations conditional upon reforms of their existing Agricultural Produce Marketing Committee laws. Once a few states start showing positive results, others will follow. Experience with recent Finance Commissions and the Jawaharlal Nehru Urban Renewal Missions show that incentives work with states if they are not subject to political renegotiation. They should be made more formula based.

A fiscal deficit (FD) implies a government's expenditure exceeds its revenues. Large FDs in India are thought to create excess demand that drives Indian inflation. But Table 3.2 shows large demand compression during inflationary episodes. Given high private savings, relatively low government debt, and growth prospects, current deficits are manageable, provided there is a credible fiscal consolidation path (Goyal 2011b). Improvements in institutions and laws such as the FRBM Act did succeed in reducing deficits, especially in the states where they were complemented with incentives.

Many western countries have much higher deficits and debt with worse growth prospects. If the composition of government spending changes towards building human capacity,[12] including improvements in public service delivery, it can deliver inclusive growth, remove the fear of unsustainable deficits, and improve supply response. Strengthening institutions and thickening democracy are imposing more continuous accountability. State elections are also rewarding better governance.

Better systems are required. Formula, based pricing in the oil sector could reduce political pressures that lead to lags in adjustment to external price shocks, yet deliver some smoothing and burden sharing even as regulatory capacity and competition are encouraged. That fuel prices in India rise but rarely fall is one feature that turns a temporary supply shock into a persistent one. This could change.

If improvements in governance reduce cost pressures on inherently elastic supply, monetary policy can support demand. Monetary–fiscal coordination will improve reducing the cyclicality seen in Indian growth rates.

CONCLUSION

To the extent supply-side issues dominate inflation contractionary demand policies they should be used with moderation, although they have a role in anchoring inflation expectations. Headline inflation can have persistent effects in India but needs to be reduced through short- and long-term policies that impact the supply-side.

Key contributions of the analysis include the idea that aggregate supply is elastic but subject to frequent upward shocks. It provides a new way of understanding how supply constraints affect the economy. Output turns out to be demand determined but supply shocks and propagation mechanisms that make them persistent create inflation. Certain relative prices—including food prices and the exchange rate—play a critical role in the propagation process as do price setting behaviour and failures of governance.

A standard macroeconomic analysis requires adaption to context. Else mistakes are made. In summer 2011 there was a crescendo in international pressure: India was said to be overheating, when it was clear that industry was already slowing (Table 3.1, 2011–12, Q2). A July 2011 *Economist* article, based on IMF research, put India among the 'sizzling 7' countries, on highly contestable grounds,[13] even as advanced countries were encouraged to try innovative policy mixes for unemployment much lower than that in EMs. Indian policy has always reacted strongly to high inflation; as interest rates were raised further, output crashed. Instead, as the sharp post-GFC rise in oil prices was partly responsible for EM inflation, the IMF should have sought to plug regulatory gaps in advanced countries that allow 'innovative' excess liquidity to raise commodity prices, and created an emerging market fund to compensate for excessive volatility in capital flows driven by external events.

REFERENCES

Basu, K. (2011), 'Understanding Inflation and Controlling It', *Economic and Political Weekly*, 46(41): 50–64.

Bicchal, M., N. Kumar, and B. Kamaiah (2013), 'Different Statistical Core Inflation Measures for India: Construction and Evaluation', *Macroeconomics and Finance in Emerging Market Economies*, forthcoming. Accessed in March 2012. Available at http://www.tandfonline.com/doi/abs/10.1080/17520843.2012.682339.

Gali, Jordi (2008), *Monetary Policy, Inflation and the Business Cycle: An Introduction to the New Keynesian Framework*. Princeton and Oxford: Princeton University Press.

Gokarn, S. (2011), 'The Price of Protein', *Macroeconomics and Finance in Emerging Market Economies*, 4(2): 327–35.

Goyal, A. (2008), 'Incentives from Exchange Rate Regimes in an Institutional Context', *Journal of Quantitative Economics*, 6(1 & 2): 101–21.

———. (2010), 'Inflationary Pressures in South Asia', *Asia-Pacific Development Journal*, United Nations Economic and Social Commission for Asia and the Pacific (ESCAP), 17(2): 1–42.

———. (2011a), 'A General Equilibrium Open Economy Model for Emerging Markets: Monetary Policy with a Dualistic Labor Market', *Economic Modelling*, 28(3): 1392–1404.

———. (2011b), 'Sustainable Debt and Deficits in Emerging Markets', *International Journal of Trade and Global Markets*, 4(2): 113–36.

---

[12] Romar Correa pointed out the distinction between soft and hard government expenditures and their differential effectiveness. A poor composition of expenditure is also a failure of governance, but can be captured in a more standard macroeconomic variable.

[13] For example, it used 20-year trends which are incorrect for countries undergoing structural change. The variables included amounted to putting responsibility for external shocks on domestic policy.

Goyal, A. and S. Arora (2012), 'Deriving India's Potential Growth from Theory and Structure'. IGIDR Working Paper no. WP-2012-018, available at http://www.igidr.ac.in/pdf/publication/WP-2012-018.pdf. Last accessed in September 2012.

Goyal, A. and S. Tripathi (2011), 'New Keynesian Aggregate Supply in the Tropics: Food Prices, Wages and Inflation', *International Journal of Monetary Economics and Finance*, 4(4): 330–54.

IMF [International Monetary Fund] (2011), 'Asia and Pacific: Navigating an Uncertain Global Environment While Building Inclusive Growth', *Regional Economic Outlook*, October. Available at http://www.imf.org/external/pubs/ft/reo/2011/apd/eng/areo1011.pdf. Last accessed in March 2012.

Jha, R. and T.N. Dang (2012), 'Inflation Variability and the Relationship Between Inflation and Growth', *Macroeconomics and Finance in Emerging Market Economies*, 5(1): 3–17.

Krishnan, R. and R.R. Vaidya (2013), 'Is Fiscal Policy in India Pro-cyclical?', Chapter 5 in S. Mahendra Dev (ed.), *India Development Report 2012–13*. New Delhi: IGIDR and Oxford University Press: 59–78.

Ministry of Finance (2011), *Economic Survey 2010–11*. Government of India. Available at http://indiabudget.nic.in, last accessed on 30 March 2011.

———. (2012), *Economic Survey 2011–12*. Government of India. Available at http://indiabudget.nic.in/, last accessed on 10 April 2012.

RBI [Reserve Bank of India] (2011), *Annual Report 2010–11*. Mumbai. Available at http://rbidocs.rbi.org.in/rdocs/AnnualReport/PDFs/0RBIAN250811_F.pdf. Last accessed in March 2012.

Tripathi, S. (2012), 'Dynamics of Oil Prices in Emerging Market Economies', Unpublished PhD thesis, Mumbai: Indira Gandhi Institute of Development Research.

Tripathi, S. and A. Goyal (2011), 'Relative Prices, the Price Level and Inflation: Effects of Asymmetric and Sticky Adjustment', Working Paper 2011-026. Mumbai: Indira Gandhi Institute of Development Research.

4

Fiscal Deficits, Credibility, and Inflation Persistence
Lessons from Thatcher and Volcker Disinflations[†]

Pankaj Kumar, Pratik Mitra, and Naveen Srinivasan[*]

INTRODUCTION

Since the global financial turmoil of 2008, the Indian economy has grappled with high and persistent inflation. The headline inflation measured by the wholesale price index (WPI) hovered in the range of 9–10 per cent in every month between February 2010 and November 2011, way above the Reserve Bank of India's (RBI's) implicit inflation target of around 4–5 per cent. To deal with the inflationary pressure, the Reserve Bank cumulatively raised the cash reserve ratio (CRR) by 100 basis points and the policy rate (the repo rate) 13 times by 375 basis points between January 2010 and October 2011. Despite these policy actions the inflation rate continues to remain persistently high. It is no surprise, therefore, that this issue has been at the forefront of public policy debates in recent years.

What explains our current inflation predicament? It is often claimed that stubbornly high inflation is because of 'temporary factors or cost shocks' such as an increase in oil or commodity prices. According to this widely held view, inflation is largely a non-monetary phenomenon: it is driven by 'cost-push' factors, and these factors dominate the behaviour of inflation regardless of what course monetary or fiscal policy takes.[1] It has also become fashionable in certain circles to assert that the way to deal with the problem is by microeconomic policy—the panoply of controls

---

[†] Any opinions, findings, and conclusions or recommendations expressed in this chapter are those of the authors and do not necessarily reflect the views of the institutions they represent.

[*] We are grateful to Romar Correa, Vikas Chitre, K.L. Krishna, and K. Kanagasabapathy for helpful comments and suggestions.

[1] For example, Balakrishnan (1991) concluded that inflation in India was driven mainly by supply shocks. Structuralists argue that inflation occurs because of structural bottlenecks in the agricultural sector. Sectoral imbalances (caused by a rapid growth of the industrial sector) lead to an excess demand for agricultural goods and, consequently, a rise in agricultural commodity prices. The increase in raw material prices and the indexation of money wages to the consumer price index results in the transmission of the rise in agricultural prices to industrial prices as firms simply pass on the increase in costs to the consumers.

and subsidies associated with a different era.[2] The former Chief Economic Adviser to the Finance Ministry, Kaushik Basu on the other hand believes that inflation can be brought down by reducing (not increasing) interest rates.[3] All this talk is ill-informed and diverts attention away from the real cause of persistent inflation. This chapter is an attempt to explain why, based on lessons of economic history and commonsense economic analysis.

Economic theory teaches us that inflation persistence is a product of the forcing processes (shocks) interacting with the policy regime. It is perfectly reasonable to find that these shocks are themselves autocorrelated. These processes will propagate themselves through all the endogenous variables and be a natural source of persistence. Monetary authorities (in the absence of fiscal constraints) could choose to close this persistence down if they wish by credibly committing to price stability. In fact, major inflation episodes around the world have ultimately resulted from fiscal problems, and it is hard to think of a fiscally sound country that has ever experienced high and persistent inflation. So long as the government's fiscal house is in order, people will naturally assume that the central bank should be able to stop a small uptick in inflation. Conversely, when the government's finances are in disarray, inflation expectations can become 'unanchored' very quickly. But this link between fiscal and monetary expectations is too often ignored by both policymakers and the popular press.[4]

The basic point is that deficits today must be paid for by taxes, money expansions or lower expenditure tomorrow (the government's inter-temporal budget constraint). If one assumes any reasonable termination of the rising debt/GDP ratio, whether because of a limit on incentive damaging taxes, then money financing is eventually required in the absence of quite implausibly severe cuts in public expenditure. This means a rise in future inflation worse than the moderation in current inflation from the current money-supply restraint. This analysis was spread widely by Sargent and Wallace in their well-known paper, 'Some unpleasant monetarist arithmetic' (1981). Hence the 'unpleasant' policy lesson that the budget deficit must also be cut back to make a monetarist inflation-control programme work. By implication contractionary monetary policy signalling the authorities' wish to halt inflation may not be credible unless accompanied by a coordinated reduction in budget deficits.

In this regard we believe that the experience of the Thatcher government in the UK and the Volcker regime in the US in the early 1980s are full of lessons about our own, less drastic predicament with inflation. Our reason for studying these episodes is that they are laboratories for the study of policy regime changes. The idea is to stand back from our current predicament and to examine the measures that successfully brought inflation under control in these countries.

The rest of the chapter is organized as follows. The next section provides an overview of Mrs Thatcher and Paul Volcker's disinflation programme in the early 1980s. In the next section, we empirically evaluate the link between policy regime credibility and inflation persistence. Our empirical methodology, data used in the analysis, and our empirical results are also discussed. The last section provides a conclusion.

ESTABLISHING ANTI-INFLATIONARY CREDIBILITY: LESSONS FROM THATCHER AND VOLCKER DISINFLATIONS

Mrs Thatcher's Economic Policies

In 1979 Margaret Thatcher inherited a monetary mess. Inflation was rising rapidly in the UK as the policy of wage controls that had been put in place to hold it down crumbled in the 'winter of discontent' of that year when graves went undug and rubbish piled up in the streets. Large public sector pay increases had been promised by the Clegg

---

[2] Milton Friedman, writing in 1978, observed that in diagnosing the inflation problem, there were many factors other than money that politicians, economists, and journalists write about... '[They] attribut[e] the acceleration of inflation to special events—bad weather, food shortages, labor-union intransigence, corporate greed, the OPEC cartel...' (cited in Nelson 2005: 2). Recalling this period a quarter-century later, Friedman argued: Central banks performed badly prior to the 80s ... because they [had] a wrong theory. ... Inflation, according to this vision, was produced primarily by pressures on cost that could best be restrained by direct controls on prices and wages.

[3] '... I believe that is something (reduction of interest rate) which ought to be considered. When you have high inflation, the central bank's standard response is to increase the interest rate and my view is that we have done it. It had some impact, but not at the level which we had expected,' Basu said in an interview to Karan Thapar on the programme, 'Devil's Advocate', aired on news channel CNN-IBN. The Reserve Bank, he said, needs to think out-of-the-box and come out with steps to tackle high inflation. 'We are in a new world. Many countries are facing this problem. We have to try a different policy, because we don't want to damage India's growth story,' Basu added.

[4] There are exceptions of course. In fact, in its 'Third Quarter Review of Monetary Policy 2011–12 on 24 January 2012', the Reserve Bank of India notes that 'the anticipated fiscal slippage, which is caused largely by high levels of consumption spending by the government, poses a significant threat to both inflation management and, more broadly, to macroeconomic stability.' It further states that 'strong signs of fiscal consolidation, which will shift the balance of aggregate demand from public to private and from consumption to capital formation, are critical to create the space for lowering the policy rate without the imminent risk of resurgent inflation.' (RBI 2012: 15)

Commission under the previous Labour government. The budget was in crisis and was expected to deteriorate further with these pay awards on top of the usual spending pressures (see Minford 1991).

The return of the Conservative government in May 1979 signalled a milestone in the history of UK post-war macroeconomic policy. Prior to this date, British post-war administrations, whether Conservative or Labour, had pursued policies which could broadly be described as Keynesian in their orientation and philosophy. In sharp contrast, the Thatcher government adopted a decidedly monetarist stance in which fiscal policy became subordinate to meeting money supply targets.

The key problem was seen to be the lack of long-term credibility in counter-inflation policy.[5] As Minford (1991) argues, if the central bank had been constitutionally independent or even fiercely committed to price stability in practice, with a high profile Governor with respect for monetary probity, matters could have been very different. However, the Bank of England commanded no such position; formally an executive arm of the Treasury, it was staffed by Keynesians and had as Governor a lawyer whose main personal interest was regulation and who had no intuitive grasp of monetary theory. In order to achieve durability, policy was cast in the form of a Medium-Term Financial Strategy (MTFS). This consisted of a commitment to a five-year rolling target for gradually decelerating £M3 backed by parallel reduction of the PSBR/GDP ratio—the Public Sector Borrowing Requirement, the usual measure of deficit in the UK. Although the previous Labour administration had also endorsed the concept of money supply targets, this was seen not much as a conversion but rather as a necessary sop to placate the IMF.

Clearly, the new policy framework was aimed at securing a reduction in inflationary expectations. It was the first convincing indication that the theoretical niceties of the rational expectations revolution in macroeconomics were beginning to influence the menu of policy choice (see Shaw 1983). In brief, MTFS represented the antithesis of the Keynesian demand management philosophy.[6] Logic,

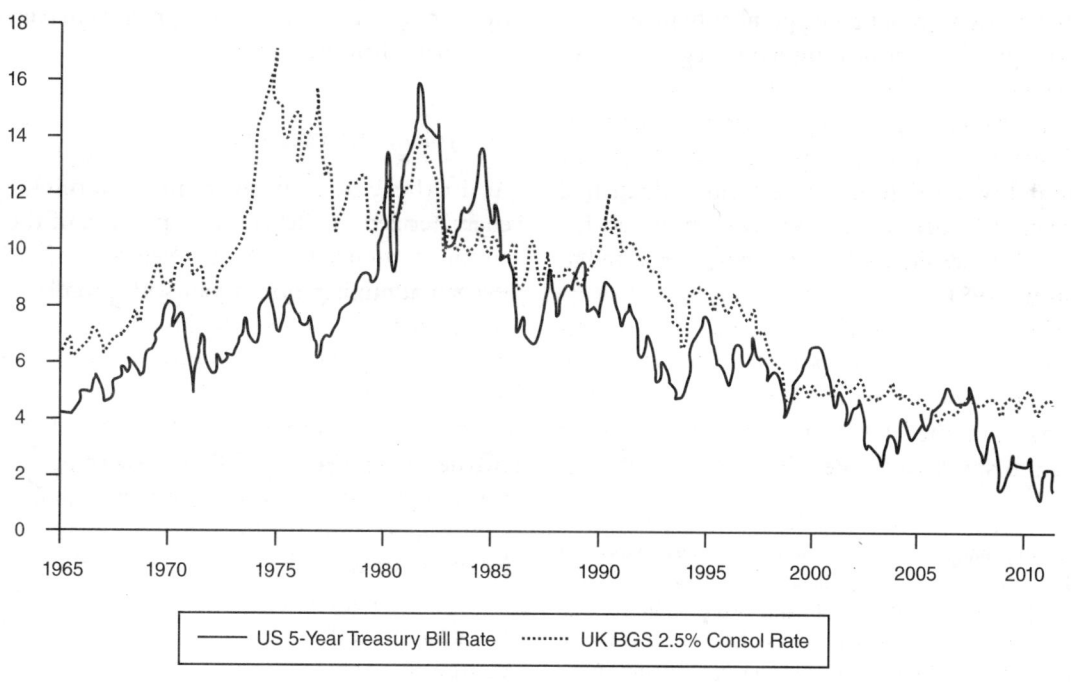

Figure 4.1 US and UK Long-term Interest Rate
Source: Federal Reserve Economic Data and Office for National Statistics, UK.

---

[5] It is widely recognized that the key factor governing the cost of disinflationary policies is the degree of policy regime credibility. Credibility is important because it influences the public's expectations about future inflation. These expectations, in turn, affect the current state of the economy because they are incorporated into wages via forward-looking labour contracts and into the level of long-term nominal interest rates, which govern borrowing behaviour.

[6] It was readily conceded that the stated policy would curtail demand and deepen the recession already underway. Yet the control of inflation was given precedence in the belief, doggedly maintained and sometimes dogmatically asserted, that this policy alone would be able to create the conditions for future growth and prosperity.

however, was not enough; MTFS not only failed to command immediate credibility, it also failed to be carried out in its own literal terms. In response, long-term interest rates rose initially—indicating a lack of confidence in the government's ability to control inflation (see Figure 4.1).

To enhance credibility, the budget of 1981 'perversely' raised taxes by 2 per cent of GDP to cut PSBR even though the recession still had not ended. This was very unpopular, not least among the economics profession. In fact, 364 economists (including Nobel Prize-winning economist Amartya Sen) were signatories to a letter which was published by *The Times* protesting against the government's fiscal and monetary policy in general and against the 1981 budget in particular.[7] The signatories to the letter were signing up to a statement on economic policy which is given in Box 4.1.[8]

Nevertheless, this approach to policy was unequivocally vindicated by events. We now know that the bottom of the cycle occurred very shortly afterwards. There is no evidence that the budget of 1981 'deepened the recession' as 364 economists confidently predicted at the time. In fact, it turned out to be a significant tipping point both in terms of the public's acceptance of the determination of government policy and economic performance. The tax rise brought inflation (and inflation expectations) down decisively and was crucial in finally creating market confidence in the policies' durability. Long-term interest rates which had fluctuated around 14 per cent for two years began to fall at last during 1981 (see Figure 4.1).[9] Output also started to recover in spring 1981.

The Thatcher revolution teaches us that a prudent anti-inflation policy includes containing the deficit to an amount that can be comfortably financed without printing money. It was felt that, provided the basic source of monetary temptation so to speak was bolted down, then control of

---

Box 4.1 Statement on Economic Policy

'We, who are all present or retired members of the economics staffs of British universities, are convinced that:

(a) there is no basis in economic theory or supporting evidence for the Government's belief that by deflating demand they will bring inflation permanently under control and thereby induce an automatic recovery in output and employment;

(b) present politics will deepen the depression, erode the industrial base of our economy and threaten its social and political stability;

(c) there are alternative policies; and

(d) the time has come to reject monetarist policies and consider urgently which alternative offers the best hope of sustained recovery.

---

money supply itself would be easier over the long term and, most importantly, market confidence in that control would be assured. This was the primary maxim of Margaret Thatcher's disinflation policy.

The Volcker Disinflation

As in the UK, a programme of monetary restraint characterized the deflationary package of the Republican administration in the US, also elected to office in 1979. The Reagan administration began with promises of a supply-side revolution. Lower inflation, lower taxes, and a smaller government were going to boost productivity and growth. Most evident was a general change in policy away from inflationary accommodation which had been evident for two decades previously.[10] This was accompanied with what was seen as an important change in operating procedures—a shift from interest rate to money stock targets. This change in emphasis was seen, in part, as a deliberate attempt to gain public confidence in the planned monetary contractions and to endorse the administration's anti-inflationary commitment.

---

[7] There is a story that, not long after *The Times* published its letter from the 364 economists, Margaret Thatcher was asked in a House of Commons debate whether she could name two economists who agreed with her. Margaret Thatcher replied that she could, and named Alan Walters and Patrick Minford. On returning to Downing Street, a civil servant said to her, 'It is a good job he did not ask you to name three.' This anecdote illustrates how much opposition there was in 1981 to the new policy framework.

[8] Those who signed include: (a) 76 present or past professors; (b) a majority of the chief economic advisers to the government since the war: James Meade, Roberthall, Alec Cairncross, Bryan Hopkin, and Fred Atkinson; (c) the President; nine of the Vice-Presidents, and the Secretary-General of the Royal Economic Society.

[9] Matthews and Minford (1987) argue that the tax rise was entirely deliberate. The cuts in deficits were intended to signal the seriousness of the government's resolve to hold down monetary growth in the long term. The severe demand squeeze of the period was necessary to overcome the 'inflationary psychology' and to generate credibility.

[10] In 1980, Paul Volcker explained: 'In the past, at critical junctures for economic stabilization policy, we have usually been more preoccupied with the possibility of near-term weakness in economic activity or other objectives than with the implications of our actions for future inflation ... The result has been our now chronic inflationary problem ... The broad objective of policy must be to break that ominous pattern ... Success will require that policy be consistently and persistently oriented to that end. Vacillation and procrastination, out of fears of recession or otherwise, would run grave risks' (cited in Romer and Romer 2004: 145).

A casual inspection of the data may leave one in little doubt that the Volcker Fed suffered from a serious lack of credibility. One might reasonably have expected the aggressive funds rate actions beginning in October 1979 that brought inflation down from almost 10 per cent in 1981–2 to about 4 per cent in 1983–4 to reduce long-term interest rates by quickly stabilizing long-term inflation expectations at a low rate. Yet, as Figure 4.1 reveals, the reverse was true. The five-year Treasury bill rate rose about 7 percentage points from a trough in June 1980 to its 15.9 per cent peak in September 1981. The long rate continued its rise in early 1984, moving up from the 10.6 per cent level it had maintained since the previous summer to a 13.5 per cent peak in June 1984. Amazingly, this was only about 2.5 percentage points short of its September 1981 peak, even though by 1984 inflation was 6 percentage points lower than in 1981—indicating a lingering lack of confidence in the Fed. In fact, we now know that it took until 1988 for the long-rate volatility to disappear.

These events appear extremely odd, especially given the rhetoric that surrounded the anti-inflationary policy and the strong ideological commitment of the Reagan administration to inflation control (see Blackburn and Christensen 1989). Something fundamental was preventing the public from believing the anti-inflationary programme. How could two seemingly identical policies in the UK and US produce such different results? Indeed, it seems likely that the Fed's commitment to reducing inflation was viewed with considerable scepticism by the public. Fears had been fuelled, in particular in the spring and summer of 1980, by the decrease in short nominal rates in the face of a recession. The Volcker Fed behaved in a manner consistent with prior experiences. It had undertaken restrictive monetary policy in the face of rising inflation, but it had promptly reversed course to fight the recession. Goodfriend and King (2005) argue that this policy reversal likely hurt the Fed's credibility and thereby contributed to the ultimate costliness of the disinflation.

Perhaps more importantly, unlike the Thatcher administration which had instituted fiscal reform, the Reagan administration allowed the budget deficit to rise far beyond the wildest early projections. US fiscal policy during the Reagan administration was characterized by large and growing federal budget deficits which, if projected forward might have been seen to imply the need for future monetization of the debt to maintain solvency of the government's intertemporal budget constraint.[11] As a result public confidence in the Fed's future capacity to control the money supply was severely dented. The Reagan tax cuts put the Fed in a familiar bind. In the past, it was understood that the Fed would accommodate rather than resist an expansionary fiscal policy designed to stimulate growth. This time, however, the Fed did not back off. While challenging the government to implement reforms in order to make the transition to low inflation as painless as possible, the Volcker Fed was willing to fight inflation by itself if necessary. The Fed, faced with a high deficit decided to maintain high real interest rates in order to gain counter-inflationary credibility. But this proved costly. During this period, the US experienced two recessions generally attributed to tight monetary policy. The civilian unemployment rate peaked at about 11 per cent in 1982—the highest level observed in the US economy since the Great Depression.

EMPIRICALLY EVALUATING THE LINK BETWEEN POLICY REGIME CREDIBILITY AND INFLATION PERSISTENCE

Evidence from UK and US Disinflation

Our empirical strategy is to establish the link between policy regime credibility and inflation persistence. To this end we estimate the path of the time-varying persistence parameter. We track inflation persistence by estimating the autoregressive process in our inflation reduced form treating inflation as an observable variable and the inflation persistence parameter (and the intercept) as an unobserved time-varying state variable. The derivation of the inflation reduced-form (equation A4.6) is shown in Appendix A4. The model links regime credibility with inflation persistence. The model for inflation is couched in annual terms. To preserve this interpretation we estimate the model with 12-month-ended inflation data but at a monthly frequency. We estimate the following model:

$$\pi_t = \alpha_t + \rho_t \pi_{t-1} + u_t + \sum_{j=1}^{q} \theta_j u_{t-j},$$
$$\alpha_t = \alpha_{t-1} + \xi_t,$$
$$\rho_t = \rho_{t-1} + \gamma C_t + \eta_t,$$

where π is the inflation rate and u is the disturbance term assumed to be normally distributed with zero mean and constant variance. The order-q moving-average (MA)

---

[11] This can be seen by looking at 'baseline projections' constructed by the Congressional Budget Office (CBO) before and after the Reagan tax cuts were voted in 1981 and implemented over the following three years (see Blanchard 1987). These projections assumed roughly no change in the current tax structure and in the level of real spending. Previously, those projections always showed very large surpluses over the long run. Since 1981, however, the projections for each year show no improvement as the horizon increases.

error term is motivated by the use of year-ended data. The first equation represents the *measurement* equation and the remaining two equations are *transition* equations. The disturbances ξ_t and η_t are serially uncorrelated disturbances with zero mean and constant variances, and are assumed uncorrelated with each other in all time periods.

The variable C_t is the month-on-month change in long-term interest rate—our proxy for credibility.[12] When credibility is low (characterized by substantial month-on-month variation in the long rate) we would expect substantial inflation inertia, higher ρ_t. In contrast, when a policy regime is credible and inflation expectations are well anchored (characterized by lower month-on-month variation in the long rate) we would expect inflation persistence to drop significantly, lower ρ_t. These equations represent a state space form, in which the unknown parameters γ, σ_ξ^2, and σ_η^2 can be estimated by maximum likelihood techniques. The Kalman filter recursions can then be applied to yield optimal estimates of the state variable sequence. The resulting estimate of γ should be positive: the lower the credibility (substantial month-on-month variation in the long rate), the higher will be the inertial effect on inflation.

Data and Estimation Results

The state-space model described above is estimated with monthly observations of year-ended inflation data for the US and UK (all items consumer price index) from 1963:1–2010:12. This data is collected from the Bureau of Labour Statistics and OECD respectively. For US long-term interest rates we use the five-year constant maturity Treasury bill rate from the FRED database and for the UK we use British Government Securities 2.5 per cent consols gross flat yield from the Office for National Statistics.

Table 4.1 reports our estimates of $\hat{\gamma}$ (asymptotic standard error in parentheses) based on MA(12) process for the errors. The coefficient is positive for both countries, as predicted by the model, and highly significant. Figure 4.2 plots our estimates of persistence for both the US and UK along with our proxy for credibility—month-on-month change in the long rate. The standard error bands around these estimates are not plotted to avoid visual clustering.

The pattern of time variation in inflation persistence is largely consistent with a reading of US and UK policy history, with inflation persistence high and more volatile

Table 4.1 Maximum Likelihood Estimates

	$\hat{\gamma}$	$\hat{\sigma}_\xi^2$	$\hat{\sigma}_\eta^2$
US	1.22 (0.69)	4.99×10^{-2}	9.6×10^{-4}
UK	2.19 (0.85)	5.91×10^{-2}	36.8×10^{-4}
India	0.04 (0.02)	4.06×10^{-3}	4.22×10^{-5}

Source: Authors' own calculations.

during the 1970s and early 1980s than in surrounding years. In both the countries the long rate exhibits substantial variation during this period, indicating a lack of confidence in the government's ability to control inflation.

In the UK the budget of 1981 (that 'perversely' raised taxes by 2 per cent of GDP to cut PSBR) was a significant turning point in establishing credibility. The tax rise brought inflation persistence down decisively (see Figure 4.2) and was crucial in finally creating market confidence in the policies' durability.

Although a programme of monetary restraint characterized the deflationary package of the Republican administration in the US as well, yet President Reagan's policies contrast sharply with Margaret Thatcher's. The budget deficit was allowed to rise and the consequences for money supply control were shrugged off by the White House resulting in a collapse of confidence in the Fed's future capacity to control money supply. This was sufficient to prevent the persistence parameter from falling markedly. In fact, it took until the late 1980s for inflation persistence to drop and public confidence in the counter-inflation policy to be firmly established.

Policy Regime Credibility and Inflation Persistence—The Indian Evidence

The state-space model described above is estimated with monthly observations of year-ended inflation data for India (all commodities WPI with base year 1981–2=100) from 1981:4–2011:11. The data is collected from the Office of the Economic Adviser, Ministry of Commerce and Industry, Government of India. For India our proxy for credibility is the gross primary deficit of the central and state governments as the percentage of GDP.[13] The data

---

[12] Minford (1991) and Goodfriend and King (2005) also use the behaviour of long-term interest rates as an indicator of credibility. They argue that both the Thatcher administration in the UK and the Volcker Fed in the US regarded long-term interest rates as a key indicator of inflation expectations and of their disinflation policy credibility.

[13] During most of the 1980s, the debt market in India was dominated by government securities primarily due to large fiscal deficits and banking regulations that forced banks to invest in government securities. The interest rate on government debt was administered and there was hardly any secondary market for these securities. Although a significant degree of deregulation has taken place in the

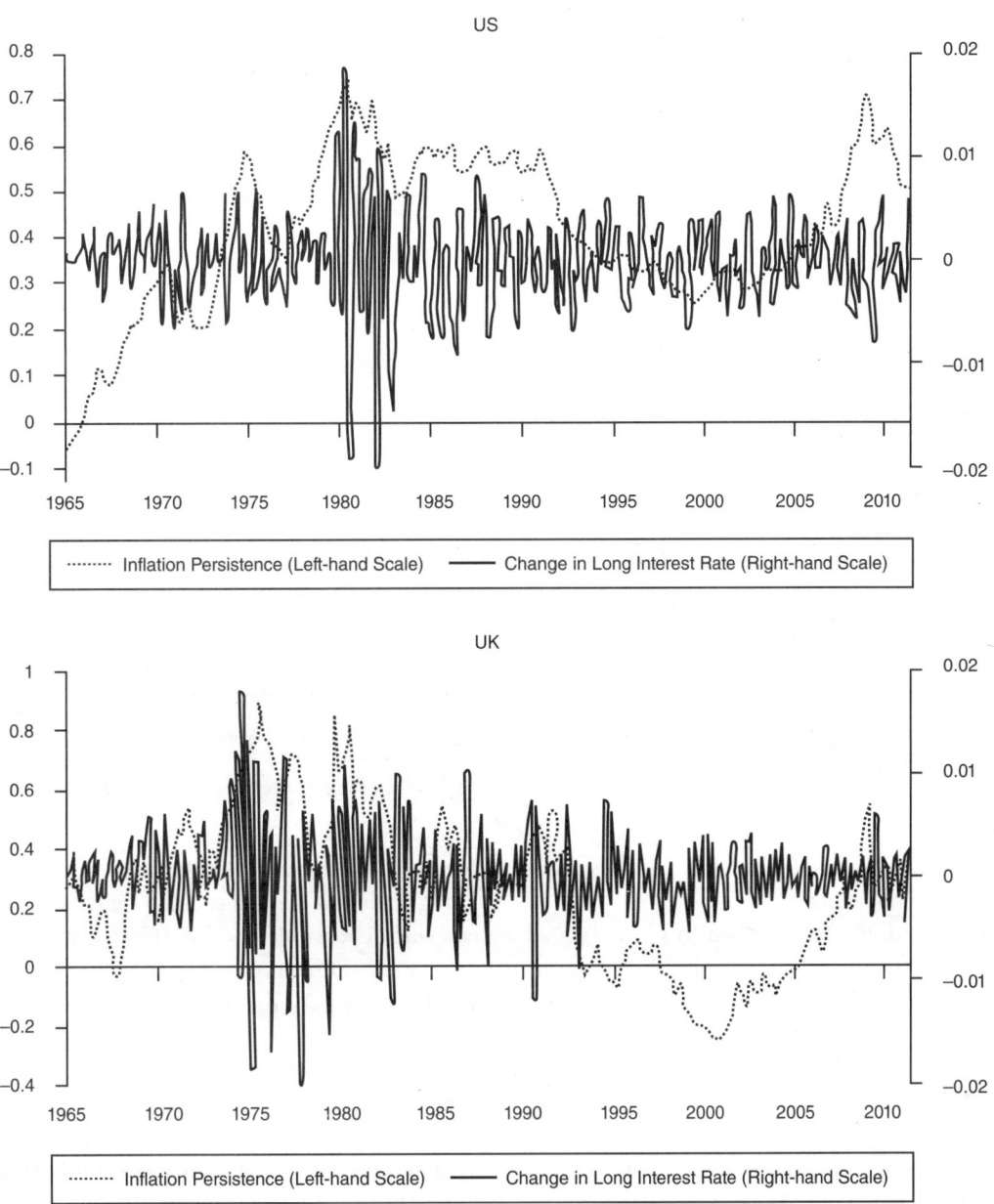

Figure 4.2 Inflation Persistence and Month-on-Month Variation in Long Interest Rate

Source: Authors' own calculations.

on combined gross primary deficit is obtained from RBI's *Handbook of Statistics on Indian Economy 2010–11*. This data is available at annual frequency, which is converted to monthly frequency by using cubic spline interpolation.

recent past, there is still captive demand for government debt. Nearly 70 per cent of the debt is owned either by the RBI or by the banking system which remains dominated by state-owned lenders. As a result it would be inappropriate to use bond yields as a proxy for credibility in the Indian case.

From an empirical standpoint the credibility hypothesis predicts that when the government's finances are in disarray (characterized by persistent primary deficits) and are projected to get worse, the central bank's inflation target enjoys very low credibility. In this case we should expect substantial inflation inertia. Conversely, when the government's fiscal house is in order the basic source of monetary temptation so to speak is bolted down, then control of money supply itself would be easier over the long term and, most importantly, market confidence in that control would be assured. We would expect inflation

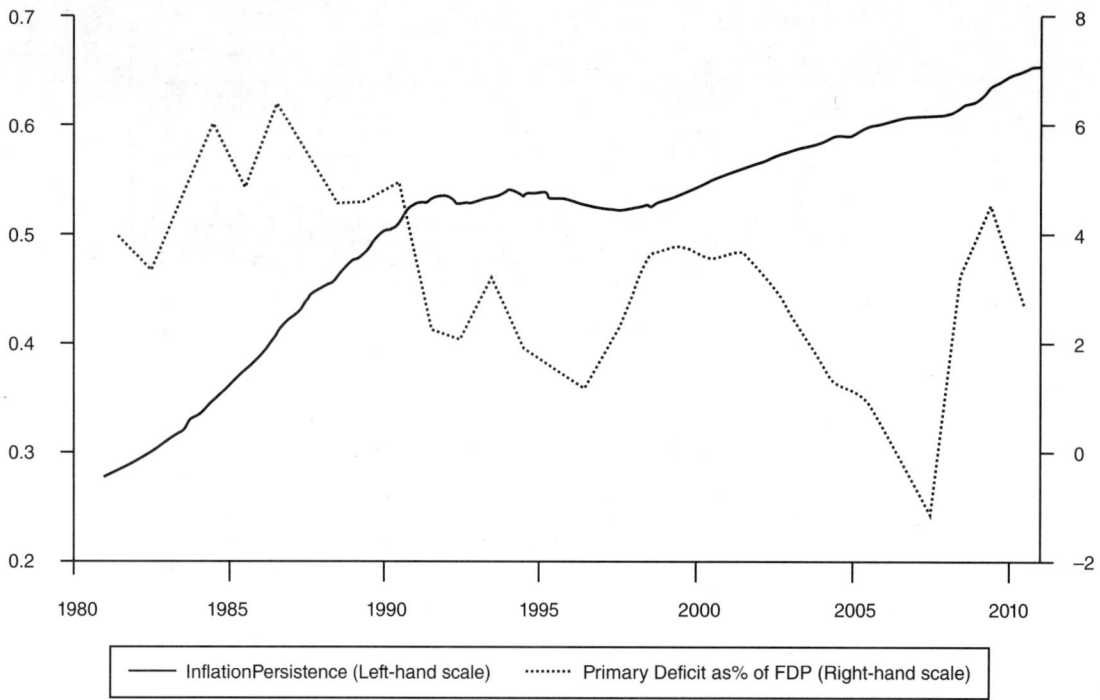

Figure 4.3 Inflation Persistence and Primary Deficit to GDP Ratio

Source: Authors' own calculations.

persistence to drop significantly. Therefore, the resulting estimate of γ should be positive.

Kalman filter recursions were applied to yield optimal estimates of the state variable sequence. Table 4.1 reports our estimates of $\hat{\gamma}$ (asymptotic standard error in parentheses) based on MA (12) process for the errors. The coefficient γ is positive, as predicted by the model, and highly significant.[14] Figure 4.3 plots our estimates of persistence along with our proxy for credibility—primary deficit as the percentage of GDP. The estimates of the persistence coefficient indicate significant variation over the sample period. Specifically, the persistence coefficient started to drift up in the 1980s. It rose steadily until the early 1990s, before stabilizing thereafter. It started to drift up during the late 1990s. After the financial crisis of 2008 we once again witnessed an upward drift. So what explains the time-variation in inflation persistence?

In the 1980s fiscal controls weakened and deficits mounted. An increasingly expansionist fiscal stance spilled over to the external sector, requiring growing recourse to external borrowing on commercial terms. Against a background of rising trade and current account deficits and a deteriorating external debt profile, the 1990 Gulf War and consequent oil price spike tipped India's balance of payments into crisis in 1990–1. This period is associated with a substantial rise in inflation persistence. In 1991 the new Congress government seized the opportunity offered by the crisis to launch an array of long overdue and wide-ranging economic reforms. They encompassed fiscal consolidation and reform of the tax system, which kept a check on government borrowings. The persistence coefficient stabilized during this phase. This was followed by a period of steady deterioration in government finances during the late 1990s. Our persistence estimate starts to drift up during this phase.

Finally, in the aftermath of the global financial crisis of 2008 we see a significant deterioration in government finances (mainly due to large public sector pay increases following the Sixth Pay Commission and the Mahatma Gandhi National Rural Employment Guarantee Act [MNREGA]). In response to the financial crisis, monetary and fiscal policies were eased by allowing for a pause in the fiscal consolidation process enjoined by the FRBM Act of 2003. Moreover, there are increasing indications that meeting the targets adopted in the revised roadmap for fiscal consolidation as recommended by the Thirteenth Finance Commission would pose a formidable challenge. In sum, government finances are once again in disarray and are not

---

[14] When we estimated the model for a longer sample, the coefficient was positive but not significant. This is consistent with the view that until the beginning of the 1980s the overall fiscal situation was under control with very low deficits (see Chelliah 1996). In fact, it was only during the 1980s that the fiscal situation steadily deteriorated. This resulted in increasing additions to unproductive debt and the interest burden on the general budget began to grow exponentially.

expected to improve over the foreseeable future. This has clearly undermined public confidence in the RBI's ability to stabilize inflation going forward. We see a rise in inflation persistence during this phase. In sum, it is insufficient to announce and maintain restrictive monetary policies unless accompanied by a coordinated reduction in budget deficits. This is what history teaches us. Today's debate about inflation largely misses this point, and therefore, fails to contend with the greatest inflation danger that we face.

LESSONS AND CONCLUSIONS

The policy implications of this chapter are quite clear. A prudent anti-inflation policy includes containing the deficit to an amount that can be comfortably financed at steady interest rates without printing money. Large contemporary government deficits unaccompanied by concrete prospects for future government surpluses promote realistic doubts about whether monetary restraint must be abandoned sooner or later to help finance the deficit. It is insufficient to announce and maintain restrictive monetary policies. Agents will also look at fiscal policy in their attempt to determine whether the 'reform' can be sustained. If fiscal policy is incompatible with the 'reform' in monetary policy, agents will attach positive probability to the event that the reform will be abandoned in the future. The result will be an increase in inflationary expectations. If so, agents will try to get rid of money today—driving up the prices of goods, services, and eventually wages across the entire economy. Our economy will be primed for it as long as our fiscal trajectory is unsustainable. International evidence reported here supports the hypothesis that close adherence to a policy of reducing the monetary growth rate combined with deficit reduction can result in dramatic reductions in inflation. These considerations are pertinent in assessing the state of our economy today and that of the UK and US in the 1980s.

Appendix A4

A MODEL OF CREDIBILITY, LEARNING, AND INFLATION PERSISTENCE

Following Bomfim and Rudebusch (2000) we define monetary policy credibility through the relationship between inflation targets and inflation expectations. Their definition of central bank credibility is straightforward. At period $t-1$ the central bank announces its inflation target for period t, denoted, π^*. The private sector must evaluate the future reliability of this target. Agents must judge the central bank's credibility of intent, that is, whether the target represents the true goal of the central bank and its credibility of action, that is, whether the central bank has the ability to meet the target even if it wants to (say, in the face of fiscal constraints).[1] Overall credibility is measured by the extent to which the pronouncement of a target is believed by the private sector in the formation of their inflation expectations. Specifically, we assume that period $t-1$ expectations of the inflation target at time t, that is, perceived inflation target denoted, π_t^p, are a weighted average of the announced target π^* and the current period's inflation rate:

$$E_{t-1}\pi^* = \pi_t^p = \lambda \pi^* + (1-\lambda)\pi_{t-1} \qquad (A4.1)$$

The parameter λ (with $0 \leq \lambda \leq 1$) indexes the target credibility of the central bank. For analytical convenience we assume that this learning parameter is constant in what follows.[2] If $\lambda = 1$, there is perfect credibility, and the private sector's perceived inflation target will be equal to the announced target. If $\lambda = 0$, there is no credibility, and the announced target is ignored in the formation of expectations. Intermediate values of λ represent partial credibility for the announced target. The policymaker's loss function is:

$$L(\pi_t, u_t) = 1/2[b(\pi_t - \pi^*)^2 + (u_t - ku^n)^2], \qquad 0 < b < 1$$
$$(A4.2)$$

where π_t is the inflation rate in period t, u_t is the unemployment rate and ku^n represents the central bank's target level of unemployment. We assume that $k < 1$, in which case the central bank's target unemployment rate is below the natural rate. The constraint facing the policymaker is given by an expectations augmented short-run Phillips curve:

$$u_t = u^n - \alpha\left(\pi_t - \pi_t^e\right) + \varepsilon_t, \quad \alpha > 0 \qquad (A4.3)$$

where u^n is the natural rate of unemployment assumed to be a constant and ε_t is a random shock to supply assumed to be normally distributed with zero mean and constant variance.

---

[1] The importance of the fiscal regime in determining the credibility of disinflationary policies is emphasized by Sargent (1982, 1983) and Baxter (1985).

[2] Credibility of the announced target as indexed by λ is unlikely to be exogenous. In fact, a major contribution of learning literature is to show that credibility is established by outcome. That is, the weight that agents place on the announced target reacts to developments in the economy. If past inflation matches the inflation target, then the announced target is given more weight by the private sector in the formation of expectations of future inflation.

The policymaker's optimal choice of inflation at time t, that is, the inflation rate that equates the marginal benefit from inflation surprise to the marginal cost is given by:

$$\pi_t = \left(\frac{b}{b+\alpha^2}\right)\pi^* + \left(\frac{\alpha(1-k)}{b+\alpha^2}\right)u^n +$$

$$\left(\frac{\alpha^2}{b+\alpha^2}\right)\pi_t^e + \left(\frac{\alpha}{b+\alpha^2}\right)\varepsilon_t, \quad (A4.4)$$

where π_t^e represents the private sector's expectations of period t inflation. The private sector in this framework knows the model, including the policymaker's objective function. So the private sector expects inflation to be:

$$\pi_t^e = \lambda\pi^* + (1-\lambda)\pi_{t-1} + \frac{\alpha(1-k)}{b}u^n. \quad (A4.5)$$

Under discretion the central bank cannot credibly manipulate inflation expectations. So the central bank takes private sector inflation expectations as given when it solves its optimization problem. Substituting (A4.5) in (A4.4) for π_t^e yields the reduced-form solution for inflation:

$$\pi_t = \left(a_0\pi^* + a_1 u^n\right) + a_2\pi_{t-1} + a_3\varepsilon_t, \quad (A4.6)$$

where:

$$a_0 = \left(\frac{b+\alpha^2\lambda}{b+\alpha^2}\right), \; a_1 = \left(\frac{\alpha(1-k)}{b}\right),$$

$$a_2 = \left(\frac{\alpha^2(1-\lambda)}{b+\alpha^2}\right) \text{ and } a_3 = \left(\frac{\alpha}{b+\alpha^2}\right).$$

The reduced-form solution for inflation in this model has an ARMA(p,q) representation. The source of persistence in this model is imperfect credibility ($0 \leq \lambda < 1$). Time-variation in inflation persistence can arise in this model because of learning on the part of the private sector. That is, if the announced inflation target lacks credibility (say, because of fiscal constraints), then inflation expectations will not be significantly affected. Facing imperfect credibility, the policymaker perceives a quick disinflation to be extremely costly and consequently, finds it optimal to gradually reduce inflation–higher persistence. From an empirical standpoint credibility literature predicts that the degree of inflation persistence should negatively co-vary with policy regime credibility.

REFERENCES

Balakrishnan, Pulapre (1991), *Pricing and Inflation in India*. New Delhi: Oxford University Press.

Baxter, Marianne (1985), 'The Role of Expectations in Stabilization Policy', *Journal of Monetary Economics*, 15: 343–62.

Blackburn, K. and M. Christensen (1989), 'Monetary Policy and Policy Credibility: Theories and Evidence', *Journal of Economic Literature*, 27(1): 1–45.

Blanchard, Olivier J. (1987), 'Reaganomics', *Economic Policy*, 5: 15–56.

Bomfim, Antulio N. and Glenn D. Rudebusch (2000), 'Opportunistic and Deliberate Disinflation Under Imperfect Credibility', *Journal of Money, Credit, and Banking*, 32: 707–21.

Chelliah, Raja J. (1996), *Towards Sustainable Growth: Essays in Fiscal and Financial Sector Reforms in India*. New Delhi: Oxford University Press.

Goodfriend, Marvin and Robert G. King (2005), 'The Incredible Volcker Disinflation', *Journal of Monetary Economics*, 52: 981–1015.

Matthews, Kent and Patrick Minford (1987), 'Mrs. Thatcher's Economic Policies 1979–87', *Economic Policy*, 5: 57–102.

Minford, Patrick (1991), *The Supply Side Revolution in Britain*. Aldershot, UK and Brookfield, USA: Edward Elgar.

Nelson, Edward (2005), 'The Great Inflation of the Seventies: What Really Happened?', *Advances in Macroeconomics, Berkeley Electronic Press*, 5(1): 1–48.

Reserve Bank of India [RBI] (2012), *Third Quarter Review of Monetary Policy for 2011–2*, Mumbai: Reserve Bank of India.

Romer, Christina and David H. Romer (2004), 'Choosing the Federal Reserve Chair: Lessons from History', *Journal of Economic Perspectives*, 18(1): 129–62.

Sargent, Thomas J. (1982), 'The End of Four Big Inflations', in Robert E. Hall (ed.), *Inflation, Causes and Effects*. Chicago: University of Chicago Press, pp. 41–97.

———. (1983), 'Stopping Moderate Inflations: The Methods of Poincare and Thatcher', in Rudiger Dornbusch and Mario Henrique Simonsen (eds), *Inflation, Debt, and Indexation*. Cambridge, Massachusetts: MIT Press, pp. 54–98.

Sargent, Thomas J. and Neil Wallace (1981), 'Some Unpleasant Monetarist Arithmetic', *Federal Reserve Bank of Minneapolis Quarterly Review*, 5(3): 1–17.

Shaw, G.K. (1983), 'Fiscal policy under the first Thatcher administration—1979–83', *Public Finance Analysis*, 41: 312–42.

5

Is Fiscal Policy in India Pro-cyclical?

*R. Krishnan and Rajendra R. Vaidya**

INTRODUCTION

The purpose of this chapter is to empirically verify the generalization in literature that fiscal policy is pro-cyclical in developing economies, by analysing exclusively the fiscal behaviour of India over the period 1950–2008. A pro-cyclical fiscal policy simply means that developing economies adopt an expansionary fiscal policy in booms but follow a contractionary policy during recessions. This is contrary to the conventional wisdom of reducing expenses and increasing savings during good times and utilizing such savings to reduce taxes and increasing expenditure during recessions and thus smoothen out the business cycle fluctuations. A finding of such a pro-cyclicality of fiscal policy was first observed in Latin American countries by Gavin and Perotti (1997) and subsequently it was established that developing countries in general exhibited pro-cyclicality (see Talvi and Veigh 2005) and advanced countries followed an a-cyclical or a counter-cyclical fiscal policy. However, evidence of pro-cyclicality has been reported in sub-components of government spending and in overall discretionary government spending in developed countries as well (see Hallerberg and Strauch 2002; Gali and

Perotti 2003; and Lane 2003). Buiter and Patel (2010) narrate how even advanced countries like the UK, France, and the US blatantly followed pro-cyclical fiscal policies in some instances. This suggests that the problem of a pro-cyclical fiscal policy is not strictly confined to the developing world. Some cross-country empirical studies do point out that Indian fiscal policy, too, has indeed been pro-cyclical (see, for example, Kaminsky et al. 2004).

Why should countries follow a counter-cyclical fiscal policy? Such counter-cyclical fiscal policies intend to smooth business cycle fluctuations and reduce adverse welfare consequences. Pallage and Robe (2000) have shown that estimates of such welfare loss are about 15 to 30 times higher in developing countries—which typically have higher output variability—than comparable estimates pertaining to the US economy. Portier and Puch (2006) have argued that in an economy with non-clearing markets, a feature observed in most developing countries, welfare costs of business cycles are substantially higher compared to economies which operate in a frictionless environment, an observation likely to hold good in advanced economies. Lucas (1987), for instance, concludes that in the context of the US economy, welfare costs of business cycle fluctuations are minimal and this prompted him to suggest that governments should abandon counter-cyclical policies. To our best knowledge, no study that quantifies such welfare costs exists in the Indian context.

However, studies conducted exclusively on India recorded episodes of pro-cyclical behaviour, based on

---

* We gratefully acknowledge the comments on an earlier draft by Romar Correa, V.S. Chitre, K.L. Krishna, S.L. Shetty, and Kanakasabhapathi. Comments by the participants of the IDR workshop are also gratefully acknowledged. We would like to thank Vikash Gautam for excellent research assistance. Remaining errors, if any, are ours.

which questions on the government's ability to smooth out cyclical swings had arisen (see Shah and Patnaik 2010 and Raj, Kundrakpam, and Das 2011). In particular, during good times, government spends more and its deficits increase and during recessions it spends less but the deficits also come down, thus aggravating the recession. Should this turn out to be true in a country where fiscal policy dominates, there is a possibility that fiscal policy may have fallen far short of the potential that it has to stabilize output during downturns. The introduction of the Fiscal Responsibility and Budget Management Bill, 2003 (FRBMA) in India, did result in some fiscal consolidation both at the centre and in the states, but evidence of savings during good times is still not clear. For example, during the fiscal years 2006 and 2007, actual GDP outgrew potential GDP, resulting in actual deficits declining faster than the adjusted deficits (see Herd and Leibfritz 2008). Even FRBMA does not have an explicit provision to encourage counter-cyclical fiscal policies (Buiter and Patel 2010). If such pronouncements about the pro-cyclicality of fiscal policy are further confirmed by a more rigorous empirical inquiry using a larger dataset, which is what this chapter aims to do, then we will have good reason to be very concerned about the future of the macroeconomic stability of our economy.

Theoretical literature identifies various reasons ranging from credit constraints, lack of strong institutions, social pulls, political pressures, and corruption, for the presence of pro-cyclicality. But applied literature mostly using panel data, has used different variables for different countries to explain such pro-cyclicality, with very few explanatory variables being in common in such studies. However, our endeavour in this chapter is a modest one. We do not intend to test or empirically verify any competing hypotheses to explain pro-cyclicality. We aim to address the pro-cyclicality issue in general. We use a dataset different from the usual aggregate government expenditure or consumption data that is generally employed in such studies and adopt a different approach to measuring fiscal cyclicality. Using data from the 'Economic and Functional Classification' of the budget over the period 1950–1 to 2008–9 and employing a popular tool used in business cycle literature to measure synchronization of cycles, we find overall evidence suggesting that the Indian fiscal policy, measured by total expenditure, can be termed at best as a-cyclical. However, this has to be tempered with the observation that some important components of government expenditure do show clear signs of pro-cyclicality. On the whole, this finding suggests that we still lack a fiscal policy design that encourages a counter-cyclical policy. In the next section, we list out the various issues involved with fiscal policy. The section that follows explains the methodological approach adopted in this chapter and discusses the data used and the empirical evidence. The last section concludes the chapter.

FISCAL CYCLICALITY—CONCEPTUAL, THEORETICAL, AND METHODOLOGICAL ISSUES

In this section we discuss the reasons for the pro-cyclicality of fiscal policy, how to measure fiscal policy, and the conceptual issues behind them.

Why Fiscal Pro-cyclicality? Theory and Empirics

Given that a pro-cyclical fiscal policy contradicts both Barro's (1979) concept of the tax smoothing principle for fiscal stabilization and Keynesian stabilization policies, researchers have laid out some possible reasons for the presence of the pro-cyclicality of fiscal policy. Two such reasons are: (i) credit constraints faced by developing economies, especially during recessions as advanced by Gavin and Perotti (1997); and (ii) political and economic considerations prevalent in developing economies, as advanced by Tornell and Lane (1999), Talvi and Veigh 2005; and Alesina et al. (2008). According to the former, in good times developing economies are able to borrow at low interest rates, resulting in increased public spending and wide deficits. Alternatively, during recessions, countries cannot borrow at reasonable interest rates to finance the deficits and the only way to reduce deficits is to cut spending. Gavin and Perotti (1997) provide evidence of the role of such borrowing constraints while establishing pro-cyclicality in Latin American economies using data over a period of 25 years. They find that fiscal policy, especially public spending, is particularly pro-cyclical during bad macroeconomic times. Kamnisky et al. (2004) adopt different measures of cyclicality to establish that fiscal policy in OECD countries is a-cyclical or counter-cyclical while in developing economies it is pro-cyclical. Thornton (2008) in his study on 37 African countries over the period 1960–2004 finds real government consumption to be overwhelmingly pro-cyclical.

In the latter strand, pro-cyclicality of fiscal policy arises because of competition among powerful coalition partners to demand more funds in a boom, out of a fear that the extra income generated during the boom would otherwise go to wasteful spending, resulting in a 'voracity effect' according to Tornell and Lane (1999). These authors suggest that in democracies, pro-cyclicality of fiscal deficit arises because of a lack of transparency in fiscal policies. Voters have difficulty in understanding the budget and hence evidence of pro-cyclicality is negatively associated with budget transparency but positively associated with corruption.

Assuming that political pressures dictate tax-breaks in good times, they conclude that while economic upturns in industrialized countries are associated with higher inflation, these peaks during economic busts for developing countries. Alesina et al. (2008) using an unbalanced panel find that both government expenditure and revenues exhibit pro-cyclicality but expenditure shows clearer signs of pro-cyclicality. Besides these, other factors like difficulties in assessing economic cycles (Akitoby et al. 2004) which can result in untimely implementation of fiscal programmes and the small proportions of transfers in government expenditure (Lane 2003) also have been quoted as evidence for a pro-cyclical fiscal stance. According to Woo's (2009), theoretical model, greater heterogeneity of preferences of different social groups causes fiscal policy to be more pro-cyclical. Using income inequality and dispersion of educational attainment as indicators of the divergence of preferences, Woo finds these variables to be consistently significant in his cross-country tests of fiscal pro-cyclicality.

The above mentioned studies used government expenditure to measure fiscal policy. Not much work has been done using government revenue, because of paucity of quality data. Talvi and Veigh (2005) tackle this problem by considering inflation tax as a proxy for all taxes and their finding also concurs with that of the above studies in finding pro-cyclical fiscal policy; they attribute this to the existence of political pressures that demand tax breaks in good times so that governments will find it politically correct to reduce both conventional taxes and inflation tax during booms.

Measures of Fiscal Policy

Such divergent views on the existence of a pro-cyclical fiscal policy, make selecting an appropriate variable to measure fiscal policy a difficult issue. Many studies that have provided overwhelming evidence on fiscal pro-cyclicality focus on government expenditure. For example, Kaminsky et al. (2004) have persuasively argued that it is only government expenditure (and its components) that would allow an unambiguous answer to this question. They caution that tax revenues and the primary balance (defined as tax revenues minus government expenditures [excluding interest payments]) could be particularly misleading. Let us assume that fiscal policy is in fact a-cyclical and tax rates are constant over the business cycle. The tax base is likely to increase during booms and decrease during busts. Given that tax revenues are defined as tax base multiplied by tax rates, this would mean that tax revenues would rise during booms and fall during busts even if the fiscal policy stance is a-cyclical. This biases the results towards finding pro-cyclicality. The same conclusion would hold true in case of the primary balance. Government expenditures and tax rates do not suffer from this shortcoming. Since obtaining consistent data on aggregate tax rates is extremely difficult, most of the empirical literature focuses on government expenditure and its components. This chapter also employs government expenditure as a measure of fiscal policy but employs it in a way that differs from the earlier studies. A detailed explanation of our fiscal measure is offered in the results section.

Measuring Fiscal Cyclicality

Applied literature employs a variety of cyclical indicators ranging from the simple correlation to non-parametric procedures to quantify a cycle. We outline briefly the various methods used in literature to measure the cyclical component. Often a high correlation coefficient between the cyclical component of the fiscal policy variable, mostly government expenditure, and the reference series, the GDP series, is used as an indicator of a pro-cyclical fiscal stance.

In regression-based studies of cyclical measures, a variety of fiscal policy measures like government expenditure, government consumption or revenue are used as dependent variables and the main independent variables like GDP, are themselves measured differently. Here both the fiscal variable and the output variable are transformed in different ways to extract the cyclical component. Fiscal policy variables are defined either as a de-trended series or defined as GDP-deflated growth rates—which are first differences of logs of such fiscal policy variables as a proportion of GDP. Similarly, the most common independent variable is the growth rate of GDP or output gap, defined as deviations from the Hodrick-Prescott (H-P) filter. Regressing the cyclical component of the fiscal measure on that of the output is the norm in studies that employ such regression methods. A positive and significant coefficient is an indication of the existence of pro-cyclicality.

In this chapter we employ both the regression method and a time series method, where we use a measure of the cycle that is quite popular in business cycle literature and then quantify pro-cyclicality by measuring the degree of synchronization of the two cycles. To aid this we use a non-parametric tool called the concordance index. We describe our methodology in detail in the next section.

EMPIRICAL RESULTS

We start the discussion on the empirical part by first explaining the fiscal policy measure that we have used.

Measure of Fiscal Policy

The fiscal policy measure that we have used is government expenditure, but it differs from the other studies in that we have used a disaggregated expenditure data structure. We use data from 'An Economic and Functional Classification of the Central Government Budget' published by the Ministry of Finance, Department of Economic Affairs, and consider the expenditures incurred under the 'Administrative Departments and Departmental Commercial Undertakings' separately. Our time period under consideration is 1950–1 to 2008–9. This classification provides separate data for current expenditures of the central government under two broad sub-accounts—administrative departments (comprising all the ministries of the central government) and departmental commercial undertakings. Data on capital expenditures, unfortunately, is available only as an aggregate and not available under these two heads. In addition there have been definitional changes with regard to capital expenditures which render constructing a disaggregated series a difficult exercise. Hence for our analysis we have used data only on *current* expenditures of both government administration and departmental commercial undertakings. However, data for the years 1993–4 was not available and has been interpolated. Data on various individual categories as well as the total expenses under both these heads have been utilized for estimation purposes. The rationale for doing this is:

1. The budget of the central government covers expenditure of the government on both capital and current accounts. Expenses on capital accounts have been omitted from both the above mentioned sub-accounts, since proposals on capital expenditures committed in earlier years are expected to be met at all times and they form a substantial part of total expenditures. We argue that including them may obscure the cyclicality findings.
2. Coming to the current account part of the budget, we notice that it covers both the expenditures of government administrative departments and departmental commercial undertakings. Departmental commercial undertakings (including the Indian Railways, Post and Telegraph, Opium Factories and Alkaloid Works, Transport Schemes, Power Projects including Atomic Power Stations, Forests, and the Delhi Milk Scheme) can be viewed as business activities of the government. In principle, expenditures by departmental commercial undertakings are not made out of tax revenues, but out of the revenues earned by these undertakings by the selling goods and services that they produce. It could be argued that the expenditures of these commercial enterprises would by their very nature be pro-cyclical. During an economic upswing the expenditures of, say, the Indian Railways, which is by far the largest departmental commercial undertaking, would automatically rise as it transports more people and goods. In any case, the amount of discretion the government would have to use these expenditures to counter the business cycle would be limited as these are commercial enterprises and are normally expected to cover costs. Expenditures of the administrative departments on the other hand would by their very nature have a much larger discretionary component.

The expenses are analysed under the headings given in Table 5.1

Table 5.1 Components of Expenditures of the Central Government

Total Expenditure of the Central Government
1. Total expenditure
2. Wages and salaries
3. Expenditure on commodities and services
4. Interest payments
Expenditure of Administrative Departments
1. Total expenditure
2. Expenditure on commodities and services
3. Interest payments
4. Subsidies
5. Total grants
5. Grants to states
7. Grants to local bodies and others
Of which 7a. grants to local bodies
7b. grants to others
Expenditure of Departmental Commercial Undertakings
1. Total expenditure
2. Expenditure on commodities and services
3. Interest payments

Source: Ministry of Finance (various years).

3. While most of the categories of expenditures are self-explanatory, the categories of subsidies and grants of the administrative departments need some clarifications. Subsidies include assistance for export promotion and market development schemes, fertilizer subsidy, and others. The percentage of subsidies in the total expenditure of the administrative departments has been rather volatile over the years and

in recent years they contributed about 12 to 16 per cent to total expenditures. A well-designed system of subsidies will by its very nature be counter-cyclical. In a boom (bust) the number of people eligible (and amounts) for these subsidies would drop (rise), leading to counter-cyclicality.

4. Grants consist of statutory grants and other non-plan and plan grants to states and union territories. Grants to others comprise grants made to institutions like the Council of Scientific and Industrial Research, the Indian Council of Agricultural Research, and the University Grants Commission. The ratio of the total grants to total expenditure of administrative departments was about 9 per cent in the 1950s which has risen to over 25 per cent in recent years. The percentage of grants to states and union territories has remained fairly stable over the years ranging between 10 to 13 per cent. Grants to local bodies have contributed to about 1 to 4 per cent of total expenditures over the years. Grants to others constituted about 2 per cent of total expenditures in the early 1960s and have risen substantially to about 14 per cent in recent years. Grants are likely to be influenced by political factors. Khemani (2003) has argued that plan grants from the centre to the states have a large amount of discretion (that is, they are not completely determined according to a pre-agreed formula) and thus are open to political manipulation. If the central government finds it politically difficult to deny demands to states in good times they could well be pro-cyclical.

With these explanations, we next embark on our empirical exercise. In our empirical exercise we consider real counterparts (obtained by deflating using the GDP deflator) of the above mentioned variables. Data on real GDP is obtained from the Reserve Bank of India website.

Measure of Fiscal Cyclicality

Next we explain how we have measured fiscal cyclicality. We have used both the regression and time series methods to measure pro-cyclicality. We first explain the time series method.

We have employed a simple methodology adopted in business cycle literature to measure cycles in a time series and a non-parametric tool to measure how cycles in two or more time series are synchronized with each other to pass conclusions on pro-cyclicality.

Graphs of time series data often seem to move in tandem, with a recurrent pattern of many inflections in the plotted series. Such inflections are sometimes termed turning points. Figures 5.1 to 5.3 plot the H-P filtered expenditure components used in this study. One can easily see the various turning points with the co-movements between the plotted series. In business cycle literature, the existence of such

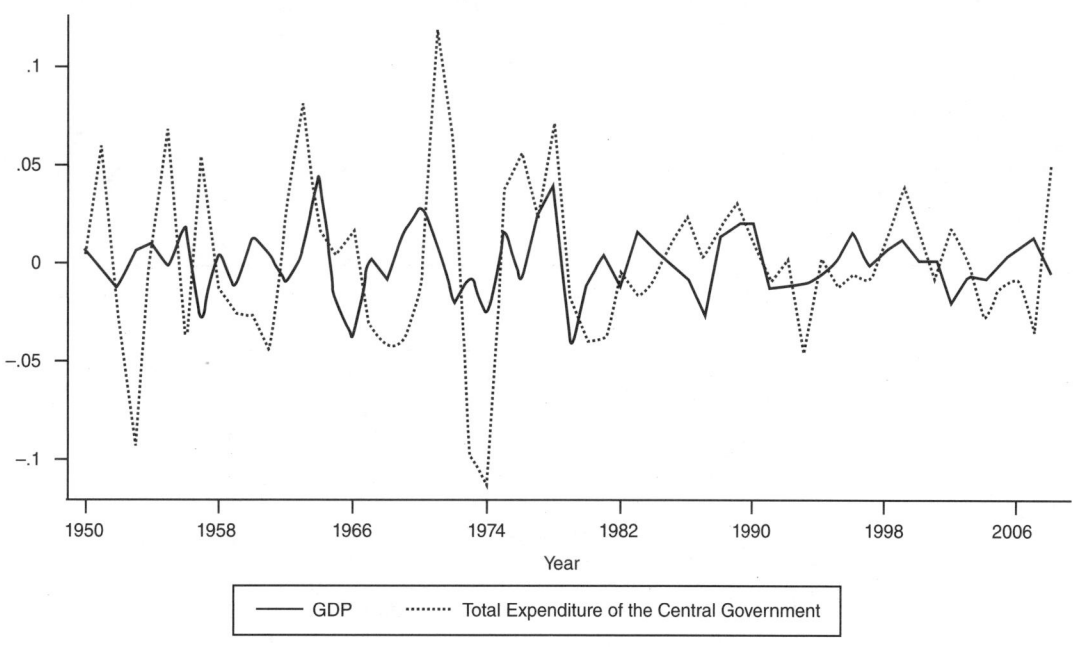

Figure 5.1 Total Expenditure of the Central Government

Source: Authors' own calculations.

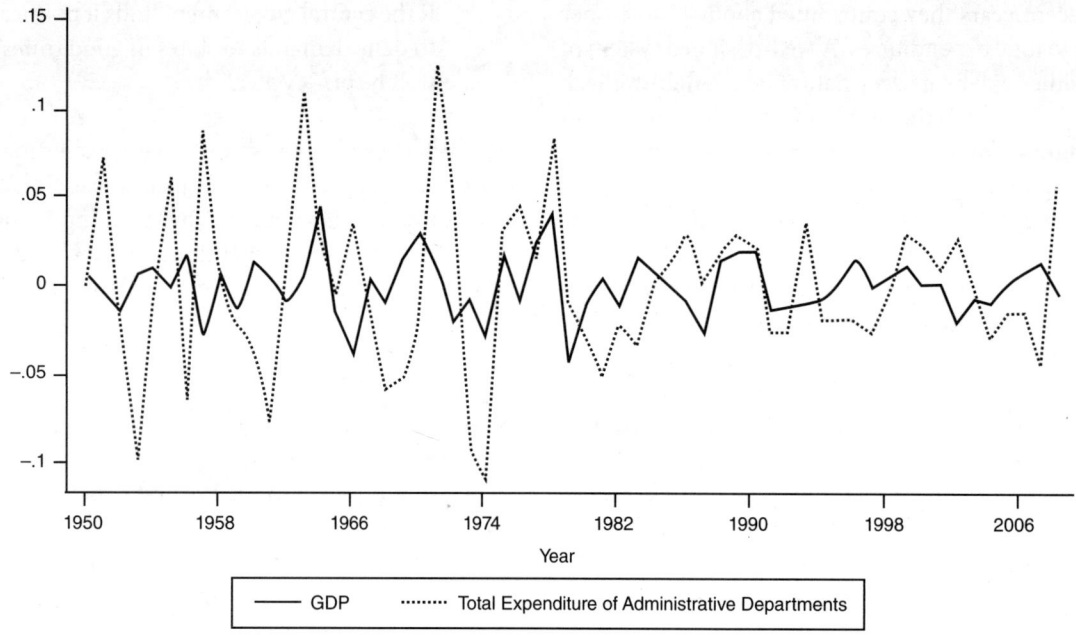

Figure 5.2 Total Expenditure of Administrative Departments
Source: Authors' own calculations.

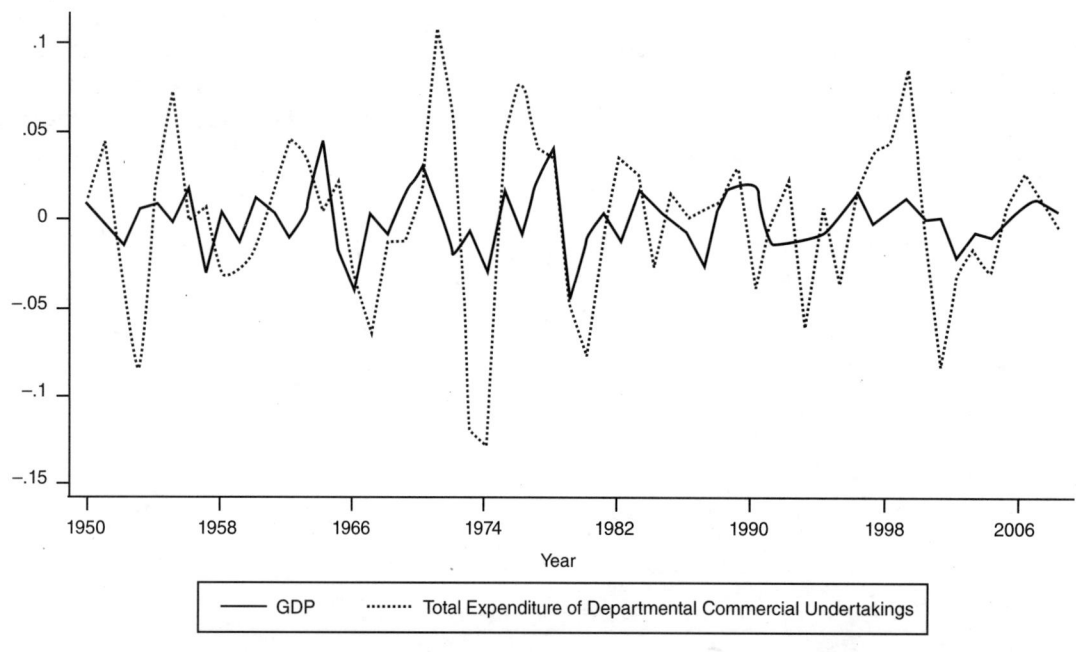

Figure 5.3 Total Expenditure of Departmental Commercial Undertakings
Source: Authors' own calculations.

turning points is associated with the idea of cycles in a series. And if we find many such turning points of two or more series clustered together and occurring at the same time, we then say that there could be synchronized movements amongst the series. Intrinsic to an understanding of such synchronization is defining turning points in terms of *peaks* and *troughs*. We use the simple rule on the basis of the National Bureau of Economic Research (NBER) procedures summarized in the Bry and Boschan (1971) algorithm. This algorithm is used by NBER in its business cycle research and has a universal appeal for its simplicity. It is normally used on monthly or quarterly data and we use the so-called *calculus rule*. And the rule for any time series is that the derivative (less) greater than zero to the (right) left of a local (peak) trough provides the starting point for locating turning points in a series. A discrete analog to the above rule is that a *peak* occurs in a time series if at time t, z_t exceeds z_s for $t-k < s < t$ and $t+k > s > t$ where k is some symmetric window in time around t. (Harding 2007). A trough can be defined similarly. The value of k is set to five for monthly observations and is set to two for quarterly observations. But for annual data k is invariably set to one. Then we have the following definition for peak and trough for annual observations:

we have a peak at time t if $\quad \Delta z_t > 0 \quad$ and $\Delta z_{t+1} \leq 0$, and
we have a trough at time t if $\Delta z_{t+1} \geq 0$ and $\Delta z_t < 0$

The main purpose of deriving such cycles is to understand the business cycle characteristics of an economy, where we study how cycles in specific macro time series behave in relation to cycles in some *reference* series, which will mostly be the GDP series. Since we have used only the *levels* of a time series in defining these rules, the resulting cyclical pattern is sometimes called the *levels cycle*, also called the classical cycle. Another popular cycle identified using the time series, obtained after removing the permanent component, either by using the H-P filter or first differencing, is called the growth cycle.

One can use such a definition of cycles to understand how any two or more series *co-move* or how *synchronized* such movements are. Let z_{jt} and z_{rt} be two time series, of which z_{rt} is labelled as the reference series. We are interested in measuring how synchronized z_{jt} is with the reference series. We do that by finding the degree of *concordance* or *co-movement* between the *cycles* of two time series. Concordance will be quantified by the fraction of time that both the series are simultaneously in the same state. To enable that, we define the following two binary time series. For example let S_{jt} be equal to one when the series z_{jt} is in expansion and zero when it is in contraction. Similarly define the series S_{rt}. Perfect synchronization between the two series will occur when $S_{jt} = S_{rt}$.

In many instances, series are just synchronized, but not perfectly so. So we need a measure to quantify the degree of synchronization between the two series. It is in this connection that we derive the *concordant index* (CII) recommended by Harding and Pagan (2006) which gives us a simple metric to decide how synchronized two or more time series are. While the details are available in their paper, we present here the important equations. The concordance index is a simple non-parametric statistic to measure how close S_{jt} and S_{rt} are.

Mathematically, the concordant index is written as:

$$\hat{I}_{jr} = T^{-1} [\sum_{t=1}^{T} S_{jt} S_{rt} + \sum_{t=1}^{T} (1 - S_{jt})(1 - S_{rt})] \quad (5.1)$$

where T is the sample size. We can re-parameterize the above equation as:

$$\hat{I}_{jr} = 1 + \frac{2}{T} [\sum_{t=1}^{T} S_{jt} S_{rt} + \sum_{t=1}^{T} (1 - S_{jt})(1 - S_{rt})]$$
$$= 1 + 2\hat{\sigma}_{S_{jt} S_{rt}} + 2\hat{\mu}_{S_{jt}} \hat{\mu}_{S_{rt}} - \hat{\mu}_{S_{jt}} - \hat{\mu}_{S_{rt}} \quad (5.2)$$

where $\hat{\sigma}_{S_{jt} S_{rt}}$ is the estimated co-variance between S_{jt} and S_{rt}. Noting that and are binary series, the estimated standard deviations take the form $\sqrt{(\hat{\mu}_{S_{jt}} - \hat{\mu}_{S_{jt}}^2)}$, and hence (5.2) can be re-written as follows, which is convenient to interpret:

$$\hat{I}_{jr} = 1 + 2\hat{\rho}_s \left(\hat{\mu}_{S_{jt}}(1 - \hat{\mu}_{S_{jt}})\right)^{1/2} \left(\hat{\mu}_{S_{rt}}(1 - \hat{\mu}_{S_{rt}})\right)^{1/2} +$$
$$2\hat{\mu}_{S_{jt}} \hat{\mu}_{S_{rt}} - \hat{\mu}_{S_{jt}} - \hat{\mu}_{S_{rt}} \quad (5.3)$$

where $\hat{\rho}_s$ is the estimated correlation between S_{jt} and S_{rt}. With this expression it is easy to show that the concordant index has a maximum value of 1 when $S_{jt} = S_{rt}$ and zero when $S_{jt} = (1 - S_{rt})$. For example, note that, when $S_{jt} = S_{rt}, \hat{\sigma}_{S_{jt}} \hat{\sigma}_{S_{rt}} = \hat{\sigma}_{S_{jt}}^2$. So from (5.3) simple algebra tells us that a $\hat{\rho}_s = 1$ value of corresponds to a concordance index of one. Similar arguments show that a value of $\hat{\rho}_s = -1$ corresponds to a concordance index of zero. Harding and Pagan however suggest that one should use the estimated correlation between the two binary time series rather than the concordance index. How to calculate the correlation then? Harding and Pagan suggest the following simple regression based on the method of moment estimator:

$$\hat{\sigma}_{S_{jt}}^{-1} \hat{\sigma}_{S_{rt}}^{-1} S_{rt} = a_1 + \rho^s \hat{\sigma}_{S_{jt}}^{-1} S_{jt} + u_t \quad (5.4)$$

Under the null of $\rho^s = 0$ there will be strong serial correlation in u_t's. So in applications we have to report the standard errors that are adjusted for serial correlation and possible heteroscedasticity, called HAC standard errors. A popular method is to use the Newey-West estimator with Bartlett weights. The resulting t ratio is called the robust t ratio.

Regression methods that are employed in studies testing pro-cyclicality are simple. They involve running the following simple linear regressions:

$$\Delta \log G_t = a_0 + b_0 \Delta \log (GDP_t) + e_{1t} \quad (5.5)$$

$$\log G_{HP, t} = a_1 + b_1 \log (GDP_{HP, t}) + e_{2t} \quad (5.6)$$

where log G_t refers to the logs of various components of government expenditure listed above, and log GDP_t refers to log of real GDP. Similarly, log $G_{HP,t}$ and log $GDP_{HP,t}$ refer to H-P filtered expenditure components and output gap, respectively. A high and significant estimated value of b will indicate strong pro-cyclical behaviour between that component of expenditure and the cycle in reference series GDP. Similarly a negative is interpreted as evidence for counter-cyclicality and a coefficient not significantly different from zero is interpreted as evidence in favour of a-cyclicality.

Next we shall analyse the results.

Synchronization in Classical Cycles between GDP and Government Expenditure

Beginning with time series evidence, Table 5.2 displays the concordance index, calculated using (5.1), and the correlations obtained using (5.4), between the states of GDP and the various components of government expenditure. Mean of S_j is reported in the third column. High concordance index values seem to suggest that many components are in as same a state of the *classical cycle* as GDP has been. But such concordance values may be biased towards accepting pro-cyclicality; because in a large sample, it is most likely that the variables are in a state of expansion for a longer period. So Harding and Pagan suggest that a better statistic is to use a mean-corrected concordance index value, which is what the regression estimate, $\hat{\rho}_s$, gives. Consequently, if we check the pair-wise correlations, $\hat{\rho}_s$, most of the values are very small, and turn out to be insignificant, suggesting that high concordance values, in the light of equation (5.3), supports Harding and Pagan's conviction that one should use the mean corrected concordance index. Since there is invariably a high serial correlation in the binary time series describing the two states—expansionary and contractionary—of the cycle, we need to use the Newey-West heteroscedasticity-autocorrelation (HAC) adjusted standard errors.

Table 5.2 Concordant Index and Correlations of Cycles (Classical Cycle)

Variables	Raw Correlation $\hat{\rho}$ with GDP	Mean S_j	Concordance Index	Estimated Correlation of Cycles		
				$\hat{\rho}_s$	Student's t-statistic	HAC Adjusted t-statistic
Total Expenditure of the Central Government						
Total expenditure	0.990*	0.847	0.847	0.182	2.038	1.285
Wages and salaries	0.975*	0.729	0.729	0.078	1.058	0.870
Expenditure on commodities and services	0.977*	0.661	0.627	−0.027	0.383	0.409
Interest payments	0.986*	0.898	0.864	0.110	1.008	0.655
Expenditure of Administrative Departments						
Total expenditure	0.987*	0.814	0.814	0.140	1.679	1.150
Wages and salaries	0.975	0.763	0.763	0.098	1.275	0.988
Expenditure on commodities and services	0.969*	0.678	0.644	−0.022	0.314	0.333
Interest payments	0.983*	0.898	0.864	0.110	1.008	0.655
Subsidies	0.930*	0.678	0.644	−0.022	0.314	0.333
Total grants	0.966*	0.814	0.814	0.140	1.679	1.150
Grants to states	0.948*	0.763	0.763	0.098	1.275	0.983
Grants to local bodies and others	0.948*	0.797	0.797	0.124	1.531	1.094
Grants to local bodies	0.058	0.695	0.661	−0.018	0.243	0.251
Grants to others	0.979*	0.780	0.780	0.110	1.397	1.003
Expenditure of Departmental Commercial Undertakings						
Total expenditure	0.978*	0.780	0.780	0.110	1.397	1.038
Wages and salaries	0.953*	0.712	0.712	0.070	0.960	0.780
Expenditure on commodities and services	0.983*	0.746	0.712	−0.002	0.020	0.020
Interest payments	0.893*	0.712	0.712	0.070	0.960	0.812

Notes: * Indicates significance at 5 per cent level.
Source: Authors' own calculations.

Table 5.2 displays both the conventional student-statistics in column 6 and the *t* values obtained using the HAC standard errors in column 7. One can see that there is a stronger support that there is little concordance between GDP and the components of government expenditure.

In summary, the evidence of pro-cyclicality amongst the various components of government expenditure and Gavin-Perotti, using the classical cycles approach, is not that strong.

Considering the long time period of our sample, we also calculate the rolling as well as the recursive concordance

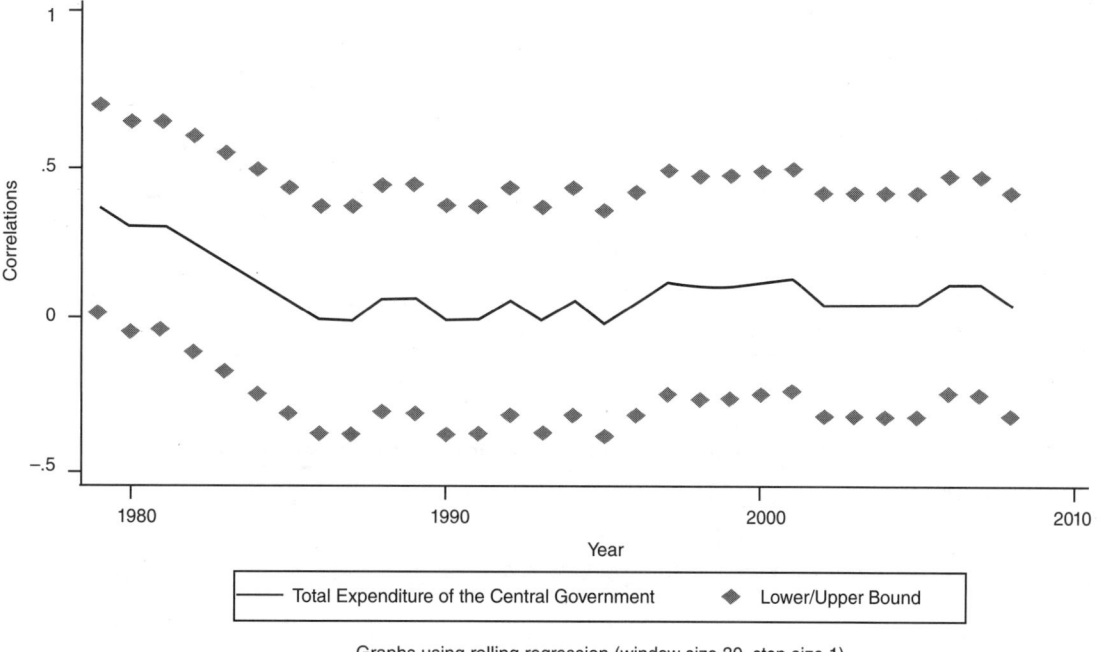

Figure 5.4 Total Expenditure of the Central Government (Rolling Correlations)

Source: Authors' own calculations.

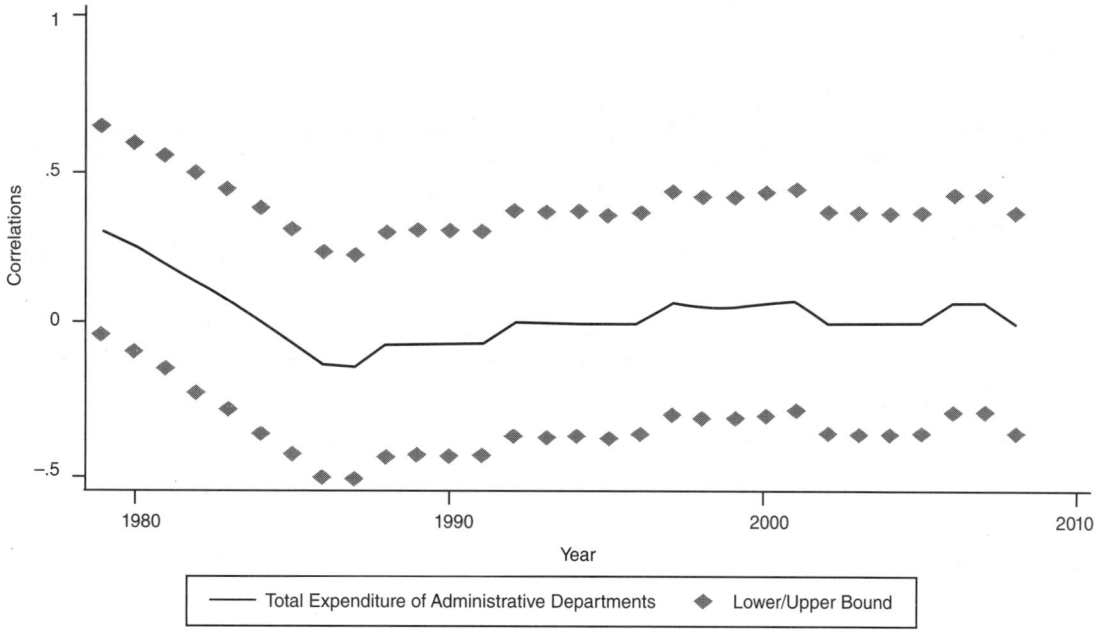

Figure 5.5 Total Expenditure of Administrative Departments (Rolling Correlations)

Source: Authors' own calculations.

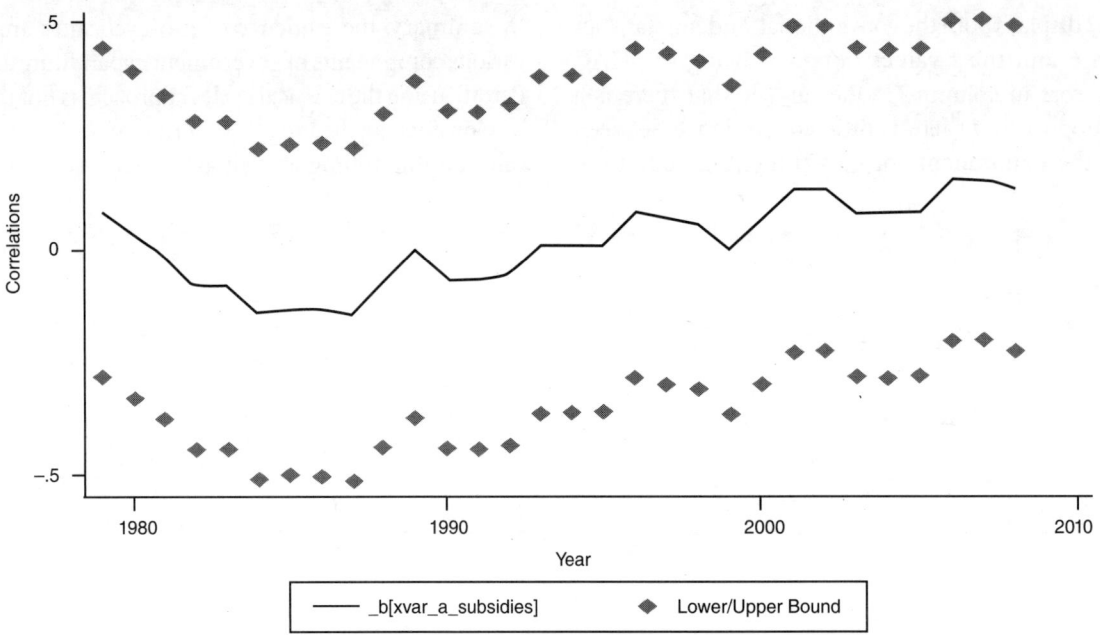

Figure 5.6 Subsidies of Administrative Departments (Rolling Correlations)

Source: Authors' own calculations.

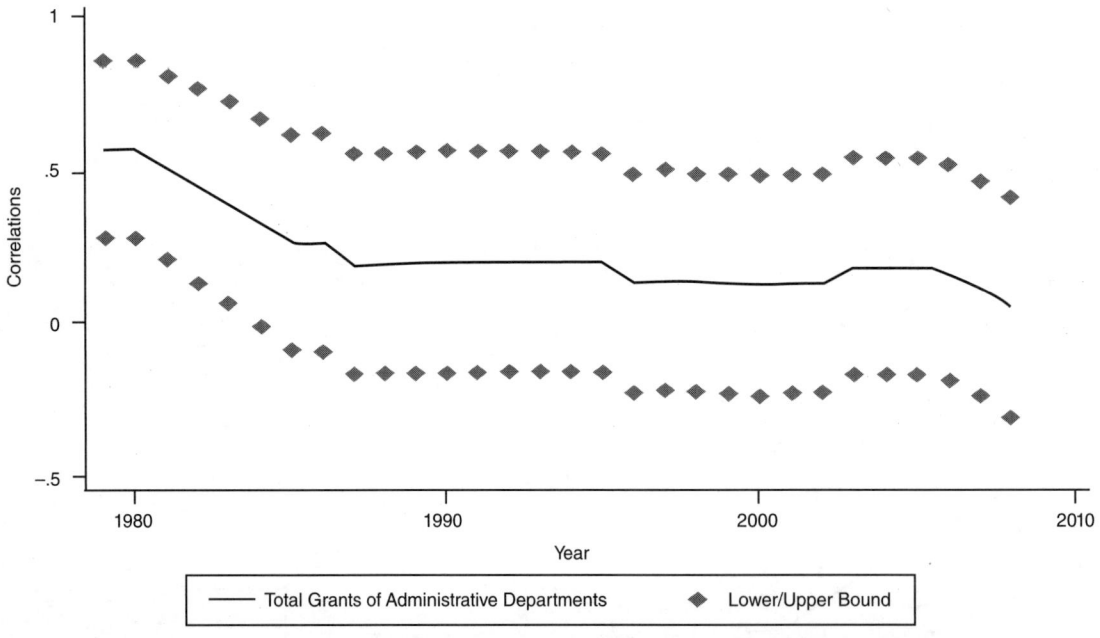

Figure 5.7 Total Grants of Administrative Departments (Rolling Correlations)

Source: Authors' own calculations.

estimates with a window of 30 years and a step size of one year, to check for any possible time varying pattern in the correlation of states. And the associated correlation values have been plotted in Figures 5.4 to 5.21. There is no dramatic change in the results, though many of the correlations, which were negative in the initial years, turn positive around year 1990, suggesting that pro-cyclical tendencies started manifesting in the later stages of the sample. Only subsidies of administrative departments show a visible time-changing pattern of correlation values.

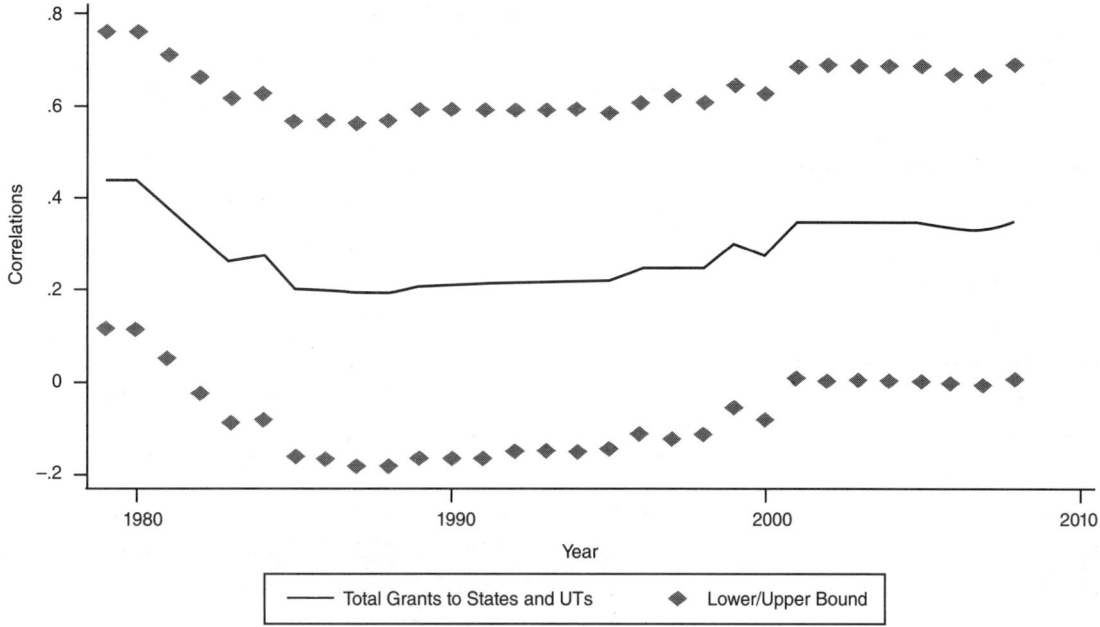

Figure 5.8 Total Grants to States and UTs (Rolling Correlations)

Source: Authors' own calculations.

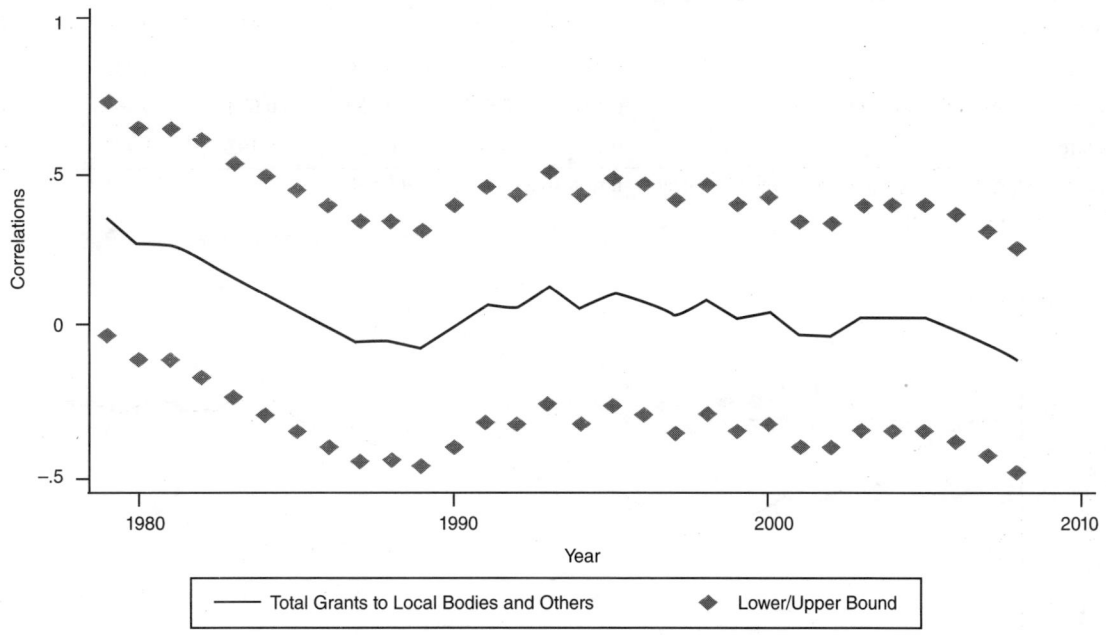

Figure 5.9 Total Grants to Local Bodies and Others (Rolling Correlations)

Source: Authors' own calculations.

Synchronization in Growth Cycles between GDP and Government Expenditure

We also checked for the possibility of concordance in the *growth cycle* by estimating the concordance index and the associated pair-wise correlations between output gap and cyclical components of expenditure, obtained by employing the Harding-Pagan filter. These results are displayed in Table 5.3 and, though the numerical values of concordance index have become smaller, we do not find any significant evidence of pro-cyclicality between expenditure and GDP.

Table 5.3 Concordant Index and Correlations of Cycles (Growth Cycle)

Variables	Raw Correlation $\hat{\rho}$ with GDP	Mean S_j	Concordance index	Estimated Correlation of Cycles $\hat{\rho}_s$	Student's t-statistic	HAC adjusted t-statistic
Total Expenditure of the Central Government						
Total expenditure	0.212	0.576	0.610	0.186	1.461	1.505
Wages and salaries	0.113	0.492	0.492	−0.013	0.099	0.099
Expenditure on commodities and services	0.067	0.492	0.593	0.191	1.519	1.364
Interest payments	0.122	0.542	0.508	−0.005	0.036	0.033
Expenditure of Administrative Departments						
Total expenditure	0.139	0.542	0.576	0.132	1.036	1.027
Wages and salaries	0.066	0.508	0.542	0.080	0.630	0.655
Expenditure on commodities and services	0.053	0.525	0.593	0.174	1.379	1.497
Interest payments	0.046	0.559	0.458	−0.117	0.910	0.917
Subsidies	−0.167	0.559	0.559	0.090	0.699	0.831
Total grants	0.274*	0.559	0.661	0.296	2.409**	2.213**
Grants to states	0.223	0.525	0.695	0.378	3.200**	3.164**
Grants to local bodies and others	0.094	0.678	0.576	0.071	0.520	0.515
Grants to local bodies	0.167	0.661	0.593	0.117	0.868	0.868
Grants to others	0.283*	0.627	0.627	0.203	1.563	1.553
Expenditure of Departmental Commercial Undertakings						
Total expenditure	0.298*	0.610	0.542	0.030	0.230	0.261
Wages and salaries	0.086	0.627	0.559	0.058	0.437	0.428
Expenditure on commodities and services	0.127	0.593	0.559	0.074	0.568	0.555
Interest payments	0.120	0.661	0.627	0.192	1.447	1.155

Notes: * Indicates significance at 5 per cent level. ** Indicates significance at 1 per cent level.
Source: Authors' own calculations.

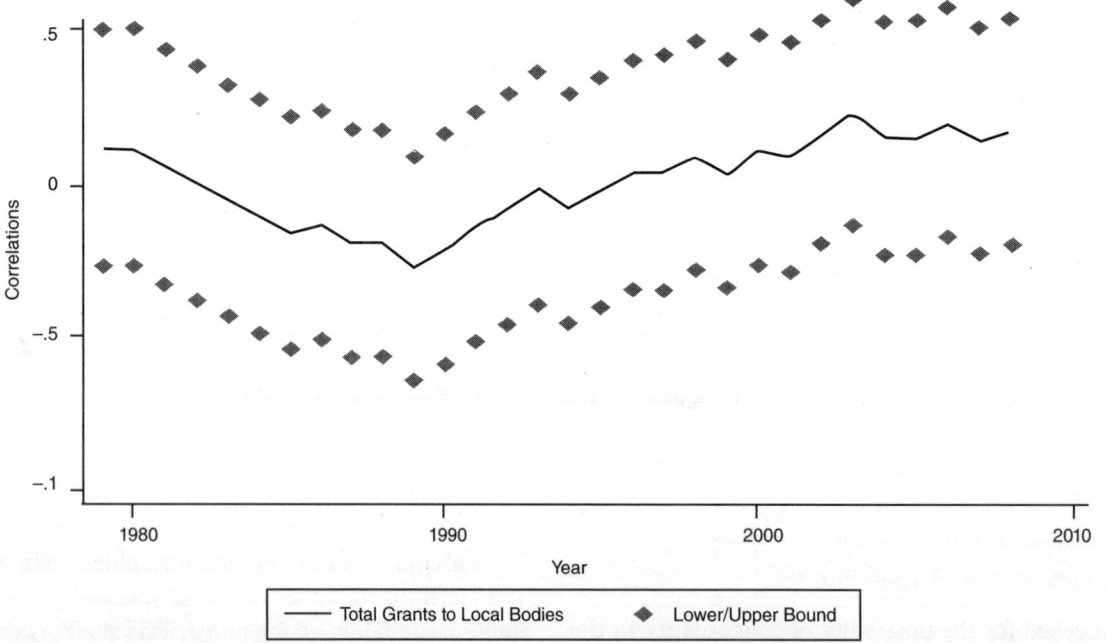

Figure 5.10 Total Grants to Local Bodies (Rolling Correlations)
Source: Authors' own calculations.

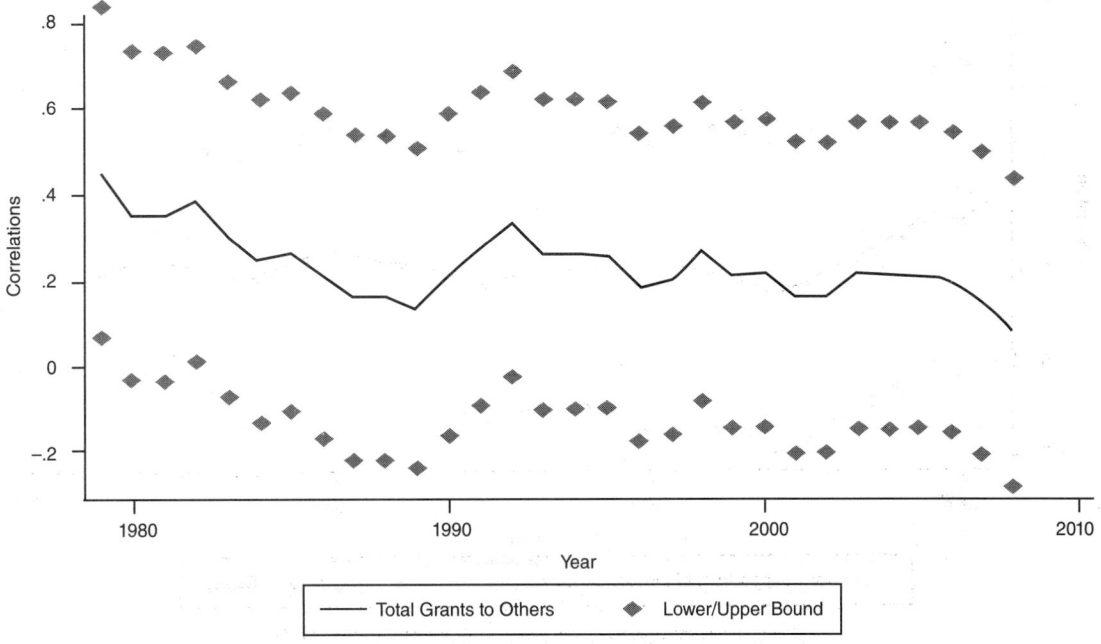

Figure 5.11 Total Grants to Others (Rolling Correlations)

Source: Authors' own calculations.

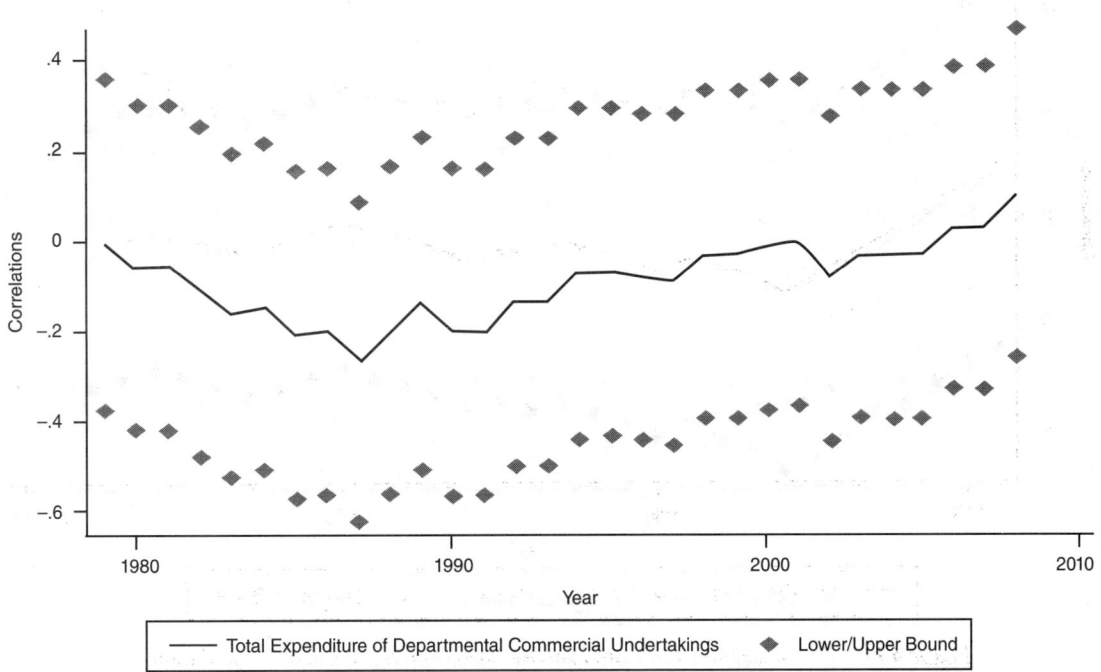

Figure 5.12 Total Expenditure of Departmental Commercial Undertakings (Rolling Correlations)

Source: Authors' own calculations.

Of course, there is some stronger evidence of pro-cyclicality involving grants to states than what was reported using the classical cycle. Correlation coefficients between total grants and a sub-component, grants to states, and GDP are positive and significant, which is clear evidence of pro-cyclical behaviour. More importantly, the significant correlation coefficient between grants to states and GDP suggests the fact that states do successfully extract a fair

72 INDIA DEVELOPMENT REPORT

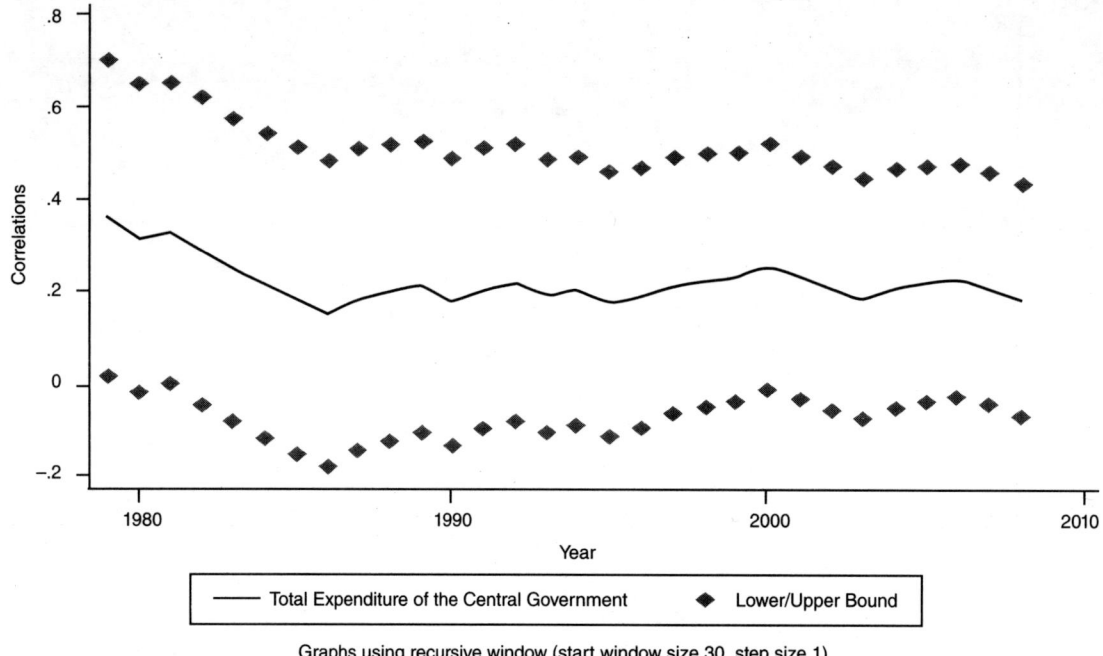

Figure 5.13 Total Expenditure of the Central Government (Recursive Correlations)
Source: Authors' own calculations.

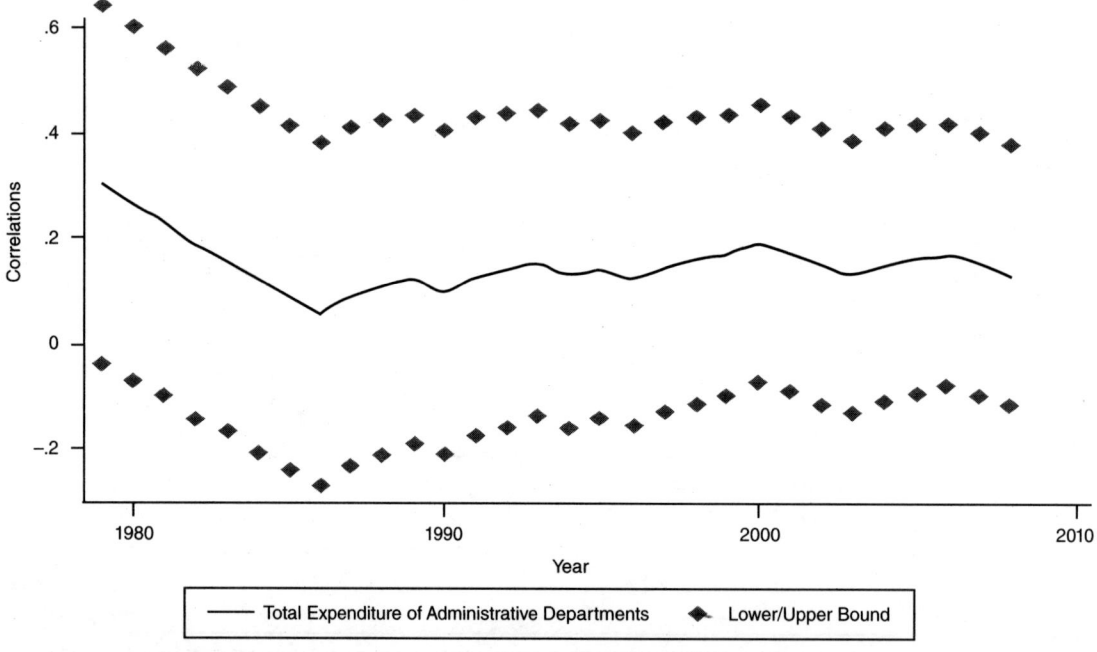

Figure 5.14 Total Expenditure of Administrative Departments (Recursive Correlations)
Source: Authors' own calculations.

share of revenue, accruing during the good times, from the central government.

Evidence of Synchronization from Regressions

We estimate equations (5.5) and (5.6) using a two-step standard procedure to correct for autocorrelation. These are estimated using both the growth rates of various components of government expenditures and the growth rate of real GDP (classical cycles) and with the cyclical components of these variables obtained after using the Harding-Pagan filter (growth cycles). The results are presented in Table 5.4. The first column presents the coefficient and *t* statistic of the

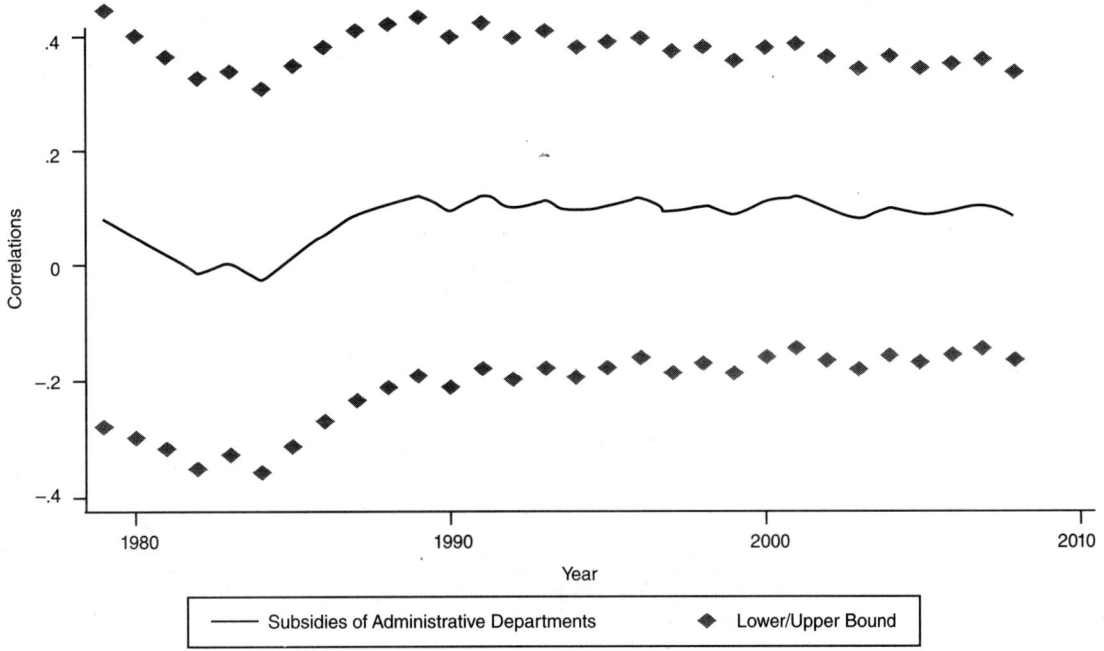

Figure 5.15 Subsidies of Administrative Departments (Recursive Correlations)

Source: Authors' own calculations.

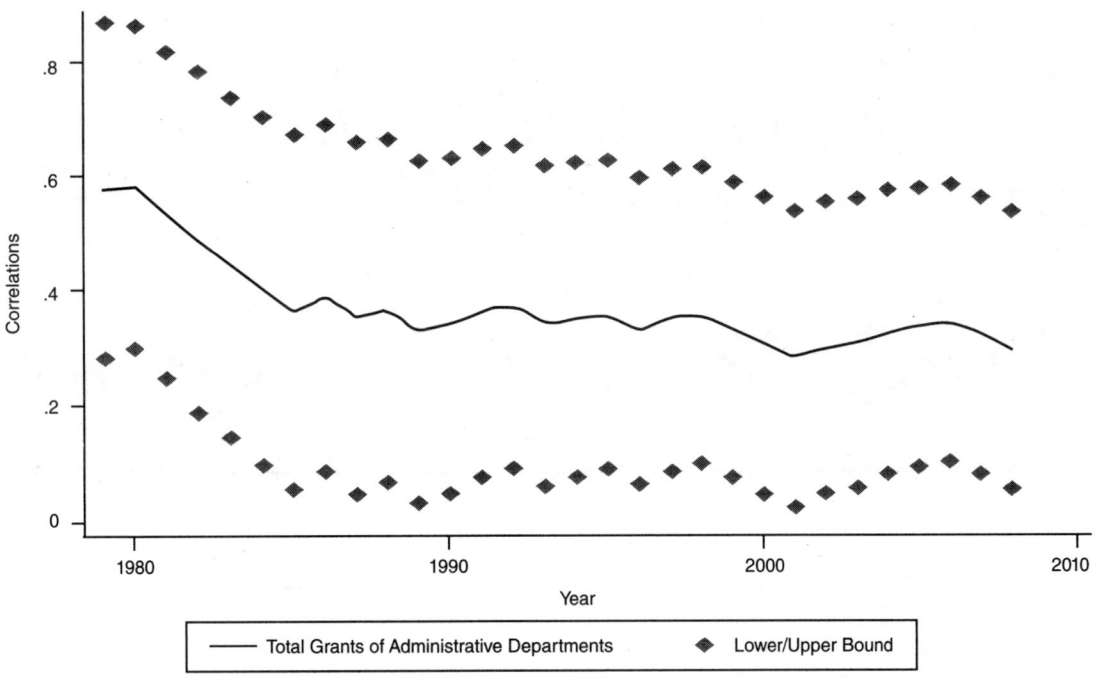

Figure 5.16 Total Grants of Administrative Departments (Recursive Correlations)

Source: Authors' own calculations.

b coefficient using (5.5). In this specification none of the coefficients is significant, except the coefficient for grants to others which is significant. This is generally consistent with the results obtained regarding correlations, $\hat{\rho}_s$, with respect to the classical cycles reported in Table 5.2. This implies that fiscal policy in general can be said to be a-cyclical on the basis of this specification.

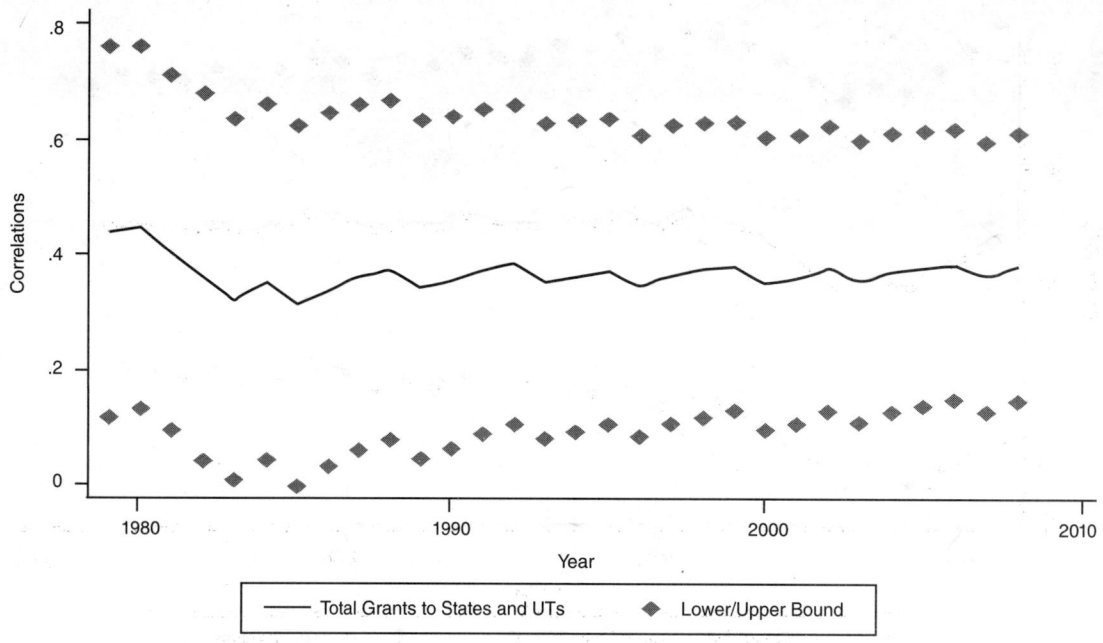

Figure 5.17 Total Grants to States and UTs (Recursive Correlations)

Source: Authors' own calculations.

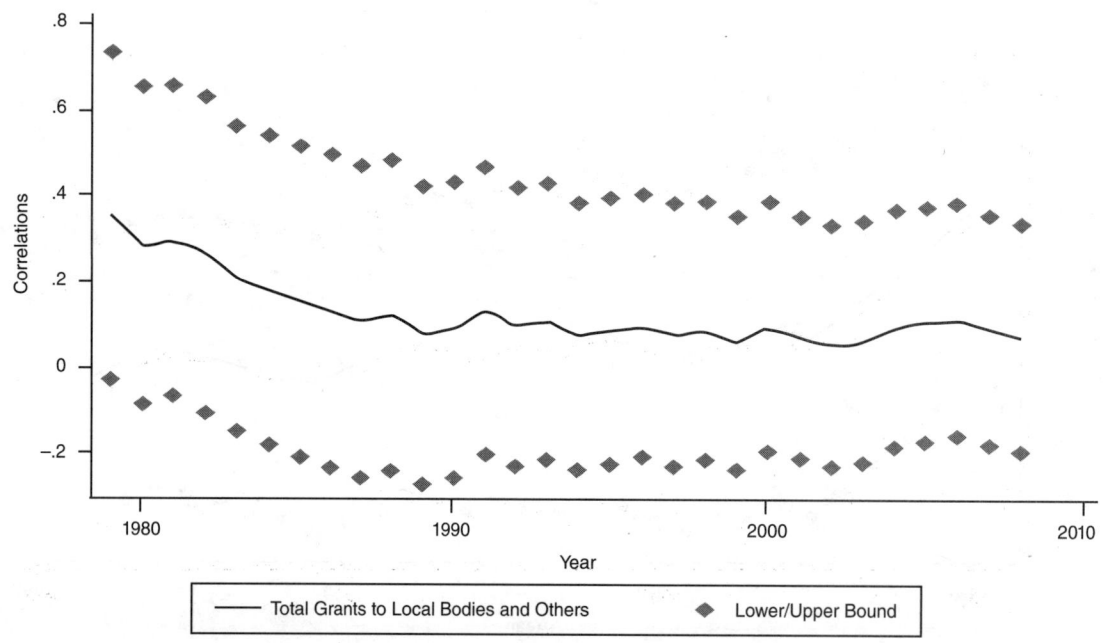

Figure 5.18 Total Grants to Local Bodies and Others (Recursive Correlations)

Source: Authors' own calculations.

Column 2 of Table 5.4 presents estimates based on equation 5.6 (growth cycles). Here total grants, grants to others have a positive and significant coefficient at the 5 per cent level, while grants to states have a positive and significant coefficient at the 10 per cent level of confidence and all other components of government expenditure have coefficients which are not significant. While most components of government expenditure are a-cyclical, these three components (total grants, grants to states, and grants to others) shows distinct pro-cyclicality. We obtained similar

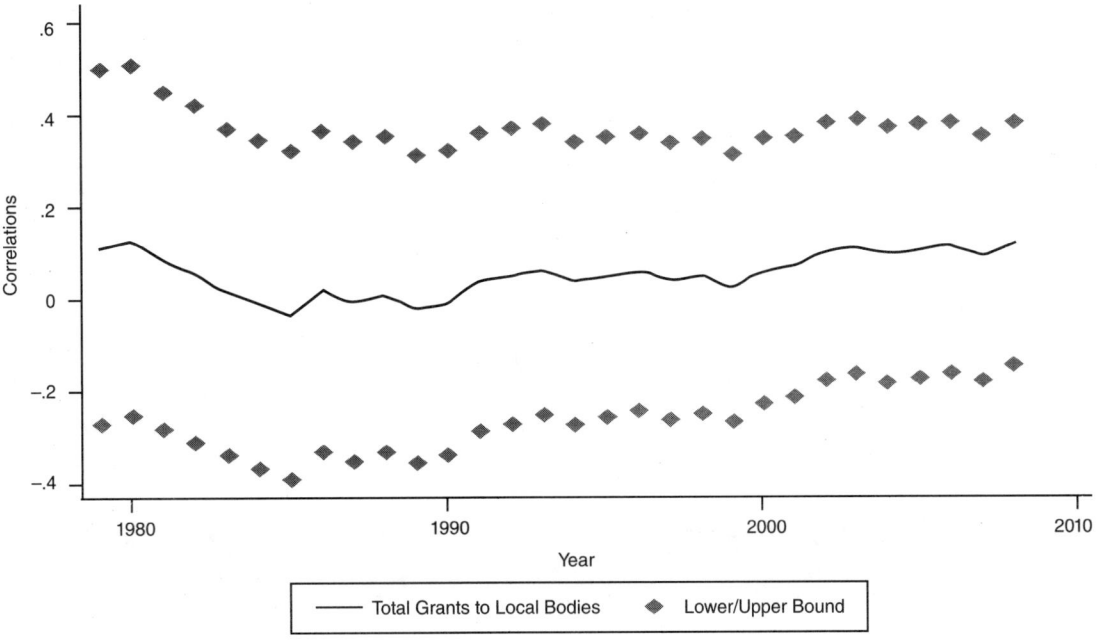

Figure 5.19 Total Grants to Local Bodies (Recursive Correlations)

Source: Authors' own calculations.

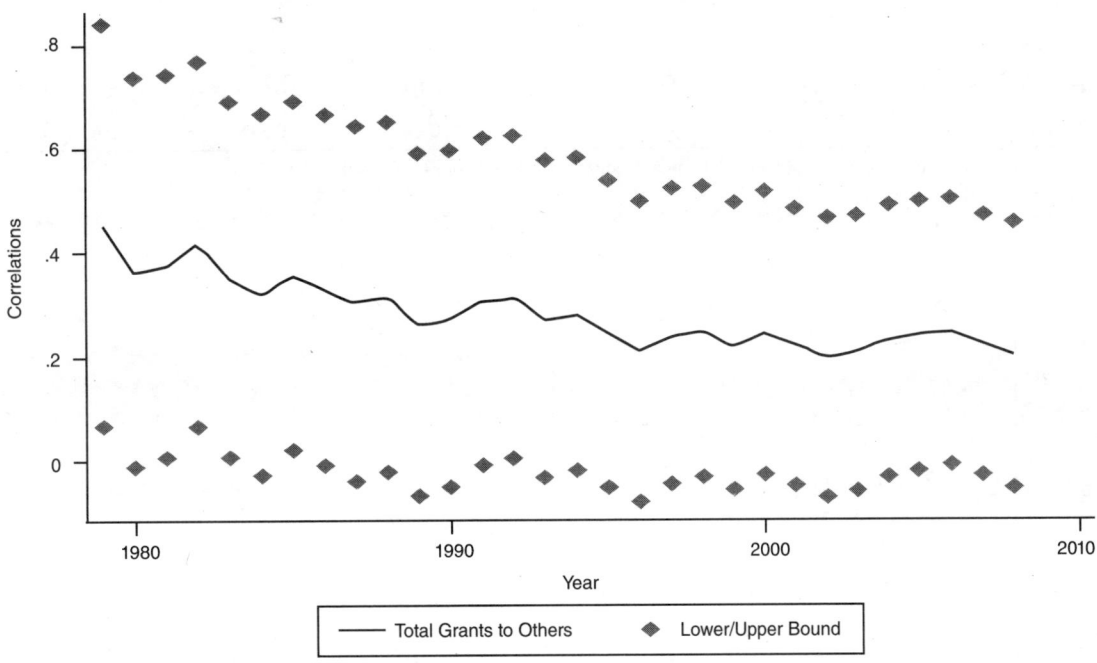

Figure 5.20 Total Grants to Others (Recursive Correlations)

Source: Authors' own calculations.

results with time series methods, displayed in Table 5.3, with the correlation between the category grants to states and grants to others and GDP showing strong pro-cyclicality. Thus total expenditures of the central government and most of their components are a-cyclical but total grants, grants to states, and grants to others turn out to be pro-cyclical. This may be construed as some support for the voracity effect, where states successfully force the central government to make higher grants during good times.

Table 5.4 Regression Estimates after Correcting for First Order Autocorrelation

Variables	Without HP Filter		With HP Filter	
	Coefficient	Student's t-statistic	Coefficient	Student's t-statistic
Total Expenditure of the Central Government				
Total expenditure	0.128	0.462	0.354	1.169
Wages and salaries	0.272	0.862	0.285	0.768
Expenditure on commodities and services	−0.249	0.525	0.136	0.240
Interest payments	−0.079	0.329	0.182	0.787
Expenditure of Administrative Departments				
Total expenditure	0.014	0.045	0.265	0.788
Wages and salaries	0.238	0.662	0.200	0.471
Expenditure on commodities and services	−0.407	0.742	0.027	0.041
Interest payments	−0.226	0.752	0.078	0.274
Subsidies	−2.854	1.375	−2.715	1.434
Total grants	0.779	1.527	1.048	2.053*
Grants to states	0.481	0.704	1.152	1.778
Grants to local bodies and others	0.794	1.543	0.789	0.769
Grants to local bodies	1.587	0.712	2.803	1.216
Grants to others	1.523	2.246*	1.436	2.696**
Expenditure of Departmental Commercial Undertakings				
Total expenditure	0.122	0.427	0.582	1.707
Wages and salaries	0.276	0.687	0.289	0.611
Expenditure on commodities and services	0.015	0.039	0.342	0.892
Interest payments	0.209	0.318	0.676	0.819

Notes: * Indicates significance at 5 per cent level. ** Indicates significance at 1 per cent level.
Source: Authors' own calculations.

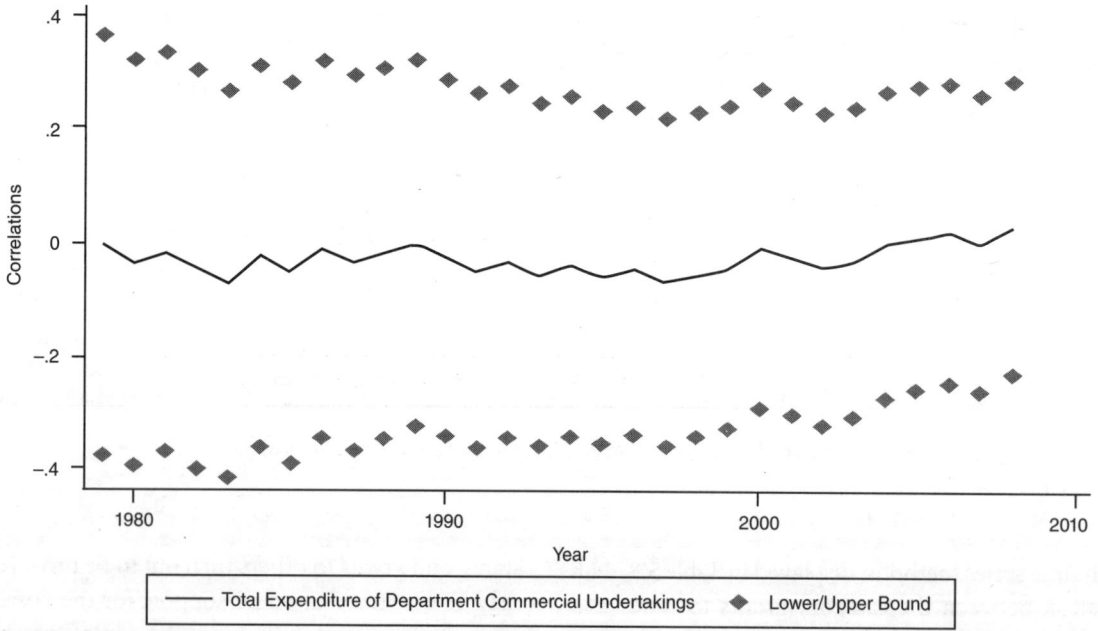

Figure 5.21 Total Expenditure of Departmental Commercial Undertakings (Recursive Correlations)
Source: Authors' own calculations.

We also find that the central government is not averse to liberal funding of research and higher education in good times, but also resorts to cutting the funding during bad times as is evident from the significant coefficient of grants to others in Table 5.4. However, it will be incorrect to attribute this to the voracity effect, since the institutions that fall under this category are by no means political pressure groups. To check for any possible time varying pattern in regression relations, we estimated recursive least squares with a window of years and step size of one year. Since there was no dramatic change in the results, we have not reported these.

Our study also highlights an issue that has not received much attention in literature. That is, the methodology adopted to measure fiscal cyclicality does result in disparate results. For example, correlation estimates, $\hat{\rho}_s$, of classical cycles show that same states do not show strong synchronization. But in the case of growth cycles, we see such synchronization taking place.

Considering all the results on hand, we can categorize fiscal policy in India to be, at best, as a-cyclical. This is in stark contrast with the evidence found in other developing countries. The evidence provided by this exercise also questions conventional wisdom that a country with a polarized society and a federal set-up such as ours, is prone to follow a pro-cyclical fiscal policy.

We, however, notice that significant cyclical behaviour did manifest, but only in one component of government expenditure—grants to states.

CONCLUSION

This chapter aimed to quantify cyclical behaviour, with the intention of answering the specific question: if the fiscal stance in India has been pro-cyclical over the period 1950 to 2008 using a dataset on expenditure of the central government that is more disaggregated than normally used. Our results show that the fiscal policy has been generally a-cyclical over the period of study, with most of the major expenditure components showing a-cyclicality. The exception to this finding is the expenditure component of total grants, especially grants to states and grants to others, which show pro-cyclical behaviour. This evidence shows that our fiscal policy has not been blatantly pro-cyclical as has been the case with many developing countries.

At this juncture, it is equally important to realize that our study has not produced a strong evidence of a counter-cyclical fiscal stance given that India experienced a number of booms and busts over the period of study. This could be considered a matter of concern, since this suggests that our fiscal measures have not been aimed at smoothening business cycle fluctuations, which are generally believed to have adverse welfare consequences.

Graduating from an a-cyclical fiscal stance to a counter-cyclical stance is an important challenge that the Indian economy will have to face in the coming decades. From a policy perspective, strict adherence to acts like the FRBM Act should be a good beginning to design a fiscal policy that incentivizes the government to adopt a counter-cyclical fiscal policy. From a research perspective, we suggest that a first step in this direction will be to quantify the benefits of adopting a counter-cyclical fiscal stance.

REFERENCES

Akitoby, B., B. Clements, S. Gupta, and G. Inchauste (2004), 'The Cyclical and Long-Term Behavior of Government Expenditures in Developing Countries', International Monetary Fund, Working Paper No. WP/04/202.

Alesina A., F.R. Campante, and G. Tabellini (2008), 'Why is Fiscal Policy Often Procyclical?', *Journal of the European Economic Association*, 6(5): 1006–36.

Barro, R.J. (1979), 'On the Determination of the Public Debt', *Journal of Political Economy*, 87: 940–71.

Bry, G. and C. Boschan (1971), *Cyclical Analysis of Time Series: Selected Procedures and Computer Programs*. New York: National Bureau of Economic Research.

Buiter, W.H. and U.R. Patel (2010). 'Fiscal rules in India: Are they effective?', available at: http://www.nber.org/papers/w15934, last accessed on 13 September 2012.

Gali, J. and R. Perotti (2003), 'Fiscal Policy and Monetary Integration in Europe', *Economic Policy*, 18(37): 533–72.

Gavin, M. and R. Perotti (1997), 'Fiscal Policy in Latin America', *NBER Macroeconomics Annual*, 12: 11–70.

Hallerberg, M. and R. Strauch (2002), 'On the Cyclicality of Public Finances in Europe', *Empirica*, 29: 183–207.

Harding, D. (2007), 'Australian Business Cycle—A New View', MPRA Working Paper No. 3698.

Harding, D. and A. Pagan (2006), 'Synchronization of Cycles', *Journal of Econometrics*, 132: 59–79.

Herd, R. and W. Leibfritz (2008), 'Fiscal Policy in India: Past Reforms and Future Challenges', *OECD Economics Department Working Papers*, No. 595, OECD Publishing. Available at: http://dx.doi.org/10.1787/244241786035, last accessed on 20 March 2012.

Kaminsky G.M., C.M. Reinhart, and C.A. Vegh (2004), 'When it Rains, it Pours: Pro-cyclical capital flows and macroeconomic policies', *NBER Macroeconomics Annual*, 19: 11–53.

Khemani, S. (2003), 'Partisan Politics and Intergovernmental Transfers in India', Policy Research Working Paper 3016, The World Bank, Washington DC.

Lane, P.R. (2003), 'The Cyclical Behavior of Fiscal Policy: Evidence from OECD', *Journal of Public Economics*, 87(12): 2661–75.

Lucas R.E. (Jr.) (1987), *Models of Business Cycles*. Oxford: Basil-Blackwell Ltd.

Ministry of Finance (various years), *An Economic and Functional Classification of the Central Budget*. New Delhi: Economic Division, Ministry of Finance.

Pallage, S. and M.A. Robe (2000), 'Welfare Costs of Business Cycles in Developing Countries', Center for Research on Economic Fluctuations and Employment (CREFE), Working Paper No. 124.

Portier, F. and L.A. Puch (2006), 'Welfare Costs of Business Cycles in an Economy with Non-Clearing Markets', *Topics in Macroeconomics*, 6(3): article 7.

Raj, J., J.K. Khundrakpam, and D. Das (2011), 'An Empirical Analysis of Monetary and Fiscal Policy Interaction in India', Reserve Bank of India, Working Paper No. 15/2011.

Shah, A. and I. Patnaik (2010), 'Stabilizing the Indian Business Cycle', in Sameer Kochhar (ed.), *India on the Growth Turnpike: Essays in Honour of Vijay L. Kelkar*. New Delhi: Academic Foundation, pp. 137–53.

Talvi, E. and C.A. Veigh (2005), 'Tax Base Variability and Pro-cyclical Fiscal Policy', *Journal of Development Economics*, 78: 156–90.

Thornton, John (2008), 'Explaining Procyclical Fiscal Policy in African Countries', *Journal of African Economies*, 17(3): 451–64.

Tornell, A. and P.R. Lane (1999), 'The Voracity Effect', *American Economic Review*, 89: 22–46.

Woo, J. (2009), 'Why do More Polarized Countries Run More Pro-cyclical Fiscal Policy?', *The Review of Economics and Statistics*, 91(4): 850–70.

6

Performance and Key Policy Issues of Indian Agriculture

S. Mahendra Dev and Vijay Laxmi Pandey

INTRODUCTION

The agriculture sector employs 52.9 per cent of the total workforce (NSSO 2011), and 46 per cent of the total geographical area, making it a vital element for the inclusive and sustainable growth of the Indian economy. The fact that approximately 41.8 per cent of the rural population lived below the poverty line in 2004–5 emphasizes the need for high growth in the agriculture sector. The share of agriculture and allied sectors in gross domestic product (GDP) declined steadily from 38.8 per cent in 1980–1 to 14.2 per cent in 2010–11 (Ministry of Finance 2012). Till the Eighth Five Year Plan (FYP) period, observed growth in this sector was higher than the targeted growth rate (though the target itself was low, less than 3.5 per cent) but from the Ninth Five Year Plan (1998–2002) onwards that momentum was lost and the observed growth rate was below the targeted one. In the Ninth FYP, agriculture recorded only 2.5 per cent growth rate (MoA 2012a) as against a target of 3.9 per cent. There is a growing divergence between overall economic growth and agricultural growth and this might have serious implications for inter-sectoral equity. A lot of distress was felt in the farming sector in the early 2000s, becoming a cause of concern for policymakers. To add to this concern, the NSS 59th round (NSSO 2006) reported that approximately 27 per cent of the farmers were not interested in farming as it was not profitable and 40 per cent of all the farmers wanted to quit the farming profession if they had a choice.

To address these issues of inclusive growth and for releasing agriculture from the clutches of distress and disinterest, the Indian government took many steps to revive the sector from the mid-2000s, the launch of Bharat Nirman in 2005–6 being a step in this endeavour. The main objectives of the Eleventh Five Year Plan (2007–12) were achieving a 4 per cent rate of growth in agriculture and ensuring that the growth and benefits achieved were distributed more widely across regions. This was a major challenge due to the fact that Indian agriculture is undergoing lot of structural changes because of an altering local and global scenario and the integration of global and local markets. Therefore, it is imperative to understand the performance of agriculture and the association of this sector with key policy initiatives for high productivity, enhancing livelihoods, and for the sustainability of agriculture.

PERFORMANCE OF AGRICULTURE

To understand temporal and spatial performance, agricultural growth rates were compared in three different periods—the pre-reform period (1980–1 to 1989–90), the reform period (1990–1 to 1999–2000), and the recent decade (2000–1 to 2010) at the all-India level and also at state levels. However, to look into the performance more closely, the growth rates were also estimated at an interval of five-year periods. Economic reforms were initiated in the early 1990s by opening up of the economy to external competition, liberalization of the trade, and deregulation of inputs and other sub-sectors. This was supposed to give a boost to the agriculture sector also. In order to capture the changes in the growth rate, a semi-log model was fitted to the three-year moving average data of agriculture GDP.

The analysis shows that the overall performance of agriculture and its allied sectors was not up to the mark during the period 2000–1 to 2010–11, considering the fact that much of the emphasis was laid on this sector from 2005 onwards. The trend growth rate of this sector was only 2.79 per cent (Table 6.1) while the growth recorded during the reform period (1990–1 to 1999–2000) was 3.21 per cent. However, the overall economy experienced a robust growth of 7.83 per cent during the 2000s. Growth rate depends on the years chosen for estimates. For example, if we take the decade from the mid-1990s to the mid-2000s, agriculture growth was only around 2 per cent per annum. This period of ten years may have masked some of the changes. Therefore, an analysis at five-year intervals shows (Figure 6.1) that there was a steep deceleration in agriculture and allied sectors after 1999–2000 and the growth rate declined from 3.4 per cent during 1994–5 to 1999–2000 to 1.8 per cent during 2000–1 to 2004–5. A major setback was observed for the crop and livestock sectors during 2000–1 to 2004–5 when it dropped to 1.22 per cent. However, the agriculture sector showed signs of revival. The growth rate rose from 1.77 per cent in 2000–1 to 2004–5 and to 2.89 per cent during 2005–6 to 2010–11 with the growth rate in agriculture and allied sectors being 2.89 per cent. This might be due to the corrective action taken by the government since 2004–5.

Table 6.1 Trend Growth Rate of Agriculture Sector and Overall Economy (at 2004–5 prices)

	Agriculture & Allied	Overall GDP
1980–1 to 1989–90	2.99	5.17
1990–1 to 1999–2000	3.21	6.45
2000–1 to 2010–11	2.79	7.83

Source: CSO (2012a and 2012b).

The fishery sector was at its peak during 1990–1 to 1994–5 with a growth rate of 7.09 per cent and faced a major decline during 1995–6 to 1999–2000 when the growth rate was only 3.42 per cent. However, subsequently this sector showed an increasing trend. Rise in the growth rate was observed for the forestry sector throughout the period. During the Eleventh FYP period (2007–12) the estimated average annual growth rate for agriculture and allied sectors was 3.3 per cent (Ministry of Finance 2012), which though significantly higher than the growth rate observed during the Tenth FYP (2.4 per cent) (MoA 2012a), was less than the targeted growth rate of 4 per cent.

It is evident from Figure 6.1, that the crop and livestock sectors recorded the lowest growth rate during 2000–1

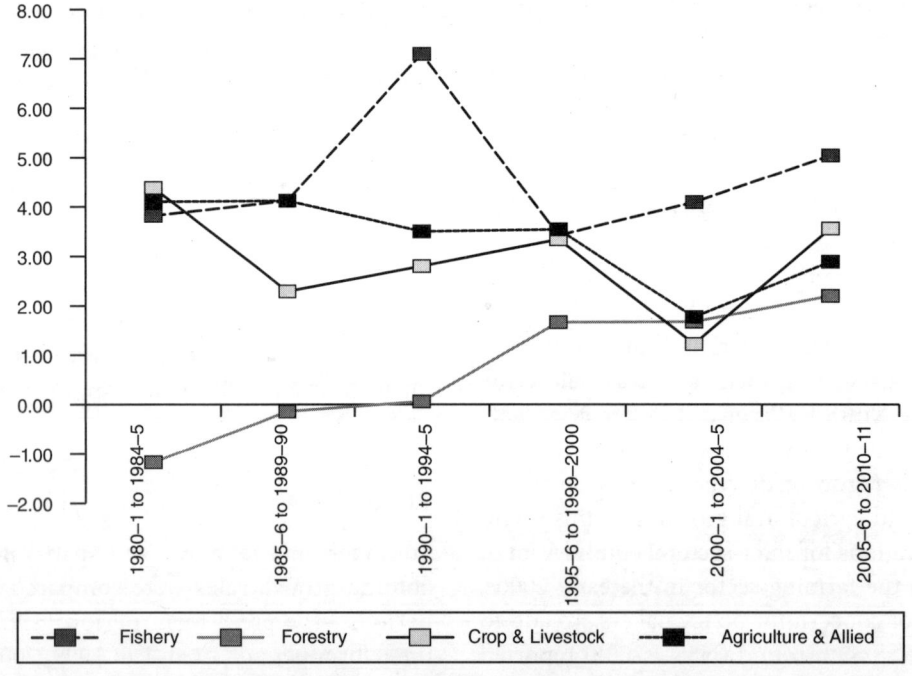

Figure 6.1 Growth in the Agriculture Sector

Source: CSO (2012a and 2012b).

to 2004–5. Therefore, to understand the performance of the different sub-sectors of agriculture, we looked at the growth in the value of output by crops and crop groups. The growth rate of cereal crops showed a continuous decline in all the three periods. Paddy and wheat crops registered the lowest growth in 2000–1 to 2009–10. However, maize crops registered a significant improvement in the growth rate of value of output from 1.59 per cent in the 1980s to 4.92 per cent in the 2000s. The value of output of cotton grew about three-fold during 2000–1 to 2009–10 as compared to the 1990s (Table 6.2). This growth might be attributed to adopting of Bt cotton in a large area, due to which productivity of cotton improved significantly. Government initiatives to promote oilseeds and pulses through programmes like the National Pulses Development Project, Integrated Scheme of Oilseeds, Pulses, Oil Palm and Maize (ISOPAM), and National Food Security Mission (NFSM) also had a positive impact. Growth rate of both these crops improved in the 2000s as compared to the 1990s. Fruits and vegetables recorded the highest growth rate in the value of outputs during 1990–1 to 1999–2000. In the livestock sector, the meat and fish group observed an improvement in 2000–1 to 2009–10 over 1990–1 to 1999–2000.

Table 6.2 Trend Growth Rate in the Value of Output

	1980–1 to 1989–90	1990–1 to 1999–2000	2000–1 to 2009–10
All cereals	2.76	2.02	1.25
Paddy	3.31	1.80	1.13
Wheat	3.85	3.54	1.16
Maize	1.59	2.35	4.92
Pulses	1.97	0.56	1.55
Oilseeds	4.33	2.76	4.28
Sugar cane	2.43	2.86	1.90
Cotton	0.61	3.02	10.90
Fruits & vegetables	2.73	5.50	3.00
Milk group	5.57	4.20	3.35
Meat group	4.93	3.68	4.38
Eggs	7.82	4.28	5.25

Source: CSO (2012a and 2012b).

It was observed that total growth in the production of cereals occurred mostly due to growth in yield rather than area growth (Table 6.3). The highest growth in the yield of wheat and rice was observed during the 1980s when the

Table 6.3 Growth Rate of Area, Production, and Yield of Major Crops

Crop	1980–1 to 1989–90			1990–1 to 1999–2000			2000–1 to 2010–11		
	A	P	Y	A	P	Y	A	P	Y
Rice	0.41	3.62	3.19	0.68	2.02	1.34	−0.1	1.51	1.61
Wheat	0.46	3.57	3.10	1.72	3.57	1.83	1.28	2.16	0.87
Jowar	−0.99	0.28	1.29	−3.53	−3.07	0.48	−3.27	−0.54	2.82
Bajra	−1.05	0.03	1.09	−1.46	0.95	2.44	−0.26	2.4	2.66
Maize	−0.20	1.89	2.09	0.94	3.28	2.32	2.81	5.65	2.77
Coarse cereals	−1.34	0.40	1.62	−2.12	−0.02	1.82	−0.75	2.8	4.24
Total cereals	**−0.26**	**3.03**	**2.90**	**0.04**	**−0.02**	**1.59**	**0.09**	**2.01**	**3.19**
Gram	−1.41	−0.81	0.61	1.26	2.96	1.68	4.61	6.32	1.64
Tur	2.30	2.87	0.56	−0.66	0.89	1.55	1.18	2.05	0.87
Total pulses	**−0.09**	**1.52**	**1.61**	**−0.6**	**0.59**	**0.93**	**1.62**	**3.35**	**1.9**
Total food grains	**−0.23**	**2.85**	**2.74**	**−0.07**	**2.02**	**1.52**	**0.37**	**2.12**	**2.89**
Sugarcane	1.44	2.70	1.24	−0.07	2.73	1.05	1.12	1.64	0.52
Groundnut	1.67	3.76	2.06	−2.31	−1.25	1.08	−0.87	1.24	2.13
Rapeseed and mustard	1.95	7.28	5.22	0.71	0.78	0.07	3.05	5.37	2.26
Sunflower	25.69	21.32	−3.47	−2.97	−3.2	−0.24	0.19	2.31	2.12
Soybean	17.10	17.96	0.73	10.23	13.06	2.56	5.35	9.14	3.6
Nine oilseeds	2.47	5.36	2.49	0.17	1.42	1.42	2.13	5.16	3.01
Cotton	−1.25	2.80	4.10	2.71	2.29	−0.41	2.6	13.8	10.91
Potato	2.90	5.17	2.20	3.84	5.44	1.54	4.76	5.28	0.49
All principal crops	0.10	3.19	2.56	0.27	2.29	1.33	0.91	2.5	3.25

Source: MoA (2012b).

green revolution had matured and was extended to more areas. However, in the 1990s and 2000s, growth in wheat production was mostly on the account of an expansion in area. This growth in area is likely to have occurred due to the deceleration in the area under coarse cereals (Table 6.3), especially jowar and bajra. Thus the growth in the production of coarse cereals can be attributed to growth in yield which was mostly because of new seed technology. Maize crops recorded an exceptional growth in production on account of growth in both area and in yield during 2000–1 to 2010–11. Growth in the production of oilseeds and pulses was also very impressive during 2000–1 to 2010–11 on account of growth in both area and yield. However, remarkable growth was observed in the case of cotton production (13.8 per cent), which was mostly due to an increase in the yield. The highest growth in area was observed for sunflower (25.69 per cent) followed by soybean (17.1 per cent) during the pre-reform period. For all principal crops, the highest yield growth was observed during the decade of the 2000s.

Growth in output is due to many factors such as growth in input use, adopting improved technology, infrastructure, and institutions. Total factor productivity (TFP) is generally estimated to segregate the effect of growth of inputs from other factors. A study by Sivasubramonian (2004) shows that TFP growth in agriculture was the highest in the 1980s at 1.89 per cent per annum but declined to 1.68 per cent in the post-reform period (Table 6.4). One remarkable result is that in spite of lower growth in agricultural GDP, TFP contributed more than 50 per cent to GDP in agriculture whereas in non-agriculture its contribution was less than 30 per cent during the 1980s and 1990s. It shows the importance of TFP growth for agriculture in the last two decades. Crop-wise TFP growth rate was estimated by Chand et al. (2011) for the two time periods 1986–95 and 1996–2005. The estimates show that TFP growth rate has increased for crops like coarse cereals (maize, bajra), gram, moong, barley, groundnut, soybean, and cotton in the period 1996–2005. But TFP growth has decelerated for rice, wheat, rapeseed, and mustard during the period 1996–2005, whereas, a negative growth rate in TFP was observed for jowar, arhar, urad, etc. during the period 1996–2005. To understand the impact of technological innovation on different crops, Chand et al. (2011) have also observed the share of TFP growth in the output growth of various crops. The same study shows that wheat had registered the highest share of TFP growth in output growth (68.3 per cent and 60.4 per cent) as compared to other cereals (for example, rice had a 23.5 per cent and 43.5 per cent share of TFP growth) in both the periods respectively (Table 6.5). This implies that wheat had the highest advantage of technology innovation.

Performance at the State Level

Performance of agriculture at the all-India level gives a picture of underperformance in the decade of 2000–1 to 2010–1 with growth picking up since 2004–5. However, since agriculture is a state subject, state-specific policies and actions are critical for the growth and productivity of this sector. Therefore, it is important to examine how states have performed in the different periods.

An analysis of the trend rate of growth in state agricultural GDP shows an improvement from the pre-reform period to 2000–1 and 2010–11 in Andhra Pradesh, Bihar, Gujarat, Karnataka, Madhya Pradesh, Maharashtra, and Odisha (Figure 6.2). However, in the 1990s most of the states registered a significant decline from their respective pre-reform period growth rates except for Gujarat, Karnataka, Kerala, and Madhya Pradesh. Agricultural performance was disappointing in some of the most progressive states, especially in Punjab and West Bengal during 2000–1 to 2009–10. The highest growth rate was recorded by Gujarat (5.42 per cent) followed by Andhra Pradesh (4.98 per cent)

Table 6.4 Total Factor Productivity (TFP) in Agriculture and Non-agriculture

	1950–1 to 1960–1	1960–1 to 1970–1	1970–1 to 1980–1	1980–1 to 1990–1	1990–1 to 1999–2000
Agriculture					
Growth rate in GDP (%)	3.03	2.31	1.50	3.43	2.97
Growth rate in TFP (%)	1.65	0.88	−0.35	1.89	1.68
% of TFP share in GDP Growth	54.5	38.1	−23.3	55.1	56.6
Non-Agriculture					
Growth rate in GDP (%)	5.34	5.30	4.38	6.77	7.14
Growth rate in TFP (%)	0.88	0.89	0.01	1.98	2.04
% of TFP share in GDP growth	16.5	16.8	0.22	29.3	28.6

Source: Sivasubramonian (2004).

Table 6.5 Annual Growth Rate in TFP and Share of TFP Growth in Output Growth

Crop	TFP growth rate (%)		Share of TFP growth in output growth (%)	
	1986–95	1996–2005	1986–95	1996–2005
Rice	0.74	0.40	23.5	43.5
Wheat	2.51	1.61	68.3	60.4
Maize	0.67	1.64	11.6	31.0
Jowar	0.74	−0.42	47.7	(−)
Bajra	0.39	1.50	9.4	55.9
Barley	0.44	0.61	30.5	(−)
Gram	0.09	0.34	5.7	71.4
Moong	−0.59	1.70	(−)	17.8
Arhar	0.21	−0.54	33.8	(−)
Urad	−0.22	−0.73	(−)	(−)
Soybean	0.83	0.63	4.6	6.7
Groundnut	0.55	1.30	25.4	30.8
Rapeseed and mustard	0.74	0.08	8.0	7.7
Sugarcane	−1.32	−0.65	(−)	(−)
Cotton	0.92	0.80	21.5	46.0

Source: Chand et al. (2011).

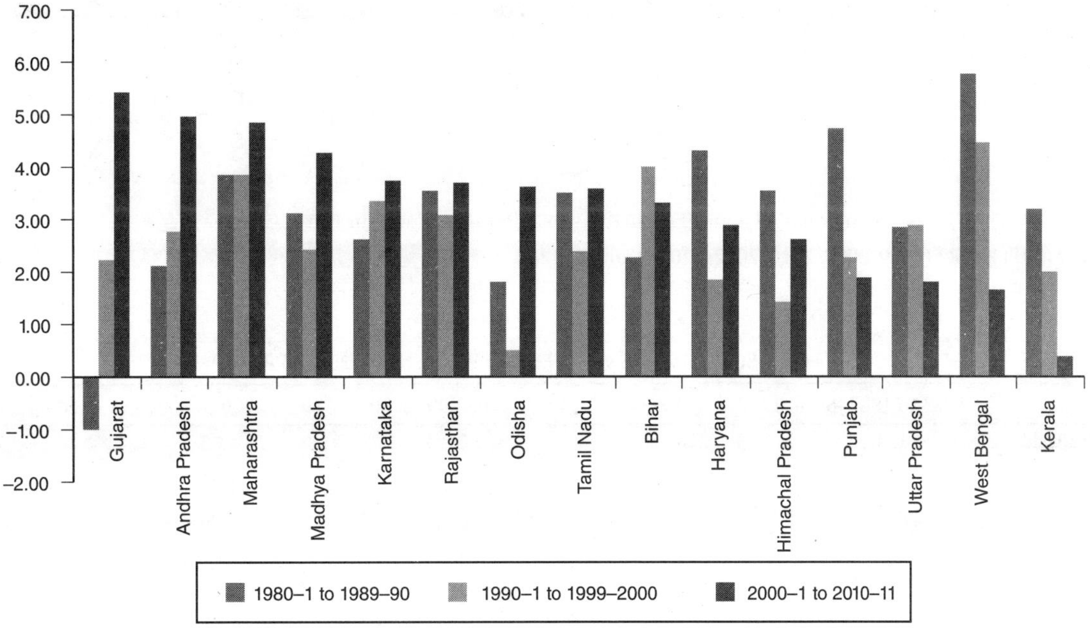

Figure 6.2 State-wise Growth in Agricultural GDP at 2004–5

Sources: CSO (1999, 2007, 2010, 2012a, 2012b, and 2012c).

and Maharashtra (4.84 per cent) in the period 2000–1 to 2010–11.

Land and Labour Productivity

Apart from growth rates, productivity levels are also important for improving the living standards of the people dependent on agriculture. A comparison of productivity (workforce and land) across the states shows large variations. GSDP from agriculture was used to compute the productivity of workers and land in different time periods. These periods for the analysis of worker productivity were taken on the basis of the NSS quinquennial rounds which fall in the years 1983, 1987–8, 1993–4, 1999–2000, 2004–5, and

2009–10 as data for the workforce in agriculture is available for these years. The three-year average GSDP was taken such that the NSS quinquennial round years were in the middle.

The highest level of labour productivity was observed in Punjab (Rs 24,017) followed by Kerala (Rs 22,204) and Haryana (Rs 18,234) in the three-year average period of 2008–11. The lowest productivity per worker was observed in Bihar (Rs 3,402) (Figure 6.3). Growth in labour productivity across the states indicates improvements in farm incomes in all the states except Kerala, Punjab, Rajasthan, and West Bengal during 2004–5 to 2009–10 as compared to 1983 to 1987–8 (Table 6.6). Continuous improvements in growth of worker productivity were observed in Andhra Pradesh for all the periods under consideration. Gujarat showed large fluctuations in the growth rate of worker productivity across the periods (Table 6.6).

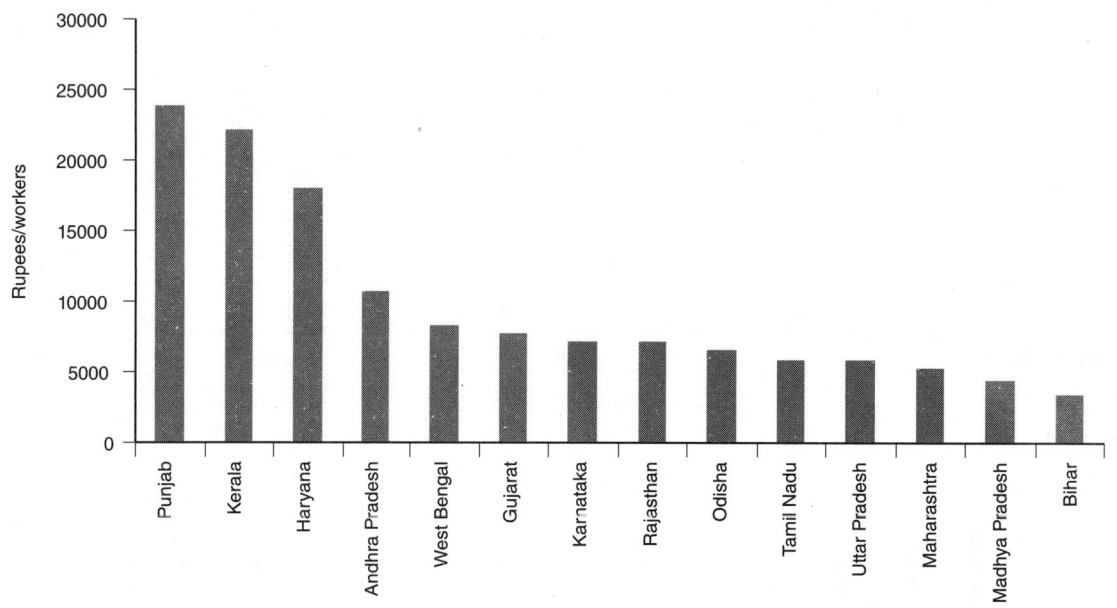

Figure 6.3 Labour Productivity in 2009–10 at Constant Prices (2004–5)
Sources: NSSO (2011); CSO (1999, 2007, 2010, 2012a, 2012b, and 2012c).

Table 6.6 State-wise Growth in Labour Productivity (2004–5 Prices)

State	1983 to 1987–8	1987–8 to 1993–4	1993–4 to 1999–2000	1999–2000 to 2004–5	2004–5 to 2009–10
Andhra Pradesh	−1.49	1.70	2.01	4.03	5.59
Bihar	3.55	−2.92	1.94	1.03	3.87
Gujarat	−6.01	2.67	−1.63	7.29	0.62
Haryana	0.81	6.52	−0.44	2.85	1.99
Karnataka	1.27	2.62	2.25	−4.84	4.52
Kerala	4.71	8.32	3.93	1.35	4.21
Madhya Pradesh	0.53	1.89	0.41	1.15	1.74
Maharashtra	0.47	5.80	0.72	2.70	4.29
Odisha	2.35	−3.64	−1.26	5.24	2.35
Punjab	5.60	2.93	1.51	4.59	1.02
Rajasthan	0.94	2.42	0.61	4.17	0.01
Tamil Nadu	2.29	6.19	1.54	−3.00	3.61
Uttar Pradesh	−0.84	1.56	1.56	1.39	0.50
West Bengal	4.43	4.84	1.88	2.03	0.44

Sources: NSS reports (various rounds); CSO (1999, 2007, 2010, and 2012a, 2012b, and 2012c).

Nevertheless, marginalization of agricultural workers was observed over the years. The percentage of agricultural labourers increased, whereas the percentage of cultivators in total agriculture reduced from 62 per cent in 1981 to 54 per cent in 2001 (MoA 2012b). The dependence of the workforce on agriculture in rural areas was still a high 66.5 per cent even in 2004–5. There is a need for growing the rural non-farm sector (RNFS) for reducing the pressure on land. Past studies show that the growth in RNFS contributed to diversification of employment opportunities in the post-reform period. This shift of employment from agriculture to non-agriculture was too slow to employ large surplus agricultural labour (Radhakrishna 2002).

Productivity of land estimated as GSDP per net sown area was the highest in Kerala mainly due to the production of cash crops (Figure 6.4) followed by West Bengal and Haryana. However, the average annual growth rate was the highest in Gujarat for 2001–2 to 2006–7, followed by Madhya Pradesh, Maharashtra, Odisha, and Rajasthan (Figure 6.5).

Instability

The above analysis suggests that Indian agriculture is marked with a lot of temporal fluctuations and it is important to understand if these fluctuations increased or decreased over a period of time. This was also analysed by Mehra (1981), Hazell (1982), Ray (1983), Dev (1987), and Chand and Parappurathu (2011) for different periods. We have used Ray's method of calculating instability (that is, SD of $LN(Y_{t+1})/(Y_t)$), where Y_t in our study is taken as the net domestic product from agriculture.

The analysis shows that at the all-India level, instability reduced (4.6 per cent) in the 1990s but in the latest decade of 2000–1 to 2009–10, volatility in the agriculture sector increased to the level of the pre-reform period (5.8 per cent) (Table 6.7). The growth in GDP from agriculture during 2000–1 to 2009–11 was low and this coupled with higher instability would have led to more vulnerability and distress to the farming sector. The growth rate in the latter half of the 2000s was higher than that in the first half of the 2000s. Farmers must have benefited from the growth in the last five years.

A comparison across states in net state domestic produce (NSDP) reveals that in all the states, except in Madhya Pradesh, Karnataka, Maharashtra, Rajasthan, and Tamil Nadu, instability reduced in the latest decade. In the decade of the 1980s, highest instability was observed in Gujarat (48 per cent), followed by Rajasthan (26 per cent). However, in the latest decade of the 2000s the highest instability was observed in Rajasthan (29.4 per cent), followed by Madhya Pradesh (21.7 per cent), and the lowest in Uttar Pradesh (1.3 per cent) (Table 6.7).

KEY POLICY ISSUES

The above analysis shows that during the initial years of the 2000s agricultural growth was very sluggish; however

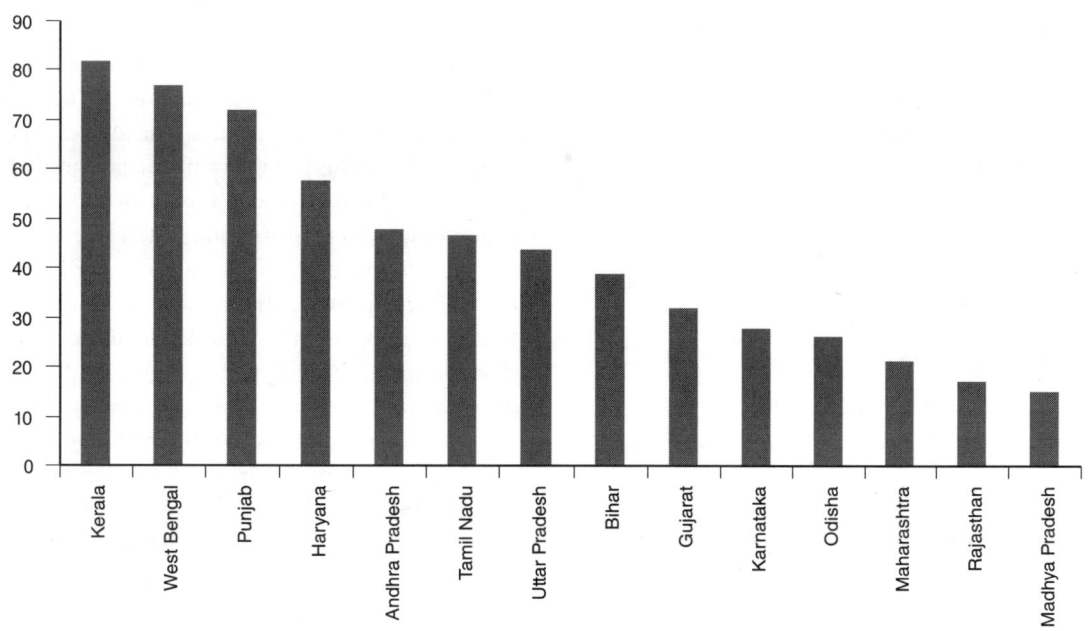

Figure 6.4 Land Productivity in the Year 2006–7 (000' Rs/Ha of NSA)

Sources: CSO (2007); MoA (2012b).

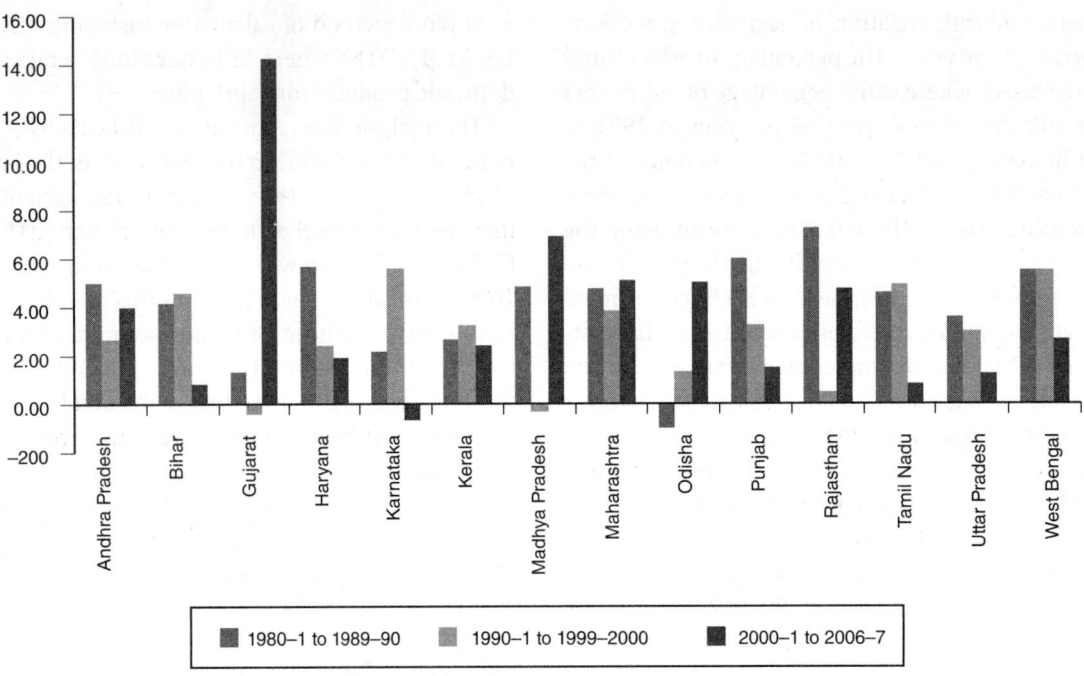

Figure 6.5 Average Annual Growth in Land Productivity
Sources: CSO (1999, 2007, and 2010); MoA (2012b).

Table 6.7 State-wise Instability in NSDP from Agriculture at 2004–5 Prices (%)

State	1980–1 to 1989–90	1990–1 to 1999–2000	2000–1 to 2009–10
Andhra Pradesh	11.5	11.9	9.3
Bihar	13.1	15.5	12.8
Gujarat	47.9	29.7	19.3
Haryana	14.5	6.5	5.2
Himachal Pradesh	14.2	5.3	11.6
Karnataka	8.9	9.2	11.8
Kerala	7.1	10.1	5.8
Madhya Pradesh	9.7	9.0	21.7
Maharashtra	14.0	16.7	12.2
Odisha	16.0	18.3	14.0
Punjab	4.9	4.3	2.0
Rajasthan	26.0	18.6	29.4
Tamil Nadu	16.2	8.8	13.4
Uttar Pradesh	3.4	4.8	1.3
West Bengal	9.6	6.1	4.4
All-India	5.8	4.6	5.8

Source: CSO (1999, 2007, 2010, and 2012c).

government initiatives from 2005 onwards in the form of Bharat Nirman, RKVY, and NFSM are showing signs of revival amid an increased volatility especially in the rainfed areas. The goal for the Twelfth Plan is attaining more inclusive faster and sustainable growth. Such a goal is not possible without focusing on growth in the agriculture sector, and particularly, small and marginal farm-holders covering 80 per cent of the total holdings and rainfed agriculture which accounts for about 60 per cent of the total cropped area. For sustainability of this growth more focus is needed to increase production and also a focus after growth on environmental resources and its conservation. Therefore, the key supply-side factors for attaining 4 per cent agricultural growth in the Twelfth Five Year Plan are: (a) land management, (b) water management, (c) market for agricultural products, (d) new and improved technologies, and (e) investment for infrastructure. They also cover four 'Is': Infrastructure, institutions, incentives, and information. Besides these key factors, other factors such as price policy, access to credit, climate change, and issues related to women farmers are also very important and cannot be ignored.

Land Management

Good soil ensures proper retention and release of water and nutrients, promotes and sustains root growth, and maintains the soil biotic habitat. Indian soils are gradually degrading because of soil erosion, loss of organic carbon, nutrient imbalance, compaction, and salinization. Existing policies of MSP and input subsidies have encouraged inappropriate use of fertilizers and water (Pingali and Shah 1999), led to inefficiency in production, and caused hindrances crop production that are not effectively covered under minimum support price (MSP). Overuse of highly subsidized chemical fertilizers lead to nutrient imbalance and deficiency of micro-nutrients. The recommended dose of nitrogenous, phosphatic, and potassium (N, P, and K) fertilizers have the ratio of 4:2:1. In 2005–6 it was 5.27: 2.2:1 and after government measures, it improved to 4.55:1.96:1 in 2008–9 (Ministry of Finance 2010). Adoption of HYV has led to increased use of pesticides, further, which results in soil and water contamination in case of inefficient and careless application.

There are many land-related issues in agriculture. It is generally argued that small size of farms is responsible for the low profitability of agriculture. However, the experience of China and other East Asian countries show that it is not a constraint. On the land market, the 'Report of the Steering Committee' recommended that, 'Small farmers should be assisted to buy land through the provision of institutional credit, on a long-term basis, at a low rate of interest and by reducing stamp duty. At the same time, they should be enabled to enlarge their operational holdings by liberalizing the land lease market. The two major elements of such a reform are: security of tenure for tenants during the period of contract; and the right of the land owner to resume land after the period of contract is over' (Planning Commission 2007a: 52). Basically, we have to ensure land leasing and create conditions including access to credit, whereby the poor can access land from those who wish to leave agriculture. There are some emerging land issues such as an increase in the demand for land for non-agricultural purposes including special economic zones and displacement of farmers, tribals, and others due to development projects. There is a need for careful land acquisition. Land alienation is one of the serious problems in tribal areas.

Irrigation and Water Management

Water is the leading input in agriculture. Development of irrigation and water management are crucial for raising levels of living in rural areas.[1] Major areas of concern in irrigation include a decline in real investment, thin spread of investment, low recovery of costs, a decline in the water table, wastages and inefficiencies in water use, and non-involvement of users (Planning Commission 2007b). Both investments and efficiency in the use of water are needed. Major areas of reforms needed in irrigation include stepping up and prioritizing public investment, raising profitability of groundwater exploitation and augmenting ground water resources, rational pricing of irrigation water and electricity, involvement of user farmers in the management of irrigation systems, and making groundwater markets equitable (Rao 2005). In a recent study, Shah et al. (2009a) indicate that the impact of the 2009 drought is expected to be less severe than the 2002 drought due to groundwater recharge in the last few years. Groundwater can be exploited in a big way in the eastern region. Watershed development and water conservation by communities are needed under water management. New watershed guidelines based on the Parthasarathy Committee's recommendations were accepted by the central cabinet in March 2009. Their implementation has to be stepped up in order to obtain benefits in rainfed areas. The National Rainfed Area Authority has a big responsibility in matters relating to water conservation and watershed development. Assets created under National Rural Employment Guarantee Scheme (NREGS) can help in improving land and water management.

Agricultural Markets

An assured market and remunerative prices are very important for agricultural growth. The MSP policy should lead to diversification in cropping patterns toward non-cereals. The development of markets and post-harvest infrastructure were not able to keep pace with the growth in agricultural production over time. In many states agricultural markets are underdeveloped and farmers have to sell even rice and wheat crops at much below the MSP. Because of market imperfections there is a strong asymmetry in transmission of prices between the retail, wholesale, and farm levels.

Over time, farmers have diversified production towards high value crops, especially fruits and vegetables (Joshi et al. 2007; Chand et al. 2008; Dev 2008). The share of fruits and vegetables in the total value of crop output increased from 16 per cent in 1980–1 to 28 per cent in 2009–10 with its share in total gross cropped area being about 7.3 per cent in 2009–10 (Table 6.8). The share of food grain crops in the total value of output was only 33.5 per cent although it occupied about 63 per cent of the gross cropped area in 2009–10 (Table 6.8). Therefore, the value of output from per unit of land for fruits and vegetables is about five times that of food grains. The percentage area under sugarcane, cotton, and fruits and vegetables increased in the post-reform period as compared to the pre-reform period (Table 6.8).

---

[1] On land and water management, see Vaidyanathan (2006).

Table 6.8 Crop Group's Share in Value of Output at 2004–5 Prices

Crop group	1980–1	1990–1	2000–1	2009–10
Cereals	37.2 (59.5)	34.5 (54.5)	32.8 (53.2)	29.1 (51.2)
Pulses	6.4 (13.5)	6.8 (12.4)	4.5 (11.6)	4.4 (11.7)
Oilseeds	8.4 (10.7)	12.9 (14.2)	6.9 (11.9)	9 (13.8)
Sugarcane	5.7 (1.8)	4.8 (2.1)	4.6 (2.3)	3.6 (2.4)
Cotton	3.6 (4.5)	3.7 (4.2)	2.6 (4.8)	4.5 (4.8)
Fruits and vegetables	15.9 (2.8)	17.2 (4.6)	25.3 (5.4)	27.8 (7.3)

Note: Figures in parenthesis are % of gross cropped area under the crop.

Sources: CSO (2012a and 2012b); Indiastat (2012); and MoA (2008 and 2012b).

The diversification of agriculture is primarily led by diversification of diet. However, to sustain diversification towards high-value commodities and leveraging it towards benefiting the farmers, good infrastructure in terms of an assured market, better road connectivity, cold storage, post-harvest technology, and a supportive policy to attract private players are required. Participation of the private sector is very crucial for developing these agriculture sub-sectors as huge investments are required to improve and upscale backward and forward linkages with the farmers (Gulati and Ganguly 2010). Farmers can hedge against price risk by opting for contract farming in the context of increasing the number of supermarkets and food processing companies (Birthal et al. 2007; Singh 2008).

Further, vertical integration of services related to farming, warehousing, and other logistical, processing, and retailing can help direct farm-firm linkages by lowering transaction and transportation costs and strengthening the supply chain to enhance value addition. Earlier such direct linkages were not permitted as agricultural produce transactions outside regulated markets (mandis) were restricted. Nevertheless, to promote diversification of agriculture and the participation of private players, an amendment to the Agriculture Produce Marketing Committee (APMC) Act known as 'APMC Model Act' was enacted in 2003. This amendment allowed direct transactions between producers and retailers in several states through various institutional mechanisms such as cooperatives, producers' associations, and contract farming. Reservations on many products for small-scale industry were recently relaxed and fiscal incentives such as reduction in excise and corporate taxes were given to food processing industries (Birthal et al. 2007). However, the Model Act is not yet been fully implemented by all the state governments. Only a few states have amended the legislation significantly, for example, Andhra Pradesh, Karnataka, and Maharashtra and several other states have acted but have not notified the rules. States like Jammu and Kashmir, Meghalaya, Pondicherry, Uttar Pradesh, Uttarakhand, and West Bengal are yet to amend their APMC Acts. The rules proposed under the Warehousing (Development & Regulation) Act 2006, still need to be notified for introducing a regulated system of warehouses (CACP 2011). Further, it is being reported that most of the markets lack basic infrastructure and charge very high taxes and commissions on fresh and processed agri-produce (Planning Commission 2010).

In India, a major share of food retailing is still confined to the unorganized sector with small traders, kirana stores, hawkers, and wet markets. However, organized food retail is slowly becoming popular and the top ten Indian food and grocery retailers grew at average annual rates of above 70 per cent per annum during 2002 to 2007. This trend is likely to continue for next 10–15 years (Gulati and Ganguly 2009).

With the presence of supermarkets, the concept of rural business hubs is emerging. It is like a rural mall where agri-input suppliers and service providers come close to the farmers to meet their demands. It also offers facilities for procuring consumer durables, medical services, and groceries. Given the fact that demand of High Value Crops (HVCs) is increasing, the demand for input services have also risen. Private players like ITC (Choupal Saagar), DSCL (Hariyali Kisan Bazaar), Tata (Kisan Sansar), and the Future Group (Aadhaar) are some key players operating in this segment of agri-food system.

To reap the benefit of increased production and diversification towards HVCs, good and improved infrastructure is required in the form of road connectivity, cold storage, and irrigation. To encourage participation of private partners, the policy framework should not be a hindrance. Therefore, there is a need to implement the APMC Model Act and the Warehousing Act and cut down on taxes and commissions on fresh produce to give a boost to high value agriculture. To ensure the inclusion of small farm-holders in the new supply chain, tenancy reforms, and clear regulations for contract farming should be evolved and implemented. Food retail trade is a major economic activity and needs attention to ensure the livelihood of the poor.

Technology

A new and efficient technology is essential for agricultural growth. Studies have shown that at least one-third of the future growth in productivity should come through innovations in crop technologies. Generally, private sector research and the seed industry focus on crops and varieties with massive commercial markets and scope. Public sector research needs to take into the account the farmers' need for crops as per prevailing agro-climatic conditions. One of the reasons for low growth in total factor productivity in India, as compared to countries like Brazil, Indonesia, and China, relates to less focus on science and technology in agriculture in India in comparison to these countries. Public sector investment for agriculture research and development and education in India is only 0.6 per cent of the agricultural GDP which needs to be raised to at least 1 per cent as is being invested by most of the developing countries.

Seeds are the carriers of technology and hence play a vital role in improving and sustaining the growth of agriculture, especially under constraints of scarce and fixed land and water resources. The technology of High Yielding Varieties (HYV) seed production was a major contributor in making India self-sufficient in food grains during the green revolution period. It has been estimated that the direct contribution of quality seeds in total production is about 15–20 per cent depending upon the crop. This can be further raised up to 45 per cent with efficient management of other inputs (seednet India 2012). There is a proposal for a new seed bill 2011, with the main objective of increasing production and supply of quality seeds to meet future requirements for sustainable agriculture production. As it was experienced in the case of Bt cotton and hybrid maize, the role of the private sector in technological innovation, dissemination, and adoption is very important. A spectacular performance especially in the case of Bt cotton was possible due to the active participation of the private companies.

Therefore, the participation of the private sector should be solicited in the development and dissemination of new and improved technologies. Some of the improved technologies include zero tillage, laser levelling, micro-irrigation, raised bed, system of rice intensification, and non-pesticide farm management etc. However, before taking the technologies to the farmers' field, there is a need to understand and analyse them for local adaptation.

Subsidies and Investment in Agriculture

Another issue that needs to be focused on for agricultural growth relates to reducing the pressure of subsidies and escalating investment. As discussed in the earlier sections, agricultural subsidies encourage inefficiency in the use of resources, which leads to environmental degradation. There is a tradeoff between subsidies and investment and it is being shown that returns to investment are three times higher than those on subsidies (Fan et al. 2008). Hence it is important to rationalize subsidies and enhance investment. The share of gross capital formation in agriculture and allied sectors (GCFA) to total gross capital formation (GDCF) in the economy declined during 1980–1 to 1989–90. With a slight recovery in the initial period of reforms, it further

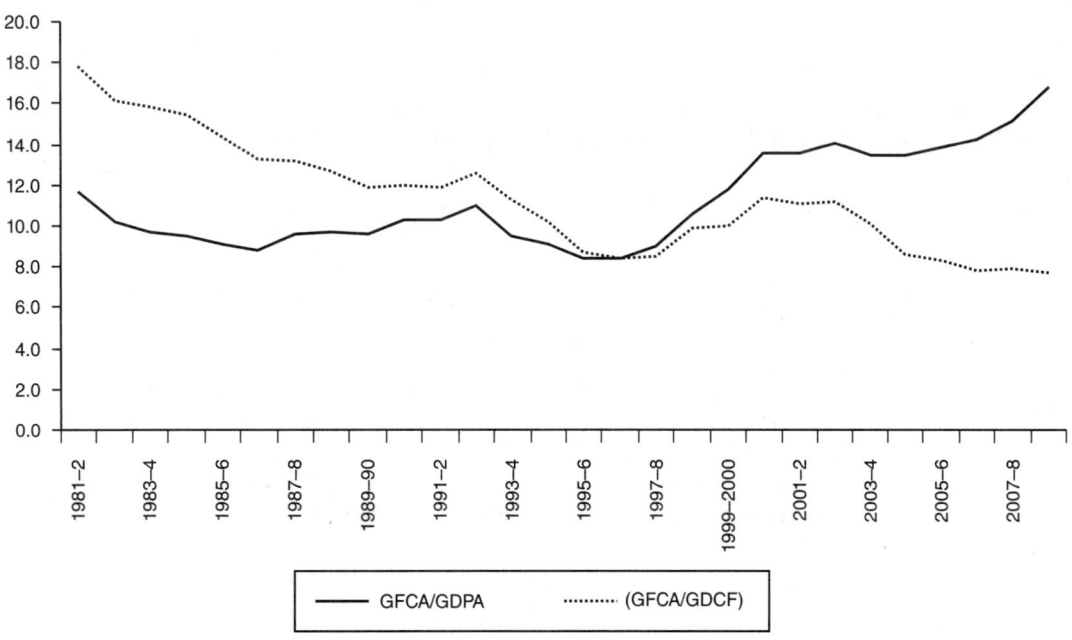

Figure 6.6 Investment in Agriculture

Source: CSO (2012b).

declined drastically during the late 1990s and early 2000s. The ratio of GCFA to GDCF was 7.7 per cent in 2009–10 which had declined from around 11.7 per cent in 2001–2 (Figure 6.6), signifying less investment in the agriculture sector as compared to the non-agriculture sector. Decline in investment is linked to a slowdown in agriculture (Dev 2008). Fortunately, the ratio of GCFA to agriculture GDP is showing signs of improvement and this ratio has improved from 12 per cent in the mid-2000s to 20 per cent in 2009–10.

Both public and private investment is required for the growth of agriculture. Public investment in agriculture as a percentage of GDP agriculture peaked at 3.71 per cent in 2006–7and got stagnant thereafter at around 3.5 per cent. However, in the Eleventh Five Year Plan it was envisaged that for achieving 4 per cent growth in agriculture, public investment as a percentage of agricultural GDP should be 4 per cent (Planning Commission 2010).

About 90 per cent of the public sector investment for agriculture covers investment for irrigation in the Central Statistical Organization (CSO)data. This does not give a correct picture and underestimates the investment in agriculture. Many researchers have expanded this series by using a broader series of investment that also includes expenses such as rural development and rural infrastructure (Chand 2001; Gulati and Bathla 2002). In the early 1980s, the share of public sector and private sector investment (including the household sector) in gross capital formation in agriculture was almost equal but from the early 2000s, the share of private sector has been much higher than the share of the public sector. These analyses are based on CSO data which make assumptions for corporate private investment on the basis of term loans. However, the entire term loan may not be utilized for capital formation. Bisaliah and Dev (2011) have used Commission on Agriculture Cost and Prices (CACP) cost of cultivation data for analysing private investment. They have shown that there is not much improvement in private investment for agriculture in selected states. It was estimated that only 10 per cent of the investment was from corporate bodies and the remaining 90 per cent of the investment was made by farmers on their farms. A shift in the composition of on-farm investment is being observed as farmers are putting more money for improving irrigation and buying farm machinery than investing on animal capital. A sudden increase in corporate private investment was seen in 2011 but this was mainly due to two major projects, Sankhrail Agro and Agro Allied Products in West Bengal and the Lunej Demonstration Project in Gujarat (Reddy 2011). Most of these corporate private investments are coming in food processing and dairy sub-sectors.

Countries like China, Brazil, and Indonesia have invested much more than India in rural infrastructure and education. India needs to invest more in agriculture and rural areas in order to increase productivity in agriculture and for achieving rural transformation.

OTHER ISSUES

Regional Experience in Agriculture Growth

There are significant variations in the experience of agricultural growth across the states. As was seen earlier, agricultural performance was disappointing in some of the most progressive states like Punjab, whereas Gujarat demonstrated a phenomenal performance in the 2000s. To understand the reasons for this, the story of agriculture in these two states of Gujarat and Punjab is given in Box 6.1. It is clear from Box 6.1 that the initiatives taken by the state government along with civil society organizations, farmers and the private sector, amending the APMC Act, and adopting Bt cotton boosted agricultural growth in Gujarat.

Climate Change

Climate change is associated with global warming and increasingly fluctuating weather cycles with unpredictable cold waves, heat waves, floods, and exceptionally heavy single-day downpours. It is estimated that a global warming by 1°C will result in yield losses in the production of wheat, soybean, mustard, groundnut, and potato by 3–7 per cent in India (MOEF 2009). Climate change will have a greater impact on rainfed agriculture and most of the rainfed land is in arid and semi-arid zones where the annual rainfall is meagre and prolonged dry spells are quite usual even during the monsoon season. Therefore, farmers need enabling technologies to cope up with climate change risk. Realizing this, the National Action Plan on Climate Change was launched in 2008, with the aim of developing technologies to help rainfed agriculture adapt to changing climate patterns.

Agriculture and Nutrition

Another emerging issue is the relationship between agriculture and nutrition. Malnutrition is very high in India with one-third of the children born with low birth weights. About 43 per cent of the children below five years of age are underweight, 48 per cent are stunted, and 20 per cent are wasted (Ministry of Health and Family Welfare 2007). The stunting rate in India is two-to-seven fold of that in the other BRIC countries. Micronutrient deficiencies are also very high. Growth in agriculture can influence nutrition through many diverse and interconnected pathways (Gillespie and Kadiyala 2011). However, agricultural growth per se cannot always reduce malnutrition and this

PERFORMANCE AND KEY POLICY ISSUES OF INDIAN AGRICULTURE 91

> **Box 6.1** Story of Gujarat and Punjab Agriculture
>
> **Gujarat**
>
> Gujarat recorded the highest growth rate of agricultural GDP (5.42 per cent) during the decade of the 2000s (Figure 6.2). There was a major jump in the growth rate from the decade of the 1980s owing to the diversification of agriculture into high-value agriculture. Yield growth was the highest for cotton (12.24 per cent) followed by arhar (9.78 per cent) and gram (8.05 per cent). Land productivity in the decade of the 2000s was about 14 per cent which reached this level from a negative growth in the decade of the 1980s. In fact, adopting Bt cotton and other supportive policies and programmes helped farmers.
>
> It is being reported that the state government has taken many initiatives along with civil society organizations, farmers, and the private sector to ensure adequate irrigation, encourage water-use efficiency, and groundwater recharge. Programmes like the Sardar Sarovar Project, micro-irrigation, and watershed programmes have helped in this endeavour. To improve groundwater recharge and the power situation Gujarat combined feeder separation with an extensive watershed programme. Another driver of growth is technology development—Bt cotton and diffusion by the private sector. For improving nutrition-use efficiency there are 20 soil testing laboratories with a total capacity to analyse around 2,40,000 soil samples per year. The state government has also promoted new institutional arrangements like contract farming and aggressively encouraged the private sector to participate in agricultural exports, organized food retail, and agro-processing etc. For this purpose the state government has given many incentives, subsidies, and legislative support by amending the APMC Act (Shah et al. 2009b). Thus, implementation of these programmes and developing better infrastructure such as roads, cold storages, and warehouses have given a boost to agriculture in Gujarat.
>
> **Punjab**
>
> The growth rate of agricultural GDP in Punjab has slowed down since the decade of the 1980s (Figure 6.2). Intensive agriculture in terms of land, nutrients, water, capital, energy, and other inputs is practised in the state. The cropping intensity has been continuously rising and was 189.8 per cent in 2008–9 as against 184.5 per cent in 2002–3, putting additional stress on the already stressed soil and water resources. The major crop system followed in the state is rice-wheat farming which is degrading soil and water resources and thereby threatening environmental sustainability (Ladha et al. 2003). The prevailing policies for MSP and input subsidies have encouraged inappropriate land and input use (Pingali and Shah 1999), especially water and fertilizers. Intensification and mechanization of agriculture has further aggravated environmental degradation. Currently combined harvesting technologies are being used in Punjab, which leave behind large quantities of straw in the field. This residue when burnt in the open not only results in air pollution but also affects soil quality. Crop residue if added to the soil improves its quality. Due to the power subsidy the groundwater resources have been extensively exploited over the period. Subsequently out of 137 blocks in the state, 103 blocks are over-exploited, 5 blocks are critical, 4 blocks semi-critical and only 25 blocks are in the safe category (Gupta 2011). It is being reported that the water table is going down by 50–100 centimetres each year in Punjab (Planning Commission 2007b).
>
> Farmers in Punjab are very enthusiastic and can adapt to new technologies or cropping systems provided they are assured of market and remunerative prices. To give a boost to agricultural growth and to regenerate natural resources, especially water and soil, Punjab farmers will have to move away from the intensive rice-wheat farming system and diversify to other non-cereal crops. For ensuring livelihoods, assured prices, and markets, the state government needs to amend the APMC Act fully. Right now it is only partially amended in the state.

disconnect is visible in many states which have very high agricultural growth rates but no significant reduction in malnutrition, for example, Gujarat and Rajasthan. Therefore, to address the nutrition problem, agricultural policies should also aim at inclusiveness and equity.

SUMMING UP

Indian agriculture is showing signs of revival since the mid-2000s due to different initiatives taken by the government. However, the higher growth rate during 2005–6 to 2010–11 has not been able to curb high food inflation. There are significant spatial and temporal differences in the performance of agriculture in different states. The states which were doing very well before the reforms are showing signs of stagnation or deceleration in the post-reform period, especially Haryana, Punjab, Tamil Nadu, and Andhra Pradesh. However, Gujarat recorded a remarkable growth rate in the 2000s which may be partly attributable to the adoption of Bt cotton and developing good infrastructure.

For achieving more inclusive, faster, and sustainable growth along with 4 per cent growth in the agriculture sector during the Twelfth Five Year Plan, there is need to give more emphasis on issues related to land and water management, rainfed agriculture, agricultural markets, new and improved technologies, and investment in agriculture. Therefore, developing land lease markets and widespread plans for development of degraded land, adopting integrated farming systems, adopting best practices, and rationalization of input subsidies are all needed. To revitalize rainfed agriculture a comprehensive programme is required at the local level with active participation of all the stakeholders as per Integrated Watershed Management Programme (IWMP)guidelines. For efficient and equitable management of water, water user associations (WUAs) should be formed in line with performance improvement measures (PIMs).

The strategies have so far concentrated on rice and wheat in irrigated areas. Future growth will need to rely on a dual strategy of diversification into non-cereal high-value crops like pulses, fruits, vegetables, milk, and meat and a focus on rainfed areas and small farmers. The focus should also be on the eastern region.

Agriculture is diversifying towards HVCs, therefore, to reap the benefits of diversification and increase in production, there is need to develop better infrastructure, institutional and pricing reforms for water and energy-use efficiency, and notification of the APMC Model Act and Warehousing (Development & Regulation) Act by all the states. The high rates of taxes and commissions on fresh and processed agricultural produce need to be cut down. Production and marketing of HVCs require a supportive infrastructure that can be achieved through active public-private participation. As the food retail trade forms a very large segment of economic activity it needs special attention to ensure the livelihood of poor people. For making agricultural production sustainable and profitable, there has to be an emphasis on increasing investment, assured quality, and timely access to inputs, improving technology, and ensuring environmental sustainability. Yields of many crops in India are low compared to many developing countries. Total factor productivity growth in India is also low as compared to countries like Brazil, China, and Indonesia. This shows that there is lot of opportunity for India to improve yield levels and total factor productivity in the future without compromising on sustainability. This can be achieved through encouraging investment from the private sector for improving infrastructure, research, and developing technologies and their wider dissemination.

REFERENCES

Bhalla, G.S. (2007), *Indian Agriculture Since Independence*. New Delhi: NBT Publications.

Birthal, Pratap Singh, P.K. Joshi, Devesh Roy, and Amit Thorat (2007), *Diversification in Indian Agriculture Towards High-value Crops: The Role of Smallholders*. IFPRI Discussion Paper 727. Washington DC: International Food Policy Research Institute (IFPRI).

Bisaliah, and S. Mahendra Dev (2011), 'Private Investment in Indian Agriculture: Farm Level Evidences and Policy Directions', Paper presented in the workshop on 'Policy Options and Investment Priorities for Accelerating Agricultural Productivity and Development in India', organized by IGIDR, Mumbai and IHD, New Delhi at the India International Centre, New Delhi, 10–11 November 2011.

Commission on Agriculture Cost and Prices (CACP) [2011], *Report on Price Policy for Kharif Crops 2011–12*, available at http://cacp.dacnet.nic.in/RPP/Kharif_Report-2011-12.pdf, last accessed on 3 June 2012.

Central Statistical Organization [CSO] (1999), *State Domestic Product, 1980–81 Series*. New Delhi: Ministry of Statistics and Programme Implementation, Government of India. Available at http://mospi.nic.in/Mospi_New/upload/NAS12.htm, last accessed on 16 May 2012.

———. (2007) *State Domestic Product, 1993–94 Series*. New Delhi: Ministry of Statistics and Programme Implementation, Government of India. Available at http://mospi.nic.in/Mospi_New/upload/NAS12.htm, last accessed on 18 May 2012.

———. (2010) *State Domestic Product, 1999–2000 Series*. New Delhi: Ministry of Statistics and Programme Implementation, Government of India. Available at http://mospi.nic.in/Mospi_New/upload/NAS12.htm, last accessed on 18 May 2012.

———. (2012a), *National Accounts Statistics 2011* (back series). New Delhi: Ministry of Statistics and Programme Implementation, Government of India. Available at http://mospi.nic.in/Mospi_New/upload/back_series_2011.htm, last accessed on 12 March 2012.

———. (2012b), *National Accounts Statistics, 2011*. New Delhi: Ministry of Statistics and Programme Implementation, Government of India. Available at http://mospi.nic.in/Mospi_New/upload/NAS12.htm, last accessed on 12 March 2012.

———. (2012c) *State Domestic Product, 2004–05 Series*. New Delhi: Ministry of Statistics and Programme Implementation, Government of India. Available at http://mospi.nic.in/Mospi_New/upload/NAS12.htm, last accessed on 18 May 2012.

Chand, Ramesh (2001), 'Emerging Trends and Issues in Public and Private Investments in Indian Agriculture: A Statewise Analysis', *Indian Journal of Agricultural Economics*, 56(2): 161–84.

Chand, Ramesh, S.S. Raju, and L.M. Pandey (2008), 'Progress and Potential of Horticulture in India', *Indian Journal of Agricultural Economics*, 63(3): 299–309.

Chand, Ramesh and S. Parappurathu (2011), 'Historical and Spatial Trends in Indian Agriculture: Growth Analysis and National and State Level'. Paper presented during the workshop on 'Policy Options and Investment Priorities for Accelerating Agricultural Productivity and Development in India' from 10–11 November 2011 at the India International Centre, New Delhi, organized by the Indira Gandhi Institute of Development Research, Mumbai and the Institute for Human Development, New Delhi. Available at http://www.igidr.ac.in/newspdf/srijit/PP-069-03a.pdf, last accessed on 21 May 2012.

Chand, Ramesh, Praduman Kumar, and Sant Kumar (2011), 'Total Factor Productivity and Contribution of Research

Investment to Agricultural Growth in India', Policy Paper No. 25, National Centre for Agricultural Economics and Policy Research, New Delhi.

Dev, S. Mahendra (1987), 'Growth and Instability in Food-grains Production: An Interstate Analysis', *Economic and Political Weekly*, 22(39): A82–A92.

———. (2008), *Inclusive Growth in India: Agriculture, Poverty, and Human Development*. New Delhi: Oxford University Press, p. 399.

Fan, Shenggen, Ashok Gulati, and S. Thorat (2008), 'Investment, Subsidies, and Pro-poor Growth in Rural India', *Agricultural Economics*, 39: 163–70.

Gillespie, S. and S. Kadiyala (2011), 'Exploring the Agriculture-Nutrition Disconnect in India, 2020', Conference Brief 20, prepared for the IFPRI 2020 International Conference on 'Leveraging Agriculture for Improving Nutrition and Health', 10–12 February, New Delhi.

Gulati, Ashok and Kavery Ganguly (2009), 'Transforming Agri-food System: Role of Organized Retail in India', International Food Policy Research Institute, Mimeo.

———. (2010), 'The Changing Landscape of Indian Agriculture', *Agricultural Economics*, 41: 37–45.

Gulati, Ashok and S. Bathla (2002), 'Capital Formation in Indian Agriculture: Trends, Composition and Implications for Growth', National Bank for Agriculture and Rural Development, Occasional Paper 24, Mumbai.

Gupta, Sushil (2011), *Ground Water Management in Alluvial Areas*. New Delhi: Central Ground Water Board, available at http://cgwb.gov.in/documents/papers/incidpapers/Paper%20 11-%20sushil%20gupta.pdf, last accessed on 11 April 2012.

Hazell, Peter B.R. (1982), *Instability in Indian Food Grain Production*. Washington DC: Food Policy Research Institute, Research Report No. 30.

Indiastat (2012), *Area under Crops in India (1950–1951 to 2010–2011)*, available at http://www.indiastat.com/agriculture/2/agriculturalarealanduse/152/areaundercropsinindia19501951to20102011/448934/stats.aspx, last accessed on 15 March 2012.

Joshi, P.K., A. Gulati, and R. Cummings (2007), 'Agricultural Diversification in South Asia: Beyond Food Security', in P.K. Joshi, A. Gulati, and R. Cummings (eds), *Agricultural Diversification and Smallholders in South Asia*. New Delhi: Academic Foundation, pp. 46–86.

Ladha, J.K., D. Dawe, H. Pathak, A.T. Padre, R.L. Yadav, Bijay Singh, Yadvinder Singh, Y. Singh, P. Singh, A.L. Kundu, R. Sakal, N. Ram, A.P. Regmi, S.K. Gami, A.L. Bhandari, R. Amin, C.R. Yadav, E.M. Bhattarai, S. Das, H.P. Aggarwal, R.K. Gupta, and P.R. Hobbs (2003), 'How Extensive are Yield Declines in Long-term Rice–Wheat Experiments in Asia?', *Field Crops Research*, 81: 159–80.

Mehra, Shakuntala (1981), *Instability in Indian Agriculture in the Context of the New Technology*, International Food Policy Research Institute, Research Report No. 25, Washington DC.

Ministry of Agriculture [MoA] (2012a), *State of Indian Agriculture 2011-12*. New Delhi: Government of India. Available at: http://agricoop.nic.in/SIA111213312.pdf, last accessed on 11 May 2012.

———. (2012b), *Agriculture Statistics at a Glance, 2011*. New Delhi: Government of India. Available at: http://eands.dacnet.nic.in/latest_2006.htm, last accessed on 11 April 2012.

———. (2008), *Agriculture Statistics at a Glance, 2008*, New Delhi: Government of India, available at http://eands.dacnet.nic.in/At_Glance_2008/hpcrops_new.html, last accessed on 15 January 2012.

Ministry of Environment and Forests [MoEF] (2009), *Vulnerability of Indian Agriculture to Climate Change: Current State of Knowledge*. Available at: http://moef.nic.in/downloads/others/vulnerability_PK%20Aggarwal.pdf. Last accessed on 19 Many 2012.

Ministry of Finance (2010), *Economic Survey 2009–2010*. New Delhi: Government of India.

———. (2012), *Economic Survey 2011–2012*. New Delhi: Government of India.

Ministry of Health and Family Welfare (2007), *National Family Health Survey 2005-6*. New Delhi: Government of India.

National Sample Survey Organization (NSSO) (2006), *Some Aspects of Operational Holdings in India 2002–03*. New Delhi: National Sample Survey Organization, Ministry of Statistics and Programme Implementation, Government of India, Report No. 492.

———. (2011), *Key Indicators of Employment and Unemployment in India 2009–10*. New Delhi: National Sample Survey Organization, Ministry of Statistics and Programme Implementation, Government of India.

Parthasarathy Committee Report (2006), *Report of the Technical Committee on Watershed Programme in India*. New Delhi: Department of Land Resources, Ministry of Rural Development, Government of India.

Pingali, P.L. and M. Shah (1999), 'Rice-wheat Cropping Systems in the Indo-Gangetic Plains: Policy Re-directions for Sustainable Resource Use', in P. Pingali (ed.), *Sustaining Rice-wheat Farming Systems: Socio-economic and Policy Issues*, New Delhi: Rice-Wheat Consortium for the Indo-Gangetic Plains, pp. 1–13.

Planning Commission (2007a), *Report of the Steering Committee on Agriculture and Allied Sectors for Formulation of 11th Five Year Plan, 2007–12*, p. 52. Available at: http://planningcommission.nic.in/aboutus/committee/strgrp11/str11_agriall.pdf., last accessed on 3 January 2012.

———. (2007b), *Report of the Expert Group on Ground Water Management and Ownership*. Available at: http://planningcommission.nic.in/reports/genrep/rep_grndwat.pdf., last accessed on 3 January 2012).

———. (2010), Mid-term appraisal of Eleventh Five Year Plan, Chapter 4, p. 85. Available at: http://planningcommission.nic.in/plans/mta/11th_mta/chapterwise/chap4_agri.pdf. Last accessed on 5 January 2012.

Radhakrishna, R. (2002), 'Agricultural Growth, Employment and Poverty: A Policy Perspective', *Economic and Political Weekly*, 37(3): 243–50.

Rao, C.H.H. (2005), *Food Security, Poverty and Environment, Essay on Post Reform India*. New Delhi: Oxford University Press.

Ray, S.K. (1983), 'An Empirical Investigation of the Nature and Causes for Growth and Instability in Indian Agriculture: 1950–80', *Indian Journal of Agricultural Economics*, 38(4): 459–74.

Reddy, Bhaskar (2011), 'Private Investment in Agriculture', Paper presented during the workshop on 'Policy Options and Investment Priorities for Accelerating Agricultural Productivity and Development in India', organized by the Indira Gandhi Institute of Development Research, Mumbai and the Institute for Human Development, New Delhi at the India International Centre, New Delhi on 10–11 November 2011.

Seednet India (2012), *Indian Seed Sector*, available at http://seednet.gov.in/material/IndianSeedSector.htm., last accessed on 7 March 2012.

Shah, Tushaar, Avinash Kishore, and P. Hemant (2009a), 'Will the Impact of the 2009 Drought be Different from 2002?', *Economic and Political Weekly*, 44(37): 11–14.

Shah, Tushaar, Ashok Gulati, Hemant Pullabhotla, G. Shreedhar, and R.C. Jain (2009b), 'Secret of Gujarat's Agrarian Miracle after 2000', *Economic and Political Weekly*, 44(52): 45–55.

Singh, Harbir and Ramesh Chand (2011), 'The Seed Bill 2011: Some Reflections', *Economic and Political Weekly*, 46(51): 22–5.

Singh, S. (2008), 'Marketing Channels and their Implications for Smallholder Farmers in India', in E.B. McCullough, P.L. Pingali, and K.G. Stamoulis (eds), *The Transformation of Agrifood Systems: Globalization, Supply Chains, and Smallholder Farmers*. Rome: Food and Agricultural Organization; and London: Earthscan, pp. 279–310, chapter 14.

Sivasubramonian (2004), *Sources of Economic Growth in India*. New Delhi: Oxford University Press, pp. 307–21.

Vaidyanathan, A. (2006), *India's Water Resources: Contemporary Issues on Irrigation*. New Delhi: Oxford University Press, p. 287.

7

Sectoral Linkages, Multipliers, and the Role of Agriculture

*G. Mythili and Nitin Harak**

INTRODUCTION

The agricultural sector in India was growing at a rate of about 3 per cent till 1997. Since then the rate has gone down to a meagre 2 per cent. Reduction in public and private sector investments, a slowdown in major irrigation projects, misdirected subsides in fertilizers resulting in land degradation, and institutional constraints such as a weak credit delivery system are some of the reasons cited for the falling growth (Acharya 2009). However, since the population depending on agriculture is still standing at 60 per cent, it is imperative that policies identify the key factors that can directly or indirectly provide the stimulus required for the agricultural sector. Policies which focused on agriculture itself could not achieve the expected momentum due to the complex nature of inter-dependence among the various sectors of the economy.

Knowledge of the magnitude of linkages of non-agricultural sectors with the agricultural sector is one prerequisite for designing right policies to tackle the low growth in agriculture. Studies in the 1980s and 1990s reported a weakening linkage of agriculture with the rest of the sectors. Lack of demand for agricultural goods, a decline in the share of agro-based industries, and slow employment growth in industry were held responsible for the weakening linkage between agriculture and industry; for instance, limited demand linkages reported in Rangarajan (1982); weak supply linkage in Bhattacharya and Rao (1986) and Chowdhury and Chowdhury (1995); and Sastry et al. (2003) maintained that while forward linkages had been declining, backward linkages had become stronger during 1981–2 to 1999–2000.

The structural transformation of agriculture and the shift in demand patterns among households triggered a new interest in an analysis of inter-sectoral linkages. In the recent years, factors such as the increasing demand for high-value crops, the rise of agricultural supply chains and the contract farming system, and the increasing demand for processed products are expected to strengthen the linkage of agriculture with other sectors. Moreover, with the increasing contribution of the service sector in overall growth, it would be interesting to see how the linkages will change over time. There is ample evidence that the demand for services such as storage, transport, communication, banking, roads, and trade will increase with the transformation of agriculture and consumer preferences and hence it is expected to strengthen the linkages between agriculture and the service sector considerably (Saikia 2009).

---

* We are thankful to A. Ganesh-Kumar, Professor, IGIDR, for sharing with us the SAM database for 2006–7 and giving us valuable inputs on details and descriptions of SAM.

An analysis of sectoral linkages using the social accounting matrix (SAM) based multipliers has recently become popular due to its ability to provide an overall impact unlike linkage measures provided by the conventional input–output matrix. This chapter proposes to determine the linkage measures using the latest data available and compare themse with the earlier years to see how they have been transforming over the years. This will have an important policy implication since the linkage measures not only indicate which sectors should get priority for stimulating overall growth but also to determine if the key sector is to be targeted directly or through the sectors which have high production and demand linkages with the concerned sector.

The next two sections of the chapter present the scope and objectives of the study respectively. The next section gives a few statistics which reflect the structural changes that occurred in the economy from 1997–8 to 2006–7. This is followed by a literature survey on sectoral linkages. The next section focuses on the theoretical and analytical aspects of SAM multipliers. This section also gives the database and the methodology. The section that follows presents an analysis of the results. Finally, the chapter concludes with a summary and the possible way forward.

SCOPE OF THE STUDY

According to the conventional input–output (I–O) analysis, a sector depends on other sectors for its input requirements and its own product demand. In this framework, only the activity account is endogenized. This reveals only a part of the linkage measure. SAM multipliers can go beyond this to show how the factors' income and household demand for products can also be translated into linkage multipliers. SAM multipliers capture the triangular interaction; they start with production activities and consider the links with factor income, household income, and then back to production. There are broadly four techniques available for finding sectoral inter-dependence: (1) input–output method, (2) the SAM approach, (3) computable general equilibrium (CGE) model, and (4) the econometric approach. This chapter uses the SAM approach for the reason that the first method does not give the full impact and in the other two methods, even though they are more flexible in terms of forming models, the results are often very sensitive to the specification of the model.

OBJECTIVES

In this chapter, it is proposed to compute and compare various growth and income multipliers, direct and indirect, using SAM in India for the period 1997–8 and 2003–4 and the latest one for 2006–7. Decomposition of linkages into within and between effects is also attempted. Inferences drawn from the results and their policy implications are also discussed.

Specifically, the following questions were asked: 1) Does agriculture still play a significant role in influencing other sectors' growth and institutional income in spite of its declining share in the GDP and, 2) Is the structural inter-dependence between the sectors in the economy weakening over time?

SECTORAL COMPOSITION AND GROWTH RATE

The Indian economy has been witnessing major structural changes in the last two decades. The composition of sectoral value added measured at factor cost in current prices presented in Table 7.1 shows the structural transformation taking place in the Indian economy over time; moving from agriculture to manufacturing and service-oriented growth. Among the sub-sectors, the share of construction continuously increased from 1997–8 to 2006–7. Capital-intensive manufacturing goods sharply increased their share from 2003–4 to 2006–7. Services other than transport and electricity saw a jump in their proportion to total value added by about 6 per cent between 1997–8 and 2003–4 but did not register much increase in the next period. The magnitude of decline in the ratio of agriculture and allied sectors was about 9 per cent during the entire period of analysis.

Table 7.1 Sectoral Value Added* Composition and the Growth Rate

Sectors	Sectoral Composition (%)		
	1997–8	2003–4	2006–7
Food	7.38	5.40	4.21
Non-food	12.22	9.86	8.64
Dairy & animal products	7.47	6.32	5.39
Primary products	3.48	3.56	3.42
Agro-processing	1.77	2.05	1.60
Labour-intensive manufacturing	4.15	3.08	2.94
Petro-chemical	2.02	1.64	1.59
Capital-intensive manufacturing	7.92	7.64	9.76
Construction	5.70	6.22	8.43
Electricity	2.14	1.73	1.54
Transport	5.48	6.18	5.65
Other services	40.26	46.33	46.82
Total	100	100	100

Note: *Value added at factor cost at current prices.

Source: Authors' calculation from the SAM of respective years.

The annual growth of value added depicted in Figure 7.1 shows the annual growth for the period 1997–8 to 2006–7. The construction sector was the front runner registering about 16.5 per cent per annum growth. This was followed by capital-intensive manufacturing, other services, and transport which recorded around 14, 13.5, and 12 per cent growth respectively. Agro-processing also grew faster with an annual rate of 10.5 per cent. Apart from agriculture and allied sectors, the labour-intensive manufacturing sector also recorded slow growth.

Many empirical studies tried to find out the reason for the faster growth of the service sectors and sub-sectors. Notable among them is Bhagwati's (1984) study which attributed service sector growth to more specialization and splintering of activities. In particular, the study noted that many service components of manufacturing like accounting, research and development, and logistics are splintered-off and outsourced to other firms and hence treated as the service sector's contribution instead of that of the manufacturing sector. This was supported by the findings of Gordon and Gupta (2004) based on the changes in service input coefficients in agriculture and manufacturing, which confirmed that the coefficient had increased significantly in the 1980s to add 0.5 per cent points to service sector growth in the decade. However Singh (2006), when trying to repeat the exercise for data on the 1990s did not observe a similar pattern and the reason for this, he states, is that the methodology was suitable only for domestic splintering and did not take into account cross-country splintering which became very significant in the 1990s. The second reason attributed to the increasing share of services was the higher average income elasticity of demand (Singh 2006). The other reason cited was the policy of liberalization, in particular telecommunication reforms, which is associated with the faster growth of ITs.

AN OVERVIEW OF SECTORAL LINKAGES

The concept of 'sectoral linkages' was first introduced by Hirschman's (1958) theory of 'unbalanced growth' where it was argued that the expansion of sectors with larger linkage measures can increase growth faster through their interdependence with other sectors than by alternative means. In particular, he pointed out that agriculture could not become a leading sector in developmental strategies due to its weak backward linkages. Since then, agriculture–industry interactions have been researched by a large number of scholars as the findings have crucial policy implications. Contrasting Hirschman's views are the popular propositions of Kalecki (1960) and Kuznets (1968) which emphasize that agriculture development is essential for a successful industrialization strategy and hence technological advances

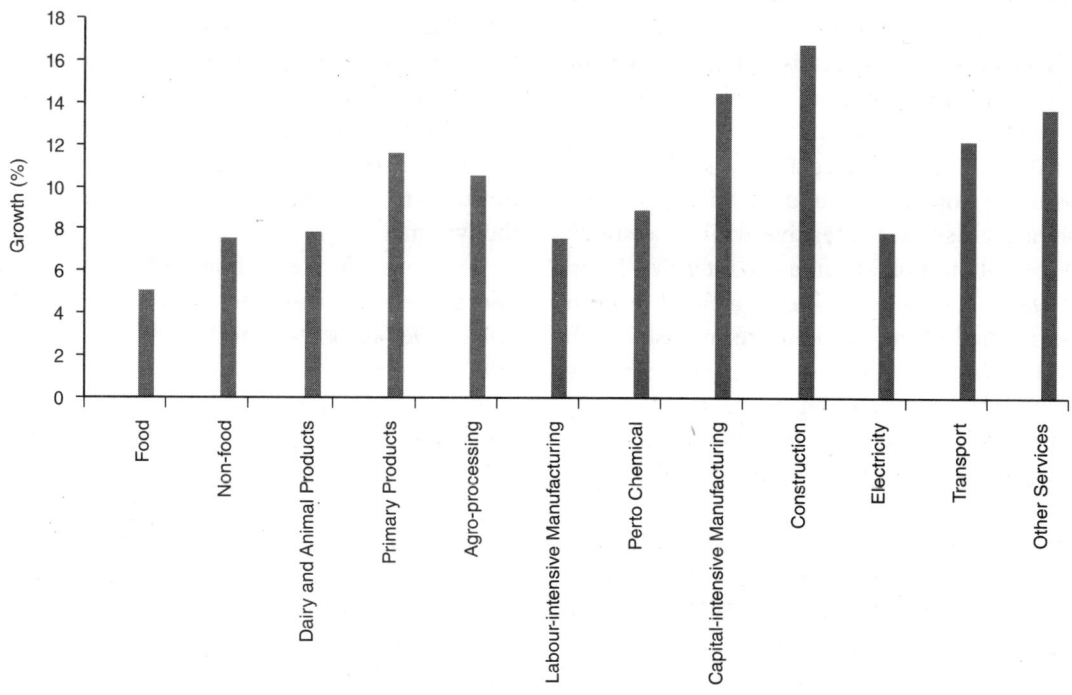

Figure 7.1 Value Added* Annual Growth Rate from 1997–8 to 2006–7 (%)

Note: *Value added at factor cost at current prices.
Source: Authors' calculation from the SAM of respective years.

in agriculture are indispensable for modern economic growth.

Bhaduri et al. (2007) examined agriculture–industry interactions using data for 1950–2000. In particular, this study revisited the contrasting views of Lewis (1954) and Kaldor (1967) in explaining the role of the terms of trade in agriculture–industry interactions. Lewis maintained that agriculture surplus—food available to the industrial sector—determines industry growth; an increase in the terms of trade in favour of agriculture and hence higher food prices would push up the industrial wage rate and reduce industrial profit and growth. In contrast to this, Kaldor emphasized the demand-driven theory where the growth of the agriculture sector due to a favourable shift in terms of trade would increase the potential demand for industrial goods and hence industry growth. Kaldor's model treated the shift in terms of trade as autonomous. The econometric exercise employed by Bhaduri et al. (2007) reinstated Kaldor's demand-driven explanation for industry growth. However, it revealed the invalidity of the assumptions of autonomous agriculture growth and the terms of trade as have been maintained in the Kaldor and Lewis models.

Singh (2006) examined the agriculture–industry–service sector's interaction using an input-output framework. He updated the data used in Sastry et al.'s (2003) study, by including the year 1998–9. The findings suggest that over the period 1968–9 to 1998–9, agriculture was more industry- and service-intensive, while industry became less agriculture-intensive and more service-intensive. Applying this technique at a more disaggregated level for 1993–4, Hansda (2001) found that industrial activities were very service-intensive. This was updated by Singh (2006) for 1998–9 with further disaggregation, and the results are: manufacturing, construction and electricity, gas, and water supply are all service-intensive while transport, storage, and communication are industry-intensive. From 1993–4 to 1998–9, service intensities increased in both absolute and relative terms. Agriculture intensity with respect to both industry and services remained relatively low. Using a new index of vertical integration, Hansda (2001) found that the service sector gave the largest multiplier effect on the other sectors of the economy based on data for 1993–4.

Rakshit (2007) examined the trend in direct and direct-cum-indirect input–output coefficients between the two periods of 1979–80 to 1993–4 and 1993–4 to 1998–9. While the impact of a unit increase in the final demand for agriculture and industry sector goods on service sector GDP increased significantly in the former period, it showed a decline in the latter period. In other words, direct and indirect service intensity of agriculture and industry decreased significantly in the latter period. Rakshit attributed the decline to structural changes in the composition of the sector and hence these could be treated as transitory in nature. As India has been witnessing service-led GDP growth since 1990, Rakshit expressed concerns about the highly volatile nature of service exports and the sustainability of service-led growth. In this context, he argued that the inefficient credit delivery system and infrastructural facilities and the failure of agriculture and industry enterprises to make use of services like information technology fully to increase their efficiency could be the reasons behind the reversal of the trend. He is of the view that the policies must ensure that the role of services should be enhancing the productivity of agriculture and manufacturing.

Studies Based on SAM

While Hirschman's concept was based on technological inter-dependence, through 'forward and backward linkage' the SAM approach takes into account not only production activities but also the various agents of the economy. SAM is being widely used as a conceptual framework for policy purposes. Even though the original idea of SAM is due to Stone (1966) for his work on social accounts, SAM was popularized by subsequent works of Pyatt and Thorbecke (1976) and Pyatt and Round (1979). SAM also provides a very useful framework for a multiplier analysis and serves as baseline data for computable general equilibrium models (Pyatt 1988). Since SAM covers the socioeconomic system with disaggregated household classes, it is also widely used for analysing income distributional impacts. The principal aim of the SAM multiplier analysis is to examine the extent of impact of an exogenous injection of income in one account of the economic system on the functional and institutional distribution of income on all the accounts of the system.

There are a limited number of studies on SAM multiplier analysis: Pyatt and Round (1979), Hayden and Round (1982), Defourny and Thorbecke (1984), Thorbecke et al. (1992), and Powell and Round (2000). The first attempt at constructing SAM for India was by Sarkar and Subbarao (1981) for 1979–80 and later by Sarkar and Panda (1986) for 1985–6; other attempts are de Janvry and Subbarao (1986) for 1977–8 and Pradhan and Sahoo (1996) for 1989–90. After 2000, two SAMs were constructed—one for 2003–4 by Saluja and Yadav (2006) and the other for 2006–7 by Kumar and Panda (2010).

Few research studies are available on SAM multiplier analysis for India. Pradhan and Sahoo (1996) made a detailed decomposition of SAM multipliers using 1989–90 SAM for India. Pradhan et al. (2006) studied the multiplier for three more years—1997–8, 1998–9, and 2002–3. Pal et al. (2012) used extended SAM for 2006–7 to find the environmental impact of economic growth. Based on an extended SAM for 2002–3, Pieters (2010) studied the impact of sectoral growth on inequality. The wage account in SAM was split into three educational levels and 10 employment sectors. The results indicated that only agricultural growth reduced inequality and growth in the industry and service sectors increased inequality. The standard SAM gives a different result that any sector growth reduces inequality. This signified the importance of extension in the existing SAM database.

There is a dearth of studies conducted on a detailed analysis of SAM multipliers using data from post-2000 in India. Even data for 2003–4 have not been researched adequately for multipliers. Since large changes have occurred in the economy in the last decade, there is a need for updating SAM multipliers which this study focuses on.

THEORETICAL AND ANALYTICAL ASPECTS OF SAM

SAM Structure and Assumptions

SAM provides an economy-wide account of various activities and agents and shows the transaction flows between different accounts of the economy. It displays the structural inter-dependence between different accounts and sectors. Macro identities are reflected in SAM: which are aggregate demand equals aggregate supply; total investment equals total savings; and current account deficit equals net foreign savings.

SAM assumes a Keynesian demand-driven economy. In this chapter it is assumed that supply increases to meet the rise in demand keeping the prices constant. Supply is assumed to be perfectly elastic. Hence there are no supply constraints in the model and the prices are fixed. SAM is used to understand the real side of the economy and the effects of price changes are not included in the system. Moreover, the feedback effect of any single change within the exogenous accounts is also not accounted for in this model.

On SAM Multipliers

SAM multipliers give both the first and subsequent rounds of impacts of any change in the exogenous account on production and income. For instance, a new investment expenditure can trigger an increase in the production of certain commodities and thereby increase factor income and then household income. This is the first round impact. The incremental income will influence higher demand for goods, as a result of which there is a second round increase—induced influence in production activities. In the next round, this will generate further increase in demand for goods in many sectors. This will continue till the effects get smaller and smaller and eventually vanish. SAM takes into account all the effects.

Induced effects in the activity account are those effects which are over and above Leontief's input–output multipliers. These effects are part of output multipliers in SAM which flow from household incomes to commodity outputs explained by the Keynesian income-expenditure multipliers (Robinson 1989). In input–output multipliers, only the activities are endogenized, whereas the SAM multipliers endogenize household demand also and hence SAM output multipliers give greater indirect feedback effects. It would be interesting to analyse the changes in induced effects over time and the sectors that cause more induced effects.

SAM's accounting multipliers are different from its fixed price multipliers; the difference depends on whether the agents' responses are considered on the average or on the margin. While the former uses average propensity to consume, the latter uses marginal propensity. Hence the accounting multipliers, in effect, have an implicit assumption of unitary expenditure elasticity. This chapter is confined to accounting multipliers.

Features of the India SAM Used for the Study

SAMs used for the study pertain to the periods 1997–8, 2003–4, and 2006–7.[1] The aggregation of sectors in SAM has a balance representation between the agriculture sector and the non-agriculture sectors. The I–O matrix in SAM is a commodity x commodity matrix. The households are classified into two groups, rural and urban. The final SAM consists of 12 sectors, two factors of production (labour and capital), and four institutions (rural and urban households, private, and public enterprises). SAM for each year is aggregated in a manner so as to ensure consistency between different years. The final SAM database used for the study is provided in the Appendix A7.3a to A7.3c.

Of the 12 sectors, three sectors represent agriculture and allied, six represent industry, and three sectors represent the service sector. The detailed classification is given in Appendix A7.2.

---

[1] The source for the data for 2006–7 is the 130 sector Activity x Commodity (A × C) SAM for India by Kumar and Panda (2010); for 2003–4, the 73 sector Activity x Commodity (A × C) SAM for India by Saluja and Yadav (2006); for 1997–8, the 60 sector Activity x Commodity (A × C) SAM for India by Pradhan et al. (2006). The unit of the numbers in SAM used in our study is factor cost at current prices.

The final sectors are:

1. Food crops
2. Non-food crops
3. Animal husbandry, fishery, and other animal products
4. Primary products
5. Agro-processing
6. Textiles and labour-intensive manufacturing products
7. Petroleum, fertilizers, and pesticides
8. Capital-intensive manufacturing
9. Construction
10. Electricity
11. Transport
12. Other services

Schematic Representation of SAM

The first step in the analysis is deciding the endogenous and exogenous accounts of SAM. In this study there are three endogenous accounts—production activities, factors of productions, and institutions (households and enterprises). The other accounts comprising government, capital, and the rest of the world are treated as exogenous.

Table 7.2 shows the partition of SAM into endogenous and exogenous accounts and the transformation matrices. These matrices are: T_{11} gives intermediate input requirements (that is, the input–output transactions matrix), T_{21} allocates the value added generated by the various production activities into income accruing to the factors of production, T_{32} maps the factorial income distribution into household income distribution, T_{33} captures the income transfers within and among household groups, and finally, T_{13} reflects the expenditure pattern of the various institutions (households in our model) for the different goods (production activities) which they consume. Exogenous accounts—government expenditure, investment, and exports have been combined together in the Xs. X_1 represents the total exogenous income accruing to production activities, X_2 is the exogenous demand for factors, and X_3 is exogenous income to households. The L_is are leakages representing transfer income sent abroad, savings, taxation, and imports. More the leakages from the system, lesser will be the multiplier effect. The column and row totals are represented by Y with Y_1 representing the total demand for goods and services produced by activities; Y_2, the total factor income; and Y_3, the total institutional income.

SAM can be expressed as a set of algebraic equations from which one can derive the multipliers as:

$$Y = T+X$$
$$A_{ij} = T_{ij}/Y_j$$
$$Y = AY + X = [I-A]^{-1} X = MX$$

where M is the SAM multiplier matrix. The representative element m_{ij} is the total (direct and indirect) impact on account i of an exogenous injection in account j. The diagonal elements of M indicate direct multipliers while the off-diagonal elements are indirect multipliers. This matrix has been referred to as the accounting multiplier matrix because it is based on the average expenditure propensities for household consumption in matrix A. This implies the unitary elasticity of the demand for goods. It is preferable to use marginal expenditure propensities, which relaxes this assumption. However, it has not been attempted in this chapter due to paucity of data for the commodity groups used in the study. Pieters (2010: 279) has noted that for the periods 1997–8 and 2003–4, the multiplier matrices are not much affected '… by using the marginal instead of average expenditure propensities, indicating that the indirect distributive effect via increased consumption expenditure is relatively unimportant'.

In order to understand the exact nature of the linkages, within and between accounts, SAM multiplier decomposition is required. Following Pyatt and Round's (1979) method, SAM multipliers of income distribution effects were decomposed into: (1) own direct effect (M_1), (2) cross effect (M_2), and (3) circular flow effects (M_3). The first one is similar to the input–output multiplier effect for activities. This refers to 'within own account'. The second effect (cross effect), shows what is the direct effect of injec-

Table 7.2 Schematic Social Accounting Matrix

		Endogenous Accounts			Exogenous	Total
		Activities	Factors	Institutions		
Endogenous	Activities	T_{11}	0	T_{13}	X_1	Y_1
	Factors	T_{21}	0	0	X_2	Y_2
	Institutions	0	T_{32}	T_{33}	X_3	Y_3
Exogenous	Leakages	L_1	L_2	L_3		
	Total	Y_1	Y_2	Y_3		

tion into one set of accounts (for example, activity) on the other accounts (for example, households) of the economy, but not the reverse effect. Hence it is an 'open loop' effect. Circular effect is the full effect of the exogenous injection going round the system of accounts and back to the origin. Hence it is a 'closed loop' effect. M_3 gives only the 'between accounts' effects net of within accounts. The benefits of exogenous shock are indirect in the circular flow and hence it is significant to analyse these numbers to see which sectors have more income-generating potential for different factors and household groups that work through other accounts, which are otherwise not visible. Since the cross effect pattern was more or less similar to the circular flow effect, we present only the circular effect in this chapter. The break up in matrix is given by:

$M = M_3 M_2 M_1$

where M is a full multiplier matrix.[2]

ANALYSIS AND RESULTS

Output and Income Multipliers

Table 7.3 shows sector-wise SAM multipliers for an impact on the three broad production sectors. The multipliers tell us the direct and indirect impact of an exogenous increase in the jth sector on the ith sector. For instance, a one unit injection in the food crop sector increases the total output of agriculture by 1.85 (refer the number corresponding to the first row and first column in Table 7.3). The own output multipliers are higher in the industry and service sectors as compared to the agriculture sector. Multipliers in the sectors other than their own depict indirect linkages. An exogenous injection in the agriculture sector has a higher influence on the output of the industry and service sectors than the impact of an exogenous change in the industry and service sectors on agriculture. In other words, the backward linkage of agriculture is stronger than its forward linkage. The linkage pattern is similar across time. This indicates the significant role of the agricultural sector for other sectors' growth. This is in contrast to the findings of Singh (2006) which came out with the result that the service sector had a larger influence on the rest of the sectors by using the input–output (I-O) linkage measures for 1998–9. Since the I-O linkage measure ignored the circular flow transactions, it does not reveal the full effect.

Among the non-agricultural sectors, the exogenous increase in agro-processing had the highest impact on the agriculture sector. The industry and service sectors exhibited higher output linkages against each other. Comparison across the time period indicates that services exhibited increases in multipliers between 1997–8 and 2003–4 for a unit injection in four out of the 12 sectors, while industries showed an increase in multipliers in four out of the 12 sectors between 2003–4 and 2006–7 for a unit exogenous injection. The agriculture sector revealed an increase in the multiplier in the latter period for a unit injection only in the food crops sector. Except for this, agriculture multipliers consistently decreased in both the periods. Technological improvements and the compositional changes within a broad sub-sector were partly the reasons for the declining trend of the multipliers over time. Rakshit (2007) has observed that from 1993–4 to 1998–9, direct and indirect services intensity fell significantly and also the intensity of all the three sectors' inputs into the production of the service sector. This was in contrast to the increasing trend noted for the previous period from 1979–80 to 1993–4. Rakshit attributed it to compositional changes and more importantly, to factors such as inefficiency in the credit delivery system, infrastructural constraints, and the inability of agriculture and industries to take full advantage of the service sector boom, particularly of the IT sector, to enhance their efficiency by splintering and outsourcing.

The total income multipliers broken into urban and rural displayed a declining trend over time for a unit injection in every sector (Table 7.4). Particularly, a sharp decline was observed for urban households from 2003–4 to 2006–7. Regarding factor demand multipliers, all declined over time except for capital for the period from 2003–4 to 2006–7 where it increased sharply for a unit exogenous injection in almost every sector. Labour demand multipliers recorded a steep decline in the same period. Agriculture followed by services exhibited more income-generating potential. Among the industries, the agro-processing sector generates the maximum income for both types of households.

Table 7.5 gives the summary measures of all the multipliers for various accounting sectors. The agro-processing industry made the highest impact on the gross output of the economy in the first two periods; the multipliers respectively being 4.11 and 3.88. This implies that an exogenous injection of one unit in the sector generated about a four-unit increase in the total output of the economy. For the last period, 2006–7, this sector was pushed to the number three spot with the multiplier at 3.50. Value added (GDP growth) multipliers showed that agriculture followed by the service sector were important sectors for influencing the overall growth of the economy. Among the industries,

---

[2] A complete scheme of break up is available in Pyatt and Round (1979). An application for India with a detailed scheme is available in Pradhan and Sahoo (1996). The analytical steps of decomposition are given in Appendix A7.1.

Table 7.3 Sectoral Output Multipliers

Sectors	Crop Sector		Dairy & Animal	Primary Prod.	Agro-process	Labour-int. Manuf.	Petro-chem.	Capital-int. Manuf.	Constrn	Electricity	Trnspt	Other Service
	Food	Non-food										
1997–8												
Agriculture	1.85	1.74	1.83	0.38	1.06	0.63	0.47	0.41	0.59	0.53	0.56	0.62
Industry	0.98	0.86	0.82	1.55	1.94	2.18	2.15	2.06	2.20	1.03	1.02	0.85
Services	1.08	0.97	0.96	0.61	1.10	1.19	0.93	0.93	1.16	2.39	2.11	1.99
2003–4												
Agriculture	1.54	1.48	1.60	0.17	0.81	0.40	0.21	0.24	0.37	0.35	0.32	0.40
Industry	0.89	0.79	0.74	1.35	1.92	2.03	2.06	1.93	2.10	1.08	0.95	0.77
Services	1.07	1.01	1.02	0.45	1.15	1.08	0.62	0.81	1.13	2.32	2.07	2.04
2006–7												
Agriculture	1.73	1.41	1.45	0.11	0.70	0.33	0.15	0.17	0.26	0.29	0.27	0.33
Industry	1.04	0.71	0.65	1.30	1.90	2.14	2.06	1.92	2.15	1.20	1.12	0.67
Services	0.93	0.70	0.77	0.28	0.90	0.88	0.45	0.57	0.79	2.32	1.82	1.75

Source: Authors' calculation from the SAM of respective years.

Table 7.4 Full Income Multipliers

Labour and HH	C1	C2	C3	C4	C5	C6	C7	C8	C9	C10	C11	C12	Total
1997–8													
Labour	1.10	1.10	1.07	0.60	0.93	0.91	0.60	0.63	1.02	0.82	0.90	0.98	10.65
Capital	1.14	1.13	1.11	0.72	1.02	0.86	0.82	0.76	0.87	1.02	0.86	1.08	11.37
HH rural	1.05	1.05	1.03	0.62	0.91	0.84	0.65	0.64	0.90	0.85	0.83	0.96	10.35
HH urban	0.82	0.82	0.80	0.48	0.71	0.66	0.50	0.50	0.71	0.66	0.65	0.75	8.06
2003–4													
Labour	1.05	1.06	1.09	0.40	0.91	0.76	0.43	0.52	0.95	0.96	0.81	0.91	9.84
Capital	0.95	0.95	0.95	0.48	0.84	0.71	0.63	0.57	0.69	0.68	0.71	0.92	9.06
HH rural	0.86	0.87	0.88	0.38	0.76	0.63	0.46	0.47	0.70	0.70	0.65	0.80	8.17
HH urban	0.79	0.80	0.82	0.32	0.69	0.58	0.37	0.41	0.69	0.69	0.61	0.71	7.48
2006–7													
Labour	0.61	0.43	0.44	0.13	0.39	0.35	0.17	0.20	0.27	0.33	0.34	0.42	4.10
Capital	1.16	1.25	1.27	0.49	1.04	0.91	0.64	0.62	0.99	1.17	0.96	1.19	11.67
HH rural	0.79	0.72	0.73	0.26	0.61	0.54	0.34	0.34	0.52	0.63	0.56	0.69	6.74
HH urban	0.56	0.52	0.52	0.19	0.44	0.39	0.24	0.25	0.38	0.46	0.40	0.49	4.84

Note: The first three sectors pertain to agriculture and allied, the next six sectors cover industry, and the rest are service sector (for details of the sectors refer to Table 7.1 and 'Features of the India SAM Used for the Study' in the text).

agro-processing turned out to be the most significant one for value added growth. Income multipliers figures also show that agriculture followed by other services and agro-processing were the important income-generating sectors for households in that order. The income multiplier was about 1.8 for a unit exogenous increase in the agricultural sector for 1997–8 which went down to about 1.3 in 2006–7, but was still the highest in terms of ranking of all the sectors.

Induced effects in the total output multiplier were computed by taking the difference between SAM multipliers and input–output multipliers and are presented in Table 7.5. These effects for activities capture induced effects on the factors and household income for an exogenous increase and back to the outputs increase due to Keynesian income-expenditure multipliers. Induced effects were stronger in the agricultural sector, particularly non-food and others

Table 7.5 Total Output and Income Multipliers

Particulars	Crop Sector		Dairy & Animal	Primary Prod.	Agro-process	Labour-int. Manuf.	Petro-chem.	Capital-int. Manuf.	Constrn	Electri-city	Trnspt	Other Service
	Food	Non-food										
1997–8												
Total output multiplier	3.90	3.58	3.61	2.55	4.11	4.00	3.54	3.40	3.95	3.96	3.69	3.46
Value-added multiplier	2.23	2.23	2.18	1.32	1.95	1.77	1.42	1.39	1.89	1.83	1.76	2.05
HH income multiplier	1.87	1.87	1.83	1.09	1.63	1.50	1.16	1.14	1.61	1.51	1.48	1.71
Induced effects	2.26	2.26	2.21	1.32	1.96	1.81	1.40	1.38	1.95	1.82	1.79	2.07
as % to total output multiplier	57.91	63.00	61.16	51.76	47.71	45.23	39.42	40.68	49.27	45.99	48.59	59.76
2003–4												
Total output multiplier	3.50	3.28	3.36	1.98	3.88	3.51	2.90	2.98	3.61	3.75	3.34	3.21
Value-added multiplier	1.99	2.01	2.03	0.88	1.75	1.46	1.06	1.09	1.64	1.64	1.51	1.84
HH Income multiplier	1.65	1.67	1.69	0.71	1.45	1.21	0.83	0.88	1.39	1.39	1.26	1.51
Induced effects	1.96	1.98	2.01	0.84	1.72	1.43	0.99	1.05	1.65	1.65	1.49	1.78
as % to total output multiplier	55.99	60.22	59.70	42.42	44.22	40.84	34.01	35.10	45.81	44.14	44.70	55.61
2006–7												
Total output multiplier	3.70	2.82	2.87	1.69	3.50	3.35	2.66	2.66	3.20	3.81	3.22	2.76
Value-added multiplier	1.77	1.69	1.71	0.62	1.43	1.26	0.81	0.81	1.26	1.50	1.30	1.61
HH Income multiplier	1.35	1.24	1.26	0.45	1.05	0.93	0.58	0.59	0.90	1.08	0.95	1.18
Induced effects	1.61	1.47	1.49	0.53	1.25	1.10	0.69	0.70	1.07	1.28	1.13	1.40
as % to total output multiplier	43.40	51.89	51.81	31.35	35.66	32.85	25.91	26.39	33.50	33.65	35.19	50.78

comprising dairy, fishing, and other animal products, ranging more than 60 per cent of the total output multiplier in 1997–8. This was around 52 per cent in 2006–7. This implies that the demand for agricultural commodities through the income effect had a bigger influence on agricultural growth than the production linkage. Services also had a good share of about 50 per cent induced influence in the total output multiplier for 2006–7.

Table 7.6 presents the summary table of 3×3 sector SAM multipliers. Though the direct multipliers were higher for non-agricultural sectors as compared to the agricultural sector (indicated by diagonal elements in the activities), Table 7.6 clearly demonstrates that agriculture had a strong backward linkage (0.89 with industry and 1 with services) and weak forward linkages (0.56 with industry and 0.57 with services) with other sectors. This result supports the findings of Vogel (1994) based on SAM multipliers for 1977 for India. The technological revolution in agriculture generated more demand for inputs from industries. The data in Table 7.6 also show how agriculture became more and more capital-intensive; capital multipliers sharply increased between 2003–4 and 2006–7 from 0.94 to 1.24, and there was a sharp decline in the labour multiplier from 1.09 to 0.48. By analysing the SAM multiplier for groups of countries classified as low and high income, developing and developed, Vogel (1994) puts forth an interesting point that the increasing divergence between agriculture's forward and backward linkages is a reflection of the transformation of the economy's production structure and of its agricultural technology and consumption pattern during the development process. By decomposing the output multipliers, Vogel found that the divergence was due to the efficiency gains from specialization as the economy grew.

If we look at the rows corresponding to rural and urban households (HH), it is clear that agriculture had the highest income-generating potential followed by the service sector. As expected, agriculture growth influenced rural income the most. But surprisingly, agriculture had a greater influence on urban income than manufacturing and service sectors. For rural income, even though agricultural sector growth turned

Table 7.6 3×3 Sectoral Output, Factor, and Household Income Multipliers

Endogenous Accounts	Agriculture	Industry	Services	Labour	Capital	HH Rural	HH Urban
1997–8							
Agriculture	1.76	0.56	0.57	0.70	0.48	0.78	0.61
Industry	0.89	2.09	0.91	0.90	0.61	0.92	0.87
Services	1.00	1.03	2.05	1.03	0.70	1.02	1.05
Labour	1.10	0.81	0.97	1.71	0.48	0.73	0.67
Capital	1.11	0.84	1.02	0.73	1.50	0.76	0.70
HH rural	1.05	0.78	0.94	1.23	0.86	1.70	0.64
HH urban	0.82	0.60	0.73	0.98	0.65	0.55	1.50
2003–4							
Agriculture	1.51	0.36	0.37	0.45	0.29	0.46	0.45
Industry	0.81	1.98	0.83	0.81	0.52	0.82	0.80
Services	1.05	0.94	2.08	1.18	0.70	1.02	1.30
Labour	1.09	0.71	0.92	1.67	0.42	0.63	0.71
Capital	0.94	0.66	0.87	0.62	1.38	0.57	0.65
HH rural	0.88	0.59	0.78	0.97	0.80	1.52	0.59
HH urban	0.82	0.54	0.71	1.10	0.50	0.48	1.54
2006–7							
Agriculture	1.49	0.25	0.30	0.39	0.25	0.43	0.34
Industry	0.77	1.99	0.78	0.77	0.49	0.82	0.70
Services	0.79	0.67	1.80	0.85	0.55	0.82	0.92
Labour	0.48	0.25	0.40	1.26	0.17	0.26	0.26
Capital	1.24	0.79	1.15	0.74	1.48	0.75	0.73
HH rural	0.74	0.44	0.66	1.03	0.64	1.43	0.42
HH urban	0.53	0.32	0.48	0.69	0.48	0.31	1.30

Source: Authors' calculation.

out to be more beneficial, the service sector also became important. Table 7.6 also shows income multiplier effects that include both direct transfer as well as the indirect effect of an exogenous increase in the income of the households effected through the other accounts of SAM and back to the households. Income transfers to one group of households lifted the income of both the groups of households. The results show that the rural income multiplier effect is more than that of urban income for a given increase in any one of the activity sectors. Exogenous increase in urban income percolates to the rural area more than the benefits flowing to the urban area due to the same increase in the income of the rural. In order to further probe the income redistribution paths, it is required to decompose the total multiplier into direct effect, cross effects, and circular effects.

Direct effects are simple input–output multipliers and cross effects show the income originating from one sector and finally ended up in a different sector. The circular flow effect is the most important as this shows how the income originating in one sector goes through different accounts before finally reaching the same account. Own accounts are netted out from this, and the between account effects are presented in the next section.

Circular Flow Multipliers

This effect gives the impact of exogenous injection into the activity account on income distribution that works through other accounts and back to the point of start. The circular flow effect (M_3) given in Table 7.7 clearly demonstrates the higher influence of agriculture and other services on the demand for factors, labour and capital, and income of both rural and urban household groups. A comparison across the time period reveals that the labour demand effect declined sharply in all sectors during 2006–7, while the capital demand effect varied only marginally over time, except for non-food and animal products sectors where they increased sharply in 2006–7, from about 0.4 to 0.6. The non-food crops sector recorded the highest indirect effect on income for both rural and urban going by the circular flow multiplier component.

SUMMARY AND POLICY IMPLICATIONS

Summary

The agricultural sector is the most influencing sector for overall growth as well as household income for both rural and urban in terms of ranking for all the three periods under analysis. This is revealed by an analysis of SAM multipliers which measure the extent of impact of a unit injection by the exogenous accounts consisting of government, capital, and the rest of the world, on various endogenous accounts. The induced effects highlight that the institutional final demand makes a significant contribution to the production linkage in agriculture. The results also indicate a strong backward

Table 7.7 Circular Flow Multiplier (between Accounts) M_3

Labour and HH	C1	C2	C3	C4	C5	C6	C7	C8	C9	C10	C11	C12	Total
1997–8													
Labour	0.20	0.25	0.21	0.15	0.06	0.08	0.04	0.06	0.13	0.09	0.12	0.21	1.61
Capital	0.22	0.26	0.23	0.15	0.06	0.09	0.05	0.07	0.14	0.10	0.13	0.23	1.71
HH rural	0.11	0.13	0.11	0.08	0.03	0.04	0.02	0.03	0.07	0.05	0.06	0.11	0.86
HH urban	0.08	0.10	0.09	0.06	0.02	0.03	0.02	0.03	0.05	0.04	0.05	0.09	0.67
2003–4													
Labour	0.21	0.24	0.22	0.10	0.05	0.07	0.04	0.05	0.13	0.11	0.11	0.20	1.54
Capital	0.20	0.23	0.21	0.10	0.05	0.07	0.04	0.05	0.12	0.11	0.11	0.19	1.47
HH rural	0.09	0.10	0.10	0.04	0.02	0.03	0.02	0.02	0.06	0.05	0.05	0.08	0.67
HH urban	0.08	0.09	0.09	0.04	0.02	0.03	0.02	0.02	0.05	0.04	0.05	0.08	0.61
2006–7													
Labour	0.07	0.10	0.09	0.04	0.02	0.03	0.02	0.02	0.04	0.04	0.04	0.09	0.58
Capital	0.19	0.26	0.24	0.10	0.05	0.08	0.05	0.05	0.11	0.10	0.12	0.24	1.58
HH rural	0.05	0.07	0.06	0.02	0.01	0.02	0.01	0.01	0.03	0.03	0.03	0.06	0.40
HH urban	0.03	0.05	0.04	0.02	0.01	0.01	0.01	0.01	0.02	0.02	0.02	0.04	0.29

Note: The first three sectors pertain to agriculture and allied, the next six sectors cover industry, and the rest are service sector (for details of the sectors, refer to Table 7.1 and the section on 'Features of the India SAM Used for the Study' in the text).

Source: Authors' calculation.

and weak forward linkage of agriculture with other sectors based on SAM multipliers. A unit exogenous expenditure in the industry and service sectors, respectively, generated a multiplier of 0.25 and 0.30 in the agriculture sector, whereas a unit injection in the agriculture sector generated a significant, 0.77 and 0.79 respectively in the industry and service sectors for 2006–7 (Table 7.6). The circular flow effect which includes the two-way transaction from one account to another also gave the same pattern. A temporal comparison of the multipliers revealed a declining trend of most of the multipliers. Urban income and labour demand multipliers declined sharply from 2003–4 to 2006–7.

The scope of the empirical exercise was limited. Due to the limitation of SAM, the results should be considered utmost as indicative.

Inferences and the Way Forward

Inter-sectoral dependence and the circular flow of income indicate that the agriculture sector still retains its significance for its income-generating potential in all the sectors and household accounts, in spite of the fact that the economy has seen a structural transformation over the past two decades with an increasing contribution of the service sector to overall growth. That service sector growth could not influence household income to the same extent as agriculture is consistent with arguments in literature (Rakshit 2007) that employment growth in the service sector is lagging far behind the sector's growth and hence the sustainability of the service sector growth per se is questioned.

Declining multipliers over time indicate that the economy, particularly agriculture, could not take full advantage of the service sector boom to enjoy spillover benefits. Hence the policy should focus on ways to increase the efficiency of the agriculture and industry sectors by appropriate use of services, including IT. Strengthening rural infrastructure, credit delivery, expansion of irrigation, and phasing out of misdirected subsidies are some of the measures to improve agriculture growth directly.

Among the industry sub-sectors, agro-processing turned out to be the most significant one for output multipliers, GDP multipliers, and income multipliers. Addressing the constraints in this sector would not only help in the expansion of the sector to meet increasing demand but also strengthen the forward linkage of the agricultural sector and thereby gain in multipliers.

Appendix A7

A7.1 MULTIPLIER DECOMPOSITION

The multiplier matrix M can be expressed as the product of three multipliers M_3, M_2, and M_1.

$$M = M_3 M_2 M_1 \qquad \text{A7.1}$$

To carry out decomposition, we define the Matrix A and A* such that equation (A7.1) can be expressed as:

$$A = \begin{bmatrix} A_{11} & 0 & A_{13} \\ A_{21} & 0 & 0 \\ 0 & A_{32} & A_{33} \end{bmatrix} \text{ and } \tilde{A} = \begin{bmatrix} 0 & 0 & A_{13} \\ A_{21} & 0 & 0 \\ 0 & A_{32} & A_{33} \end{bmatrix}$$

where:

$$A_{ij} = \frac{T_{ij}}{Y_j}$$

$$M_1 = (I - A_{11})^{-1}$$
$$A^* = M_1 * \tilde{A}$$
$$M_2 = (I - A^{*4})^{-1}$$
$$M_3 = (I + A^* + A^{*2} + A^{*3})$$
$$M = (I - A_{11})^{-1} (I - A^{*4})^{-1} (I + A^* + A^{*2} + A^{*3}) \qquad \text{A7.2}$$

The SAM multipliers M have been decomposed into own direct effect (M_1), cross effect (M_2), and circular flow effects (M_3).

Appendix A7.2 Detailed Classification of the Sectors

Sector No.	Name	Classified Sectors
C1	Food	Cereals and pulses
C2	Non-food	Crops other than cereals and pulses including plantation crops
C3	Dairy & animal products	Dairy, fishing, poultry, and other animal products
C4	Primary products	Forestry and logging, fossil fuel, minerals and metals
C5	Agro-processing	Sugar, food products, vegetable oil, beverages, and tobacco products
C6	Labour-intensive manufacturing	Textiles and garments, furniture and wood products, paper and paper products, newsprint, printing and publishing, leather and leather products, rubber products, and plastic products
C7	Petro-chemicals	Fertilizers, pesticides, and petroleum products
C8	Capital-intensive manufacturing	Chemicals, coal tar products, cement, iron and steel, paints, drugs and medicines, soap, cosmetic and synthetic fibres, non-ferrous basic metals, equipment and machinery, machine tools, electrical products, electrical appliances, electronic equipments, transport equipment, ship, boat, aircraft and spacecraft, rail, bicycle, motor vehicles, watches and clocks, medical equipment, gems and jewellery and miscellaneous manufacturing
C9	Construction	Construction
C10	Electricity	Electricity
C11	Transport service	Railways and other transport services
C12	Other services	Water supply, storage and warehousing, trade, hotels and restaurants, communication, banking, insurance, education and research, medical and health, and other services

(Rs in billion)

Appendix A7.3a   Social Accounting Matrix, 1997–8

Sectors	C1	C2	C3	C4	C5	C6	C7	C8	C9	C10	C11	C12
Food	181	41	26	0	53	0	1	0	0	0	10	36
Non-food	2	62	213	0	347	127	62	4	41	1	39	53
Dairy and animal	60	67	7	0	115	21	4	9	3	0	0	55
Primary production	0	0	0	6	17	57	275	188	86	152	10	29
Agro-process	0	1	21	0	74	2	3	1	0	0	0	35
Labour-int. manuf.	2	1	12	4	29	407	65	132	69	6	84	123
Petro-chemicals	129	99	6	18	22	148	218	95	5	9	174	142
Capital-int. manuf.	5	3	9	26	27	81	159	1260	449	34	132	194
Construction	14	9	1	8	3	5	3	16	16	3	44	128
Electricity	34	18	0	17	13	77	52	176	29	204	110	92
Transport	51	42	22	11	72	203	100	202	153	73	50	122
Other services	57	43	65	26	161	290	163	560	256	117	323	712
Labour	527	872	516	202	99	386	28	395	614	100	484	2580
Capital	499	827	522	281	148	191	253	705	178	198	278	3016
HH rural	0	0	0	0	0	0	0	0	0	0	0	0
HH urban	0	0	0	0	0	0	0	0	0	0	0	0
Pvt. & Pub.	0	0	0	0	0	0	0	0	0	0	0	0
Tax	–99	–69	4	9	37	67	71	244	61	9	148	99
Govt	0	0	0	0	0	0	0	0	0	0	0	0
Capital a/c	0	0	0	0	0	0	0	0	0	0	0	0
Rest of world	23	15	1	339	43	126	198	795	0	0	94	147
Total	1485	2029	1426	948	1257	2189	1655	4784	1960	905	1980	7564

(*Contd.*)

Appendix A7.3a (*Contd.*)

(Rs in billion)

Sectors	Labour	Capital	HH Rural	HH Urban	Pvt & Pub	Tax	Govt	Capital a/c	ROW	Total
Food	0	0	792	308	0	0	3	3	32	1485
Non-food	0	0	682	343	0	0	2	2	49	2029
Dairy & animal	0	0	655	364	0	0	17	21	30	1426
Primary production	0	0	43	53	0	0	1	14	18	948
Agro-process	0	0	554	421	0	0	2	41	102	1257
Labour-int. manuf.	0	0	486	341	0	0	25	103	301	2189
Petro-chemicals	0	0	189	188	0	0	53	91	70	1655
Capital-int. manuf.	0	0	213	148	0	0	118	1438	488	4784
Construction	0	0	0	0	0	0	80	1631	0	1960
Electricity	0	0	32	40	0	0	11	0	0	905
Transport	0	0	338	293	0	0	28	77	142	1980
Other services	0	0	1458	1526	0	0	1309	128	370	7564
Labour	0	0	0	0	0	0	0	0	-2	6800
Capital	0	0	0	0	0	0	0	0	-130	6966
HH rural	3742	2752	0	0	0	0	646	0	99	7238
HH urban	3058	2002	0	0	0	0	340	0	339	5739
Pvt. & Pub.	0	574	0	0	0	0	51	0	0	626
Tax	0	0	292	217	0	0	24	205	-9	1312
Govt	0	132	235	227	200	1312	0	0	0	2107
Capital a/c	0	1505	1269	1271	425	0	-602	0	-114	3754
Rest of world	0	0	0	0	0	0	0	0	0	1782
Total	6800	6966	7238	5739	626	1312	2107	3754	1782	

Appendix A7.3b Social Accounting Matrix, 2003–4

(Rs in billion)

Sectors	C1	C2	C3	C4	C5	C6	C7	C8	C9	C10	C11	C12
Food	159	35	32	0	168	0	0	1	0	0	6	80
Non-food	1	40	315	0	687	196	0	88	72	0	16	203
Dairy & animal	62	117	6	0	167	21	0	19	2	0	0	56
Primary production	0	0	1	7	38	61	1,110	388	176	177	1	111
Agro-process	0	1	31	0	210	2	0	5	0	0	0	122
Labour–int. manuf.	4	2	15	6	72	533	9	217	107	7	123	198
Petro-chemicals	202	203	8	15	30	18	123	178	54	99	583	126
Capital-int. manuf.	4	3	14	55	115	332	82	2657	931	81	174	852
Construction	12	8	1	15	8	6	2	17	22	8	59	213
Electricity	35	16	0	21	24	120	31	271	54	205	210	156
Transport	45	56	19	24	123	159	37	333	242	99	123	347
Other services	81	75	73	34	414	403	122	1073	481	158	641	1771
Labour	759	1387	903	341	287	414	34	753	1285	377	982	5580
Capital	603	1102	694	557	231	363	381	1176	284	59	578	6117
HH rural	0	0	0	0	0	0	0	0	0	0	0	0
HH urban	0	0	0	0	0	0	0	0	0	0	0	0
Pvt. & Pub.	0	0	0	0	0	0	0	0	0	0	0	0
Tax	−80	−66	1	19	34	80	127	439	174	25	288	243
Govt	0	0	0	0	0	0	0	0	0	0	0	0
Capital a/c	0	0	0	0	0	0	0	0	0	0	0	0
Rest of the world	20	33	4	1219	135	329	123	2286	0	0	275	479
Total	1908	3012	2116	2313	2744	3039	2181	9900	3883	1295	4059	16654

(Contd.)

Appendix A7.3b (*Contd.*)

(Rs in billion)

Sectors	Labour	Capital	HH Rural	HH Urban	Pvt & Pub	Tax	Govt	Capital a/c	ROW	Total
Food	0	0	955	316	0	0	6	78	72	1908
Non-food	0	0	634	574	0	0	3	59	123	3012
Dairy & animal	0	0	848	682	0	0	14	71	51	2116
Primary production	0	0	185	32	0	0	1	−27	52	2313
Agro-process	0	0	1436	654	0	0	10	144	126	2744
Labour-int. manuf.	0	0	739	345	0	0	34	−3	631	3039
Petro-chemicals	0	0	107	211	0	0	29	35	160	2181
Capital-int. manuf.	0	0	374	323	0	0	215	2067	1621	9900
Construction	0	0	0	0	0	0	151	3361	0	3883
Electricity	0	0	62	106	0	0	24	−39	0	1295
Transport	0	0	1033	832	0	0	75	86	427	4059
Other services	0	0	2927	4332	0	0	2649	305	1116	16654
Labour	0	0	0	0	0	0	0	0	−31	13072
Capital	0	0	0	0	0	0	0	0	−110	12035
HH rural	5362	5495	0	0	0	0	1733	0	783	13373
HH urban	7710	2223	0	0	0	0	698	0	265	10896
Pvt. & Pub.	0	1419	0	0	0	0	0	121	0	1540
Tax	0	0	324	293	0	0	69	509	−16	2462
Govt	0	362	220	415	610	2462	0	0	−25	4044
Capital a/c	0	2536	3530	1782	930	0	−1666	0	−343	6769
Rest of the world	0	0	0	0	0	0	0	0	0	4903
Total	13072	12035	13373	10896	1540	2462	4044	6769	4903	

Appendix A7.3c Social Accounting Matrix, 2006–7

(Rs in billion)

Sectors	C1	C2	C3	C4	C5	C6	C7	C8	C9	C10	C11	C12
Food	711	72	16	0	184	0	0	9	0	0	0	142
Non-food	41	174	267	0	804	255	1	63	107	3	96	222
Dairy & animal	139	112	28	0	207	39	0	23	60	1	0	131
Primary production	0	0	0	9	14	100	1839	873	409	206	0	14
Agro-process	7	1	31	0	431	4	1	51	0	1	2	247
Labour-int. manuf.	6	2	15	9	109	912	12	462	111	9	241	165
Petro-chemicals	395	271	16	24	46	69	254	303	114	161	1257	108
Capital-int. manuf.	22	5	16	144	120	696	197	6819	2830	141	484	780
Construction	55	28	1	43	34	52	24	232	379	38	148	393
Electricity	76	21	0	25	27	117	44	435	109	520	79	95
Transport	118	58	58	38	174	283	86	669	485	97	338	480
Other services	173	97	230	67	616	668	151	2100	1015	235	835	2151
Labour	787	813	509	215	189	385	74	755	360	90	616	4616
Capital	810	2463	1534	1079	417	729	529	2945	2836	495	1524	13131
HH rural	0	0	0	0	0	0	0	0	0	0	0	0
HH urban	0	0	0	0	0	0	0	0	0	0	0	0
Pvt. & Pub.	0	0	0	0	0	0	0	0	0	0	0	0
Tax	−256	−159	−17	26	77	153	180	1022	247	−180	290	125
Govt	0	0	0	0	0	0	0	0	0	0	0	0
Capital a/c	0	0	0	0	0	0	0	0	0	0	0	0
Rest of the world	3	111	5	2528	268	316	319	6270	0	0	48	788
Total	3086	4069	2709	4208	3718	4778	3712	23030	9062	1816	5958	23588

(Contd.)

Appendix A7.3c (*Contd.*)

(Rs in billion)

Sectors	Labour	Capital	HH Rural	HH Urban	Pvt & Pub	Tax	Govt	Capital a/c	ROW	Total
Food	0	0	1449	357	0	0	21	6	118	3086
Non-food	0	0	1119	703	0	0	13	120	82	4069
Dairy & animal	0	0	1123	674	0	0	34	45	93	2709
Primary production	0	0	204	30	0	0	3	-17	524	4208
Agro-process	0	0	1892	621	0	0	40	142	248	3718
Labour-int. manuf.	0	0	1077	349	0	0	92	215	992	4778
Petro-chemicals	0	0	254	345	0	0	42	-244	296	3712
Capital-int. manuf.	0	0	769	545	0	0	152	5698	3613	23030
Construction	0	0	134	84	0	0	74	7346	0	9062
Electricity	0	0	93	112	0	0	64	0	0	1816
Transport	0	0	1470	838	0	0	103	198	465	5958
Other services	0	0	3919	4543	0	0	3573	494	2720	23588
Labour	0	0	0	0	0	0	0	0	18	9427
Capital	0	0	0	0	0	0	0	0	402	28893
HH rural	5732	10516	0	0	0	0	2164	0	750	19163
HH urban	3652	8058	0	0	0	0	1475	0	511	13696
Pvt. & Pub.	0	4487	0	0	0	0	0	0	0	4487
Tax	0	0	1292	975	1443	0	59	876	80	6233
Govt	0	787	0	0	0	6233	0	0	0	7019
Capital a/c	0	4370	4369	3521	3044	0	-908	961	482	15839
Rest of the world	43	675	0	0	0	0	18	0	0	11393
Total	9427	28893	19163	13696	4487	6233	7019	15839	11393	

REFERENCES

Acharya, Shankar (2009), 'India's Growth: Past and Future', in Natalia Dinello and Shaoguang Wang (eds), *China, India and Beyond: Development Drivers and Limitations*. UK: Edward Elgar Publishing Limited, pp. 23–45.

Bhaduri, Amit, Ashok Parikh, and Rune Skarstein (2007), 'The Dual Role of the Terms of Trade: The Indian Experience of Agriculture–Industry Interactions, 1950–51 and 2000–01', in A. Vaidyanathan and K.L. Krishna (eds), *Institutions and Markets in India's Development, Essays for K.N. Raj*. New Delhi: Oxford University Press, pp. 224–41.

Bhagwati, Jagdish N. (1984), 'Splintering and Disembodiment of Services and Developing Nations', *World Economy*, 7(2): 133–43.

Bhattacharya, B.B. and C.H.H. Rao (1986), 'Agriculture-Industry Interrelations: Issues of Relative Prices and Growth in the Context of Public Investment', Theme 18, Eighth World Economic Congress of the International Economic Association, New Delhi.

Chowdhury, K. and M.B. Chowdhury (1995), 'Sectoral Linkages and Economic Growth in Asia: Evidence from Granger Causality Test', *Indian Economic Journal*, 42: 59–75.

Defourny, J. and E. Thorbecke (1984), 'Structural Path Analysis and Multiplier Decomposition within a Social Accounting Matrix Framework', *Economic Journal*, 94(373): 111–36.

de Janvry, A. and K. Subbarao (1986), *Agricultural Price Policy and Income Distribution in India*. New Delhi: Oxford University Press.

Ganesh-Kumar, A. and Manoj Panda (2010), 'SAM for India 2006–07', unpublished document.

Gordon, James and Poonam Gupta (2004), 'Understanding India's Services Revolution', *IMF Working Paper WP/04/171*, September.

Hansda, Sanjay K. (2001), 'Sustainability of Services-led Growth: An Input–Output Analysis of Indian Economy', *RBI Occasional Papers*, 22(1, 2 and 3), pp. 73–118.

Hayden, C. and J.I. Round (1982), 'Developments in Social Accounting Methods as Applied to the Analysis of Income Distribution and Employment Issues', *World Development*, 10: 451–65.

Hirschman, A.O. (1958), *The Strategy of Economic Development*. New Haven: Yale University Press.

Kaldor, N. (1967), Strategic Factors in Economic Development. Ithaca: Cornell University Press.

Kalecki, M. (1960), 'Unemployment in Underdeveloped Countries', *Indian Journal of Labour Economics*, 3(2): 59–61.

Kuznets, S. (1968), *Toward a Theory of Economic Growth with Reflections on the Economic Growth of Nations*. New York: Norton.

Lewis, W.A. (1954), 'Economic Development with Unlimited Supplies of Labour', *The Manchester School*, 22(2): 139–91.

Pal, B. Deb, S. Pohit, and J. Roy (2012), 'Impact of Economic Growth on Climate Change: An Environmentally Extended Social Accounting Matrix-based Approach for India', available at: http://mpra.ub.uni-muenchen.de/36540, last accessed on 14 March 2012.

Pieters, Janneke (2010), 'Growth and Inequality in India: Analysis of an Extended Social Accounting Matrix', *World Development*, 38(3): 270–81.

Powell M. and J.I. Round (2000), 'Structure and Linkage in the Economy of Ghana: A SAM Approach', in E. Aryeetey, J. Harrigan, and M. Nissanke (eds), *Economic Reforms in Ghana: Miracle or Mirage*. Oxford: James Currey Press, pp. 68–87.

Pradhan, B.K. and A. Sahoo (1996), 'Social Accounting Matrix and its Multipliers for India', *Margin*, 28(2): 153–69.

Pradhan, B.K., M.R. Saluja, and S.K. Singh (2006), *A Social Accounting Matrix for India, Concepts, Construction and Applications*. New Delhi: Sage Publications.

Pyatt, G. (1988), 'A SAM Approach to Modelling', *Journal of Policy Modelling*, 10(3): 327–52.

Pyatt, G. and J.I. Round (1979), 'Accounting and Fixed Price Multipliers in a SAM Framework', *Economic Journal*, 89: 850–73.

Pyatt, G. and E. Thorbecke (1976), *Planning Techniques for a Better Future*. Geneva: ILO.

Rakshit, M. (2007), 'Services-Led Growth: The Indian Experience', *Money and Finance*, February: 91–126.

Rangarajan, C. (1982), 'Agricultural Growth and Industrial Performance in India', Research Report 33, International Food Policy Research Institute, October.

Robinson, S. (1989), 'Multisectoral Models', in Hollis Chenery and T.N. Srinivasan (eds), *Handbook of Development Economics*, Vol. II. Amsterdam: Elsevier, pp. 885–947, chapter 18.

Saikia, D. (2009), 'Agriculture-Industry Interlinkages: Some Theoretical and Methodological Issues in the Indian Context', available at: http://mpra.ub.uni-muenchen.de/27820, last accessed on 23 January 2012.

Saluja M.R. and B. Yadav (2006), *Social Accounting Matrix for India—2003–04*. Gurgaon: India Development Foundation.

Sarkar, H. and M. Panda (1986), 'Quantity-Price Money Interaction in a CGE Model', *Margin*, 18(3): 31–47. New Delhi: NCAER.

Sarkar, H. and S.V. Subbarao (1981), 'A Short-term Macro-forecasting Model for India: Structure and Use', *Indian Economic Review*, 16(1–2): 55–80.

Sastry, D.V.S., B. Singh, K. Bhattacharya, and N.K. Unnikrishnan (2003), 'Sectoral Linkages and Growth Prospects: Reflections on the Indian Economy', *Economic and Political Weekly* 38(24): 2390–7.

Singh, Nirvikar (2006), 'Service-led Industrialization in India: Assessment and Lessons', MPRA, Paper No. 1276, November.

Stone, J.R.N. (1966), 'The Social Accounts from a Consumer Point of View', *Review of Income and Wealth*, 12(1), pp. 1–33.

Thorbecke, E., R. Downey, S. Keuning, D. Roland-Holst, and D. Berrian (1992), *Adjustment and Equity in Indonesia*. Paris: OECD Development Centre.

Vogel, S.J. (1994), 'Structural Changes in Agriculture: Production Linkages and Agricultural Demand-Led Industrialization', *Oxford Economic Papers*, New Series, 46(1): 136–56.

8

Services-led Growth, Employment, Skill, and Job Quality

A Study of Manufacturing and Service Sectors in Urban India

*K.V. Ramaswamy and Tushar Agrawal**

CONTEXT AND FOCUS

Labour market outcomes are critical for an evaluation of economic policy. Growth in jobs, earnings, job quality in terms of worker status like regular wage work, casual wage, or self-employment, and access to social security benefits tell us much about the well-being of a workforce in an economy. Urban labour markets in particular merit a separate focus as urban agglomerations play an important role as drivers of economic transformation in the process of growth and development. This transformation is expected to provide large productive employment opportunities to absorb additions to the labour force. In the broader context of economic development and structural change, the observed sequence was that manufacturing followed agriculture while the service sector became prominent only at a later stage. India's experience appeared to be different with the share of the service sector in GDP sharply going up in the 1990s, beginning with a share of 43 per cent in 1990–1 to reach a high share of 57 per cent in 2009–10. This raised expectations in development policy discussions of the possibility of India skipping the traditional sequence and the service sector assuming the role of the lead sector in India's growth path (Eichengreen and Gupta 2011; Gordon and Gupta 2004; Singh 2006). In this scenario, labour shifting out of agriculture gets directly absorbed in services rather than in manufacturing. While there is broad agreement about the dynamism of the service sector, questions have been raised about the sustainability of services output growth by many others on several grounds (Acharya 2002; Bosworth et al. 2007; Nagaraj 2009; Panagariya 2008 among others). Dominance of the informal sector and the associated low productivity of the service sector is a key concern undermining the optimistic viewpoint. Others have pointed out the statistically significant contribution of modern segments of services to GDP growth and have suggested a complementary relationship between manufacturing and services as both are required to absorb India's large additions to the labour force (Eichengreen and Gupta 2011). In this context, a study of employment growth, structure, and changes in the skill/education composition of the workforce in urban

---

* We thank K.L. Krishna, Vikas Chitre, and R.N. Bhattacharya for their comments and suggestions on an earlier draft of this chapter. We are solely responsible for the remaining errors.

India in the last decade can throw more light on recent developments and future prospects.

In the decade of 2001–11, the population in urban India grew by 2.76 per cent per annum and its share of the total population increased to 31.1 per cent in 2011 from 27.8 per cent in 2001.[1] Two leading sectors in particular are studied in detail in this chapter—manufacturing and services. The growth performance of the manufacturing sector in India since 1991, the year of trade and industrial policy liberalization, has been creditable with an estimated growth rate of 6.5 per cent per annum during 1992–2008. There was a manufacturing sector boom during 2003–4 to 2007–8 with an average growth rate of 9.4 per cent. However, the employment creation aspect (jobless growth), slow growth rate of formal sector employment (so-called 'good jobs'), and the continuing 'duality' with most of the job creation taking place in the informal sector have been a matter of serious concern and debate. While analysing the urban sector we pay particular attention to the following sectors: manufacturing and services.[2] The service sector is defined as a sum of the following sub-groups: retail and wholesale trade, hotels and restaurants, transport and storage, financial intermediation, real estate, public administration, education, and community and social services. In the following discussion we refer to these two segments as simply manufacturing and services. The other sectors are referred to depending on the context. These two categories together have an employment share of 81 per cent in the total urban employment.[3]

An issue not much discussed is the quality of jobs in urban areas. The quality of jobs is hard to define but easier to observe in terms of contractual conditions and access to social security benefits. Using the National Sample Survey (NSS) data for 1999–2000 (55th Round) and 2009–10 (66th Round), we undertake a comparative study of manufacturing and services in urban India in terms of employment growth, job quality, earnings distribution, skill (education levels), and access to social security benefits. The survey results of 2004–5 (61st Round) are referred to sparingly as there is some suggestive evidence that they suffer from overestimation of employment numbers (Himanshu 2011). Following this introduction, this chapter is divided into five sections. The next section presents a discussion of employment growth and structure in urban India relative to that at the all-India level. The following section contains a discussion of earnings inequality and distribution by educational levels. A short discussion of worker status in terms of contracts and access to social security is provided in the next section. The last section concludes with some broad remarks on the way forward.

EMPLOYMENT GROWTH AND STRUCTURE

Growth of Service Sector GDP: Causal Factors

It is useful to begin first by noting the output or GDP growth rates in various sub-sectors of the Indian economy and the associated change in the structure of GDP during the reference period of our study, that is, 1999–2000 to 2009–10 (Table 8.1). Service sector output grew rapidly since 1990 and by 2005 the share of services in GDP had reached well above the international norm that corresponds to the average share of services in countries with similar per capita GDP.[4] Our estimates based on National Accounts Statistics (NAS) data indicate that the service sector clocked an average annual compound growth rate of 8.7 per cent between 1999–2000 and 2009–10 as against 7.7 per cent achieved by manufacturing during the same period.[5] Within the service sector the group transport, storage, and communications grew the fastest at 11.8 per cent. This largely reflects the rapid growth of communication services that grew at more than 20 per cent.[6] This was followed by trade and hotels at 8.5 per cent and other business services at 7.9 per cent. What factors explain the rapid growth of the service sector in India?

Both demand-side and supply-side factors have been shown to have played important roles in this 'services revolution' (Rakshit 2007). Two types of demand for services are the final demand from consumers (both domestic and exports) and the intermediate demand for services from the other two sectors of the economy of industry and agriculture. Faster growth of the final demand for service sector output is indicated by growth in private household consumption

---

[1] See Bhagat (2011). The decade of the 2000s showed signs of a reversal of the declining urbanization trend of the 1990s.

[2] In terms of National Industrial Classification (1998), we study the following sections: Manufacturing (Section D) and the services sector equals the sum of the following sections (Retail and Wholesale Trade), H (Hotels and Restaurants) + I (Transport and Storage) + J (Financial Intermediation) + K (Real Estate) + L (Public Administration) + M (Education) + O (Community and Social Services).

[3] An industry *excluded* with a significant employment share is the construction sector with a little more than a 10 per cent share as we believe that this needs separate treatment.

[4] The critical question to ask, they point out, is whether this is just a structural convergence correcting the earlier neglect or a distinctive pattern of structural transformation (Eichengreen and Gupta 2011: 4).

[5] This matches closely with growth rates reported in the Reserve Bank of India, *Annual Report 2010–11*, for the period 2000–1 to 2008–9 excluding the construction sector.

[6] This is Eichengreen and Gupta's (2011: 7) estimate. They further argue that the contribution of communications, business services, and financial services has in fact risen to the point where it contributes more to the growth of GDP than manufacturing.

Table 8.1 Structure of GDP and Growth Rate (%): 1999–2000 and 2009–10

Sector	GDP Share 1999–2000	GDP Share 2009–10	Average Annual Growth Rate
Agriculture	23.30	14.60	2.30
Mining and quarrying	3.00	2.30	4.40
Manufacturing	15.10	15.90	7.70
Electricity, water, etc.	2.30	2.00	5.70
Construction	6.50	7.90	9.30
Trade (retail+ wholesale),	14.60	16.40	8.50
Hotels and restaurants, transport, storage, and communications	6.60	10.20	11.80
Other services like financial, business, public administration, education, etc.	28.70	30.70	7.90
Above three services	49.90	57.30	8.70
All sectors	100.00	100.00	

Source: National Income Statistics, Central Statistical Office (CSO).

expenditure and a rapid growth of export of services.[7] During the time period 1995–2005 private consumption of services grew at an average of 8.6 per cent and export of services grew at 19.1 per cent that are much higher than the growth rate of services GDP (8 per cent). Household income elasticity demand for services averaged 1.5 per cent for the 10-year period (Rakshit 2007). A key supply-side factor widely mentioned has been the 'splintering' of production activity. This refers to 'outsourcing' of activities previously carried out 'in house' by industrial firms like marketing, legal services, transport, security, repair, and maintenance. This outcome of the splintering process gets reflected in the greater service input per unit of output (intensity of use of services) in industry. Available evidence suggests that the intensity with which services are used in industry and agriculture has not changed much over time (Eichengreen and Gupta 2011). Therefore, the growth in the intermediate demand for services is largely attributed to increasing output and not to outsourcing by manufacturing firms. A supply factor of importance has been technological change or total factor productivity growth (TFPG) in the service sector. Indirect evidence in support of this factor is the declining incremental capital-output ratio and increasing labour productivity growth in the service sector since 1995. Real GDP estimates by sector are not available separately for rural and urban segments in India. However, as most of the manufacturing and services activities are dominated by the urban sector, it can be safely assumed that similar high output growth rates were achieved in the urban sector as a whole.

Employment

In Tables 8.2 and 8.3, our estimates of employment growth rates by sector are shown for India and for urban India separately for easy reference.[8] Manufacturing employment in urban India grew at a faster rate (2.8 per cent) relative to all-India (1.8 per cent) over the period 1999–2000 and 2009–10. Its growth rate was higher relative to the earlier period of 1993–9. In contrast, service sector employment in urban India grew at the same rate (2.5 per cent) as that of all-India (rural + urban). A marginal slow down in service employment growth rate (all-India) relative to the earlier period (2.6 per cent versus 2.9 per cent) can be attributed to the sharp fall in employment growth of trade and hotel industries during the 2000s. Employment in the business services segment that includes financial, real estate, and software services grew the fastest in urban India with a growth rate of 3.4 per cent. However, its share in total urban employment went up by less than 2 percentage points. What we find is that the service sector's share (58 per cent) in urban employment in 2009–10 was stagnant at the level that it had been in 1999–2000 (Table 8.4). An alternative way of understanding the importance of the urban sector in job creation is by examining its contribution to employment in terms of absolute numbers (Table 8.5). A little less than 50 per cent of the employment created in India was accounted for by the urban sector in the 2000s. More than 85 per cent of the jobs created in business services and more than 80 per cent of the jobs in total manufacturing were in the urban sector.

---

[7] See Rakshit (2007) for an excellent analytical discussion and supporting empirical evidence on demand and supply factors. This paragraph borrows much, including the statistics cited from this chapter.

[8] Employment is estimated using the NSS worker–population ratios and the mid-year population estimates for the survey years. Employment refers to all workers, that is, usual principal status (ps) and subsidiary status (ss) combined. The NSS worker–population ratios are taken from the NSS reports (National Sample Survey Organization 1997, 2001, 2006a, and 2006b).

Table 8.2 Employment Growth Rates (%) by Sector in India: 1993–4 to 2009–10

Sector	1999–2000 over 1993–4	2009–10 over 1999–2000	2009–10 over 1993–4	Share in Total Employment 2009–10
Agriculture	0.10	−0.10	0.00	52.30
Mining and quarrying	−2.80	2.70	0.60	0.60
Manufacturing	1.60	1.80	1.70	11.50
Electricity, water, etc.	−4.80	1.90	−0.60	0.30
Construction	6.40	9.70	8.40	9.70
Trade (retail + wholesale), hotels and restaurants	6.30	2.40	3.80	11.40
Transport, storage, and communications	5.30	3.40	4.10	4.50
Other services like financial, business, public administration, education, etc.	−0.70	2.40	1.20	9.80
Above three services	2.90	2.60	2.70	25.70
All sectors	1.00	1.40	1.30	100.00

Note: Average Annual Compound Growth Rate. Employment is measured by the number of workers by usual status (ps+ss).
Source: NSS employment and unemployment surveys adjusted for population censuses (see footnote 8 in this chapter).

Table 8.3 Employment Growth Rates (%) by Sector in Urban India: 1993–4 to 2009–10

Sector	1999–2000 over 1993–4	2009–10 over 1999–2000	2009–10 over 1993–4
Agriculture	−3.40	1.10	−0.60
Mining and quarrying	−3.70	0.20	−1.30
Manufacturing	1.60	2.80	2.40
Electricity, water, etc.	−4.20	2.10	−0.30
Construction	6.30	5.30	5.70
Trade (retail+ wholesale), hotels and restaurants	8.00	1.60	4.00
Transport, storage, and communications	3.90	2.70	3.20
Other services like financial, business, public administration, education, etc.	−0.70	3.40	1.80
Above three services	3.40	2.50	2.90
All sectors	2.30	2.70	2.60

Note: Same as that for Table 8.2.
Source: NSSO surveys 55th and 66th Rounds adjusted for population censuses.

Table 8.4 Structure of Urban Employment by Sector (%)

Sector	1999–2000	2009–10
Agriculture	8.70	7.50
Mining	0.80	0.60
Electricity	0.70	0.60
Construction	7.90	10.20
Manufacturing	22.70	23.00
Trade, hotels, and restaurants	26.90	24.20
Transport, storage, communications	8.70	8.70
Other services like financial, business, etc.	23.50	25.20
Above three services	59.20	58.10
All sectors	100.00	100.00

Note: Same as that for Table 8.2.
Source: NSSO surveys 55th and 66th Rounds adjusted for population censuses.

Table 8.5 Distribution of Absolute Employment Change by Sector (in million, 2009 over 1999)

Sector	Total	Urban	Urban share (%)
Agriculture	−2.52	0.97	−38.40
Mining	0.67	0.02	2.40
Manufacturing	8.42	6.88	81.60
Electricity, water, etc.	0.22	0.15	69.40
Construction	26.56	5.02	18.90
Trade, hotels, and restaurants	10.80	4.48	41.50
Transport, storage, and communications	5.78	2.53	43.80
Other services like financial, business, etc.	10.32	8.78	85.10
Above three services	26.91	15.79	58.70
All sectors	60.27	28.83	47.80

Source: NSSO surveys 55th and 66th Rounds adjusted for population censuses.

Similarly, the urban sector's share was more than 40 per cent in the two service sectors of trade and hotels and transport, storage, and communications. The three service sectors in urban India taken together accounted for more than 58 per cent of the total jobs created in India in these three sectors. This establishes the relative quantitative importance of services and manufacturing in urban employment growth. What has been the quality of the jobs created is a question that we attempt to understand in the next section.

STRUCTURE OF URBAN WORKFORCE, WORKER STATUS, AND JOB QUALITY

Urban Workforce Growth and Dependency Ratio Change

In 2009–10 the estimated size of the urban labour force (those with jobs plus those seeking jobs) was 126.9 million persons of which 122.6 million persons had jobs constituting the workforce or those employed. This gives us an unemployment rate of a little more than 3 per cent. The urban workforce grew at the rate of 2.7 per cent per annum over the period 1999–2000 to 2009–10 (Table 8.3).[9] Sector-wise distribution did not undergo much change with the construction sector increasing its share to 10 per cent (Table 8.4). The sector broadly called 'Other business services' increased its share marginally as it is the only sector other than the construction sector that achieved growth rates higher than the economy wide average growth rate during this period. In absolute terms, more than 28 million additional jobs were created in urban India during this period. Urban India is expected to absorb additions to the labour force at a much faster rate. What is the status of urban workers in term of types of jobs, education, earnings, and social security benefits? Has it improved or deteriorated in the last decade? These questions deserve attention from the viewpoint of workers' well-being as well as potential growth. The reason for the latter (potential growth) is derived from the fact that urban India is relatively better positioned in terms of demographic dividend. Our estimates based on successive rounds of NSS surveys suggest that relative to the rural sector, the dependency ratio, the ratio of dependent population to working-age population, in urban India declined from 0.6 in 1993–4 to 0.5 in 1999–2000 both for males and females. Conversion of this demographic 'gift' into real economic dividend depends on the implementation of several structural and institutional reforms. Otherwise it remains as a growth potential not realized.[10]

Employment Status: Structure and Change

Three types of activity status within the category of those 'employed' can be distinguished and which can help one to differentiate between the job quality of the workforce. They are regular wage workers, casual wage workers, and those who are self-employed. In other words, two types of employment status get attention. They are wage employment and self-employment. Wage employment includes those with regular jobs (regular wage and salaried) (hereafter RWS), and those with casual wage jobs (CW). RWS refers to those who work in other enterprises and receive salaries/wages on a regular basis (not on a daily basis or a periodic renewal

---

[9] It is similar to the growth rate of the urban labour force at 2.6 per cent for this period.

[10] See Bloom and Williamson's (1998) discussion in the East Asian context.

of contract). It is important to understand that the term 'regular' means only 'continuous' employment. Workers employed as contract workers may report as regular workers and not as casual wage labourers who are employed on a daily wage basis or on a periodic renewal of work contract. Casual wage workers are the most vulnerable category as they lack social security benefits and are least covered by labour regulations including minimum wage rules. The self-employment (SE) category consists of three types of workers: (1) own-account workers running a household enterprise without hiring labour, (2) employers who run enterprises by hiring labour, and (3) helpers in household enterprises. Income data is not reported for the SE category. This makes it harder to judge job quality differences between SE and RWS. Often SE takes the form of subsistence entrepreneurship due to lack of regular job opportunities. Downsizing and restructuring by formal sector enterprises (that involves retrenchment or voluntary retirement schemes) could force RWS to take up self-employment. We begin by looking at all workers above the age of 15 years and their distribution in three key categories of employment—self-employment (SE), regular workers (RWS) and casual workers (CW). Casualization of the workforce would be the first indicator of any deterioration in the job quality of the urban workforce.

Casualization

Casualization refers to an increase in the incidence of casual labour within an industry and this incidence is measured by the share of casual workers in the total workforce in that industry. A widely held perception is that there has been a secular decline in the share of regular workers and a corresponding increase in the share of casual workers in the urban sector. Contrary to this perception, employment shares in the urban sector have remained stable, with a marginal rise in the share of regular male workers and a significant increase in the share of female regular workers from 33 per cent in 1999–2000 to 39 per cent in 2009–10. The latter change has been largely a shift out of self-employment as the share of casual jobs shows a decline of merely 1.8 percentage points. For workers of all ages the incremental contribution (share in the absolute change in total urban workers) of regular workers is 46 per cent as against 17 per cent for casual workers. Further, the growth rate of regular workers of all ages is 2.9 per cent per annum similar to that of casual workers (3 per cent) but more than the growth rate of SE (2.7 per cent). It is possible that casualization would have increased in particular industries (Pais 2002) but it was not a sector-wide phenomenon in the last decade. The observed decline in the share of casual and self-employed female workers needs to be counted as a welfare gain. It is possible to have a life-cycle pattern in employment that could account for the shift out of one category to another with urban males and females showing different types of movements (Glinskaya and Jalan 2006).[11] For example, young age workers (either regular/casual) may move to SE on reaching middle age having accumulated seed capital and female workers may shift out from self-employment to regular work perhaps after gaining more experience. This possibility is likely to be identified more clearly within sectors by using the age-specific distribution of SE, RWS, and CW over the 11-year period.

Manufacturing versus Services

In Table 8.6, age specific distribution of workers by work-status for the two survey years separated by a gap of 10 years is presented. The data covers all workers (ps+ss: principal and subsidiary status).[12] Similar distribution for ps workers was estimated but it is not presented here to save space. The following results emerge from Table 8.6:

1. In manufacturing, young male workers (15–30 years) increased their share of regular jobs. Both middle age workers (31–50 years) and older workers (51 years and above) lost some share of their regular jobs but their share of casual jobs went up substantially suggesting that they were vulnerable to losing their regular jobs perhaps due to enterprise restructuring and/or technological change. Perhaps they also moved to take up SE. For all males, the share of casual jobs showed a marginal increase. Female workers' distribution was stable.

2. Younger male workers in services increased their share substantially. Middle age workers lost regular jobs and increased their share of SE. The service sector turned out to be a boon for female workers. Both young and middle age female workers increased their share in regular jobs significantly; casual jobs and SE declined for females of all ages. The service sector created a greater number of regular jobs for female workers. This was a welcome development

---

[11] This is based on the empirical findings of Evans and Jovanovic (1989) for the US. They found that young workers may be more prone to risk taking and take up work as self-employment; it is the older workers who are likely to enter using accumulated savings as capital.

[12] We estimated similar distribution for only principal status (ps) workers. We observed that for manufacturing when subsidiary status (ss) workers were added, the share of casual workers went up, the share of regular workers did not change, and the share of SE workers declined in 2009–10. This suggested that casual work status dominates ss workers.

Table 8.6 Age-specific Distribution (%) by Worker Status and Gender in Manufacturing and Services: 1999–2000 and 2009–10

Gender /Age Group	1999–2000				2009–10			
	SE	RWS	CW	Total	SE	RWS	CW	Total
Manufacturing								
Male								
15–30	26.41	37.36	36.23	100.00	21.19	42.57	36.24	100.00
31–50	31.10	45.03	23.87	100.00	29.55	38.98	31.47	100.00
Above 51	40.9	40.87	18.23	100.00	39.41	37.50	23.09	100.00
Total	30.03	41.24	28.73	100.00	26.97	40.37	32.66	100.00
Female								
15–30	51.83	23.36	24.81	100.00	53.90	21.76	24.34	100.00
31–50	53.67	18.84	27.50	100.00	57.45	14.72	27.83	100.00
Above 51	74.46	9.31	16.23	100.00	57.94	12.61	29.45	100.00
Total	54.57	20.12	25.31	100.00	56.04	17.41	26.55	100.00
Services								
Male								
15–30	46.95	40.94	12.11	100.00	42.84	48.30	8.86	100.00
31–50	44.52	49.15	6.34	100.00	48.06	46.26	5.68	100.00
Above 51	49.80	45.26	4.94	100.00	54.22	41.49	4.29	100.00
Total	46.08	45.6	8.31	100.00	47.23	46.24	6.53	100.00
Female								
15–30	37.12	51.84	11.05	100.00	23.07	69.48	7.45	100.00
31–50	36.60	53.03	10.37	100.00	29.28	62.15	8.57	100.00
Above 51	48.28	41.14	10.57	100.00	38.27	50.79	10.94	100.00
Total	38.27	51.11	10.62	100.00	28.32	63.19	8.49	100.00

Note: SE, RWS, and CW denote self-employed, regular wage and salaried, and casual workers, respectively.

Source: Unit level data from NSSO surveys 55th and 66th Rounds.

in the sense that the demographic dividend was expected to result in greater female labour supply.
3. The share of SE in the workplace decreased for males in manufacturing and for females in services. It increased for females in manufacturing and for males in services. This suggests an increasing number of female home-workers in manufacturing and male home-workers in services as the status of self-employment is essentially household employment.

Location of Workplace

Indirect evidence of the conditions of work is the location of the workplace of the different categories of workers. In Table 8.7 estimates of the proportion of the three types of workers—self-employed, regular, and casual—in terms of locations of their workplace are presented.[13] The following points may be noted:

1. Ninety per cent of the self-employed worked in their own-dwelling/own-enterprise office suggesting the dominance of home-based workers in self-employment irrespective of the sector in which they worked—either manufacturing or services.
2. Ninety-four per cent of the regular workers worked in shops or offices that were outside the employer's dwelling.
3. The share of casual home workers in manufacturing increased. The share of casual workers who worked

[13] See Appendix A8 for the concordance between location codes in NSS surveys.

Table 8.7 Distribution of Workers (%) of Each Status by Location of Workplace: Manufacturing and Services

Location	1999–2000				2009–10			
	SE	RWS	CW	Total	SE	RWS	CW	Total
Manufacturing								
Own-dwelling or own-office	90.70	3.00	3.00	35.10	89.90	4.30	12.40	36.80
Employer's dwelling or employer's shop/office	5.10	94.20	92.00	61.30	4.30	93.30	80.20	58.90
Street with fixed location	1.30	1.10	1.20	1.10	3.60	1.30	3.30	2.40
Construction site	0.90	0.30	1.80	0.70	1.00	0.40	2.50	0.90
Others	2.00	1.50	2.10	1.80	1.30	0.70	1.70	1.00
Total	100	100	100	100	100	100	100	100
Services								
Own-dwelling or own-office	75.70	2.70	3.90	33.00	78.80	3.20	5.20	32.90
Employer's dwelling or employer's shop/office	4.70	88.90	78.80	53.20	5.00	93.10	82.90	58.10
Street with fixed location	8.10	2.50	4.60	5.00	10.40	1.70	5.10	5.30
Construction site	0.40	0.20	2.00	0.40	0.70	0.10	1.50	0.40
Others	11.10	5.80	10.60	8.40	5.20	1.80	5.30	3.40
Total	100	100	100	100	100	100	100	100

Note: SE, RWS, and CW denote self-employed, regular wage and salaried, and casual workers, respectively.

Source: Unit level data from NSSO surveys 55th and 66th Rounds.

at an employer's office declined by 10 percentage points. At the same time the share of casual workers who worked in their own dwellings went up by 9 percentage points. This is a clear sign of increasing production by home-workers—a phenomenon widespread in tobacco, garment, and food industries.

4. In contrast, in the service sector the proportion of casual workers who worked in an employer's offices went up significantly. Casualization equally increased in the service sector.

Informal Employment and Enterprise Size

An idea related to that of casualization is that of informality. Informal employment refers to jobs in enterprises that are not covered by labour and social security regulations. In the Indian context it refers to employment in the unorganized sector. Workers in informal enterprises are not covered by regulations related to conditions of work, retrenchment, and minimum wages. They are vulnerable and often bear the burden of economic shocks. However, informality is much harder to capture in employment statistics. Often it is measured by the sum of the shares of CW and SE workers in the total employment in a sector. This is based on the argument that self-employment as captured in own account enterprises and self-employed owners who hire outside workers are often small enterprises which escape labour and tax regulations. RWS is a proxy for organized sector employment. As noted earlier, regular employment does not imply employment in the covered sector or access to labour or social security regulations. RWS only suggests continuous wage employment (see more on this below). The combined share of CW and SE workers in both manufacturing and services remained stable in the period under consideration for both principal and all (ps+ss) workers. An alternative approach for capturing informality is by considering employment distribution by the enterprise size of the worker. NSS surveys collect this information by asking the surveyed workers about the number of workers in the enterprise in which they work. We have tabulated this data separately for manufacturing and services and presented it in Table 8.8.[14] The following results emerge:

1. In manufacturing, a higher proportion of regular workers worked in the formal sector, in enterprises with more than 10 workers, than in services.
2. A significantly higher proportion of casual workers worked in the informal sector, in enterprises with less than 10 workers, in services compared to manufacturing.

---

[14] This is tabulated only for principal status (ps) workers. The percentage worker response for the category 'not known' is not shown here. It probably comes from firms with more than 10 workers as labour regulations begin to bite those firms.

3. These two together imply that the incidence of informality or informal employment was more widespread in the service sector than it was in manufacturing.
4. Taking all workers together, services had a significantly higher proportion of workers in informal enterprises (66 per cent) than in manufacturing (55 per cent) in 2009–10.
5. As the relative incidence of informality was not showing signs of decline, it is arguable whether the service sector is likely to offer better employment status to the urban workforce than manufacturing.

Table 8.8 Distribution of Workers (%) by Enterprise Size: Manufacturing and Services

Sector	Less Than 10		More Than 10	
	1999–2000	2009–10	1999–2000	2009–10
Regular				
Manufacturing	29.30	28.40	55.10	58.90
Services	39.30	39.90	42.90	46.10
Casual				
Manufacturing	52.00	53.60	33.00	32.00
Services	76.10	77.40	10.20	11.90
All Workers				
Manufacturing	56.90	55.50	33.00	35.40
Services	67.80	66.00	22.00	25.20

Source: Unit level data from NSSO surveys 55th and 66th Rounds.

WAGE INEQUALITY, EDUCATION, AND SOCIAL SECURITY

Measures of Wage Inequality

Inequality measures attempt to capture the extent of disparity in the distribution of income (wages or earnings in our context). Several estimated measures of inequality are presented in Table 8.9 for both the sectors. The evidence is clear that wage inequality among regular workers increased over time in both manufacturing and services.[15] This is not surprising as we find a mix of formal and informal enterprise workers in both the sectors. The key suggestive indicator is that the Mean Log Deviation that gives more weight to changes in the lower end of the distribution was much higher in services than it was in manufacturing in both 1999 and 2009. Wage inequality below the median (log difference between the 50th and 10th percentile) was higher in the service sector relative to manufacturing (Table 8.9). It did not reduce over time leading to higher overall inequality in the service sector (log difference between the 90th and 10th percentile).[16]

The real daily wage per male worker at 1999–2000 prices increased at the average annual compound rate of 1.3 per cent in manufacturing as against 2.4 per cent in services. The increase in the mean wages was heavily influenced by wage increases at the upper end of the wage distribution, particularly in services. Figure 8.1 plots the distribution of the mean real daily wage for regular workers in manufacturing and services by deciles for 1999–2000 and 2009–10.[17] The stark difference between the two sectors is obvious with the two-lines, representing the two years separated by a 10-year gap in manufacturing almost coinciding until we reach the poorest (or least-skilled) 80 per cent of the workers.

A substantive change that goes beyond the difference between the least skilled and the most skilled emerges when we plot, for each sector, the log real daily wage changes between 1999–2000 and 2009–10 by *deciles* in Figure 8.2.[18] The log difference is interpreted as the percentage change between the two years.[19] Two striking outcomes emerge: (i) firstly, the growth rate of real wages is actually falling for the workers below the median wage in manufacturing (except for the bottom 20 per cent who have gained). It is more or less constant for workers below the median in services. In manufacturing, the decline continues for workers with incomes in the bottom 70 per cent. The least skilled received the lowest wage increases; (ii) secondly, in services the growth rate of real wages was sharp for those workers with income levels above the median. In manufacturing, in contrast, real wages increased sharply only for those in the income group of the top 20 to 30 per cent (see Figure 8.2). The implication is clear. The most skilled experienced the highest wage increases in both manufacturing and services. It was substantially higher for the higher skilled workers in

---

[15] Earnings inequality was not computed for the category of casual workers as we did not observe large human capital differences among them.

[16] This is consistent with the finding based on quintile regression coefficients for 1999–2000 that tertiary sector has greater duality, net earnings gap between the lowest quintile and the higher quintiles for regular wage earners, than in manufacturing (Mazumdar and Sarkar 2009: 241–42).

[17] We have plotted the mean daily wage by percentiles and obtained similar results (not reported here to save space).

[18] This analysis is directly comparable to that of Kijima (2006). Kijima carried out the analysis for the entire urban sector and used the log weekly wage differences for the period 1983 and 1999. She argues that wage inequality started increasing even before the economic reforms of 1991. She found that wage inequality grew faster in urban India after 1993. Our results are more striking as explained in the text.

[19] For each percentile we subtract the log real wage per day in 1999–2000 from that in 2009–10.

Table 8.9 Wage Inequality among Regular Workers in Urban India: 1999–2009

Measures	Manufacturing			Services		
	1999–2000	2004–5	2009–10	1999–2000	2004–5	2009–10
Gini coefficient	0.41	0.43	0.45	0.42	0.45	0.46
Theil index (GE(a), a = 1)	0.28	0.33	0.36	0.29	0.34	0.34
Mean Log Deviation (GE(a), a = 0)	0.28	0.31	0.34	0.34	0.39	0.40
90–10 Log Wage Difference	1.89	NE	2.02	2.28	NE	2.48
90–50 Log Wage Difference	1.04	NE	1.27	0.95	NE	1.17
50–10 Log Wage Difference	0.85	NE	0.75	1.34	NE	1.32

Note: Daily wage rates were used with the data trimmed by 0.1 per cent of highest and lowest wage. NE: not estimated.

Source: Unit level data from NSSO surveys 55th, 61th, and 66th Rounds.

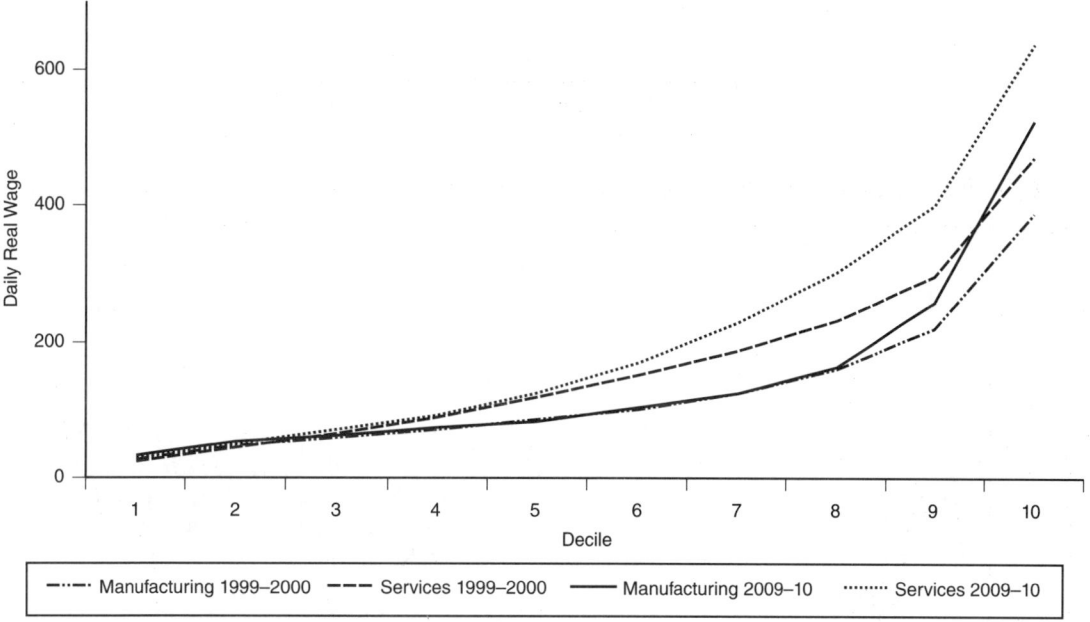

Figure 8.1 Average Daily Real Wage (in Rs) by Deciles in Manufacturing and Services

Source: Unit level data from NSSO surveys 55th and 66th Rounds.

services. Over time, the service sector experienced greater skill shortages and the growth in the service sector was relatively more skill demanding than manufacturing at higher skill levels. Skill-biased technical change perhaps bites more over time in the service sector.[20] This finding is consistent with earlier studies of sectoral growth and income inequality that suggest growth in the services sector raises income inequality (Pieters 2010).[21]

These conclusions are further confirmed when we plot the log real wage changes between 1999–2000 and 2009–10 by *percentile* groups in Figure 8.3. The plot exhibits more fluctuations but it is consistent with our earlier finding. In manufacturing the decline continued for workers with incomes below the 80th percentile. This further sharpens the above finding that in manufacturing the least skilled received the lowest wage increases relative to services.

Skill or Educational Level Differences

The observed wage inequalities could be a reflection of greater skill/education level differences in the workforce. This leads us to examine the distribution by educational levels over time in these two sectors. We distinguish only

---

[20] Greater use of information technology by the service industry could be an important reason. This proposition needs a separate study.
[21] This study by Pieters shows that services sector growth increases household wage income inequality using an extended social accounting matrix (SAM) that takes into account wage and education distribution within different sectors for 2002–3.

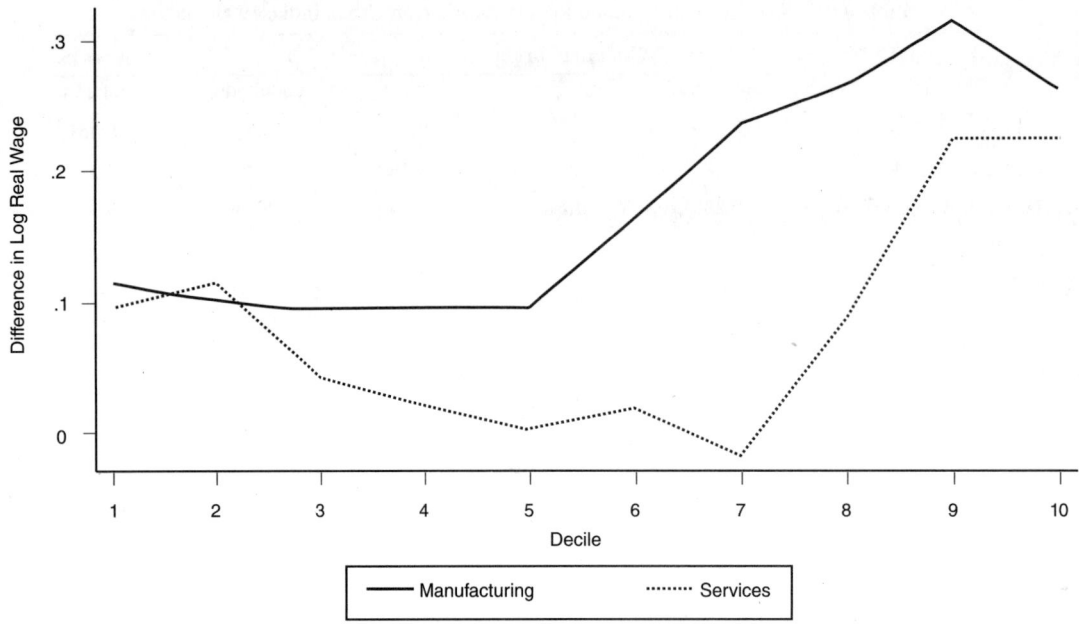

Figure 8.2 Difference in Log Real Wage between 1999 and 2009 by Deciles: Manufacturing versus Services
Source: Unit level data from NSSO surveys 55th and 66th Rounds.

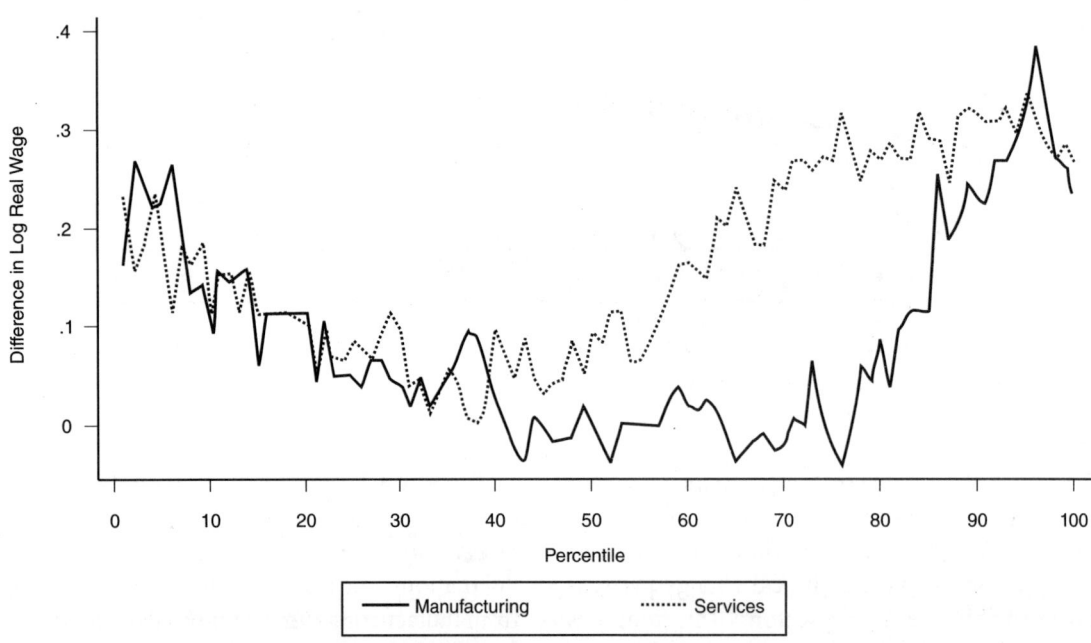

Figure 8.3 Difference in Log Real Wage between 1999 and 2009 by Percentiles: Manufacturing versus Services
Source: Unit level data from NSSO surveys 55th and 66th Rounds.

four levels—those with below primary education that includes not literate, middle school education, those with above secondary school that includes those with a diploma, and those with above graduate level education. The distribution is presented separately for males and females (Table 8.10). The uneven change over time in the service sector compared to manufacturing is evident. The proportion of male workers with above secondary education was significantly higher (61 per cent) in services compared to manufacturing (46 per cent) in 2009–10. The share of

Table 8.10 Distribution of Male and Female Workers by Level of Education (%)

Educational Level	Manufacturing		Services	
	1999–2000	2009–10	1999–2000	2009–10
Males				
Below primary	39.20	32.50	31.80	22.60
Middle	19.80	21.20	18.90	16.20
Secondary	27.20	32.10	28.60	33.70
Graduate	13.80	14.20	20.70	27.40
Total	100.00	100.00	100.00	100.00
Females				
Below primary	68.80	55.80	46.20	34.50
Middle	15.20	20.80	8.80	9.60
Secondary	11.90	17.70	20.0	20.20
Graduate	4.00	5.70	24.90	35.70
Total	100.00	100.00	100.00	100.00

Source: Unit level data from NSSO surveys 55th and 66th Rounds.

workers with graduate education and above among males was almost twice as that of manufacturing in 2009–10. This is not to deny the argument that over time the skill mix in manufacturing and services would become increasingly similar (Eichengreen and Gupta 2011). However, if current education-skill distribution is taken as the correct reflection of the underlying skill-demand structure then manufacturing would be the first destination for a majority of labour force who are expected to move into the modern sector. Manufacturing has much greater capacity to absorb labour with lower levels of education.

What was happening to the educational attainment of the population over this time period? We would be interested in knowing the changes in the proportion of the educated in the age group 15 years and above in the urban population. Here we define educated as those with secondary education and above. A comparison of the change in the proportion of educated population between 1999–2000 and 2009–10 reveals the following: among urban males, the proportion of the educated increased from 46 per cent (1999–2000) to 56 per cent (2009–10). Among urban females the corresponding change was from 22 to 32 per cent. The supply of educated labour certainly did not decline. The problem was more of a mismatch between demand and supply of different and diverse skill levels.[22] It is fairly well established by econometric studies that returns to education by levels of education in India have been increasing in recent years (Agrawal 2011). In Figure 8.4, we show the log wages per day of workers with five different levels of education for 2009–10. They are: (i) not literate, (ii) literate and up to middle, (iii) secondary and higher secondary, (iv) diploma/certificate, and (v) graduate and above. This is plotted for six selected sectors.[23] Three service sectors, education and health, business and finance, and transport and real estate had relatively higher returns.[24]

Access to Social Security and Job Contract Status

Our findings are based on individual worker responses to questions asked for the time in the NSS employment and unemployment survey in the 61st Round (2004–5) and repeated in the 66th Round (2009–10). The question on access to social security benefits asked whether the worker was eligible for provident fund, pension, healthcare, and gratuity benefits. One could tabulate the proportion saying 'Yes' and those saying 'No' to the above question. In manufacturing we find that only 36 per cent of the workers reported that they had access to social security benefits.[25] The service sector fared better with 52 per cent saying yes to

---

[22] Labour market mismatch could originate from different sources that require a separate analysis.

[23] Manufacturing (traditional) includes industry divisions 15–22 and manufacturing (modern) includes industry divisions 23–37. PA denotes Public Administration.

[24] This is only a broad approximate gross indicator as we have not controlled for many other worker attributes like experience.

[25] This refers to the 2009–10 survey.

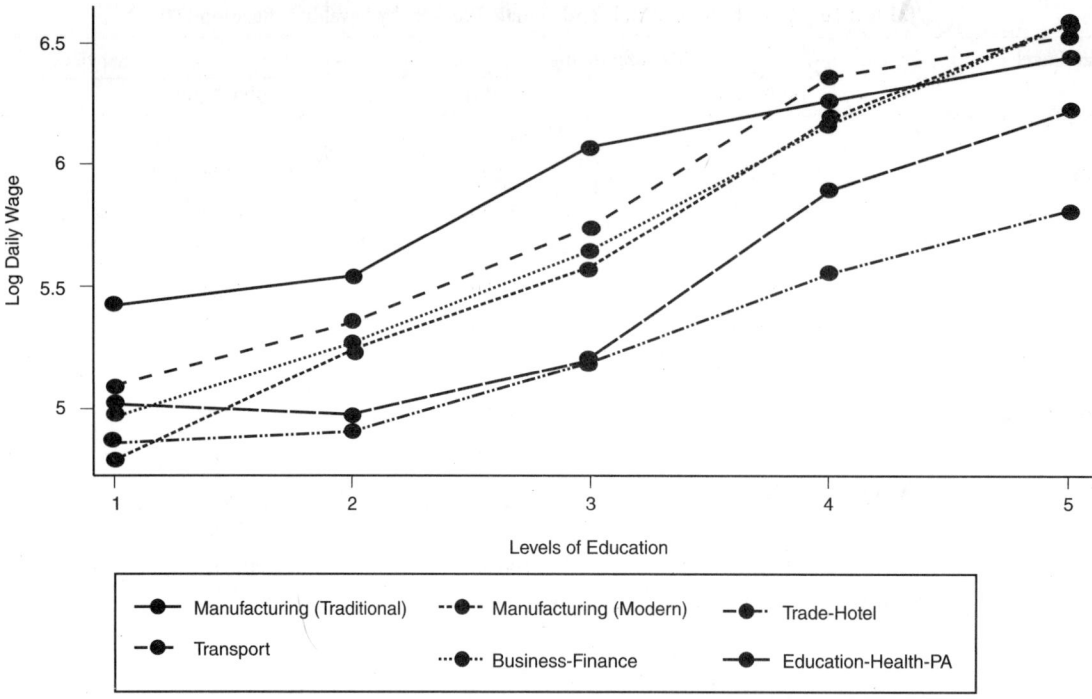

Figure 8.4 Returns to Education by Industry: 2009–10
Source: National Sample Survey Organization (2011: A504, Table 46). See footnote 23 in this chapter.

the question. However, the averages are misleading due to large deviations. We have tabulated the responses of workers classified into 69 three-digit industry groups within the service sector and those in 59 three-digit industry groups in manufacturing. The results are shown in Table 8.11. We find that in less than 17 per cent of the 69 service industries, more than 75 per cent of the workers said that they had access to social security benefits. Similarly, in less than 12 per cent of the 59 manufacturing industries, more than 75 per cent of the workers said that they had access to such benefits. The situation seems to improve somewhat in manufacturing over time. Overall, there is nothing much to show that services offered better access to social security benefits.

The NSS surveys had also asked the workers about the type of job contract they worked out with their employers. In manufacturing, only 20 per cent of the estimated workers reported that they had more than a three-year contract and this percentage was better in services (35 per cent). Correspondingly, nearly 80 per cent of the manufacturing workers reported that they had no written contract and in services this percentage was less at 59 per cent. We have tabulated the distribution of responses (workers who indicated that they had more than three years of contract) within three-digit industry groups for the question (Table 8.12). The evidence suggests that contractual conditions were broadly similar between services and manufacturing.

CONCLUSIONS

We studied employment growth, structure, and job quality outcomes in urban India between 1999–2000 and 2009–10. This was a period of dynamic growth of the service sector in India. We did not find any acceleration in service sector employment growth relative to manufacturing in the urban areas in India. The good news is that young males increased their share of regular employment both in manufacturing and services. The service sector turned out to be a boon for female workers. Both young and middle age female workers increased their share in regular jobs. However, we find greater duality in the service sector in terms of informality and wage inequality. The incidence of informality or informal employment was more widespread in the service sector than it was in manufacturing. A large number of such workers would be in low productivity activities. Similarly wage inequalities were relatively higher in services and those with more skills received significantly higher increases in real wages. The skilled in the service sector gained proportionately more in terms of real wage growth. In other words, the service sector experienced greater skill shortages and the growth in the service sector was relatively more skill demanding than it was in manufacturing at higher skill levels. We showed that the skill composition of the workforce was significantly different between the two sectors

Table 8.11 Access to Social Security Benefit: Industry Distribution 2004–5 and 2009–10

Percentage of Workers Saying YES (Y)	No. of Industries–Manufacturing		No. of Industries–Services	
	2004–5	2009–10	2004–5	2009–10
Y≤25	26	21	26	26
25< Y≤ 50	15	17	16	18
50<Y≤ 75	11	13	15	13
Y>75	7	8	12	12
Total (3-digit) industries*	59	59	69	69

Note: *National Industrial Classification [NIC] (1998).

Source: Unit level data from NSSO surveys 61st and 66th Rounds.

Table 8.12 Workers with Job Contracts for More Than Three Years: Industry Distribution 2004–5 and 2009–10

Percentage of Workers Saying YES (Y)	No. of Industries–Manufacturing		No. of Industries–Services	
	2004–5	2009–10	2004–5	2009–10
Y≤25	29	38	20	39
25< Y≤ 50	17	17	1	18
50<Y≤ 75	8	4	14	11
Y>75	4	0	4	1
Total (3-digit) industries*	58	58	69	69

Note: *National Industrial Classification [NIC] (1998).

Source: Unit level data from NSSO surveys 61st and 66th Rounds.

with services clearly skill biased. Social security conditions were not found to be relatively much superior in services. Our results strongly suggest that the service sector would be an unlikely destination for the millions of low-skilled job seekers. India needs to focus on the manufacturing sector to provide large-scale employment. Manufacturing has the capability because it has stronger backward linkages unlike the service sector. We cannot afford to neglect manufacturing at this stage of development. Policy signals have to clearly say that we stand to support manufacturing activity in a big way. Manufacturing has the potential to grow as fast as services.

The Way Forward

The share of manufacturing in GDP and employment has been stagnating since 1999–2000 at 15 to 16 per cent and 11 per cent, respectively. The National Manufacturing Policy has set an ambitious and unrealistic target of raising the GDP share to 25 per cent by 2022 and aims to create 100 million jobs. However, the policy actions that it has advocated in terms of establishing industry clusters like National Manufacturing and Investment Zones (NIMZ), exit mechanisms for inefficient firms, and compensation measures to offset job losses due to industry restructuring and skill upgrading programmes, among other things, are unassailable. Carrying out these policy actions and giving them operational content are a huge challenge. Land and labour, the two critical areas in this context, are in the domain of the states. Coordination issues between the central and state governments pose difficult problems and suggested new institutions like the Manufacturing Industry Promotion Board (MIPB) may take years to become functional. Meanwhile, the broad policy should focus on supporting and accelerating current manufacturing growth rates by facilitating incentives to invest in manufacturing by providing access to institutional credit and solving infrastructure bottlenecks like power and transport. Capital market imperfections continue to limit access to finance for small and medium enterprises (SMEs) and macroeconomic policy has pushed up the cost of credit in recent years. The higher cost of credit and infrastructure costs (a negative pecuniary externality!) together adversely affect SMEs. They drive up the cost of production relatively more in existing SMEs preventing scaling up of operations and at the same time inhibit the new entry of SMEs into manufacturing. This will severely constrain the potential job-creating capacity of the manufacturing sector. SMEs are important both as exporters as well as suppliers in the expanding domestic market in a wide range of industries. Economic policy can aid employment creation by reducing costs of doing business for SMEs in manufacturing.

Appendix A8 Concordance between Location Codes in NSS Surveys

1999–2000	2009–10
Own-dwelling (21) plus own-enterprise office but outside own dwelling (22)	Own-dwelling unit (20)+structure attached to own-dwelling unit (21)+open area adjacent to own-dwelling unit(22)+detached structure adjacent to own-dwelling unit(23)+own-office but away from dwelling
Employer's dwelling(13)+employer's shop/office but outside employer's dwelling (24)	Same (25+26)
Street with fixed location (25)	Street with fixed location (27)
Construction site (26)	Construction site (25)
Others (29)	Others (29)

Note: Figure in brackets refers to location codes used in the respective NSS surveys.

REFERENCES

Acharya, S. (2002), 'Macroeconomic Management in the Nineties', *Economic and Political Weekly*, 37(16): 1515–38.

Agrawal, T. (2011), *Returns to Education in India: Some Recent Evidence*. Mumbai: Indira Gandhi Institute of Development Research.

Bhagat, R.B. (2011), 'Emerging Pattern of Urbanisation in India', *Economic and Political Weekly*, 46(34): 10–12.

Bloom, D.E. and J.G. Williamson (1998), 'Demographic Transitions and Economic Miracles in Emerging Asia', *World Bank Economic Review*, 12(3): 419–55.

Bosworth, B., S.M. Collins, and A. Virmani (2007), *Sources of Growth in the Indian Economy*. Cambridge, MA: National Bureau of Economic Research, NBER Working Paper 12901.

Eichengreen, Barry and Poonam Gupta (2011), 'The Service Sector as India's Road to Economic Growth in India', *India Policy Forum: 2010–11* (Vol. 7). New Delhi: Sage Publications.

Evans, D.S. and B. Jovanovic (1989), 'An Estimated Model of Entrepreneurial Choice under Liquidity Constraints', *Journal of Political Economy*, 97(4): 808–27.

Glinskaya, E. and J. Jalan (2006), 'Quality of Informal Jobs in India', in Conference Papers of 'India: Meeting the Employment Challenge', Conference on Labour and Employment Issues in India, organized by the Institute of Human Development, New Delhi, 27–29 July.

Gordon, J and P. Gupta (2004), 'Understanding India's Services Revolution'. Washington DC: International Monetary Fund.

Himanshu (2011), 'Employment Trends in India: A Re-examination', *Economic and Political Weekly*, 46(37): 43–59.

Kijima, Y. (2006), 'Why Did Wage Inequality Increase? Evidence from Urban India 1983–99', *Journal of Development Economics*, 81(1): 97–117.

Mazumdar, Dipak and Sandip Sarkar (2009), *Globalization, Labor Markets and Inequality in India*. London and New York: Routledge.

Nagaraj, R. (2009), 'Is Services Sector Output Overestimated? An Inquiry', *Economic and Political Weekly*, 44(5): 40–5.

National Sample Survey Organization (1997), Employment and Unemployment Situation in India, 1993–1994. NSS 50th Round, Report No. 409. New Delhi: Government of India.

———. (2001), Employment and Unemployment Situation in India, 1999–2000. NSS 55th Round, Report No. 458. New Delhi: Government of India.

———. (2006a), Employment and Unemployment Situation in India, January–June 2004, NSS 61st Round, Report No. 515, Part I. New Delhi: Government of India.

———. (2006b), Employment and Unemployment Situation in India, January–June 2004, NSS 61st Round, Report No. 515, Part II. New Delhi: Government of India.

———. (2011), Employment and Unemployment Situation in India 2009–10, NSS Report No. 537(66/10/1). New Delhi: Government of India.

Reserve Bank of India (2011), *Reserve Bank of India Annual Report 2010–2011*. Available at www.rbi.org.in, last accessed on 15 October 2011.

Pais, J. (2002), 'Casualisation of Urban Labour Force: Analysis of Recent Trends in Manufacturing', *Economic and Political Weekly*, 37(7): 631–52.

Panagariya, Arvind (2008), *India: The Emerging Giant*. New Delhi: Oxford University Press.

Pieters, J. (2010), 'Growth and Inequality in India: Analysis of an Extended Social Accounting Matrix', *World Development*, 38(3): 270–81.

Rakshit, M. (2007), 'Services-led Growth: The Indian Experience', *ICRA Bulletin Money & Finance*, 3(1): 91–126.

Singh, N. (2006), *Services-Led Industrialization in India: Prospects and Challenges*. Stanford, CA: Stanford University.

9

The 'Miracle' Still Waiting to Happen
Performance of India's Manufactured Exports in Comparison to China

*C. Veeramani**

INTRODUCTION

At the end of the 1950s, India turned to a strategy of industrialization based on import substitution. China, too, adopted the heavy-industry-oriented development strategy (also known as the leap forward strategy) during the early 1950s. Both the countries introduced a battery of trade and exchange controls, which severed the link between domestic and world relative prices. Exchange rates were overvalued, creating a bias against exports in both the countries (Lal 1995). By contrast, the East Asian tiger economies adopted export-promoting policies (Weiss 2005). Thus, India's 'Hindu rate of growth' under import substitution was often contrasted with the growth 'miracle' that the East Asian tigers had experienced under export-promoting policies.

As the East Asian 'miracle' gained widespread attention and as doubts about the effectiveness of import substitution arose in other countries, it became a common practice to recommend the East Asian model for other countries wishing to accelerate the pace of their industrialization and economic growth (Bhagwati 2002). China started its trade liberalization process in earnest in 1978, while India introduced 'cautious' liberalization during the 1980s, focusing on internal deregulation rather than on trade liberalization. The most pronounced overhaul of India's trade policy regime occurred during the early 1990s in response to a severe balance of payment crisis. The post-1991 policy changes in India have gone a long way towards product market liberalization by easing entry barriers for domestic and foreign firms in manufacturing industries. However, it must be noted at the outset that India's factor markets (labour and land) are still plagued by severe distortions and policy-induced rigidities.

Subsequent to market-oriented reforms, both India and China have been successful in achieving a turnaround in their economic growth rates. Today, India and China are among the fastest growing economies of the world. However, certain important contrasts are evident in the growth process in the two countries. China's growth pattern exhibits striking similarities with the manufacturing-based export-oriented growth of the East Asian tigers while Indian growth reveals some notable idiosyncrasies. China followed the conventional pattern of shifting labour from agriculture to labour-intensive manufacturing. By contrast, India seems to be skipping the intermediate stage of industrialization and directly moving to the final stage of services-led growth.

---

* I am thankful to K.L. Krishna and Vikas Chitre for helpful comments on an earlier draft of this chapter.

During the last two decades (1990–2010), the share of manufacturing in India's GDP remained low in the range of 14–17 per cent as against 30–33 per cent for China. International comparisons suggest that the *actual* manufacturing share of GDP for India was lower than what was *predicted* while the opposite is the case for China (ADB 2007).[1] Further, in contrast to employment-intensive growth in China, India's manufacturing growth followed a relatively capital-intensive path.[2] The share of manufactures in India's merchandise exports declined from about 70 per cent in 1990 to 63 per cent in 2010. In contrast, the share of manufactures in China's merchandise exports increased from 71 per cent in 1990 to 94 per cent in 2010. Unlike in China, exports have not yet become a major engine of growth in India's manufacturing sector. Between 1990 and 2010, China's share in the world exports of manufactures steadily increased from about 2 per cent to a whopping 15 per cent while India's share increased from 0.5 per cent to just 1.4 per cent.

The lack of dynamism in labour-intensive manufacturing has considerably slowed down the process of transferring the large pools of India's surplus labour from agriculture into the well-paying modern sectors.[3] Agriculture accounted for 17 per cent of India's GDP in 2009, but employed 52 per cent of the total workforce. Thus, Indian growth has not been effective in reducing poverty on the scale that was possible in China and other industrialized countries of East Asia. The experience of the successful East Asian countries shows that rapid industrialization, based on the expansion of labour-intensive manufactured exports in the early phase of development is crucial for employment generation and sustained poverty reduction (Islam 2008).

Drawing upon the experience of China's export success in manufacturing, this chapter attempts to provide explanations for India's lacklustre performance. The chapter highlights certain idiosyncrasies pertaining to the pattern of specialization, structure of trade, and the nature of inward foreign direct investment in Indian manufacturing.

The remainder of the chapter is organized as follows. The next section briefly discusses the relative contribution of the manufacturing sector to aggregate GDP and merchandise exports in India and China. As shown by the Heckscher–Ohlin model, the workhorse of international economics, a country's export structure is intrinsically linked to its relative factor endowments. Therefore, in order to put the empirical analysis in perspective, the next section discusses trends in relative factor endowments (physical capital, arable land, human capital etc.) in the two countries. In the section that follows, we analyse the changes in the commodity pattern of exports and interpret the findings in light of the observed changes in relative factor endowments in the two countries. The next section discusses the extent to which India's manufacturing industries are linked to the vertically integrated global production networks. The next section deals with the geographical direction of manufacturing exports from India and China. Finally, the last section provides a conclusion and draws some policy implications.

RELATIVE CONTRIBUTION OF THE MANUFACTURING SECTOR TO GDP AND EXPORTS

The decade-wise average growth rates of GDP across sectors in India and China during the period 1970–2010 are depicted in Figures 9.1 and 9.2 respectively. It is clear that throughout the period the service sector was the fastest growing sector in the Indian economy followed by industry. A similar trend can be observed in China during the 1970s and 1980s, but industry emerged as the fastest growing sector in that country during the more recent decades of the 1990s and the 2000s.

During the period 1950–2 to 1964–6, India's registered manufacturing output grew at a rate of about 5 per cent per annum, which is substantially below the growth rates recorded by a number of other comparable countries (Brazil, Mexico, Pakistan, Philippines, and Taiwan) during this period (Little et al. 1970). The years since the early 1970s witnessed some improvement with a growth rate of 6 per cent per annum for 1973–2003, but the trend growth rate during the post-1991 reform period showed little change (Gupta et al. 2010). Overall, this growth performance is respectable, but pales in comparison with the performance recorded by East Asian NIEs and China (Weiss 2011). During 2000–10, manufacturing GDP grew at a rate of 8.7 per cent per annum in India while it grew at a much higher rate of 11.6 per cent in China.

The major contrasts between the economies of India and China are clearly evident in Table 9.1, which presents the

---

[1] Predicted shares are calculated from a cross-country regression of manufacturing shares on GDP per capita, GDP per capita squared, population and foreign trade to GDP ratio. For 2000, the predicted shares are about 20 and 27 per cent respectively for India and China while the actual shares are 16 per cent for India and 35 per cent for China (ADB 2007: 294).

[2] That India's manufacturing growth followed a relatively capital-intensive path is evident from the much smaller growth rate of employment than capital stock and value added. During 1973–2003, registered manufacturing employment grew slowly (1.3 per cent per annum) while capital stock grew faster (7.3 per cent per annum) than manufacturing value added (6 per cent) (see Gupta et al. 2010).

[3] Typically, employment in manufacturing only requires on-the-job training whereas employment in formal service sectors (such as banking, insurance, finance, communications, and information technology) requires at least college-level education.

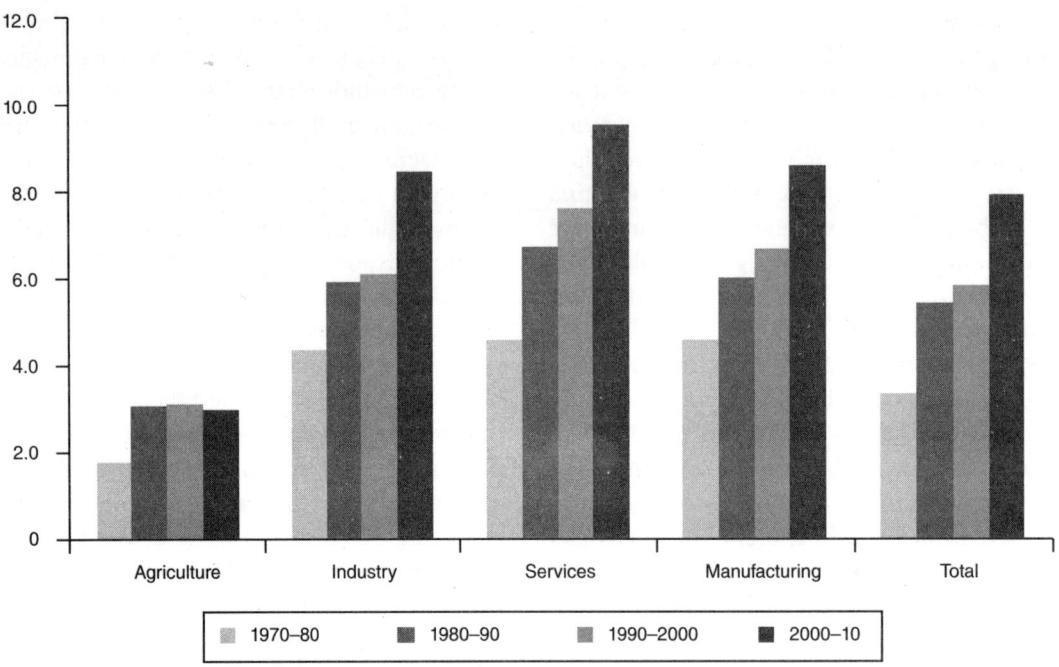

Figure 9.1 Average Annual Growth Rates across Sectors, India, 1970–2010
Source: *World Development Indicators*, The World Bank.

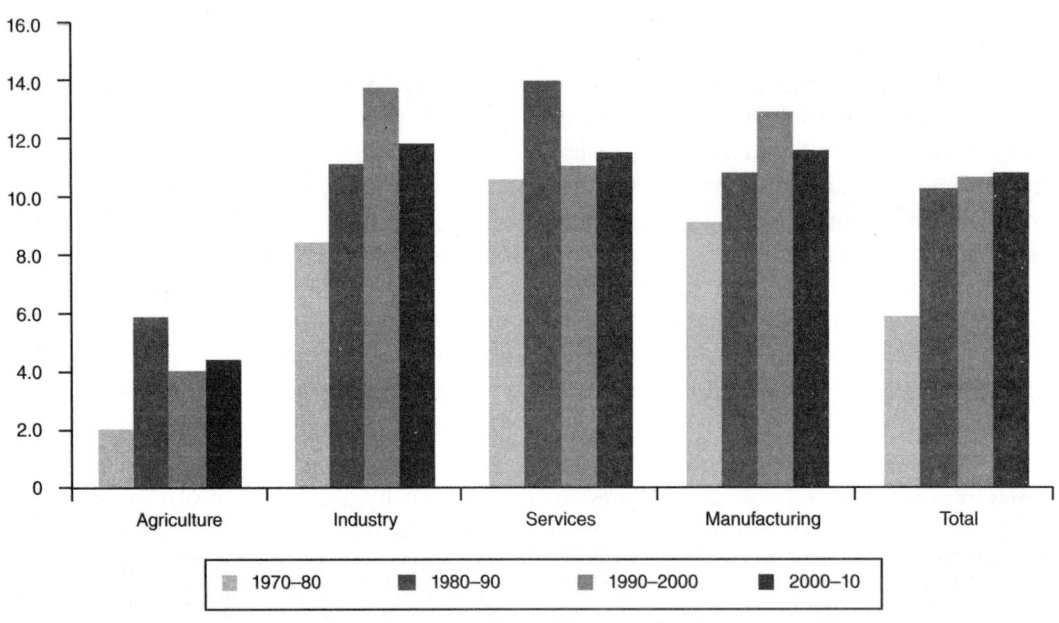

Figure 9.2 Average Annual Growth Rates across Sectors, China, 1970–2010
Source: *World Development Indicators*, The World Bank.

sectoral composition of GDP in the two countries. In contrast to China, where the industrial sector always accounted for the largest share of GDP, services held the dominant share in India's GDP (except in 1970 when agriculture was the leading sector). As one would expect, the share of agriculture declined with growth in both the countries. The share of manufacturing in India's GDP virtually remained constant in the range of 14–17 per cent during 1970–2010. During the same period, manufactures' share in China's GDP was in the much higher range of 30–40 per cent. In 2010, manufacturing accounted for about 14 per cent of India's GDP while its share was 30 per cent for China.

Table 9.1 Sectoral Composition of GDP (% shares)

	India					China				
	1970	1980	1990	2000	2010	1970	1980	1990	2000	2010
Agriculture	42.3	35.7	29.3	23.4	19.0	35.2	30.2	27.1	15.1	10.1
Services	36.9	39.6	43.8	50.5	54.7	24.3	21.6	31.5	39.0	43.1
Industry	20.8	24.7	26.9	26.2	26.3	40.5	48.2	41.3	45.9	46.8
of which Manufacturing	14.2	16.7	16.7	15.6	14.2	33.7	40.2	32.7	32.1	29.6
Total	100	100	100	100	100	100	100	100	100	100

Source: World Development Indicators, The World Bank.

Table 9.2 Sectoral Composition of Employment (% shares)

	India				China					
	1994	2000	2005	2010	1980	1990	1994	2000	2005	2008
Agriculture	61.9	59.8	55.8	51.1	68.7	60.1	54.3	50.0	44.8	39.6
Services	22.4	24.1	25.2	26.5	13.1	18.5	23.0	27.5	31.3	33.2
Industry	15.7	16.1	19.0	22.4	18.2	21.4	22.7	22.5	23.8	27.2

Source: Key Indicators of the labour market, ILO.

While services and industry accounted for the largest shares of output in India and China respectively, agriculture contributed to the largest share of employment in both the countries (Table 9.2). However, consistent with its declining share in GDP, workers moved out of agriculture, but the decline in the share of employment in agriculture was much larger for China. Agriculture's share in employment declined from 62 per cent in 1994 to 51 per cent in 2010 in India while it declined faster, from 54 per cent in 1994 to 40 per cent in 2008, in China.[4] The contributions of the industrial and service sectors in total employment was higher for China than for India.

Since manufacturing output is far more tradable than services, India's low share of manufacturing output resulted in a low trade to GDP ratio. Thus, exports of goods and services as a percentage of GDP was much lower for India (average of 21 per cent for 2006–10) compared with China (average of 34 per cent for 2006–10). Likewise, as Panagariya (2007: 234) noted 'in labour-abundant economies such as China and India, the direct foreign investment is attracted principally to the manufacturing sector to take advantage of lower wages'. Thus, India's low share of manufacturing output also means less foreign direct investment (FDI). Hence, the differences in the share of manufacturing output are part of the explanation for why China is able to attract much higher inward FDI flows compared with India.[5]

Figure 9.3 shows the changes in the share of manufacturing in total merchandise exports. It is interesting to note that during the 1980s, manufacturing accounted for a higher share of India's export than that of China's. However, this pattern got reversed since the early 1990s, with the share of manufacturing in China's exports showing steady increases and remaining considerably higher than that of India's. In 2010, manufacturing constituted about 94 per cent of China's merchandise exports while the similar figure for India was 63 per cent.

Table 9.3 reports the average annual growth rates for different categories of exports—manufacturing, non-manufacturing, and services—for India, China, and the world. Compared to the previous two decade of the 1980s and 1990s, India's total exports (merchandise plus services) grew at a faster rate of 22 per cent per annum during the first decade of the 21st century, matching the growth rates of China for the first time. During 2000–10, India's service exports registered a higher growth rate than China's while India's merchandise exports registered a lower growth rate.

---

[4] It is likely that China's statistics significantly overestimate its employment share in agriculture because a significant proportion of migrant workers employed in cities may be reporting their occupation as agriculture.

[5] Inward FDI inflows as a percentage of GDP was 2.5 per cent for India (average for the period 2006–10) while the corresponding figure was nearly 4 per cent for China (estimated from *World Development Indicators*, The World Bank).

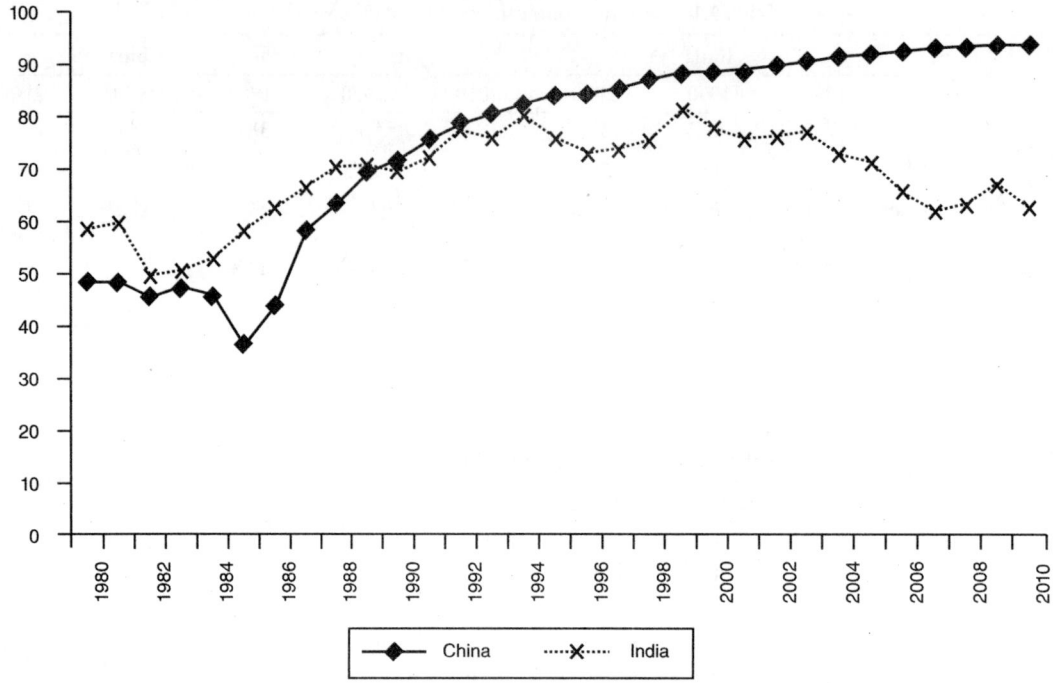

Figure 9.3 Share of Manufacturing in Total Merchandise Exports

Source: Estimated from the WTO database.

Table 9.3 Average Annual Growth Rates of Exports, Values in US$

	Merchandise		Total Merchandise	Services	Total Merchandise plus Services
	Manufactures	Non-manufactures			
India					
1980–90	10.6	2.1	7.3	4.7	6.7
1990–2000	10.2	7.1	9.5	13.8	10.5
2000–10	17.1	27.1	20.0	26.0	21.9
China					
1980–90	17.8	6.1	12.8	11.6*	14.4*
1990–2000	16.7	4.8	14.5	18.2	14.8
2000–10	23.2	14.6	22.4	20.3	22.2
World					
1980–90	9.2	0.8	5.9	8.0	6.3
1990–2000	7.4	5.1	6.8	6.8	6.8
2000–10	9.4	14.2	10.9	11.5	11.0

Note: * For the period 1982–90.

Source: Estimated from the WTO database.

Within the merchandise sector, India recorded a lower growth rate than China in manufacturing exports while the opposite was true for non-manufacturing exports. In short, during the last one decade, services and non-manufactured exports grew faster in India than in China while manufactured exports continued to grow faster in China. It is remarkable that China is able to sustain rapid growth despite the fact that its base export value today is about seven times higher than that of India.

Figures 9.4 and 9.5 show the changes in the world market shares of India and China in different categories of exports. India accounted for a meagre 0.5 per cent or less in total

PERFORMANCE OF INDIA'S MANUFACTURED EXPORTS 137

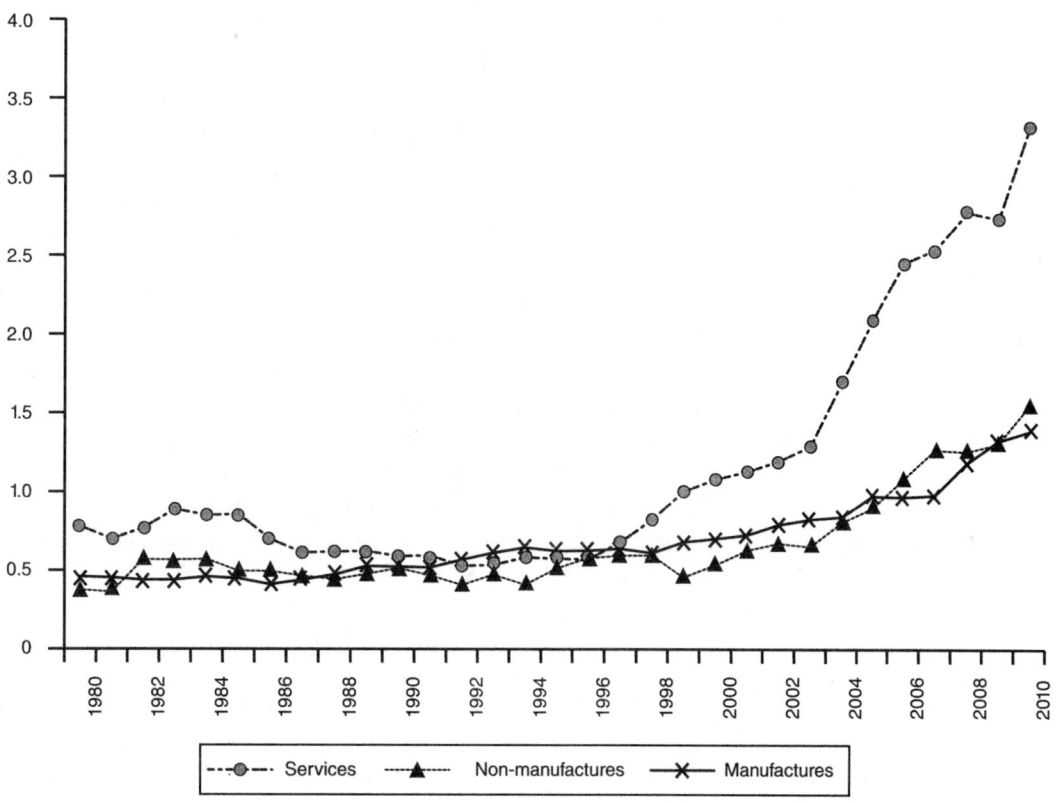

Figure 9.4 World Market Shares of Exports, India

Source: Estimated from the WTO database.

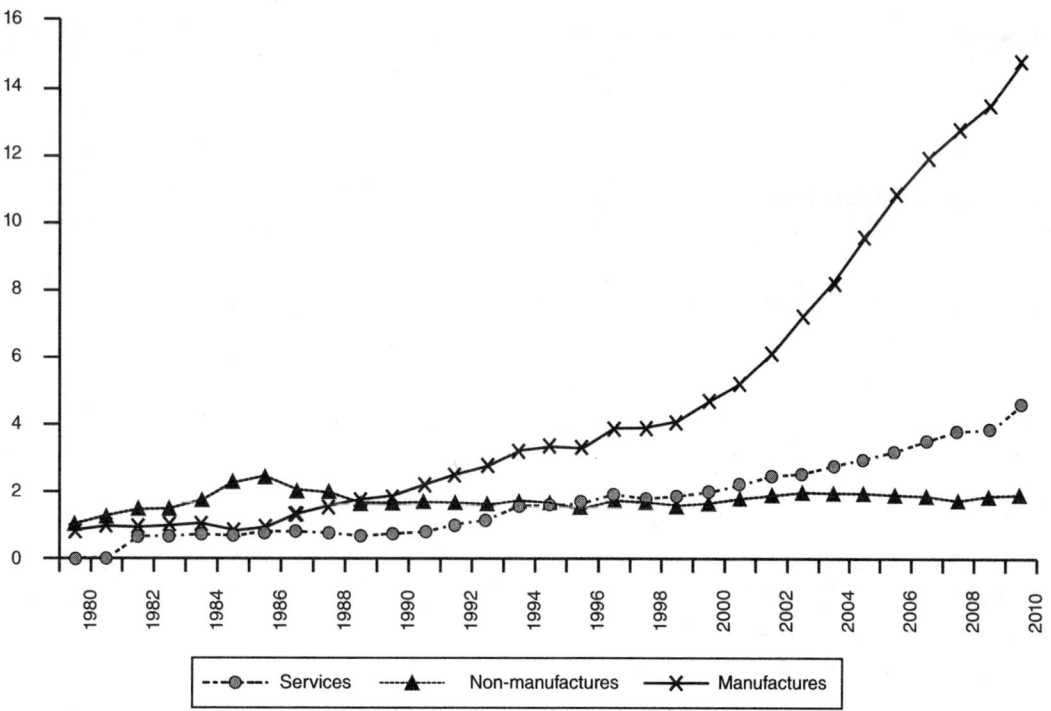

Figure 9.5 World Market Shares of Exports, China

Source: Estimated from the WTO database.

world exports of manufactured products during the 1980s, which increased marginally to 0.6 per cent in 1992 and remained at that level until 1998 before showing a relatively faster increase during the 2000s. In 2010, India accounted for 1.4 per cent of world exports of manufactures while China's share was a whopping 15 per cent. China's shares were higher than India's in services and non-manufactures as well, but the difference was not noticeably high as in the case of manufactured exports.

RELATIVE FACTOR ENDOWMENTS

The Heckscher–Ohlin model of international trade explains the specialization patterns of countries based on their relative factor endowments. According to this model, a country will specialize in and export products that are intensive in the use of the factor that is abundant in that country. Thus, for example, a country with an abundant supply of labour has a comparative advantage in labour-intensive products. In order to put the empirical analysis that follows in perspective, this section analyses the available data on relative factor endowments in India and China.

Tables 9.4 and 9.5 compare the relative endowment of physical capital, human capital, and arable land in India and China. Based on the availability of data, the periods covered in these tables are: 1961 to 2003 in Table 9.4 and 1960 to 2010 in Table 9.5. The tables also report the mean relative endowments of four groups of countries classified according to income: low income, lower-middle income (excluding India and China), upper-middle income, and high-income Organization for Economic Corporation and Development (OECD). It is evident that physical capital and skilled labour are relatively scarce in both India and China compared to upper-middle income and high-income countries. Even compared to the group of lower-middle income countries, India was capital scarce throughout the period and China was capital scarce till the early 2000s.

In 1970 and 1980, India recorded a slightly higher value of capital stock per worker than China. However, during the subsequent years, China's physical capital endowment

Table 9.4 Relative Endowments

	1961	1970	1980	1990	2003
Physical capital stock per worker					
India	1,398	2,058	2,735	3,679	5,883
China	1,682	1,626	2,571	4,709	14,386
Low-income countries	2,438	2,519	2,974	2,677	2,641
Lower middle-income countries	7,539	9,574	13,184	14,271	13,909
Upper middle-income countries	19,139	21,951	25,602	24,073	29,113
High-income OECD	39,775	58,825	79,743	92,487	111,968
Human capital (average years of schooling)					
India	1.46	1.90	2.71	3.68	4.77
China	2.80	3.18	3.61	5.23	5.74
Low-income countries	0.78	0.98	1.43	2.04	2.57
Lower middle-income countries	2.22	2.42	3.17	4.15	5.08
Upper middle-income countries	3.40	3.84	4.88	5.91	6.81
High-income OECD	6.40	6.97	8.15	8.86	9.51
Arable land hectares per worker					
India	0.77	0.67	0.54	0.45	0.36
China	0.30	0.24	0.18	0.18	0.18
Low-income countries	1.43	1.13	0.78	0.65	0.58
Lower middle-income countries	1.18	1.00	0.86	0.66	0.53
Upper middle-income countries	1.10	1.08	0.85	0.69	0.57
High-income OECD	1.46	1.33	1.04	0.92	0.75

Note: China and India are excluded from the group of lower middle-income countries; simple averages are calculated for income groups.
Source: Cadot et al. (2009).

Table 9.5 Educational Attainment

	1960	1970	1980	1990	2000	2010
No schooling						
India	72.1	66.2	66.3	51.6	43.0	32.7
China	58.3	41.9	27.1	22.2	11	6.5
Korea	42.6	24.3	13.1	11.4	5.9	3.6
Low-income countries	73.4	67.6	59.6	49.9	42.3	34.6
Lower middle-income countries*	56.0	47.8	37.8	30.5	24.0	18.2
Upper middle-income countries	38.4	30.1	21.9	15.0	10.0	6.8
High-income OECD	8.0	6.2	4.7	4.5	3.7	2.6
Primary education						
India	24.8	27.1	12.6	18.7	19.7	20.9
China	28.7	36.9	38.4	34.5	30.4	24.1
Korea	36.9	39.1	28	22	11.8	9.4
Low-income countries	21.4	24.2	26.5	30.6	33.5	35.6
Lower middle-income countries*	31.0	33.8	35.1	35.2	35.8	33.0
Upper middle-income countries	46.7	47.2	43.3	38.1	31.3	25.7
High-income OECD	63.4	54.0	43.3	35.6	25.7	19.0
Secondary education						
India	2.5	5.6	18.7	25.6	32.9	40.7
China	12.3	20.3	33.6	41.3	54.1	60.4
Korea	17.8	30.8	49.8	47.8	52	46.8
Low-income countries	4.5	7.3	12.4	17.4	21.8	26.7
Lower middle-income countries*	11.4	16.2	23.3	28.8	32.9	39.7
Upper middle-income countries	13.0	19.7	29.8	39.0	48.2	53.8
High-income OECD	23.9	33.0	41.5	45.1	51.2	55.4
Tertiary education						
India	0.6	1.1	2.3	4	4.5	5.8
China	0.7	0.8	0.9	1.9	4.6	9
Korea	2.6	5.8	9.1	18.8	30.2	40.1
Low-income countries	0.7	0.9	1.5	2.1	2.4	3.2
Lower middle-income countries*	1.7	2.3	3.9	5.5	7.1	9.1
Upper middle-income countries	1.9	3.0	5.1	8.0	10.6	13.7
High-income OECD	4.6	6.8	10.5	14.8	19.4	23.1
Per capita income (constant 2000 US$)						
India	145	214	229	318	453	823
China	105	122	186	392	949	2425

Note: *China and India are excluded from the group of lower middle-income countries; simple averages are calculated for income groups.
Source: Barro and Lee (2010).

was much higher than that of India's, which was expected due to the faster economic growth in the former compared to the latter since the early 1980s. As expected, the average years of schooling in both India and China were much below the level in high-income OECD and upper-middle income countries. Compared to the lower-middle income countries, the average years of schooling were better in China but worse in India.

Highly skilled workers, that is, those with more than a secondary education were relatively scarce in both India and China. In 2010, about 23 per cent of the population in high-income OECD countries and about 14 per cent in upper-middle income countries had attained tertiary education while these figures in China and India were about 9 per cent and 6 per cent respectively. The attainment of tertiary education in India was less than the mean attainment ratio in lower-middle income countries. In terms of secondary level education, China consistently ranked above India and other lower-middle income countries. In 2010, about 60 per cent of the population in China and 41 per cent of the population in India had attained secondary-level education.

In terms of population without schooling, India has always been similar to the low-income economies. In 2010, about 33 per cent of India's population was without schooling compared to 6.5 per cent in China. Thus, unskilled labour, defined as those with no schooling, is more abundant in India as compared to China. The pattern remains the same even if unskilled labour is instead defined as those with no schooling or with only primary attainment. More than half of India's population had either no schooling or only primary attainment while 70 per cent of China's population had attained education either till the secondary level or above. In addition to being relatively skill and capital scarce, India and China are relatively land scarce compared to other countries (Table 9.4). However, land is relatively abundant in India than in China.

In sum, compared to high-income and middle-income countries, physical capital, skilled labour, and land are relatively scarce both in India and China but unskilled labour is relatively abundant. This is particularly true for India than for China. Therefore, it is beyond doubt that the true comparative advantage of India would lie in industries that intensively use unskilled labour rather than physical capital and skilled labour. For the more recent years, based on relative factor endowments, India's comparative advantage in unskilled labour-intensive goods appears particularly strong compared to China's.

PATTERN OF EXPORT SPECIALIZATION

Accumulation of factor endowments, such as human and physical capital, that characterize economic growth can bring about a dynamic process of changing comparative advantages. For example, the road to export success of the Newly Industrialized Countries (NICs) in Asia started with labour-intensive and low technology manufactures. However, as investments in physical and human capital rose and as labour costs increased with the accumulation of skills, relatively more sophisticated manufacturing activities expanded in these countries at the expense of traditional labour-intensive manufactures. This pattern of initial specialization in labour-intensive activities followed by a move up the ladder of comparative advantage, as relative resource endowments change, is precisely the sequence envisaged in the 'stages of comparative advantage' thesis postulated by Balassa (1977).

In the light of the observed differences in relative factor endowments between India and China at given points in time and their changes over time, as shown above, we now analyse the commodity pattern of exports from the two countries. We are particularly interested in assessing the extent of congruence between the evolution of relative factor endowments and commodity specialization in the two countries.

In order to view the dynamics of specialization through the lens of the Heckscher–Ohlin model, we classify traded products according to factor intensities. First, using relatively aggregate data at the one and two-digit level of the Standard International Trade Classification (SITC), we classify products into two broad categories: labour-intensive and capital-intensive. Second, using the factor intensity classification of the International Trade Centre (ITC), adapted by Hinloopen and van Marrewijk (2008), we classify the traded products into five specific categories: natural resource-intensive, unskilled labour-intensive, human capital-intensive, technology-intensive, and unclassified. The latter classification makes use of data disaggregated at the three-digit level of SITC (Revision 2).[6]

Based on the aggregate classification scheme mentioned above, the shares of different commodity groups in the export baskets of the two countries are shown in Table 9.6. It is evident that throughout the period 1962–92, labour-intensive products accounted for more than three-fourths of both India and China's total manufacturing exports. Between 1992 and 2008, however, the share of labour-intensive products declined from 78 per cent to 47 per cent in China while it declined from 84 per cent to 63 per cent in India.

World market shares of the two countries in different broad groups of commodities are shown in Table 9.7. It is evident that India's world market share in labour-intensive products was higher than China's in 1962. India's share declined from 1.6 per cent in 1962 to 0.9 in 1972. In 1982,

---

[6] The classification is available at: (http://www2.econ.uu.nl/users/marrewijk/eta/intensity.htm, accessed on 15 October 2011). A total of 240 items, at the three-digit SITC level, have been grouped into five categories (number of items in each category in parentheses): primary (83), natural resource-intensive (21), unskilled labour–intensive (26), human capital-intensive (43), technology-intensive (62), and unclassified (5). For our purpose, we define an additional category, called the capital-intensive category, by adding human capital-intensive and technology-intensive categories.

Table 9.6 Composition of Exports

	Labour-intensive					Capital-intensive			
	Resource-based Products (SITC 6)	Textile (SITC 65)	Misc. Manufacturing (SITC 8)	Clothing & Footwear (SITC 84+85)	Total (SITC 6+8)	Chemicals (SITC 5)	Machinery (SITC 71+72)	Transport Equipment (SITC 73)	Total (SITC 5+7)
1962									
India	89.4	73.4	4.8	2.9	94.2	3.4	2	0.3	5.7
China	79.6	39.4	10.5	5.4	90.1	8	1.3	0.7	10
1972									
India	80.3	47.8	9	5.7	89.3	3.3	5.2	2.3	10.8
China	57.5	35	25.8	12.5	83.3	11.5	4	1.2	16.7
1982									
India	57.5	19.1	27	20.2	84.5	3.6	7.3	4.6	15.5
China	42.3	24.6	39.2	25.8	81.5	11.8	5.7	1	18.5
1992									
India	52.2	17.5	31.8	25	84	8.1	5.4	2.5	16
China	17.9	9.2	59.6	31.8	77.5	4.3	16.9	1.2	22.4
2002									
India	48	14.3	24.8	16.2	72.8	16.1	8.8	2.4	27.3
China	14.2	4.7	44.7	17	58.9	3.6	36.1	1.5	41.2
2008									
India	43.1	8.1	19.4	11.6	62.5	18.4	14.8	4.2	37.4
China	16.3	3.2	30.7	11.1	47	5.2	45.4	2.4	53

Source: Estimated from COMTRADE-WITS using partner country import records (mirror exports).

China accounted for over 2 per cent of the world exports of labour-intensive products, while India's share was below 0.9 per cent. China's share increased dramatically to about 8 per cent in 1992, 15 per cent in 2002, and to a whopping 20 per cent in 2008 while India's share increased marginally to about 2 per cent by 2008. In 2008, China accounted for 41 per cent of the world exports of clothing and footwear, while India's share was a mere 3 per cent. China also recorded a significant increase in its world market share of capital-intensive products, particularly machinery. China's share in the total world exports of machinery items increased from almost zero to as high as 20 per cent in 2008. By contrast, India's market share in machinery was a mere 0.5 per cent.

Table 9.8 reports the commodity composition of the two country's exports according to the more detailed factor intensity classification. Panel A shows the shares of the various factor intensity categories within aggregate merchandise exports while panel B shows the results for manufactured exports. A steady increase in the share of technology-intensive products (within aggregate merchandise as well as manufacturing) is a trend that is common for both India and China. This trend, however, is more pronounced for China than for India: the share of technology-intensive products in India's manufactured exports increased from 10 per cent in 1980 to 33 per cent in 2010 while it increased from 17 per cent to as high as 57 per cent for China. Between 1980 and 2010, the share of human capital-intensive goods in India's manufactured exports increased from 14 per cent to 21 per cent while it declined from 19 per cent to 16 per cent for China.

In 1980, consistent with the two countries comparative advantages, unskilled labour-intensive goods constituted the largest share of manufacturing exports both in India (49 per cent) and China (58 per cent). However, the share of this category declined significantly in both the countries in subsequent years, with the latest share being 22 per cent in India and 25 per cent in China. It must be noted that though the share of unskilled labour activities declined in both the countries, the decline occurred from a much higher starting point for China than for India. This decline in the share of the unskilled labour-intensive category is broadly consistent with the steady decline in the endowment of

Table 9.7 World Market Shares

	Labour-intensive					Capital-intensive			
	Resource-based Products (SITC 6)	Textile (SITC 65)	Misc. Manu-facturing (SITC 8)	Clothing & Footwear (SITC 84+85)	Total (SITC 6+8)	Chemicals (SITC 5)	Machinery (SITC 71+72)	Transport Equipment (SITC 73)	Total (SITC 5+7)
1962									
China	1.03	2.33	0.48	0.80	0.91	0.33	0.02	0.03	0.09
India	1.89	7.07	0.36	0.71	1.55	0.23	0.06	0.02	0.09
1972									
China	0.93	2.69	0.90	1.31	0.92	0.48	0.07	0.04	0.15
India	1.17	3.31	0.28	0.54	0.89	0.12	0.09	0.07	0.09
1982									
China	1.80	6.08	2.71	5.41	2.15	1.00	0.22	0.07	0.35
India	0.94	1.80	0.71	1.61	0.85	0.12	0.11	0.12	0.11
1992									
China	3.42	8.82	12.49	20.08	7.75	1.40	2.18	0.31	1.53
India	1.28	2.16	0.85	2.02	1.08	0.34	0.09	0.09	0.14
2002									
China	7.42	14.60	23.47	29.81	15.43	2.40	9.37	0.96	5.98
India	2.19	3.86	1.14	2.46	1.67	0.93	0.20	0.13	0.34
2008									
China	12.72	24.00	29.97	40.59	20.39	5.01	19.64	2.82	12.61
India	2.63	4.73	1.48	3.32	2.12	1.39	0.50	0.39	0.70

Source: Estimated from COMTRADE-WITS using partner country import records (mirror exports).

unskilled labour (that is, those with either no schooling or just primary education) in both the countries (see Table 9.5). Similarly, the increase in the share of capital-intensive goods (that is, the combined share of technology and human capital-intensive goods) is consistent with the increase in the endowment of physical capital per worker and skilled labour in both the countries.

Overall, the evolution of industrial specialization in India and China seems consistent with the changes in their relative endowments. However, a comparison of the trajectories in the two countries brings out the fact that industrial specialization in India is disproportionately biased towards capital- and skill-intensive industries than in China (also see Krueger 2010; Kochhar et al. 2006; Panagariya 2008). The following observations make this argument clearer.

First, between 1980 and 2010 both the countries experienced an equal rate of decline in the share of unskilled labour-intensive goods in exports (that is, about 56 per cent) though the corresponding decline in the share of unskilled labour in the total workforce was faster in China (53 per cent) than in India (32 per cent). Thus, compared to China the extent of decline in the share of unskilled labour-intensive goods in India's exports seems disproportionately higher. Second, during the same period, the share of capital-intensive goods in India's exports more than doubled from 24 per cent to 54 per cent while it increased less rapidly from 37 per cent to 73 per cent in China. In contrast, the endowment of physical capital stock per worker increased significantly faster in China (from $2,571 in 1980 to $14,386 in 2010) than in India (from $2,735 to $5,883 in 2010). Thus, compared to China, the extent of increase in the share of capital-intensive goods in India's exports is disproportionally higher than what would be explained by the growth in the endowment of physical capital stock per worker.

Third, a recent study, using finely disaggregated 10-digit-level US bilateral import data, has shown that India's export bundle to the US is becoming increasingly more similar to that of the high-income OECD countries (Veeramani and

Table 9.8 Export Composition according to Factor Intensity Classification

	India					China				
	1980	1990	2000	2005	2010	1980	1990	2000	2005	2010
Panel A: Total Merchandise										
Primary	38.7	28.5	20.7	23.2	30.1	51.4	19.4	7.3	4.9	3.6
Natural resource-intensive	16.2	24.3	20.0	20.0	17.5	3.4	2.9	3.1	3.3	2.6
Unskilled labour-intensive	30.2	30.6	29.1	20.0	14.3	27.8	46.5	39.3	28.2	24.4
Capital-intensive	14.8	16.5	30.1	35.2	35.4	17.3	31.1	49.3	63.6	69.3
human capital-intensive	8.5	9.1	14.0	16.8	13.8	9.2	15.5	14.4	15.6	14.9
technology-intensive	6.3	7.4	16.1	18.4	21.6	8.1	15.6	35.9	48.0	54.4
Unclassified	0.0	0.0	0.0	1.7	2.7	0.1	0.0	0.0	0.0	0.0
Total	100	100	100	100	100	100	100	100	100	100
Panel B: Manufacturing										
Natural resource-intensive	26.3	33.5	24.3	24.3	24.3	5.3	2.6	2.4	2.4	1.8
Unskilled labour-intensive	49.4	43.2	37.2	27.4	21.8	58.3	58.3	42.8	30.0	25.5
Capital-intensive	24.3	23.3	38.5	48.2	54.0	36.5	39.0	54.8	67.5	72.6
human capital-intensive	14.0	12.8	17.9	23.0	21.1	19.4	19.5	15.7	16.5	15.6
technology-intensive	10.3	10.5	20.6	25.2	32.9	17.1	19.5	39.1	51.0	57.0
Total	100	100	100	100	100	100	100	100	100	100

Note: Shares of the capital-intensive category have been obtained by adding the shares of human capital-intensive and technology-intensive categories.

Source: Estimated from COMTRADE-WITS using partner country import records (mirror exports) and the factor intensity classification of ITC, adapted by Hinloopen and van Marrewijk (2008).

Saini 2011).[7] It has been noticed that in a majority of the cases, the 10-digit-level export unit values of India in the US market are higher than that of China. The higher export unit values of India may reflect its undue specialization in capital- and skill-intensive varieties and production process. For, it may be argued that, the higher the level of capital and skill embodied in a variety/product line, the higher the price (unit value) that it commands in export markets.[8]

Finally, as discussed in detail in the next section, there are strong reasons to believe that Tables 9.6 and 9.8 overestimate the share of capital-intensive exports and underestimate the share of labour-intensive exports for both the countries, but significantly more so for China than for India. In other words, it is likely that the actual share of labour-intensive exports was much bigger than what is shown in Tables 9.6 and 9.8 for China while this discrepancy was relatively smaller for India.

GLOBAL PRODUCTION NETWORKS AND VERTICAL SPECIALIZATION

China's export promotion policies since the 1990s have relied heavily on a strategy of integrating its domestic industries with global production networks. Global production networks refer to the links between a lead or a key firm and its suppliers in different countries (Weiss 2011). In certain industries, such as electronics and automobiles, technology makes it possible to sub-divide the production process into discrete stages. In such industries, the fragmentation of the production process into smaller and more specialized components allows firms to locate parts of the production in countries where intensively used resources are available at lower costs.

A high level of fragmentation- (vertical specialization) based trade, which occurs when countries specialize in particular stages of a good's production sequence rather

---

[7] Specifically, an export similarity index (ESI), which captures the extent of product structure overlap between India and the high-income OECD countries has been computed using finely disaggregated (10-digit-level) US bilateral import data. The rationale behind the use of ESI is the idea that the OECD countries hold comparative advantages in products that are most sophisticated and, therefore, an increase in the value of ESI would imply catching up by India with the OECD (Schott 2008).

[8] A higher price that results from 'distorted' specialization, however, does not translate into an overall higher volume of exports.

than in the entire good, has been an important factor in driving the East Asian export growth (Athukorala 2012; Athukorala and Yamashita 2006). This type of trade is the result of increasing inter-connected production processes that form a vertical trading chain stretching across many countries, with each country specializing according to factor intensities involved at the different stages in production. Labour-abundant countries like China tend to specialize in low skilled labour-intensive activities involved in the production of a final good while the capital and skill-intensive activities are carried out in countries where those factors are abundant. Thus, international firms might retain skill- and knowledge-intensive stages of production (such as R&D and marketing) in the high-income headquarters (for example, the US, EU, and Japan) but locate all or parts of their production in a low wage country (for example, China or Vietnam).

The major driving forces behind the steadily increasing vertical specialization-based trade during the last two decades include: (i) world-wide reduction of tariff barriers, (ii) spatial inter-dependence and production sharing of multinational firms, and (iii) expansion of transportation and communication networks.

A manifestation of China's participation in global production networks is the growing importance of machinery items in its export basket (see Tables 9.6 and 9.7). In 2008, machinery contributed about 45 per cent of Chinese exports and China accounted for about 20 per cent of the world exports in this product category. The fast growth of China's machinery exports has been driven by its high degree of integration with regional and global production networks (Athukorala 2012).

In particular, based on imported parts and components, China has emerged as a global hub for electrical and electronic goods assembly. Typically, China imports the parts and components from other parts of East Asia and exports the finished goods to the US and Europe. Since this strategy involves processing or assembly of imported parts and components, the net domestic value added *per unit* of the exported good is generally not very high. However, since the scale of operations is usually very large, the *total* domestic value addition from these activities is considerably high, contributing to employment generation for a large number of migrant workers in China.

Though, machinery as a whole may be considered as a capital-intensive category, certain stages of production or tasks (such as low-end assembly activities) within this category are highly labour-intensive. The data disaggregated at the three-digit level does not fully capture these heterogeneities. The calculations shown in Table 9.8 ignore the fact that within the three-digit industries, that are grouped under the capital-intensive category, China largely specializes in process and product lines that are mainly labour-intensive. Therefore, Tables 9.6 and 9.8 may significantly overestimate the shares of capital-intensive exports and underestimate the shares of labour-intensive exports from China. This discrepancy, however, is likely to be smaller for India since it remains a minor player in fragmentation-based trade.

A proxy variable for measuring the intensity of vertical specialization-based trade is the share of parts and components (henceforth referred to as 'components' for brevity) in total manufacturing trade. Based on estimates by Athukorala (2012), Table 9.9 reports the components shares for India, China, and several other countries for two time points, 1992–3 and 2006–7. That a growing share of world trade is based on vertical specialization and fragmentation is evident from the fact that the share of components in world manufacturing exports increased sharply from 19 per cent in 1992–3 to 27 per cent in 2006–7. This share increased at a much faster rate in developing Asian countries, from 17 per cent to 34 per cent.

Table 9.9 Share of Parts and Components in Manufacturing Trade (%)

	Exports		Imports	
	1992–3	2006–7	1992–3	2006–7
Developing Asia	17.3	34.0	29.0	44.2
China, PR	7.4	25.6	20.4	44.0
Hong Kong SAR	15.8	33.3	24.1	48.5
Taiwan	24.7	44.2	29.5	38.9
Korea, RP	18.1	47.3	30.1	31.9
ASEAN 6	22.7	44.2	36.0	47.9
Indonesia	3.8	21.5	27.0	21.8
Malaysia	27.7	53.6	40.5	50.0
Philippines	32.9	71.7	32.6	61.3
Singapore	29.0	49.3	39.9	60.4
Thailand	14.1	29.9	30.6	36.1
Vietnam	—	11.0	—	19.1
India	3.0	10.4	17.5	22.9
Memo items				
East Asia	20.2	34.1	27.2	42.1
Japan	23.9	34.4	19.3	29.9
NAFTA	28.4	31.2	37.4	28.8
EU 15	18.3	22.4	21.2	23.2
World	19.3	27.1	19.6	27.3

Note: shares for 1992–3 have been computed using the average trade values for the years 1992 and 1993 and analogously for 2006–7.

Source: Athukorala (2012).

For China, the components share in exports increased from 7 per cent to 26 per cent and its share in imports increased from 20 per cent to 44 per cent between 1992–3 and 2006–7. That the components share in China's manufacturing imports (44 per cent in 2006–7) was much larger than the corresponding share in its exports (26 per cent) is consistent with our earlier observation that China has emerged as a global hub for the final assembly activities in manufacturing.[9]

Despite its intrinsic comparative advantage in unskilled labour-intensive activities, India still remains a minor player in global production networks and vertical specialization-based trade. Table 9.9 reveals that India's components share, both in exports and imports, was much lower than the world average and the corresponding shares for all the regional groups and all the individual countries in Asia (with the exception of Indonesia and Vietnam in the import share in 2006–7). The share of components in India's exports increased from a paltry 3 per cent in 1992–3 to 10 per cent in 2006–7 while the components share in its imports increased from about 18 per cent to 23 per cent.

Using input–output tables, Hummels et al. (2001) proposed an index of vertical specialization, which is defined as the share of imported intermediates embodied in a country's exports. This index for country k is given as:

$$VS_k = uA^M [I-A^D]^{-1} X/x_k,$$

where u is $1 \times n$ vector of 1's, A^M is the $n \times n$ imported coefficient matrix (share of imported intermediate goods in total inputs by n sectors), A^D is the $n \times n$ domestic coefficient matrix, I is the identity matrix, X is an $n \times 1$ vector of exports, x_k is a scalar that denotes the aggregate value of exports from country k and n is the number of sectors. The numerator of the above equation measures all the imported inputs that are needed to produce the exports of country k from all n sectors. Dividing this by the amount of aggregate exports yields the share of country k's exports attributable to imported inputs—that is, the share of foreign value added in exports. Recently, Koopman et al. (2010) have proposed a more comprehensive framework for measuring the foreign value added share of a country's exports taking into account the back-and-forth trade of intermediates across multiple borders.

OECD provides the estimates of the VS index for all the member countries as well as for selected non-member countries for three time points—the mid-1990s, early 2000s, and the mid-2000s. Table 9.10 reports the VS indices for India and other Asian countries for which OECD estimates are available. It is evident that the import content of India's manufactured exports increased from 13 per cent in the mid-1990s to 27 per cent in the mid-2000s. Between the same periods, this share increased from 17 per cent to 30 per cent in China. India's VS values were significantly lower (except for Indonesia in the mid-2000s) than other Asian countries shown in Table 9.10. The VS values were much above 40 per cent for Singapore, Taiwan, Thailand, Korea, and Vietnam.

Table 9.10 Vertical Specialization in Manufacturing across Selected Asian Countries (import content of exports), VS indices

	Manufactures		
	Mid-1990s	Early 2000s	Mid-2000s
China	0.17	0.21	0.30
India	0.13	0.17	0.27
Indonesia	0.23	0.28	0.23
Korea, RP	—	0.41	0.42
Singapore	0.69	0.70	—
Taiwan	0.40	0.43	0.55
Thailand	—	—	0.48
Vietnam	—	0.46	—

Source: OECD StatExtracts.

Using more detailed data, Dean et al. (2008) have estimated the VS index for China for 2002. Depending upon the definition used, they show that about 25 to 46 per cent of the value of China's total merchandise exports to the world was attributable to imported inputs, with some individual sectors accounting for as much as 52–95 per cent. In general, vertical specialization was much higher in China's manufacturing sector accounting for over 50 per cent in many industries, and is growing over time.[10]

About half of China's exports represent processing trade with no tariffs charged on intermediate imports. The estimates for 2004 by Koopman et al. (2010), using a more comprehensive framework, showed that the share of foreign value added in China's processing exports was as high as 57 per cent. This share in China's non-processing exports was only 15 per cent and hence the average share stood at 36 per cent. Their estimate for India was 20 per cent which is the lowest in Asia and below the world average (22 per cent).

---

[9] China imports the parts and components mostly from other parts of East Asia and exports the finished goods to the US and Europe. Therefore, China records long-run trade deficits with the former group and long-run trade surplus with the latter group.

[10] Another proxy for fragmentation-based trade is the Grubel-Lloyd index of intra-industry trade. Veeramani (2009) reports relatively lower levels of intra-industry trade for India compared to China in manufacturing (excluding diamonds and precious stones) during the period 1990–2005.

Vertical specialization is not a phenomenon restricted to East Asia alone. Between 1970 and 1990, growth in vertical specialization related exports accounted for about 30 per cent or more of the growth in overall exports of 10 OECD and four emerging market countries (Hummels et al. 2001).

Inward FDI was instrumental in integrating China's manufacturing with global vertical production chains. The bulk of the FDI flows to the manufacturing sector in China and other East Asian developing countries are vertical (export-promoting) in nature. Vertical FDI represents international fragmentation of the production process by multinationals, locating each stage of the production in the country where it can be done at the least cost. The contribution of foreign-funded enterprises in total Chinese exports steadily increased from less than 9 per cent in 1989 to 55 per cent in 2010.[11]

In contrast, inward FDI into India was primarily horizontal (domestic market seeking) rather than vertical. FDI was much less important in driving India's export growth, accounting for less than 10 per cent of manufacturing exports. A recent OECD Investment Policy Review for India observes: 'despite the government's intention of promoting export-oriented FDI projects, the main objective of foreign investment in India was domestic market seeking and foreign-invested enterprises were characterised by a generally poor export performance, though no less poor than their domestic counterparts' (OECD 2009: 31). Krueger (2010: 424) notes that '… India has not succeeded in attracting foreign investors to use India as an export platform in many of the unskilled-labour intensive industries that have been attracted to east and southeast Asia.'

China, through specialization in labour-intensive processes, tasks, and product lines, has successfully integrated its manufacturing sector with global production networks. In contrast, India has been locked out of the vertically integrated global supply chains in manufacturing industries mainly because the country's incentive structures are not in alignment with its comparative advantage in unskilled labour-intensive activities. We elaborate on this in the concluding section.

GEOGRAPHICAL DIRECTION OF EXPORTS

The disproportionate bias of India's export specialization towards capital and skill-intensive product lines and the resulting disconnect with global production networks have a bearing on the geographical pattern of India's exports. Arguably, India's product specialization patterns provide it with a comparative advantage in relatively poorer markets (such as Africa) but at the cost of losing market shares in the richer countries.

In the past, traditional developed country markets (comprising Australia and New Zealand, Europe, Japan, and North America) accounted for a major share of India's export basket. But their dominance has been steadily declining over the last two decades. The aggregate share of these markets in India's merchandise exports declined from about 63 per cent in 1993 to 35 per cent in 2010 (Veeramani 2012). The remaining group of countries (which include South and Central America, the Caribbean, and the various regions of Asia and Africa), accounted for nearly two-thirds of India's merchandise exports in 2010.

The share of the high-income OECD countries in India's total manufacturing exports declined sharply from 58 per cent in 2000 to 41 per cent in 2010. For China, the corresponding decline in the share of high-income OECD countries was relatively slow from 62 to 53 per cent. In contrast to India, China continues to show a high trade orientation with traditional developed country markets.

What explains India's declining trade intensity with traditional developed country markets? A possible explanation for this trend lies in India's idiosyncratic pattern of specialization. India's capital- and skill-intensive products are unlikely to make inroads into the quality-conscious richer country markets. These products from India, however, may enjoy a competitive advantage in the relatively poorer country markets.

That the nature of specialization has a bearing on the geographical direction of exports is evident from the fact that the high-income OECD countries account for a much smaller share in India's total exports of capital-intensive products (for example, 'machinery and transport equipment') compared to their share in India's total exports of labour-intensive products (for example, 'textiles'). In 2010, the high-income OECD countries accounted for about 52 per cent of the total exports of 'textiles' from India while their share in 'machinery and transport equipments' was much smaller at 38 per cent (see Table 9.11). For China, however, the high-income OECD countries accounted for much above 50 per cent of its exports in both these product groups. The high share of OECD countries in China's exports of 'machinery and transport equipment' is consistent with its high degree of vertical specialization in the labour-intensive production stages within these industries.

A concrete example that should make our arguments clearer is related to India's export pattern of passenger motor vehicles (HS 8703), a capital- and skill-intensive product

---

[11] The shares were 32 per cent in 1995 and 50 per cent in 2001. These shares (except for 1989) have been computed using data from the various issues of the *Chinese Statistical Yearbook* published by the National Bureau of Statistics of China. The share for the year 1989 is taken from the *World Investment Report, 2003*, published by UNCTAD.

Table 9.11 Share of High-income OECD Countries in Exports from India and China

	India			China		
	1990	2000	2010	1990	2000	2010
Manufactures	48.9	58.1	40.8	29.9	61.8	53.2
Textiles	53.9	66.1	51.7	37.0	57.6	55.1
Machinery and transport equipment	17.4	46.7	38.3	12.8	59.1	51.6

Source: Estimated using COMTRADE-WITS database.

group. India's exports of passenger motor vehicles increased remarkably from $151 million in 2002 to $4,511 million in 2010, registering a growth rate of 44 per cent a year. Low and middle-income countries were the major destinations for these exports from India. In 2010, the high-income countries accounted for only 8 per cent of Indian exports of passenger motor vehicles while Sub-Saharan Africa accounted for 11 per cent. By contrast, the high-income countries accounted for 58 per cent of India's total exports of HS 6105 ('men's or boys' shirts, knitted or crocheted')—a traditional labour-intensive group—while Sub-Saharan Africa accounted for just 1 per cent. Clearly, changes in specialization have bearings on the geographical direction of exports. In general, India's movement out of labour-intensive industries implies a loss of comparative advantage in the richer country markets.

It is important to note that, despite their continued expansion, the overall size of developing country markets remains much smaller than traditional developed country markets.[12] Therefore, the undue dependence on developing country markets may put a natural limit on India's volume growth of exports. It is beyond doubt that India holds a huge unexploited export potential in traditional developed country markets despite the recent slow down in these countries. The general perception, however, is that India should necessarily diversify to new markets in the developing world if it has to increase its export volume. Consistent with this perception, the Indian government recently announced an export incentive scheme providing explicit financial supports for market diversification.[13] The recent slow down in the developed countries may provide a short-term rationale for this diversification strategy. Viewed through the lens of the Heckscher–Ohlin model, however, the declining trade intensity with traditional richer country markets is symptomatic of distortions in India's specialization patterns in favour of capital-intensive industries. In order to exploit the export potential in developed country markets, it is imperative to realign India's specialization on the basis of its intrinsic comparative advantage in labour-intensive manufacturing.

CONCLUDING REMARKS AND THE WAY FORWARD

The road to the success of exports in the East Asian countries started by specializing in low skilled labour-intensive and low technology manufactures. In contrast, the pattern of India's industrial growth, though still at the early stage, shows a bias in favour of relatively skill- and capital-intensive industries. The fast-growing exports from the country are either skilled labour-intensive (such as drugs and pharmaceuticals and fine chemicals) or capital-intensive (such as automobiles and parts). The share of capital-intensive products in India's manufacturing export basket more than doubled from about 23 per cent in 1990 to nearly 54 per cent in 2010 while the share of unskilled labour-intensive products nearly halved from 43 per cent to 22 per cent.

The lack of dynamism in labour-intensive manufacturing is a matter of concern because it is this sector that holds the potential to absorb the large pools of unskilled surplus labour from India's agriculture sector. Thus, Indian growth has not been effective in reducing poverty on the scale that was possible in China and other industrialized countries of East Asia. The experience of East Asian countries shows that export-led industrialization based initially on labour-intensive industries is crucial for sustained employment generation and poverty reduction. India seems to be skipping this important intermediate stage of industrialization and moving directly to the next stage based on capital- and skill-intensive industries.

That India's export basket is biased towards capital- and skill-intensive products is an anomaly given the fact that the country's true comparative advantage lies in unskilled labour-intensive activities. While India's import substitution policy regime created a bias in favour of capital and skill-intensive manufacturing, the reforms since 1991 have not been comprehensive enough to remove this bias. Though

---

[12] The countries in the traditional group accounted for about 70 per cent of world exports in 2002 and 58 per cent in 2010.

[13] See the 'Foreign Trade Policy 2009–14', Ministry of Commerce and Industry, Department of Commerce, Government of India, available at: http://dgft.gov.in/exim/2000/policy/ftp-plcontent0910.pdf, accessed on 1 November 2011.

the post-1991 policy changes have gone a long way towards product market liberalization by easing entry barriers, factor markets (labour and land) are still plagued by severe distortions and policy-induced rigidities. Arguably, government interventions in factor markets have had the unintended consequence of creating a bias in the incentive structure against labour-intensive manufacturing. Trade liberalization by itself does not guarantee specialization in line with the comparative advantage of a country if other policies militate against the efficient pattern of resource allocation.

In particular, India's archaic labour laws create severe exit barriers and hence discourage large firms from choosing labour-intensive activities and technologies (Krueger 2010; Kochhar et al. 2006; Panagariya 2007). A provision in the Industrial Disputes Act (IDA), 1948 stipulates that firms employing 100 or more regular workers must seek prior consent of the state government before any retrenchment or closure of firms.[14] Based on a labour market survey and comparable research in other countries, an OECD report (2007: 13) notes that 'laws governing regular employment contracts in India are stricter than those in Brazil, Chile, China and all but two OECD countries'. Nagaraj (2011), however, questions the hypothesis that labour market rigidities are holding up India's industrial growth. He argues that the exemptions and loopholes built into the labour laws provide sufficient flexibilities to firms to retrench workers. It has also been argued that in order to surpass stringent labour laws, firms are increasingly using non-regular contract labour (for example, see Sharma 2006).

While illegal retrenchments and use of contract workers are not ruled out, the main charge against this legislation is that it raises the implicit cost of employing workers (including the costs of litigation and bribes to politicians and trade union leaders in the event of illegal retrenchments) and reduces the freedom of firms to decide the optimal way of choosing their product lines and employing the workers.[15] These costs can be prohibitive especially in labour-intensive segments where firms generally operate with low margins in a highly competitive international environment. Overall,

the legislation has created an incentive for firms to choose skill- and capital-intensive product lines that employ relatively more white collar workers who are not classified as 'workmen' and therefore do not enjoy employment protection under the IDA.

A number of econometric studies have attempted to analyse the impact of labour laws on employment and firm performance in India. Such attempts have been encumbered by difficulties in properly measuring the extent of labour market rigidities. Some recent studies, exploiting state-level variations in labour policies, suggest that labour market rigidities have constrained employment, firm performance, and industrial growth in India (see, for example, Hasan et al. 2007 and Aghion et al. 2008).[16]

Until the reforms, China had severe distortions in all its factor and commodity markets (Lal 1995). The Chinese labour market was characterized by direct allocation of jobs and administrative control of wages. China gradually liberalized the labour market, particularly in the non-state sector, providing greater flexibility in the allocation of resources (Brooks and Tao 2003; Meng 2000). Firms in special economic zones, in the very early stage of opening, had the authority to hire and fire. The government then extended this policy to other areas in the country (Panagariya 2007).

A flexible labour market, with appropriate social safety nets, is a crucial necessary condition for the growth of labour-intensive manufacturing in India. Other constraints that stand in the way of manufacturing growth include inadequate supply of physical infrastructure (especially power, roads, and ports) and a highly inefficient and cumbersome land acquisition procedures. Faced with power shortages, capital- and skill-intensive industries such as automobiles and pharmaceuticals, might be in a position to rely on the high-cost internal sources of power. This option, however, is not affordable to firms in the labour-intensive segments that generally operate with low margins.

A high level of vertical specialization-based trade, which occurs when countries specialize in particular stages of a good's production sequence rather than in the entire good, has been an important factor in driving the East Asian export growth. China, through specialization in labour-intensive processes and product lines, has successfully integrated its manufacturing sector with global production networks. Inward FDI has been instrumental in integrating China's manufacturing with global vertical production chains. The bulk of the FDI flows to China's manufacturing sector has been vertical (export-promoting) in nature,

---

[14] The original post-independence legislation allowed employers to retrench workers as market conditions required, subject to minimum levels of protection through stipulated notice periods, severance payments etc. The legislation was tightened in 1976 for firms employing over 300 workers by making it mandatory for firms to obtain government permission to retrench workers. In 1982, this restriction was extended to all firms employing 100 or more workers.

[15] Leaving the debate on the specific effect of IDA aside, it has been generally agreed that the 'Indian labour laws are so numerous, complex and even ambiguous that they promote litigation rather than the resolution of problems related to industrial relations' (Sharma 2006: 2078).

[16] Bhattacharjea (2006) provides a critical review of these studies.

which represents international fragmentation of the production process by multinationals.

In contrast, due to its idiosyncratic specialization, India has been locked out of the vertically integrated global supply chains in manufacturing industries. Inward FDI into India is primarily horizontal (market seeking) rather than vertical in nature. FDI has been much less important in driving India's export growth, accounting for less than 10 per cent of manufacturing exports.

What explains the fact that India has been attracting horizontal rather than vertical FDI while the opposite has been the case for China? The factors responsible for this are broadly the same as those that explain the relatively low degree of India's vertical specialization in general. First, there existed a powerful incentive for multinationals to undertake tariff jumping horizontal investment as Indian tariff rates, despite the reduction since 1991, remained relatively high until 2007. Higher tariff rates would have made India a relatively undesirable destination for vertical investments.

Second, vertical specialization has been discouraged in India also on account of labour laws, inefficient infrastructure, a burdensome regulatory environment, an inefficient land acquisition process, and poor trade facilitation.[17] The World Bank's annual 'Doing Business 2012' ranked India 132nd out of 183 countries in ease of doing business while China's rank stood much better at 91st. The Logistic Performance Index (LPI) database of the World Bank, ranks countries on the basis of the quality of trade-related logistic provisions.[18] According to the latest LPI index, India's rank stood at 47 out of 155 countries while China's rank was higher at 27.

Recognizing the importance of a strong manufacturing sector for employment generation, the Indian government recently announced the National Manufacturing Policy (NMP).[19] This policy aims to create 100 million additional jobs and to increase the share of manufacturing in India's GDP to 25 per cent by 2022. A major ingredient of this policy is the plan to establish national investment and manufacturing zones, with the units in the zones being given single-window clearance, a liberal exit policy, and certain tax exemptions. The good part of the policy is that it addresses, at least partly, some of the rigidities in the factor (labour and land) markets.

However, there has been little or no effort to situate NMP in the context of growing global production networks in manufacturing industries. Failing to recognize the importance of integrating domestic manufacturing industries with the vertically integrated global production networks, NMP erroneously assumes that a significant local value addition is a necessary condition for manufacturing to increase its size. The policy aims to improve domestic value addition by encouraging the local availability of most of the components, spare parts, and raw material (Mani 2011). This strategy will possibly result in realizing a higher net domestic value added *per unit* of the good produced but at the cost of a lower *total* domestic value addition if the domestic industries continue to be locked out of global production networks.

The grand idea of building a self-contained indigenous industry with local value chains is meaningless in the current landscape of international commerce, where countries engage in production and trade by specializing at the level of distinct product lines and processes within each industry. What is important is the creation of an environment that allows entrepreneurs to freely search and identify opportunities in the vertically integrated global supply chains of various industries. A deliberate strategy of promoting greater integration of domestic industries with global production networks will accelerate the process of shifting the surplus labour engaged in India's agriculture to labour-intensive manufacturing. Increased participation in global production networks must form an essential part of the strategy for achieving inclusive growth in India.

REFERENCES

ADB (2007), *Asian Development Outlook*. Manila: Asian Development Bank.

Aghion, Philippe, Robin Burgess, Stephen J. Redding, and Fabrizio Zilibotti (2008), 'The Unequal Effects of Liberalization: Evidence from Dismantling the License Raj in India', *American Economic Review*, 98(4): 1397–412.

Athukorala, Prema-chandra (2012), 'Asian Trade Flows: Trends, patterns and Prospects', *Japan and the World Economy*, 24(2): 150–62.

Athukorala, Prema-chandra and Nobuaki Yamashita (2006), 'Production Fragmentation and Trade Integration: East Asia

---

[17] For a long period, India had had a small-scale reservation (SSR) policy under which a number of industrial activities (mostly unskilled labour-intensive) were 'reserved' for small-scale units (see Mohan 2002 for a detailed analysis). Reduction in the list of SSR industries started in 1997 and continued till the late 2000s. Krueger (2010: 422–3) pointed out that 'because exporting many unskilled-labor intensive goods requires considerable fixed costs and fairly large scales of output, it is possible that there will be a delay between the time SS regulations are relaxed and exporting activity increases'. It may also be noted that the stringent labour laws applicable to the larger firms may act as a major disincentive for firms to expand in the de-reserved industries. In the absence of labour reforms, de-reservation alone is unlikely to generate significant growth in labour-intensive production and exports.

[18] For details see http://info.worldbank.org/etools/tradesurvey/Mode1a.asp, last accessed on 18 September 2012.

[19] See Mani (2011) for a critical evaluation of NMP.

in a Global Context', *North American Journal of Economics and Finance*, 17(3): 233–56.

Balassa, Bela (1977), *A Stages Approach to Comparative Advantage*. Washington, DC: The World Bank, World Bank Staff Working Paper No. 256.

Barro, Robert and Jong-Wha Lee (2010), 'A New Data Set of Educational Attainment in the World, 1950–2010', NBER Working Paper No. 15902.

Bhagwati, Jagdish N. (2002), *The Wind of the Hundred Days: How Washington Mismanaged Globalization*. Cambridge, Mass: MIT Press.

Bhattacharjea, Aditya (2006), 'Labour Market Regulation and Industrial Performance in India: A Critical Review of the Empirical Evidence', *Indian Journal of Labour Economics*, 49(2): 211–32.

Brooks, Ray and Ran Tao (2003), 'China's Labour Market Performance and Challenges'. Washington, DC: IMF Working Paper No. 03/210.

Cadot Olivier, Bolormaa Tumurchudur, and Miho Shirotori (2009), 'Revealed Factor Intensity Indices at Product Level', UNCTAD Publication series on 'Policy Issues in International Trade and Commodities'.

Dean, Judit M., K.C. Fung, and Zhi Wang (2008), 'How Vertically Specialized is Chinese Trade', Office of Economics Working Paper No. 2008-09-D, US International Trade Commission. Aailable at: http://usitc.gov/publications/332/working_papers/ec200809d.pdf, last accessed on 18 September 2012.

Gupta, Poonam, Rana Hasan, and Utsav Kumar (2010), 'What Constraints Indian Manufacturing', in Barry Eichengreen, Poonam Gupta and Rajiv Kumar (eds), *Emerging Giants: China and India in the World Economy*. New York: Oxford University Press, pp. 307–39.

Hasan, Rana, Devashish Mitra, and K.V. Ramaswamy (2007), 'Trade Reforms, Labor Regulations, and Labor-Demand Elasticities: Empirical Evidence from India', *Review of Economics and Statistics*, 89(3): 466–81.

Hinloopen, J. and C. van Marrewijk (2008), 'Empirical Relevance of the Hillman Condition for Revealed Comparative Advantage: 10 Stylized Facts', *Applied Economics*, 40(18): 2313–28.

Hummels, David, Jun Ishii, and Kei-Mu Yi (2001), 'The Nature and Growth of Vertical Specialization in World Trade', *Journal of International Economics*, 54: 75–96.

Islam, Rizwanul (2008), 'Has Development and Employment Through Labor Intensive Industrialization Become History?', in Kaushik Basu and Ravi Kanbur (eds), *Arguments for a Better World: Essays in Honor of Amartya Sen*, Vol. 2. New York: Oxford University Press, pp. 387–410.

Kochhar, Kalpana, Utsav Kumar, Raghuram Rajan, Arvind Subramanian, and Ioannis Tokatlidis (2006), 'India's Pattern of Development: What Happened, What Follows', *Journal of Monetary Economics*, 53(5): 981–1019.

Koopman, Robert, William Powers, Zhi Wang, and Shang-Jin Wei (2010), 'Give Credit where Credit is Due: Tracing Value Added in Global Production Chains', NBER Working Paper 16426.

Krueger, Anne O. (2010), 'India's Trade with the World: Retrospect and Prospect', in Sharkar Acharya and Rakesh Mohan (eds), *India's Economy: Performance and Challenges*. New Delhi: Oxford University Press, pp. 399–429.

Lal, D. (1995), 'India and China: Contrasts in Economic Liberalization?', *World Development*, 23(9): 1475–94.

Little, I., T. Scitovsky, and M. Scott (1970), *Industry and Trade in Some Developing Countries*. London and New York: Oxford University Press.

Mani, Sunil (2011), 'National Manufacturing Policy: Making India a Powerhouse?', *Economic and Political Weekly*, 46 (53): 16–19.

Meng, Xin (2000), *Labour Market Reform in China*. New York: Cambridge University Press.

Mohan, Rakesh (2002), 'Small-scale Industry Policy in India: A Critical Evaluation', in Anne O. Krueger (ed.), *Economic Policy Reforms and the Indian Economy*. Chicago: University of Chicago Press, pp. 213–97.

Nagaraj, R. (2011), 'Industrial Performance, 1991–2008: A Review', in D.M. Nachane (ed.), *India Development Report 2011*. New Delhi: Oxford University Press, pp. 69–80.

Organization for Economic Corporation and Development (2007), *OECD Economic Surveys: India*, Vol. 2007/14. Paris: OECD.

———. (2009), *OECD Investment Policy Reviews: India*. Paris: OECD.

Panagariya, Arvind (2007), 'Why India Lags Behind China and How it Can Bridge the Gap', *World Economy*, 30(2): 229–48.

———. (2008), *India: The Emerging Giant*. New York: Oxford University Press.

Schott, Peter K. (2008), 'The Relative Sophistication of Chinese Exports', *Economic Policy*, 23(53): 5–49.

Sharma, Alakh, N. (2006) 'Flexibility, Employment and Labour Market Reforms in India', *Economic and Political Weekly*, XLI (21): 2078–85.

Veeramani, C. (2009), 'Specialisation Patterns under Trade Liberalisation: Evidence from India and China', in Natalia Dinello and Wang Shaoguang (eds), *China, India and Beyond: Development Drivers and Limitations*. Edward Elgar, Cheltenham, pp. 73–97.

———. (2012), 'Anatomy of India's Merchandise Export Growth, 1993–94 to 2010–11', *Economic and Political Weekly*, 47(1): 94–104.

Veeramani, C. and K. Gordhan Saini (2011), 'India's Export Sophistication in a Comparative Perspective', in D.M. Nachane (ed.), *India Development Report 2011*. New Delhi: Oxford University Press, pp. 187–95.

Weiss, John (2005), 'Export Growth and Industrial Policy: Lessons from the East Asian Miracle Experience', ADB Institute Discussion Paper No. 26. Available at: http://www.adbi.org/files/2005.02.dp26.eastasia.govt.policy.pdf, last accessed on 18 September, 2012.

———. (2011), *The Economics of Industrial Development*. London and New York: Routledge.

10

Borrowing by Indian Firms

*Renuka Sane and Susan Thomas**

THE ISSUES

One of the key functions of a financial system is to deliver external capital (that is, capital from outside the firms) to high-quality firms. In a flourishing financial system, equity and debt capital is raised by firms which have sound prospects but poor cash flows.

The Indian equity market was a major focus of economic reforms from 1992 onwards. By and large, while substantial success was achieved in building the equity market, India fared badly in the area of debt. This was high on the agenda of the Percy Mistry and Raghuram Rajan reports (Mistry 2007; Rajan 2008), which mapped the landscape of financial sector reforms. Both these reports highlighted the problems that have held back the 'Bond-Currency-Derivatives nexus' (BCD nexus), the tightly inter-linked web of fixed income and currency markets with both spot and derivatives markets fully integrated through arbitrage. In addition, the need for deep and liquid sources for financing of infrastructure projects has led to a renewed policy focus on this issue.

In this chapter, we describe the borrowing of firms. On the one hand, the narrative is descriptive. But there is also a normative narrative alongside, where we use certain features of firm financing and the functions of the debt market to illustrate where there is a lack of sophistication in the Indian financial system. We hope that this will also serve to illustrate the kind of changes that are required to improve the quality and sophistication of the debt markets in India.

At the simplest, it is possible to interpret corporate financial choice of the firms in India as reflecting the optimal decisions of firms to the problems of taxation, bankruptcy costs, and agency problems. This would be an appropriate perspective in a well-functioning financial system.

However, India is far from a well-functioning financial system. As an example, the Financial Development Report of the World Economic Forum carries out a detailed measurement of the capability of the financial system. In 2010, the overall rank for India was 37th out of 57 countries. While India has made enormous progress on the equity market, with the establishment of Securities and Exchange Board of India (SEBI), National Stock Exchange (NSE), and National Securities Depository Limited (NSDL) in the 1990s, market institutions that matter for the borrowing of firms are quite weak. The banking system stands at a rank of 41, while the bond market stands at a rank of 35.

We start the analysis of what makes for a sophisticated financial system that enables borrowing by firms, by sketching three key elements:

1. A key element in a well-developed financial system is whether lenders are able to lend based on their

---

* We thank Suhasini Subramaniam and the IGIDR Finance Research Group for research support. The chapter benefited from some very useful comments and suggestions from Ajay Shah, Mahesh Vyas, and the participants of the IGIDR 'India Development Report 2012' workshop, 3–4 May 2012. All errors and omissions are our own.

assessment of the future prospects of a firm. This assessment allows them to allocate capital based on this calculated soundness of the health of alternative borrowers. Financial systems where this ability is wanting depend instead on collateralized lending: where the borrower will be financed depending upon its ability to put up security.

Thus, a fundamental difference between an underdeveloped and sophisticated financial system is how much of the credit that is given out is secured (collateralized) and how much is unsecured. Secured borrowing is based on an assessment of the liquidation value of the security offered as collateral. Lending against collateral merely requires an analysis of the collateral. Unsecured borrowing is based on an assessment of the future prospects of the firm. Unsecured borrowing involves a sophisticated financial process, where lenders offer capital to firms which may not have assets to pledge as securities but which can demonstrate the ability to repay the loan. It requires lenders to understand who they are lending to. To the extent that this can take place, this can give rise to firms which can vigorously compete with incumbent lending firms. While both are forms of lending, they reflect profoundly different institutional capabilities.

In India, the legal framework governing the rights of a creditor has been improved with secured credit: the Securitization and Reconstruction of Financial Assets and Enforcement of Security Interest (SARFAESI) Act improved creditors' rights by improving the expected liquidation value of physical assets after a default. This is expected to help improve the institutional environment for secured borrowing. Comparable improvements have not taken place in the structure and reliability of the bankruptcy process through which insolvent firms are closed down and residual value given to the lenders.

It is easy for financial firms to create processes to give out secured credit. Requirements of internal information and incentive problems are profoundly different when it comes to unsecured credit, which requires the discretionary judgment of a loan officer. This takes us to incentive arrangements within a financial firm. In an unsophisticated financial system, such complex incentive structures would not be set up, and secured credit would dominate. The prime bottleneck for a financial firm to achieve a larger scale in giving out credit is the internal organizational and agency problems of the firm itself rather than information asymmetry with the firm that wants to borrow. For large borrowing firms (particularly those with a balance sheet size of above Rs 1,000 crore) it is fairly easy to construct estimates of default probabilities by using listed stock prices. India's success in building a vibrant equity market can be utilized for the purpose of information processing about the financial health of firms whose shares are actively traded. The real problem of increasing the amount of credit in the system (to even these large firms) lies within the financial firm, reflecting a combination of problems of regulation, corporate governance, and HR processes.

2. The second key element of sophistication is the shift from bank financing to market-based financing. The process of lending in primitive economies is dominated by banks which give out illiquid and opaque loans. In more sophisticated financial systems, a bulk of the financing of large corporations moves out to the bond market. Banks then focus on giving loans to smaller firms which do not have the sheer size which is required to raise finances in the bond market. As a thumb rule in India, under reasonable assumptions about the size of a bond issue that can become liquid, a firm with a balance sheet of less than Rs 1,000 crore is unlikely to be able to issue a bond. The normative idea then is that firms with balance sheets of above Rs 1,000 crore will primarily rely on the bond market and that the rest will depend on banks for loans.

3. A sophisticated financial system is one that is integrated with international markets and where significant borrowing takes place from these markets. The key factor driving this is the lower required rate of return for foreign lenders, who are diversified across many countries. In addition, rich countries are likely to have larger capital stock which typically implies that they have a lower cost of capital. Access to such lenders can help lower the cost of borrowing for Indian firms.

There is one critical distinction in foreign borrowing: the currency in which the bonds are denominated. While borrowing in dollar-denominated bonds is easy, it poses new challenges because large rupee depreciations can induce adverse balance sheet effects. The best form of foreign borrowing is when a local Indian firm can issues bonds in the local bond market (which are denominated in rupees), and these are purchased by foreign investors. Under this arrangement, the foreign investor bears currency risk. At the same time, the use of the local bond market ensures that maximal liquidity and information processing are obtained in India.

When these three elements are in place, non-financial firms will have access to ample credit, and debt will play a large role in the balance sheet structure.

In contrast, when these three elements are not in place, many firms will suffer from constraints in their ability to borrow. This will have far-reaching consequences:

1. Internal capital markets. One response that has been observed in India is that large firms run internal capital markets. Large firms raise equity and debt capital, and then give it out to subsidiaries or related firms or supply chain firms as equity and/or debt. To some extent, this reflects superior information in the hands of a large firm (for example, a large car company lending to a component manufacturer). To some extent, this reflects regulatory arbitrage: when formal financial firms are prohibited from doing economically rational things, these activities move off to the treasuries of non-financial firms. Financing activities by non-financial firms is generally considered an aberration and a reflection of the infirmities of the financial system.

   When firms run large internal capital markets, this impinges on corporate governance. An ideal corporate governance arrangement is one where all net profit is paid out to the shareholders, and every capital investment proposed by managers is scrutinized by the board, which then authorizes a rights issue or a seasoned equity offering (SEO) or borrowing in order to finance it. Through such corporate actions that increase the breadth and diversity of shareholding, the board and the financial system increases the scrutiny on the investment proposals of the firm. To the extent that the firm operates an internal capital market, there is much less transparency of these transactions since they take place directly among the subsidiaries of the firm, which could be a source of lower payout ratios. Given this lack of scrutiny either by the board or the broader general financial system, these could ultimately lead to inferior utilization of capital.

2. Difficulties with financing different kinds of firms. The three elements outlined earlier can have substantial cross-sectional variations. A financial system may be effective in dealing with a firm with a trillion-rupee balance sheet, but it may fail when attempting to deal with a billion-rupee balance sheet (that is, cross-sectional variation by size). A financial system may liberally give out secured credit to firms in industries where there are many tangible assets on the balance sheet, but it may fail when dealing with industries with low tangible assets (that is, cross-sectional variation by asset tangibility).

   The hardest financing challenge is typically the most important one: the ability of a financial system to deliver capital to firms with high prospects when they are young and have low tangible assets. To the extent that a financial system is able to do this, competition in the economy is fostered. In this manner, financial sector policy is integral to competition policy.

   As an example, banks in India largely shunned software companies in India until the mid-1990s, when their business model was proven. Prior to this, the emergence of the software industry in India was dominated by equity financing. If a more capable financial system had existed, the software industry may have risen more rapidly and grown to scale faster. Conversely, if the Indian equity market had not been as capable in the 1990s, this may have severely retarded the emergence of the software industry in that decade.

3. Infrastructure financing. Similarly, borrowing for infrastructure projects is a particularly difficult puzzle. Borrowing in dollars is not feasible since the cash flows of these projects are in rupees. Borrowing from banks is also not feasible since the cash flows of the project are very long-dated. The only genuine solution to the financing problems in infrastructure is an onshore long-dated corporate bond market. In this fashion, the financial sector policy is integral to infrastructure policy.

   In India, in the desire to enable infrastructure financing, bank regulation has tolerated maturity mismatches on bank balance sheets. Infrastructure companies are tolerating currency mismatches on their balance sheets. The desire to build infrastructure, which has not been matched by the desire to build a bond market, is inducing fragility in the balance sheets of both banks and infrastructure companies.

EVIDENCE OF FINANCING FROM FUNDING SOURCES

Firms' balance sheets are a key data source for understanding their financing. A critical element is termed the 'sources and uses of funds statement' which is the difference between two successive balance sheets. This shows what new resources came into the corporation in the year, and for what purposes these new resources were put to use. The aggregated information for all non-financial firms observed

Table 10.1 Sources of Funds Aggregated for All Non-financial Firms

(in %)

	Three-year Averages, Centred Around	
	1991–2	2009–10
Equity	22.60	34.87
Retained earnings	10.56	21.05
Fresh issuance	12.04	13.82
Depreciation	17.64	9.69
Borrowing	35.32	29.48
Banks	17.14	17.83
Bonds	7.87	3.94
From firms	1.28	2.28
Foreign	5.51	3.22
Current liabilities	24.42	24.19

Source: CMIE Prowess database.

in the Centre for Monitoring Indian Economy (CMIE) database is compiled and presented in Table 10.1.

The outstanding feature of this data is the increased reliance by Indian firms on equity financing over the last two decades. In 1991–2, which was the start of the financial reforms process, 22.6 per cent of the funds were raised from equity financing,[1] which had risen to 34.87 per cent by the end of 2010. There can be two reasons for this shift. The first is the success of equity market reforms (including capital account liberalization on the equity market), which gave firms a better functioning mechanism through which financing could be obtained. The second is that during this time, India became a more market-based economy, which inevitably faced greater uncertainty. When economic risk rises, the tendency of firms is to undertake a reduction of leverage which will mean higher levels of equity and lower levels of debt.

A closer look at the remaining elements of Table 10.1 shows that remarkably little else changed between the start and the end of the sample period. In a more sophisticated financial system, there would be a shift away from banks towards market-based financing. However in India, banks continued to be a steady source of debt financing, with a slight rise from 17.14 per cent to 17.83 per cent. In fact, other sources of debt financing decreased. Bond financing went down significantly from 7.87 to 3.94 per cent. The nascent long-dated bond market in 1991–2 had collapsed by 2009–10. India was supposed to have opened up the capital account in the post-reforms period, but foreign financing of debt actually dropped from 5.51 to 3.22 per cent.

[1] Equity in a firm is a sum of retained earnings and fresh issuance of equity.

All these show that the move to a more market-based debt financing has not happened in India, and is consistent with the failures of policy reforms in the fields of banking, the bond market, and capital account liberalization for corporate bonds.

A sophisticated financial system is one in which:

1. Non-financial firms have access to ample debt financing;
2. The bond market is active, and banks play a less important role in the financing of large corporations;
3. Greater borrowing takes place from abroad; and
4. Non-financial firms stick to non-financial businesses; less corporate financial activity flows through corporate balance sheets.

The last is directly related to a badly performing financial system: where real sector firms increasingly take on the burden of undertaking financing activities. Evidence shows that this is increasingly the case in India, with a slight rise in borrowing from 1.28 to 2.28 from other firms.[2]

From 1991–2 to 2009–10, it therefore appears that India made little to no progress on these four notions of sophistication, with some of the elements having regressed.

EVIDENCE FROM THE STRUCTURE OF LIABILITIES

The sources of fund statements in the previous section showed the flow of new resources going into a firm. Next, we do a more conventional analysis of the stock of liabilities of firms. The sample remains the same set of all non-financial firms in the CMIE database, with a focus on the share in total liabilities (that is, total assets). Once again, we report the three-year average centred on 1991–2 and 2009–10 in Table 10.2.

A dramatic deleveraging of non-financial firms can be seen in this data, as was seen in the sources of funds statements. From the aggregates in Table 10.2, the growth in equity (from 29.45 per cent of the balance sheet in 1991–2 to 38.74 per cent of the balance sheet in 2009–10) is associated with a decline in the role of borrowing. However, within these various sources of borrowings, banks have held their own at roughly 18 per cent of the balance sheet. In contrast, the bond market has seen a steep decline (from 6.86 to 2.24 per cent), while foreign sources of debt capital have also declined somewhat.

[2] This is mirrored in the uses of funds, where there was a slight rise in loans and advances given out from 3.24 per cent in 1991–2 to 3.71 per cent in 2009–10.

Table 10.2 Structure of Liabilities of Indian Non-financial Firms

(in %)

	Three-year Averages, Centred Around	
	1991–2	2009–10
Equity	29.45	38.74
Total borrowings	44.90	32.00
Banks	17.61	18.00
Bonds	6.86	2.24
Foreign	5.66	4.02
From firms	2.61	2.57
Current liabilities	25.64	26.87
Structure of borrowing, secured	25.40	19.31
Unsecured	19.50	12.69

Source: CMIE Prowess database.

On the problem of secured versus unsecured credit, the evidence shows a sharp decline in unsecured borrowings, from 19.5 per cent of the balance sheet to 12.69 per cent. Secured borrowings also fell from 25.4 to 19.3 per cent. There is no evidence of an improvement in the quantum of unsecured borrowings, which would suggest the emergence of a more sophisticated financial system.

CROSS-SECTIONAL HETEROGENEITY BY FIRM AGE

An important litmus test of a financial system lies in its ability to deliver debt to young firms. Young firms tend to have low tangible assets, and therefore, present significant challenges of informational asymmetry to financial firms when they approach them for financing. The problems of information asymmetry are characteristic of a less developed financial system. This is an amalgamation of poor standards of information disclosure from firms and weak legal processes of the definition and resolution of bankruptcy. Thus, in such markets it is relatively easy for a conservative lender to focus on the financing requirements of older firms.

One way to address these issues is to examine the borrowings that are accessible by old and well-established firms and young firms. The principle here is that the financial system will have much lower levels of information asymmetry with respect to the older firms, both because they have likely had financial interactions with these firms for longer, as well as because these firms have a longer history of observed track record. Young firms, on the other hand, have a much shorter track record of the nature that the financial systems typically use to evaluate the financial health of a firm. Therefore, such firms are likely to pose higher information asymmetry to the financial system. In order to assess how the financial system treats this problem of information asymmetry, we analyse the structure of firm financing and firm borrowing across age quartiles. We define the young quartile as firms with age below 12; Q2 with age from 12 to 19; Q3 with age from 19 to 33; and the old quartile with firms of age above 33. We examine the borrowings of these different quartiles at the oldest point with strong data (1990–2) and the most recent time point (2009–11). The results are shown in Table 10.3.

Table 10.3 Variation across Age

	Quartiles by Firm Age			
	Young	Q2	Q3	Old
Average of 1990–2				
Share of unsecured debt	35.15	58.88	27.78	21.78
Share of banks	38.75	21.20	53.70	48.01
Share of bonds	25.54	17.73	11.67	28.50
Share of foreign	20.71	15.42	8.30	3.28
Average of 2009–11				
Share of unsecured debt	32.39	20.68	29.50	54.88
Share of banks	61.36	52.29	63.87	55.04
Share of bonds	7.00	17.31	7.14	12.41
Share of foreign	19.31	18.01	21.90	19.90

Note: This is a comparison of the borrowings pattern of firms categorized into quartiles by age, which are defined as follows: • Young: age < 12 years; • q2: 12 < age ≤ 19; • q3: 19 < age ≤ 33; • Old: age > 33
Source: CMIE Prowess database.

We find that most age quartiles lacked substantial unsecured debt at either time point. The important exception was old firms in 2010, where over half of the borrowings were unsecured. In 2010, the financial system appeared to be willing to lend based on the analysis of the forward-looking prospects of firms, but only for those above age 33. Foreign borrowings were more visible by 2010, particularly for old firms. The bond market was an important source of financing in 1991 but not in 2010.

Thus, if a better developed and sophisticated financial system is one where large firms shift away from bank financing to market financing, then the reverse movement appears to have taken place in India over the last 20 years. More recently, however, there have been institutional changes that have taken place to improve problems of information asymmetry between the borrower and the lender in India, namely in the corporate bond market.

THE CORPORATE BOND MARKET

In India, bonds issued by all entities other than the central government make for the 'corporate' bond market. Bonds fall under two categories by maturity: (a) short-term contracts of maturity under a year, which is also called commercial paper (cp), and (b) long-term contracts with maturity more than a year, called bonds or debentures. These bonds are typically privately placed, have very low trading, and suffer from a severe lack of transparency in pricing and liquidity.

The Raghuram Rajan and Percy Mistry reports mapped out the deeper changes to macroeconomic and financial policy that are required to obtain a well-functioning BCD nexus. An element of these reforms includes a shift of all bond market activity from Reserve Bank of India (RBI) to SEBI regulation, so that market institutions and regulatory structures which delivered success on the equity market can be reused for the bond market. Implementation of these proposals has been slow. The RBI Amendment Act, 2006 marks a reversal of the direction of reforms by entrenching some of these functions with RBI.

Macroeconomic policy has a major role to play in enabling a bond market through two important features: financial repression and a focus on price stability. Financial repression refers to the forced capture of assets from financial firms into the hands of the government. When financial firms are forced to give resources to the exchequer, this dampens the price discovery of a government bond yield curve. The second issue is price stability. When inflation is high and variable, the inflation risk premium required for a nominal-rupee bond investment becomes very high. In India, both fiscal and monetary policies have been part of the reason for the lack of emergence of a bond market, with a combination of financial repression and the failure to deliver price stability.

In a fledgling economy, the bond market typically develops from the short end, for a variety of reasons:

1. Lack of trust in forecasts of inflation. This makes lenders focus more on undertaking short-dated contracts. When a rollover takes place, the interest rates on the contract are indexed to current inflation rates.
2. When information processing about a borrower is difficult, lenders are willing to take on the credit risk only for a short period at a time.

Based on these reasons, a substantial amount of short-dated papers have been issued in recent years, making short maturity instruments a key feature of the corporate bond market. Further, this has been primarily about issuance by financial firms. Financial firms which lack access to households appear to be paying other financial firms (who have access to households) for the privilege of obtaining debt capital. For non-financial firms, the bond market is a very small source of financing, as is visible in the tables in this chapter.

While the bond market has failed to emerge—reflecting deeper problems of law, regulation, and macroeconomic policy—some policy initiatives of recent years (Patil 2005) have aimed at addressing technical problems of market design in the corporate bond market, some limited outcomes of which have been:

1. In April 2007, SEBI permitted both Bombay Stock Exchange (BSE) and NSE to have in place corporate bond trading platforms to enable efficient price discovery and reliable clearing and settlement facilities in a gradual manner.

    BSE operationalized its reporting platform in January 2007 and NSE did it in March 2007. Permission for corporate bond trading platforms was given to BSE and NSE in April 2007 and the platforms became operational in July 2007.
2. The clearing and settlement of trades in corporate bonds have been done through the National Securities Clearing Corporation or the the Indian Clearing Corporation from 1 December 2009.

    This has resulted in a far higher level of transparency about corporate bond trades compared to the earlier market situation.
3. Foreign Institutional Investors (FII) investment into rupee-denominated corporate bonds has commenced, though it remains sharply circumscribed by quantitative restrictions (QRs).

As Table 10.4 shows, slight progress has come about in the corporate bond market through these initiatives. The two factors that appear to have mattered the most are improvements in clearing at NSE and BSE, and the participation of foreign investors. At the same time, it is important to emphasize that the magnitudes involved thus far are tiny, and the activity on this market has been dominated by bonds issued by financial firms.

Table 10.4 Corporate Bond Trades

	No. of Trades	Turnover (Rs billion)
2007–8	19,079	9,588.9
2008–9	22,683	1,481.7
2009–10	38,230	4,011.9
2010–11	44,060	6,052.7
2011–12	51,533	5,937.8

Source: SEBI (2012).

FOREIGN FINANCING

In 1991–2, 5.5 per cent of the sources of funds were from foreign sources. This declined to 3.22 per cent in 2009–10.

Right from the outset, Indian capital controls have been rooted in concerns about foreign borrowing. The current overall component of foreign borrowings comprises two parts: (1) Dollar-denominated debt—where India borrows in foreign-currency-denominated debt through government borrowing (both bilateral and multilateral), external commercial borrowing (ECB) by firms including foreign currency convertible bonds (FCCB), and fully repatriable Non-resident Indian (NRI) deposits. (2) Rupee-denominated debt—where foreign investors buy bonds in the Indian debt market, all of which are denominated in rupees.

There is much flexibility with dollar denominated borrowing by Indian firms (which takes place outside India). In contrast, rupee-denominated debt is constrained by a series of QRs. Unfortunately, present Indian capital controls, that have been put into place to protect India from the volatility of foreign fund flows, end up exacerbating these problems.

A more careful examination of the evidence focuses on the currency in which the borrowing has been done (Hausmann and Panizza 2003). Suppose, an Indian entity (either government or corporation) borrows in US dollars at a time when the rupee is at Rs 40/dollar. When the rupee depreciates to Rs 60/dollar, the liabilities of the borrower increases by 50 per cent. It is likely that several borrowers will go bankrupt when faced with such events of extreme movements. When a borrower has a 'currency mismatch', there is the possibility of dramatic 'balance sheet effects' when a large depreciation takes place. As an example, during the East Asian crisis of 1997–8, a large number of corporations across East Asia were driven to bankruptcy when large depreciations took place.

In comparison to the previous example, suppose that an Indian firm issued bonds in the Indian debt market and an FII bought the rupee-denominated bond when the exchange rate was at Rs 40 to the dollar. When the exchange rate depreciates to Rs 60 to the dollar, the 50 per cent loss is borne entirely by the FII; there is no impact on the Indian borrower since local currency borrowing implies that the balance sheet is not affected when a large depreciation takes place. Yet the evidence shows that even the limited foreign borrowing that is taking place in India today is being increasingly channelled into dollar-denominated borrowing, most likely as a consequence of the strong restrictions against rupee-denominated debt.

An additional issue is the problem of engaging with global capital. In the equity market, India does not have restrictions that are as stringent, while India has QRs on the bond market. This has far-reaching consequences for the behaviour of global financial firms.

In the equity market, global financial firms have built India-related businesses with large staff teams that study India and connect Indian firms seeking capital with global investors seeking to deploy resources. In the area of corporate bond investments, QRs have prevented the emergence of India-related businesses. Global financial firms occasionally embark on building teams that study Indian firms and play a role in connecting Indian firms that seek to sell rupee-denominated bonds with global investors. However, there is a cap on foreign investment in rupee-denominated bonds set by policy. This cap implies a very low ceiling on permitted investments, which is rapidly met, after which the teams are unable to do any business. This forces disbanding of the teams and loss of organizational capital.

Under the present policy framework, global financial firms are unlikely to invest in system-building that is required to study companies, forecast credit risk, optimize portfolios, etc. The lack of strong teams in global financial firms that work on Indian corporate bond investment can have substantial consequences. Such teams are not likely to assess the risks of a firm accurately, which will end in access to capital that is likely to be limited to a few large firms who are well-known world-wide. Further, the presence of low knowledge and analytical capability among these firms is likely to lead to less educated responses when news events in India unfold. Thus, the present policy framework appears to induce behaviour on the part of foreign capital that is feared the most by emerging market policymakers rather than inhibit it, such as decisions to enter or exit investments that are based on short-term returns rather than long-term gains.

As with many other aspects of financial reforms, we see a distinct contrast between the successful strategies for reforms seen in the equity market as opposed to the continued lack of effective reforms for the problems that bedevil the bond market. As in other areas, the way forward will be greatly helped by adopting several ideas that have been refined on the equity market. For one, FII investments in corporate bonds need to be freed of QRs. This will combat asymmetric information by supporting stable teams and investments in research and data systems. It will make possible a deep engagement between the global financial system and the financing needs of Indian firms. In an environment where many other elements of firm financing have exhibited serious problems, this is one area where progress can be easily achieved.

One of the focus areas for policy analysis about capital controls lies in the encouragement for dollar-denominated borrowing. While foreign participation in India has been largely blocked, Indian firms have borrowed in London and in Singapore, on a large scale, with dollar-denominated bonds. A modest-sized credit derivatives market has emerged in London, where protection can be obtained against default by an Indian issuer. These developments have two negative aspects. First, the development of market structures and liquidity, of the nature of a credit derivatives market, should ideally have taken place within India. It is a striking indictment of financial policy in India that the credit default swap (CDS) on Reliance Industries trades in London but not in India.[3] Second, the large scale of borrowings denominated in dollars exposes Indian firms to balance sheet risks when large rupee depreciations arise, as has happened from early 2008 onwards.

CONCLUSIONS

The key argument of this chapter is that a sophisticated financial system is one where borrowings by firms have three features:

1. Access to unsecured credit is readily available, rooted in the institutional capability of financial firms to judge their future prospects, and backed by a strong bankruptcy code.
2. Large firms primarily borrow through the bond market, while banks lend to firms with a balance sheet of below Rs 1,000 crore.
3. Debt capital comes readily and reliably into the country from abroad, mostly through foreign investment in rupee-denominated bonds in the local bond market.

The evidence presented in the chapter shows comprehensive failure on all these dimensions:

1. Financial firms in India today are ill-equipped to make discretionary judgments about the future prospects of borrowing firms. This reflects a combination of poor HR practices in the public sector, coupled with low-quality regulations such as prohibitions on investing in bonds which are not highly rated.
2. The bankruptcy process is very weak, so that the loss given default is roughly 100 per cent.
3. The bond market is minuscule.
4. Foreign capital flowing into rupee-denominated bonds has been blocked by capital controls.

Features of borrowings by firms which are a cause for concern include: the emergence of internal capital markets through which large non-financial firms perform financing functions so as to overcome the weaknesses of financial firms and markets; difficulties in financing young firms; difficulties in financing firms with low tangible assets; and difficulties in infrastructure financing.

India has obtained substantial policy reforms in certain areas, such as telecom and the equity market. The main argument of this chapter is that the mechanisms through which firms borrow constitutes a failure story, where the policy reforms from 1991–2 till 2011–12 either delivered no change or a worsening of conditions.

These failures have important consequences. The Indian financial system finds it difficult to finance long-term projects with rupee cash flows, as in infrastructure. Financing is constrained for young firms, particularly for firms which have low tangible assets that can be pledged. These constraints have far-reaching consequences for investment and competition in the economy. Addressing these problems requires fresh work in policy reforms in four directions:

1. The ownership and regulation of financial firms requires substantial change, so as to support and enable the emergence of sophisticated financial firms where the internal staff analyses the forward-looking prospects of firms and takes decisions about lending;
2. Policy should focus on developing a sophisticated bankruptcy code that is enshrined in company law, so that failures of payment by a firm trigger off expropriation of shareholders, and handing over control of the firm to lenders;
3. The numerous policy problems that have held back the BDS nexus require resolution; and
4. Capital controls which hold back participation in the onshore rupee-denominated bond market need to be removed.

REFERENCES

Hausmann R. and U. Panizza (2003), 'On the Determinants of Original Sin: An Empirical Investigation', *Journal of International Money and Finance*, 22(7): 957–90.

Mistry, P. (2007), *The Report of the High Powered Expert Committee on Making Mumbai an International Financial Centre*. New Delhi: Ministry of Finance.

Patil, R.H. (2005), *The Report of the High Level Expert Committee on Corporate Bonds and Securitization*. New Delhi: Ministry of Finance.

Rajan, R. (2008), *Report of the Committee on Financial Sector Reforms: A Hundred Small Steps*. New Delhi: Planning Commission.

SEBI (2012), *Trading in Corporate Bonds* (Rs in Cr) Archive. Available at: http://203.199.12.51/debt/corpbondsarchivesnew.html, last accessed on 2 November 2012.

---

[3] Technically, CDS trading can take place in India. However, the regulatory constraints imposed upon this market ensure that market activity is near zero. In effect, the offshore market has roughly had a 100 per cent market share.

11

Sustainability of Biomass Energy in India
The Case of Biodiesel Production from Tree-borne Oils*

Vinod Kumar Sharma

INTRODUCTION

The International Energy Agency (IEA) estimates that the percentage of biomass energy within the total share of different energy sources is set to treble from 10 per cent at present to 30 per cent by 2050. It is reported that in most of the developing economies, a poor biomass resource governance results in the loss of biomass energy resources. The distribution of benefits arising from existing biomass energy business value chains is unequal. Also, inefficient biomass energy conversion and consumption prevails in many developing economies. Modern energy services are crucial to a country's social and economic development and yet globally over 1.3 billion people are without access to electricity and 2.7 billion people are without clean cooking facilities. More than 95 per cent of these people are either in Sub-Saharan Africa or in developing Asia and 84 per cent are settled in rural areas (IEA 2011; IIED 2010).

According to the US Energy Information Administration and IEA, fossil fuels will continue to provide a major part, about 80 per cent, of the global energy supplies and demand for liquid fuels will increase by more than 50 per cent in 2030. An assessment by the Intergovernmental Panel on Climate Change (IPCC) indicates that the global oil demand will rise from 75 million barrels per day in 2000 to 120 million barrels per day in 2030. Almost three-quarters of this increase in demand will be from the transport sector and oil is going to remain the fuel of choice in road, sea, and air transportation. This has spurted the demand for biomass-derived biofuels, and biodiesel and ethanol have emerged as major transport fuels. As the demand for diesel is much more than that for petrol, production of biodiesel is being given more importance than ethanol, globally.

Energy consumption in India is increasing and in the next 20 years or so the total demand for energy may be five to six times of the present demand. Currently, almost 40 per cent of the rural households in India are without electricity and, thus meeting rural energy needs is a major challenge. With a business as usual scenario, this may have several economic, environmental, and social implications. The import of petroleum products is projected to rise, from

---

* This chapter is based on the outcome of an international case study conducted by National Institute of Advanced Industrial Science and Technology (NIAIST), Japan, and ERIA, Indonesia, in four countries, including India during 2009–11. Some portions of the text are reproduced from the 'Indira Gandhi Memorial Lecture on Sustainability and Rural Livelihoods' delivered by the author at the annual conference of the Biodiesel Association of India held on 19 November 2010.

about 75 per cent at present, to about 90 per cent in 2030, which will not only increase the financial burden on the national economy but will also threaten the country's energy security. A large share of thermal power (around 65 per cent) in the country's energy mix, particularly coal-based production, is a serious environmental concern. As a response to these issues, several government agencies have framed policies and initiated activities for promoting various forms of renewable energy, including biomass energy. Thus, promotion of bioenergy in India is aimed at achieving energy security and gaining from its various socioeconomic and environmental benefits.

India is endowed with vast natural and environmental resources, which possess a huge potential for biomass energy. More than 600 million tonnes of biomass based on agricultural residues is generated in the country annually. Encouraging the use of biomass and other natural resources will help India achieve its growth targets with a much lesser negative impact on society and the environment. The various forms of bioenergy promoted in the country may be categorized into two major forms—biogas and liquid biofuels. Biogas is generated through either biomass thermal gasification or biomass anaerobic digestion. Biodiesel and bioethanol are two major liquid biofuels that are being produced. Development of biofuels may satisfy the growing energy needs of the country by supplying clean, economic, and eco-friendly fuels. As diesel forms a major portion of fuels for rail and road transport and agricultural activities, production of biodiesel is being considered at a much larger scale than any other form of bioenergy.

As of December 2011, of the total 23,000 MW of renewable power produced in India, the share of biopower was almost 16 per cent that included power from biomass gasification, bagasse cogeneration, and urban and industrial wastes. However, biopower potential in India is around 20,000 MW and so far only 5 per cent has been exploited. The Ministry of New and Renewable Energy (MNRE) plans to cover about 10,000 villages with biomass-based systems and over 1,000 villages with solar power by 2022. Tree oil-based production of biodiesel is being given priority over ethanol because of two main reasons: a) increasing ethanol production may have a negative impact on food (sugar) security, and b) diesel consumption in the country is above 75 per cent of all liquid and gaseous fuels used in the transport sector and other activities (CEA 2011; MNRE 2011).

In view of the above, biomass derived fuels (BDFs) such as biodiesel are being promoted world-wide. The reasons for the large-scale promotion of BDFs include energy security from fluctuating fossil fuel prices, environmental benefits of reduced emissions, and large-scale generation of employment in rural areas. Biodiesel can be blended with conventional diesel fuel in any proportion and used in diesel engines without significant engine modifications. However, the process for production of biodiesel is country-specific and depends on the availability of raw material, technology, and skilled manpower available in the country. Various raw materials such as palm oil, coconut, and jatropha seeds are used for biodiesel production. Selection of raw materials mainly depends on the sustained availability and price of oil or oilseeds. Some of the feed stocks used in various countries/regions of the world are listed in Table 11.1.

Table 11.1 Global Feed Stocks for Biodiesel Production

Country/Region	Feed Stock
US	Soybeans
Europe/EU	Rapeseed, sunflower
Africa	Jatropha
India	Jatropha, pongamia
Malaysia/Indonesia	Palm
Philippines	Coconut
Spain	Linseed Oil
Greece	Cottonseed

Source: ALTP (2010).

The estimated potential for tree-borne oils (TBOs) in India is 5 million tonnes annually of which only about 10 per cent is being exploited. In a country like India, where a major part of fossil fuels is being imported, promotion of liquid biofuels makes both economic and ecological sense. Rising crude oil prices are putting an extra financial burden on the economy and their increased use is also deteriorating the environmental quality in the country. Both these problems can be tackled to a great extent if biofuel blended fossil fuels are used in transportation and other activities (Sharma 2007, 2010).

Biodiesel Demand in India

The projected demand for diesel in 2011–12 and 2016–17 may be about 66.9 and 83.6 million tonnes (MT) respectively. Accordingly, the demand for biodiesel at various blending rates (5, 10, 15, and 20 per cent) is shown in Figure 11.1.

The Government of India (GoI) formed the National Biodiesel Mission (NBM), which set an ambitious target for biodiesel production in the country. NBM proposed to introduce 5 per cent and 10 per cent blends of biodiesel by 2007 and 2008 respectively, which would have gradually increased to 20 per cent in 2011–12. In order to achieve these targets through domestic production, the government had planned to bring a minimum of 2.19 million hectares of land under plantation by oilseed feed stock in 2006– and

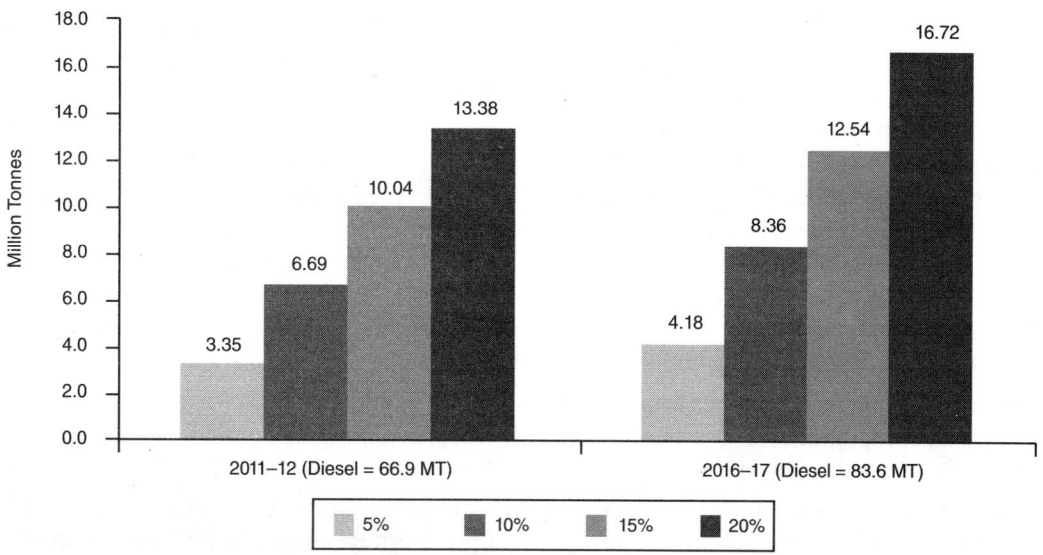

Figure 11.1 Biodiesel Demand in India at Various Blending Rates

Note: Plantation area is calculated on the basis of plantation density of 2,500 per hectare, seed production of 1.5 kg per tree, or of 3.75 T of seed per hectare corresponding to 1.2 T of oil per hectare of plantation.
Data Source: Based on data from Committee on Biofuels, GoI.

raising it to 11.2 million hectares by 2011–12 (MoA 2006). However, none of these targets were achieved and the GoI formulated the National Biofuel Policy (NBP) in 2009.

NBP envisages benefits to all stakeholders involved in biofuel production and consumption. The use of waste land for growing non-edible oilseed plantations is the main feature of NBP. These steps would not only be environmentally beneficial but will also be socially desirable, keeping in mind the global debate on 'food versus fuel'. Employment generation, particularly in rural areas, and achieving energy security and self-sufficiency for the nation are also the objectives of the policy. Under NBP, the revised target of 20 per cent blending rate is to be achieved by 2016–17, which may require 16.7 million tonnes of biodiesel and correspondingly the area under oil tree plantation should be 11.2 million hectares. However, given the progress on earlier targets under NBM, achieving these targets will require tremendous effort and coordination among various stakeholders of the biodiesel production and consumption chain.

BIOENERGY CASE STUDIES IN EAST ASIA

In January 2007, the second East Asian Summit (EAS) held in Cebu, was attended by East Asian energy ministers and their representatives. During the summit, the Energy Co-operation Task Force (ECTF) in EAS countries was formed. The ministers requested ERIA (Economic Research Institute for ASEAN and East Asia) to develop a methodology to assess the environmental, economic, and social sustainability in production and utilization of biofuels. ERIA, with the help of an international expert work group, framed the 'Guidelines for Sustainability Assessment of Biomass Utilisation' in East Asia. Based on these guidelines four case studies were conducted in select East Asian countries. The objective of these studies was to assess the sustainability of biofuels' production using various feed stocks. The studies included 'biodiesel production from tree oils in India and Indonesia'; 'biodiesel production from coconut oil in the Philippines'; and 'ethanol production from cassava in Indonesia and Thailand'. All the studies followed the life cycle approach for estimating the economic, environmental, and social impacts of biofuels during their production chain (ERIA and AIST 2007–11).

The ERIA methodology essentially includes estimating three sets of indicators—economic indicators such as total or gross value added; environmental indicators, such as savings in green house gases (GHGs); and social development indicators such as increase in employment and personal income and access to modern biomass energy. Whether an increase in the personal incomes of households resulted in an improvement in their living standards, access to basic necessities, spending on health and education, and lifestyle was also investigated.

INDIAN STUDY ON BIODIESEL

The case study in India focused on biodiesel production using non-edible TBOs such as oils from the seeds of jatropha and pongamia during 2009–11. The study included a field survey of biofuel plantations and biodiesel producers at three sites in the state of Andhra Pradesh. This state is among the foremost states which has initiated biodiesel production using various non-edible tree oils, the major being jatropha curcas. Among all renewable power, the share of biomass power in Andhra Pradesh ranks quite high. For instance, while at the national level biomass power is about 11 per cent of all renewable power, it is about 48 per cent for Andhra Pradesh (INDIASTAT 2011).

The state government supports farmers and landless labourers in cultivating biodiesel plantations by paying for the maintenance from programmes under the National Rural Employment Guarantee Act, for the first three years. However, jatropha cultivation can be taken up only on cultivable land with existing farmers, which seems to be a deviation from GoI's NBP suggesting cultivation of oil trees on waste land only (PCRA 2011). As per the state government policy, concerned authorities plan to promote contract farming for buy back of jatropha seeds with a minimum price based on the quality and quantity of the produce. A special department called the Rain Shadow Area Department has been created for planning, coordination, monitoring, and implementing biodiesel programmes. The state government proposes to encourage jatropha plantations in the ten districts of Ananthapur, Kurnool, Kadappa, Chitoor, Mehboobnagar, Nalgonda, Ranga Reddy, Prakasam, Medak, and Nellore. A state-level task force has been formed that will evaluate expressions of interest for setting up new biodiesel plants in Andhra Pradesh (RSADD 2011).

Description of Sites

The three sites selected in Andhra Pradesh include two oil tree plantation farms situated near Zaheerabad town in Medak district, namely, Tree Oils India Limited (TOIL), and Nandan Biomatrix Limited (NBL) and one biodiesel production plant located in Nalgonda district, namely Southern online Bio Technologies Limited (SBTL). Each of these companies are involved in at least one stage of the biodiesel production chain and were identified to capture, as much as possible, the major part of the life cycle of biodiesel production, that is, from jatropha cultivation to biodiesel production. A brief introduction of the companies is now given.

TOIL has various oil tree plantations on about 120 acres of waste land (a barren land with rocky soil), which include pongamia on about 60 acres, jatropha on about 40 acres, amla on about 15 acres, and others (simaroba, madhuca, neem, soapnut, calophyllum, Chinese talo, candle nut, and camelina) in about five acres. Thus, the maximum focus is on pongamia and jatropha plantations. In addition to the main product, that is, oilseeds, the company has developed several ancillary activities on the farm which include growing various vegetables as inter-crops, producing manure, apiculture, animal rearing, poultry, vermiculture, composting, and biogas from animal dung. On the one hand, these activities cater to the daily needs of farm workers and on the other hand, they are generating some revenue for the company from the first year itself. Thus, the company is able to survive without any revenue from its core business, that is, the sale of oil tree seeds or tree oil, during the gestation period of 5–7 years.

NBL's oil tree plantations (mainly jatropha) and main research and development (R&D) facility is located in Zaheerabad. It has developed jatropha hybrid varieties, which may yield upto 7 tonnes of seeds per hectare and upto 3 tonnes of oil per hectare, which are almost twice the yield from a normal jatropha variety. NBL has been awarded four global patents for jatropha varieties. The company is using advanced approaches in crop improvements like mutagenesis (radiation induced and chemical induced), hybridization of high-yield varieties of oilseeds, and developing proper agronomical practices. NBL is involved in contract farming, direct benefit through estate farming, partnership with panchayats, and farming in forest land. The company is also providing many support services to farmers such as high-quality planting material and cultivation technology; financial assistance for crop cultivation through bank tie-ups, crop insurance through insurance companies, and continuous monitoring of the crop and buy back of oilseeds.

SBTL's biodiesel production plant is situated in an area which has easy access to the availability of oilseeds and other raw materials. The plant uses multi-feed stock techniques for biodiesel production with existing raw materials such as palm stearin oil and animal talo. The company projects itself as an eco-friendly greenfield company, which is involved in biodiesel production by developing waste lands and employing tribal and rural people, thereby generating rural employment, saving foreign exchange on diesel imports, and reducing pollution levels by substituting biodiesel for fossil diesel. During the survey, the company reported that the available quantity of jatropha and other oil tree seeds for the plant at Nalgonda was not enough or cost-effective, hence as an alternative, presently the company uses a combination of various feed stocks such as non-edible vegetable seed oils, fish oils, animal fat, fatty acid, and used cooking oil to produce biodiesel and glycerin.

Major Outcomes

The field survey and an analysis of the data collected from the above sites revealed very limited success on economic, environmental, and social aspects of the biodiesel production chain. Some of the major findings of the case study are:

(i) On the economic front, the cost incurred during the cultivation stage is much higher than the revenue generated as oil tree growing companies are facing financial losses during this stage. However, economic benefits in terms of gross value added (GVA) by biodiesel producers and forex savings for the country could be substantial, which indicates that the promotion of biodiesel production may result in net economic benefits in the long run. On a small scale, such as at a village or community level, there are some examples of biodiesel production using tree oil being successful. However, major biodiesel producers in Andhra Pradesh are not able to procure enough feed stock, that is, TBOs or seeds for biodiesel production. They are surviving on various other feed stocks such as palm stearin oil, animal tallow, and waste oils. This defeats the basic purpose of biodiesel producers as well as government policies, which are focused on biodiesel production using TBOs.

(ii) On the environmental front, although data were not sufficient, preliminary estimates from available data indicated a net reduction in GHG emissions during the life cycle of biodiesel production. GHG saving was better in the production stage than in the cultivation stage. Other environmental changes such as the impact on local air pollution, water demand, and land-use change may be significant but none of the stakeholders on the sites surveyed collected data to calculate such impacts.

(iii) On the social front, in terms of employment generation, comparatively good performance is visible in all stages of the biodiesel production chain. Both during the oil tree cultivation and biodiesel production phases, good employment generation resulted in an increase in the personal incomes of people in the surrounding localities. Employee wages in the biodiesel production chain are about 50–60 per cent higher than wages in employment elsewhere. Due to the increase in wages, employees are able to spend more on their food, health, education, and living standards. Estimates of various social development indicators (SDIs) showed an overall improvement at the local and community levels. As there is a visible increase in employment and income of individuals employed in oil tree plantations as well as in other stages of biodiesel production, promoting these activities will have a positive effect on social development at the local level.

(iv) On the policy front, GoI's policy seems to encourage production of biodiesel in the country but the ground realities are different. Various activities have been initiated for production of biodiesel, which include development of high oil-yielding varieties of jatropha, planting jatropha by government-sponsored agencies, setting up of pilot plants for transesterification, successful trial runs on locomotives and road vehicles using 5 per cent biodiesel blends, and organizing seminars to increase awareness about the biodiesel programme. A comparison of the biofuel policies in the four EAS countries mentioned earlier indicates that India has the most ambitious targets of a 20 per cent blending rate, which if achieved may result in several benefits. However, in India none of the biodiesel blending targets set by government agencies have been achieved so far. Initially, blending targets of 5 and 10 per cent were to be achieved by 2007 and 2008 respectively; however, these were not met. Further, the final target of a 20 per cent blending rate was to be met by 2011–12 but this has now been revised to 2016–17, as per the National Biofuel Policy 2009. But based on facts from the field survey, considering the ground realities and feedback from various stakeholders, achieving these targets seems difficult and will require tremendous efforts from all stakeholders.

Lessons Learned

Several issues need to be tackled for ensuring the sustainability of biodiesel production in India. The main challenges for various stakeholders involved in the biodiesel production chain are the economic viability of the plantations, particularly during the non-yield period, economic viability of biodiesel production, social acceptance by farmers and other stakeholders to take up the plantations by themselves or release their lands on lease/contract farming for the same, adequate and sustained availability of feed stock (oilseeds), an appropriate pricing of raw materials used and the final product, and labour availability.

The lessons learned and problem areas revealed from the Indian case study are:

- Jatropha curcas was initially considered a miracle plant in India that would grow in any type of soil without irrigation, fertilizers, proper care, etc. But the results of the field study indicate that jatropha and other oil trees such as pongamia, need to be nurtured for their survival, particularly in the first few years of plantation. Also, for sustainable yield, regular irrigation and fertilizer applications, throughout the life span of the plantation, are essential even if they not as intensive as for food crops.

- Among various hurdles, the price of raw material (oil tree seeds) and the final product (biodiesel) seems to be the biggest limitation in promoting tree oil-based biodiesel production. During the study period (2009–11) the prevailing price of oil tree seeds of Rs 7–10 per kg and the biodiesel purchase price of Rs 26.5 per litre were not commercially viable. Thus, it is necessary that the price of both oilseeds and biodiesel are kept at a level that can sustain the biodiesel production chain.
- It was found that farmers and other stakeholders are not very interested in taking up biofuel plantations. Livelihood insecurity among farmers and their households is very high and farm and non-farm activities are likely to be attractive only if they simultaneously improve short-run welfare. Thus, it is necessary to encourage farmers to undertake jatropha and other oil tree plantations, which will be possible only by ensuring financial gains to them, particularly during the non-yield period. The study supports the idea of initiating ancillary activities such as poultry farming, vegetable and other inter-crops, rearing milk-producing animals, vermi-compost production, organic manure production, horticulture, and apiculture which were found successful in the field. In addition, mass awareness and capacity-building programmes in rural areas, financial and technical support such as interest-free loans or soft loans, easy availability of quality seeds and other inputs, and crop insurance will attract farmers towards biodiesel crops.
- There is no stakeholder who has an integrated facility exhibiting all the life cycle stages of biodiesel production and, hence estimating economic, environmental, and social impacts using a life cycle approach for each stage of biodiesel production is difficult. During the cultivation stage of oil trees, a long gestation period is a major concern for farmers and small companies. Also, lack of clarity on the GoI's biofuel pricing policy and shortage of oilseeds are other concerns. Due to lack of availability of data at the field level and throughout the value chain of biodiesel production, an exact analysis of GHG savings and carbon credits and other environmental impacts is not possible. Personal incomes of local people employed increased by about 60 per cent in the cultivation stage and by 90 per cent in the production stage. However, an increase in the number of employees was not substantial as most of the labourers/farmers employed in the cultivation of biodiesel crops were already employed elsewhere in other activities but with lesser wages.
- Social development was visible in some SDIs that were estimated using collected data. For example, the standard of living of the families staying on the plantation farms is higher than that of families living in a nearby village. Families staying on farms use biogas, a clean fuel generated by farm waste, for cooking and other household activities, they have toilets within their premises and electricity is available either through the normal grid or it is generated by biodiesel generators. Due to a rise in their incomes, families spent more on health and education, particularly on the female members, indicating better social development. However, it was observed that despite working hours being the same, women are paid only 65–70 per cent of the salary of their male counterparts. In addition, they also had to contribute much more to household chores. Such gender bias may not be good in the long run as bioenergy programmes are already facing a shortage of labourers.

CONCLUSIONS

Despite the very limited success achieved so far, biomass energy offers a sustainable alternative when compared to other forms of energy. Decentralized bioenergy generation will contribute to social development in those areas where conventional and other forms of energy are either inaccessible or not economically viable. A large part of the rural population will be able to use this energy for various domestic and commercial purposes such as cooking, irrigation, and education which may result in poverty reduction, higher literacy rates, and better healthcare.

The Indian biodiesel industry, in comparison to ethanol industry, is still in its early stages. However, the demand for diesel is about five times higher than that for petrol, and thus, more attention is required for increasing biodiesel production. Since the demand for edible vegetable oil exceeds supply, to meet the ambitious targets of a 20 per cent biodiesel blending rate by 2016–17, the GoI's decision to use non-edible oil from jatropha curcas and other oil tree seeds for biodiesel production is justified. The formation of NBM and formulation of NBP and bringing a substantial area under jatropha cultivation on non-agriculture land are steps in the right direction.

If the target of 20 per cent biodiesel blending rates is achieved at the national level, it will result in substantial economic and social gains through reduction in imports of fossil fuels, generation of large-scale employment, particularly in rural areas, improving the environment, and in gender development. The case study found a visible increase in employment and income of individuals employed in jatropha and other oil tree plantations. This marginal increase in income has improved the living standard and lifestyle of the people, as they are able to spend more on their basic needs such as food, education, and health. It also has some positive impact on female literacy and the upliftment of women in rural areas.

Biofuel crops on non-agriculture land and use of non-edible tree oils for biodiesel production will be beneficial in the long run. Utilization of waste land for biofuel plantations will augment land resources and will not have any adverse effect on arable land used for food crops. Also, since no edible oils are used as feed stock for biodiesel production, the 'food versus fuel' debate may not be of much relevance for India. Further, biofuel plantations on denuded land and land with negligible vegetation will turn them into green areas, resulting in enhanced carbon sequestration and thus a reduction in global GHG emissions.

The companies involved in biodiesel production reported a shortage of supply of oil tree seeds and to sustain production they are using various other feed stocks such as animal fats and waste oils. This defeats the basic purpose of the NBP of biodiesel production using jatropha and other tree oils and needs to be tackled on an urgent basis.

The geographical location and field conditions have a tremendous effect on survival rates of jatropha plants. Under adverse conditions, their survival rates are very low and the yield per plant is also very low. The average annual yield is 1–2 kg of seeds per plant depending on various conditions. It was observed that the frequency of irrigation, fertilizer application, and nurturing of jatropha plants can increase the yield substantially. Thus, the myth that oil trees like jatropha can grow without any care and attention should be dispelled. In fact, for better yield, jatropha and other oil trees require as much care as other crops. However, the amount of various inputs is much less than that for food crops and depends upon the location of the plantation. For example, in arid and semi-arid regions, the frequency of irrigation may be higher, particularly in the first few years of a plantation.

GVA is highest in the fifth year of the jatropha plantation and may tend to stabilize thereafter. Also, GVA during the biodiesel production stage is much higher as compared to GVA during the plantation stage. Economic benefits in terms of net profit are better at the biodiesel production stage as compared to the plantation stage. Employment generated is higher at the plantation stage than at the biodiesel production stage. Jatropha cultivation, being an agricultural activity, is labour-intensive and hence beneficial for employment and the development of rural areas. The GoI should encourage biofuel plantations by setting up more biodiesel production plants. Availability of limited data restricts the comparison of GHG reduction in various stages of the biodiesel production chain and other environmental impacts.

Policy Recommendations

The first and foremost condition for the success of biomass energy programmes is the regular and sufficient supply of biomass. The lack of community participation and transparent government policies are some of the serious concerns, which may affect the availability of biomass feedstock to bioenergy plants in India. Some of the urgent measures that are necessary for achieving the objective of biodiesel production programmes include:

- The case study focused on a small scale (village or community level) and the reality at the macro-level (state or country level) might be different. It is suggested that for a macro-scale assessment more rigorous fieldwork on a large extent of area should be undertaken. A representative sample size could cover at least 10–15 per cent of the total plantation area and about 25 per cent of biodiesel production capacity, including both small- and large-scale biodiesel production units.
- The GoI may consider diverting funds from various social schemes such as famine relief work and national rural employment schemes and using them for biofuel plantations. Since the major objective of both NBP and the Mahatma Gandhi National Rural Employment Guarantee Act (MNREGA) is to provide employment to the rural population, this mechanism will serve the purpose of these schemes and also boost biofuel crops.
- It was observed that for getting approval for biofuel schemes, corporates have to deal with several government authorities, groups, and individuals such as authorities at the district, block or panchayat levels and even local groups and people. It is suggested that for accelerating and enhancing biofuel crop production through government intervention, there should be a minimum number of such approvals and interferences.
- Generally, it is presumed that biofuels are carbon-neutral. However, if we consider all inputs and outputs throughout the life cycle of biofuel production and consumption, this may not be true. Two of the most controversial arguments on environmental sustainability of biofuels are land-use changes and emissions of GHGs from energy used in the production and transportation of biofuels. Land-use changes for the production of bioenergy crops should be aimed at maximizing environmental benefits and improving livelihood. Also, measures should be taken to ensure that the net impact on the reduction of GHG emissions from biofuel programmes is positive.

- To maximize environmental benefits, the distance between the point of the availability of feed stock and the biofuel production point and also that between biofuel production and consumption points should be minimized. Research and action through policies should benefit the poor farmers and labourers, be environmentally sustainable, provide energy security, accelerate agricultural productivity, and use advanced energy crop farming techniques. At the same time, it should be ensured that automation does not reduce the labour-intensive character of biofuel crop production activities.
- As of now, the economic viability of biofuel production is questionable as the profit margins of the producers are very low. It is advisable to rationalize various tax structures and at least up to the targeted 20 per cent blending rates, biodiesel could be exempted from various duties, taxes, etc. It is necessary that the buy-back guarantee is assured to the producers of biofuel feed stocks as well as producers of biofuels. Some of the ways of achieving this could be similar to the system existing between sugarcane producers and sugar mills.
- As studies have observed a shortage of raw materials for biodiesel production, we could consider importing feed stock with either nil or the least possible duties and taxes so that the biodiesel industry can survive until enough indigenous feed stock is available. In addition to jatropha, plantation of other non-edible oil trees should be encouraged as some of them are native to India such as pongamia, mahua, neem, and simaroba and they may have better survival rates than jatropha.
- The price of biomass feed stock and biodiesel should be such that it results in overall benefits to all the stakeholders including growers/biomass farmers, biodiesel producers, and even oil marketing companies (OMCs). The government has taken the right steps in gradually removing or reducing subsidies on petroleum products but if the benefits of these steps are borne in the form of the burden of extra cost of biofuels, the net effect on OMCs may be either nil or negative. Thus, OMCs should be ensured that they will not be burdened with additional costs, which makes the marketing of such fuels unattractive for them. The price at the end-use of blended fuels should be lower than fossil fuels to increase the social acceptability of biofuels. Investigations through Indian field studies have shown that the oil-seed purchase price of about Rs 15–17 per kg and the biodiesel purchase price of about Rs 37 per litre in 2010–11, seemed commercially viable. This price may be reviewed and, if required, revised each year.

REFERENCES

ALTP (2010), *Profiting from the Alternative Energy Revolution*. Available at http://www.altprofits.com/, accessed in December 2010.

Central Electricity Authority [CEA] (2011), *Power Scenario at Glance*. New Delhi: Central Electricity Authority, January.

ERIA and AIST (2007–11), Various Reports of the Expert Working Group of ERIA, Indonesia and AIST, Japan, published by ERIA during 2007–11, Jakarta, Indonesia (editor, M. Sagisaka of AIST).

IEA (2011), Website of International Energy Agency. Available at http://www.eia.doe.gov/cabs /India/Oil.html, accessed on 11 February 2011.

International Institute for Environment and Development [IIED] (2010), 'Biomass energy—optimising its contribution to poverty reduction and ecosystem services', a report on the international workshop of IIED and ESPA (Ecosystem Services for Poverty Reduction), Edinburgh, UK, October.

INDIASTAT (2011), *Details on Biomass Power*. Available at http://www.indiastat.com/, accessed during March–June, 2011.

Ministry of Agriculture [MoA] (2006), *Report of the National Oilseeds and Vegetable Oil Development Board*, New Delhi: Ministry of Agriculture.

Ministry of New and Renewable Energy [MNRE] (2011), *Annual Report 2010-11*. New Delhi: Ministry of New and Renewable Energy, Government of India. Available at http://www.mnre.gov.in/annualreport/2010_11_English/index.htm, last accessed on 6 June 2011.

Petroleum Conservation Research Association [PCRA] (2011), Website of PCRA. Available at http://www.pcra-biofuels.org/ap.htm, accessed on 16 May 2011.

RSADD (2011), Rain Shadow Area Development Department, Andhra Pradesh, http://rsad.ap.gov.in/, accessed on 5 May 2011.

Sharma, Vinod K. (2007), 'Social Aspects of Biomass Utilisation', in M. Sagisaka (ed.), *Sustainable Biomass Utilisation Vision in East Asia*. Chiba Shi, Japan: The Institute for Development Economies, JETRO, and ERIA.

———. (2010), 'Sustainability Assessment of Biomass Energy Utilisation in Selected East Asian Countries', (editors) ERIA Working Group on 'Sustainability Assessment of Biomass Utilization in East Asia, ERIA Research Project Report 2009-12, ERAI, Jakarta, Indonesia.

UNEP (2001), *State of the Environment, India 2001*. Thailand: Regional Resource Centre for Asia and the Pacific.

12

Access to Modern Energy Services
The Road Not Taken

B. Sudhakara Reddy

*The test of our progress is not whether we add more
to the abundance of those who have much,
it is whether we provide enough for those who have too little.*

—Franklin D. Roosevelt

MODERN ENERGY—PLANNED SCARCITY

In the age of iPhones, Facebook, and Twitter, there is instant access to information and constant means of communication. It is difficult to imagine life without these 'luxuries', but they are just that, luxuries. For a large portion of the population in developing countries, particularly those at the bottom of the pyramid, these technologies are not only a rarity, but an impossibility as there is no access to electricity (Relich 2011).

In the case of India, even as recently as 2010, only 65 per cent of the households had electricity connections, though almost 90 per cent of the villages have been electrified and 70 per cent have no access to gaseous fuels for cooking (Anonymous 2011a). The benefits of modern energy services[1] are not reaching them for two reasons: (i) '*inaccessibility*',[2] and (ii) '*unaffordability*'.[3] Many factors contribute to this deficiency but there are ways to overcome them, some of which, however, are overlooked in conventional planning (Anonymous 2010a, 2011b; IEA 2011; UNDP 2009).

While energy is a basic necessity, it is not universally accepted as one. There are a limited number of actors in the field who consider energy more a commodity from which money can be made. In the 'socialistic regime', electricity or gas was supplied entirely by state utilities that owned both generation systems and distribution networks. The governments set the rate of return of profit for the utilities, planned for future energy needs, and helped ensure that rates were fair and based on the cost of the service. However, as time passed, the practice of earning even limited returns, was often given a go by because of political compulsions and capacity to influence policy decisions. In many instances, tariffs were so low that in the absence of competition they encouraged a culture of complacency leading to poor performance. Structural inefficiencies and political interference combined with agricultural subsidies landed most state utilities in serious financial crises. Thus, the national grid

---

[1] Modern energy services are the desired and useful processes/services that result from the use of modern energy such as gas or electricity to produce heat for cooking; power for transport, water pumping, and grinding; and air cooling.

[2] Accessibility indicates whether the available energy service can reach the household, which is usually indicative of infrastructure.

[3] Affordability is indicative of the purchasing ability of households for a particular energy service.

has become weak and its extension slow and underfinanced. The trend is unsustainable and there is lack of political will to shift policies to expand the consumer base. For these reasons, power has failed to reach the targeted communities in rural regions and also the urban poor.

Given the multiplicity of challenges faced by state-owned utilities and the unwillingness of private players to supply power to rural areas, the issue is to what extent these energy governance issues help in improving energy access for a majority of the rural poor. To make energy accessible it is important to take into account the characteristics of the issues discussed above and incorporate them in strategies. Fortunately, several experiences that provide useful lessons are available in literature (Balachandra 2012; UNDP 2009; UNEP 2008).

The question often asked is, how will physical access to modern energy be achieved? Yes, it can be done by including three main ingredients in the implementation mechanism: (i) integrating energy access into the rural energy development approach, (ii) combination of an off-grid decentralized and centralized energy system approach, and (iii) public–private partnerships for rural energy infrastructure development.

The aim of this chapter is, therefore, to design a framework to help households attain *development through modern energy services*, which is widely seen as having three essential components: availability, accessibility, and affordability (AAA). The data collected by the National Sample Survey Organization (NSSO) as well as Census 2011 provide the base for a cross-sectional study for rural as well as urban households on cooking and lighting energy carriers (Anonymous 2011; NSSO 2007).

HOUSEHOLD ENERGY USE IN INDIA—THE WOOD, THE BAD, AND THE UGLY

A large share of the 37 per cent of the total primary energy used by the household sector in India comes from non-commercial fuels such as fuel wood and dung (Reddy and Srinivas 2009). The use of modern sources of energy has increased significantly over the decades, particularly in urban regions, but the share of traditional use of biofuels for cooking, heating, etc. is still far larger and is a noticeable feature. The use of biofuels is reflective of non-uniform availability of modern energy carriers and uneven access to infrastructure to avail them. Even if the required energy carrier is available and accessible, households simply cannot afford it. Biofuels (fuel wood, charcoal/coal, dung, etc.) are a major source for cooking in rural areas, while in urban areas, LPG, along with kerosene, is the dominant fuel. In many households, the same energy carrier is used for both cooking and water heating. Similarly, multiple carriers are used for a particular end use. However, the carrier that is being used most is the main one while the rest are referred to as 'auxiliary fuels/carriers'. Between 1950 and 2010, the primary energy use increased by nearly two times, from 62 to 175.8 MTOE reflecting a change in the fuel mix. By 2010, the share of oil and gas in secondary energy use increased while that of biofuels reduced (Table 12.1).

A household's total energy consumption and mix of energy sources is the result of its attempt to meet its various energy needs. LPG is the fuel of choice for cooking because it is easy to use, clean, efficient, and economical. Firewood is the most widely used fuel among rural households and it is obtained by gathering twigs and fallen branches or cutting of public trees. It is the original biofuel as used in the discovery of fire and a firm favourite for millions of years. It is different from its counterparts in many respects. Unlike others, it is a dirty fuel, emits smoke, requires a large storing space, and its preparation (collection, transportation, cutting, etc.) is done by households themselves with the primary responsibility falling on women and children. Electricity is the most preferred carrier for lighting (Table 12.2). With increasing incomes, households climb the energy ladder and thereby the comfort ladder. The

Table 12.1 Household Energy Consumption (1950–2010)

Year	Percentage Share of Various Energy Carriers					Total (MTOE)
	Biofuels	Coal/Charcoal	Kerosene	Gas/Electricity	Others	
1950	97.0	1.10	1.8	0.0	0.1	62.0
1960	96.0	1.2	2.6	0.0	0.2	77.5
1970	93.1	2.8	3.2	0.5	0.4	92.7
1980	88.9	3..8	4.2	2.5	0.6	113.9
1990	81.2	4.1	5.3	7.7	1.7	136.0
2000	71.0	3.5	5.5	13.2	2.8	158.0
2010	66.1	1.2	2.7	27.2	4.8	175.8

Source: Anonymous (2011).

Table 12.2 End Uses and Rationale for Using Various Energy Carriers

Energy Carrier Used	End Use	Rationale for Using the Fuel	Reasons for Not Using
Fuel wood	Cooking Water heating	(i) Available in plenty (ii) Accessible (iii) Low cost (iv) Possibility of collecting free (v) More appropriate for cooking traditional meals (iv) Inefficiency of usage (vi) No access to modern fuels	(i) Provides smoke (ii) Pollution/respiratory ailments/irritations (iii) Not easy to use
Kerosene	Cooking Lighting	(i) Available in small shops and markets (ii) No access to electricity	(i) Not a good light source (ii) Increasing cost (iii) Smoke
LPG	Cooking	(i) Ease of use (ii) Efficient (iii) Clean	(i) Limited access (ii) Prohibitive cost (iii) Frequent shortage
Electricity	(i) Lighting (ii) Appliances (iii) Mechanical power	(i) Easy to use (ii) Availability (iii) Comfort (iv) Efficient	(i) Inaccessible (ii) High connection cost (iii) Frequent shortage (iv) Prohibitive price for poor households

Source: Survey by the author.

energy ladder describes the transition from the use of traditional fuels/technologies like wood to modern and more sophisticated fuels/technologies and services as household incomes increase. The high-income group households use more electricity plus some liquid and gaseous fuels with advanced technologies for a much wider range of energy services (cooking/heating, transport, cooling and refrigeration, Information and Communications Technology [ICTs], etc. (Figure 12.1).

ACCESS TO ENERGY SERVICES—THE TARGETS

According to our estimate, nearly 180 million households lack gaseous fuels for cooking and 80 million households lack access to electric lighting. This basic human need is not met for a significant percentage of India's population and for a much higher percentage from the poorer sections of the society. Inadequate access to modern energy services contributes to the loss of employment opportunities, staggering burden of health effects, and personal productive time, with widespread economic effects, especially affecting vulnerable groups such as women, children, poor people in rural areas, and slum dwellers. Problems associated with poor-quality fuels are significant barriers to development, both human and economic. Despite growing attention to energy access, investment in energy services in India remains low.

Energy Services—Cooking

In spite of an expanding energy infrastructure, the shares of modern energy carriers for cooking[4] and lighting[5] are low among rural and urban poor households. For example, a significant proportion of the households lives just yards away from electricity transmission lines but cannot get power connections because of poverty.

There is a distinct difference in access to modern energy between urban and rural areas. In mega cities, 90 per cent of the households have access to LPG, whereas 85 per cent in metros have access to it. The share is down to 75 per cent in case of smaller cities and only 50 per cent in towns. In rural regions, the reach is only 11 per cent. The total number of households in India that need access to gaseous fuels are 177 million (Table 12.3).

Energy Services—Lighting

Although lighting uses relatively less energy in comparison to cooking, it is an important household energy service. This

---

[4] As a proxy for lack of clean cooking, the use of biofuels such as fuel wood, cow dung, and agricultural waste measures deprivation of cooking services provided by modern energy carriers.

[5] Kerosene is being used as a source of lighting by poor households. The proxy for the lack of access to modern energy for lighting could be households using kerosene as the primary source of lighting.

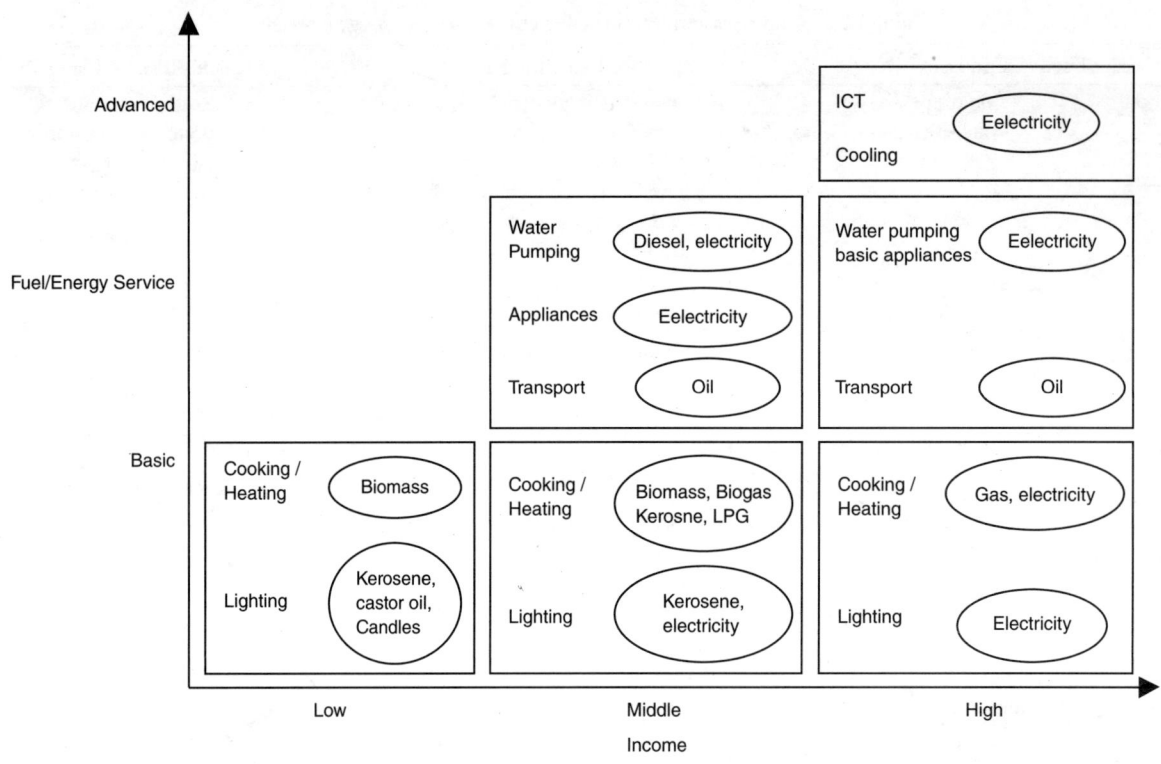

Figure 12.1 Household Energy Transition

Source: Modified version of Hammond (2007).

Table 12.3 Energy Accessibility for Cooking (2010)

Population (million)	Urban	Population (million)	Households (million)	Share of HH Having Access to LPG/Biogas (%)	Current Level of Access (%)	Target (million)
Urban	Mega (more than 10 million) cities	53	10.6	90		
	Metros (5–10 million)	32	6.4	85		
	Other cities (0.5–5 million)	101	20.2	75		
	Small towns (less than 0.5 million)	191	38.2	50		
	Total	330	84		65	29
Rural		830	167	11	11.0	148

Source: Anonymous (2011).

is because lighting usually involves the use of commercial energy and often not many alternatives exist. Nearly 0.4 billion people in India—more than the world's population in Edison's time—still have no access to electricity. Estimates show that the population growth rate is exceeding the electrification rate (Reddy et al. 2010) resulting in an increase in the number of people without electric light, the majority being in rural areas. This was probably not the lighting future imagined by Edison.

Access to electricity in India is rather unusual. Over 90 per cent of the villages have access to power, but only 55 per cent households have electric connections owing to the high cost of power. As seen in Table 12.4, the percentage of villages electrified increased significantly until 1991, steeply fell thereafter and the same is the case with household electrification. By the end of 1970, nearly one-fifth of the villages had been electrified, but only 5 per cent of the households had electricity connections. Thereafter the momentum picked up, and by 1991, 88 per cent of the villages and about a third of the rural households had the benefit of electricity. However, the number of households without electricity increased from 61 million in 1951 to 75 million in 2011.

Table 12.4 Electricity Accessibility

Year	Village Electrification			Households Electrification							
	Villages Electrified	% Share	CAGR (%)	Rural Households (million)	Electrified (%)	CAGR Rural (%)	Urban Households (million)	Electrified (%)	Total HH (million)	Electrified (%)	CAGR (Total) (%)
1947	1,500	0.28									
1951	3,061	0.57	8.20	61	0.02		13	8	74	1.3	
1961	21,750	4.03	24.34	68	1.5	1.2	18	21	85	5.0	1.5
1971	1,06,931	19.81	19.36	78	5.1	1.5	24	40	100	12.1	1.8
1981	2,73,906	50.75	11.02	92	14.7	1.9	35	62.5	123	26.2	2.3
1991	4,74,982	88.00	6.31	114	30.5	2.4	47	75.8	153	42.4	2.5
2001	4,81,124	89.14	0.14	137	43.5	2.1	64	87.6	194	55.8	2.7
2011	4,93,240	91.38	0.28	167	55.0	2.2	84	92.7	250	65.0	2.9

Source: http://www.powermin.nic.in, last accessed in February 2011.

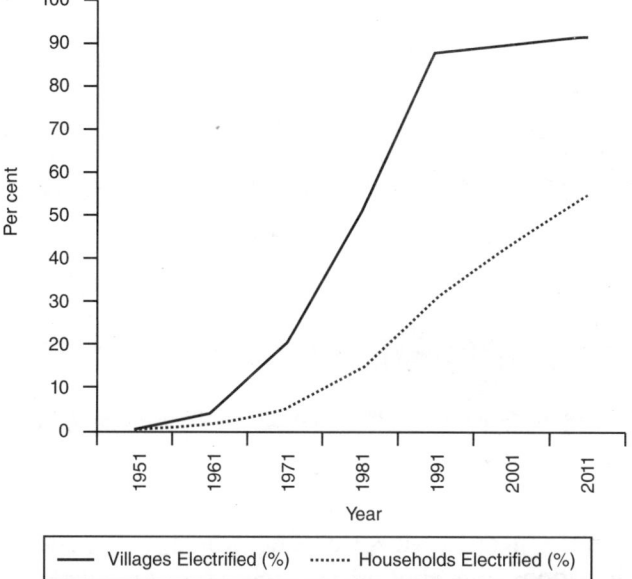

Figure 12.2 Electricity Access (1951–2001) (Village and Household Levels)

Source: Anonymous (2010b).

Rural Electrification

In the 1950s and 1960s, state electrification efforts were directed at cities and towns (Modi et al. 2005). No special efforts were made to improve access to modern cooking fuels. The Rural Electrification Corporation (REC) was created in 1969 with a mandate to facilitate the provision of electricity in rural and semi-urban areas. However, due to resource constraints, many of these programmes have not taken off. High Transmission and Distribution (T&D) losses and non-rational tariffs have resulted in financial losses to many state-owned utilities. Because of this, their focus has shifted to urban and industrial consumers while neglecting rural supply and electrification (Reddy and D'Sa 1995). Box 12.1 provides information on village electrification programmes.

The extent of rural electrification varies widely from state to state, for example, about 50 per cent of the households in north India and in the north-eastern hill states are not served by grid electricity. States like Andhra Pradesh, Kerala, Haryana, and Punjab have achieved 100 per cent village electrification. Many other states also have a high rate of

---

Box 12.1 Village Electrification Programmes

Kutir Jyothi—The government bears the entire cost of the service connection and internal wiring and is provided to the states as a grant.

REC programmes—Facilitated electrification of 62 per cent of the Indian villages and 59 per cent of electrified irrigation pump sets.

Prime Minister's Village Development Programme (Pradhan Mantri Gramodaya Yojana)—The scheme offers financing through loans (90 per cent) and grants (10 per cent). The states have the flexibility to decide the allocation among six basic services.

Minimum Needs Programme—100 per cent loans from the central government for last mile connectivity for rural electrification projects in less electrified states.

Accelerated Rural Electrification Programme—Designed for electrification of non-electrified villages. States can borrow funds from financial institutions and receive interest subsidies from the central government.

Rajiv Gandhi Grameen Vidyutikaran Yojana launched in 2005—The government provides 90 per cent of the capital cost as grant. Projects will be managed by franchisees, which can be local-level organizations (such as NGOs and rural committees) or private entrepreneurs.

Table 12.5 Village and Household Electrification Rates among Various States (2010)

State	Elec. Consumption (KWh/HH/year)	Villages Electrified (%)	HH Electrified (%)		
			Urban	Rural	Total
Andhra Pradesh	920	100	95	60	70.9
Assam	250	78.6	80.6	16.54	36.4
Bihar	120	61.3	74.1	5.13	26.5
Chhattisgarh	650	94	92.2	46	60.3
Delhi	1,650		99.4	85.5	89.8
Gujarat	1,500	99.7	97.5	72.1	80.0
Goa	2,263		98.3	92.4	94.2
Haryana	1,320	100	97.5	78.5	84.4
Himachal Pradesh	970	98.2	99.4	94.5	96.0
Jammu & Kashmir	850	98.2	99.4	74.5	82.2
Jharkhand	800	31.1	90.8	10	35.0
Karnataka	900	99.9	96.5	72.2	79.7
Kerala	500	100	94.5	65.5	74.5
Madhya Pradesh	680	96.4	95.1	62.3	72.5
Maharashtra	1,000	88.3	97.4	65.2	45.3
Odisha	800	62.6	83.9	19.3	13.6
Punjab	1,600	100	98.2	89.5	62.1
Rajasthan	750	71.5	95.7	44	30.7
Tamil Nadu	1,080	100	93.8	71.2	78.2
Tripura	500		91.8	31.8	50.4
Uttaranchal	1,112		95.0	50.3	64.2
Uttar Pradesh	400	88.3	85.4	19.8	40.1
West Bengal	500	99.5	89.6	20.3	41.8
North-east	300	82.2	80.0	40	27.6
All-India	700	95	92.7	55.3	65.0

Source: Anonymous (2011).

electrification. However, in the case of household electrification, states like Uttar Pradesh, West Bengal, Odisha, and Assam have achieved only 40–60 per cent household electrification. In per capita use, Gujarat consumes the highest with 1,500 KWh/year, while in Bihar it is just 120 KWh/year (Table 12.5).

Affordability[6]—Energy Use across Different Income Groups

Energy is a basic household good and it is not possible to live without fuel for cooking and lighting. Hence, the interaction between welfare and energy use is significant. A high budget share for energy services makes households vulnerable to fluctuations in energy prices. Table 12.6 shows data on households using various energy carriers for cooking and lighting in poor and non-poor households from rural and urban regions. There is a strong positive relationship between income and household demand for commercial fuels. High-income households have a greater choice in selecting an energy carrier and many opt for cleaner, comfortable, and more efficient modern energy carriers such as electricity or LPG. Thus, the demand for electricity and LPG tends to increase with income, reflecting an increasing desire for comfort and discretionary energy consumption. The high cost of electric connections in urban areas ensures that subsidized kerosene remains the dominant fuel for the poor.

Energy Services and Household Budgets

Energy is a basic need and the share of income spent on energy services at various income levels varies. Data indicate

---

[6] Affordability in the context of modern energy services means whether the households can afford to have LPG and electricity connections and after having them whether they can actually use them regularly. This depends on the household incomes, cost of connection, and the price of LPG/electricity.

Table 12.6 Energy Affordability among Different Income Groups (2010*)

Region		% Share of HH Using Various Fuels		
		Poor	Non-poor	Total
Rural	Solid	93.5	66.4	75.1
	Liquid	3.7	11.5	8.9
	Gas/Elec.	1.1	21.3	14.7
	No cooking	1.7	0.8	1.1
	Total households (million)	52	110	167
Urban	Solid	85.5	32.3	47.5
	Liquid	6.7	4.5	5.1
	Gas/Elec.	4.5	62.1	45.7
	No cooking	3.3	1.1	1.7
	Total households (million)	25	59	84

Source: (*) Estimates based on NSSO (2007).

(Table 12.7) that lower-income households spend their limited resources on energy services. In fact, poorer households often pay higher per unit cost for energy services because they can only afford to buy fuel in smaller quantities or have less efficient equipment. Similarly, lighting sources that are used by low-income households provide very low levels of illumination and are very inefficient. The inefficiency is so high that the cost of energy will be 20 times higher (per unit of light) compared to that of electric devices (ESMAP 2004). Thus, these households not only use low-efficiency devices but pay higher costs for their use. Energy costs thus have a significant impact on how basic needs are satisfied: for example, how much disposable income is available for education or healthcare.

Table 12.7 Average Budget Share of All Household Energy (in %)

Income Group	Share of Expenditure on Energy	
	Rural (*)	Urban
Low	10.5%	12.6
Medium	8.9	10.2
High	5.1	6.3
Average	9.0	9.5
Value of consumption in 1987 (Rs) (**)	11.77	16.7
Value of consumption in 2007 (Rs)	60.41	109

Note: (*) including the value of home-grown, collected, and purchased fuels
** CPI = 100

Source: NSSO (2007).

Among rural poor, 10.5 per cent of the expenditure goes for energy while in urban regions it is 12.6 per cent. In the case of high-income groups the share of expenditure on energy is around 9 per cent (in rural and urban regions). The poor households pay much more in terms of health impacts, collection time, and energy quality for the equivalent level of energy services as their rich counterparts.

There is a high degree of variation in electricity use between rural and urban regions, both in quantity as well as quality. Of the total use, two-thirds of the electricity is consumed by urban households and the rest by rural regions, even though the rural population constitutes 70 per cent of the total. This is expected because the share of households living in rural regions that have access to grid electricity is significantly less than those in urban areas. That is why the per capita consumption of an urban household is three times more than that of its rural counterpart. Added to this is the unreliability in the supply of electricity. During 2010, on an average, 18 hours of electricity was available in urban areas while it was only seven hours in rural areas (World Bank 2010). This despite the fact that between 1975 and 2010 electricity prices increased by a factor of 30 for rural households but only eight times for urban households (Table 12.8).

COLLECTIVE SELF-RELIANCE—A NEW BUSINESS MODEL

The general perception is that to provide electricity to about a million homes, significant resources are needed. Simply producing more will not solve the problem. It will be used by urban households and high consumers like big malls. Even though economic growth is necessary, basic human needs must guide the direction and function of markets, and not the other way around. There is a need to invest in those programmes that have the most positive impact on rural regions, and on the poor in particular.

In any given scenario of overall income and price levels, an innovative marketing mechanism has to be devised which plays a significant role in providing energy access. One such mechanism is encouraging social entrepreneurs[7] at the grassroots to facilitate large-scale diffusion of sustainable energy technologies (SETs).[8] It is important

---

[7] Social entrepreneurs have a 'social mission' and seek to generate 'social value' rather than profits. They have the potential to transform people' lives with innovative solutions to society's most pressing problems (Oteh 2009).

[8] The technologies that can be considered are gaseous fuels (LPG and biogas) for cooking, and electricity (centralized and decentralized) for lighting. They are relatively easy to deploy leading to a 'win-win-win' situation (where the entrepreneur gets profits, consumers get a modern energy service, and society gets a clean environment).

Table 12.8 Rural–Urban Disparities in Electricity Use and Service Provision

Details	1975		2010	
	Rural	Urban	Rural	Urban
Share in total consumption (%)	14.6	85.4	24.4	75.6
Consumption per HH (KWh/year)	48	137.5	310	1372.5
Consumption per capita (KWh)	8	25	65	305
End use shares (%)				
Lighting	76	36	46	28.1
Entertainment	3.5	17	20.1	15.7
Kitchen appliances	6.1	15.6	7.8	21.8
Heating/cooling	14.4	31.4	26.1	34.4
Price (Rs/KWh)	0.05	0.25	1.7	2.8
Supply (hours/day)	12	16	7	18

Source: World Bank (2010).

that the government be engaged at an early level and also participate in the activity. 'Access' to modern energy services can thus be provided through a micro-enterprise energy service delivery system with the government providing the necessary infrastructure. This can result in reliable, high-quality, sustainable, and continuous access to modern energy carriers (Reddy et al. 2010). A large number of such enterprises can provide employment to rural youth. This will also result in long-term reduction in social healthcare costs due to cleaner energy substitution, and improved self-respect and confidence among the poor due to a better quality of life. These strategies will also help in achieving other planning objectives such as reduction in resource use, savings in imported fuels, improved safety and health, energy conservation, and reduction in pollution.

In the present study we propose an entrepreneur-centred approach to support rural households and urban poor to provide modern energy services (Box 12.2) for which innovative institutional, financial, and policy mechanisms are needed. This should operate on three dimensions:

(i) Geographic dimension—geographic availability of service (nation-wide provision wherever and whenever required).
(ii) Distribution dimension—accessibility of the energy service to rural households (non-discrimination in terms of service and quality).
(iii) Equity dimension—affordability of the service to low-income households (should be priced in such a way that most users can afford it).

Box 12.2 Options for Modern Energy Supply

Lighting—*Shifting from kerosene to electricity*

Grid extensions—Extending electricity grids is capital-intensive and requires on-going maintenance.

Small-scale hydropower systems—Have high capital costs but relatively low maintenance costs, a long service life, high operational reliability (given availability of water), and low environmental impact. Location and seasonality issues.

Solar energy systems (photovoltaic and solar thermal)—High capital costs and no environmental impact. Maintenance and replacement may be difficult in remote places.

Small-scale wind energy systems—High capital but low running costs. Supply is intermittent and so energy storage is necessary for reliability. Location and seasonality issues.

Hybrid systems—Provide a mix of energy sources for electricity generation and can frequently reduce costs, and ensure a reliable supply (for example, wind and grid extensions).

Biomass power systems—Capital costs are not high and neither are running costs. Biomass storage is necessary for reliability.

Cooking—*Shifting from biofuels and kerosene to biogas*

Biogas—Low capital costs and fuel is available in plenty.

How Much to Pay and to Whom?

People without access to central grid services live mainly in the most remote and sparsely populated regions with limited access to roads, markets, and other services. In these areas, renewable energy technologies such as biomass power systems, wind energy, and photovoltaics are the most technically viable and in many cases, the most cost-effective options. For cooking and heating, biogas is the best option. It should be noted that technology in itself is not the cure-all to developmental issues. In fact, installation of the same technology within different contexts can often yield contrasting results. There is no best-fit solution to energy needs, and carriers must be weighed carefully against the local situation, capabilities, and preferences. However, provision of these services must be on a sustainable basis, economically, socially, and environmentally, if it is to ultimately improve living standards and lift people out of poverty.

Cooking Energy Services

According to our approach, modern energy services for cooking, biogas in rural areas, and LPG/biogas in peri-urban regions have to be made available to all the target households. The estimated cost is about Rs 1,040 billion (Table 12.9). The capital cost and investments for rural areas is around 80 per cent of the total because of the need for higher coverage. The piping cost is 8–10 per cent of the installation cost.

Electricity for Lighting

The prevailing mode of electricity generation and distribution is grid-based electricity, generated in large power plants and distributed on high-voltage transmission lines, transformed and distributed to households. For this reason, many people see electrification as synonymous with the extension of the national grid. We use a variety of technologies to provide households with clean and affordable energy. With regard to the business model, the connection type is more important than the way in which the energy is produced. Table 12.10 shows the costs and investments for lighting.

There are three types of households that need to be targeted. Type 1 consists of those households that are in villages in hilly regions which are inaccessible and hence grid electricity cannot reach them. These villages can be electrified by setting up small power plants that provide enough energy for the village's household and productive needs. Mini-grids are usually run by a local entrepreneur but larger companies can also find a business case here. The technologies used to generate the power range from biomass/biogas to hydro to solar energy, or in some cases, a combination of different sources or the application of hybrid systems (a combination of technologies). In some cases, mini-grids cannot be operated profitably in these areas due to the small number of potential customers, geographical location, or income structure of the community. In such cases, off-grid systems such as solar home systems (installed on rooftops) or solar-powered lamps can play a key role. These products can be produced locally and marketed. For such villages, to ensure that households achieve the universalization target, the additional installed capacity required is 92 MW with an investment of Rs 23 billion to provide electricity to 0.75 million households. This cost includes the generation, transmission, as well as the cost of meters. The second type is households that stay in villages that are yet to be electrified. These are in plain areas and grid electricity can be extended to these areas. The cost of generation, T&D, as well as meter installation works out to Rs 73 billion. Type 3 households are those where the village is electrified but the houses are not. These households are reasonably close to existing transmission and distribution lines, so getting connected to the grid may be the best and most economical option. Households get the initial connection for free and thereafter pay monthly charges based on the electricity that they consume. Providers of these services are state utilities. There are approximately 60 million such households in India. In terms of investment, the capital cost, and other infrastructure costs as well as meters works outs to Rs 722 billion. Since unconnected households in urban regions are mostly unauthorized and include pavement dwellers, estimates for providing them electric connection is not included here.

Table 12.9 Cost Estimates of Providing Cooking Services for Households

	Rural	Urban	Total
Total no. HH (million)	167	84	251
HH deprived (million)	148	8	156
cost of biogas (per m^3) plant Rs	5,000	8,000	
Requirement of gas per HH (m^3)	1	1	1
Total installation cost (Rs billion)	743	67	810
Piping requirement (m) per HH	25	15	25
Piping cost per km (Rs)	60,000	60,000	60,000
Piping cost (Rs billion)	166	11	176
Total cost (Rs billion)	965	75	1,040

Source: Reddy et al. (2010).

Table 12.10 Cost Estimates for Providing Electricity Connections

	Type 1	Type 2	Type 3	Total
Total villages	25,000	72,000	4,96,000	5,93,000
Households to be electrified (million)	0.75	3.6	69.5	74
Demand (MW)	92	480	7,200	7,772
Need/village (kW)	4	6.7	14.5	
Capacity/village (kW)	10	10	20	
Capital cost (Rs/kW)	79,000	61,000	60,000	
T&D cost Rs/kW	11,000	36,000	9,000	
Cost/meter (Rs)	750	750	750	
Total cost/village (Rs)	9,22,500	10,07,500	14,55,000	
Total cost (Rs billion)	23	73	722	817
Street lighting (Rs billion)	1.38	3.96		
Grand total (Rs billion)	24	77	722	823

Source: Author's estimates.

THE IMPLEMENTATION—WHAT CAN 'THEY DO' AND WHAT CAN 'I' DO?

To achieve the goal of making the energy services *available*, we should focus on the 'market efficiency gap' which refers to currently unserved markets which are commercially viable and ensure that these markets are served within a radius of a few kilometres. This gap can be bridged through service provision by local entrepreneurs so long as policymakers ensure a level playing field among all market participants and create a positive business climate. This will allow operators and service providers to be able to serve a much broader area and its inhabitants and thus close the market efficiency gap. In the case of making the services accessible, one should focus on the 'access gap' which refers to currently unserved markets which are not commercially viable in the foreseeable future without outside intervention. The reasons include: hilly terrains, low population density, high cost of supply, and low household incomes. Access to energy increases people's productivity, but realizing this potential requires access to markets for one's products. Affordability is generally seen as depending on two major factors: (i) household income levels, and (ii) energy price levels. These calculations are based on current energy costs and what the households would be able to save by switching to the new energy source. Subsidies are a regular feature in energy markets. To make energy services affordable, we can have: (i) a 'subsidy mechanism' in which markets could become commercially self-sustaining within a few years, if they receive initial support (a 'smart subsidy') from the government, and (ii) 'providing infrastructure' in which outside support is needed for providing permanent infrastructure (typically laying gas pipe lines to households and installing biogas plants exceeding what a small rural community can pay).

Providing energy access in low-income markets is a difficult proposition. Limited infrastructure, lack of financial services, and increased transaction costs limit the applicability of standard business models. How can the customer use gasous fuels if they have never heard of biogas? For this, an interface with the customer is essential. How can payments be ensured when customers lack access to bank accounts and have limited cash flows? The payment schedule can be adjusted to customers' cash flows. For example, farmers might prefer to pay energy bills after the harvest (Gradl and Knobloch 2011).

In the proposed approach, innovative institutional, financing, and pricing mechanisms are suggested. They include: (i) changing from an 'investment subsidy' to 'incentive-linked' delivery of services; (ii) selling a 'package of energy services' instead of the 'quantum of energy carriers', and (iii) making 'entrepreneurs' diffusion targets and not millions of 'end-users'. If implemented, it will result in a win-win-win situation for all: consumers will benefit through improved access to modern energy services, governments will advance social and economic development objectives, and private enterprises and equipment manufactures will expand business opportunities. Figures 12.3 and 12.4 show the proposed mechanism and the involvement of various actors.

Role of the Government

The role of the government is to lay the groundwork for investment in energy access. In this model, the government will tender and license entrepreneurs, who

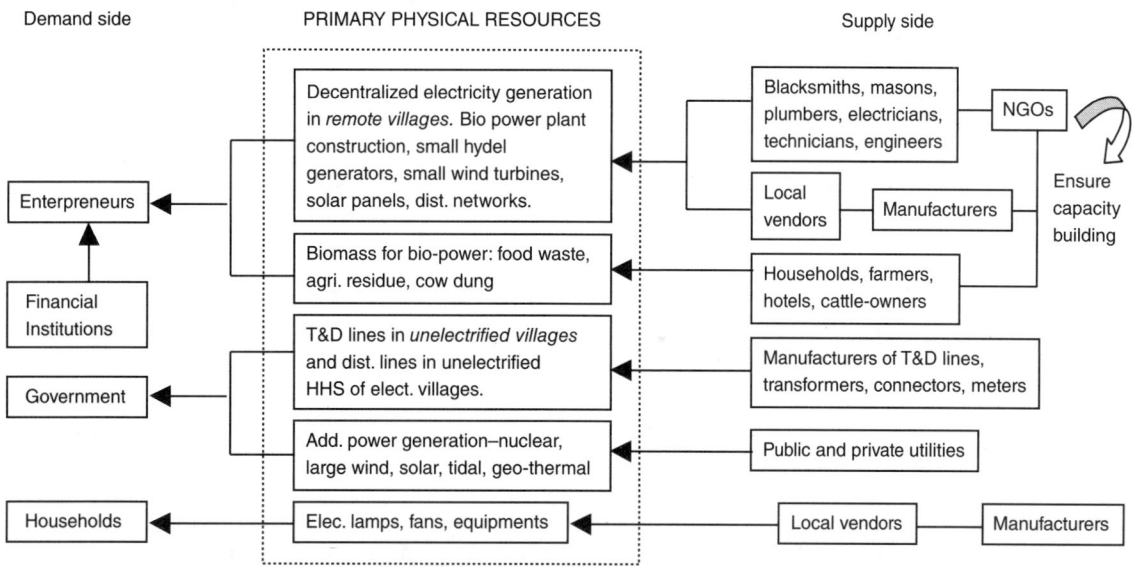

Figure 12.3 Primary Physical Resources and Actors Mapping

Source: Author's own.

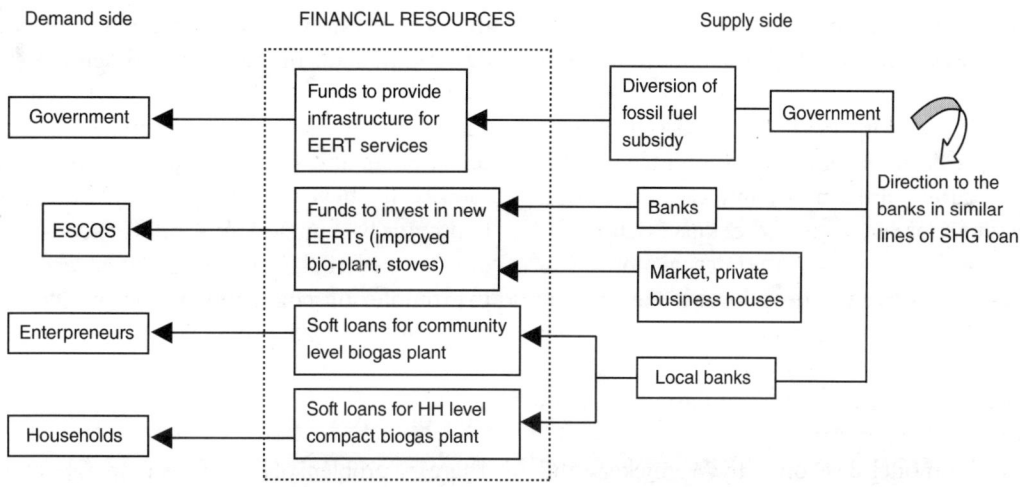

Figure 12.4 Financial Resources and Actors Mapping

Source: Author's own.

will provide modern energy services to households. It will create the required infrastructure such as biogas pipes to households, roads for LPG transport, and build the electricity infrastructure through state electricity utilities. An energy empowerment (EE) fund has to be established by diverting funds from the kerosene subsidy.[9] The cost of setting up the infrastructure has to be borne by the government through the EE fund, while the responsibility of operating and maintaining the connection facilities can be with entrepreneurs. Finally, the government must make a provision in financial institutions for low-interest loans to entrepreneurs. From the policy perspective, the government should formulate national policies that can influence the emergence of local markets for energy access. It should also coordinate various ministries, donors, and other sector actors to support policies that encourage local entrepreneurial activity and promote investment. There are various rural electrification programmes (both at the

---

[9] Nearly Rs 150 billion is spent on kerosene subsidy (2010 data). The number of households that use kerosene for cooking (thereby the quantity of kerosene) is significantly lower than official figures. This means that subsidized kerosene is being diverted to other uses, mainly for use as transport fuel, where it greatly increases air pollution (see Shelar et al. 2007).

state as well as the central levels) and rural development programmes whose efforts have to be integrated.

Strategic partnerships can be a critical part of an entrepreneur's business model. If properly structured, they offer businesses a long-term competitive advantage. The government should coordinate the capacity-building process to deal with decentralized supply options (how to provide Operation and Maintenance (O&M) at a minimum cost; how to work with communities; how to sub-contract local agents to provide an electricity service such as NGOs, municipalities, community associations; how to respond to regulator rules and surveying; and possibilities on how to bill, among others).

Role of Entrepreneurs

These grassroots entrepreneurs act as agents of change, invent new approaches, and disseminate sustainable solutions that create social value. They are the strongest link in the present initiative. Programmes aimed at increasing access to modern energy services should leverage the innovative power of entrepreneurs, especially local or indigenous ones. Presently, there is a wealth of entrepreneurial talent in the country as can be seen from running cable networks to Public Call Offices (PCOs) and cell-phone-recharging services. More importantly, they focus exclusively on serving rural communities and the urban poor. These entrepreneurs possess many of the skills essential for operating a successful enterprise such as internal motivation and work ethics, risk tolerance, deep knowledge of their products, competition, and finally, the passion to succeed. What they lack, however, is not only working capital, but also technical skills in finance, and other basic aspects of running a commercial enterprise.

According to the model developed by Wennekers and Thurik (1999), determinants of entrepreneurship can be examined from three distinctive levels—the individual, the firm, and the macro level. The origin of entrepreneurial activity is always by necessity the individual. Entrepreneurship is induced by an individual's attitudes or motives, skills and psychological endowments. However, while entrepreneurship originates at the individual level, realization is achieved at the firm level. Corporations are vehicles for transforming personal entrepreneurial qualities and ambitions into actions. Hence, it is important for the government to foster entrepreneurship among individuals who have skills and have a strong desire to succeed (Oteh 2009).

Role of Financial Institutions

One of the main barriers to the development of small enterprises and consequently, entrepreneurship relates to access to finance and in many instances the inability to obtain loans at reasonable interest rates. Most financial institutions consider lending to small enterprises a risky business because of inadequate guarantees. Financial institutions like commercial banks can set up micro-credit services to cater to these enterprises. Through this, they can provide soft loans to the manufactures who supply equipment to entrepreneurs to deliver the services. The financial sources available to entrepreneurs depend on the legal structure (for-profit versus non-profit) and their business models. They should not only provide capital but also the management and advisory services necessary to make them self-sufficient. This results in maximizing an entrepreneur's ability to scale up energy access (IFC 2010).

Role of Local Manufacturers

The general perception is that many technologies should be imported which depend on international supply chains. They are also subjected to importation taxes, storage and handling fees, regulatory approvals, etc. resulting in delays. However, local production of energy technology components or entire technologies exists in India (for example, solar panels). The government and investors should encourage local manufacturers to decrease reliance on imports and increase local competition. The model foresees the development of a cadre of trained technicians to provide backup/service support to consumers which was often an element lacking in various government approaches to promote non-conventional energy, thereby discouraging the public from adopting these programmes.

Role of NGOs

There is a problem of lack of awareness about modern energy services or the risk of disease from the use of biofuels. In general, social and behavioural attitudes influence households' decisions about the energy they use. Acceptability of some technologies/services may be poor if their use requires a change in habits or introduces time or resource demands. Efforts to expand energy access are doomed to fail due to lack of understanding of the target population or the market segment's behavioural attitudes. NGOs should play a unique role in this exercise due to their flexibility, accessibility, and creativity (for building Energy Efficient and Renewable Energy Technologies [EERT] awareness among consumers) since there is a need for capacity building at all levels, ranging from training for poor rural women to rural entrepreneurs. They should lead awareness campaigns with innovative marketing programmes about modern energy services to raise awareness among rural households and the urban poor.

Role of Markets

Many rural areas and slums in urban regions may not be readily accessible for the distribution of energy services. Insufficient development of a viable supply chain for energy access hinders these processes. Reaching rural markets often means partnering with an organization with significant experience and distribution channels in the area. NGOs, groups such as self-help groups (SHGs), or local governments may help with rural marketing and distribution/logistics.

It is important to know that adopting business approaches and encouraging entrepreneurs to provide rural energy services are essential for ensuring the sustainability of the systems in the long run. There are numerous examples of projects which are developing sustainable and business-oriented approaches to rural energy supply (Greenpeace 2003).[10] The underlying assumption of the traditional approach is that rural electrification should focus on the provision of technology, and that its sustainable operation, management, and financing would follow almost automatically. Recent research has shown that a new development paradigm is emerging where the adoption of more egalitarian and participatory, less-polluting, and wasteful lifestyles will help the poor in developing countries, thereby avoiding social disintegration.

The model is based on the premise that the financing of basic social services—not necessarily their provision—is a fundamental task of the government. Experience has shown that high levels of social benefits are found in countries where the state played a central role in guaranteeing the financial resources to achieve them. Private provision of services based on particular needs or price incentives and without state intervention has fallen short of the level of intervention required to produce widespread benefits (Lewis 1999). This does not mean that we do not recognize the importance of other stakeholders including civil society in energy access but stress the responsibility of the government for its financing and management.

BEYOND THE REHEARSALS

In India, about 0.4 billion people lack access to electricity, and about 0.8 billion people use traditional biomass for cooking. Without access to modern energy sources it is impossible to achieve the Millennium Development Goals (MDGs). The goal of ensuring energy access for the unreached and the vulnerable sections of society is not only morally imperative but also economically rational. The total cost, about Rs 1,900 billion (only 2 per cent of GDP) is really moderate which ensures every individual an opportunity to lead a healthy and productive life. Access to modern, affordable, and reliable energy services helps to serve basic needs and improve the livelihoods of people which in turn helps achieve economic prosperity. These are inter-linked and it is important that planners and policymakers should address these issues through relevant policies and instruments.

To supply sustainable energy services to meet local needs and to stimulate enterprises and job creation, the government should enhance its support to energy access programmes. This should be done through stimulation of markets for local renewable energy systems, technology transfer, and applied research into renewable energies. It should step up assistance to address the various barriers in implementing energy supply and services at the local level.

The government should encourage local entrepreneurs for energy service delivery. It should try to cooperate with local actors (in particular, local authorities), other local bodies in charge of energy development, the private sector (in particular small and medium-sized enterprises or SMEs), local micro-finance institutions, and civil society organizations. There is also a need to enhance capacity building (including energy education) at the local level. This can be achieved with the involvement of NGOs. Models of cooperation should be built on best practices and may include twinning arrangements and other institutional support programmes at various levels. There is also a need to strengthen long-term sustainable energy supply policies and have conducive legal, regulatory, and institutional frameworks.

The involvement of grassroots entrepreneurs is important in the processes of integrating energy planning into the development processes. By raising awareness and improving linkages and the working relationship among stakeholders this will eventually create the necessary conditions that raise demand for energy access interventions. This approach, conceptualized as entrepreneur-based energy planning, will enable rural communities to identify and envision their developmental needs, map the resources for achieving those needs, and scale up over time. This will ensure that energy is integrated from the beginning into all development sectors at the grassroots level in a manner that avoids duplication or formation of unnecessary new structures.

---

10 WWF initiated a programme of small credit loans for rural households to promote small-scale biogas systems in rural areas of HuBei province in China. The W. Jones Foundation and Shell Foundation have supported a small-scale biogas programme in remote areas of Yunnan province, and the Greenstar Solar Community Centre has initiated a joint venture entity with villagers in Tibet to deliver solar-powered handicrafts for sale internationally, to ensure the economic viability of the solar power systems.

If we wish to overcome the gloom of the immediate future, we have to learn from the new development paradigms. Human society has reached a point where it cannot extract any more natural resources; it is then better to learn how to distribute them fairly and sustainably. If this is done, all humans can develop to their full potential in harmony with nature.

REFERENCES

Anonymous (2010a), *Poor People's Energy Outlook 2010*, Rugby: Practical Action, Warwickshire.

———. (2010b), *Annual Report: 2009–10*. New Delhi: Ministry of Power, Government of India.

———. (2011a), *Distribution of Households by Source of Lighting*. Census of India, Registrar General of the Census. New Delhi: Government of India.

———. (2011b), 'Access to Energy for the Poor: The Clean Energy Option', Action Aid International, Oil Change International, and Vasundhara Foundation India.

Balachandra, P. (2012), 'Energizing India: Expanding electricity access in rural areas', in *Towards an Energy Plus Approach for the Poor: A Review of Good Practices and Lessons Learned from Asia and the Pacific*. Bangkok: UNDP, Asia–Pacific Regional Centre.

Energy Sector Management Assistance Programme [ESMAP] (2004), *Annual Report, Energy Sector Management Assistance Program*. Washington, DC: The International Bank for Reconstruction and Development, The World Bank Group.

Gradl, Christina and Claudia Knobloch (2011), *Energy Business Model Generator for Low-Income Markets*. Berlin: Endeva Publications.

Greenpeace (2003), *A Sustainable Pathway to a Clean Energy Future*. Rio, Brazil: Greenpeace International.

Hammond, A.B. (2007), 'Challenges to Increasing Access to Modern Energy Services in Africa', Background paper, Forum of Energy Ministers of Africa, Conference on Energy Security and Sustainability, Maputo, Mozambique, 28–30 March.

International Energy Agency [IEA] (2011), *Energy for All-financing the Access for the Poor, World Energy Outlook*. France: International Energy Agency.

International Financial Corporation [IFC] (2010), *Safe Water for All: Harnessing the Private Sector to Reach the Underserved*. International Financial Corporation. Washington DC: World Bank Group.

Lewis, S. (1999), 'Achieving Universal Access to Basic Social Services', *International Social Science Journal*, 51(162): 547–57.

Modi, V., S. McDade, D. Lallement, and J. Saghir (2005), *Energy Services for the Millennium Development Goals*. Energy Sector Management Assistance Programme, United Nations Development Programme. New York: UN Millennium Project and World Bank.

Ministry of Power [MoP] (2010), http://www.powermin.gov.in. New Delhi: Government of India. Last accessed on 2 March 2012.

National Sample Survey Organization [NSSO], (2007), *Results of the National Sample Survey*. New Delhi: NSSO.

Oteh, A. (2009), 'The Role of Entrepreneurship in Transforming the Nigerian Economy', Seventh Convocation Lecture, Igbinedion University, Okada, Edo State, 4 December.

Reddy, A.K.N. and A. D'Sa (1995), 'The Enron and Other Similar Deals vs the New Energy Paradigm', *Economic and Political Weekly*, 30(24): 1441–8.

Reddy, Sudhakara B., Balachandra P., and Hippu Salk Kristle Nathan (2010), 'Universalization of Access to Modern Energy Services in Indian Households—Economic and Policy Analysis', *Energy Policy*, 37(11): 4645–57.

Reddy, Sudhakara B. and T. Srinivas (2009), 'Energy Use in Indian Household Sector—An Actor-Oriented Approach', *Energy—The International Journal*, 34(6): 992–1002.

Relich, N. (2011), 'Solving the Energy Poverty Problem', *Opinion, American Energy for Leadership*, 28 February 2011.

Shelar, Mahesh, S.D. Barahate, M.R. Rathi, and V.D. Pethkar (2007), 'Energy Stamps to Discourage Inefficient Use of Kerosene and Reduce Emissions from Autorickshaws: A Case-study from Maharashtra, India'. *Energy for Sustainable Development*, 11(4): 74–7.

UNDP [United Nations Development Programme] (2009), *The Energy Access Situation in Developing Countries: A Review Focusing on the Least Developed Countries and Sub-Saharan Africa*. Nairobi: United Nations Development Programme.

UNEP (2008), *Green Jobs—Towards decent work in a sustainable low-carbon world*. Nairobi: United Nations Environment Programme.

Wennekers, S. and R. Thurik (1999), 'Linking Entrepreneurship and Economic Growth', *Small Business Economics*, 13: 27–55.

World Bank (2010), *Empowering Rural India: Expanding Electricity Access by Mobilizing Local Resources*. Washington, DC: South Asia Energy Unit, the World Bank.

13

Provision of Civic and Environmental Services in the Urban Centres of India
Present Trends and the Way Forward

*Sudhakar Yedla**

INTRODUCTION

India is the second most populous country in the world with a population of 1.21 billion in 2011. It has been experiencing one of the fastest urbanizations in the world with the share of the urban population increasing from 17.3 per cent in 1951 to 31.2 in 2011. Table 13.1 presents the transformation of rural India into semi-urban India.

This increasing share of urbanization has resulted in an increasing number of large-sized cities in the country. With more employment opportunities and higher per capita incomes compared to the national average, these cities have been attracting a large number of migrants from the surrounding rural areas. This migration has resulted in urban sprawls and an increasing number of slums. Metropolitan cities such as Mumbai have 50 per cent of its population living in slums (ADB 2009; Water Aid India 2005).

The provision of basic civic and environmental services to these varying sections of society is a challenge for city administrators. Basic services that are traditionally provided by the state include:

- Water supply
- Sewage collection and disposal
- Solid waste management (SWM)
- Public healthcare and hygiene
- Sanitation
- Street lighting
- Maintenance of city roads

This chapter considers three basic civic services that are particularly relevant to the environmental well-being of people—water supply, sewage and sanitation, and municipal solid waste management.

Water supply and sanitation coverage varies across the regions in the world. While the North has developed a near perfect water supply and sanitation coverage, the South is still limping with below par standards as presented in Figure 13.1. Asia as a region is the last on the list with only 31 per cent of the rural population having sanitation services available. Overall sanitation is also as low as less than 50 per cent. The global average for water supply is only 80 per cent and sanitation coverage is as low as 60 per cent. There is a significant gap between urban and rural sanitation

---

* The author is thankful to the reviewers K.L. Krishna and Gopal Kadekodi for their valuable comments and suggestions.

Table 13.1 Share of Urban Population in India (1951–2011)

Year (1)	Total Population (in million) (2)	Urban Population (in million) (3)	Rural Population (in million) (4)	% of Urban Population (5)	% of Rural Population (6)
1951	361.1	62.4	298.7	17.3	82.7
1961	439.2	78.9	360.3	18	82
1971	548.2	109.1	439.1	19.9	80.1
1981	683.3	159.4	523.9	23.3	76.7
1991	846.3	217.6	628.7	25.7	74.3
2001	1028	287.6	740.4	28	72
2011	1210.1	377.1	833	31.20	68.80

Source: Census 2011; MoUD (2012).

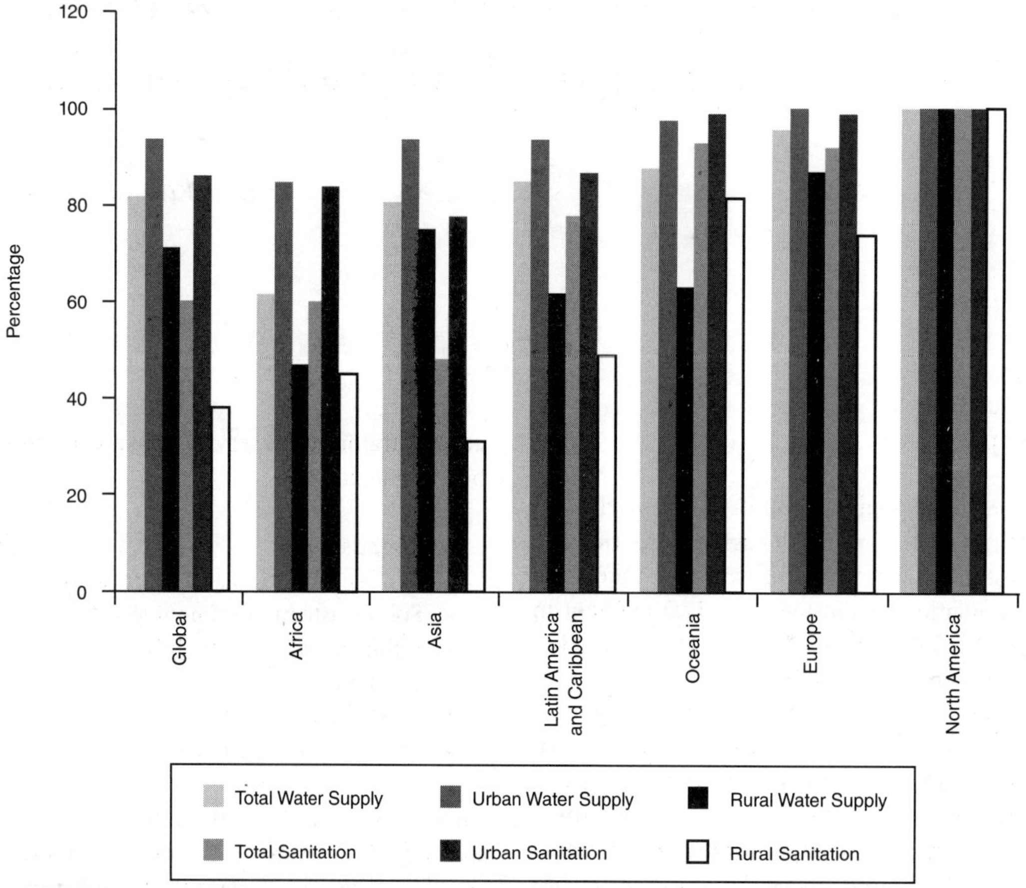

Figure 13.1 Water Supply and Sanitation Coverage by Region, 2000

Source: Compiled using data from Gleick (2009).

situations both in global average as well as in low-income regions such as Asia and Africa (Gleick 2009).

WATER SUPPLY

Along with material inputs, water plays an important role in all sectors—agriculture, domestic, industry, power, commercial, and others. While the industrial sector dominates water usage in industrialized countries, agriculture remains the dominant sector using up a major share of water in developing countries, particularly agriculture based countries like India. Table 13.2 gives the sectoral share in water consumption till 2050, as projected by the standing sub-committee of the Ministry of Water Resources (MoWR)

Table 13.2 Sectoral Share of Water Demand in India, 2010–50

Sector	Standing Sub-committee of MoWR			NCIWRD		
Year	2010	2025	2050	2010	2025	2050
Irrigation	84.62	83.26	74.08	78.45	72.48	68.39
Drinking water	6.89	6.68	7.05	6.06	7.35	9.41
Industry	1.48	2.10	4.35	5.21	7.95	6.86
Energy	0.62	1.37	8.98	2.68	3.91	5.93
Others	6.40	6.59	5.53	7.61	8.30	9.41
Total	100	100	100	100	100	100

Source: Data taken from CPCB (2009).

and the National Council for Integrated Water Resources Development (NCIWRD) (CPCB 2009; CSE 2004). In both the estimates it is clear that agriculture will continue to dominate the share of water consumption for the next forty years. The Ministry of Water Resources estimates predict that the industry and energy sectors will grow into more water-demanding sectors.

With India aiming to continue with its rapid economic growth, industries are expected to increase their production and hence will need increased consumption of water. With increasing energy needs, the power generation sector is also expected to have more demand for water in the years to come. It is established that rapid economic growth will foster expansion of urban centres, putting more stress on water supply and sewage management systems as well.

Adding to the increasing stress, is the per capita water availability for the country as a whole, which is reducing with increasing population over the years. Water consumption by sectors such as industries has two dimensions to its use—water usage and water pollution. It is believed that every one litre of wastewater discharged by an industry makes 5–8 litres of water unusable for most human usages (CSE 2004). With this aspect of industrial waste water discharge and with increasing water usage by this sector, water availability is expected to reduce even faster. Table 13.3 gives the forecast of water availability per capita till 2025. Per capita water availability got reduced by about a fraction of three during 1951–2001 and is expected to reduce further during 2001–50.

In India about 78 per cent of the urban population had access to safe drinking water and 38 per cent of the population had access to sanitation services in 2008. While some states fare relatively better in water supply, states like Tamil Nadu and Andhra Pradesh face a severe water crisis as shown in Table 13.4. Among all the states Maharashtra, and Punjab recorded a higher per capita water supply. A study conducted by CPCB in 2008 reported that the average per capita water supply to Class I cities was 179 lpcd where as for the class II cities it was 120 lpcd.

Table 13.3 Per Capita Water Availability in India, 1951–50

Year	Population (Million)	Per Capita Water Availability (m^3)
1951	361	5177
1955	395	4732
1991	846	2209
2001	1027	1820
2025	1394	1341
2050	1640	1140

Source: www.indiastat.com, last accessed on 14 January 2012.

As per the norms of water supply suggested by the Central Public Health and Environmental Engineering Organization (CPHEEO), cities with a piped water supply and sewage collection systems should have a maximum water supply per capita of 130 litres per day. For metropolitan cities this is considered as 150 lpcd. Though, with an overall per capita water supply of 149.5 lpcd, Indian cities look sufficiently supplied for water, the share of non-domestic use and also wide deviations (as in the case of class I cities in Goa, Tamil Nadu, and the majority of class II cities) from the mean per capita water supply are alarming. Figures 13.2 and 13.3 give water supply differentials between class I and class II cities in Indian states.

The dominance of category A indicates a water scarce situation and predominant category B indicates water sufficiency. Andhra Pradesh, Tamil Nadu, and Rajasthan are among the water scarce states.

Other criteria for assessing water supply systems are the source of water quality and the supply duration. While states and union territories like Chandigarh, Delhi, Puducherry, and Punjab have a major percentage of the households getting water from reliable (quality) sources such as taps, hand pumps, and tube wells, other states

Table 13.4 State-wise Water Supply in Class I Cities in India, 2008

S.No.	State/Union Territory	No. of Class I Cities	Water Supply in Class-I Cities (in MLD)	Per Capita Water Supply (lpd)
1	Andaman & Nicobar	1	15.0	139.9
2	Andhra Pradesh	47	2,205.0	109.5
3	Assam	5	427.7	301.7
4	Bihar	23	1,262.2	218.2
5	Chandigarh	1	537.2	540.0
6	Chhattisgarh	7	438.1	174.2
7	Delhi	1	4,346.0	292.5
8	Goa	1	12.2	100.1
9	Gujarat	28	2,101.2	143.2
10	Haryana	20	783.4	142.6
11	Himachal Pradesh	1	36.2	221.3
12	Jammu & Kashmir	2	267.4	140.0
13	Jharkhand	14	1,038.1	209.1
14	Karnataka	33	2,238.0	148.2
15	Kerala	8	719.0	190.3
16	Madhya Pradesh	25	1,560.9	144.6
17	Maharashtra	50	12,482.9	310.1
18	Manipur	1	43.4	173.8
19	Meghalaya	1	26.1	140.0
20	Mizoram	1	39.6	140.0
21	Nagaland	1	24.1	140.0
22	Odisha	12	825.9	247.6
23	Puducherry	2	70.6	140.0
24	Punjab	19	1,837.2	290.2
25	Rajasthan	24	1,728.0	179.8
26	Tamil Nadu	42	1,346.5	79.9
27	Tripura	1	30.0	140.0
28	Uttar Pradesh	61	4,382.6	170.1
29	Uttrakhand	6	221.2	177.1
30	West Bengal	60	3,723.5	187.9
	Total	498	44,769.1	179.0

Note: lpd: litres per day.
Source: CPCB (2009).

as Assam, Kerala, Manipur, Meghalaya, Mizoram, Odisha, Rajasthan, and Jharkhand rely mostly on other sources of water. As shown in Figure 13.4, urban households are well supplied with tap water and other more reliable sources of water.

Tube wells are the major source of water for the country as a whole. While urban centres are well-connected with municipal tap water compared to rural areas, villages rely mostly on tube wells and hand pumps for their water needs.

Though open wells are the third-largest reported prime source of water both for rural and urban areas, the share of HH using it as a prime source is not significant. Some cities and towns draw water from rivers and others (particularly mountainous areas) rely on springs. Table 13.5 shows the share of households using different sources for their water needs.

Among metropolitan cities, Delhi, Mumbai, and Pune had (in 2008) the best per capita supply of water with

PROVISION OF CIVIC AND ENVIRONMENTAL SERVICES 185

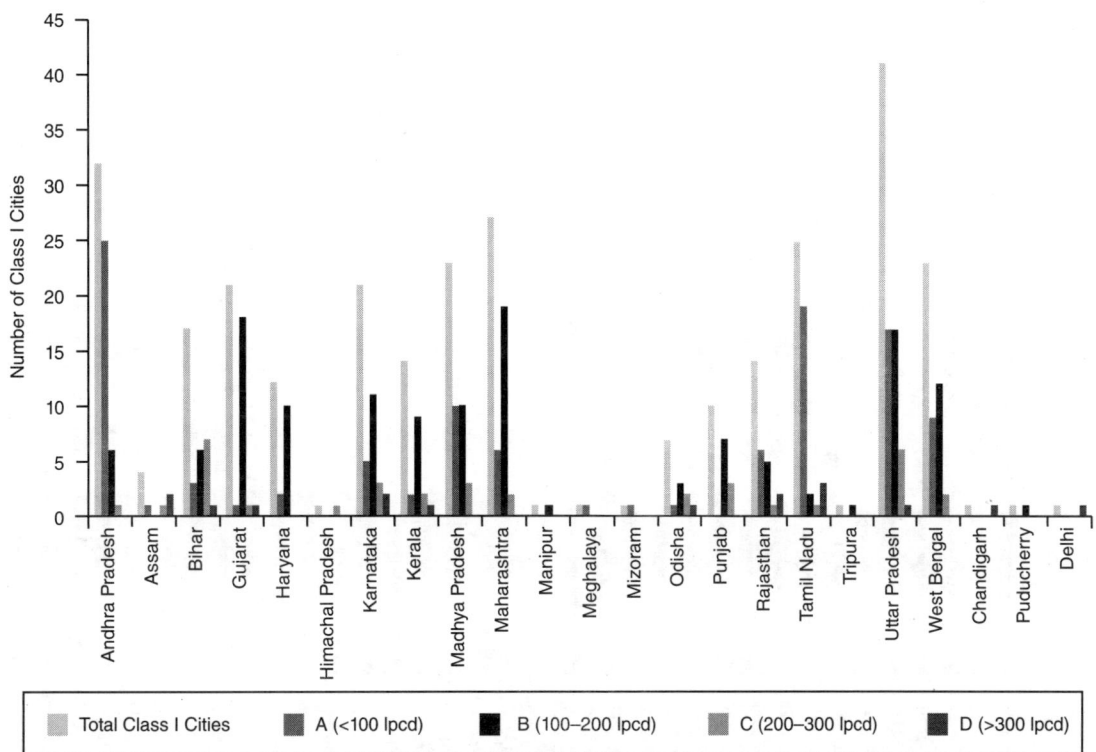

Figure 13.2 Number of Class I Cities in Different States having Different Levels of Water Supply, 2008
Source: Compiled using the data from Indiastat.com and CPCB (2009).

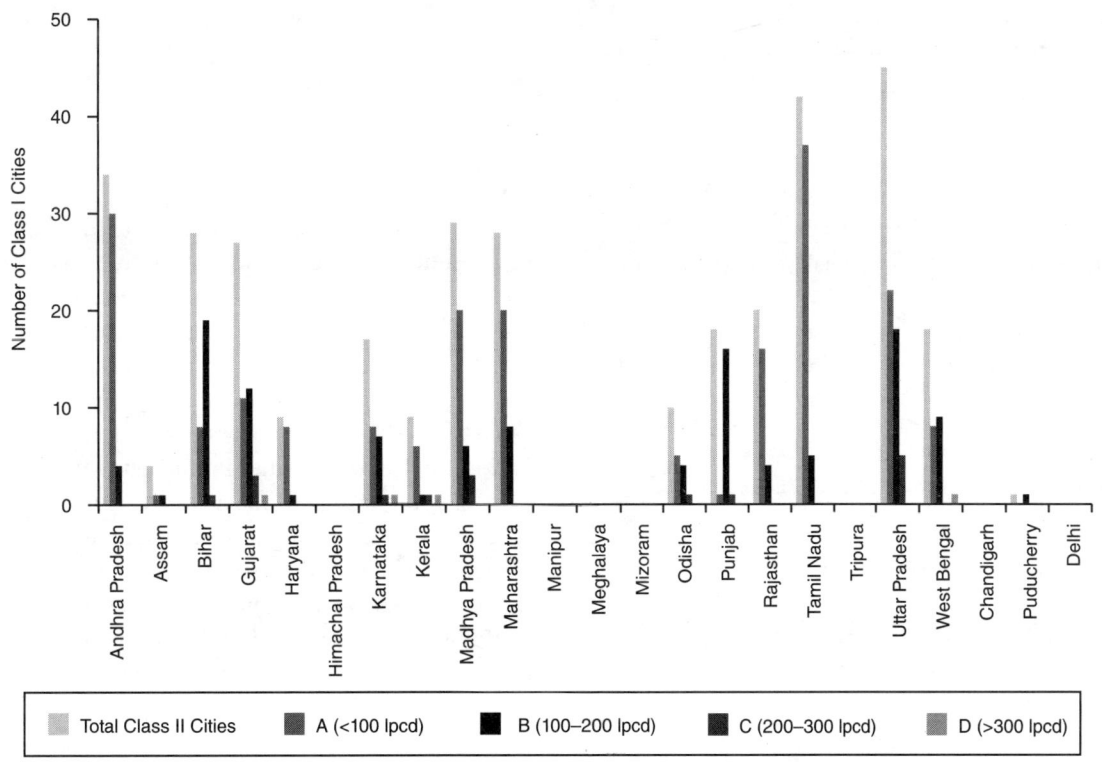

Figure 13.3 Number of Class II Cities in Different States having Different Levels of Water Supply, 2008
Source: Compiled using the data from Indiastat.com and CPCB (2009).

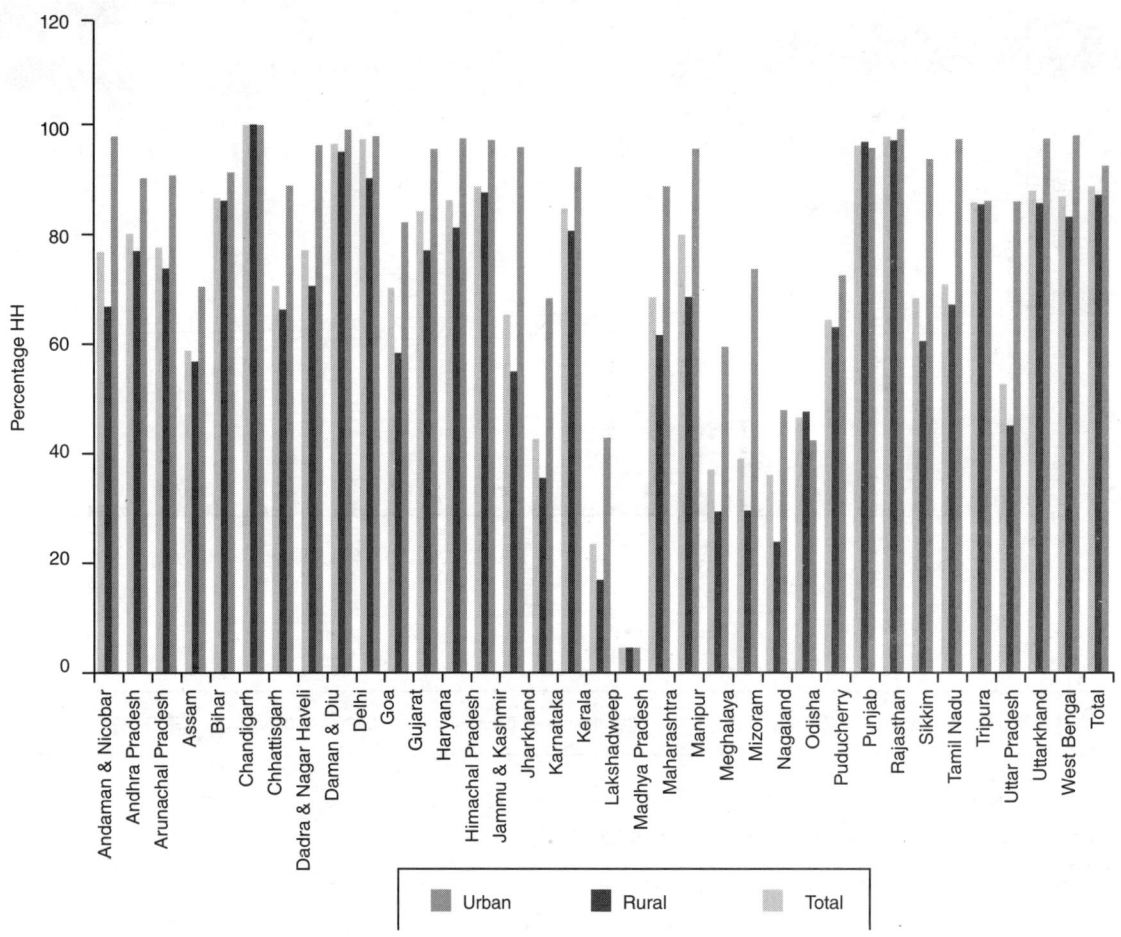

Figure 13.4 Households Access to Safe Drinking Water, 2008–9 (Tap/Hand Pump/Tube Well) in India
Source: NSS (2010).

Table 13.5 Prime Source of Drinking Water in Rural and Urban Areas in India (distribution per 100 HH), 2008–9

Prime Water Source of Drinking Water	Total	Rural	Urban
Tap	405	275	736
Tube well/hand pump	423	513	196
Well	143	179	51
Tank/pond (reserved for drinking)	7	8	2
Other tank/pond	3	4	0
River/canal/lake	8	11	1
Spring	6	8	1
Others	6	3	13

Source: NSS (2010).

218, 268, and 283 litres of water supply per capita per day. Madurai, Chennai, and Coimbatore with their respective water supply of 88, 108, and 108 lpcd are the least water supplied cities in the country. Figure 13.5 gives the per capita water supply in metropolitan cities. While the western cities, blessed with a strong monsoon are better supplied, most of the southern cities are water scarce. Some cities such as Delhi, Mumbai, Pune, Hyderabad, Kolkata, and Bengaluru have a predominant non-domestic share in their per capita water supplied and that could probably explain the increasing stress for water for domestic use. Figure 13.6 shows the share of water between domestic and non-domestic uses in various metropolitan cities in the country.

It is interesting to observe that some metropolitan cities, in spite of having low per capita water supply, have longer water supply compared to other well supplied cities. Bengaluru, Kolkata, Ludhiana, Pune, and Varanasi seem to be doing better compared to the other cities. However, the maximum water supply duration is reported as 12 hours which is only 50 per cent of the water supply duration in cities in industrialized countries such as Japan, North America, and Europe. Figure 13.7 gives the water supply duration and number of supplies in different metropolitan cities in India.

PROVISION OF CIVIC AND ENVIRONMENTAL SERVICES 187

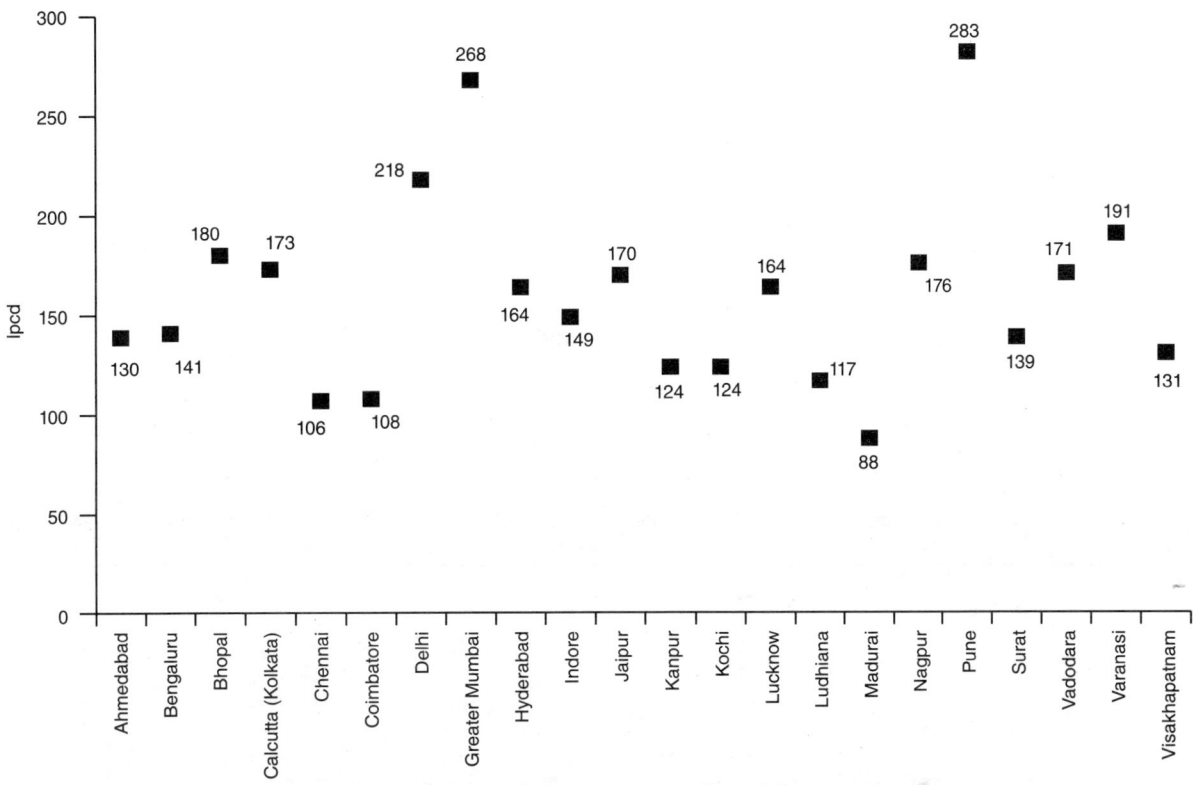

Figure 13.5 Per Capita Water Supply in Metropolitan Cities, 2005
Source: Compiled with data from NIUA (2005).

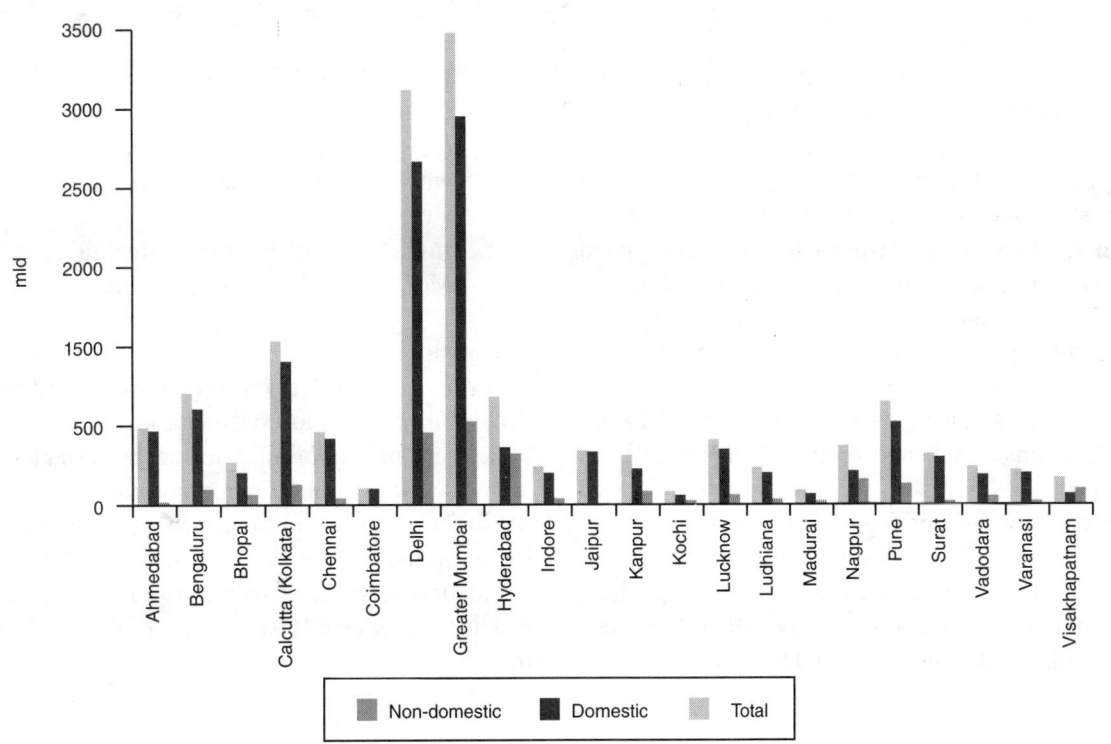

Figure 13.6 Share of Domestic and Non-domestic Use of Water Supplied in Metropolitan Cities
Source: Compiled with data from NIUA (2005).

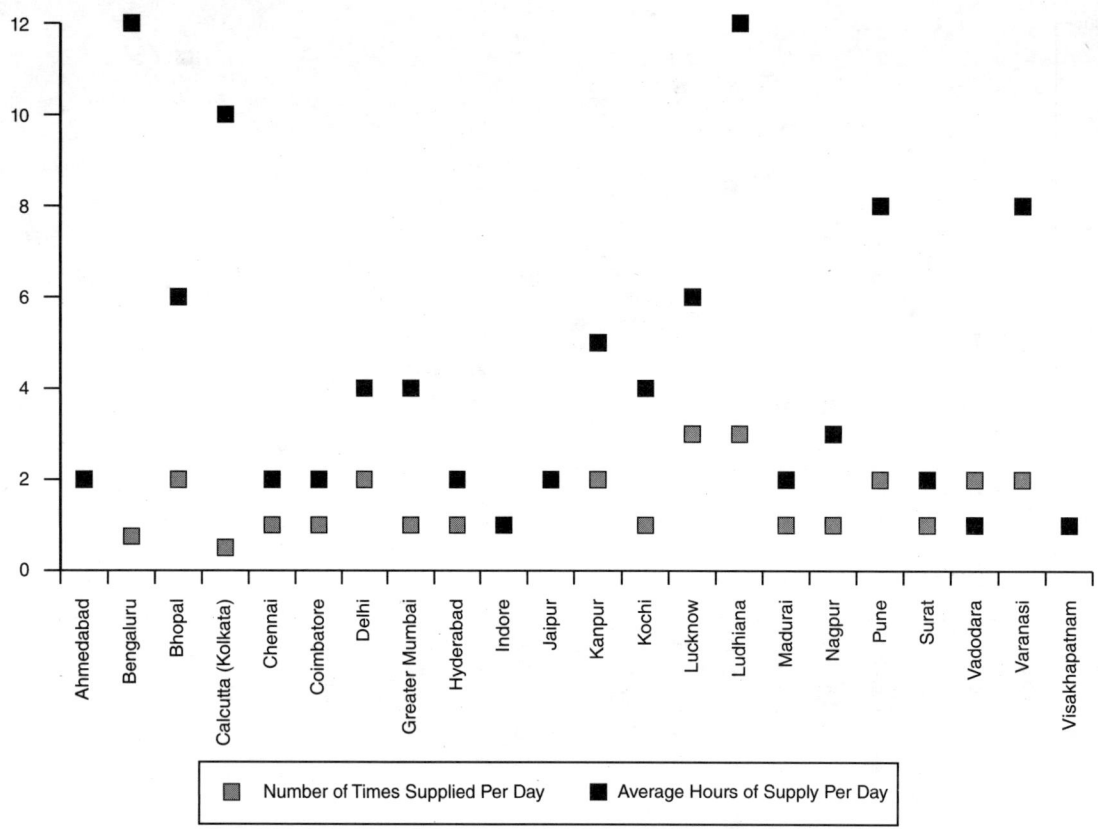

Figure 13.7 Water Supply Duration and Frequency in Metropolitan Cities, 2005
Source: Data compiled from www.Indiastat

Average water supply in metropolitan and other class I cities in India matches the national standard for drinking water supply. However, the water supply duration and frequency remain a concern. Particularly in water scarce cities such as Chennai, and Hyderabad, water is supplied once in two days and for very short durations. Further, water supply in unauthorized settlements (slums) is a major concern in metropolitan cities. Mumbai has about 50 per cent of its population living in slums (both notified and unnotified); water supply to unauthorized residential areas in general remains a challenge in most of the urban areas in the country.

As per the most recent report from the Ministry of Urban Development, 71.2 per cent of the urban population had drinking water within their premises and another 20.7 per cent of the population had it near their premises. No city had 24×7 water service (MoUD 2012).

SANITATION

Sanitation services in India are driven by the following two targets:

1. Goal 7 of the Millennium Development Goals (MDGs) 'halve, by 2015, the proportion of people without improved sanitation facilities (from 1990 levels)'
2. India's goal of Sanitation for all by 2012 under MoUD's Total Sanitation Campaign.

Sanitation services are one of the very basic civic and environmental services traditionally provided by the state. Provision of sanitation has been identified as one of the basic needs and important priorities by the national government as well as by international agencies. MDGs and the national objectives as presented above describe such a priority set on this basic civic service. By 2008, the percentage population with access to improved sanitary service had reached 31 per cent (54 per cent in urban and 21 per cent in rural areas).

The situation of water supply in India has improved significantly during 1990–2010 due to various national initiatives taken up by the Government of India (MoUD 2011c). Access to sanitation in rural areas also improved from a mere 1 per cent in 1990 to 21 per cent in 2008

(MoSPI 2011). According to an ADB report on sanitation (ADB 2009), with a similar rate of improvement (1990–2002), India is expected to have safe sanitation for 48 per cent of its rural population and up to 80 per cent of its urban population by 2015. In spite of these achievements in the past decade, the Indian population's access to safe sanitary facilities is still far low as compared to North American and European countries and even when compared to countries with lower per capita GDP. An estimated 55 per cent of all Indians, close to 600 million people, still do not have access to any kind of toilet (Gleick 2009). An alarming fact is that a major share of this population is living in urban slums and in rural environments. The fact that about 74 per cent of the rural population in India still defecates in the open reflects the poor sanitation infrastructure in place for these sections of society.

While infrastructure for sanitation remains poor, lack of or an inadequate sewage collection system further adds to complications in urban centres. Inadequate sewage systems lead to overflow of raw sewage, which in turn, becomes a major source of water contamination and various water-borne diseases. Figures 13.8 and 13.9 present the situation of sewage generated in different states and metropolitan cities and their respective treatment capacities. The figures show the gap between sewage generation and its treatment.

Maharashtra generates a large quantity of sewage (10,000 MLD) with less than 50 per cent of it treated before its final disposal. Many states fall short of this figure and most of the untreated sewage reaches natural water bodies. This sewage is one of the major sources of surface water contamination in the country. The degree of sewage treatment in states such as Karnataka, Bihar, and Rajasthan is alarmingly low.

Delhi generates close to 4,000 MLD of sewage a day whereas only 2,500 MLD is treated before its final disposal. Mumbai is the next Indian city with a large quantity of sewage generation of which more than 50 per cent goes untreated. Other than a few metropolitan cities such as Hyderabad and Ahmedabad most of the other cities fail to treat even 50 per cent of their sewage. The main reason for this is lack of infrastructure in the form of sewage treatment plants (STPs).

According to MoUD's latest report in 2010–11, only 32.7 per cent of the urban population had access to a piped sewer system and 12.6 per cent still defecated in the open. While the installed sewage treatment capacity is only 30 per cent, the actual operation load is a mere 20 per cent (MoUD 2012).

SOLID WASTE MANAGEMENT

India, with its huge population of 1.2 billion and an urban share of more than 30 per cent, is estimated to produce 68.8 million tonnes of municipal solid waste per year (Annepu

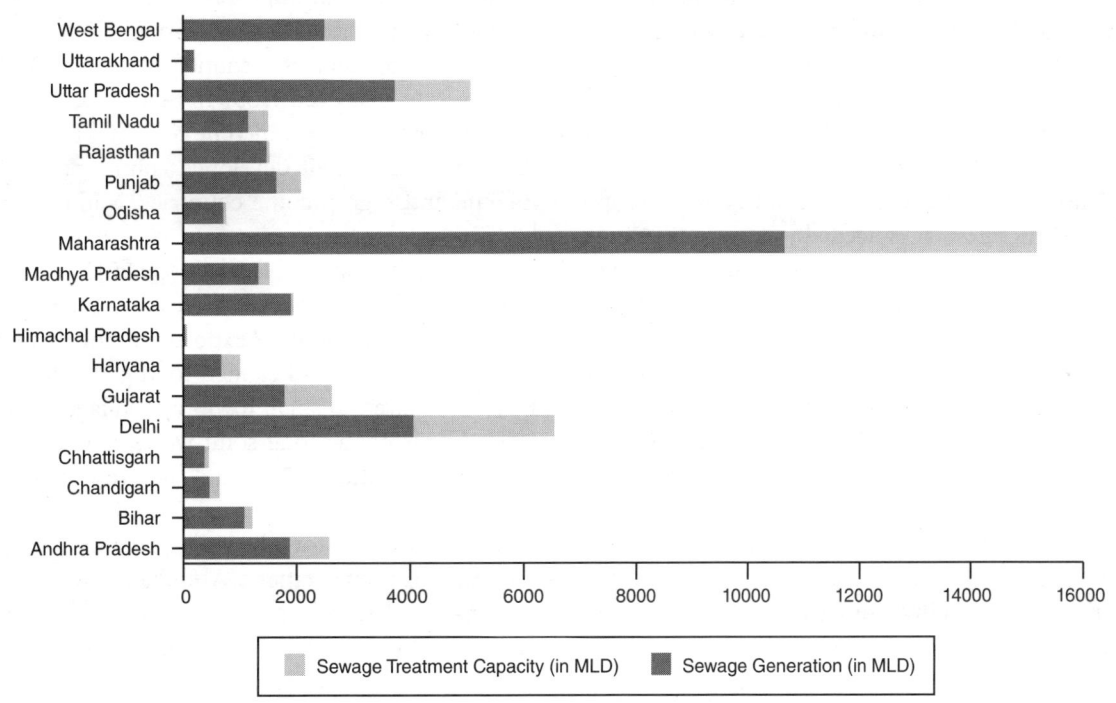

Figure 13.8 Sewage Generation and Treatment Capacity in Different States, 2010

Source: Data compiled from MoSPI (2011).

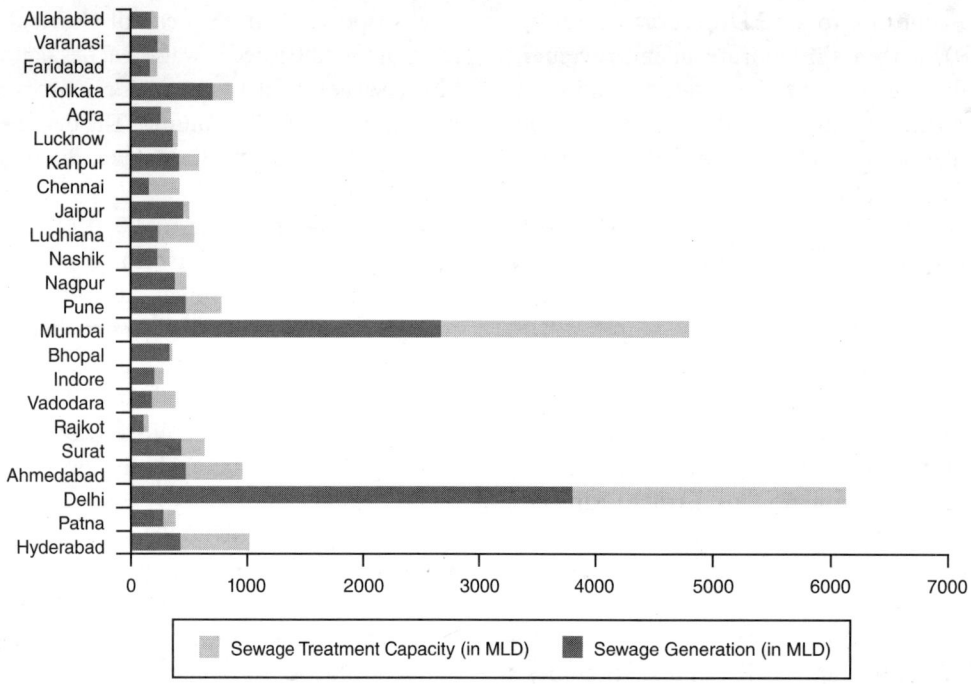

Figure 13.9 Sewage Generation and Treatment Capacity in Different Metropolitan Cities, 2010
Source: Data compiled from MoSPI (2011).

2012). Due to its rapid economic growth, India's per capita waste generation rate increased from 440 gm/person/day in 2001 to 500 gm/person/day in 2011. The average reported waste generation per capita for India is 370 grams (CPCB 2009). This is still far less than the per capita waste generation rates of western countries and for even China (700 gm/person/day). Metropolitan cities together generate a total of 86,000 tonnes of municipal solid waste per day, which amounts to 31.5 million tonnes per year. India, still in transition into becoming a developed country, fails to cope with the infrastructure that is needed to handle this huge quantity of waste generated (Yedla 2011). Figure 13.10 gives the situation of solid waste generation in different states in India. Maharashtra, Gujarat, Andhra Pradesh, Tamil Nadu, Uttar Pradesh, and West Bengal lead the list with waste generations ranging from 25,000 tpd to 55,000 tpd.

Waste collection is by and large inefficient in Indian cities. While big cities collect about 70–90 per cent of the waste generated, smaller cities collect only 50 per cent of the garbage generated (MoSPI 2011; NIUA 2005). Over and above these dismal numbers uncollected waste is littered all over garbage bins and in open areas making the streets unhygienic. Open dumping is a major method of waste disposal in almost all the cities in the country, accounting for about 90 per cent of the waste generated being dumped. While landfills catching fire is the most common way accounting for about 10 per cent of the garbage being burnt, garbage left uncollected is also burnt, leading to significant air pollution. Annepu (2012) reported that such burning accounted for an annual emission of about 22,000 tonnes of pollutants into the atmosphere in Mumbai city alone.

Waste generation rates are strongly linked to the economic development of a country/state/city (Yedla 2006). This can be observed from the fact that the per capita waste generation in low income countries is as low as 0.675 kg compared to their developed counterparts of middle-income and high-income countries. Middle-income and high-income countries generate an average waste of 0.81 kg and 3.08 kg respectively (Annepu 2012).

Cities with higher per capita incomes as compared to the national average and their exposure to the western culture of shopping malls and canned food generate much more waste compared to small towns and villages. Figure 13.11 gives details of the total solid waste generated in Indian metropolitan cities in 2011 and their respective per capita waste generation.

The top six spots for total waste generation were taken by the six metropolitan cities of Mumbai, New Delhi, Kolkata, Chennai, Hyderabad, and Bengaluru in 2008–9 as reported by CPCB. Three out of these six metropolitan cities generated over 11,000 tonnes of municipal solid waste every day. Per capita waste generation in Indian cities ranged between 0.2–0.87 kg/day. Some smaller cities recorded higher per capita waste generation as compared to bigger metropolitan

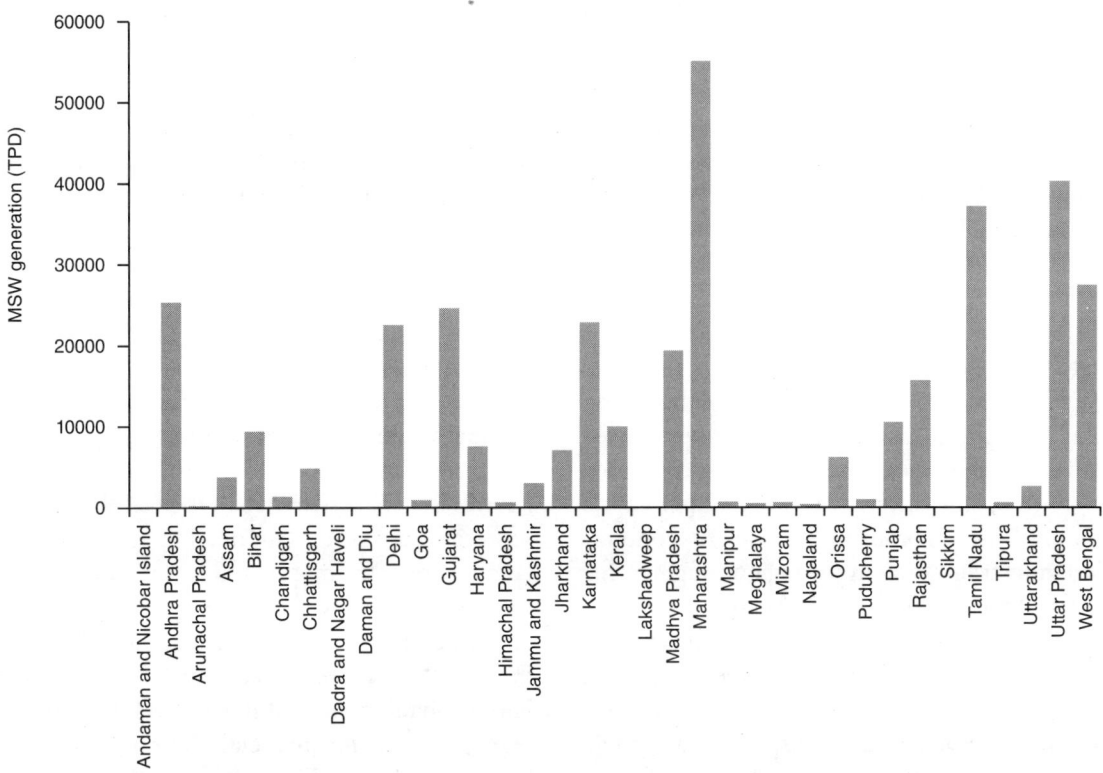

Figure 13.10 Municipal Solid Waste Generation in Different States of India, 2009–10

Sources: Data compiled from CPCB (2009); MoSPI (2011).

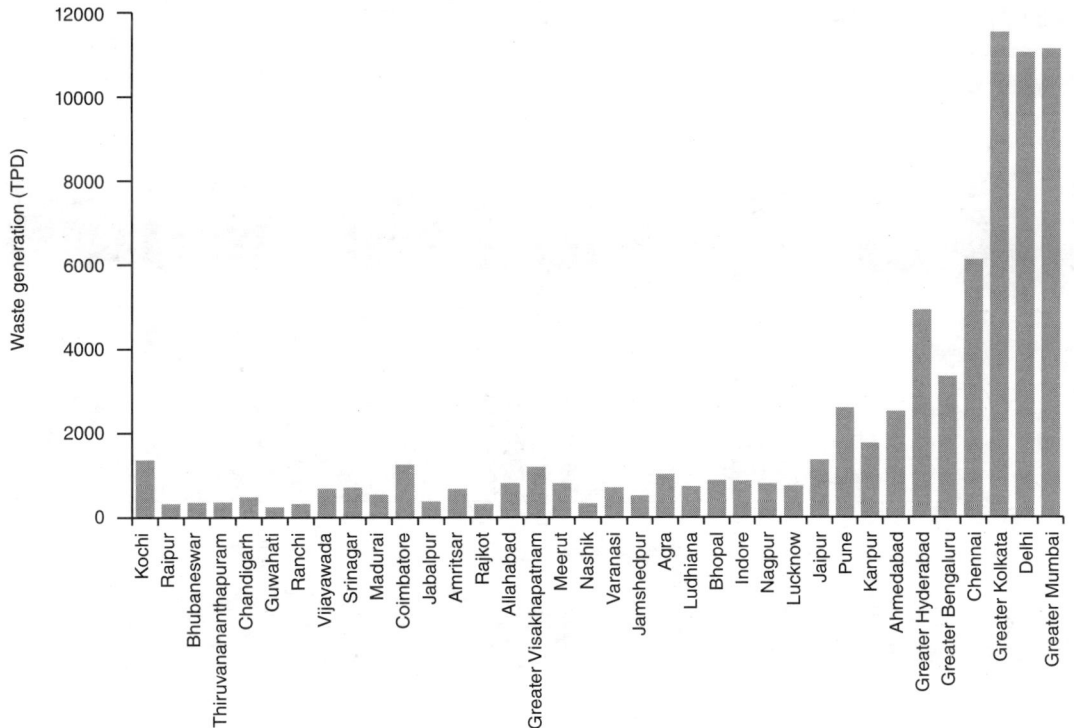

Figure 13.11 Waste Generation Rates in Metropolitan Cities, 2010–11

Sources: Data compiled from Annepu (2012); MoSPI (2011).

cities. Kochi, Coimbatore, Greater Visakhapatnam, Agra, Greater Hyderabad, Chennai, Greater Kolkata, and Delhi recorded higher per capita waste generation. Cities from central India reported relatively lesser per capita waste generations.

From Figure 13.12 it can be observed that among the metropolitan cities Chennai recorded the lowest waste generation (6,200 TPD) but the highest per capita waste generation (0.708 kg). Among the states, Arunachal Pradesh reported the lowest MSW generation and Maharashtra the highest waste generation. Goa recorded the highest per capita waste generation while Manipur reported the lowest. A study conducted by the Columbia University reported that east India as a region is less MSW loading compared to the west, both on the criteria of total and per capita waste generation. This can probably be linked to economic activities and industrialization in the region. Augmenting this observation, it was also reported that metropolitan cities have a higher average per capita waste generation at 0.605 kg/person/day as compared to the class I cities' average of 0.45 kg.

The predominant means of waste disposal in almost all Indian cities is open dumping. At the reported rate of waste generation it is expected that land requirements for waste disposal will rise substantially, making it essential to find alternative and more scientific means of disposal. (Annepu 2012; GoI 2009).

Indian municipal solid waste management has a predominant presence of the informal sector (Imura et al. 2005; Yedla 2011). Many studies in the past have reported the evaluated estimate of the rag-picking activity. With augmented recycling done by the formal sector, however small it is, the recyling achieved in India is comparable to the best in the world.

Many alternative methods for the disposal of organic waste such as aerobic composting, anaerobic composting, bio-methanation, and waste-to-energy (WTE) have been attempted in the past. However, there have been more failures than successes due to the fact that the waste is not segregated at source. Out of all these alternatives, aerobic composting is the most common method and it is reported that about 6 per cent of MSW collected is composted at various facilities. India has about five refuse derived fuel (RDF) facilities located in Hyderabad, Vijayawada, Jaipur, Chandigarh, and Rajkot. Due to poor governance, coordination, and financial planning, these alternatives have been facing difficulties in their incubation and implementation.

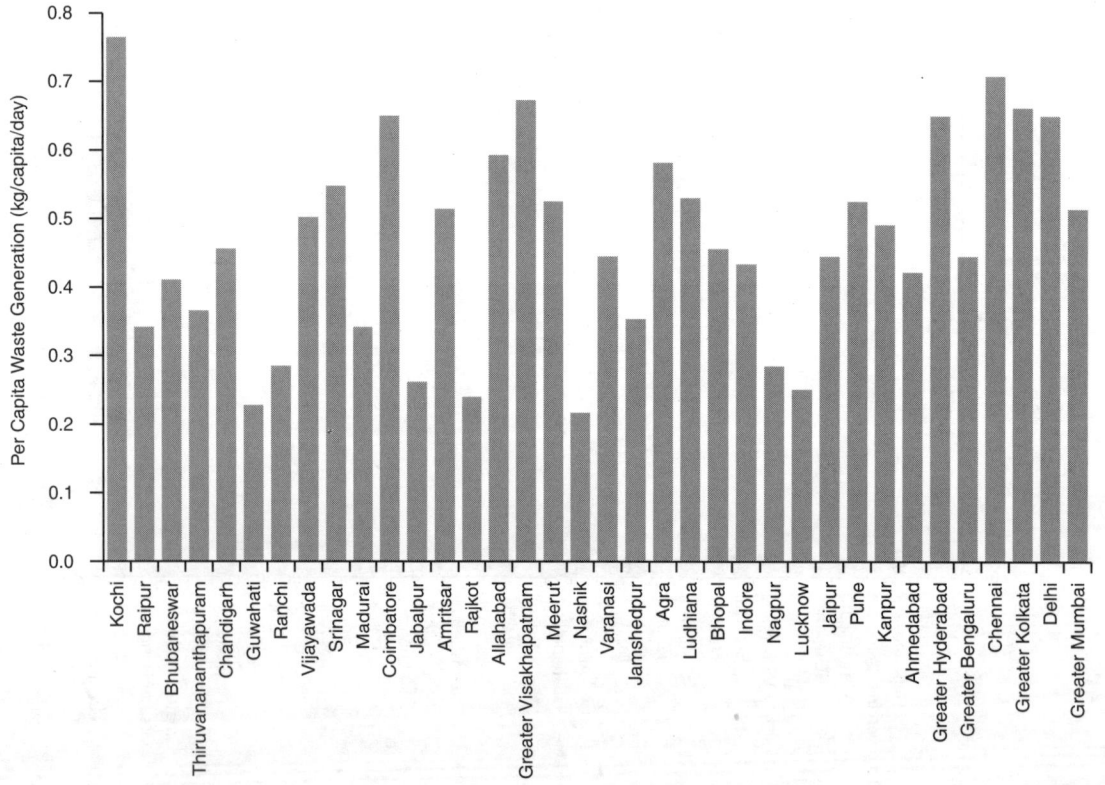

Figure 13.12 Per Capita Waste Generation in Metropolitan Cities, 2010

Source: Data compiled from the CPCB database.

The government of India has come up with Municipal Solid Waste (Handling and Management) Rules, 2000 which required all urban local bodies (ULBs) to handle their MSW as per the given guidelines by 2003 (MoEF 2000). However, due to lack of financial resources and poor public participation these rules were not effectively implemented. Even after a decade, the state of MSW management in most of the cities remains a concern.

INITIATIVES FACILITATING/AUGMENTING THE PROVISION OF SERVICES IN URBAN AREAS

With increasing population, urbanization, migration, consumption rates and waste (water and solid) generation rates, it becomes a Herculean task for city administrators to provide basic civic and environmental services. The existing system of provision of these services is plagued by the following issues:

- Poor infrastructure.
- Lack of financial capacity of ULBs.
- Lack of community participation in conserving the resource.
- Poor choice of technological alternatives.
- Poor governance.
- Inefficient/insufficient institutional structure.
- Lack of partnership between the state, the private sector, and community organizations.

In order to serve the millions of urban dwellers with a reliable water supply and safe sanitation service, it is essential to adopt a multi-pronged approach as explained in Figure 13.13.

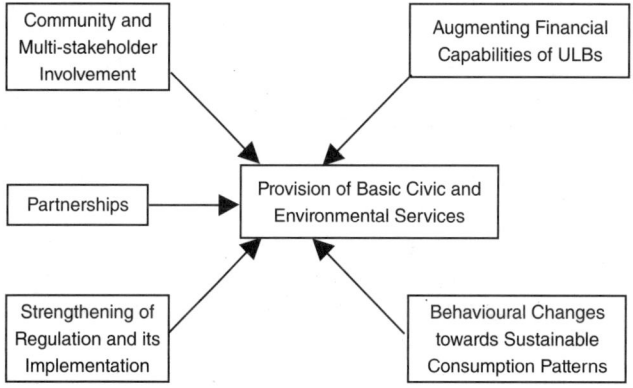

Figure 13.13 A Multi-pronged Approach to the Provision of Basic Civic and Environmental Services in Urban Areas
Source: Author's own.

While financial capabilities of ULBs are augmented, it is also essential to strengthen the regulatory regime and governance, foster partnerships, involve the community and other stakeholders in the dialogue and the process, and most importantly, work towards a behavioural change towards sustainable consumption patterns.

The government of India has taken up initiatives in these lines and the following are a few such initiatives leading to the provision of better civic and environmental services to urban dwellers (GoI 2012; MoUD 2010, 2011a; and MoWR 2012):

- Grants for ULBs under the Thirteenth Finance Commission's recommendations.
- The Jawaharlal Nehru National Urban Renewal Mission (JNNURM) scheme.
- Urban Infrastructure Scheme for Small and Medium Towns (UIDSSMT).
- Infrastructure Development Scheme for Satellite Towns, North Eastern Region Urban Development Programme (NERUDP), Backward Regions Grant Fund.
- Rajiv Gandhi National Drinking Water Mission.
- National Urban Sanitation Policy.
- Municipal Solid Waste (Handling & Management) Rules, 2000.
- National Water Policy, 2012.

On the one hand, the government has been making necessary regulations to promote the efficiency of service provision in urban centres in the country, and on the other hand—more so in the recent times—attempts have also made to augment the financial capabilities of cities. The following section discusses such initiatives.

Augmenting Financial Capabilities of ULBs

Urban centres are the drivers of economic growth contributing a major share of the national GDP. In spite of being the drivers of growth, the urban centres failed to get attention from the central government until the JNNURM was initiated in 2005. According to a High Powered Committee serving the Planning Commission on Financing Urban Infrastructure (HPEC), in 2009–10, the government invested about Rs 75,000 crore in the rural sector while the share for the urban sector under JNNURM was mere Rs 8,000 crore (MoUD 2012). This explains the fact that the urban sector has been neglected over the years, which has left the urban sector facing the huge challenge of providing infrastructure for the new population and also dealing with the backlog from the past. ULB are not equipped with such finances and nor does the private sector show any interest in issues like water supply, sanitation, and solid waste due to their low viability.

It has been reported that the total municipal revenue in India accounts for about 0.75 per cent of the country's GDP whereas for countries like Brazil it is 5 per cent (MoUD 2012). A study by the Reserve Bank of India (RBI) in 2007 revealed that the total revenue of municipalities was growing at a lower rate compared to combined central and state government revenues. With both revenue and expenditure accounting for only 2 per cent of the countries' GDP, the ULBs in India are a lot weaker financially when compared to the cities in the developed world.

Realizing the need to reinvent the drive for augmenting much-needed infrastructure development in urban centres—the drivers of growth—the government has come up with the following mission:

Jawaharlal Nehru National Urban Renewal Mission (JNNURM)

The urban share of population in India is projected to touch 40 per cent by 2021 and the share of urban centres in GDP is likely to be as high as 65 per cent. MoUD (2011a) estimates that ULBs will need an investment of Rs 1,20,536 crore over a period of seven years from 2005–6. That makes it an annual requirement of Rs 17,219 crore. This includes the following 63 cities covering the entire country:

- Seven cities with population more than 4 million.
- Twenty-eight cities with population between 1–4 million.
- Twenty-eight selected cities with population less than 1 million.

It was felt by the government that such investments need the following reform initiatives:

- Harnessing the potential of reforms in urban infrastructure.
- Need for national-level reform-linked investments.
- Need for sustainable infrastructure development.
- Need for efficiency enhancement.

Following this view, and with the objectives of: a) focused attention to integrated development of infrastructure services in selected cities; b) establishing linkages between asset-creation and asset-management through a series of reforms for long-term project sustainability; c) ensuring adequate funds to meet the deficiencies in urban infrastructural services; d) planned development of identified cities including peri-urban areas, outgrowths, and urban corridors leading to dispersed urbanization; e) scaling-up delivery of civic amenities and provision of utilities with emphasis on universal access to the urban poor; f) special focus on an urban renewal programme for old city areas to reduce congestion; and g) provision of basic services to the urban poor including security of tenure at affordable prices, improved housing, water supply and sanitation, and ensuring delivery, the government earmarked a fund of Rs 100,000 crore under the national JNNURM in December 2005 (MoUD 2011a). The duration of the missions is seven years from 2005–6. The sectors considered under this mission are:

1. Urban.
2. Water supply and sanitation.
3. Sewage and solid waste management.
4. Construction and improvements of drains and storm water drains.
5. Urban transportation including roads, highways, expressways, MRTS, and metro projects.
6. Parking lots and spaces based on public–private partnerships (PPP).
7. Developing heritage areas.
8. Prevention and rehabilitation of soil erosion and landslides only in cases of special category states where such problems are common.
9. Preservation of water bodies.

Activities covered for funding under this national mission are: 1) assistance for capacity building, city development plan (CDP), detailed project reports (DPRs), community participation, information, education and communication (IEC), and 2) investment support component.

Component under the sub-mission of urban infrastructure and governance (UIG) include urban renewal, water supply, sanitation, sewage and solid waste management, urban transportation, and preservation of water bodies. Revised allocation for UIG for the seven-year period was Rs 31,500 crore. For 2011–12 it was Rs 6,423 crore. As on February 2012, more than 98 per cent of the allocation of Rs 31,500 crore had been committed (GoI 2012). All the selected cities under the UIG component have prepared CDPs charting out their long-term visions and goals in urban governance and development.

So far 546 projects have been approved under JNNURM. While some have already been completed the rest are being executed. Figure 13.14 gives details of sectoral projects completed so far in specific states. While some states put more emphasis on water supply, others used this funding to augment their sewage and transport systems. Out of 126 JNNURM projects completed so far, 37 are for water supply, 16 for sewage system, 41 for roads, and 12 for drainage.

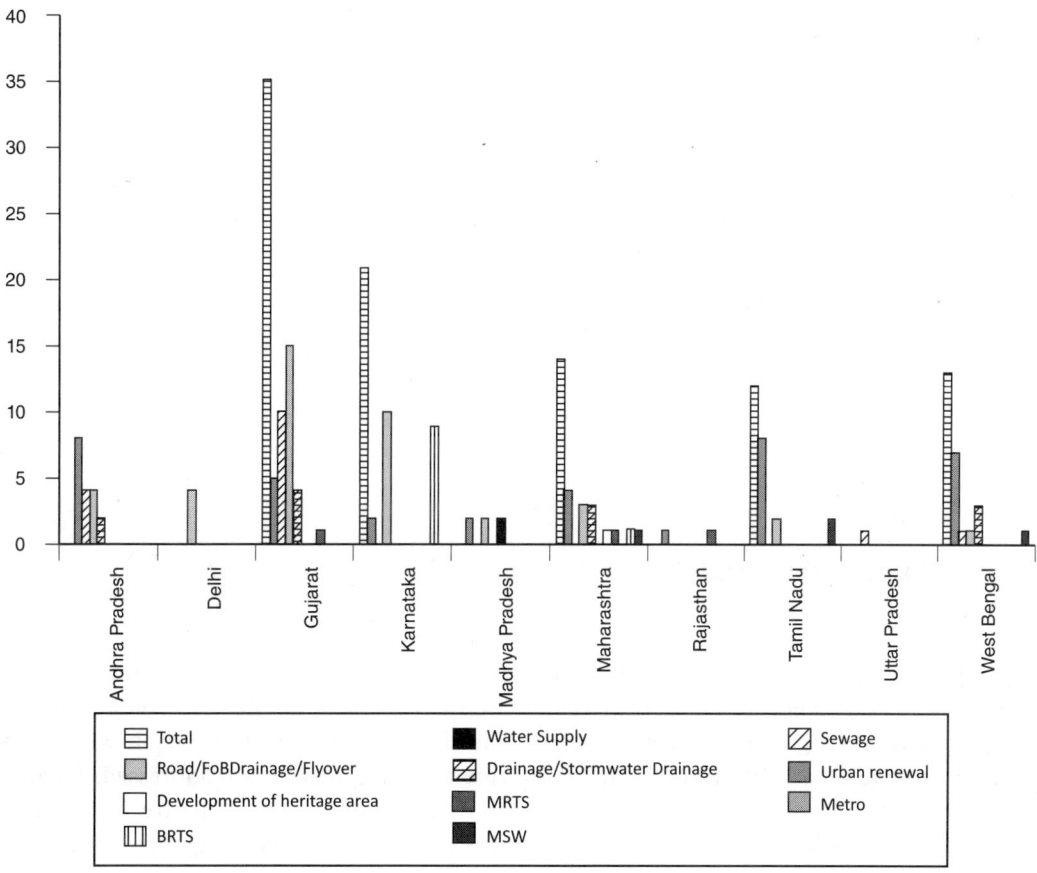

Figure 13.14 Details of JNNURM Projects Completed in Different States and for Different Sectors
Source: MoUD (2011a and 2011b).

Financial outlay for the service sector under the Five Year Plan programme has been incremental and Table 13.6 gives details of the funds required as projected for the Eleventh Five Year Plan.

Table 13.6 Projected Funds Requirement for the Eleventh Five Year Plan

Sub-sector	Estimated Amount (in Rs crore)
Urban water supply	53,666
Urban sewerage and sewage treatment	53,168
Urban drainage	20,173
Solid waste management	2,212
MIS	8
R&D and PHE training	10
Total	129,237

Source: MoUD (2011a).

While the centre contributes the major share, the remaining part is contributed by state sector outlays through national financial institutions such as the Life Insurance Corporation (LIC), the Housing and Urban Development Corporation (HUDCO) and Infrastructure Leasing & Financial Services (IL&FS), and from mobilization of funds from external agencies such as the World Bank, JBIC, ADB, and others.

The water supply and sewage sectors are capital-intensive and need huge funds. As per the High Powered Expert Committee (HPEC) estimates, the per capita investment costs for water supply, sewage, and solid waste management are Rs 5,099, Rs 4,704, and Rs 391 (Mathur et al. 2007; MoUD 2012). The urban sector outlay for the states for the last four years of the Eleventh Five Year Plan increased from 16.8 per cent to 27.9 per cent. Table 13.7 gives the projected capital and revenue expenditure during the Twelfth Five Year plan.

HPEC has estimated that the total urban sector infrastructure for its eight core services would need Rs 39.2 lakh crore in the next 20 years beginning from Twelfth Five Year Plan in 2012 (MoUD 2012). In addition to this, an estimated Rs 18.1 lakh crore is required for its operations and maintenance. Realizing the huge investments required for the development of infrastructure for the provision of civic and

Table 13.7 Projected Capital and Revenue Expenditure for the Twelfth Five Year Plan

Sector	Capital Expenditure	Revenue Expenditure	Total
Water supply	33,390	74,774	108,164
Sewerage	25,042	25,738	50,780
Solid waste	5,137	25065	30,202
Urban roads	179,149	37,367	216,516
Mass transit	46,553	25,065	71,618
Traffic mgmt. systems	10,274	1,377	11,651
Storm water drains	19,905	4,337	24,242
Street lighting	1,926	550	2,476
Other sectors	73,050	19,428	92,478
Total	394,428	213,701	608,129

Source: MoUD (2012).

environmental services in urban centres and the difficulty in mobilizing these resources, the government has been strategically promoting the private sector's involvement by means of PPPs. The government estimates that about 20 per cent of the total investment requirements for the Twelfth Plan could be derived potentially through PPP. The government has demonstrated the potential of PPPs in infrastructure development by employing the same in the case of Delhi Airport wherein the government did not incur any costs and instead the project gives sustained revenue due to a revenue-sharing agreement between the government and the builder. A number of such partnerships have been attempted in many cities for the provision of sanitation services, water supply, and municipal solid waste management. Table 13.8 gives a few PPP initiatives from different cities. Though their numbers are small they possess tremendous potential to further contribute to the provision of urban infrastructure and services. As recommended by the HPEC working group, it is necessary for the government to facilitate the PPP model by aggressively promoting the PPP model projects and take up a number of PPP-friendly initiatives across all tiers of the government. Capacity building for ULBs in fostering partnerships could also play an important role in promoting PPPs.

THE WAY FORWARD

Improvements in the provision of basic civic and environmental services has been attempted in the last two Five Year Plans by increasing capital and revenue expenditure. The most recent strategy has been promotion of partnerships. As a result, water supply service has improved and we may as well be set to meet the MDG targets. However, the situation of sanitation is far from anybody's comfort with millions of urban dwellers still without proper sanitation facilities even if we meet the MDG and national targets (ADB 2009).

Municipal solid waste management, in spite of having one of the best regulatory frameworks in the world, is far too poor and needs a lot of catching up in terms of technology, governance, and public participation/perception.

Improvement in these services involving individuals need a multi-pronged approach wherein all aspects of the service provision are addressed. Financial provisions for augmenting infrastructure is, of course, the most important aspect and the government is responding well by means of increasing allocation in its investment plans and facilitating states through JNNURM and other national missions/initiatives. Fostering partnerships plays a key role and the government has rightly put a priority on involving partnership models in infrastructure development for the provision of civic and environmental services.

It is important to empower ULBs by enhancing their capacity for fostering partnerships and involving the private sector while maintaining social equity. ULBs need to be trained at different levels in a way to uplift the governance. This would help in transmitting the financial and administrative efforts delivered at the national level through important missions such as the JNNURM to the local implementation.

The role of NGOs needs to be mainstreamed as they are better equipped to bridge the gap between the formal and informal sectors, especially when the presence of the informal sector is dominant and intertwined with a sensitive issue of social equity—as in the case of municipal solid waste management.

Water and sewage tariffs as a means to strengthen cities: Water and sewage tariffs are an important means of augmenting the financial capabilities of the cities. It is always recommended to have all connections metered so as to improve revenues from water supply as also to monitor supplies. Metering is the only way to charge the users based on actual consumption. However, Indian cities are not

Table 13.8 Some of the PPP Initiatives (Indicative) Implemented in Indian Cities for the Provision of Services

Sector	City	Project	Awarded Year	Term of Contract	Revenue Model
MSW	Ulhasnagar, MH (300 tpd)	Collection and transportation	October 2007	10 years	Management contract
	Greater Noida (50 tpd)	Collection and transportation	August 2007	3 years	Management contract
	Coimbatore, TN (400 tpd)	Integrated MSW system, setting up transfer stations, waste processing, and SFL	November 2007	20 years	BOT and JNNURM funds
	Hyderabad, AP (3800 tpd)	Integrated MSW system, setting up transfer stations, waste processing, and SFL	February 2009	25 years	BOOT
	Delhi (1000 tpd)	Integrated MSW system, setting up transfer stations, waste processing, and disposal	January 2008	20 years	BOOT
	Asansol, Durgapur	Integrated waste processing and sanitary landfill	January 2007	20 years	BOT
	Thiruvananthapuram, Kerala	Only sanitary landfill at Vilasilpala		20 years	BOT
Water supply & distribution	Latur and Chandrapur	Distribution-cum-revenue collection	June 2005	5/10 years	Performance management contract
	Salt Lake City	Underground network of water supply and sewage services	February 2008	30 years	BOT
	Chennai	Development of sea water desalination plant	January 2007	25 years	DBOOT
	Cluster of ULBs, Karnataka	Augmentation-cum-O&M of distribution system		3.5 years	Management contract
	Haldia	Augmentation of water treatment system-cum-O&M of water supply system	2008	25 Years	BOT
	Thiruppur	Providing water and sewage services	1993		BOOT

Source: Extracted from GoI (2009).

effectively metered for their water consumption. According to a survey conducted in 2007 under JNNURM by ADB, only 25 per cent of the customers in the 20 city utilities considered for the survey were metered. Most other customers were charged at a flat rate independent of their consumption levels. This is a deterrent in recovering production costs and also for water conservation. While Bengaluru and Pune were the most metered cities for water, Kolkata did not bill residents for their water consumption (ADB 2007).

In 2008, the average tariff for all the customers, which includes industries, commercial, and residential was Rs 4.90 (USD 0.09) per cubic metre (ADB 2007). Commercial users were mandated to have meters. However, due to the non-functional meters, most of the times they were charged flat rates which are always less efficient for cost recovery. Monitoring of industrial water usage has always been inefficient and so is their water tariff.

Unaccounted-for water (UFW) is a major issue in the Indian water supply system, which accounts for about 40–50 per cent loss while the acceptable level is 15 per cent as per CPHEEO. Unaccounted-for water in the three largest metropolitan cities (Mumbai, Chennai, and New Delhi) was between 20–26 per cent of the total supply in 2004 (NIUA 2005). Many city administrations found it difficult to estimate UFW and lack of meters and non-functional meters only added to the difficulty. These losses affect the overall efficiency of the system as they fail to recover the cost of production.

Therefore, it is essential to derive an appropriately dynamic and equitable tariff system for water and sewage users in different categories and make the necessary institutional arrangements to enforce these tariffs (TERI 2010). Similarly, enforcing a differentiated and equitable waste collection fee for municipal solid waste management would add to the financial strength of the city administration and also help citizens reduce waste generation.

The water-energy-carbon nexus—A call for integrative action: Food security is a major concern for the next few decades all over the world. This concern has its bases in the projected world population for the next 30 years and the resulting food requirements. Agriculture as a sector is the largest consumer of water and, therefore, it can transform the increasing food insecurity issue into a problem of an intense water crisis. The fact that agriculture is energy-intensive makes it clear that food security implies ensuring water and energy security.

Producing more water to meet the needs of agriculture and other sectors involves considerable energy inputs. Production of energy to meet the needs of agriculture and the other sectors is highly water-intensive. Using more water for the generation of energy and not meeting the water demands of the other sectors could potentially jeopardize food security and other ecological aspects, leading to serious consequences. Addressing sectoral issues independently leads to inefficiencies, and hence it is important that planning and investment in energy and water infrastructure take into account the nexus between water, energy, and carbon. According to the G-Science Academies Statement–2012, the impending challenges central to humanity—the need for affordable and environmental friend energy, need for water, and need for food security—are strongly linked. In order to address the issue of water and energy in tandem it may be necessary to plan and implement an integrated water and energy programme at the national level (G-Science 2012). In addressing these issues one needs long-term planning in a systems approach within the boundary of regional circumstances. There is an emerging nexus between water, energy, and carbon and this needs to be addressed through an integrated approach. Accounting for all the energy inputs in water production in a life cycle analysis (LCA) framework not only helps improve the energy efficiency of the system but also helps in realizing the true cost of water production and supply and that in turn helps in devising an appropriate and effective tariff structure for water use and conservation.

Most of the national initiatives target the provision of infrastructure by augmenting financial mechanisms. However, it is equally important to change consumption patterns of people. While the provision of a better water supply network is certainly the need of the day and on immediate terms, provision of better water supply could in turn lead to more consumption of water, leading to its scarcity, unless citizens are made aware of scarce water resources and the need to conserve them. A similar argument can be put forward for sewage and municipal solid waste management services as well. National initiatives such as JNNURM fail to address the issue of augmenting the source such as watershed management, water harvesting etc. As it enters the second phase it may be appropriate and timely for JNNURM to include in its portfolio aspects of 'water and sewage metering', the 'water-energy-carbon nexus', and 'means/mechanisms to change consumption patterns towards resource conservation'.

Due to the peculiarity of the Asian growth model, where the cities are faced with both the quality and quantity aspect of the same problem at the same time, the conventional model of 'grow first and then clean' may prove to be very costly (Yedla 2011). Therefore, it is necessary to have an integrated approach to the problem. Unhealthy consumption patterns can lock our infrastructure into unsustainability, turning our cities into centres of unsustainability. Therefore, in order to provide quality environmental and civic services to all citizens, it is essential to have an integrated approach with equal emphasis on financial mechanisms for providing infrastructure, improving governance and the capacity of ULBs, equity in the provision of services, and changes in consumption and civic patterns of the population.

REFERENCES

Annepu, Ranjit Kharvel (2012), 'Sustainable Solid Waste Management in India', (Masters' thesis), Earth Engineering Center, Columbia University, USA.

Asian Development Bank [ADB] (2007), '2007 Benchmarking and Data Book of Water Utilities in India', in a Partnership between the Ministry of Urban Development, Government of India, and Asian Development Bank.

———. (2009), *Indian's Sanitation for All—How to Make it Happen*. Water for All Series 18. Manila: Asian Development Bank.

Center for Science and Environment [CSE] (2004). Available at: http:www.cseindia.org/dte-supplement/industry20040215/non-issue.htm, last accessed on 12 March 2012.

Central Pollution Control Board [CPCB] (2009), 'Status of water supply, wastewater generation and treatment in class-I cities & class-II towns of India', Control of Urban Pollution Series: CUPS/70/2009–10, New Delhi.

Gleick, Peter H. (2009), *The World's Water 2008–2009: The Biannual Report on Fresh Water Resources*. USA: Pacific Institute for Studies in Development, Environment and Security.

Government of India [GoI] (2009), *Position Paper on the Solid Waste Management Sector in India*. New Delhi: Department of Economic Affairs, Ministry of Finance.

———. (2012), *Economic Survey 2011–12*. New Delhi: Ministry of Finance, Government of India.

G-Science Academies Statements 2012 (2012), *Energy and Water Linkage: Challenge to a Sustainable Future*, statement signed by the apex science academies of the G-20 nations.

Imura, H., S. Yedla, M.M. Memon, and H. Shirakawa (2005), 'Urban Environmental Issues and Trends in Asia: An Overview', *International Review of Environmental Strategies* (IGES, Japan), 5(2): 357–82

Indiastat (2012), data base available at http://www.indiastat.com. Last accessed on 12 March 2012.

Mathur, M.P., R. Chandra, and S. Singh (2007), *Norms and Standards of Municipal Basic Service in India*. New Delhi: National Institute of Urban Affairs, NIUA WP 07–01.

Ministry of Environment and Forests [MoEF] (2000), *Solid Waste (Handling and Management) Rules, 2000*. New Delhi: Government of India.

Ministry of Statistics and Programme Implementation [MoSPI] (2011), *Compendium of Environmental Statistics, India 2011*. New Delhi: Central Statistics Office, MoSPI, Government of India.

Ministry of Urban Development [MoUD] (2010), *National Urban Sanitation Policy*. New Delhi: Government of India.

———. (2011a), *Jawaharlal Nehru National Urban Renewal Mission—Overview*. New Delhi: Government of India.

———. (2011b), *Project Implementation Status: UIG—Jawaharlal Nehru National Urban Renewal Missions*. New Delhi: Ministry of Urban Development, Government of India.

———. (2011c), *Handbook of Service Level Benchmarking*. New Delhi: Ministry of Urban Development, Government of India.

———. (2012), *Report of the Sub-committee on Financing Urban Infrastructure in the 12th Five Year Plan*. New Delhi: High Level Committee on Financing Infrastructure, Ministry of Urban Development, Government of India.

Ministry of Water Resources [MoWR] (2012), *Draft National Water Policy (2012)*. New Delhi: Government of India.

National Institute of Urban Affairs [NIUA] (2005), *Status of Water Supply, Sanitation and Solid Waste Management in Urban Areas*. New Delhi: Central Public Health and Environmental Engineering Organization (CPHEEO), Ministry of Urban Development (MoUD), Government of India.

National Sample Survey [NSS] (2002), *Housing Conditions in India: Household Amenities and Other Characteristics*. Report No. 489, Ministry of Statistics and Programme Implementation (MoSPI), Government of India.

———. (2010), *Housing Condition and Amenities in India: 2008-9*. Report No. 535, MoSPI, Government of India.

The Energy Resources Institute [TERI] (2010), *Review of current practices in determining user charges and incorporation of economic principles of pricing of urban water supply*. Project Report No. 2009/IA/02. New Delhi: The Energy Resources Institute.

Water Aid India (2005), *Drinking Water and Sanitation Status in India—Coverage, Financing and Emerging Concerns*. New Delhi: Water Aid India.

Yedla, S. (2006), 'Dynamics of Environmental Problems in Mumbai', *Journal of Cleaner Technologies and Environmental Policy*, 8(3): 182–7.

———. (2011), 'Dynamic of Environmental Problems—Why are the Waste Management Problems Unique in the Developing Cities of Asia?', Proceedings of the 2nd International Conference on Solid Waste Management (ICON MSW), Kolkata, India, 9–11 November.

14

On the Internal Mobility of Indians
Knowledge Gaps and Emerging Concerns

*S. Chandrasekhar and Ajay Sharma**

INTRODUCTION

Jan Breman, who studied the transition in the rural economy of southern Gujarat over a span of 30 years, not only documented the changing importance of non-agricultural activities in rural India, but also highlighted the mobility of workers in search of work. He found that on account of slow growth and stagnation in job creation in agriculture, rural workers were moving towards the urban economy. Much of what he talked about in his book—seasonal migrants and footloose labour (workers commuting daily for work)—has become extremely relevant today in the context of understanding the mobility of India's workforce (Breman 1996). In the recent past, these issues have also received their fair share of column inches in newspapers. Veteran journalist P. Sainath, in his columns,[1] has described a trip from Mahbubnagar in Andhra Pradesh to Mumbai. According to him, in 1993 there was one bus every week. Ten years later, not including private bus services, there were as many as 42 to 45 buses a week. The increase in bus services was to keep pace with the increase in the number of individuals migrating to Pune and Mumbai in search of improved livelihoods. Sainath also writes that since 2008, the Mahatma Gandhi National Rural Employment Guarantee Scheme (MGNREGS) has had a salutary effect and people have found work in their villages. The proof of the pudding being that the number of buses from Mahbubnagar to Mumbai declined to 28 per week. The migration stream from Uttar Pradesh and Bihar to Haryana and Punjab, which used to be very high at one time, has reduced in the past few years because of the cumulative effect of the MGNREGS and also the development observed in the origin states.

It is also true that seasonality in availability of jobs means that in addition to migration, workers seek opportunities on a daily basis and commute to where the jobs are available. Breman, too, shed light on this phenomenon in his book. Data from official sources indicate that in 2009–10, 8.05 million workers not engaged in agriculture commuted from rural to urban areas for work, while 4.37 million workers not engaged in agriculture commuted from urban to rural areas for work. In addition, there were 5.03 million rural and 7.17 million urban residents without a fixed place of work (Chandrasekhar 2011).

The long and short of it is that there are large numbers of Indians, in particular workers, who are mobile. The Indian Railways have had to provide for the increase in demand

---

* We are grateful to Vikas Chitre and K.L. Krishna for useful comments on an earlier draft of this chapter. This chapter is written as part of the 'Strengthen and Harmonize Research and Action on Migration in the Indian Context' (SHRAMIC), an initiative by Sir Dorabji Tata Trust and Allied Trusts (SDTT&AT). SHRAMIC is anchored by IGIDR and is in collaboration with NIUA, CPR, IRIS-KF, and the Tata Trusts' Migration Programme partners.

[1] Sainath (2003, 2008).

from the migrant and commuter populations. In 2011, Northern Railways alone ran 74 trips of special trains to clear the rush of passengers travelling on account of the Chhat festival. In 2012, Southern Railways ran special trains during Pongal to cater to the increase in the number of passengers. Western Railways is yet to meet the long-standing demand of commuters to have local trains run from Churchgate in Mumbai to Dahanu which is 125 km away. Presently, the local trains run till Virar and commuters have to wait for a considerable time for the connecting train to Dahanu.

Anecdotal evidence and case studies apart, there are many aspects of the phenomenon of mobile workers that we are yet to come to grips with. We can ill-afford not to have a comprehensive understanding of this phenomenon. This chapter focuses on the different forms of mobility, provides their estimates based on data from official sources, identifies data and knowledge gaps, and then highlights emerging concerns in the context of India's mobile population.

DEFINING MOBILITY AND THE EXTENT OF MOBILITY

There are two aspects of mobility: migration and commuting. Migration by itself is of various types—temporary, permanent, return, and short-term (see Box 14.1). In addition there is distress migration, a phenomenon that is not captured in official datasets and hence not well understood. In the context of this chapter, we define commuting as one where the place of work (rural, urban, no fixed place) differs from the usual place of residence (rural, urban). We first discuss the issue of migration and then move to the issue of commuting.

There are two sources of data on migration: Census of India and surveys of the National Sample Survey Office (NSSO). Since information from the Census of India 2001 is dated we provide estimates based on NSSO's survey on employment and unemployment and migration conducted over July 2007–June 2008.[2] Further, information on short-term migrants and return migrants is not available as part of the Census of India data. The kind of information available in the two datasets is different (see Box 14.1).

Migration can be in the context of the entire household or specific individuals. Recognizing this distinction, NSSO in its surveys seeks details on: whether the household migrated to the village/town of enumeration during the last 365 days, whether any former member of the household migrated out at any time in the past (out-migrants who are not currently

---

Box 14.1 Definition of Key Terms Related to Migration

Census Definitions

Migrant: A person who has moved from one politically defined area to another similar area. In the Indian context, these areas are generally a village in rural areas and a town in urban areas. Thus a person who moves out from one village or town to another village or town is termed as a migrant provided his/her movement is not of a purely temporary nature on account of casual leave, visits, tours, etc.

Non-migrants (immobiles): People who are seen living their entire life-time and die in the same village/town in which they were born, are defined as immobiles or non-migrants.

Birth Place Migrant: If at the time of Census enumeration, there is a change in the usual place of residence of an individual with reference to his/her birth place, he/she is defined as a migrant in accordance with 'birth place' concept.

Last Residence Migrant: If at the time of Census enumeration, a change in the usual place of residence of an individual is noted with reference to his/her previous usual residence, he/she is termed as a migrant in accordance with 'last residence' concept.

Migration Rate: It is taken as the ratio of total migrants counted in the Census to its total population multiplied by 1,000. While discussing the migration result, the term 'population mobility' is taken as a synonym for migration rate.

NSSO definitions

Migrant: As per the NSSO definition, a migrant is defined based on the last place of residence, that is, for an individual if the place of residence at the time of the enumeration differs from the last place of residence at the time of the survey.

Temporary and Permanent Migrants: Migration is temporary in nature, if a migrant intends to move again to the last usual place of residence or to any other place. If a migrant, in normal course, is likely to stay at the place of enumeration and does not plan to move out of the place of enumeration, it is treated as a permanent migration. Those who migrate temporarily, are further categorized in two groups—those with expected duration of stay less than 12 months and those with expected duration of stay 12 months or more.

Return Migrants: Those migrants who had reported that the present place of enumeration was the usual place of residence any time in the past are considered return migrants.

Short-term Migrants: Persons who had stayed away from the village/town for a period of a month or more but less than six months during the last 365 days for employment or in search of employment are termed as short-term migrants.

Sources: http://censusindia.gov.in/Metadata/Metada.htm#Mig and NSSO (2010).

---

[2] NSSO integrated the collection of migration data with the quinquennial survey on employment and unemployment. Before the 65th Round survey conducted in 2007–8, migration particulars were collected as part of the 38th Round (January 1983–December 1983), 43rd Round (July 1987–June 1988), and 55th Round (July 1999–June 2000). The 49th Round collected information on housing conditions and migration in India.

members of the household), and migration particulars of household members.

A total of 2.07 million households residing in rural areas and 2.11 million households residing in urban areas reported having moved to their current residence location in the 365 days preceding NSSO's survey in 2007–8. These households constitute 1.3 and 3.3 per cent of rural and urban households respectively.

Considering all households, we find that among rural and urban households, 95.4 million and 21 million individuals respectively migrated out any time in the past. These out-migrants were not currently members of the households who were surveyed. Among rural (urban) households with out-migrants, 36.5 (24) per cent of the households report receiving remittances. The average remittance received by a rural household with an out-migrant was Rs 20,700 per year and the average remittance received by an urban household with an out-migrant was Rs 43,600 per year. This information by itself is not very useful when we want to understand the issue of diversification of sources of income. Davis et al. (2007) find that in Asia the proportion of rural households classified as migration/transfers-oriented varied from 1.2 per cent in Vietnam to 11.5 per cent in Indonesia. In Latin America, it varied from 0.9 per cent in Nicaragua to 5.9 per cent in Guatemala; and in Africa it varied from 1 per cent in Nigeria to 3.4 per cent in Ghana.[3] These figures show that the proportion of migration or transfers-oriented households is still not sizeable. Our lack of understanding of sources of income of households is in our opinion an emerging concern and a knowledge gap.

Whether a member of a household is considered as a migrant or not is inferred based on the response to a question on whether the place of enumeration differs from the last usual place of residence. A migrant is an individual whose place of enumeration is different from the last usual place of residence. Overall, in 2007–8, 26.1 per cent of the rural residents and 35.4 per cent of the urban residents could be classified as migrants. There were over 193 million migrants in rural and 94 million migrants in urban areas (Table 14.1). Given that women moving on account of marriage are considered migrants, it is not surprising that they account for bulk of the migrants in India.

Table 14.1 Size of Migrant Population

Gender	Migrants	Short-term Migrants	Return Migrants
Rural			
Male	20,618,579	10,671,627	4,894,476
Female	173,193,548	1,912,980	18,357,100
Total	193,812,127	12,584,607	23,251,576
Urban			
Male	35,705,919	876,633	4,161,885
Female	58,325,264	159,891	6,093,890
Total	94,031,183	1,036,524	10,255,775

Source: Calculations based on unit level data from NSSO's survey on employment, unemployment, and migration (2007–8).

A total of 12.5 million rural residents and 1 million urban residents could be classified as short-term migrants. The interesting point to note is that short-term migrants were overwhelmingly men and this was because men were relatively more mobile than women in search of work. Estimates of short-term migrants have been contested by some commentators and researchers. For instance, Deshingkar and Akter (2009) put out an estimate of 100 million short-term migrants. They arrived at this number by adding the number of child workers (estimates by the International Center on Child Labor and Education to be roughly 25–30 million where as Census 2001 states this figure to be around 12 million), workers employed in the brick kiln industry (10 million), the textile industry (35 million), and construction industry (30 million). The way this number is arrived at does not seem to be very realistic and needs to be reconsidered, given that not all these workers can be migrants. But still the numbers estimated from NSSO surveys do seem to be very low. We identify the issue of undercounting of short-term migrants as an emerging concern and a knowledge gap.

The phenomenon of return migration is sizeable. Return migrants are those who report their present place of enumeration as their usual place of residence any time in the past. In rural and urban areas, there were 23.2 million and 10.2 million return migrants respectively. There is a valid perception that return migration is on the rise. Newspaper reports indicate that over 50,000 workers in Surat, Gujarat, working in the textile and diamond industry have returned to their homes in Ganjam, Odisha on account of a variety of reasons, including dispute over wages. The fact that employment-related reasons are an important driver of return migration is also evident from NSSO data. Of course, there is anecdotal evidence to suggest that discrimination at the destination may force migrants to return to their place of origin. The large size of return migration calls for

---

[3] They proposed a typology of rural households based on the sources of a household's income: farm-oriented (more than 75 per cent of total income from farm production); farm, market-oriented (more than 50 per cent of agricultural production sold in the market); farm, subsistence (<= 50 per cent of agricultural production sold in the market); labour-oriented household (more than 75 per cent of the total income from wage or non-farm self-employment); migration/transfers-oriented household (more than 75 per cent of total income from transfers/other non-labour sources); and diversified households.

a careful analysis of this phenomenon in order to get a clearer picture.

When feasible, an alternative to moving permanently, that is, to migrate, is to commute long distances to work. This is particularly so in the current context where the seasonality in availability of jobs and anaemic growth in non-farm employment has meant that workers seek opportunities on a daily basis and commute to where the jobs are available. Sainath has written about the hundreds of women in Gondia district of Maharashtra 'who spend just four hours a day at home and travel over 1,000 km each week (by train)—to earn Rs 30 daily'.[4] In the context of workers engaged in non-agricultural activities and commuting across rural–urban boundaries on a daily basis, Mohanan (2008: 61) writes, '... movement of rural workers to urban areas is somewhat reinforced by the daily picture of overcrowded trains and buses bringing people to the cities and towns from the surrounding areas, sometimes called the floating population'.

Estimates of the commuting workforce are available from NSSO's survey on employment and unemployment (66th Round, 2009–10), which has a question on location of workplace (rural, urban, and no fixed place) for all workers engaged in non-agricultural activities. The size of workers residing in rural areas but working in urban areas is 8.05 million, accounting for 8.16 per cent of the rural workforce being engaged in non-agriculture; whereas urban residents working in rural areas are 4.37 million constituting 4.94 per cent of the urban workforce. It should be noted that 5.03 million rural residents and 7.17 million urban residents report not having any fixed workplace[5] (Table 14.2). So, we have 24 million workers who commute on a daily basis across rural and urban boundaries for employment purposes. Of course, these numbers do not reflect the distance travelled by a commuting worker.

Typically, the size of the rural (urban) workforce is set equal to the number of workers living in rural (urban) areas. Mohanan (2008) and Chandrasekhar (2011) have argued the need for adjusting the size of the rural and urban workforce to reflect commuting workers. If one were to ignore the workers with no fixed place of work, then for 2009–10, the urban workforce needs to be adjusted upwards by

---

[4] Sainath (2007).

[5] These numbers have been calculated using unit level data from NSSO's 66th Round (2009–10) survey on 'Employment and Unemployment'. The survey provides information on commuting by workers engaged in non-agricultural activities (National Industrial Classification divisions 02–99 and industry groups 012, 013, 014). Information is available on location of residence (urban, rural) and location of workplace (rural, urban, no fixed location). Even though, we know the district and state of residence of workers, information about the district and state of work location is not available.

Table 14.2 Estimated Size of the Non-agricultural Workforce Based on Sector of Residence and Place of Work (all-India)

Sector of Residence	Place of Work			
	Rural	Urban	Not Fixed	Total
Rural	85,556,220* (86.73)	8,050,036 (8.16)	5,035,493 (5.1)	98,641,749 (100)
Urban	4,370,678 (4.94)	76,947,337 (86.95)	7,177,731 (8.11)	88,495,746 (100)
Total	89,926,898 (48.05)	84,997,373 (45.42)	12,213,224 (6.53)	187,137,495 (100)

Note: Values in bracket are in percentage. Workers in NIC div. 02–99, industry group 012,014,015. * Number and percentage of workers living in rural areas but working in urban areas. Similarly for others.
Source: Author's calculation based on NSSO 'Employment and Unemployment Survey', 2009–10 (66th Round).

3.68 million (8.05 million rural–urban commuters less 4.37 million urban–rural commuters) and the rural workforce will have to be adjusted downwards by a similar magnitude.

Chandrasekhar (2011) points out that a disaggregation of the number of commuter workers by state reveals patterns that fit popular perceptions. The states adjoining the national capital territory of Delhi, that is, Punjab, Haryana, Rajasthan, and Uttar Pradesh have a large number of rural residents reporting working in urban areas. The National Sample Survey regions adjoining Delhi from these four states have a sizeable number of workers reporting living in rural but working in urban areas. These four states account for nearly 35 per cent of the workers (all-India) living in rural areas but working in urban areas. The data does suggest interesting commuting dynamics (rural–urban and urban–rural) in these four states and this need to be explored in detail in the future. The four southern states of Andhra Pradesh, Karnataka, Kerala, and Tamil Nadu account for nearly 25 per cent of such workers, while Maharashtra and Gujarat account for 11 per cent of the workers living in rural but working in urban areas. These averages are not surprising since these states not only have higher levels of urban population, but also sizeable urban centres that would attract commuter workers. Individuals might be inclined to live in rural areas to take advantage of lower costs of living, in particular housing. The four southern states account for 27 per cent of urban residents working in rural areas, while the share of Maharashtra and Gujarat is 16 per cent. Thus, the movement of workers across the rural–urban or urban–rural corridor is in the urbanized states of India or where large urban centres act as magnets.

Which sectors are the commuting workers employed in? Around 60 per cent of commuting workers are concentrated in the three sectors: manufacturing, construction, and wholesale and retail trade, repair. Among rural residents working in urban areas, construction has the highest share (31 per cent) of workers, whereas 28 per cent urban residents work in the wholesale, retail and repair industries in rural areas. The fact that there are not enough jobs in manufacturing is evident from the large share of the construction industry.

Coming back to estimates of the commuting workforce, using NSSO data we can differentiate the workers in terms of rural to urban and urban to rural streams, as well as workers with no fixed location. This ignores the urban to urban and rural to rural stream of commuters, who also constitute a large share of the commuting workforce. The limitation of NSSO surveys which only collect information on the workplace (rural, urban, and no fixed place) leads to the lack of a discourse on these streams. If information on these commuting streams were collected, the size of the commuting workforce is likely to be higher than the estimates of 24 million.

TO MIGRATE OR TO COMMUTE

Migration and commuting are both aspects of mobility. The question is which of these two aspects is likely to become more prominent in this decade. This question is important given the perception that India's cities are unwelcoming for migrants. India's Vice President Mohammad Hamid Ansari surely thinks so. Delivering the Yusuf Meherally Memorial Lecture 2011,[6] Vice President Ansari said:

Our urban spaces and governance mechanisms have become the theatres for political conflicts and economic struggles. 'Exclusionary' urbanization is benefitting certain social groups to the detriment of others, and directing resources to large metropolises depriving small and medium towns of funds needed for infrastructure and essential services.

Exclusionary urbanization can be defined as forced or market-driven deprivation of a part of the urban residents from basic urban amenities such as clean water, affordable housing, sanitation, sewage facilities, as well as legal citizenship in cities and large urban settlements. Urban exclusion has been documented in the context of Brazil and China (Cai 2006; Feler and Henderson 2011).

Five indicators—one anecdotal and the other four based on official data—suggest that the phenomenon of exclusionary urbanization is evident in India.

There has been extensive media coverage on discrimination against migrants. Provocative statements made by certain politicians against migrants living in Mumbai are a cause for concern. This goes against the spirit of Article 15 of the Constitution of India which prohibits discrimination on any grounds. On paper the rights of migrant workers are protected under labour laws, including the Inter-State Migrant Workers (Regulation of Employment and Conditions of Service) Act, 1979.[7] Two core parts of this Act focus on the role of contractors in the employment of migrant workers and the minimum benefits that should be ensured to migrant workers. The contractor is required to keep a record of the name and place of the establishment wherein the workman is employed; the period of employment; the proposed rates and modes of payment of wages; the displacement allowance payable; the return fare payable to the workman on the expiry of the period of his employment and in such contingencies as may be prescribed and in such other contingencies as may be specified in the contract of employment; deductions made; and such other particulars as may be prescribed. The contractor is also required to furnish details in respect of every inter-state migrant workman who ceases to be employed. The law also specifies the wages, welfare, and other facilities to be provided to the inter-state migrant worker. Are migrant workers aware of the responsibilities of the contractor and do they receive a passbook with all the necessary information? Does the contractor fulfill the requirements as required under the law? There is valid scepticism over whether migrant workers actually receive their entitlements. Newspapers not only routinely report discrimination against migrant workers but also on the increasing number of wage disputes.

Viewed along certain dimensions, life in the cities is deteriorating for newcomers. Moving on to indicators from official statistics, the first indicator is urbanization of poverty. India is no exception to the phenomenon of urbanization of poverty. Over the period 1983–2004, the number of Indians in rural areas living below the poverty line declined by 12.3 per cent (31.03 million), while the total number of urban poor increased by 13.9 per cent (9.86 million) (GoI 2002, 2007). Due to paucity of data it is not possible to understand what proportion of the increase in the number of urban poor is attributable to rural–urban migration. Whether it is the rural poor or non-poor who migrate to urban areas has

---

[6] Ansari (2011).

[7] In addition they are covered under many laws including: the Minimum Wages Act, 1948; the Contract Labour (Regulation and Abolition) Act, 1970; the Equal Remuneration Act, 1976; the Building & Other Construction Workers (Regulation of Employment and Conditions of Service) Act, 1996; the Building & Other Construction Workers' Welfare Cess Act, 1996; the Workmen's Compensation Act, 1923; the Payment of Wages Act, 1936; the Child Labour (Prohibition & Regulation) Act, 1986; and the Bonded Labour Act, 1976.

implications for the incidence of poverty among non-migrants in rural areas. Consider two possible extreme scenarios. In Scenario A, only the poor migrate from rural areas, other things constant. In this scenario there is a reduction in the incidence of rural poverty as measured by simple a head count. In Scenario B, only the non-poor migrate, other things constant. In this scenario there is an increase in the incidence of rural poverty. In reality, both the poor and the non-poor migrate, and scenarios A and B set the bounds for change in rural poverty if migration were the only pathway to improved livelihoods. Decomposing the reduction in rural poverty suggests that over the period 1993–2002, migration accounted for only 19 per cent of the reduction in world-wide rural poverty while 81 per cent of the reduction could be ascribed to improved rural livelihoods (World Bank 2007). This suggests that in the Indian context migration is not necessarily the most important pathway to reducing rural poverty and rural anti-poverty programmes have an important role to play. In fact, the total number of urban poor is expected to increase further in India. As per one estimate, the total number of urban poor could increase to 113.60 million by 2020 (Mathur 2009).

The second indicator pertains to the proportion of the population living in slums and in slum-like conditions. Recently, a committee appointed by the government considered moving to a regression-based approach to count slum dwellers using indicators of household conditions. The committee estimated that 75.26 million (26.31 per cent of the urban population) lived in slums in urban India in 2001 and projected that 93.06 million would be living in slums in 2011 (GoI 2010). Based on their analysis of temporal changes in poverty and well-being in Indian cities during the period 1993–2002, Chandrasekhar and Mukhopadhyay (2010) find that evidence on improvements in well-being in urban India is mixed. They compare the joint distribution of monthly per capita expenditure (a private good) and access to drainage (a public good) in slums and non-slum areas in Indian cities to understand changes in well-being. Not only do they not find evidence of improvement in the well-being of slum dwellers over time, they also do not find that non-slum urban dwellers were better-off in 2002 as compared to 1993. Due to the paucity of data neither are we able to understand the phenomenon of urbanization of poverty at any depth nor are we able to understand in a coherent fashion the evolution of livelihoods in the slums and non-slum areas of Indian cities.

The third indicator pertains to migration streams and migration rates. Given that the quality of cities is not necessarily improving for one and all, it is not surprising that during 2001–11 nationally representative surveys in India did not record a large increase in rural–urban migration. Based on 2007–8 data, the share of the four migration streams were: rural–rural (62 per cent), rural–urban (19 per cent), urban–rural (6 per cent), and urban–urban (13 per cent) (NSSO 2010). This distribution was the same when we examined data from NSSO's survey conducted in 1999–2000 (NSSO 2001). Migration is predominantly movement of workers within the same state rather than across state boundaries. Comparison at two points in time 1999–2000 and 2007–8 reveals that among rural–urban migrants the share of inter-state migrants increased from 19.6 to 25.2 per cent (Table 14.3). This is the one important change that is evident from the data. Overall, there has not been any discernable increase in the migration rate, that is, the proportion of migrants in the population.

Table 14.3 Distribution of Internal Migrants by Last Usual Place of Residence for Each Component of Rural–Urban Migration Streams

Migration Streams	Intra-state			Inter-state	All
	Intra-district	Inter-district	(Intra-district+ Inter-district)		
55th Round (1999–2000)					
Rural-to-rural	75.3	20.1	95.4	4.6	100
Rural-to-urban	43.8	36.5	80.3	19.6	100
Urban-to-rural	46.5	33.5	80.0	20.0	100
Urban-to-urban	36.6	43.5	80.1	19.9	100
64th Round (2007–8)					
Rural-to-rural	72.4	23.2	95.6	4.4	100
Rural-to-urban	41.2	33.6	74.8	25.2	100
Urban-to-rural	48.8	33.8	82.6	17.5	100
Urban-to-urban	27.9	49.2	77.1	22.9	100

Source: NSSO (2010).

There was a marginal increase in migration rates in rural and urban India between 1999–2000 and 2007–8 (Table 14.4). However, this increase in migration rate was only driven by increased female migration in both rural and urban areas, guided by non-economic factors. Male migration rates decreased in rural areas (6.9 to 5.4 per cent) whereas urban areas showed a minuscule increase (25.7 to 25.9 per cent). We do find that there is a decrease in migration to urban areas if we take 1993 as the reference year. Do these patterns indicate a reduction in the mobility of male workers, that is, away from migration? One will have to wait for data from NSSO's next round before being able to say anything beyond doubt.

Table 14.4 Migration Rates from Different NSSO Rounds

Round (year)	Category of Persons		
	Male	Female	Person
Rural			
64th (2007–8)	5.4	47.7	26.1
55th (1999–2000)	6.9	42.6	24.4
49th (1993)	6.5	40.1	22.8
43rd (1987–8)	7.4	39.8	23.2
38th (1983)	7.2	35.1	20.9
Urban			
64th (2007–8)	25.9	45.6	35.4
55th (1999–2000)	25.7	41.8	33.4
49th (1993)	23.9	38.2	30.7
43rd (1987–8)	26.8	39.6	32.9
38th (1983)	27.0	36.6	31.6

Source: NSSO (2010).

The fourth indicator pertains to return migration. Comparison of data for 1993–4 and 2007–8 clearly indicate an increase in the rates of return migration (see Table 14.5). The return migration rate is calculated as the ratio of the total number of return migrants to the total number of migrants. Note that given the way the question is asked, a return migrant is also a migrant. Overall, in rural India, the return migration rate almost doubled from 6.5 per cent in 1993–4 to 12 per cent in 2007–8. Similarly, in urban India the return migration rate increased from 5.4 to 10.9 per cent.

The fifth indicator pertains to the rate of growth of cities. The share of the urban population increased marginally from 27.8 to 31.1 per cent over 2001–11. This increase however masks important undercurrents and this brings us to the issue of an increase in the population of urban agglomerations. Two predominantly urban states of Delhi and Chandigarh and few important urban agglomerations (Chennai, Hyderabad, Kolkata, and Ahmedabad) reported

Table 14.5 Return Migration Rate

Sector	1993–4			2007–8		
	Male	Female	Person	Male	Female	Person
Rural	19.6	4.3	6.5	23.7	10.6	12.0
Urban	6.1	4.9	5.4	11.7	10.4	10.9
Rural + Urban	12.2	4.4	6.2	16.1	10.6	11.6

Source: NSSO (2010).

their lowest ever population growth rate over the period 2001–11 while Mumbai recorded an absolute decline in its population. In this context, Kundu (2011) points out that lower net birth rates cannot explain the dynamics of urban population change. So that leaves two plausible explanations: out-migration from cities and a reduced rate of in-migration to the cities. Commenting in *The State of World Population* (UNFPA 2011: 78–9), Amitabh Kundu, observes, that:

some of India's major cities are experiencing 'degenerative peripheralization'—where the people are driven out by the high cost of living and the scarcity of jobs that pay a decent wage to live in ad hoc settlements on the periphery of metropolitan areas. In those peripheral settlements, people have lost the advantages of both urban and rural life. Big cities are losing the poor because they can't afford to live there. Earlier, people would pick up something like 1,000 rupees [about $22] and come to Delhi and look for a job for a month. Now with 1,000 rupees you can't stay for a week. We are sanitizing our cities. Sanitization means making the environment clean, … clearing the slums, pushing out the low-income colonies. And in the process, cities' miss out on any opportunity to transform the urban poor into drivers of growth and development and instead perceive illiterate, unskilled workers only as liabilities to health, hygiene and law and order.

In a scenario where cities are unwelcoming of migrants and there is an anaemic employment growth in the agricultural and non-farm sectors, an alternative, albeit effective, livelihood strategy is commuting daily from rural to urban areas for work. And this is the reason why we think that the debate will increasingly be along the lines: to commute or to migrate.

Writing in *The State of World Population* (UNFPA 2011: ii–iii), Osotimehin observes that 'while some countries are attracting more people to emerging mega-cities where jobs are plentiful and the cost of living is high, others are seeing waves of migration from city centres to peri-urban areas where the cost of living may be lower but basic services and jobs may be in short supply'. In the same publication, F. Ram (p. 69) points out that India should expect an increase in number of commuting workers: 'Even though people on marginal or even middle class incomes have been pushed out of Mumbai city, they still want to work there. He said there are commuters coming into the city from numerous outlying areas, including Pune, 163 kilometres to the southeast of Mumbai, where population growth has also been rapid. Pune is now connected to Mumbai by a six-lane motorway that cuts travel time for those with cars or money for intercity buses'.

For more reasons than one, during this decade we expect that there could be an increase in the number of commuting workers. India's Five Year Plans also strive for balanced regional development. The government has strived to encourage investments in rural and backward regions. Under the industrial location policy, manufacturing units, in particular polluting industries, cannot be located within a city. Recent research provides evidence of the organized sector moving from urban to rural areas and an increase in activity in the unorganized sector in urban areas. This will induce workers to commute across rural–urban boundaries while retaining their current place of residence. Chandrasekhar (2011) argues that during the decade of 2010 three additional factors will come into play. The first factor is an increase in the number of towns from 5,161 in 2001 to 7,935 in 2011. One can observe two-way commuting among residents of the smaller towns and nearby villages if the town does not have a strong economic base to employ all its residents. The dynamics between rural and urban areas will be different between towns and villages and between urban agglomerations and their peripheral regions. Second, an expansion in construction, manufacturing, and wholesale and retail trade sectors will drive workers to cross rural–urban boundaries in search of work. The third factor is greater transport linkages between rural and urban India. The various initiatives taken by the government to increase rural–urban connectivity through the construction of rural roads (the Pradhan Mantri Gram Sadak Yojana), the Delhi–Mumbai Industrial Corridor, and the Golden Quadrilateral (Roads) Project connecting large metros, offer the option of commuting as an alternative to migration. Hence it is reasonable to conjecture that rural–urban or urban–rural commuting by workers is a viable strategy.

EMERGING CONCERNS AND KNOWLEDGE GAPS

The focus of this chapter was on two aspects of labour mobility—migration and commuting—and to provide corresponding estimates. We did not find any increase in the rural–urban migration rate. In light of this, we focused on the issue of exclusionary urbanization and provided some indicators to suggest that the concerns are not unfounded. Among the critical emerging concerns are portability of benefits and rights of migrant workers.

Portability of rights of individuals from minority groups could become a highly litigated issue in the coming years. A migrant individual from a minority group is not entitled to reservation benefits (for example, in jobs or education) in the destination state, since the reservation is given based on the state and union territory of origin. This is as per the interpretation of Articles 341 and 342 of the Constitution of India by the courts. This interpretation of Articles 341 and 342 does affect a large part of inter-state migrants, particularly those belonging to minority groups. In the recent past a few cases have been argued before the courts seeking a review of the interpretation that reservation benefits are not portable. The last word on this issue has not been said or written. A two-judge bench of the Supreme Court in the matter relating to *State of Uttaranchal* vs. *Sandeep Kumar Singh & Ors* (case filed in 2006, order in 2010) ordered that a bench of three or more judges of the Supreme Court of India should be constituted to examine the issue of portability of reservation benefits.

Some government programmes that are not specific to minority groups have the feature of portability built into them. Consider the case of the Rashtriya Swasthya Bima Yojana (RSBY), a health insurance scheme for below poverty line families. Under RSBY it is possible to issue a split card in case a member of a household is moving to another district. The split card can be used at a district different from the place of issue. The total amount covered with the two split cards is equal to the amount of coverage before the card was split. While RSBY is migrant-friendly, the same cannot be said about the ability of migrants to avail of necessary documents. The NSSO's 58th Round survey on housing amenities sought specific information from slum dwellers on the following aspects: possession of a ration card, a voter ID card, passport by the head of the household, and benefits received as a slum dweller (received allotment of land/tenement, received other benefits; received no benefit etc.). The findings from the data did reveal that a large proportion of the slum dwellers did not have ration cards, voter identity cards or received any benefits. For some inexplicable reason, NSSO's 65th Round survey on housing amenities did not collect such information similar to the 58th round. Because of this we do not know the extent to which slum dwellers and migrants suffer from some form of exclusion.

Certain government programmes need to be tailored keeping in mind the needs of migrants. The best example is that of the National AIDS Control Programme (NACP). While NACP is credited with reducing overall HIV incidence in the country, migrant workers and their spouses have emerged in the high-risk group. They are vulnerable to this infection and indeed the incidence of HIV infection is highest among migrants. Of the 1.2 lakh estimated new infections in 2009, the six high-prevalence states accounted for only 39 per cent of the cases, while Odisha, Bihar, West Bengal, Uttar Pradesh, Rajasthan, Madhya Pradesh, and Gujarat accounted for 41 per cent of the new infections. The latter states are the source of a majority of the migrants. Some of the gaps in the implementation of NACP-IV include the absence of information about the linkage between source, transit, and destination across high migration and high-HIV-prevalence states.[8]

At the outset we pointed out that there are many aspects of mobility that we do not fully understand. Before we conclude, we would like to reiterate the data and knowledge gaps that we need to address on a priority basis in order to better inform policy formulation. First, we need to understand how the sources of income of rural households in India have changed over time. We need to be able to quantify the importance of remittances by migrants and economic contributions of commuting workers as a source of income. Second, we need to understand why estimates of various types of migration flows, in particular, short-term migration flows, captured by official data are at variance with localized studies. It is important to identify and plug the source of this disconnect. Third, we do not fully understand the extent to which rural–urban migration contributes to the phenomenon of urbanization of poverty. And finally, given the concern over exclusionary urbanization we need to understand the legal and structural impediments to migration.

REFERENCES

Ansari, Hamid M. (2011), Address by the Hon'ble Vice President of India Shri M. Hamid Ansari at the Yusuf Meherally Memorial Lecture on 23rd September 2011 at 1700 Hrs at University Convocation Hall, Mumbai. Available at: http://vicepresidentofindia.nic.in/content.asp?id=346, last accessed on 15 February 2012.

Breman, J. (1996), *Footloose Labour: Working in India's Informal Economy*. London: Cambridge University Press.

Cai, F. (2006), *Floating Population: Urbanization with Chinese Characteristics*. Beijing: Institute of Population and Labour Economics.

Chandrasekhar, S. (2011), 'Workers Commuting between Rural and Urban: estimates from NSSO data', *Economic and Political Weekly*, 46(46): 22–5.

Chandrasekhar, S. and A. Mukhopadhyay (2010), 'Poverty and Well-being in Indian Cities during the Reforms Era', *Poverty & Public Policy*, 2(2): Article 7.

Davis, B., P. Winters, G. Carletto, K. Covarrubias, E. Quinones, A. Zezza, K. Stamoulis, G. Bonomi, and S. DiGiuseppe (2007), 'Rural Income Generating Activities: A Cross Country Comparison', FAO ESA Working Paper, 07-16, 2007 and background paper to the World Bank's World Development Report 2008. Available at: http://www.fao.org/es/ESA/en/pubs_wp.htm, last accessed on 15 February 2012.

Deshingkar, P. and S. Akter (2009), 'Migration and Human Development in India', Research Paper 2009/13, Human Development Report, UNDP.

Feler, L. and J.V. Henderson (2011), 'Exclusionary Policies in Urban Development: Under-servicing Migrant Households in Brazilian Cities', *Journal of Urban Economics*, 69(3): 253–72.

Government of India (2002), *National Human Development Report 2001*. New Delhi: Planning Commission.

———. (2007), *Poverty Estimates for 2004–05*. New Delhi: Planning Commission. Available at: http://www.planningcommission.gov.in/news/prmar07.pdf, last accessed on 15 February 2012.

———. (2010), *Report of the Committee on Slum Statistics/Census, Ministry of Housing and Urban Poverty Alleviation*. Available at: http://mhupa.gov.in/W_new/Slum_Report_NBO.pdf, last accessed on 15 February 2012.

Kundu, A. (2011), 'Politics and Economics of Urban Growth', *Economic and Political Weekly*, 46(20): 10–12.

Mathur, O.P. (2009), *National Urban Poverty Reduction Strategy*. New Delhi: National Institute of Public Finance and Policy.

Mohanan, P.C. (2008), 'Differentials in the Rural–Urban Movement of Workers', *Journal of Income and Wealth*, 30(1): 59–67.

National Sample Survey Organisation (2001), *Migration in India*, Report No. 470, (55/10/8), 1999–2000. New Delhi: Ministry of Statistics and Programme Implementation.

———. (2010), *Migration in India*, Report No. 533, (64/10.2/2), 2007–2008. New Delhi: Ministry of Statistics and Programme Implementation.

Sainath, P. (2003), 'The Bus to Mumbai', *The Hindu*, 1 June. Available at: http://www.hindu.com/mag/2003/06/01/stories/2003060100520100.htm, last accessed on 9 April 2012.

———. (2007), 'It's been a hard day's night', *The Hindu*, 24 January. Available at: http://www.hindu.com/2007/01/24/stories/2007012404621300.htm, last accessed on 9 April 2012.

———. (2008), 'NREGA hits buses to Mumbai', *The Hindu*, 31 May. Available at: http://www.hindu.com/2008/05/31/stories/2008053154170900.htm, last accessed on 9 April 2012.

United Nations Population Fund [UNFPA] (2011), *The State of World Population*. Information and External Relations Division, New York City: UNFPA.

World Bank (2007), *World Development Report 2008: Agriculture for Development*. Washington DC: World Bank.

---

[8] Concept note titled, 'Migrant Intervention Strategy for National AIDS Control Program IV, NACO', available at: http://nacoonline.org/upload/NACP%20%20IV/Consultation%20I%20May%202011/Reports/5.%20Concept%20note%20Migrant%20intervention%20Sub%20group%20NACP%204%20comments%20May%208%203%20pm%20clean%202011%20(2).pdf, last accessed on 8 April 2012.

15

Poverty in India and Its Decompositions
A Critical Appraisal of the New Method

*Durgesh C. Pathak and Srijit Mishra**

INTRODUCTION

The Planning Commission recently released poverty estimates across states for rural and urban areas of India for 2009–10 (GoI 2012). A matter of concern raised in the media is low poverty lines leading to a social experiment of living by spending 32 rupees only per day by young persons.[1] There have been discussions in the academia also.[2] This has revived the need to critically evaluate the *Report of the Expert Group to Review the Methodology for Estimation of Poverty* (GoI 2009). The purpose of this chapter is two-fold. First, we raise some issues with regard to the new method, which also borrows from existing literature, including some earlier work of ours (Pathak and Mishra 2011; also see Mishra 2012). Second, we use the poverty lines provided by the Planning Commission for rural and urban areas separately to compute the incidence, depth, and severity of poverty and inequality at the aggregate all-India level as also across states, social groups, religious groups, occupational groups, education-wise, and gender-wise. We also analyse poverty reduction between 2004–5 and 2009–10 at the aggregate all-India level as also for some sub-groups of the population by looking into sectoral and growth-inequality decompositions. The differential impact of the growth process between these two time points on poorer and richer sections of society is also visualized through growth incidence curves for rural and urban India.

THE NEW METHOD: SOME ISSUES

In Pathak and Mishra (2011), we had identified five issues with regard to the new method of poverty: doing away with a calorie norm, which is how poverty estimates were being computed in India till 2004–5; the use of median expenditure on health and education will be underestimates; difficulty in reproducing the estimates; the calibration of estimates to arrive at 25.7 per cent poor for urban India; and the political economy of changing poverty shares. We reiterate some of these and also point out some other concerns in this chapter.

---

* Comments from B.K. Chandra Kiran, Vikas Chitre, K.L. Krishna, Manoj Panda, V.M. Rao, and S.L. Shetty were helpful.

[1] See http://www.youthkiawaaz.com/topic/32aday/ and http://rs100aday.com

[2] A number of papers debating the pros and cons of the new method got published in a special issue of the *Indian Journal of Human Development* (2010) (See Alagh 2010; Breman 2010; Datta 2010; Kannan 2010; Raveendran 2010; Shah 2010; and Swaminathan 2010). Also see Planning Commission 2011; Rao 2010; Subramanian 2010; and Suryanarayana 2011. In recent times there have been some discussions in the pages of *Economic & Political Weekly* (See the EPW Editorial 2012; as also Krishnaji 2012; Manna 2012; and a letter by Motwani 2012). Independent of the poverty line debate, also see a discussion on the 'right not to be poor', a form of political perspective by Chandhoke (2012).

A Pragmatic Start

The expert group had three important considerations. First, the calorie norm pegged at 1973–4 may not be appropriate because of changes in age, sex, and occupational patterns and that one should go beyond calories to have a deeper understanding of nutritional requirements. In any case, the subsequent updating of poverty lines does not adhere to the calorie norm.

Second, the earlier computations of the poverty line were based on the assumption that education, health, and sanitation requirements would be provided by the state, which is no more appropriate. This is a serious observation raising the question, is India a welfare state?

Third, the consumption expenditure collected through a uniform recall period does not appropriately represent low frequency items like clothing, footwear, consumer durables, education, and institutional health.

The expert group was on an easy wicket for the last concern. The 61st Round of the National Sample Survey (NSS) in 2004–5 collected expenditure data for such items with recall of both 30 days and 365 days. The expert group used the adjusted values of the latter to make them comparable with 30 days recall of other items.

With regard to calorie requirements, the expert group implicitly conceded the need for a nuanced nutritional basis. However, in the absence of any norm they kept those concerns aside and delinked the poverty measure from any calorie norm. One hopes that the new technical committee will dwell on such issues.

Now, the expert group had to start somewhere. It is perhaps this pragmatic consideration that led it to begin with poverty estimates for urban India, as computed from the already existing method (see Alagh 2010; Datta 2010) as given, that is, a poverty ratio of 25.7 per cent. Hence, they could not bring in the health and education components into the poverty line (also see Kannan 2010; Shah 2010; Subramanian 2010; Swaminathan 2010). At the most, what it says is that under this poverty ratio or around its associated poverty line these are the budget shares of health and education expenditure. The multi-dimensional notion of poverty measurement is still open and this also needs to be given consideration by the new technical committee that has been set up.

In short, this is a pragmatic start, but one that has opened up a number of unfinished tasks. One such aspect is ideal index prices.

The Ideal Index Prices: A Black Box

The poverty ratio for urban India will have an associated poverty line. The corresponding monthly per capita expenditure (MPCE) decile class would give the budget shares or expenditure of commodity-groups. These, along with the median prices, will give the corresponding quantities (excluding rent and conveyance). Median prices will address problems of missing observations and outliers but will be underestimates for education and health, as the poor are likely to spend less and that, too, when the expenditure distribution is skewed (Subramanian 2010; Swaminathan 2010).

All-India quantities and state-specific median prices give an MPCE value/class and are used to compute state-specific budget shares and quantities. The two sets of prices and quantities are used to compute the Fisher Ideal Index (FII) of a state relative to all-India. If this computed index falls in the MPCE class we began with then this is the poverty line. Otherwise, we continue an iterative process till it matches. Subsequently, imputations for conveyance and rent are added to get the poverty lines. A similar exercise is done for all-India rural relative to all-India urban and state-specific rural relative to all-India rural. In 2009–10, updating of poverty lines has been done for rural and urban areas of each state separately.

The Planning Commission has given us the poverty lines, the number of poor, and also the poverty ratios and shares of poor (see Tables A12.3 and A12.4 provided in the Statistical Appendix to this volume). It would be difficult for others to replicate the poverty lines (Raveendran 2010), and it is this that makes it a black box. Of course, once the poverty lines are given, using unit-level data one can compute other aspects of poverty, but before that we will introduce some standard measures and concepts.

MEASURES AND CONCEPTS

The measures introduced here are of poverty, inequality, sectoral decomposition of change in poverty, growth-inequality decomposition, and the growth incidence curve. Poverty is estimated using Foster, Greer and Thorbecke (1984; hereafter FGT), an additively decomposable class of measure,

$$P_\alpha = \frac{1}{N}\sum_{i=1}^{N}\left(\frac{g_i}{z}\right)^\alpha, \ \alpha \geq \qquad (15.1)$$

where g_i if the poverty gap $(z-y_i)$ for an individual i with expenditure y_i, z, is the poverty line, N is the total number of individuals in the population, and α is a measure of sensitivity such that $\alpha = 0, 1$, and 2 refer to head count ratio (incidence), poverty gap (depth), and severity. This measure can be decomposed by sub-groups as:

$$P_\alpha = \sum_{k=1}^{K}\left(\frac{N_k}{N}\right)P_{\alpha k}, \ \alpha \geq 0 \qquad (15.2)$$

where $\frac{N_k}{N}$ and $P_{\alpha k}$ are the kth sub-groups' population share and poverty measure respectively. A sub-group poverty risk is the ratio of its share of poor to its share of the population:

$$S_k = \frac{N_k P_{\alpha k} / N P_\alpha}{N_k / N} = P_{\alpha k} / P_\alpha \tag{15.3}$$

Gini coefficient is used as an inequality measure:

$$G = 1 + \frac{1}{N} - \left(\frac{2}{mN^2}\right) \sum_{i=1}^{n} (N - i + 1) y_i \tag{15.4}$$

where N is the population, m is the mean expenditure, and y_i is the expenditure of person i. We also introduce two measures of decomposition. First is the sectoral decomposition. If the economy is divided into two sectors, rural and urban, then economic changes within the sector will impact changes in poverty (intra-sectoral effects, one for each sector). At the same time, migration between the sectors will also impact changes in poverty (population shift effects). In addition, there will also be an interaction effect. Following Ravallion and Huppi (1991), the measure is:

$$\Delta P_\alpha^{t+1} = \Delta P_{\alpha U}^{t+1} n_U^t + \Delta P_{\alpha R}^{t+1} n_R^t + \sum_{j=U}^{R} \Delta n_j^{t+1} P_{\alpha j}^t + \sum_{j=U}^{R} \Delta P_{\alpha j}^{t+1} \Delta n_j^{t+1} \tag{15.5}$$

where Δ denotes change over time such that $\Delta P_\alpha^{t+1} = P_\alpha^{t+1} - P_\alpha^t$ indicate change in poverty at over $t+1$ to t; $(\Delta P_\alpha^{t+1} * 100)$ is percentage point change and $((\Delta P_\alpha^{t+1})/P_\alpha^t * 100)$ is percentage change; $j = U, R$ denotes urban and rural respectively.

There have been various approaches to growth-inequality decomposition (Dutt and Ravallion 1992; Jain and Tendulkar 1990; and Kakwani and Subbarao 1990). In all these, poverty is represented as:

$$P_\alpha^t = f(z, m^t, G^t) \tag{15.6}$$

where P_α^t, m^t, G^t denote measure of poverty, mean expenditure, and Gini coefficient respectively at time t, and z is the poverty line. Given z, and using Datt and Ravallion (1992) the change in poverty, ΔP_α^{t+1}, can be decomposed to:

$$\Delta P_\alpha^{t+1} = (P_\alpha^{t+1/G^t} - P_\alpha^t) + (P_\alpha^{t+1/m^t} - P_\alpha^t) + E. \tag{15.7}$$

On the right hand side is the growth component, the second is the inequality or redistribution component, and the third, E, is an interaction between the two.

A final concept that we would like to introduce is the growth incidence curve (GIC). It graphically portrays the impact of the growth process across quintiles or percentiles (Haughton and Khandekar 2009). An upward sloping GIC indicates that the rich gained more relative to the poor, that is, inequality worsened. Now, we take up a discussion on recent trends and patterns.

RECENT ESTIMATES AND PATTERNS

Number of Poor and Their Share across States

Before analysing, a few caveats on the use of NSS data are its inadequate representation of higher expenditure groups, possibility of incorrect information from households, and comparability over time among others (Vaidyanathan 1986). Despite these limitations, we use the same in our poverty analysis of recent years.

In 1993–4, 40.24 crore persons were poor of which 81.5 per cent were in rural areas. The number of the poor increased to 40.72 crore persons in 2004–5 and this was largely on account of an increase in the number of poor persons in urban areas whose share increased from 18.5 to 20 per cent. This trend in urban India was reversed in 2009–10 and with a continuing decline in rural areas the total number of poor decreased to 35.47 crore persons of which 78.4 per cent were in rural areas. The share of poor has been decreasing at a lower rate than their share of population in rural India and as a result the relative risk of poverty for rural India has been increasing and was greater than unity by 10.9 per cent in 1993–4, 12.9 per cent in 2004–5, and 13.4 per cent in 2009–10. As a corollary, it is implicit that the relative risk of poverty in urban areas will be lower than unity.

The changes in the number of poor as also the changes in the shares of the poor across states could be linked to allocation and transfer of funds through centrally sponsored schemes for ameliorating poverty (Rao 2010). Any whittling down could be counterproductive because some of the reductions are because of existing schemes. Keeping this in the background, we compare the share of poor for 2009–10 with 2004–5.

The share of the poor increased in rural, urban, and at the combined level in Assam, Bihar, Chhattisgarh, Jharkhand, Manipur, Meghalaya, Mizoram, Nagaland, Uttar Pradesh, Dadra & Nagar Haveli, and Daman & Diu (Figure 15.1). It comprised most of the tribal regions, which also include five of the Northeastern states as also Chhattisgarh and Jharkhand and also the poorer states of Bihar and Uttar Pradesh. If one excludes the four smaller Northeastern states and two union territories whose combined share of the poor was less than 1 per cent, the rest comprised 46.4 per cent of the total poor from among 32.4 per cent of the total population. From the smaller entities, Manipur also had higher poverty risk. In all these states the total number of poor increased, except for Jharkhand where the number of poor decreased in total but it increased for urban areas

Figure 15.1 Change in Poverty Shares (2004–5 to 2009–10)

Note: Encircled indicates increase in share at the combined level also.
Source: Authors' computations; also see Table A12.3 in Statistical Appendix.

by 8 lakh, which was the highest across states; the number of urban poor decreased in Chhattisgarh and Dadra & Nagar Haveli.

This period witnessed some positive policy changes in Bihar, but they did not show in poverty reductions. In fact, the number of poor increased by 47.7 lakh persons, accounting for 60 per cent among the states where the rural poor increased. Inequality also increased considerably in both rural and urban areas. The reasons behind this curious case of Bihar are beyond our comprehension. In Uttar Pradesh, the number of poor increased by 0.1 lakh persons and 7 lakh persons in rural and urban areas respectively.[3]

The share of the poor decreased in the rural sector but increased in the urban sector and at the combined level in Arunachal Pradesh, Delhi, and Haryana. In Arunachal Pradesh and Haryana, the poverty risk for urban areas also increased. In all the three states, the total number of the poor increased. After Jharkhand and Uttar Pradesh, Delhi and Haryana accounted for the maximum increase in the urban poor and the increase in these two states was higher than that in Jharkhand. The increase in urban poverty in Delhi and Haryana is of concern because it is being accompanied by increased growth and economic expansion. Do these have implications on growing crime and violence that one hears of in these states? It was only in Lakshadweep that there was a decrease in the share of the poor in urban areas, but an increase in rural and also at the combined levels. In all these four states poverty risk in rural areas is lower than unity.

The number as also share of the poor decreased in rural, urban, and combined levels in the states of Andhra Pradesh, Goa, Karnataka, Kerala, Madhya Pradesh, Maharashtra, Odisha, Puducherry, Rajasthan, Sikkim, Tamil Nadu, Tripura, and Andaman & Nicobar Islands. Excluding the last one where the incidence was below 5 per cent, all the other states had reductions in incidence of poverty that were higher than the all-Indian average reduction of 7.4 percentage points. It was more than 20 percentage points in Tripura and Odisha (does this explain the popularity of these governments?), more than 15 percentage points in Sikkim and Goa, and more than 10 percentage points in Maharashtra, Puducherry, Tamil Nadu and Madhya Pradesh. Despite the reductions, Odisha and

---

[3] For a discussion on poverty in Uttar Pradesh during 1993–4 and 2004–5 using the old method see Pathak (2011).

Madhya Pradesh continued to have a poverty risk greater than unity.

Despite an increase in the number and share of urban poor, one observes a decrease in the rural and combined levels in Gujarat, Himachal Pradesh, Jammu & Kashmir, Punjab, Uttarakhand, West Bengal, and Chandigarh. The decline in the incidence was higher than the national average for Uttarakhand, Himachal Pradesh, Gujarat, and West Bengal. Increase in urban poverty, as in the case of Delhi and Haryana, needs greater scrutiny for designing appropriate public policy.

Incidence, Depth, and Severity of Poverty

The above discussion on the number and share of the poor across the states has in some sense already discussed the incidence of poverty. Now we bring in the discussion on incidence along with depth and severity as also inequality (Table 15.1). Comparing 2009–10 to 2004–5, we have the following observations.

In both rural and urban areas, the poverty risk for 2009–10 was greater than unity for incidence, depth, and severity in Chhattisgarh, Assam, Bihar, Madhya Pradesh, Odisha, Uttar Pradesh, and Jharkhand (CABMOUJ, pronounced *kab mouj*). If one recalls BIMARU (rather, BIMORU), some of these seem to be traditional pockets of poverty with the addition of Assam and the notable exclusion of Rajasthan and Uttarakhand. All these seven states do not have the same pattern with regard to poverty reduction, as discussed earlier about the curious case of Bihar or the increasing urban poverty in Jharkhand or substantial reductions in Odisha and Madhya Pradesh among others. Excluding these last two states, the poverty risk in 2009–10 was greater than that in 2004–5 for both rural and urban sectors with regard to incidence, depth, and severity in the remaining five of the CABMOUJ states.

Excluding Assam, a part of CABMOUJ and Tripura where one observed reductions in poverty, the other five Northeastern states indicate that there was an increase in incidence, depth, and severity for both rural and urban sectors in Manipur, Mizoram, and Nagaland; for the rural sector in Meghalaya; and for the urban sector in Arunachal Pradesh. In addition, Meghalaya also indicated an increase in depth and severity in the urban sector. Poverty risk was greater than unity for the rural sector in Manipur and for the urban sector in Arunachal Pradesh, Manipur, Meghalaya, and Nagaland. Further, poverty risks also increased for the three measures in both the sectors in Manipur, Meghalaya, Mizoram, Nagaland, and for the urban sector in Arunachal Pradesh. These are matters of concern because an earlier analysis points out that these states did better when it came to amelioration of poverty (Radhakrishna and Ray 2005), but are those traditional advantages being lost?

Poverty risk increased for the urban sector with regard to incidence, depth, and severity in Gujarat, Himachal Pradesh, Haryana, Jammu & Kashmir, Punjab, Uttarakhand, and West Bengal and for incidence alone in Chandigarh. This reiterates our earlier highlighted concern on the urbanization of poverty. This seems to be serious and needs to be appropriately addressed at the policy level.

The smaller entities of Dadra & Nagar Haveli, Daman & Diu, and Lakshadweep also have their own concerns. They may not matter much in terms of the aggregate statistical level, and hence, may fall out of focus from the policy parameter. However, they may fail an ethical test of neglecting the poorest, which goes against the tenets of a welfare state.

Some notable attainments with regard to the reduction of poverty risk are Maharashtra in both the rural and urban sectors, Gujarat and Tripura in the rural sector, and Karnataka, Rajasthan, and Sikkim in the urban sector.

Broadly speaking, one observes some variations like increase in poverty risks in some parts of the Northeastern states or smaller union territories, or increasing vulnerabilities in some urban pockets, or reductions in poverty in Madhya Pradesh, Odisha, and Tripura or reduction in poverty risk in Maharashtra among others. These suggest that public policy suggestions for these different groups of states should be different. It requires further probing and going down into details at the NSS regional or at a district or sub-district level, but then that should be done at the planning and implementation stages and with the use of information that goes beyond NSS data. Now, we look into sectoral as also growth-inequality decompositions at the all-India level.

Sectoral and Growth-Inequality Decompositions

Sectoral Decomposition

As per unit-level data, the rural sector comprised 74.7 per cent of the population in 2004–5, which decreased to 73 per cent of the population in 2009–10. Poverty risk for incidence in both the years was greater than unity by 11 and 30 per cent in rural and urban areas respectively. Inequality increased in both the sectors, but was higher in the urban sector for both the years. The average monthly per capita consumption expenditure (hereafter, average MPCE) for the urban sector was nearly twice that of the rural sector (Rs 1,104.6 and Rs 579.2 respectively in 2004–5 and Rs 1,856 and Rs 953 respectively in 2009–10). Keeping this in the background, let us look into the urban–rural sectoral

Table 15.1 Incidence, Depth, and Severity of Poverty and Inequality across States in India, 2004–5 and 2009–10

States	Rural									Urban								
	2004–5				2009–10					2004–5				2009–10				
	α=0	α=1	α=2	Gini	α=0	α=1	α=2	Gini		α=0	α=1	α=2	Gini	α=0	α=1	α=2	Gini	
Andhra Pradesh	32.3	7.0	2.3	0.268	22.7	4.7	1.5	0.276		23.4	4.8	1.5	0.363	17.7	3.8	1.2	0.361	
Arunachal Pradesh	33.6	7.4	2.5	0.262	26.1	5.8	2.0	0.299		23.5	4.6	1.3	0.235	24.9	6.0	2.2	0.306	
Assam	36.4	7.0	2.0	0.192	39.9	7.3	1.9	0.224		21.8	4.2	1.1	0.309	25.9	5.9	2.0	0.333	
Bihar	55.7	12.7	3.9	0.194	55.3	13.5	4.5	0.220		43.7	11.4	3.9	0.320	39.4	10.3	3.7	0.324	
Chhattisgarh	55.1	13.7	4.9	0.265	56.1	12.4	3.8	0.239		28.4	7.2	2.6	0.372	23.7	6.2	2.3	0.311	
Delhi	15.6	1.9	0.4	0.300	7.6	0.2	0.0	0.247		12.9	2.0	0.5	0.335	14.3	3.0	0.9	0.360	
Goa	28.1	5.6	1.7	0.299	11.3	1.6	0.3	0.224		22.2	4.3	1.5	0.357	6.4	1.3	0.4	0.259	
Gujarat	39.1	9.3	3.2	0.266	26.6	4.6	1.2	0.259		20.1	3.9	1.2	0.313	17.7	3.6	1.1	0.315	
Himachal Pradesh	25.0	4.2	1.1	0.289	9.1	1.4	0.4	0.290		4.6	1.1	0.4	0.283	12.5	2.4	0.7	0.361	
Haryana	24.8	4.7	1.3	0.326	18.6	3.7	1.1	0.282		22.4	4.9	1.6	0.341	23.0	4.6	1.3	0.365	
Jammu & Kashmir	14.1	2.1	0.5	0.217	8.1	1.2	0.3	0.224		10.4	2.1	0.6	0.254	12.8	1.9	0.4	0.318	
Jharkhand	51.6	11.1	3.4	0.209	41.4	9.1	2.8	0.216		23.8	5.8	1.9	0.336	31.0	7.9	2.8	0.349	
Karnataka	37.5	6.5	1.7	0.246	26.1	4.8	1.3	0.237		25.9	6.2	2.1	0.369	19.5	4.4	1.4	0.386	
Kerala	20.2	4.4	1.5	0.347	12.0	2.3	0.7	0.362		18.4	4.0	1.3	0.396	12.1	2.2	0.6	0.413	
Madhya Pradesh	53.6	12.6	4.2	0.252	42.0	10.6	3.7	0.283		35.1	8.6	2.9	0.368	22.9	5.6	1.9	0.375	
Maharashtra	47.9	11.9	4.3	0.288	29.5	5.7	1.6	0.249		25.6	6.5	2.3	0.369	18.3	4.0	1.3	0.389	
Manipur	39.3	5.7	1.3	0.152	47.4	7.0	1.5	0.163		34.5	5.1	1.0	0.165	46.4	9.0	2.6	0.197	
Meghalaya	14.0	1.4	0.2	0.150	15.3	1.6	0.3	0.174		24.7	2.8	0.5	0.261	23.9	5.0	1.3	0.248	
Mizoram	23.0	3.5	0.9	0.186	31.1	4.8	1.1	0.198		7.9	1.0	0.2	0.229	11.5	1.8	0.5	0.231	
Nagaland	10.0	1.0	0.2	0.206	19.3	2.5	0.6	0.186		4.3	0.5	0.1	0.234	24.9	3.1	0.5	0.225	
Odisha	60.8	17.4	6.6	0.266	39.2	9.0	3.0	0.253		37.6	9.6	3.5	0.340	25.9	5.3	1.7	0.386	
Puducherry	22.9	4.0	0.8	0.327	0.0	0.0	0.0	0.258		9.9	1.3	0.3	0.320	1.6	0.1	0.0	0.393	
Punjab	22.1	3.8	1.0	0.286	14.6	1.9	0.4	0.294		18.7	3.2	0.8	0.338	18.0	3.8	1.1	0.365	
Rajasthan	35.8	7.0	2.0	0.221	26.4	4.3	1.1	0.218		29.7	5.8	1.7	0.322	19.9	3.8	1.1	0.324	
Sikkim	31.8	5.6	1.4	0.254	15.2	2.2	0.5	0.265		26.0	3.4	0.9	0.246	4.2	0.7	0.2	0.188	
Tamil Nadu	37.5	7.4	2.1	0.276	21.2	3.7	1.0	0.262		19.7	4.1	1.3	0.364	12.8	2.1	0.6	0.335	
Tripura	44.5	9.6	2.9	0.212	19.6	2.4	0.5	0.202		22.5	3.8	1.0	0.314	9.5	1.6	0.4	0.291	

Uttar Pradesh	42.7	9.2	2.8	0.252	39.4	7.6	2.1	0.236	34.1	7.8	2.5	0.355	31.7	7.3	2.4	0.408
Uttarakhand	35.1	5.8	1.4	0.239	13.7	2.0	0.6	0.454	26.2	5.1	1.4	0.317	25.0	5.1	1.5	0.328
West Bengal	38.2	7.9	2.4	0.256	28.8	5.3	1.4	0.225	24.4	5.3	1.6	0.373	21.9	4.5	1.4	0.394
Andaman & Nicobar Islands	3.3	0.2	0.0	0.308	0.4	0.0	0.0	0.265	0.8	0.0	0.0	0.344	0.0	0.0	0.0	0.327
Chandigarh	29.4	6.8	2.4	0.262	10.2	1.6	0.3	0.343	10.1	2.2	0.7	0.366	9.1	1.8	0.4	0.382
Dadra & Nagar Haveli	63.6	18.0	7.1	0.336	55.6	11.4	3.2	0.220	16.8	5.0	1.6	0.311	17.7	1.5	0.2	0.228
Daman & Diu	2.4	0.5	0.1	0.254	32.0	5.4	1.1	0.303	14.4	2.1	0.3	0.247	32.7	4.2	0.8	0.272
Lakshadweep	0.3	0.1	0.0	0.258	20.6	1.5	0.1	0.321	10.3	3.8	1.8	0.264	1.0	0.2	0.1	0.280
All-India	41.8	9.2	2.9	0.281	33.3	6.8	2.1	0.283	25.7	5.8	1.9	0.364	20.9	4.5	1.4	0.381

Source: Authors' calculations using unit-level data.

Table 15.2 Sectoral Decomposition of Change in Poverty Between 2004–5 and 2009–10

(Percentage of total change in poverty)

Poverty Measure	Components of Change in Poverty			
	Intra-Sectoral Effect		Inter-Sectoral Population Shift	Interaction Effect
	Urban	Rural		
$P_{\alpha=0}$	15.65	81.60	3.58	−0.82
$P_{\alpha=1}$	14.56	83.60	2.78	−0.94
$P_{\alpha=2}$	14.06	84.59	2.35	−1.00

Note: The total intra-sectoral effect is the sum of the effects in rural and urban sectors. For it is 97.25 (=81.60+15.65).

Source: Authors' calculations using unit-level data.

decomposition of change in poverty between 2004–5 and 2009–10 for India (Table 15.2).

For all three poverty measures, both sectoral gains and population shift between sectors resulted in poverty reduction. The interaction effect, being negative, dampened these gains. In case of incidence, P_0, both the sectors gained; the rural gaining comparatively more. The inter-sectoral effect was also positive indicating that a declining proportion of the population lived in the relatively poorer rural sector in 2009–10. Overall, gains to the rural sector had a major share in reducing aggregate poverty.

Growth-Inequality Decomposition

The growth-inequality decomposition of change in poverty with regard to incidence, depth, and severity between 2004–5 and 2009–10 for rural, urban, and the all-India level are given in Table 15.3. In all the scenarios, the growth component and interaction effect were negative, indicating that they helped in the reduction of poverty while the redistribution component was positive, indicating that it halted the decline in poverty reduction. In rural India, a major part of the reduction in the incidence of poverty came from the growth component, but for depth and severity it was the interaction effect that dominated. At the same time, the countervailing impact of the redistribution component also became increasingly stronger.

The patterns were somewhat similar for urban India. The growth component was stronger than the interaction effect in reducing the incidence of poverty, but interaction was stronger for depth and severity. Compared to rural India, the impacts on incidence, depth, and severity were much stronger both by the redistribution components for halting the reduction and by the interaction component for reducing poverty. The all-India level result is closer to the rural result because of the greater population share. Overall, the results are indicative that those further away from the poverty line would have benefited relatively less. In short, mean incomes of the poor did not increase as much as the increase in inequality. These are reiterated by the growth incidence curves (Figures 15.2a and 15.2b) for rural and urban India.

As evident from Figure 15.2a, in rural India the average income of the poorest actually declined and then it increased but was lower than the average for the poorest 30 per cent. The richest 5 per cent also witnessed a decline in the average growth in their income. A plausible reason may be the failure to make productive investments or that the consumption expenditure schedule failed to capture their investments. Growth for those in the 30–95 percentile was around the

Table 15.3 Growth-Inequality Decomposition of Change in Poverty at the All-India Level

Sector	Poverty Measure	Total Change in Poverty	Growth Component	Redistribution Component	Interaction Effect
Rural	P_0	−8.53	−36.07	35.75	−8.20
	P_1	−2.42	−8.43	17.97	−11.96
	P_2	−0.89	−2.73	8.98	−7.13
Urban	P_0	−4.83	−22.22	28.04	−10.64
	P_1	−1.24	−5.25	12.59	−8.58
	P_2	−0.43	−1.75	6.26	−4.95
Total	P_0	−7.81	−33.09	34.31	−9.03
	P_1	−2.16	−7.70	17.24	−11.71
	P_2	−0.78	−2.50	8.71	−6.99

Source: Authors' calculations using unit-level data.

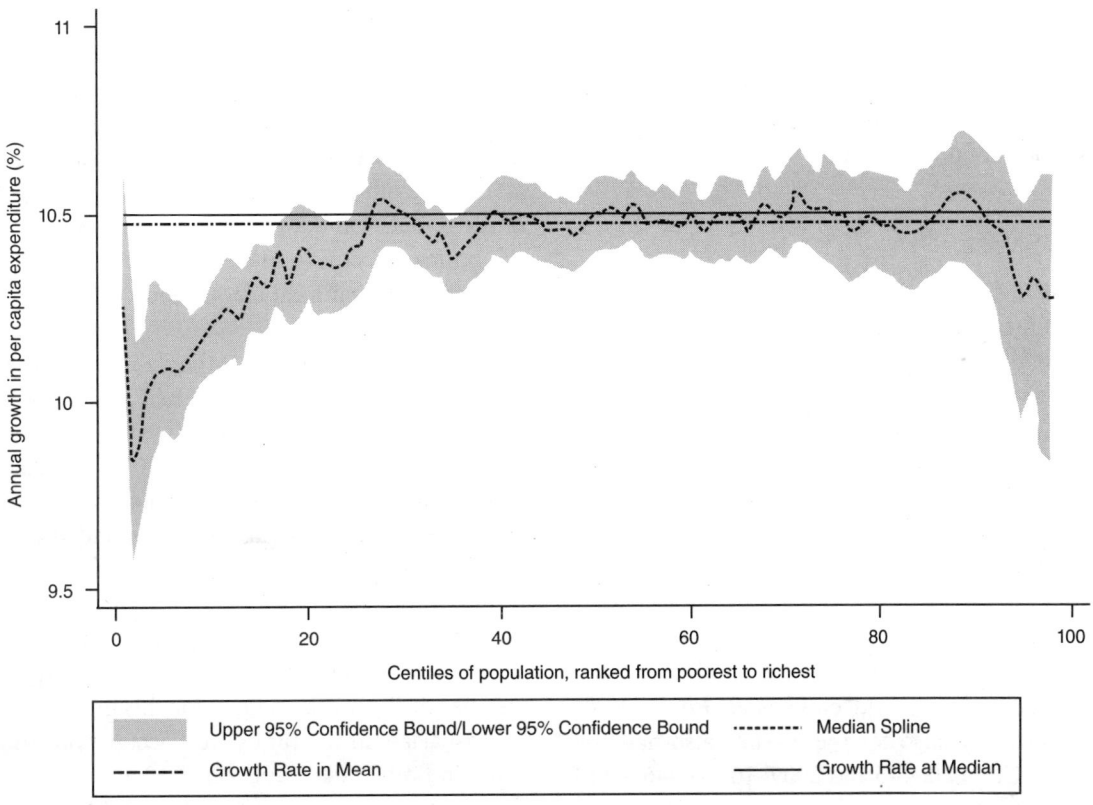

Figure 15.2a Growth Incidence Curve for Rural India (2004–5 and 2009–10)

Source: Authors' computations based on unit level data.

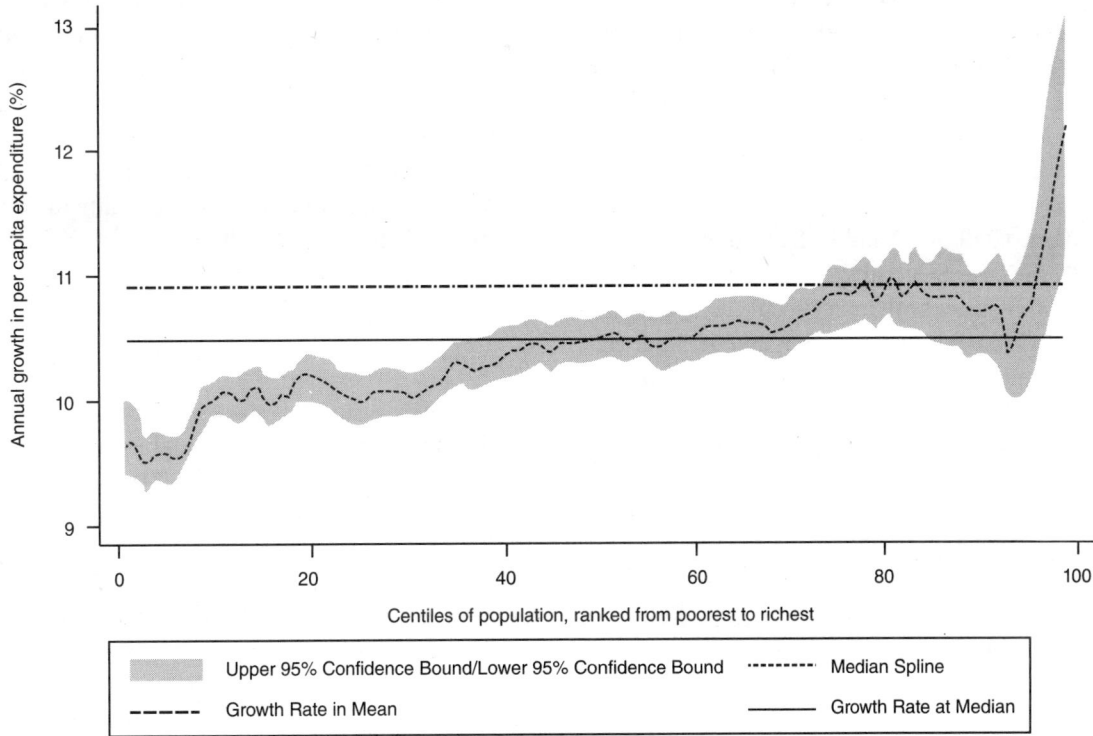

Figure 15.2b Growth Incidence Curve for Urban India (2004–5 and 2009–10)

Source: Authors' computations based on unit level data.

average. In urban India (Figure 15.2b), the poorest gained very little compared to the richest as shown by the positive slope of the growth incidence curve. From this all-India analysis, now we propose to look into some patterns across various sub-groups of populations.

Analysis across Sub-groups

At the all-India level, the incidence, depth, and severity of poverty as also inequality for 2004–5 and 2009–10 of sub-groups based on household characteristics like social group (caste), household type (occupation), religion, and size-class of land owned (rural) and of sub-groups based on individual characteristics like gender, age, and education is given in Table 15.4. Some of the observations are now discussed.

Social Groups (Caste)

Across social groups, Scheduled Tribes (STs) had the highest incidence of poverty in rural India for both the years. The highest percentage point decline as also percentage change in poverty was also for them. They also had the least average MPCE in 2004–5 and 2009–10 (Rs 446.5 and Rs 777.3 respectively). In 2009–10, the rural population share for STs and Scheduled Castes (SCs) was 10.8 and 22.2 per cent respectively whereas their share of rural poor was 15.4 per cent and 28.2 per cent respectively. Poverty risk was the highest for STs followed by that for SCs, then the Backward Classes (BCs) and then others. The least percentage change in poverty was for BCs, a group whose poverty risk increased for all the three measures. It also increased for SCs for depth and severity measures.

In urban India, average MPCE for 2004–5, was the least for SCs (Rs 794.2 and Rs 1,344.8 respectively) and the highest for others (Rs 1,366.2 and Rs 2,296.5 respectively). As is generally the case, SCs had the highest poverty levels, followed by STs, BCs, and others respectively. In 2009–10 SCs, STs, and BCs constituted 15.1, 3.5, and 38.5 per cent of the urban population but comprised 24.5, 5, and 44.8 per cent of the urban poor respectively. At the incidence level the percentage point decline for BCs was higher than that for STs, but for depth and severity the percentage point decline for STs was higher than that for SCs. In fact, this is also reflected in poverty risk, which increased for STs with regard to incidence but decreased for depth and severity. Poverty risk for BCs increased for depth and severity and that for SCs increased for incidence and depth.

Household Type (Occupation)

An analysis by household type (that is, by the major occupation of the household) indicates that in rural India the highest levels of poverty in all three measures were with agricultural labour, the next in line were other labour (manual non-agriculture) followed by self-employed in non-agriculture activities, and then by those self-employed in agriculture and then by others. In 2009–10, agriculture labour and other labour constituted 25.1 and 14.7 per cent of the population but comprised 37.2 and 17.5 per cent of the poor respectively in rural India. Poverty risk was the highest for agricultural labour and the least for the others in both the years.

In 2004–5 and 2009–10, other labour had the minimum average MPCE (Rs 434.7 and Rs 735.5 respectively) and others had the maximum average MPCE (Rs 852.6 and Rs 1,446.4 respectively). Between 2004–5 and 2009–10, inequality declined for those self-employed in non-agriculture and others. Agricultural labourers had the lowest Gini coefficient for both the years, but the increase in inequality was the maximum for this group (6.5 per cent). This indicates a serious fact: not only were agricultural labourers the poorest as a group, the distribution of expenditure was also becoming more unequal for this group.

Casual labour was the poorest occupation group in urban India in both 2004–5 and 2009–10 and its average MPCE was the lowest (Rs 598.9 and Rs 1,007.3 respectively) and was more than one-third of the average MPCE for others in 2009–10. Further, in 2009–10 casual labour and self-employed constituted 14.1 and 42 per cent of the urban population respectively but comprised 31.9 and 44.3 per cent of the urban poor. Thus, casual labour's share, in both the years was almost twice the share of the poor. The self-employed also had a poverty risk greater than unity. Regular wage/salary earners exhibited the least poverty risk. Inequality increased for all occupation groups in urban India. Others showed the highest increase in inequality in consumption expenditure followed by the self-employed (7.7 and 3.8 per cent respectively).

Religion

A religion-wise analysis shows that Buddhists (with a very small population share) had the highest incidence of poverty in rural India for 2004–5 and 2009–10. Among the other religions, Muslims had the highest incidence with Hindus following close behind. In 2009–10, the population share of Buddhists, Muslims, and Hindus was 0.52, 11.6, and 83.6 per cent and their share of poor was 0.69, 12.7, and 84.1 per cent in rural India. The least incidence of poverty was for Sikhs, a group which also registered the highest percentage decline. Sikhs had the lowest poverty risk. Inequality was highest among Christians and lowest among Muslims.

In urban India, Muslims were the poorest group and also at the highest poverty risk followed by Buddhists. In

Table 15.4 Incidence, Depth, and Severity of Poverty and Inequality across Sub-groups in India (2004–5 and 2009–10)

Sub-groups	Rural								Urban							
	2004–5				2009–10				2004–5				2009–10			
	α=0	α=1	α=2	Gini	α=0	α=1	α=2	Gini	α=0	α=1	α=2	Gini	α=0	α=1	α=2	Gini
Caste																
Scheduled tribe	62.3	17.0	6.3	0.254	47.4	11.1	3.7	0.252	35.5	9.9	3.8	0.351	30.4	7.2	2.5	0.414
Scheduled caste	53.5	12.3	4.0	0.241	42.3	9.2	2.9	0.244	40.6	9.9	3.4	0.302	34.1	7.8	2.5	0.326
Backward classes	39.8	8.2	2.5	0.265	31.9	6.2	1.8	0.268	30.6	6.7	2.1	0.326	24.3	5.3	1.7	0.349
Others	27.1	5.3	1.5	0.299	21.0	3.8	1.0	0.313	16.1	3.4	1.0	0.366	12.4	2.5	0.8	0.379
Occupation																
HHT1	36.3	7.2	2.1	0.281	28.0	5.4	1.5	0.276	27.4	6.0	1.9	0.353	22.0	4.7	1.5	0.367
HHT2	63.1	15.5	5.2	0.210	49.4	11.2	3.6	0.224	15.3	2.9	0.8	0.339	11.1	2.1	0.6	0.349
HHT3	48.6	11.1	3.6	0.256	39.6	8.3	2.5	0.260	58.7	15.5	5.6	0.246	47.2	11.4	3.9	0.253
HHT4	33.2	6.7	2.0	0.261	26.2	4.8	1.3	0.266	—	—	—	—	—	—	—	—
HHT9	21.8	4.8	1.7	0.347	14.4	2.6	0.7	0.340	15.9	3.9	1.6	0.416	12.6	2.6	0.8	0.448
Religion																
Hinduism	42.1	9.3	3.0	0.275	33.5	6.9	2.1	0.278	23.1	5.1	1.6	0.359	18.7	4.0	1.3	0.378
Islam	44.5	9.7	2.9	0.260	36.2	7.1	2.0	0.257	41.8	10.0	3.3	0.328	33.9	7.6	2.5	0.336
Christianity	28.7	6.4	2.2	0.363	23.8	4.4	1.3	0.374	14.1	2.8	0.9	0.360	12.9	2.5	0.7	0.353
Sikhism	21.7	4.0	1.1	0.289	11.9	1.6	0.4	0.303	9.5	1.4	0.3	0.331	14.5	2.9	0.8	0.382
Buddhism	63.9	16.8	6.2	0.302	44.1	11.1	3.5	0.258	40.1	11.2	4.3	0.317	31.2	7.8	2.6	0.327
Others	40.5	9.4	3.2	0.345	30.8	5.2	1.4	0.323	5.1	1.0	0.3	0.287	4.7	1.2	0.4	0.370
Land size																
Landless	47.5	11.1	3.7	0.291	37.7	8.1	2.5	0.279	25.8	5.8	1.9	0.363	20.8	4.6	1.5	0.381
Marginal	44.9	9.8	3.1	0.269	34.8	6.9	2.1	0.273	27.3	6.3	2.0	0.389	26.5	5.6	1.7	0.386
Small	35.6	7.4	2.3	0.262	29.6	5.8	1.7	0.260	25.0	4.4	1.2	0.340	18.9	3.7	1.1	0.363
Semi-medium	28.5	5.7	1.8	0.262	20.8	3.8	1.0	0.271	27.5	6.2	1.8	0.358	14.5	2.4	0.7	0.333
Medium	23.5	4.0	1.1	0.289	17.1	3.4	1.1	0.293	8.1	1.7	0.6	0.344	8.9	2.0	0.6	0.334
Large	18.9	3.0	0.7	0.320	6.1	1.0	0.2	0.346	16.0	1.7	0.4	0.374	4.1	1.9	0.9	0.262
Sex																
Male	41.8	9.2	2.9	0.281	33.6	6.9	2.1	0.288	25.5	5.7	1.8	0.363	20.7	4.5	1.4	0.382
Female	41.6	9.9	3.4	0.281	29.4	6.1	1.9	0.278	28.0	7.0	2.5	0.366	22.1	4.7	1.6	0.378

(Contd.)

Table 15.4 (*Contd.*)

Sub-groups	Rural									Urban								
	2004–5				2009–10					2004–5				2009–10				
	α=0	α=1	α=2	Gini	α=0	α=1	α=2	Gini		α=0	α=1	α=2	Gini	α=0	α=1	α=2	Gini	
Age																		
0–14	50.9	11.9	3.9	0.255	41.4	8.9	2.7	0.253		35.4	8.6	2.9	0.333	28.9	6.6	2.2	0.349	
15–29	36.8	7.8	2.4	0.283	30.4	6.0	1.8	0.294		23.3	4.9	1.5	0.359	19.6	4.1	1.3	0.395	
30–44	40.2	8.8	2.7	0.281	31.0	6.3	1.9	0.277		22.3	4.9	1.6	0.352	17.9	3.8	1.2	0.356	
45–59	32.9	6.7	2.0	0.300	26.3	5.2	1.5	0.300		18.0	3.7	1.1	0.376	15.2	3.2	1.0	0.386	
>=60	33.6	7.0	2.2	0.293	26.8	5.3	1.6	0.294		20.9	4.6	1.5	0.396	16.8	3.5	1.1	0.403	
Education																		
Illiterate	51.4	12.0	4.0	0.245	42.3	9.2	2.9	0.249		44.5	10.9	3.7	0.307	37.5	8.9	3.0	0.316	
Up to Primary	35.9	7.4	2.3	0.274	34.3	6.9	2.0	0.258		24.6	5.3	1.7	0.322	27.1	5.9	1.9	0.327	
Up to Secondary	14.9	2.5	0.7	0.336	23.0	4.1	1.1	0.284		7.1	1.2	0.3	0.330	16.2	3.2	0.9	0.326	
H. Secondary	9.9	1.5	0.4	0.352	13.2	2.3	0.6	0.355		2.9	0.5	0.1	0.341	7.2	1.3	0.4	0.378	
> H. Secondary	6.8	1.1	0.3	0.413	7.8	1.2	0.3	0.332		1.7	0.3	0.1	0.348	2.7	0.4	0.1	0.361	

Note: HHT1 through HHT9 denote self-employed in non-agriculture, agriculture labour, other labour, self-employed in agriculture, and others respectively in rural India and self-employed, regular wage, and salaried employees, casual labour, and others respectively in urban India.

Source: Authors' calculations using unit-level data.

2009–10, the population share of Muslims and Buddhists was 15.9 and 0.9 per cent and their share of the poor was 25.8 and 1.4 per cent respectively. The incidence of poverty decreased for all groups, but increased for Sikhs. The Gini coefficient also increased by about 15 per cent for Sikhs. This is commensurate with increasing poverty in urban Punjab and Chandigarh, which have a substantial Sikh population.

Size-class of Land

Size-class of land, as expected, suggested a secular decline in incidence, depth, and severity of poverty with an increase in land size in rural India. The landless class had the highest incidence of poverty, followed by marginal landowners. They constituted 41.8 and 31.9 per cent of the population and comprised 47.4 per cent and 33.4 per cent of the poor in 2009–10. The highest decline in poverty between 2004–5 and 2009–10 was for those with a large size-class of land. Inequality declined for the landless (4 per cent) and small-sized land owners (0.7 per cent) while it increased by 8.1 per cent for large landowners, by 3.1 per cent for semi-medium landowners, by 1.4 per cent for marginal landowners, and by 1.3 per cent for medium-sized landowners.

The inverse relationship between size-class and poverty seems to hold in urban India for 2009–10 if one excludes the landless. However, it was only the marginal group that constituted an incidence that was higher than the overall average. Given that almost 88 per cent of the population in urban India was landless one should be cautious in extending the size-class analysis to urban areas.

Gender

So far we have discussed household characteristics. Now we analyse individual characteristics—gender, age, and education. With regard to gender, the situation is discussed at the individual level and also about female-headed households.

Across gender, females had a slightly higher incidence of poverty than that for males for both the years under consideration in both rural and urban India. Correspondingly, the poverty risk was higher for females. For 2004–5 and 2009–10, in rural India, the incidence of poverty among female-headed households (41.6 and 29.4 per cent respectively) was lower than that for male-headed households (41.8 and 33.6 per cent respectively) whereas incidence of urban poverty in female-headed households (28 and 22.1 per cent respectively) was higher than that for male-headed households (25.5 and 20.7 per cent respectively).

For the same two years, when one takes into consideration the widow/widower or divorcee status of the head of household then the incidence of poverty in rural India was 41.8 and 32.7 per cent respectively for female-headed households and 39.9 and 32.9 per cent for male-headed households. In urban India, it was 30.6 and 25.4 per cent for female-headed households and 33.2 and 27 per cent for male-headed households.

Age-wise Classification

A curious observation about age-wise classification is that incidence, depth, and severity of poverty was the highest in the 0–14 years age group. This was true for both the time periods and for both rural and urban India. In fact, this was the only age group for which the poverty risk was greater than unity. In 2009–10, for the rural and urban sectors this age group constituted 32.2 and 20.9 per cent of the population respectively but comprised 40.1 and 36.6 per cent of the poor respectively. Though this information is based on an individual characteristic, yet it does suggest that households with this category of dependent population are at a greater risk, perhaps because of health and education requirements. Of course, this age-group would be sharing the household with other members, which is likely to spread across other age-groups. But, in rural areas, it is possible that they reside with the 30–44 years age group for whom we have a poverty risk that is less than unity but relatively higher than the other age groups. Again, in both rural and urban areas, the poverty risk was relatively higher for the 60+ years age group, another dependent category. Both these vulnerable groups will have nutritional and health implications, which is beyond the scope of this chapter.

Education-wise Classification

Like age-wise classification, education-wise classification also seems to have some broad patterns that are similar for both rural and urban sectors. There are four broad observations. First, in both the years there was an inverse relationship between incidence, depth, and severity of poverty and educational attainment; for a discussion on increasing inequality, particularly in urban India, and its link with increasing returns to education to some sections during 1993–4 and 2004–5, see Cain et al. (2010). Second, in 2004–5, poverty risk was greater than unity only for illiterates but in 2009–10, it was also greater than unity for those literate up to the primary level. This could be associated with the vulnerability of the 0–14 years age group discussed above, but this was also the case in 2004–5. The other possibility is that adults who are literate up to the primary level are losing out in the economy. Third, the poverty risk increased for all categories. This was because the poverty risk of the category for which information on educational attainment is missing has reduced. Last, but not the least, incidence, depth, and severity of poverty reduced only for illiterates (and also for up to primary in rural areas only) and increased for the rest. This reiterates our contention that some people are losing out in the economy.

CONCLUDING REMARKS

This chapter pointed out that there are some unfinished tasks that the *Report of the Expert Group to Review the Methodology for Estimation of Poverty* (GoI 2009) has implicitly mentioned. A nuanced approach is needed to go beyond calories in our understanding of nutritional norms to link them to poverty. This also assumes importance for the fact that there exists an agriculture–nutrition disconnect in India. A much more serious question that the report raises is that the state is no more able to provide some basic facilities to its citizens—be it education, healthcare needs, or sanitation. These raise a question: does India continue to be a welfare state? There is also a case to articulate the understanding of poverty by bringing in additional dimensions (see Krishnaji 2012; Radhakrishna et al. 2010), but it should not be in the form of a unidimensional money-centric measure that Guruswamy and Abraham (2006) attempted. Further, given a larger debate in the country on transparency, it is imperative that the Planning Commission gives all important data computed at the state and sector levels in the public domain through a spreadsheet. In particular, we are referring to price indices, budget shares, and quantities among others. This will take the debate in the popular as also academic discourse beyond the poverty line and help replication in some limited sense. In its absence, the computation of the poverty line remains a black box.

Our discussion on changes in the shares of the poor across states could have implications for allocation of grants from the centre for some welfare schemes. This needs to be carefully evaluated, particularly so, because of the claims of the government that the Mahatma Gandhi National Rural Employment Guarantee Scheme (MGNREGS) could have helped in ameliorating poverty. If true, then any reduction of grants because of reduction in poverty can be counterproductive because the scheme that helped reduce poverty will get withdrawn. Of course, implementation of programmes under the scheme should integrate wage-based income with asset generation that are locally relevant.

The state-wise analysis pointed out the curious case of Bihar, the increasing incidence of poverty in some states including among the Northeastern states, and the urbanization of poverty with serious implications on law and order in Delhi and adjoining areas as also other places. At the same time, we should not ignore the concerns of smaller entities. There should be specific programmes addressing their problems, as their exclusion, though statistically irrelevant, raise ethical concerns.

In sectoral decompositions, there is a positive impact at the intra-sectoral level for both rural and urban areas, with rural areas gaining relatively more, and the inter-sectoral effect also shows a positive impact due to population shift. The growth-inequality decompositions show that the growth and interaction components reduce poverty whereas the redistribution component counteracts it, which becomes stronger as we go from an analysis of incidence to that of depth and severity. These call for specific programmes for those who are far below the poverty line.

Our sub-group analysis pointed out that across social groups, vulnerabilities were higher among the STs and the SCs, the former happened to be the worst-off in rural and the latter in urban. From among occupation type of households, the agricultural labour and other labour in rural and casual labour and self-employed (read petty traders and hawkers) in urban across were the vulnerable ones. The religion-wise patterns show that Buddhists (with a small share of population), and Muslims (highest incidence in urban) are those with the greater poverty risk. One observes an inverse relationship for the incidence of poverty with land size and educational attainment. There is a greater incidence of poverty among females, particularly divorcees and widows. Moreover, the dependent population comprising children and the old seemed to be vulnerable. All these inferences raise important policy implications. However, these are aggregate figures for India as a whole. These need to be complemented with other information at the district and sub-district levels for appropriate planning and implementation of poverty alleviation programmes.

REFERENCES

Alagh, Y.K. (2010), 'The Poverty Debate in Perspective: Moving Forward with the Tendulkar Committee', *Indian Journal of Human Development*, 4(1): 33–44.

Breman, J. (2010), 'A Poor Deal', *Indian Journal of Human Development*, 4(1): 133–42.

Cain, J.S., R. Hasan, R. Magsombol, and A. Tandon (2010), 'Accounting for Inequality in India: Evidence from Household Expenditures', *World Development*, 38(3): 282–97.

Chandhoke, N. (2012), 'Why People Should Not Be Poor', *Economic and Political Weekly*, 47(14): 41–50.

Datt, G. and M. Ravallion (1992), 'Growth and Redistribution Components of Changes in Poverty Measures: A Decomposition with Applications to Brazil and India in the 1980s', *Journal of Development Economics*, 38(2): 275–95.

Datta, K.L. (2010), 'Index of Poverty and Deprivation in the Context of Inclusive Growth', *Indian Journal of Human Development*, 4(1): 45–70.

Economic and Political Weekly Editorial (2012), 'Planning Commission's Poverty Charade', *Economic & Political Weekly*, 47(14): 7–8.

Foster, J., J. Greer, and E. Thorbecke (1984), 'A Class of Decomposable Poverty Measures', *Econometrica*, 52(3): 761–6.

Government of India [GoI] (2009), *Report of the Expert Group to Review the Methodology for Estimation of Poverty*. New Delhi: Planning Commission (Chairperson: Suresh D. Tendulkar).

———. (2012), *Press Note on Poverty Estimates, 2009–10*. New Delhi: Planning Commission.

Guruswamy, M. and R.J. Abraham (2006), 'Redefining Poverty: A New Poverty Line for a New India', *Economic and Political Weekly*, 41(25): 2534–41.

Haughton, J. and S.R. Khandekar (2009), *Handbook of Poverty and Inequality*. Washington, DC: The World Bank.

Jain, L.R. and S.D. Tendulkar (1990), 'Role of Growth and Distribution in the Observed Change in Headcount Ratio Measure of Poverty: A Decomposition Exercise for India', *Indian Economic Review*, 25(2): 165–205.

Kakwani, N. and K. Subbarao (1990), 'Rural Poverty and Its Alleviation in India', *Economic and Political Weekly*, 25(13): A2–A16.

Kannan, K.P. (2010), 'Estimating and Identifying the Poor in India', *Indian Journal of Human Development*, 4(1): 91–8.

Krishnaji, K. (2012), 'Abolish the Poverty Line', *Economic and Political Weekly*, 47(15): 10–11.

Mishra, S. (2012), 'Hunger, Ethics and the Right to Food', *Indian Journal of Medical Ethics*, 9(1): 32–7.

Manna, G.C. (2012), 'On Some Contentious Issues of the New Poverty Line', *Economic and Political Weekly*, 47(15): 11–14.

Motwani, A. (2012), 'Relative Poverty' (letter), *Economic and Political Weekly*, 47(14): 5.

Pathak, D.C. (2011), *Poverty and Inequality in Uttar Pradesh: A Decomposition Analysis*. Germany: Lambert Academic Publishing.

Pathak, D.C. and S. Mishra (2011), 'Poverty Estimates in India: Old and New Methods, 2004–5', Working Paper No. WP-2011-015. Mumbai: Indira Gandhi Institute of Development Research.

Planning Commission (2011), *Statement of Shri Montek Singh Ahluwalia, Deputy Chairman, Planning Commission (Press conference on 3 October)*. New Delhi: Planning Commission.

Radhakrishna, R., C. Ravi, and C.S. Reddy (2010). 'Can We Really Measure Poverty and Identify the Poor When Poverty Encompasses Multiple Deprivations?' *Indian Journal of Human Development*, 4(2): 281–300. Or 12

Radhakrishna, R. and S. Ray (2005), 'Poverty in India: Dimensions and Character', in K.S. Parikh and R. Radhakrishna (eds), *India Development Report 2004–5*. New Delhi: Oxford University Press.

Rao, V.M. (2010), 'Upward Revision of the Poverty Line: Some Implications for Poverty Analysis and Policies', *Indian Journal of Human Development*, 4(1):143–55.

Ravallion, M. and M. Huppi (1991), 'Measuring Changes in Poverty: A Methodological Case Study of Indonesia during and Adjustment Period', *World Bank Economic Review*, 5(1): 57–82.

Raveendran, G. (2010), 'New Estimates of Poverty in India: A Critique of the Tendulkar Committee Report', *Indian Journal of Human Development*, 4(1): 75–89.

Shah, G. (2010), 'The Poor: Beneficiaries to Citizens', *Indian Journal of Human Development*, 4(1): 127–32.

Subramanian, S. (2010), 'Identifying the Income-poor: Some Controversies in India and Elsewhere', Discussion Paper, Courant Research Centre, November.

Suryanarayana, M. (2011), 'Policies for the Poor: Verifying the Information Base', *Journal of Quantitative Economics*, New Series 9(1): 73–88.

Swaminathan, M. (2010), 'The New Poverty Line: A Methodology Deeply Flawed', *Indian Journal of Human Development*, 4(1): 121–25.

Vaidyanathan, A. (1986), 'On the Validity of NSS Consumption Data', *Economic and Political Weekly*, 21 (3): 129–37.

16

Indian Inequality
Patterns and Changes, 1993–2010*

Sripad Motiram and Vamsi Vakulabharanam

INTRODUCTION

India has been growing rapidly for roughly the past two and half decades, both by its own historical standards and also as compared to other countries. By now substantial literature has accumulated on the Indian growth process and its various facets.[1] One facet that has given rise to considerable debate and controversy is inequality. On the one side are some scholars who argue that inequality is not of great concern (for example, Bhagwati 2010; Panagariya 2008), whereas on the other side are those (for example, Motiram and Sarma 2011; Vakulabharanam 2010; Weisskopf 2011) who argue that inequality is increasing, raising serious questions about the equity and sustainability of the Indian growth process. In fact, one prominent and sensitive observer of India (Guha 2011) has argued that inequality and corruption are two 'mundane and materialist' challenges that are confronting the very idea of India today.

In our contribution to the previous issue of the 'India Development Report' (IDR) (Motiram and Vakulabharanam 2011) we had provided a comprehensive overview of poverty and inequality in India since the 1980s, largely based upon the 38th (1983), 50th (1993–4), and 61st (2004–5) Rounds of the National Sample Survey (NSS) on consumption expenditure. Since then, data from another NSS (66th) Round on the consumption expenditure survey has become available. In this chapter, we use data from this round (along with data from the 50th and 61st Rounds) and findings from other studies to map changes in inequality since the 1990s, an exercise that will give us a picture of changes in roughly the past two decades.

In literature on inequality, a distinction has been made between inter-personal or 'vertical' inequality and group-based or 'horizontal' inequality and it has been argued that the latter has received unduly less attention (Stewart 2002). In light of this, we examine both inter-personal inequality and inequality among sub-groups of the population. There are different sub-groups that one could consider depending upon the cleavages that are important in a particular society. We consider four cleavages that we think are important in the Indian context—caste, sector (that is, rural versus urban), state, and class. While the first three have been widely commented upon, the last has attracted relatively less attention.

Before we proceed with a detailed analysis, it is worth presenting a summary of our main findings. We find that inter-personal inequality has increased at the rural, urban,

---

* For his comments on a previous version, we thank Professor K.L. Krishna. This chapter was written when Sripad Motiram was visiting United Nations University, World Institute of Development Research (UNU-WIDER). He would like to thank UNU-WIDER for support received during this period.

[1] For a comprehensive account of the Indian growth process, see Balakrishnan (2010).

and all-India levels since the 1990s, although changes in the latest period (2004–5 to 2009–10) are less pronounced. We also find that rural–urban inequality, inequality among states, and class-based inequality have increased since the 1990s. A closer and disaggregated examination of recent changes reveals considerable diversity—while some states have seen a decrease in inequality, others have seen an increase. Overall, the growth process has been associated with increasing inequality, both at the rural and urban levels, states that have seen higher growth rates have also seen bigger increases (or smaller reductions) in inequality. However, again there is some diversity in this link between growth and inequality.

The remaining portion of the chapter is organized in two sections. The next section presents the analysis and results, and the section that follows concludes with a discussion of our results.

ANALYSIS AND RESULTS

As mentioned earlier, in literature on inequality, a distinction has been made between inter-personal (or 'vertical') inequality and inequality among groups ('horizontal' inequality). At the outset, we summarize the main findings on inequality on both these fronts from Motiram and Vakulabharanam (2011), our contribution to the previous issue of IDR. We had used NSS consumption expenditure surveys to document a decreasing trend in inter-personal inequality during 1983 to 1993–4, and an increasing trend during 1993–4 to 2004–5. This was true at the rural, urban, and all-India levels and for most states. Inter-personal inequality in wealth (using the NSS All India Debt and Investment Survey) increased during 1991 to 2002. These increases were modest, using summary measures of inequality (for example, the Gini) but were more pronounced if we examined the expenditure or wealth of the richer groups (for example, ratio of the expenditure of an individual at the 90th percentile to the median). On horizontal inequality, we had documented considerable differences among caste groups in terms of average consumption expenditure. Using a decomposition analysis with both consumption expenditure and wealth data, we had documented increasing inequality on the dimensions of sector (rural versus urban), caste, and states. These findings have to be looked at in the context of some limitations of the NSS data—that the rich and the wealthy are undersampled and their consumption and wealth are under-represented. Given these limitations, one would tend to underestimate both the level of inequality and changes in inequality over time. Hence, our overall conclusion was that growth in the 1990s was associated with substantial and increasing disparities.

We now examine whether the above story changes if we consider the latest round of NSS consumption expenditure data. In Table 16.1 we present inequality computations using the 1993–4, 2004–5, and the 2009–10 (latest) NSS consumption expenditure surveys for India and for major states. To make the findings comparable, we use the uniform reference period (URP) data from the 61st and 66th Rounds. As we can observe, during 2004–5 to 2009–10, for the country as a whole, rural inequality fell slightly, urban inequality increased, and all-India inequality increased. The increase was less pronounced as compared to the same during the period 1993–4 to 2004–5. However, it is worth noting that in the comparison between the latest two rounds, we examine changes over only five years, whereas in the comparison between 1993–4 and 2004–5, we examined a much longer period (of 11 years). Taking roughly the two-decade period between 1993–4 and 2009–10, inter-personal inequality increased at all the levels—rural, urban, and all-India.

In light of the data limitations that we have highlighted above, it is worth looking at the consumption of the poor and the wealthy as a percentage of the median consumption. For example, the expenditure of an individual at the 90th percentile as a percentage of the median has increased since the 1990s—212.63 per cent (1993–4), 235.20 per cent (2004–5), and 234.41 per cent (2009–10). On the contrary, expenditure of an individual at the 10th percentile, as a percentage of the median has decreased steadily since the 1990s—56.67 per cent (1993–4), 56.32 per cent (2004–5), and 55.99 per cent (2009–10).

It is interesting to get a disaggregated picture by examining differences across the various states. From Table 16.1, we can observe that in most states, urban and overall inequality increased during 1993–4 to 2004–5; the observation holds for rural inequality as well, although for a lesser number of (but many) states. When we look at changes during 2004–5 to 2009–10, we witness a mixed picture. In order to illustrate this comparison better, we present Figures 16.1a–16.1c. In Figure 16.1a, for each state, we plot its rural Gini for 2009–10 as a function of its rural Gini for 2004–5. We also plot a 45-degree line, so that points lying above this line correspond to states that have seen an increase in rural inequality and those lying below this line correspond to states that have witnessed a decrease. Similarly, Figures 16.1b and 16.1c represent the comparison for urban areas and at the all-India level respectively.

From Figure 16.1a we can observe that most states saw a decrease in rural inequality during 2004–5 to 2009–10. Some cases need to be highlighted. Assam saw an increase from a low base (that is, a low level of inequality in 2004–5) whereas Kerala saw an increase from a high base. Haryana and Uttar Pradesh saw a decrease from a moderately high base.

Table 16.1 Inequality (Gini) for Major States

State	1993–4			2004–5			2009–10		
	Rural	Urban	Total	Rural	Urban	Total	Rural	Urban	Total
Andhra Pradesh	0.290	0.323	0.312	0.294	0.375	0.345	0.286	0.395	0.364
Assam	0.179	0.290	0.216	0.199	0.320	0.240	0.251	0.330	0.283
Bihar	0.225	0.309	0.253	0.213	0.355	0.259	0.234	0.358	0.273
Gujarat	0.240	0.291	0.279	0.271	0.310	0.334	0.261	0.338	0.343
Haryana	0.314	0.284	0.311	0.339	0.366	0.355	0.310	0.368	0.339
Himachal Pradesh	0.284	0.462	0.325	0.310	0.326	0.328	0.314	0.415	0.336
Jammu and Kashmir	0.240	0.287	0.270	0.247	0.249	0.260	0.240	0.315	0.266
Karnataka	0.270	0.319	0.309	0.266	0.369	0.361	0.240	0.341	0.350
Kerala	0.301	0.343	0.316	0.381	0.410	0.393	0.439	0.527	0.473
Madhya Pradesh	0.280	0.331	0.315	0.277	0.407	0.357	0.297	0.367	0.351
Maharashtra	0.307	0.357	0.376	0.312	0.378	0.393	0.276	0.423	0.409
Odisha	0.246	0.307	0.282	0.285	0.353	0.324	0.268	0.401	0.326
Punjab	0.281	0.281	0.285	0.294	0.402	0.351	0.297	0.382	0.339
Rajasthan	0.265	0.293	0.280	0.250	0.371	0.303	0.230	0.396	0.300
Tamil Nadu	0.312	0.348	0.344	0.323	0.361	0.379	0.271	0.340	0.342
Uttar Pradesh	0.282	0.326	0.302	0.291	0.367	0.327	0.281	0.367	0.322
West Bengal	0.254	0.339	0.308	0.274	0.383	0.353	0.245	0.393	0.338
All-India	0.286	0.344	0.326	0.305	0.376	0.363	0.300	0.393	0.370

Note: (i) All-India includes all the states, and not just the major states.

(ii) Bihar includes Jharkhand, Madhya Pradesh includes Chhattisgarh, and Uttar Pradesh includes Uttarakhand.

Source: Authors' computations from NSS unit-level data.

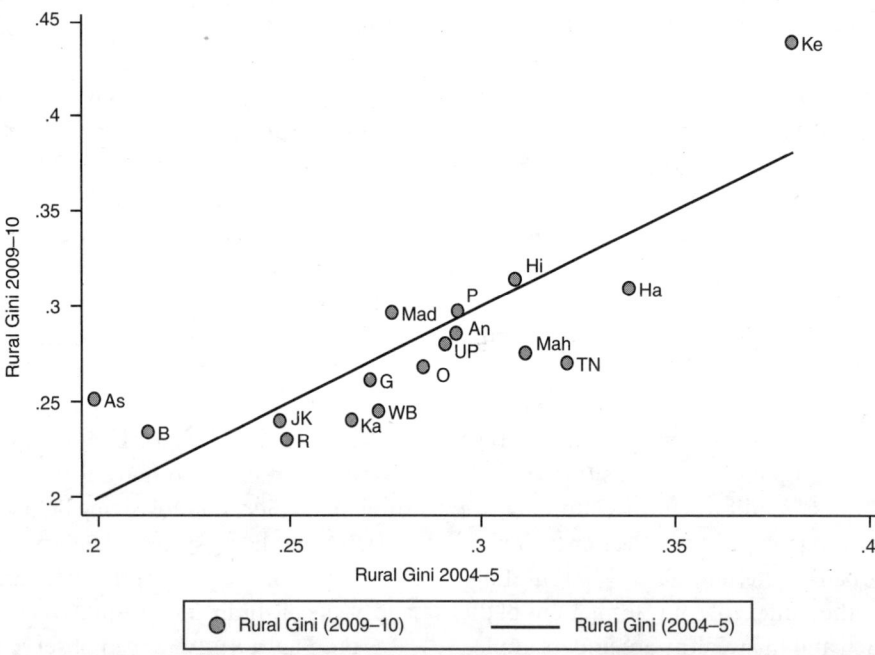

Figure 16.1a Rural Inequality for 2004–5 and 2009–10 (Major States)

Notes: (i) An: Andhra Pradesh, As: Assam, B: Bihar, G: Gujarat, Ha: Haryana, Hi: Himachal Pradesh, JK: Jammu and Kashmir, Ka: Karnataka, Ke: Kerala, Mah: Maharashtra, Mad: Madhya Pradesh, O: Odisha, P: Punjab, R: Rajasthan, TN: Tamil Nadu, UP: Uttar Pradesh, WB: West Bengal. Bihar includes Jharkhand, Madhya Pradesh includes Chhattisgarh, and Uttar Pradesh includes Uttarakhand.

(ii) On the x and y axes, we have the Rural Ginis for 2004–5 and 2009–10 respectively. The straight line is a 45-degree line.

Source: Authors' computations from NSS unit-level data.

Figure 16.1b for urban areas presents a contrasting picture to Figure 16.1a. Most states saw an increase in urban inequality during 2004–5 to 2009–10. Kerala again saw an increase from a high base, whereas Jammu & Kashmir saw an increase from a low base. Some states (for example, Odisha, Maharashtra, and Andhra Pradesh) saw an increase from a moderately high base. In contrast, Punjab and Madhya Pradesh saw a decrease from a high base.

Figure 16.1c at the all-India level presents a mixed picture between Figures 16.1a and 16.1b at the rural and urban levels respectively. The number of states that witnessed an increase in inequality lies between corresponding numbers for rural and urban areas. Cases to note are Kerala, which showed an increase from a high base; Assam, which showed an increase from a low base; and Andhra Pradesh and Maharashtra, which showed modest increases from moderate and high bases respectively. Assam, Maharashtra, and Kerala witnessed increases in inequality at the rural, urban, and all-India levels.

An interesting issue to examine is the link between growth and inequality. Are the states that are growing faster experiencing lower or higher increases in inequality? To address this question, we consider the period 2004–5 to 2009–10 and analyse the relationship between the rate of growth of real average consumption expenditure and the rate of change of inequality, separately for rural and urban areas, and for major states. We obtain the real average consumption expenditure for rural areas for each state by dividing the rural average nominal consumption expenditure by the consumer price index for agricultural labourers (CPIAL). Figure 16.2a presents the relationship between the growth rate for real average consumption expenditure and the rate of change of inequality. We also fitted a regression line and show the 95 per cent confidence interval. The growth rate for consumption expenditure is the average annual rate, derived by using the method of compounding. For the rate of change of inequality (since these changes are small), we used the simple percentage change between 2004–5 and 2009–10.

From Figure 16.2a we can discern a clear positive relationship implying that growth is associated with increases in inequality. In other words, overall, states that experienced higher growth rates also witnessed higher increases (or lower reductions) in inequality. A point to note here is that, as discussed above, many states saw a reduction in rural inequality in the period 2004–5 to 2009–10. There are some outliers worth noting—with moderate growth rates, Assam and Bihar experienced high increases in rural inequality, whereas Maharashtra and Tamil Nadu experienced higher decreases in inequality. Kerala showed both high growth and a high increase in inequality.

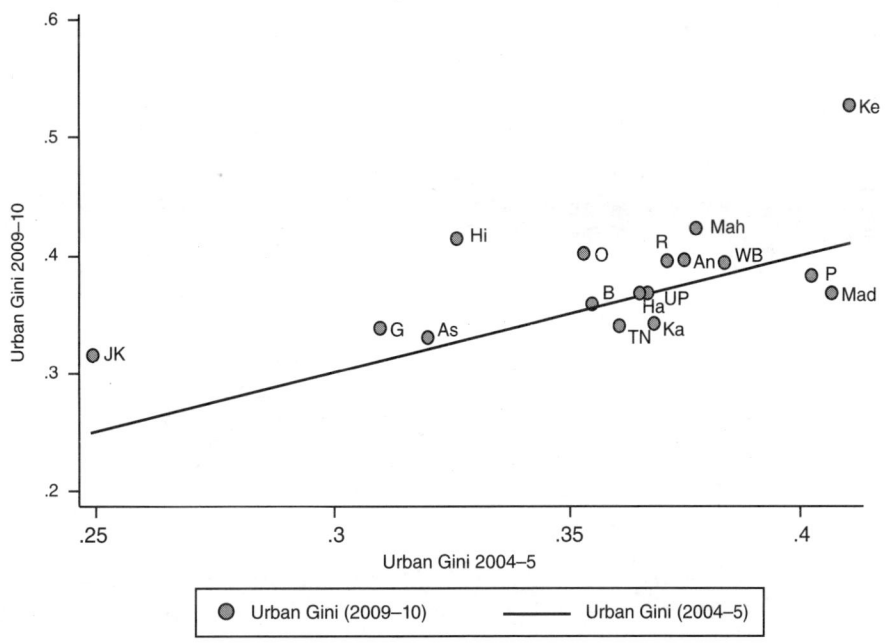

Figure 16.1b Urban Inequality for 2004–5 and 2009–10 (Major States)

Notes: (i) For the labels for various states, see notes to Figure 16.1a.
  (ii) On the x and y axes, we have the Urban Ginis for 2004–5 and 2009–10 respectively. The straight line is a 45-degree line.
Source: Authors' computations from NSS unit-level data.

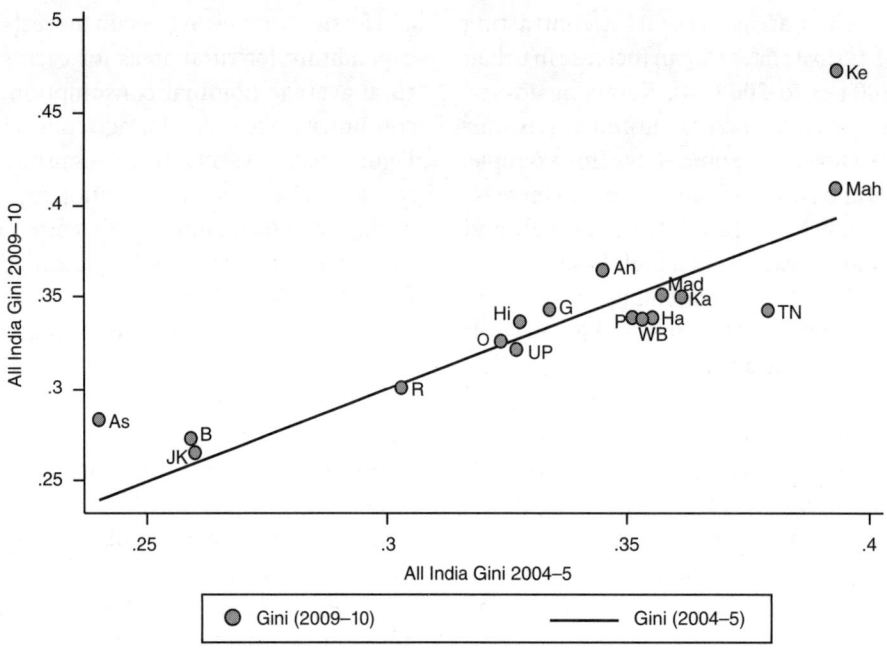

Figure 16.1c Inequality for 2004–5 and 2009–10 (Major States)

Notes: (i) For the labels for various states, see notes to Figure 16.1a.
(ii) On the x and y axes, we have the Ginis for 2004–5 and 2009–10, respectively. The straight line is a 45-degree line.
Source: Authors' computations from NSS unit-level data.

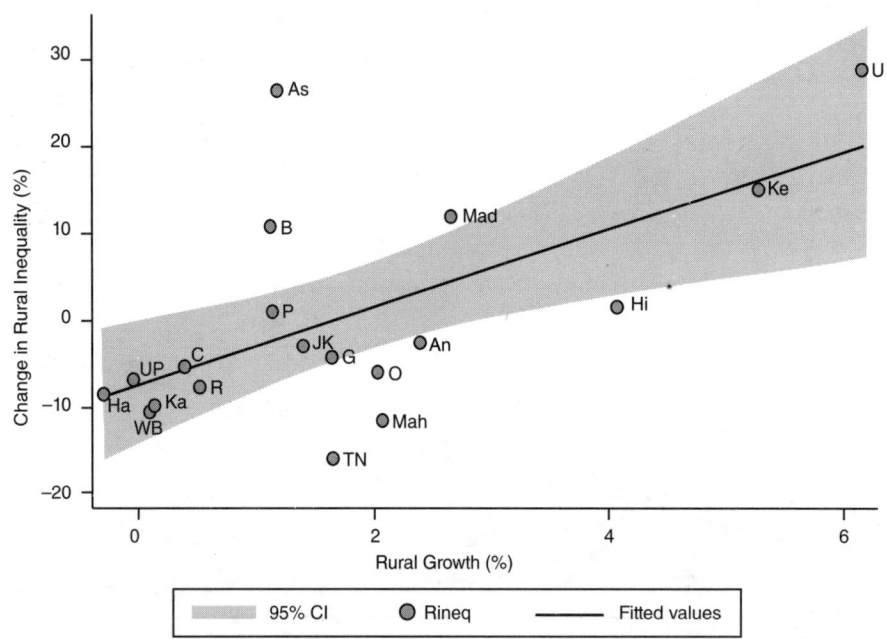

Figure 16.2a Growth and Inequality in Rural India

Notes: (i) For the labels for various states, see notes to Figure 16.1a. We have now considered Chhattisgarh (C), Jharkhand (J), and Uttaranchal (U) separately from Madhya Pradesh, Bihar, and Uttar Pradesh respectively.
(ii) On the x-axis, we have the rate of growth in real average rural monthly consumption expenditure. Real values are obtained by deflating using the CPIAL taken from data provided by the Labour Bureau. On the y-axis, we have percentage change in rural Gini.
(iii) The straight line is a fitted regression line. The estimated coefficient of growth and its robust standard errors are 4.494 and 0.941 (p-value close to zero), respectively.
Source: Authors' computations from NSS unit-level data.

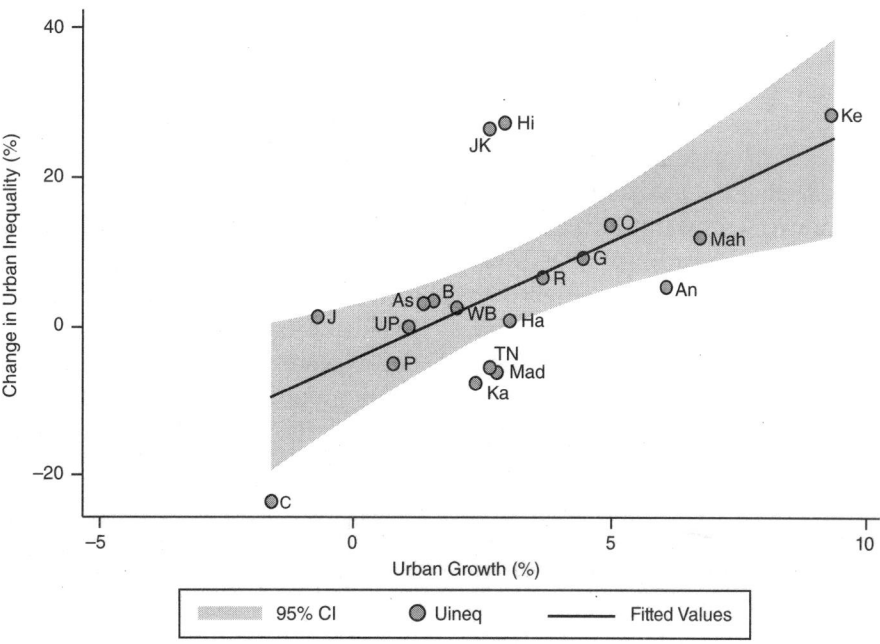

Figure 16.2b Growth and Inequality in Urban India

Notes: (i) For the labels for various states, see notes to Figure 16.1a. As in the case of Figure 16.2a, we have considered Chhattisgarh, Jharkhand, and Uttarakhand separately.

(ii) On the x-axis, we have the rate of growth in real average urban monthly consumption expenditure. Real values are obtained by deflating using CPIIW taken from data provided by the Labour Bureau. On the y-axis, we have percentage change in urban Gini.

(iii) The straight line is a fitted regression line. The estimated coefficient of growth and its robust standard error are 3.172 and 0.703 (p-value close to zero) respectively.

Source: Authors' computations from NSS unit-level data.

For urban areas, we use the same method as the one for rural areas, except that we use the consumer price index for industrial workers (CPIIW).[2] Figure 16.2b presents the relationship between growth and inequality for urban areas. As in the case of rural areas, we also fitted a regression line and show the 95-per cent confidence interval.

Again, we can discern a positive relationship, implying that states that grew faster have also experienced higher increases in inequality. It is worth noting a few cases—Jammu & Kashmir showed a high increase in urban inequality despite low growth, Andhra Pradesh showed a modest increase in inequality despite moderate growth, and Kerala showed both high growth and a high increase in inequality.

The overall picture that emerges from Figures 16.2a and 16.2b is that states that have been experiencing faster growth have also been experiencing higher increases (lower reductions) in inequality. Essentially, growth is associated with increasing inequality. We think that this is a powerful and interesting result. However, given the presence of some outliers, we would like to be cautious about this assertion, in particular about a casual linkage.

In the above discussion, we focused upon inter-personal inequality as traditionally conceived, that is, through commonly used relative inequality measures like the Gini. A recent strand in literature on inequality has emphasized 'polarization', a concept that is distinct from inequality, and that is closely related to conflict. Motiram and Sarma (2011) present an overview of literature and analyse polarization in the Indian context using NSS consumption expenditure data. We now present the basic ideas. A widely used notion of polarization is 'bipolarization', which deals with the decline of the middle class, as conceptualized by the median. Standard measures of relative inequality are constructed by imposing four principles (or axioms): symmetry, replication invariance, scale invariance, and the Pigou–Dalton

---

[2] The CPIIW is unavailable at the state-level, but available at the level of centres within each state. We therefore compute the state-level index as the weighted average of the values for various centres, with the weights being national-level weights. The base year for the CPIIW series was changed from 1982 to 2001 recently, so to achieve equivalence between 2004–5 and 2009–10, we used the linking factors that have been provided. For 2009–10, we considered only those centres for which these linking factors are available.

principle.[3] Relative measures of bipolarization retain the first three axioms, but dispense with the Pigou–Dalton principle. They replace it with two other principles—increased spread and increased bipolarity. Increased spread holds that a transformation that makes a rich person richer or a poor person poorer, without affecting the median (that is, the middle) would result in a movement away from the middle, thereby increasing bipolarization. Similarly, a transfer from a poor person to a rich person across the median will pull both the rich and poor persons away from each other (and from the middle), thereby increasing bipolarization. To illustrate increased bipolarity, consider a progressive transfer (that is, from a richer person to a poorer person) on the same side as the median. As a result of this transfer, the richer and poorer persons will come closer, with one of these moving closer to the middle and the other moving away. Increased bipolarity postulates that bipolarization increases due to this transfer. Note the distinction vis-à-vis inequality here—since this is a progressive transfer, measures of inequality that satisfy the Pigou–Dalton principle (for example, the Gini) will show a decrease, whereas bipolarization has increased.

Motiram and Sarma (2011) use NSS consumption expenditure data and several measures to show that bipolarization has increased since the 1990s at the rural, urban, and all-India levels. This is a reversal of the trend from the 1980s—during 1983 to 1993–4, bipolarization was falling.

We have so far discussed inter-personal ('vertical') inequality. Moving to 'horizontal' (group-based) inequality, we can think of several cleavages in Indian society. Four important cleavages that can be considered are caste, sector (that is, rural vis-à-vis urban), state, and class. A decomposition analysis can be used to shed light on the changes in horizontal inequality. Consider a population that consists of several sub-groups based on a particular dimension (for example, caste or ethnicity). For the entire population, we can compute the level of inequality (i) as measured by an index that belongs to the single-parameter entropy family of indices (e.g. Log mean deviation, Theil index, Square of the Coefficient of Variation, [see Shorrocks and Wan (2005), for a description of these indices]. We can then decompose this index into a sum of two components—a "within" component (w) and a "between" component (b), that is, $i = (w+b)$. The within component is a weighted sum[4] of the inequalities for (that is, within) the various sub-groups and the between component is the inequality among the sub-groups. An increase in the share contributed by the between component (that is, an increase in b/i) can be construed as an increase in inequality among sub-groups.

For example, consider a population of size n with a consumption expenditure (or income or wealth) distribution $(y_1, y_2, ..., y_n)$ with a mean consumption expenditure m. The population is divided into m sub-groups, and the consumption expenditure distribution, expenditure share, and mean of sub-group k (=1, 2, ..., m) are given by $(y_1^k, y_2^k, ...)$, s_k and μ_k, respectively. The Theil index is given as:

$$T(y_1, y_2, ..., y_n) = \frac{1}{n}\sum_{i=1}^{n}\frac{y_i}{\mu}\ln\left(\frac{y_i}{\mu}\right)$$

$$= \sum_{k=1}^{m} s_k T(y_1^k, y_2^k, ...) + \sum_{k=1}^{m} s_k \ln\left(\frac{\mu_k}{\mu}\right)$$

The first term in the above expression is the 'within component'—a weighted average of the inequalities (as measured by the Theil) within the sub-groups. Note that since the income shares (s_k) add up to 1, this is a weighted average. The second term is the 'between component'.

Table 16.2 presents the results of a decomposition of the Theil index. For caste, since the Other Backward Classes (OBCs) were not separately enumerated in 1993–4, we consider only Scheduled Castes, Scheduled Tribes and Others, that is, we include the OBCs among Others. As we can observe, for caste the share contributed by the between component increased from 1993–4 to 2004–5, but then fell in 2009–10. In 2009–10, it was slightly lower than its corresponding level in 1993–4. This is some evidence that disparities among castes have decreased since the 1990s, although this result is driven by changes in the most recent period. For sector, the share contributed by the between component increased between 1993–4 and 2004–5 and then fell slightly in 2009–10, although it was still higher than its level in 1993–4. Essentially, rural–urban inequality has increased since the 1990s. For inequality among states, the share contributed by the between component increased between 1993–4 and 2004–5 and this trend continued into the period 2004–5 to 2009–10. In other words, inequality among states has been increasing steadily since the 1990s.

Coming to class, Vakulabharanam (2010) has developed both a detailed and a simple class scheme to divide the Indian population into various classes in both rural and urban areas. In the simple scheme, two classes are identi-

---

[3] Symmetry: Only incomes (or wealth or consumption expenditures—this applies to the other axioms below) matter and not the individuals who earn these incomes; Replication invariance: Cloning the entire income distribution leaves inequality unchanged; Scale invariance: Scaling all the incomes up or down by a common factor leaves inequality unchanged; Pigou–Dalton principle: A regressive transfer from a poor person to a richer person increases inequality and a progressive transfer reduces inequality.

[4] It would be a weighted average in the case of Log mean deviation and Theil since the weights would add up to 1.

Table 16.2 Theil Decomposition Analysis

Sub-groups	Within Component	Between Component	Total
Caste			
1993–4	0.210 (95.51%)	0.010 (4.49%)	0.220 (100%)
2004–5	0.267 (95.11%)	0.014 (4.89%)	0.281 (100%)
2009–10	0.304 (95.93%)	0.013 (4.07%)	0.317 (100%)
Rural–Urban			
1993–4	0.195 (88.44%)	0.025 (11.56%)	0.220 (100%)
2004–5	0.236 (84.03%)	0.045 (15.97%)	0.281 (100%)
2009–10	0.267 (84.37%)	0.049 (15.63%)	0.317 (100%)
State			
1993–4	0.200 (90.93%)	0.020 (9.07%)	0.220 (100%)
2004–5	0.252 (89.93%)	0.028 (10.07%)	0.281 (100%)
2009–10	0.281 (88.71%)	0.036 (11.29%)	0.317 (100%)

Source: Authors' computations based upon NSS unit-level data.
Notes: (i) The decomposition is described in pp. 9–10.
(ii) Caste groups: Scheduled Castes, Scheduled Tribes, and Others.
(iii) States: Bihar includes Jharkhand, Madhya Pradesh includes Chhattisgarh, and Uttar Pradesh includes Uttarakhand.

fied in urban India: (i) the elite (owners, managers, and professionals), and (ii) workers, that is, non-professionals. Four classes are identified in rural India: (i) agricultural and non-agricultural elite (large farmers, owners, government officials, moneylenders, professionals, and absentee landlords), (ii) rural non-agricultural workers, (iii) small farmers, and (iv) agricultural workers.[5] Using NSS consumption expenditure data and these classes as population sub-groups, Vakulabharanam (2012) decomposes inequality as measured by the Gini index using the ANOGI (analysis of Gini) method of decomposition (Frick et al. 2006; Yitzhaki 1994). Decomposition of the Gini index using ANOGI (unlike decomposition of measures of the single parameter entropy family) yields an overlapping component, apart from the between and within components. However, an increase in the contribution of the between component can still be interpreted as an increase in inequality among sub-groups. Vakulabharanam (2012) shows that the contribution of the between component increased from 20.8 per cent in 1993–4 to 27.5 per cent in 2009–10, implying that class-based inequality has increased since the 1990s.

DISCUSSION AND CONCLUSIONS

In the above analysis, we used NSS consumption expenditure surveys since the 1990s to examine inter-personal inequality and inequality among groups. Our main finding on inter-personal inequality is that it has increased at the rural, urban, and all-India levels. On group-based inequality, we focused on caste, class, sector, and state and found that inequality increased on all these fronts, except for caste. Given the limitations of NSS surveys, we would expect both the levels and increases in inequality to be underestimates.

Different societies (across space and time) can tolerate different levels of and changes in inequality. So, it is difficult for us to judge whether the patterns that we have documented would lead to increased tensions and conflicts in the future. However, we do think that inequality based upon class and spaces (rural versus urban region/state) are likely to pose challenges in the future.

There are two questions that need further examination and can be the focus of future research. First, what can explain the different inequality trends in different states? Second, in the most recent period (2004–10), changes in inequality have been muted and rural and urban inequalities have shown different trends. What are the reasons for this finding?

REFERENCES

Bhagwati, J.N. (2010), 'Indian Reforms: Yesterday and Today', *The 3rd Prof. Hiren Mukherjee Memorial Annual Parliamentary Lecture*. Available at: http://www.columbia.edu/~jb38/papers/pdf/Lok-Sabha-speech-FINAL-EXPANDED-December-14.pdf, last accessed on 1 March 2012.

Balakrishnan, Pulapre (2010), *Economic Growth in India: History and Proscess*. New Delhi: Oxford University Press.

Frick, J.R., J. Goebel, E. Schechtman, G. Wagner, and S. Yitzhaki (2006), 'Using Analysis of Gini (ANOGI) for Detecting Whether Two Subsamples Represent the Same Universe: The German Socio-Economic Panel Study (SOEP) Experience', *Sociological Methods & Research*, 34: 427–68.

---

[5] The detailed class scheme comprises nine classes in urban areas: (i) Owner/manager (formal), (ii) Owner/manager (informal), (iii) Manufacturing-professional, (iv) Manufacturing-skilled, (v) Manufacturing-unskilled, (vi) Service-professional, (vii) Service-skilled, (viii) Service-unskilled, and (ix) Urban-unclassified. In the detailed class scheme, there are 12 classes in rural areas: (i) Rich farmer, (ii) Middle farmer, (iii) Small farmer, (iv) Marginal farmer/tenant, (v) Agricultural worker, (vi) Rural professional, (vii) Rural moneylender, (viii) Absentee landlord and non-agricultural self-employed, (ix) Non-agricultural self-employed, (x) Absentee landlord and others, (xi) Non-agricultural workers, and (xii) Rural unclassified.

Guha, R. (2011), 'The Nation Consumed by the State', *Outlook*, 31 January.

Motiram, S. and N. Sarma (2011), 'Polarization, Inequality and Growth: The Indian Experience', ECINEQ Working Paper 2011-225, Society for the Study of Economic Inequality.

Motiram, S. and V. Vakulabharanam (2011), 'Poverty and Inequality in the Age of Economic Liberalization' in D.M. Nachane (ed.), *India Development Report 2011*. New Delhi: Oxford University Press, pp. 59–68.

Panagariya, A. (2008), *India: The Emerging Giant*. New York: Oxford University Press.

Shorrocks, A. and G. Wan (2005), 'Spatial Decomposition of Inequality', *Journal of Economic Geography*, 5: 59–81.

Stewart, F. (2002), *Horizontal Inequality: A Neglected Dimension of Development*. (5th Annual Lecture) Helsinki: World Institute of Development Economics Research.

Vakulabharanam, V. (2010), 'Does Class Matter? Class Structure and Worsening Inequality in India', *Economic and Political Weekly*, 45 (29): 67–76.

———. (2012), 'Class and Inequality in India over Three Decades', Paper Presented at the Conference Commemorating 40 years of the School of Social Sciences at Jawaharlal Nehru University, February.

Weisskopf, T. (2011), 'Why Worry about Inequality in the Booming Indian Economy', *Economic and Political Weekly*, 46(47): 41–51.

Yitzhaki, S. (1994), 'Economic Distance and Overlapping Distributions', *Journal of Econometrics*, 61: 147–59.

17

Promoting Human Development in India
Scope for Distributive Options

*M.H. Suryanarayana and Ankush Agrawal**

INTRODUCTION

Planning in India has sought to achieve 'growth with redistribution' by reducing inequality across persons. The redistributive policy option is generally conceptualized and measured in terms of a reduction in estimates of the extent of inequality in consumption/income distribution. For instance, the Technical Note on the Sixth Five Year Plan worked out estimates of poverty reduction under alternative scenarios of: (i) 'Growth', and (ii) 'Growth with Redistribution' with reference to estimates of Gini ratios of consumption distributions (GoI 1981). This exercise facilitated quantifying the potential loss in realizing Plan targets if a country pursued an 'only growth' policy option, ignoring the extent of inequality in income distribution. In other words, it permitted verification of the scope for poverty reduction by a redistributive policy option.

One finds a similar syndrome when it comes to pursuit of human development. Though successive Plan exercises have laid emphasis on promoting achievements with respect to other dimensions of human development like education and health, India has not seriously explored the scope for reducing unequal achievements across persons in education and health,[1] which have a crucial bearing on economic growth as well as the final income distribution profile. Given the current policy emphasis on inclusive growth and eradicating multiple dimensions of deprivation,[2] this chapter seeks to quantify the extent of loss in human development due to inequality across its dimensions in different states as well as in the country as a whole. In other words, it examines the scope for promoting 'human development' by improved distribution.

Unlike an income redistributive strategy for a given income level, which would involve net transfers between

---

* The authors thank Tushar Agrawal for generating estimates of average years of schooling and inequality in education, S. Chandrasekhar for estimates of school life expectancy, Jitendra Asati for helping us in getting shape files for Indian states and K. Seeta Prabhu, K.L. Krishna, Ashwini Deshpande, Deepa Sankar, and UNDP New Delhi for comments and suggestions.

[1] The level of human development has been low in the country ever since the planning process started and this problem is compounded by skewed distribution across the states (Sen 1989, 1998).

[2] The Indian government's concern about rising inequalities and uneven distribution of the benefits of growth was reflected in the Eleventh Five Year Plan (2007–12), which placed a thrust on 'inclusive growth'. The forthcoming Twelfth Five Year Plan deepens and sharpens the focus on inequalities. While preparing the Approach Paper for the Twelfth Five Year Plan, the Planning Commission for the first time set up a dedicated web portal for involving interested stakeholders. The Commission has identified 'Twelve Strategy Challenges' to initiate the consultations that refer to some core areas, many of which aim at inclusive development.

two segments of the population by instruments like taxes and subsidies, this option on a reduction in the inequality in health and education will not involve any transfer and redistribution. Instead, an improvement in the health and education status of the deprived sections will invariably involve positive externalities for the entire community, resulting in an improvement in size as well as distribution.

The issue specified above is explored using the methodology proposed to estimate the Human Development Index (HDI) and the Inequality-adjusted Human Development Index (IHDI) in the *Human Development Report 2010* (UNDP 2010). The methodology is in fact a culmination of efforts to develop a comprehensive framework to address various issues related to human development, inequity, and inequality ever since the UNDP introduced the concept in 1990 and initiated a series of studies. UNDP's advocacy is to keep people at the centre of the development process. The first 'Human Development Report' published in 1990 proposed a concept and introduced HDI—a combined index of three dimensions of human well-being, namely, standard of living (income), education, and a long and healthy life—which has become a useful tool in welfare policy formulations across countries in the world. The human development paradigm emphasizes that the people are the real wealth of a nation and seeks to enlarge people's choices, especially in terms of their abilities to live a long and healthy life, to be educated, and to enjoy a decent standard of living (UNDP 1990).

India, too, has realized the importance of this focus as reflected in its efforts to promote 'human development' and improve 'the standard of living for the people' by ensuring 'a more equitable distribution of development benefits and opportunities, a better living environment and empowerment of the poor and marginalised' (GoI 2012: 301). Periodic human development reports (HDRs) at the national (GoI 2002; Institute of Applied Manpower Research 2011) as well as state levels to focus public and policy attention on contemporary development issues and advocate pragmatic strategies to address such issues provide evidence of the concern at the policy level.[3] In addition, there has also been individual research focus on disparities in economic and human development across states in India (Chaudhuri et al. 2007; Ram and Mohanty 2005). These attempts have provided useful estimates of disparities in different dimensions of economic and human development. However, with their concern restricted to examining only the levels, they have not been able to focus on distributive issues involving the extent of inequality in distribution of different human development dimensions.

This chapter seeks to overcome this limitation by estimating both HDI and IHDI across states in India. This is because conceptually HDI would measure the 'potential' for realizing human development when achievements across dimensions are distributed equally among the people while IHDI would capture the actual level of human development taking into account inequality in such distributions. Both HDI and IHDI would be the same when the distribution of achievements across people in society is equal. IHDI will fall short of HDI with an increase in inequality. It is this shortfall which provides a measure of the loss in potential human development due to inequality. An estimate of the loss can be bounded as a percentage of HDI.

This chapter in fact modifies on an earlier attempt (Suryanarayana et al. 2011) to provide estimates of HDIs and IHDIs for major Indian states. The earlier study estimated the average loss in human development on account of inequality to be 32 per cent in India during 2002–8. The present work extends this study in two ways. First, an attempt is made to provide IHDI estimates for minor states also.[4] Second, we contextualize IHDI with reference to domestic goalposts. However, to facilitate an international comparison we present alternative options with reference to global as well as domestic goalposts.

This study is organized as follows. The next section describes the methodology used in the chapter to contextualize HDI with reference to domestic goalposts. The next section discusses the databases. Estimates of HDI, IHDI, and their sub-indices are presented in the next section. The final section concludes.

DOMESTIC GOALPOSTS

UNDP scores corresponding to the three dimensions of human development are worked out with reference to international goalposts to facilitate ranking of countries across the world. Suryanarayana et al. (2011) follow the same procedure to examine the relative ranking of different Indian states in the global context. However, given the domestic policy focus, this study seeks to obtain scores with reference to domestic goalposts, which will provide a better picture of the relative progress of the different states in India. It will also be useful in light of the government's concern about rising inequalities and uneven distribution

---

[3] It may however be noted that the two HDRs for the country are based on the methodologies used in earlier HDRs by the United Nations. Hence, the HDIs and the ranks in this study—which uses UNDP (2010) methodology—may not be comparable with those in the HDRs.

[4] This study covers 27 of the 28 states in the country. Owing to non-availability of reliable information on the health dimension, the HDI and IHDI for Goa could not be estimated.

of the benefits of growth. This study presents findings based on both the approaches.

This section proposes a methodology to work out domestic goalposts for measures of different dimensions of human development to localize HDIs and IHDIs in the Indian context. The domestic goalposts are contextualized with reference to the profiles for *major* Indian states. Instead of extreme values of different indicators across states, the goalposts are defined with reference to the mainstream distribution of the indicators in terms of their respective box and whisker plots. In other words, the mainstream is defined with reference to the central 50 per cent of the ordered distributions. Consistent with this proposal, the goalposts may be measured in terms of the upper and lower inner fences of the box and whisker plots of the different indicators subject to the caveat that the limits for indictors, say the combined education index, are set at feasible lower and upper bounds—zero and one respectively.[5] These estimates are given in Table 17.1.

Table 17.1 Domestic Goalposts for the Human Development Index

Dimension	Upper Inner Fence	Lower Inner Fence
Life expectancy	75.7	50.7
Mean years of schooling	7.19	1.03
Expected years of schooling	10.87	8.18
Combined education index	1.00	0
Per capita income (PPP $)	5,772.23	814.68

Source: Authors' estimates.

DATA SOURCES

Income

The estimate of gross national income (GNI) per capita (PPP US$) for India is taken from HDR 2010 (UNDP 2010). Its distribution across states is worked out as per the distribution profiles of average per capita personal consumption obtained from the National Sample Survey for the year 2004–5 (GoI 2006a). This approach involves underestimation of income inequality since it ignores savings and dis-savings of the rich and poor respectively. An alternative approach could be to use estimates of state domestic product (SDP). However, this has a major limitation in that it refers to only income generated; it does not include inter-state/national remittances and actual income distribution; in addition, some of its components are based on intra/extrapolations.

Consistent with the profile on income distribution across states, estimates of intra-state personal income inequality (Atkinson's inequality indices) are estimated using NSS unit record data on personal consumption distribution for 2004–5. Such consumption inequality estimates are generated after truncating the top 0.5-percentile of the distribution and replacing zero expenditure with minimum value of expenditure of the bottom 0.5-percentile group *à la* UNDP (2010).[6]

Education

The dimension index on education is based on: (i) mean years of schooling, and (ii) expected years of schooling (school life expectancy). Mean years of schooling of the adult population (aged 25 years and above) are estimated using unit-level information from NSS data on 'Educational Status and Training in India' (GoI 2006b). The same data source is used to estimate Atkinson inequality in levels of education. To surmount computational problems in estimating inequality when there are observations with zero year of schooling, following UNDP (2010), one is added to all valid observations on years of schooling. Estimates of expected years of schooling are made based on the NSS on education in India (GoI 2010).

Health

Estimates of life expectancy for 16 major states are obtained from 'SRS Based Abridged Life Tables 2002–2006' (GoI 2008). Estimates of life expectancy for the three states formed in 2000—Chhattisgarh, Jharkhand, and Uttarakhand and the state of Jammu & Kashmir are obtained from the 'Population Projections for India and States 2001–2026' (GoI 2006c).[7] The same report also provides estimates of life expectancy for the seven states of Northeast India (that is, excluding Assam), and the same has been used as a proxy for all the seven states.

The data source for estimating inequality (Atkinson's index) in life expectancy is the 'Tables on the Life Expectancy'

---

[5] Lower and upper inner fences are defined with reference to the upper and lower hinges of the box (quartiles of the distribution). The difference between the two hinges is called H-spread and 1.5 times the H-spread constitutes a step. The upper inner fence is given by one-step beyond the upper hinge while the lower inner fence is given by one-step beyond the lower hinge (Thompson 2011).

[6] The *Human Development Report 2010* uses different data sources as household asset holding, consumption, and income for different countries to estimate inequality in income. For the Indian case, it estimates inequality from imputed income using an assets index methodology (UNDP 2010).

[7] The estimates of life expectancy for the three parent states in GoI (2008) include the new states.

across age-intervals for Indian states (GoI 2008).[8] Since the life tables are available only for 16 major states, the inequality index could only be computed for them. The inequality index for Chhattisgarh, Jharkhand, and Uttarakhand is assumed as being the same as that of their respective parent states; for the seven states in Northeast India, it is proxied by that of Assam; and for the state of Jammu & Kashmir, we have assumed it to be same as that of West Bengal.[9]

ESTIMATES AND FINDINGS

This section begins with findings based on estimates of HDI and IHDI with reference to international goalposts and then those based on domestic ones. The basic indicators are presented in Table 17.2.

HDIs Based on Global Goalposts

Table 17.3 provides relevant information on estimates of sub-indices and the inequality-adjusted sub-indices for the three different human development dimensions with reference to international goalposts.

Estimates of HDI and IHDI are shown in Table 17.4 and are plotted in Figures 17.1, 17.2, and 17.3. Distribution of global HDI across the states is shown in Figure 17.4.

The main findings are:

India Human Development Status: Global context

1. Indian achievement in terms of the normalized HDI with reference to international goalposts is 0.504. The country falls short of the world average, which is 0.624 (UNDP 2010: 155). Thus, India belongs to the category of countries with 'Medium Human Development'.
2. HDI is the highest for Kerala (0.625) followed by Nagaland (0.609) and Mizoram (0.581) and the lowest for Odisha (0.442), Bihar (0.447), and Madhya Pradesh (0.451). Kerala along with the seven Northeastern states barring Assam, Punjab, Himachal Pradesh, Haryana, Maharashtra, Tamil Nadu, Karnataka, Gujarat, West Bengal, and Uttarakhand falls under the 'Medium HDI' category. The rest of the states (nine) fall in the 'Low HDI' club.
3. As per our estimates, India's rank on global HDI is 120th; those for different states ranges from 99th for Kerala (whose global HDI estimate places it between Botswana and the Republic of Moldova) to 133rd for Odisha (whose global HDI estimate places it between Myanmar and Yemen).
4. The average loss due to inequality is 32 per cent at the all-India level. It is the highest for Madhya Pradesh (36 per cent) and Chhattisgarh (35 per cent) and the lowest for Kerala (17 per cent). Loss due to inequality is higher than the national average (32 per cent) in Madhya Pradesh, Chhattisgarh, Uttar Pradesh, Rajasthan, Jharkhand, Odisha, Uttarakhand, and Arunachal Pradesh. These are the states which need serious attention in promoting access to education and health facilities to reduce inequalities in these dimensions and reduce the loss in human development.
5. Assam, Bihar, Gujarat, Jammu & Kashmir, Meghalaya, Mizoram, Odisha, Rajasthan, Sikkim, Tripura, and West Bengal improve their rankings after adjustment for inequality while Andhra Pradesh, Arunachal Pradesh, Chhattisgarh, Haryana, Madhya Pradesh, Maharashtra, Manipur, Nagaland, Uttarakhand, and Uttar Pradesh lose their ranks. This would mean that the former sub-set of states is doing relatively better with reference to the inequality dimension on human development.

Income Dimension

1. Income indicates the opportunities dimension of human well-being. Sixteen out of the 27 states fare as good as or better than the nation as a whole in terms of the sub-index for the income dimension (0.465).
2. Average loss because of inequality in income is 16 per cent at the all-India level; it is the highest for Maharashtra (19 per cent) followed by Tamil Nadu (17 per cent) and lowest for Manipur (4 per cent). Maharashtra, which ranks eighth in the country based on the income dimension index (Table 17.3), ranks 17th after the adjustment for inequality in income is made.

---

[8] See Kovacevic (2010) for a detailed methodology on derivation of the Atkinson's inequality index for the distribution of the expected age at death.

[9] We have to rely on these proxies because the life tables are only available for 16 major states. The other demographic indicator that could have some bearing on the sub-index for the health dimension and is available for the rest of the states is the infant mortality rate. We use this information and choose a state that is closest to Jammu & Kashmir in terms of the life expectancy and infant mortality rate. By this criterion, we find West Bengal as closest to Jammu & Kashmir and use the inequality index of the former as a proxy for the latter. The same procedure could be used for the seven states in Northeast India had the information on life expectancy for each of them been available.

Table 17.2 Key Indicators: States and All-India

State	PPP Income Per Capita (PPP 2008 $)	Life Expectancy at Birth (years) (2002–6)	Mean Years of Schooling (years) (2004–5)	School Life Expectancy (years) (2007–8)
Andhra Pradesh	3,398.76	64.40	3.06	9.66
Arunachal Pradesh	3,827.03	68.54	3.56	10.69
Assam	2,883.44	58.90	3.96	9.54
Bihar	2,161.80	61.60	2.97	9.58
Chhattisgarh	2,497.00	60.24	3.39	9.31
Gujarat	3,782.87	64.10	4.54	8.79
Haryana	4,574.51	66.20	4.74	9.68
Himachal Pradesh	4,168.39	67.00	4.88	11.05
Jammu & Kashmir	4,211.40	63.84	4.07	10.54
Jharkhand	2,516.41	63.03	3.32	9.68
Karnataka	3,269.76	65.30	3.95	9.75
Kerala	5,262.89	74.00	6.19	11.33
Madhya Pradesh	2,673.76	58.00	3.47	8.95
Maharashtra	3,913.14	67.20	5.12	9.86
Manipur	3,131.51	68.54	5.75	10.37
Meghalaya	3,545.56	68.54	4.47	10.20
Mizoram	4,612.06	68.54	6.04	10.06
Nagaland	5,632.43	68.54	6.75	10.55
Odisha	2,185.84	59.60	3.34	8.74
Punjab	4,885.12	69.40	5.12	9.80
Rajasthan	3,289.27	62.00	2.96	9.19
Sikkim	3,591.16	68.54	4.17	10.08
Tamil Nadu	3,835.05	66.20	4.79	10.57
Tripura	2,731.16	68.54	4.14	9.38
Uttar Pradesh	2,910.58	60.00	3.56	9.19
Uttarakhand	3,536.13	63.96	4.97	10.23
West Bengal	3,414.08	64.90	4.36	8.87
India	3,337.00	63.50	4.10	9.62

Source: Authors' estimates.

Education Dimension

1. All the states except the economically poorer ones of Bihar, Madhya Pradesh, Rajasthan, Odisha, and Uttar Pradesh (including the newly carved states of Chhattisgarh, Jharkhand, and Uttarakhand) and Assam and Arunachal Pradesh fare as good as or as better than the nation as a whole in terms of the sub-index for the education dimension.
2. The loss in the education component on account of inequality at the all-India level is 43 per cent. The loss is the highest in Uttar Pradesh, Rajasthan, and Jharkhand (46 per cent) and lowest in Mizoram (17 per cent) and Kerala (23 per cent).
3. Loss due to inequality is more than that at the national level in Karnataka, Haryana, Chhattisgarh, Uttarakhand, Arunachal Pradesh, Jammu & Kashmir, Andhra Pradesh, Bihar, Madhya Pradesh, Jharkhand, Rajasthan, and Uttar Pradesh.

Health Dimension

1. Kerala (0.854) ranks first, followed by Punjab (0.782) and the seven states in the Northeast (0.768 each);

Table 17.3 Estimates of Sub-indices by Dimension, with and without Adjustment for Inequality: International Goalposts

State	Income (x)			Education (y)			Health (z)		
	I_x	I_{Ix}	Loss	I_y	I_{Iy}	Loss	I_z	I_{Iz}	Loss
Andhra Pradesh	0.467	0.397	15.16	0.347	0.192	44.60	0.703	0.479	31.75
Arunachal Pradesh	0.486	0.433	10.86	0.393	0.220	44.12	0.768	0.473	38.39
Assam	0.442	0.404	8.58	0.392	0.258	34.21	0.616	0.379	38.39
Bihar	0.398	0.364	8.50	0.340	0.187	45.03	0.658	0.411	37.63
Chhattisgarh	0.420	0.356	15.33	0.358	0.202	43.56	0.637	0.363	42.91
Gujarat	0.484	0.413	14.64	0.403	0.243	39.70	0.698	0.475	31.91
Haryana	0.513	0.445	13.25	0.432	0.244	43.39	0.731	0.485	33.63
Himachal Pradesh	0.499	0.433	13.22	0.468	0.287	38.80	0.744	0.527	29.17
Jammu & Kashmir	0.500	0.454	9.35	0.418	0.233	44.16	0.694	0.482	30.48
Jharkhand	0.421	0.363	13.72	0.361	0.196	45.75	0.681	0.425	37.63
Karnataka	0.461	0.387	16.17	0.396	0.226	42.85	0.717	0.503	29.76
Kerala	0.535	0.449	16.07	0.534	0.410	23.25	0.854	0.764	10.54
Madhya Pradesh	0.430	0.365	15.10	0.355	0.194	45.24	0.601	0.343	42.91
Maharashtra	0.489	0.398	18.69	0.453	0.279	38.38	0.747	0.562	24.73
Manipur	0.455	0.435	4.39	0.492	0.310	37.00	0.768	0.473	38.39
Meghalaya	0.474	0.442	6.68	0.431	0.305	29.13	0.768	0.473	38.39
Mizoram	0.514	0.467	9.22	0.497	0.413	16.99	0.768	0.473	38.39
Nagaland	0.545	0.495	9.16	0.538	0.373	30.69	0.768	0.473	38.39
Odisha	0.399	0.341	14.71	0.345	0.199	42.18	0.627	0.380	39.31
Punjab	0.523	0.455	13.05	0.452	0.265	41.40	0.782	0.572	26.86
Rajasthan	0.462	0.409	11.53	0.333	0.179	46.07	0.665	0.400	39.79
Sikkim	0.476	0.422	11.28	0.413	0.265	35.92	0.768	0.473	38.39
Tamil Nadu	0.486	0.405	16.72	0.454	0.278	38.66	0.731	0.550	24.70
Tripura	0.434	0.386	10.95	0.397	0.252	36.61	0.768	0.473	38.39
Uttar Pradesh	0.444	0.384	13.35	0.365	0.195	46.48	0.633	0.384	39.33
Uttarakhand	0.473	0.417	12.03	0.454	0.256	43.71	0.696	0.422	39.33
West Bengal	0.468	0.396	15.44	0.397	0.238	39.89	0.710	0.494	30.48
India	0.465	0.389	16.37	0.400	0.229	42.80	0.688	0.452	34.29

Source: Authors' estimates.

Note: The symbol I_j denotes the dimension index for jth dimension and I_{Ij}, the corresponding inequality-adjusted index.

Madhya Pradesh (0.601) and Assam (0.616) are the last in terms of the sub-index for health.

2. Average loss due to inequality in health is 34 per cent. It is the highest in Chhattisgarh and Madhya Pradesh (43 per cent) and the lowest in Kerala (11 per cent).

A comparison of the three HDI dimensions indicates that the country's achievements in terms of the normalized indices, both with and without inequality adjustment, are better with respect to the health dimension than for HDI as a whole and this holds good for most of the states (Figure 17.4). Loss due to inequality is the highest with respect to the education dimension (43 per cent), followed by health (34 per cent), and income (16 per cent). In other words, the potential lost due to inequality is the highest in the education sector. The rank correlation with HDI across states is the highest for income, followed by education and health (Suryanarayana et al. 2011). Further, the rank correlations between different pairs of normalized indices are positive and significant implying that achievement/deprivation in different dimensions co-vary across state.

In comparison with countries across the world, there are marked differences in the distribution of human development outcomes in India (Suryanarayana et al. 2011). Box plot profiles for global HDI and IHDI for the Indian states

Table 17.4 Estimates of Global HDI and IHDI across States

State	HDI	IHDI	Ratio	Loss (%)	Rank HDI	Rank IHDI	Difference
Andhra Pradesh	0.485	0.332	0.685	31.55	19	20	−1
Arunachal Pradesh	0.527	0.356	0.675	32.55	13	16	−3
Assam	0.474	0.341	0.718	28.17	20	19	1
Bihar	0.447	0.303	0.679	32.05	26	24	2
Chhattisgarh	0.458	0.297	0.649	35.14	24	25	−1
Gujarat	0.514	0.363	0.705	29.50	15	13	2
Haryana	0.545	0.375	0.688	31.18	8	11	−3
Himachal Pradesh	0.558	0.403	0.722	27.81	5	5	0
Jammu & Kashmir	0.525	0.371	0.706	29.40	14	12	2
Jharkhand	0.470	0.312	0.663	33.66	21	21	0
Karnataka	0.508	0.353	0.696	30.44	18	18	0
Kerala	0.625	0.520	0.832	16.78	1	1	0
Madhya Pradesh	0.451	0.290	0.643	35.73	25	27	−2
Maharashtra	0.549	0.397	0.722	27.75	7	8	−1
Manipur	0.556	0.400	0.719	28.14	6	7	−1
Meghalaya	0.539	0.400	0.741	25.86	10	6	4
Mizoram	0.581	0.450	0.774	22.57	3	2	1
Nagaland	0.609	0.444	0.729	27.07	2	3	−1
Odisha	0.442	0.296	0.669	33.11	27	26	1
Punjab	0.569	0.410	0.720	28.03	4	4	0
Rajasthan	0.468	0.308	0.660	34.02	23	22	1
Sikkim	0.533	0.375	0.705	29.51	11	10	1
Tamil Nadu	0.544	0.396	0.727	27.27	9	9	0
Tripura	0.510	0.358	0.703	29.68	16	15	1
Uttar Pradesh	0.468	0.307	0.655	34.47	22	23	−1
Uttarakhand	0.531	0.356	0.670	33.03	12	17	−5
West Bengal	0.509	0.360	0.707	29.30	17	14	3
India	0.504	0.343	0.680	32.01			

Source: Authors' estimates.

Note: 'Difference' denotes the difference between the 'Rank HDI' and 'Rank IHDI' above, and therefore denotes the gain/loss in ranking due to inequality-adjustment.

vis-à-vis countries across the world indicate that while the upper quartile for IHDI is about the median for HDI across countries, even the upper extreme value for IHDI just falls short of the median for HDI across Indian states. Thus, inequality in the distribution of human development is distinctly pronounced in India in comparison with the world scenario. Similarly, while the plots for normalized indices across dimensions bring out a progressive increase in the median from income to education and to health across countries, the order is from education to income and finally, to health across the Indian states. In other words, education is one major human development dimension which calls for serious policy attention for reducing disparities in attainment. While for income, health, and HDI (and their inequality-adjusted indices) the country lies in the inter-quartile range of cross-country distribution, it is not the case with education. With regard to education, the country stands among the bottom 25 per cent of the countries in the world (Figure 17.5). The extent of inequality in human development in India is so much that while the adjustment for inequality made little difference to the distributional profile of normalized indices for education across countries, the same brought about a radical downward shift of the box plot for Indian states. Accordingly, loss due to inequality in education is 43 per cent for India but it is much less (28 per cent) in the world as a whole and the same due to inequality

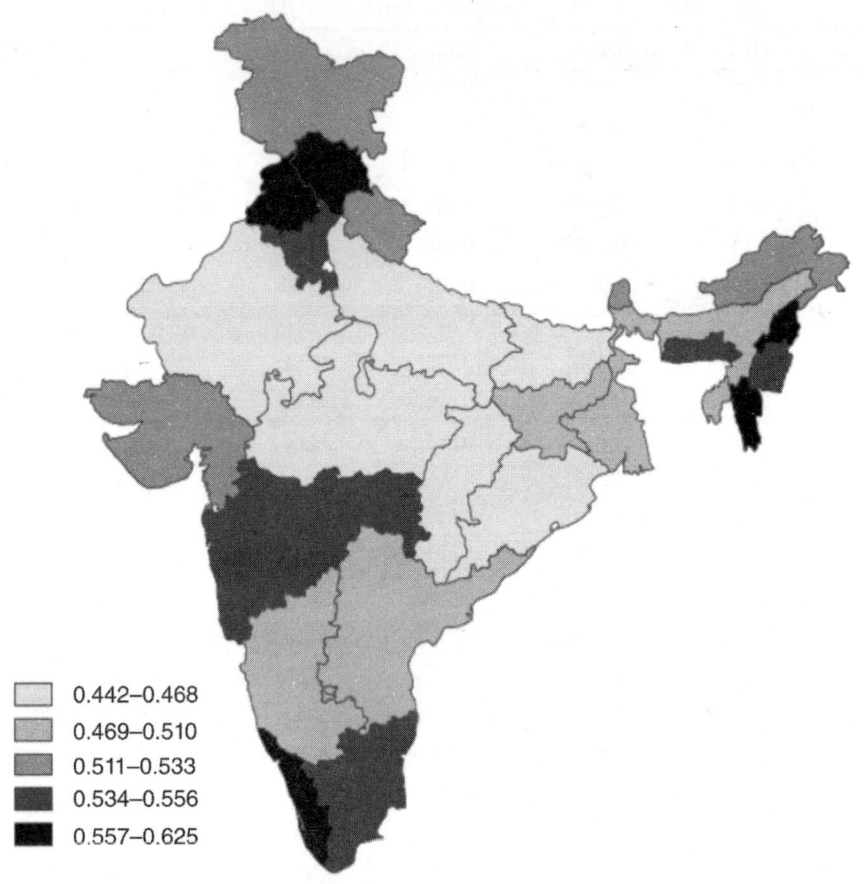

Figure 17.1 HDI across Indian States (International Goalposts)

Source: Authors' estimates.

in health is 34 per cent as compared to the world average of 21 (UNDP 2010: 155).

HDIs based on Domestic Goalposts

Normalized indices for different dimensions of human development with respect to domestic goalposts, as one would expect, throw up a profile very similar to the one based on global goalposts (Figure 17.6).[10] Since the change in goalposts does not affect the inequality-adjustment factor, the profiles of loss will remain unchanged.

Table 17.5 provides information on estimates of sub-indices and the inequality-adjusted sub-indices for the three different human development dimensions. Estimates for HDI and IHDI are shown in Table 17.6. The main findings are summarized below:

[10] Estimates of Spearman rank correlations between the two sets of indices based on alternative goalposts are positive and statistically significant, which corroborates this observation.

Aggregate HDI

1. The average achievement at the all-India level with reference to domestic goalposts is 0.576.
2. The profile of ranks across states is slightly different from the one observed for the profile based on international goalposts.

Income Dimension

1. Nagaland (0.987) ranks first in terms of the income dimension index followed by Kerala (0.953) and Punjab (0.915); the rank is the lowest for Bihar (0.498) and Odisha (0.504).
2. Remaining features remain unchanged.

Education Dimension

1. The education index is the highest for Kerala (0.915) followed by Nagaland (0.905) and Himachal Pradesh

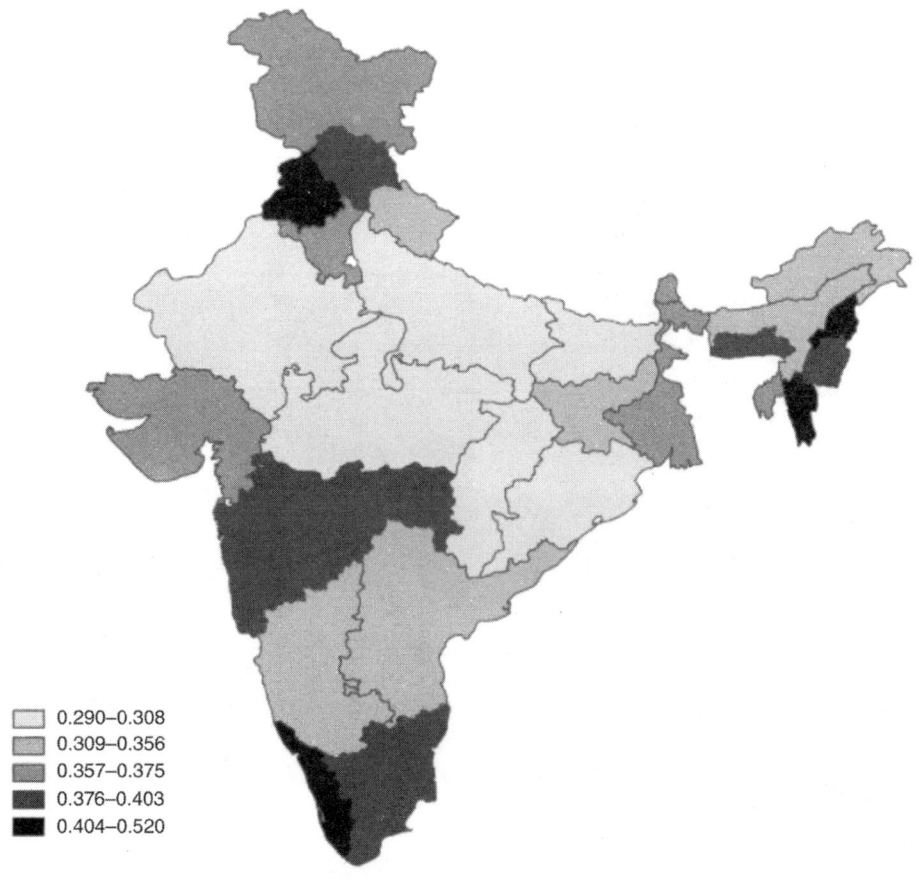

Figure 17.2 IHDI across Indian States (International Goalposts)

Source: Authors' estimates.

(0.790) and the lowest for Odisha (0.281) and Madhya Pradesh (0.337).

Health Dimension

1. Kerala (0.940) ranks first and Madhya Pradesh the last (0.294) in terms of the sub-index for health.

The results obtained from domestic goalposts differ from/tally with those from global ones in some respects. They are different in that India's achievement is better with respect to the income dimension than it is for HDI as a whole, which holds good both with and without inequality adjustment. They tally with global estimates in that the pair-wise rank correlations between the scores on different dimensions are positive and significant implying that achievement/deprivation in different dimensions co-vary across states (Table 17.7).

The relative ranking of each state under review could be examined in terms of inequality-adjusted, and unadjusted scores for the three dimensions as well as aggregate, which throws up eight different inter-state quartile-group profiles. Tabulations based on estimates in Tables 17.5 and 17.6 highlight the following features:

- Kerala is the only state in the country, which remains in 'Very High HD' with respect to all the dimensions, both with and without adjustment for inequality. In addition, Nagaland, Mizoram, and Punjab fare well by most of the indicators, with and without the adjustment for inequality.
- BIMAROU states (including the three states formed in 2000) and Assam generally belong to the 'Low HD' group by almost all the indicators, the same does not hold good for the other regions in the country. For instance, the four south Indian states, known for better levels of human development than the rest of the country, throw up a heterogeneous profile with Andhra Pradesh and Karnataka falling under 'Medium HD', Tamil Nadu mostly in 'High HD', and Kerala in 'Very High HD'. Similar is the profile for Northeastern India. A majority of the scores for Manipur, Mizoram, and

242 INDIA DEVELOPMENT REPORT

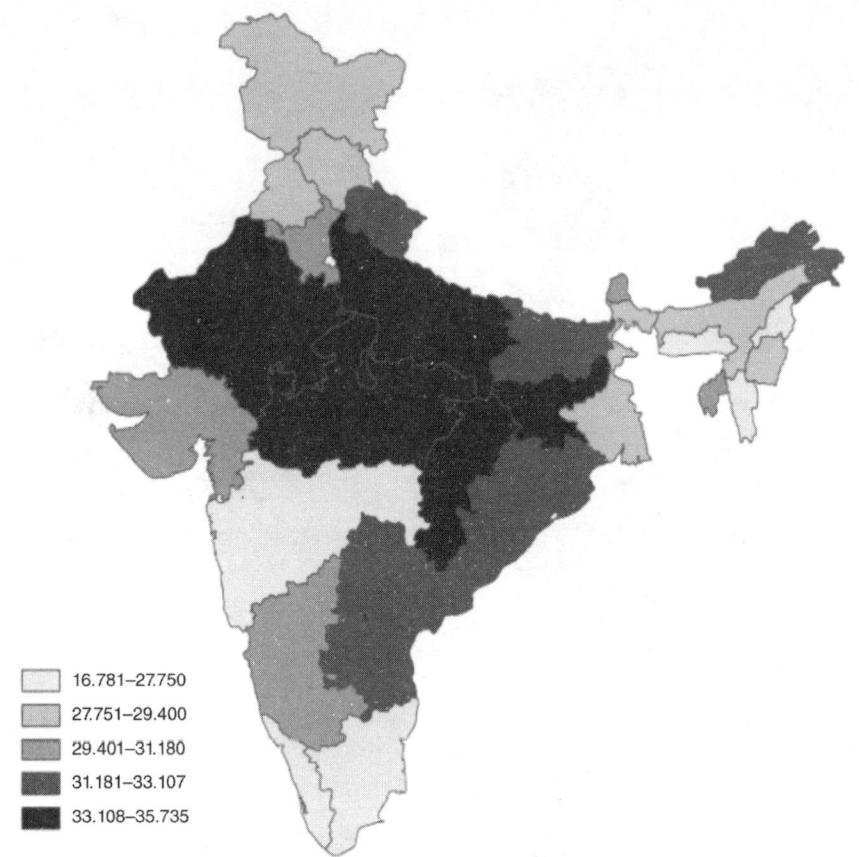

Figure 17.3 Loss in HDI due to Inequalities

Source: Authors' estimates.

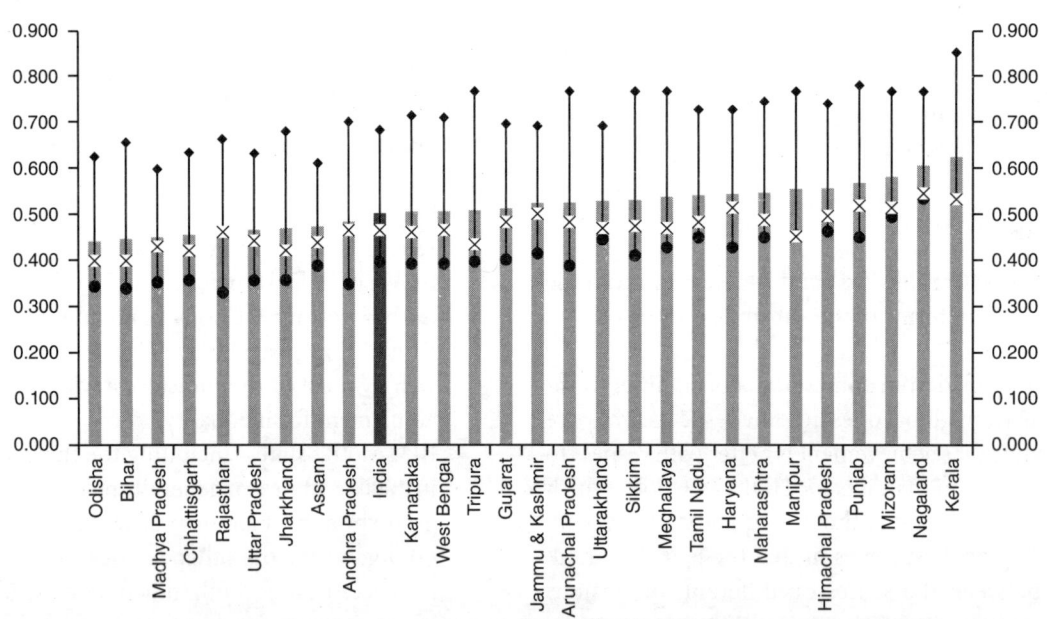

Figure 17.4 HDI and Its Dimensions: Indian States (International Goalposts)

Notes: (i) Vertical bars (light grey in colour for the states and dark grey for India) indicate HDI; dark black circles (inside the bars), the education dimension index; cross within white squares, the income dimension index; and dark black diamonds (happen to lie outside the bars), the health dimension index.

(ii) The states are arranged in ascending order of their HDIs.

Source: Authors' estimates.

PROMOTING HUMAN DEVELOPMENT IN INDIA 243

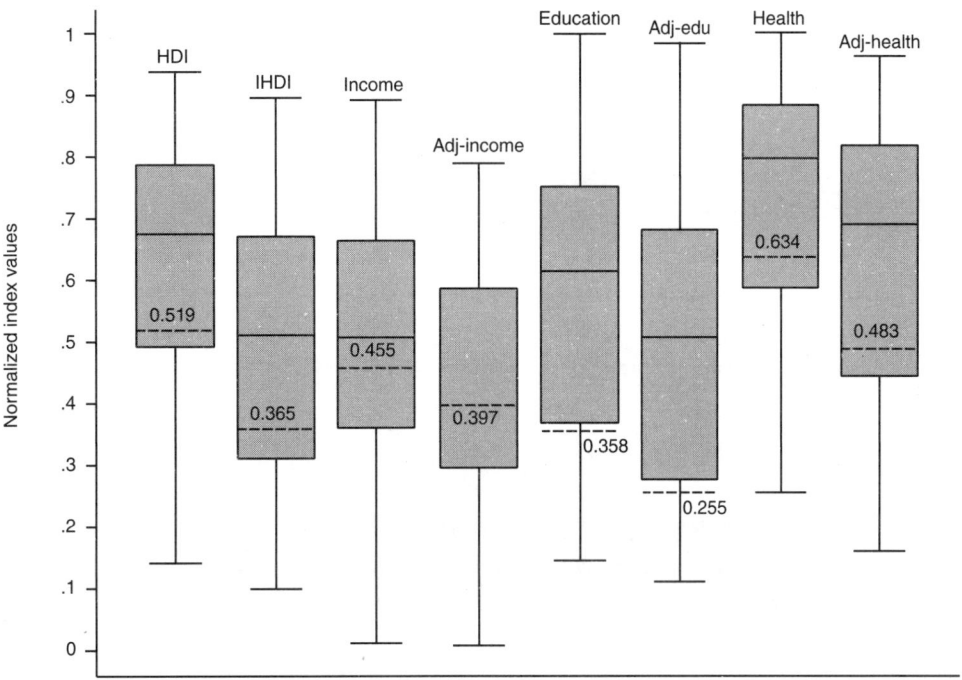

Figure 17.5 Distribution of HDI and Its Dimensions: Countries (International Goalposts)

Note: The dashed lines and the values indicated for each plot correspond to the value of index for India.
Source: Based on estimates from UNDP (2010).

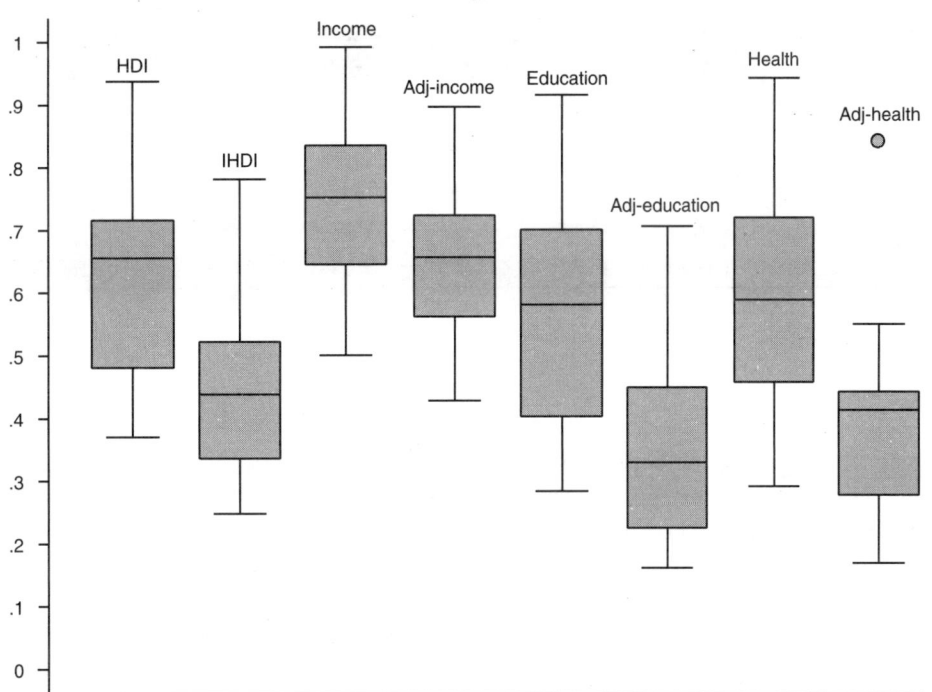

Figure 17.6 Profiles of HDI, IHDI, and Their Dimensions: Indian States (Domestic Goalposts)

Note: The dotted observation in cases of inequality-adjusted sub-index for health represents Kerala, which is an outlier among the Indian states.
Source: Authors' estimates.

Table 17.5 Estimates of Sub-indices by Dimension, with and without Adjustment for Inequality: Domestic Goalposts

State	Income (x)			Education (y)			Health (z)		
	I_x	I_{Ix}	Loss	I_y	I_{Iy}	Loss	I_z	I_{Iz}	Loss
Andhra Pradesh	0.729	0.619	15.16	0.426	0.236	44.60	0.552	0.377	31.75
Arunachal Pradesh	0.790	0.704	10.86	0.618	0.345	44.12	0.719	0.443	38.39
Assam	0.645	0.590	8.58	0.490	0.323	34.21	0.331	0.204	38.39
Bihar	0.498	0.456	8.50	0.404	0.222	45.03	0.440	0.274	37.63
Chhattisgarh	0.572	0.484	15.33	0.401	0.226	43.56	0.385	0.220	42.91
Gujarat	0.784	0.669	14.64	0.359	0.217	39.70	0.540	0.368	31.91
Haryana	0.881	0.764	13.25	0.578	0.327	43.39	0.625	0.415	33.63
Himachal Pradesh	0.834	0.723	13.22	0.790	0.484	38.80	0.657	0.466	29.17
Jammu & Kashmir	0.839	0.760	9.35	0.657	0.367	44.16	0.530	0.368	30.48
Jharkhand	0.576	0.497	13.72	0.455	0.247	45.75	0.497	0.310	37.63
Karnataka	0.710	0.595	16.17	0.526	0.301	42.85	0.589	0.414	29.76
Kerala	0.953	0.800	16.07	0.915	0.703	23.25	0.940	0.840	10.54
Madhya Pradesh	0.607	0.515	15.10	0.337	0.184	45.24	0.294	0.168	42.91
Maharashtra	0.801	0.652	18.69	0.644	0.397	38.38	0.665	0.501	24.73
Manipur	0.688	0.657	4.39	0.789	0.497	37.00	0.719	0.443	38.39
Meghalaya	0.751	0.701	6.68	0.648	0.459	29.13	0.719	0.443	38.39
Mizoram	0.885	0.804	9.22	0.754	0.626	16.99	0.719	0.443	38.39
Nagaland	0.987	0.897	9.16	0.905	0.627	30.69	0.719	0.443	38.39
Odisha	0.504	0.430	14.71	0.281	0.162	42.18	0.359	0.218	39.31
Punjab	0.915	0.795	13.05	0.632	0.370	41.40	0.754	0.552	26.86
Rajasthan	0.713	0.630	11.53	0.343	0.185	46.07	0.456	0.274	39.79
Sikkim	0.758	0.672	11.28	0.600	0.384	35.92	0.719	0.443	38.39
Tamil Nadu	0.791	0.659	16.72	0.735	0.451	38.66	0.625	0.471	24.70
Tripura	0.618	0.550	10.95	0.475	0.301	36.61	0.719	0.443	38.39
Uttar Pradesh	0.650	0.563	13.35	0.393	0.210	46.48	0.375	0.227	39.33
Uttarakhand	0.750	0.659	12.03	0.697	0.392	43.71	0.535	0.324	39.33
West Bengal	0.732	0.619	15.44	0.373	0.224	39.89	0.573	0.398	30.48
India	0.720	0.602	16.37	0.515	0.295	42.80	0.516	0.339	34.29

Note: See notes to Table 17.4.
Source: Authors' estimates.

Nagaland classify them among the better performing (High and Very High HD) categories whereas Tripura lags behind and falls into 'Low and Medium Categories'. The rest of the Northeast Indian states fall under the 'High HD' group.

SUM-UP

This study provided HDI and IHDI estimates for Indian states. IHDI estimates facilitate quantification of the potential lost due to inequality with respect to the different dimensions and hence help explain uneven human development attainments across Indian states. The findings show substantial loss in human development due to inequality in different dimensions across states. The potential lost due to inequalities is the highest in education among the three dimensions. The fact that inequalities in the education dimension are the highest is in consonance with the findings in the global context reported in the UNDP *Human Development Report 2010*. It calls for a focus specifically on areas and social groups that continue to have constraints in accessing education. Similarly, the inequalities are staggering in the case of health. Many studies have pointed out marked differences in access to healthcare and its utilization. In

Table 17.6 Estimates of HDI and IHDI across States: Domestic Goalposts

State	HDI	IHDI	Ratio	Loss (%)	Rank HDI	Rank IHDI	Difference
Andhra Pradesh	0.556	0.381	0.685	31.55	17	18	−1
Arunachal Pradesh	0.706	0.476	0.675	32.55	8	11	−3
Assam	0.471	0.338	0.718	28.17	22	20	2
Bihar	0.446	0.303	0.679	32.05	24	23	1
Chhattisgarh	0.445	0.289	0.649	35.14	25	25	0
Gujarat	0.534	0.376	0.705	29.50	19	19	0
Haryana	0.683	0.470	0.688	31.18	12	12	0
Himachal Pradesh	0.757	0.546	0.722	27.81	5	4	1
Jammu & Kashmir	0.664	0.468	0.706	29.40	13	13	0
Jharkhand	0.507	0.336	0.663	33.66	20	21	−1
Karnataka	0.604	0.420	0.696	30.44	15	15	0
Kerala	0.936	0.779	0.832	16.78	1	1	0
Madhya Pradesh	0.392	0.252	0.643	35.73	26	26	0
Maharashtra	0.700	0.506	0.722	27.75	10	9	1
Manipur	0.731	0.525	0.719	28.14	6	6	0
Meghalaya	0.705	0.522	0.741	25.86	9	7	2
Mizoram	0.783	0.606	0.774	22.57	3	3	0
Nagaland	0.863	0.629	0.729	27.07	2	2	0
Odisha	0.370	0.248	0.669	33.11	27	27	0
Punjab	0.758	0.546	0.720	28.03	4	5	−1
Rajasthan	0.481	0.317	0.660	34.02	21	22	−1
Sikkim	0.689	0.486	0.705	29.51	11	10	1
Tamil Nadu	0.714	0.519	0.727	27.27	7	8	−1
Tripura	0.595	0.419	0.703	29.68	16	16	0
Uttar Pradesh	0.458	0.300	0.655	34.47	23	24	−1
Uttarakhand	0.654	0.438	0.670	33.03	14	14	0
West Bengal	0.539	0.381	0.707	29.30	18	17	1
India	0.576	0.392	0.680	32.01			

Note: See notes to Table 17.4.
Source: Authors' estimates.

Table 17.7 Correlation between Ranks Based on Different Pairs of HDI and Its Sub-indices (Domestic Goalposts)

	HDI	IHDI	I_x	I_{Ix}	I_y	I_{Iy}	I_z	I_{Iz}
HDI	1							
IHDI	0.992*	1						
I_x	0.852*	0.842*	1					
I_{Ix}	0.875*	0.867*	0.959*	1				
I_y	0.907*	0.917*	0.708*	0.748*	1			
I_{Iy}	0.923*	0.943*	0.714*	0.757*	0.979*	1		
I_z	0.898*	0.892*	0.692*	0.726*	0.714*	0.775*	1	
I_{Iz}	0.908*	0.903*	0.742*	0.698*	0.753*	0.791*	0.930*	1

Note: See notes to Table 17.4. *indicates statistical significant correlation at the 5 per cent level.
Source: Authors' estimates

both education and health, not only is the attainment of people low but the extent of inequality, too, is high. Given the spectacular growth that the country has witnessed in the last decade, policies promoting economic growth need to be integrated with distributional dimensions of education and health. Thus, the findings provide useful policy insights calling for a strategy to promote human development by a distributive policy option that addresses inequalities across dimensions in different states in the country.

REFERENCES

Chaudhuri, Basudeb, Helene Chevrou-Severac, and Velayoudom Marimoutou (2007), 'Regional Disparities', in Kaushik Basu (ed.), *The Oxford Companion to Economics in India.* New Delhi: Oxford University Press, pp. 447–50.

Government of India [GoI] (1981), *A Technical Note on the Sixth Plan of India (1980–85).* New Delhi: Planning Commission.

———. (2002), *National Human Development Report 2001.* New Delhi: Planning Commission.

———. (2006a), *Level and Pattern of Consumer Expenditure, 2004–05, NSS 61st Round (July 2004– June 2005),* Report No. 508(61/1.0/1). New Delhi: National Sample Survey Organization, Ministry of Statistics and Programme Implementation.

———. (2006b), *Status of Education and Vocational Training in India 2004–05.* Report No. 517 (61/10/3). New Delhi: National Sample Survey Organization, Ministry of Statistics and Programme Implementation.

———. (2006c), *Population Projections for India and States 2001–2026.* Report of the Technical Group on Population Projections Constituted by the National Commission on Population. New Delhi: Office of the Registrar General & Census Commissioner.

GoI. (2008), *SRS Based Abridged Life Tables 2002–2006.* New Delhi: Office of the Registrar General, Ministry of Home Affairs.

———. (2010), *Education in India: 2007–8 Participation and Expenditure.* Report No. 532 (64/25.2/1). New Delhi: National Sample Survey Organization, Ministry of Statistics and Programme Implementation.

———. (2012), *Economic Survey 2011–2012.* New Delhi: Oxford University Press.

Institute of Applied Manpower Research (2011), *India Human Development Report 2011.* New Delhi: Oxford University Press.

Kovacevic, Milorad (2010), 'Measurement of Inequality in Human Development—A Review', *Human Development Research Paper 2010/35.* New York: UNDP.

Ram, F. and S.K. Mohanty (2005), *State of Human Development in States and Districts of India.* Mumbai: International Institute of Population Sciences.

Sen, Amartya (1989), 'Indian Development: Lessons and Non-Lessons', *Daedalus,* 118(4): 369–92.

———. (1998), 'Mortality as an Indicator of Economic Success and Failure', *Economic Journal,* 108(446): 1–25.

Suryanarayana, M.H., Ankush Agrawal, and K. Seeta Prabhu (2011), 'Inequality-adjusted Human Development Index for India's States', Discussion Paper. New Delhi: United Nations Development Programme.

Thompson, James R. (2011), *Empirical Model Building: Data, Models, and Reality* (Second edition). New Jersey: John Wiley & Sons, Inc.

United Nations Development Programme [UNDP] (1990), *Human Development Report 1990.* New York: Oxford University Press.

———. (2010), *Human Development Report 2010.* New York: Palgrave Macmillan.

18

Challenges for Right to Education in India

Preet Rustagi

The education scenario in India has been improving in terms of more enrolments and better attainment levels over time, thus narrowing some of the disparities facing the disadvantaged and hitherto excluded social groups, girls, and remote habitations and locations. With the Right of Children to Free and Compulsory Education (RTE) Act, the determination and resolve of the government to entitle every child to elementary education has been reiterated. Yet, the roadmap set out for RTE cannot be met only with financial and physical inputs. It requires addressing some structural concerns without which the move towards quality education for all children may remain difficult.

The primacy of education for human development is well established for its intrinsic and instrumental value. The influence of education within the social sector is the most widespread with implications for all types of human development outcomes (Drèze and Sen 2002) and feedback loops of these further serve as inputs to ameliorate the educational outcomes further (Mehrotra and Delamonica 2007).

The demographic change witnessed in India is gradually moving from a bottom-heavy population to an economy that is middle-heavy (GoI 2012). A very high proportion of India's population is still young (with the proportion of children under 18 years being nearly 40 per cent of the population), and will continue to be so in the near future. Retention in school education together with efforts to improve the quality and effectiveness of education is a critical factor for the demographic advantage being translated into returns—economic, social, and political. The gains made at the primary education levels over the previous decades lend confidence to the feasibility of ensuring universal coverage if appropriate approaches and policy measures are adopted with conviction.

While the issues of concern for education as a whole are currently one of access, equity, inclusion, and quality, higher education in India has been in the limelight for issues of financing, management, accountability, and regulation. The current debates of privatization and public–private partnerships raise these issues for they have implications for the quality and ethics of education. To some extent these concerns are relevant also for elementary schooling. This chapter focuses on elementary schooling since it forms the base of the educational edifice. Efforts to ensure universal elementary education have recorded gains amidst many gaps and challenges. Those who miss out on schooling in the early years are often affected by this shortcoming during their lifetime.

After the introduction, the next section briefly mentions the policies and schemes that have been operational. It lays out the roadmap for RTE with emphasis on some of its dimensions. The next section provides a brief account of the achievements and shortfalls in the spheres of school education in terms of literacy rates, current attendance, availability and access to schools, expansion of schools and the facilities therein, and the persistent inequalities, which although being bridged, continue to ail India's educational profile. Some of the issues and constraints that remain in the context of the universalization of elementary education are discussed in the next section in which the causes for non-enrolment and poor retention/dropouts/discontinuation are discussed alongside opportunity costs of child labour, school systems and management, the issue of affordability of education, teachers, quality of education, and relationships between agents. The final section summarizes the challenges and highlights a few suggestions for the universalization of elementary education.

POLICY FRAMEWORK AND PROGRAMMES FOR SCHOOL EDUCATION—BROAD CONTOURS

This section dwells briefly on major education-related policies and schemes in India while emphasizing the markers of change over the recent past. The Constitution of India in Article 45 under the Directive Principles of State Policy recognizes the importance of ensuring universal basic education for all children up to the age of 14 years. Subsequently, many documents, including every Five Year Plan, the 1968 National Policy on Education (NPE), and the 1986 National Policy on Education (revised in1992) have attempted to refine India's efforts at Universal Elementary Education (UEE).

There were important constitutional amendments as well that intended to give a boost to elementary education. The 42nd amendment to the Constitution in 1976 brought education, which was largely a state responsibility, on to the concurrent list and made universalizing elementary education the responsibility of both the central and state governments.

In 2002, the government took another significant step by making elementary education a fundamental right through the 86th constitutional amendment. Sarva Shiksha Abhiyan (SSA) was launched in 2001–2 to universalize elementary education. Prior to SSA, there were efforts such as the Operation Blackboard,[1] District Primary Education Programme (DPEP),[2] and so on.

[1] Operation Blackboard (OB) emerged out of the 1986 NPE, and was set up in 1987–8 with the aim of improving facilities in primary schools and thereby managing better retentions. The provisions specified were ensuring a building with at least two all-weather rooms and separate toilets for boys and girls; at least two teachers per school, with one of them a female as far as possible; essential teaching material, and so on. The scope of OB was enlarged to three teachers and classrooms for the primary stage, and subsequently, also extended to upper primary levels in 1992.

[2] DPEP was initiated in 1993–4 in a few districts across seven states and later spread to a wider geographical area in 18 states with the objective of ensuring universal primary education aimed at reducing dropouts to less than 10 per cent; increasing learning achievements by at least 25 per cent over a measured baseline level and ensuring basic literacy and numeracy competencies; and reducing gaps in educational

The Mahila Samkhya (MS) programme was established with a broader mandate than mere literacy with an endeavour to empower socially and economically marginalized women through mobilizing and organizing women's collectives. MS has been functioning since the late 1980s and the collectives have started to federate. Two other schemes to enhance girls' education that were launched around 2003–4 are the National Programme for Education of Girls at Elementary Level (NPEGEL) and the Kasturba Gandhi Balika Vidyalaya (KGBV). Other schemes implemented with specific objectives to improve the outreach of schooling to remote pockets and backward sections belonging to Scheduled Castes (SCs), Scheduled Tribes (STs), Other Backward Castes (OBCs), and minorities have been implemented in the new millennium.

The 2005 National Curriculum Framework (NCF) deserves mention in this section since it marks a prominent shift in the thinking and approach recommended as a plan for the implementation of educational aims. The NCF focuses on the learner and advocates for a more child-centred approach to education. The methods of teaching or teacher transactions within classrooms must also be made flexible, keeping this in mind. The curriculum needs to be made more locally relevant and in a manner to allow for plural understandings. Subsequently, through a detailed plan of action, textbooks were prepared for different grades over a period of three years.

Efforts to mainstream children with special needs (CWSN) in regular schools were made in SSA and during the Eleventh Five Year Plan. The endeavour in the Twelfth Five Year Plan would be to identify the 'hidden' CWSN and develop human resources for support services, infrastructure, and material support for inclusive education. This still remains a weak spot.

With the passing of the Right of Children to Free and Compulsory Education Act (RTE) in 2009, a legal obligation to ensure elementary education to all children in the age group 6–14 years is cast on the central and state governments. This marks the movement of India towards adopting a right-based framework in the sphere of universal elementary education. This legislation implies that every child has a right to full-time elementary education of satisfactory and equitable quality in a formal school as specified by set norms and standards. The RTE Act aims to address the persisting problems that prevent universal and effective coverage of elementary education in India. Among these are shortfalls in universal retention, reaching the unreached, and most difficult to reach sections and addressing the quality concerns.

outcomes of enrolments, dropouts, and learning across gender and social groups to less than 5 per cent.

The government has instituted many schemes and incentive measures to encourage universal cover of at least elementary education, but also beyond for completing schooling: mid-day meals and the pre-schooling element of the Integrated Child Development Services (ICDS) are the two schemes which have been universal in their spread and outreach. Other schemes include free distribution of textbooks and uniforms, student scholarships, and so on. Some of these schemes have been beneficial for the country as a whole, especially in terms of the implications that these efforts have made on the transformation of the demand for education. All reports/studies and data over the last two decades reflect the growing demand for basic education as parents and guardians recognize the importance of education and aspire towards educating their children. Infrastructural facilities have improved over the period, with gross enrolment becoming almost universal, dropout rates declining even for girls at the primary level, and many more teachers being appointed.

The capacity of India to provide education for all at the school level, that is, all children of ages 6–14 years and also those who are 15–17 years old, depends on a range of factors such as school availability; infrastructure; access dimensions; personnel, especially teachers; curriculum and pedagogy; book banks, laboratories, and playgrounds; teaching learning facilities and materials; and related aspects as reflected in the outcomes.

On similar lines to SSA, another scheme was launched in 2009—the Rashtriya Madhyamik Shiksha Abhiyan (RMSA)—extending universalization of education to the 14–18 year olds. It is guided by the principles of universal access, equality and social justice, relevance and development of curricular, and structural aspects. The vision for secondary education is good-quality education made available, accessible, and affordable to all young persons in the ages of 14–18 years.

However, unless all children of 6–14 years are in school, their continuation for further education towards secondary and higher education obviously remains limited to that extent. Also, it need hardly be reiterated that universalization of elementary education is feasible only if primary and subsequently, upper primary education is inclusive and does not miss out any children, especially those belonging to a social group, community, caste, class, or gender. The focus of this chapter is, therefore, primarily on elementary education.

Roadmap Set Out for RTE

As per the roadmap laid down, by 31 March 2013, that is, a timeframe of three years, neighbourhood schools have to be established. Provision of school infrastructure, all-weather school buildings, one teacher per classroom, and various other infrastructure such as an office-cum-store-cum-head teacher room, toilets, drinking water facilities, barrier-free access, library, playground, and fencing or boundary walls, need to be established in the neighbourhood schools. In addition, a prescribed pupil-teacher ratio (PTR) must also be attained. Training of untrained teachers has been assigned a time period of five years. This requires institutional restructuring and capacity enhancement to enroll additional persons for training since existing capacities are fairly limited.

Efforts to revamp SSA and implement RTE are guided by the following principles—holistic approach to education based on the interpretations of NCF 2005, which has implications for curriculum, teacher education, educational planning, and management; equity, access, gender concerns, centrality of teacher, moral compulsion rather than punitive processes, and moving towards a convergent and integrated system of educational management in all states as speedily as is feasible. The major challenge will be in the implementation of quality interventions and other related provisions.

ACHIEVEMENTS AND REMAINING CHALLENGES OVER THE SSA PERIOD

Near universal coverage in the primary stages has been achieved, although challenges remain in upper primary education onwards in attaining the goals of universal enrolment and retention as defined by SSA as well. The positive changes noted over the years may be summarized in five points: expansion of elementary schools—numerical and spatial; near universal levels of access and enrolment at the primary stages; reduction in the number of out-of-school children; narrowing of the gender gap in elementary education; and percentage of SC/ST children enrolled in schools being proportionate to their population. See Box 18.1 for achievements over the SSA period.

The status of education in India reflects the progress made and the challenges that still remain. Amidst narrowing gaps, there are certain persistent inequalities. Literacy rates and attendance have been improving, as have school availability and facilities across locations, yet variations and disparities prevail.

Status of Education in India

The improvements are reflected in higher literacy rates among Indians, and more emphatically among women and the other disadvantaged social groups, including Muslims among the minorities. Other parameters which also display positive developments are a gradual upward movement of the proportion of students in higher education and in

> **Box 18.1** Achievements over the SSA Period
>
> Primary school indicators are mostly positive and reflect the efforts made at multiple levels to ensure Universal Primary Education (UPE). With a decade of the mission to universalize elementary education (Sarva Shiksha Abhiyan), the impact on enrolment and to an extent even retention up to the primary level of schooling is witnessed. Upper primary or middle schooling still remains a challenge in many ways, especially in certain states and among some social groups much more than in others.
>
> A cumulative set of statistics provided by the latest *Economic Survey 2011–12* reports the additions made over the SSA period:
>
> 334,149 new primary and upper primary schools have been opened,
> 267,209 school buildings and 1,410,937 additional classrooms constructed,
> 212,233 drinking water facilities, and 477,263 toilets have been provided,
> Supply of free textbooks to 8.77 crore children on an annual basis, and
> In-service training to 19.23 lakh teachers.
>
> *Source*: GoI (2012: 320).

professional courses. Nearly 11 per cent of India's population is enrolled for higher education. While this is way lower than other countries there has been a noteworthy increase over time.

However, given the fact that only a small proportion still manage to reach the higher stages of education, the concern is to ensure that all children attain schooling at least up to the elementary stages. The pursuit to ensure equity, inclusion, and quality requires the basic education levels to improve and become universal.

Literacy Rates

Upward shifts in literacy rates are noted clearly over the last four census decades as well as in the two rounds of NSS (see Tables 18.1 and 18.2). As per Census 2011, the literacy rate was 74 per cent. This increased by 9 points from 65 per cent in 2001. It is noteworthy that female literacy rates recorded an increase of almost 12 per cent, while male literacy rates rose by only 7 per cent over the decade.

Table 18.1 Effective Literacy Rates in India

Year	Effective Literacy Rates (+7 Years)		
1981	43.6	56.4	29.8
1991	52.2	64.1	39.3
2001	64.8	75.3	53.7
2011	74.0	82.1	65.5

Source: Premi and Das (2012).

Table 18.2 Effective Literacy Rates by Social Group, and Muslims—Rural/Urban

	Year	Social Group				Muslims	All
		SC	ST	OBC	Others		
Rural							
Males	1999–2000	58.8	53.8	67.8	78.1	61.4	67.8
	2007–8	70.6	69.3	77.7	84.6	71.7	77.0
Females	1999–2000	33.6	30.1	41.1	56.7	42.1	43.4
	2007–8	49.9	47.8	55.4	68.8	55.0	56.7
Persons	1999–2000	46.6	46.6	54.8	67.7	52.1	56.0
	2007–8	60.5	58.8	66.7	76.9	63.5	67.0
Urban							
Males	1999–2000	76.0	78.1	83.5	91.4	76.7	86.5
	2007–8	83.1	86.0	88.3	93.8	80.9	89.9
Females	1999–2000	55.7	61.2	66.4	81.0	62.2	72.3
	2007–8	66.1	69.0	74.6	85.5	68.8	78.0
Persons	1999–2000	66.2	70.0	75.3	86.5	69.8	79.8
	2007–8	74.9	78.0	81.7	89.9	75.1	84.3

Source: IAMR and Planning Commission (2011); based on NSS 55th and 64th Rounds.

The gender gap has been declining over time, although it has not been eliminated. A similar change is noted in rural–urban differences, although rural literacy rates remain lower consistently, with ST girls being the worst off. The converging trend of literacy rates across social categories and states in India is discussed in the *India Human Development Reports 2011* (IAMR and Planning Commission 2011).

In spite of the improvements in literacy levels, the number of illiterates in India remains substantial. According to the UNESCO *Global Monitoring Report 2006* (p. 284–6), India's share of adult (15 plus years) illiterates was 35 per cent (that is, 267 million) among global illiterates (771 million) during 2000–4.

The previous decades from 1961 to 2001 witnessed an increase in the number of illiterates in India. However, during the last decade, the absolute numbers of illiterates have declined by 31 million between 2001 and 2011. In 2011, the absolute number of illiterates was 273 million persons above the age of seven years, with 97 million males and almost double 176 million females (Figure 18.1). This decline can be attributed to SSA's efforts and the growing demand for education across all people in India.

Regional and locational variations are, however, tremendous and are discussed in a subsequent sub-section on persistent inequities.

Years of Schooling

While the number of literates is increasing even among women and socially backward sections, what is of pertinence is educational attainment in terms of years of schooling or the level of education for its impact on the economy or gains in terms of returns to education.

On an average, the years of schooling for the population above seven years remains as low as four years (see Table 18.3). There has been a gradual improvement with the younger generations completing primary schooling of five years and studying beyond that as well. This indicator reiterates relatively poor educational attainments among STs, SCs, and Muslims (see Table 18.3). Many among the population are near-illiterates, since so few years of education and subsequently, discontinuation leads to loss of learning.

Table 18.3 Mean Year of Schooling

Year	Rural	Urban	Combined
1999–2000	2.7	5.5	3.4
2007–8	3.5	6.2	4.2
Social Group			
SC	2.9	4.6	3.2
ST	2.6	5.2	2.8
OBC	3.5	5.6	3.9
Others	4.6	7.3	5.7

Source: NSS 55th and 64th Rounds; IAMR and Planning Commission (2011).

Note: For population in the age group of 7 years and above.

Participation and Current Attendance

Even among the younger persons of 5–29 years—47 per cent of the country's population—14 per cent are illiterate,

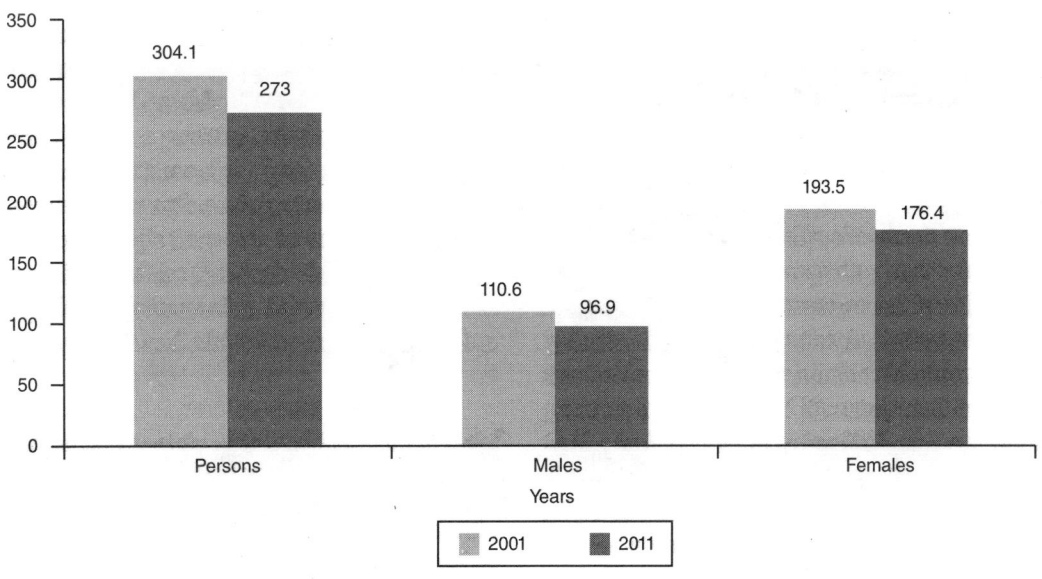

Figure 18.1 Number of Illiterates in India (in millions)

Source: Census of India (various years); Premi and Das (2012).

while a majority (53 per cent) are literate but only up to primary levels. Only 15 per cent each are at the middle and secondary levels. The graduates and above category is only 3 per cent (see Figure 18.2).

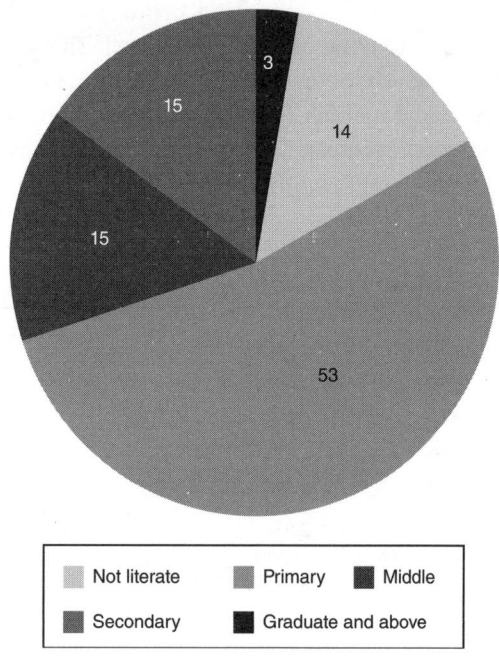

Figure 18.2 Education Status of 5–29 Year Age Group in India
Source: NSS 64th Round.

A relatively smaller proportion of 13 per cent of the 6–14 year-olds are enrolled but do not attend any educational institute. Among the 5–29-year-olds, only 52 per cent are currently attending any educational institution. Adults dropping out is often associated with the desire or need for labour market participation.

However, the out-of-participation group of persons comprises not only adults but also children. Age-specific attendance ratios reveal that while only 1 per cent (among of the 25–29 years group) are participating in education, the proportion is 18 per cent for those persons belonging to the 18–24 years group. Figure 18.3 gives primary and upper primary levels of education, where more than four-fifths of the children are attending schools. Among the 15–17-year-olds, only 59 per cent are reported to be attending any educational institute.

Variations in attendance across social groups remain (Table 18.4). As is well known, ST children face the most deprivation in terms of school attendance even among elementary school age years. By the time these ST children reach adolescence (15–17 years), a bulk of them, especially boys, are found working and therefore out of school (Rustagi et al. 2011). A similar scenario of joining the labour force is noted for the other social groups, especially among the economically backward segments, although in relatively lower proportions.

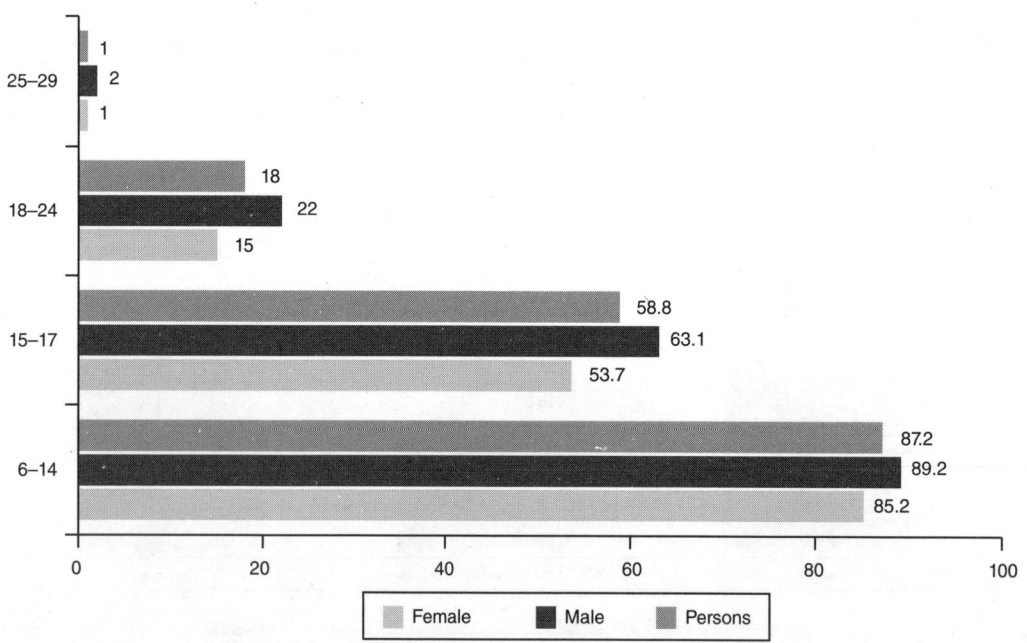

Figure 18.3 Age-specific Attendance Ratio by Age Group
Source: NSS 64th Round.

Table 18.4 Current Attendance by Age and Social Group

Social Group	6–14	15–17
ST	82.4	46.2
SC	84.1	51.7
OBC	87.1	58.4
Others	91.3	67.8
Total	87.2	58.8

Source: Estimates from NSS 64th Round.

Education as a whole should be developed as an infrastructure for the social and economic growth of the country. The issues of concern in the context of education relate to ensuring access—physical, social, and economic. Management and financial aspects are also critical. The following section examines the availability and expansion of school facilities which display the achievements over the SSA period.

Availability and Expansion of Schools and Facilities

Over the SSA period, with additional schools/classrooms being added at the elementary levels, the number of primary schools increased from 6.02 lakh in 2002–3 to 8.10 lakh by 2009–10 (Mehta 2011; MHRD 2011). The introduction of additional classrooms and upgradation of levels from primary to upper primary has witnessed a decline in the percentage of primary only schools among all elementary schools while increasing the share of the upper primary schools (see Table 18.5). Upper primary schools increased from 6 to 10 per cent over the same period (Mehta 2011).

Table 18.5 Percentage of Schools Established between 2002–3 to 2008–9

% of Total Schools by Category	Rural	Urban	Total
Primary only	18.29	16.55	18.13
Primary with upper primary	8.42	13.80	9.46
Primary with upper primary & secondary/hr secondary	13.39	8.73	11.62
Upper primary only	35.39	12.60	33.29
Upper primary & secondary/HR secondary	9.88	8.60	9.58
All schools (%)	17.81	13.91	17.31
Total number of new schools established *	199832	22672	222534

Note: *Schools may not add up due to non-responses.
Source: Mehta (2011: 31).

Information from District Information System for Education (DISE) gives a picture of the higher proportion of upper primary schools established between 2002–3 and 2008–9. What is noteworthy is that the coverage of upper primary schools in rural areas has been much more.

With the expansion in the number of schools, enrolments have also been increasing over the years. Eight million additional children were enrolled at the elementary level over three years from 2006–7 to 2009–10 (Table 18.6).

Table 18.6 Some Education-related Statistics

	2006–7	2009–10
Primary schools	7.79 lakh	8.10 lakh
Upper primary schools	4.17 lakh	4.94 lakh
Primary enrolment	132 million	133 million
Upper primary enrolment	47.5 million	54.5 million
Elementary enrolment	180 million	188 million

Source: NUEPA (2011).

With the building of additional schools over time there was near universal access to schools in terms of availability of primary level educational facilities within a proximate distance (see Table 18.7). The situation is not the same at the upper primary level, especially in rural areas, which is where a bulk of the students live and study.

Table 18.7 Distance of School

Sector	Less than 1 km	1–2 km	2–3 km	3–5 km	> 5 km
Primary	92	6.6	1.1	0.2	0.1
Upper primary	67.6	16.3	9.5	4.4	2.3
Secondary	41.6	18.2	15.7	12	12.5

Source: NSSO 64th Round (2007–8).

Nearly 7 per cent of the upper primary level schools are located beyond 3 km. Access in urban areas is relatively better than that in rural areas. Some of the gaps between rural–urban areas are gradually declining with the expansion of schools over time.

In areas where establishing schools is unviable for governments, there are proposals for alternative schooling through community initiatives such as under the Education Guarantee Scheme (EGS). Tilak (2009) raises the question whether communities can muster enough resources and whether they will be in a position to provide the much-needed school education.

Access for areas not having schools within a proximate distance are further aggravated by a lack of or inadequate infrastructural facilities such as roads, transport avenues, and so on. This is more so for children belonging to economically weaker sections, since these factors entail monetary cost implications if daily transport is involved to reach the school. The impact is of particular significance for ST, SC, and Muslim girls, for instance.

School Facilities

Facilities within schools have also been improving over time. Nevertheless, much remains to be achieved in this respect. Table 18.8 provides the number of schools which have various facilities and how the scenario has changed over the years.

Table 18.8 School Facilities Over the Years

Schools Having	2005–6	2006–7	2007–8	2008–9
Drinking water	83.1	84.9	86.8	87.8
Common toilet	52.4	58.1	62.7	66.8
Girls' toilet	37.4	42.6	50.6	53.6
Computer	10.7	13.4	14.3	14.1
Ramp	17.1	26.6	34.4	40.4
Kitchen shed (government and aided)	—	29.4	36.1	43.4
Electricity connection	—	33.2	33.3	35.6
Book bank	47.7	48.4	49.5	47.8
School development grant received	71.3	68.9	68.9	79.7
TLM grant received	67.9	66.6	61.8	71.5

Source: NUEPA (2011).

Improvements in providing girls' toilets have been remarkable—from 37 per cent in 2005–6 to 54 per cent in 2008–9. Yet in 2009–10, 4.7 lakh schools required girls' toilets (for this and other requirements, see Table 18.9). There are very few schools which have computers, ramps, kitchen sheds, book banks etc. Variations across rural–urban areas and across states are tremendous.

Table 18.9 Number of Schools Requiring Infrastructure Facilities in 2009–10 (in lakh)

Girl's toilet	4.7
Boy's toilet	2.7
Drinking water	0.7
Ramps	4.9
Boundary wall	5.4
Playground	5.4
Library	4.7
Additional classrooms	4.9

Source: NUEPA (2011).

The average number of classrooms also varies across types of school management. As compared to rural areas, urban schools have a relatively better position with more classrooms on an average. Rural areas have four classrooms, while urban areas have 7.6 classrooms on an average. Average rooms in private schools are also similar to the urban average of 7.5 rooms.

The schools are receiving grants but not in time as reported by the latest *Annual Status of Education Report* (ASER 2012). This affects the ability to utilize the grants for intended purposes.

Persistent Inequalities

In spite of the gains, many gaps remain, including persistent inequalities such as locational variations, social group differences, and gender disparities. Although some of these gaps are being bridged thanks to positive developments, these challenges will continue to affect RTE attaining its goalposts. Apart from these, the other challenges for RTE are social, economic, and physical access; school structure and management; teachers and training; and relationships and attitudes among agents.

Locational Variations

Rural–urban variations highlight the lower educational status in villages. Two illustrative cases of how varied the situation across locations is: (i) state-wise children currently attending schools, and (ii) district-wise literacy rates.

(i) Children currently attending schools across states

As per the 2007–8 NSS 64th Round, only 86 per cent of 6–14-year-olds have been attending school in rural areas, while the proportion in urban locations is 91 per cent. Across all states, Bihar in rural India and Uttar Pradesh in urban areas reported in 2007–8 the lowest proportion of children attending schools.

The percentage of children who have been attending schools is 87 per cent for the 6–14-year-olds, while it is only 59 per cent among the 15–17-year-olds. A similar scenario is witnessed in almost all the states, but with variations.

Attendance rates below the all-India average are recorded in states where poverty levels and/or the share of the ST population is high. States with low current attendance levels for children in elementary school ages (6–14 years) as per the NSS 64th Round are Bihar (75 per cent), UP (84 per cent), Odisha (85 per cent), Rajasthan (85 per cent), Arunachal Pradesh, Jharkhand and West Bengal (86 per cent each), and Gujarat (87 per cent) (see Appendix Table A18.1).

The picture varies for children in the older age cohort of 15–17 years slightly with Odisha (41 per cent), Gujarat (46 per cent), Bihar (52 per cent), Madhya Pradesh (53 per cent),

West Bengal (54 per cent), Andhra Pradesh (56 per cent), and Jharkhand/Uttar Pradesh (57 per cent each).

(ii) District-level Variations

The profile of literacy across the 640 districts in the country is disparate, with 21 districts reporting more than 90 per cent literates, while at the other end there are 59 districts which have less than 60 per cent literates (see Table 18.10). While Bihar has the lowest literacy rate and Purnia district in the state is the worst, it is interesting to note that the worse districts in the country recording a below 50 per cent literacy rate are in other states such as Madhya Pradesh, Chhattisgarh, Odisha, Uttar Pradesh, and Jharkhand (see Table 18.11). These are largely tribal-dominated areas.

Table 18.10 Distribution of Districts in 2011 by Literacy Rates

Literacy Rates	Persons	Males	Females
>90	21	105	17
81–90	158	284	59
71–90	229	194	141
61–70	173	46	191
51–60	49	10	149
Up to 50	10	1	83
Total	640	640	640

Source: Premi and Das (2012).

Table 18.11 Listing of Districts with Below 50 Literacy Rates

Rank	District	State	
1	Alirajpur	MP	Below 45
2	Bijapur	Chhattisgarh	
3.	Dantewala	Chhattisgarh	
4.	Jhabua	MP	
5.	Nabarangpur	Odisha	46–50
6.	Shrawasti	UP	
7.	Malkangiri	Odisha	
8.	Narayanpur	Chhattisgarh	
9.	Koraput	Odisha	
10.	Pakur	Jharkhand	
11.	Barwani	MP	

Source: Calculated from Census of India 2011.

Social Group Differences

It is well known that backward social groups and Muslims among the religious groups report lower educational attainments. These sections of the population are located in select states and within pockets in these states as well.

Despite the improvements in literacy across social groups over 1999–2000 to 2007–8, the SCs, STs, and Muslims among the religious groups have lower literacy rates. IAMR and the Planning Commission (2011) note how 48 per cent of STs are located in the five states of Rajasthan, Jharkhand, Odisha, Chhattisgarh, and Madhya Pradesh and they together account for 55 per cent of the illiterates among STs.

SCs are concentrated in the four states of Uttar Pradesh, Bihar, West Bengal, and Andhra Pradesh accounting for 46 per cent of the population and 52 per cent of the illiterates among SCs. What explains these low educational indicators among groups requires social mapping and further research.

Muslim illiterates are concentrated in Bihar, West Bengal, and Uttar Pradesh with a population share of 46 per cent and a 58 per cent share of illiterates.

Undertaking sub-state and sub-district level analysis can be beneficial to identify appropriate locations along with the concentration of the educationally deprived sections and groups. Clearly, all these sections of the population deserve special attention by policymakers.

Gender Gaps and Parity

Considering any dimension of education at the elementary schooling level reveals the persistence of gender disparities be it in literacy, illiterates, enrolment, and so on. Although declining consistently over the last four decades, the gender gap still persists (see Figure 18.4).

This gender gap is wider among children at the upper primary level. Relatively lower investment on girls' education, giving importance to their marriage and other parameters such as inadequate female teachers, fear for their safety, absence of functional female toilets, and so on serve

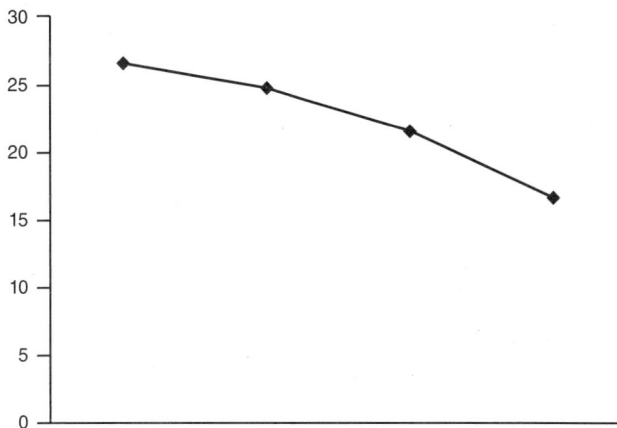

Figure 18.4 Declining Gender Gap in Literacy Rates over Four Decades (from 1981 to 2011)

Source: Premi and Das (2012); Based on Census 2011.

as deterrents to their pursuing schooling, (De et al. 2011; PROBE 1999).

Girls' participation in schooling is noted more at the primary stages and in government schools. There is a gradual improvement in enrolment of girls compared to boys, especially at the upper primary stages. The *Annual Status of Education Report* (ASER 2012 rural) also highlights the fact that the proportion of children who are currently not enrolled is declining. Rural girls, especially in the age group of 11–14 years who are the hardest to keep in school also report a decline in out-of-school figures, from 10 per cent in 2006 to 5 per cent in 2011. What is noteworthy, however, is the fact that most of the improvements in the gender parity index are recorded for government schools (see Table 18.12).

Table 18.12 Gender Parity Index in Enrolment

	I–V	VI–VII/VIII	I–VII/VIII
2000–6	0.92	0.84	0.90
2006–7	0.93	0.87	0.91
2007–8	0.93	0.89	0.92
2008–9	0.94	0.91	0.93
All Government Management			
2005–6	0.95	0.87	0.93
2006–7	0.96	0.90	0.95
2007–8	0.97	0.93	0.96
2008–9	0.99	0.97	0.98
All Private Management			
2005–6	0.80	0.81	0.80
2006–7	0.81	0.82	0.82
2007–8	0.81	0.81	0.81
2008–9	0.81	0.81	0.81

Source: Mehta (2011).

REMAINING ISSUES AND CONSTRAINTS

There are myriad issues and constraints for the universalization of elementary education which are also persistent. These range from out-of-school children to improving school effectiveness and include issues relating to teachers and different school structures and managements.

Out-of-School Children—Never Enrolled

The never enrolled and dropouts from school constitute the children who are out of school. The NSS 64th Round provides information for never enrolled persons in the 5–29 years age group (see Table 18.13). Nearly two-fifth of all children at age five remaining non-enrolled is an indication of the low proportion of pre-schooling incidence in India. This is both an outcome of low levels of interest among parents and poor facilities being available. Therefore, it is hardly surprising that the proportion of both girls and boys are reported to be quite similar at this age, of course the percentage for girls being slightly higher.

Table 18.13 Age-wise Percentage of Never Enrolled Persons in Rural–Urban Areas

Age Group (years)	Rural	Urban	Female	Male	Total
5	42	25	39	38	39
6–10	10	6	10	8	9
11–13	7	4	8	5	6
14–17	10	5	11	6	9
18–24	20	9	24	10	17
25–29	29	12	33	15	24
Total	16	8	18	10	14

Source: 64th Round NSS data (2007–8).

The proportion of out-of-school girls across different age groups remains higher as expected given the disparities and discrimination stemming from socio-economic and cultural practices. The gap among girls and boys among the 'never enrolled' increases substantially for older years, as one moves from elementary schooling ages to older ages, reflecting patriarchal norms and practices relating to marriage and child bearing that are prevalent in society.

The association of education with poverty, especially extreme poverty, continues to reveal the high levels of inequalities in our society (see Table 18.14). The difference in the proportion of students across income groups (as categorized by Sengupta et al. 2008 into six categories) attending elementary levels of schooling is narrower for 6–14-year-olds than that for 15–17-year-olds. Among the latter, it is clearly middle and high income groups who are pursuing schooling.

Discontinuation: Affordability versus Value of a Child as Labour

A combination of factors affects retention in schools. Differential facilities and managements across schools with a bulk of them affected by poor access to electricity, reading materials, space for sports and extra-curricular activities, absenteeism and inadequate training of teachers, and inadequate stimulation and creativity in teaching–learning processes often lead to disinterest and discontinuation of schooling. The Planning Commission's analysis suggests that 'a school that is far away or that does not function regularly fails to retain students. Similarly, a teacher who is absent or engaged in non-teaching work, is intimidating

Table 18.14 Proportion of Students Currently Attending by Age and Income Groups

Arjun Sengupta Categorization 2008	6–14			15–17		
	Rural	Urban	Total	Rural	Urban	Total
Extremely poor	77.7	78.4	77.9	40.8	42.3	41.3
Poor	81.5	84.6	82.1	41.8	49.3	43.4
Marginal	85.8	89.6	86.4	49.9	56.9	51.4
Vulnerable	89.9	94.9	90.9	59.2	73.9	62.5
Middle-income group	94.0	97.3	95.2	75.1	86.8	79.5
High-income group	99.7	99.4	99.5	89.8	94.7	92.8
Total	86.2	90.6	87.2	55.3	68.6	58.8

Source: Calculated from NSS 64th Round.

or uses uninteresting methods of teaching also encourages children to drop out. Often the need for children of poorer families to work also drives them away from school' (GoI 2006a: 57–8).

Even at the primary schooling level, children discontinue education. In fact the NSS 64th Round data reports that for a few, even this low level of education is the desired level of education, while many others leave before completing the level that they enrolled for. This could be due to any sudden shocks faced by the household.

Apart from these, seasonal and intermittent missing out on school attendance is quite a major factor affecting education of children, especially among the socio-economically backward and weaker sections. The compulsion of providing support to the economic base of a household often means that children have to work even while they are enrolled in school (Ramachandran et al. 2003). Children tend to miss out on attendance during peak seasons and periods, for instance when minor forest products are to be collected. Other studies have also revealed similar participation of children in economic activities for their households. Bhaskaran et al. (2010) in their study on the garment sector find that children work in home-based activities to help their families even while being enrolled in school. However, the eventual outcome of dropping out of school either because of poor performance or disinterest appears to be quite common. Similar findings have emerged from a recent survey on children working in the cotton fields in the rural areas of Punjab and Haryana conducted by the Institute for Human Development (IHD) (Nathan et al. 2012).

It is not entirely clear what distances children from schooling? Is it the syllabi and classroom transactions per se which are not appropriate and do not connect with the local context of the children, generating disinterest among them, or whether it is the disconnect ensuing after the economic compulsion-based work involvement of children for a substantial period? Since teachers in most of the schools do not come from the same social context from which the economically poorer children come they do not take a sympathetic view or put in more effort to retain the children in school, and so they may not be geared towards generating an appropriate environment for their retention. The formal school structure allows for very little flexibility to alter the routine calendar to accommodate for such fluctuations. The compulsion of having to work for survival and basic needs affects the broader understanding of the returns to investing in education and its accruals for individuals as well as for society at large.

The major reasons listed in all surveys for discontinuation or dropping out of school are either economic or opportunity cost-related (see Table 18.15). The other set of factors relate to poor quality or lack of effectiveness of education. Asadullah and Yalonetzky (2012: 1160) while examining the inequality of educational opportunities in India find that 'states with more accountable governments, greater access to finance, greater reduction in poverty, and greater inclusion of women in economic growth emerged as those that also succeeded in reducing inequality of educational opportunities'. Thus economic growth and poverty reduction are seen to have a positive association, while they find no link between educational expenditure and inequality of opportunity.

Table 18.15 Major Reasons for Discontinuance/Dropping Out

Financial constraints	21.4
Child not interested in studies	19.9
Unable to cope or failure in studies	10.3
Completed desired level or class	10.1
Parents not interested in studies	8.9
For participating in other economic activities	6.2
To work for wage or salary	5.7
To attend to other domestic chores	5.4
For helping in household enterprises	3.1
Other reasons (including marriage, etc.)	9.0

Source: NSS 64th Round.

This is a reflection of the issue of affordability of schooling on the one hand and the value of a child as labour facing many households in India on the other. Literature in the global context emphasizes that every additional year of schooling improves average earnings by approximately 10 per cent (Duflo 2001; Psacharopoulos and Patrinos 2002). The Indian reality with the intermeshing of economic conditions with social status may affect enrolment, attendance, and labour market outcomes differently; however, gains from every year of schooling are no doubt experienced.

School Systems and Management

The differences in school structures are quite firmly established. Different states in India follow either classes I–IV or I–V for the primary stages; while at the upper primary level there are four different structures—IV–VII, IV–VIII, V–VII, and V–VIII. Secondary sections again follow either of two structures—VIII–X and IX–X.

Even school managements are either government or private. Government schools also include local bodies. Government schools predominate at the elementary level while private institutions tend to be proportionately more for high school and beyond (see Table 18.16).

By and large, government schools are fully funded from state budgets, which receive support from the Government of India based on various formulas. Within government schools too, there are those run by the Department of Education, the tribal/social welfare department, local bodies, and others. For the country as a whole DISE 2009–10 reports that 56 per cent of the schools are run by the Department of Education, 19 per cent by local bodies, a few (4 per cent) by tribal/social welfare department, and 1 per cent by others (NUEPA 2011).

Private schools constitute close to 20 per cent of all schools in India as per DISE 2009–10. A bulk of the private schools are unaided, while the aided schools constitute a substantial share among all schools. Unaided private schools are in a larger proportion in Delhi (39 per cent), Puducherry (33 per cent), Chandigarh (32 per cent), Nagaland (26 per cent), Rajasthan (23 per cent), and Uttar Pradesh (21 per cent).

Apart from these, special and alternative schooling initiated under schemes/policies such as KGBV, NPEGEL, ashram schools, National Child Labour Prjoject (NCLP) schools, and so on together with the existing Kendriya Vidyalayas and a host of private schools (low cost, for profit, not-for-profit) lend schooling in India a lot of diversity.

Students are enrolled and attend schools in all types of institutions. Of those who attend private unaided institutions, more than two-thirds are in recognized institutions. However, at the primary level, 27 per cent of the children and at the middle school level 22 per cent of the children attended unrecognized institutions (NSSO 2010).

The low-cost small private schools functioning across the country will face difficulties in being recognized since this will depend on their upgrading their infrastructure to meet RTE norms. However, the pertinent question is whether RTE can attain its goals of universal cover without the additional supply of low-cost private schools.

Amidst debates to encourage private–public partnerships, what are the constraints in providing recognition to private schools? Is it a matter of basic requirements and regulations or is it an issue of elementary education being a public good which must be provided by the state or at best by non-profit private institutions?

Since a large part of the education is supplied through government schools, the need to move towards quality education requires preparing basic norms for public schools and these can be applied to private institutions as well. Strict audit and monitoring systems are required to facilitate provision of education rather than using these to constrain it.

Education: How Free? Do Incentives Help?

Only a portion of all the children participating in schools avail of free education even in the limited sense of the

Table 18.16 Number of Institutions by Management

School Category	Government		Private		Total
	Government	Local Bodies	Aided	Unaided	
Pre-primary	49	27	3	21	100
Primary	58	28	6	8	100
Middle	56	18	9	17	100
High	30	9	26	35	100
Pre-degree/junior colleges/ higher sec. schools	46	0.5	18	36	100

Source: SES (2009–10) (P).

definition of free of fees (see Table 18.17). In spite of efforts to make education free for the poorer people, there remain substantial costs of sending children to school or to any institution. While education without charge of any fee as well as the supply of subsidized books is becoming relatively common for elementary schooling, the other incentives such as scholarships, subsidized stationery, concession in transport fares, and so on are quite thinly spread (Table 18.18).

Table 18.17 Proportion of Students Availing Free Education

School	Rural	Urban	Total
Primary	80	40	71
Middle	75	45	68
Sec/HS	54	35	48

Source: NSS 64th Round.

Table 18.18 Proportion of Students Getting Educational Incentives

	Percentage
Scholarship/stipend	14 (rural—17; urban—6)
Free/subsidized books	51 (rural—58; urban—29)
Free/subsidized stationery	7 (rural—8; urban—5)
MDM from government	Primary—67; middle—29
Concession in transport fare	4.6

Source: NSS 64th Round.

The efforts introduced for SC, ST, and minority communities through a bouquet of educational schemes in the form of free or subsidized books, scholarships, and free coaching have benefited quite a few students who were deprived of facilities due to income constraints. Efforts are being made to improve transparency in the transfer of scholarship amounts through bank accounts. However, recent field studies[3] highlight the myriad problems faced by identified beneficiaries in attaining this financial inclusion since banks are not keen on opening and managing no-frill accounts on zero balance.

The central government's mid-day meal scheme is among one of the relatively successful schemes and has over the years emerged as an incentive for improving enrolment across the country. There is little doubt that such an intervention is bound to also have an impact on the hunger and nutrition dimensions of children in poor and backward areas in the country. However, the fact that children are seen walking to school with a plate and often without any books or a bag, footwear, or proper attire highlights the poor quality of education or the poverty and deprived conditions of children seeking schooling. In other words, children are affected adversely from income deficiencies, unequal treatments meted out at school as well as other factors stemming for social inequities, all of which can push them away from pursuing education.

The cost of education over the years has been increasing substantially (see Table 18.19). For the economically weaker sections, unless some monetary support in the form of fee waivers, educational loans, or scholarships is provided, access to these courses will remain remote. An effort to impose 25 per cent seats for economically weaker students as specified by RTE is one such attempt at being inclusive. How this can be made effective will critically depend on many factors such as students' interactions, peer group behaviour, and so on. The most crucial role will be of the school management and teachers.

Teachers

The stipulated PTR desirable as per RTE is 1:30 but for schools that have more than 200 students, PTR should not exceed 40 (excluding the head teacher). As per DISE 2009–10 PTR has been declining gradually. However it remains at 32 for all schools. Nearly 12 per cent of all the schools, even primary schools, report having PTRs that are greater than 60 students per teacher (NUEPA 2011). Bihar and Jharkhand are the worst with the highest PTRs.

The number of teachers in government schools has been increasing and this has improved PTR from 36:1 in 2006–7 to 33:1 in 2009–10. An analysis of school-wise information from DISE 2009–10 reveals that 46 per cent primary and 34 per cent upper primary schools had adverse PTR. The extent of variation is reflected in the fact that even in states with reasonable PTRs, there are many schools that display an adverse ratio. Filling up vacancies and rationalizing teacher deployment are immediate needs.

SSA stipulates a norm of recruiting 50 per cent female teachers, which has resulted in increasing the proportion of female teachers from 42 in 2006–7 to 45 in 2009–10. This also increased the proportion of schools with at least one female teacher from 72 per cent in 2006–7 to 75 per cent in 2009–10.

SSA provides for 20 days annual in-service training for teachers, 20 days induction training for new recruits, and 60 days training for untrained teachers, for which financial provisions are made. These will be enhanced appropriately to meet RTE requirements for augmenting training capacities for different levels of teaching personnel.

The specifications for teachers under RTE will necessitate the induction of at least 10 lakh teachers within a short period

---

[3] IHD did field studies in districts in seven states for an evaluation of educational scholarship schemes of the Ministry of Minority Affairs in 2011–12.

Table 18.19 Average Annual Expenditure Per Student Per Year by Level of Education

Level of Education	Rounds	Rural	Urban	Total		
				Female	Male	Persons
Primary	52	297	1,149	494	507	501
	64	826	3,626	1,308	1,501	1,413
Middle	52	640	1,529	933	904	915
	64	3,019	7,212	4,140	4,503	4,351
Sec/HS	52	1,180	2,219	1,619	1,552	1,577
	64	3,019	7,212	4,140	4,503	4,351
Above HS (General)	52	2,294	3,304	2,995	2,879	2,923
	64	6,327	8,466	7,324	7,386	7,360
General Education (All)	52	570	1,686	882	919	904
	64	1,551	5,128	2,293	2595	2,461

Source: NSS 64th Round.

of time and also the parallel step to initiate training at various levels, professional, induction and in-service. It is estimated that nearly 10.6 lakh teachers require professional training in the next five years that is, by 2015 (www.indg.in/primary-education/.../rte_ssa_final_report.pdf, last accessed in April 2012).

Professional qualifications as notified by the National Council for Teacher Education (NCTE) are mandated under the RTE Act. DISE 2009–10 reports that there were 6.7 lakh untrained teachers spread throughout the country. A bulk of these untrained teachers were located in four states: Bihar (1.6 lakh), Uttar Pradesh (1.2 lakh), Jharkhand (0.6 lakh), and West Bengal (0.6 lakh). This is partly an outcome of the induction of para-teachers.

If NCF, 2005 principles are to be followed and teachers trained in that mode to develop capabilities such that they are able to follow appropriate pedagogical methods for child-centred learning and so on, then the curriculum and pedagogy for teachers' training itself may require substantial revisions. Inadequacies in teaching personnel and their training deficiencies are among the most significant problems which cannot be addressed easily. These may be viewed as the second order problems in comparison to the other infrastructure-related issues which may be relatively easier to address if financial allocations are made for them.

It is relatively easier to estimate the financial allocations based on the number crunching exercises as per the norms set by RTE so as to meet the notions of minimum quality standards. But the challenge that remains is with regard to appropriate higher education and motivation to take up the profession of teaching and pursuing it as a career and sustaining it. Take the requirement that female teachers are desirable to encourage enrolments among female students. This requires adequate participation of female students at higher education levels and their pursuing teaching as a profession. A bulk of the gap in teaching personnel is in rural areas, where transport, access, and security are all issues of concern especially in the context of female teachers.

Very few female teachers choose to serve in schools located in remote and backward habitations, since access, transport, and security are issues. Relocation to the place of duty is also not an option since most female teachers, if married, will also have the responsibility of taking care of their families and households.

Since care activities continue to remain the unpaid work responsibilities undertaken by women, with minimal market provisioning of such services, especially in rural areas, this continues to remain a major issue. For the poor and gender-role bound women, the option of hiring care services, even where these may be available remain bleak.

There have been some positive changes such as the decline in percentage of single teacher schools from 2005–6 to 2008–9 by 4 points, in the proportion of schools with at least one classroom per teacher, and improving teacher attendance (ASER 2012; NUEPA 2011).

Growing dependence on tuitions by most students at all levels and resorting to guidebooks instead of designated textbooks are a reflection of the lack of confidence that the students have in the existing system. Ironically, these practices have been growing over time, with more and more students across school types and standards willing to pay the additional costs.

However, the performance of students in an assessment of their reading, comprehension, and mathematics abilities continues to be poor. ASER 2012 reports a decline in reading and arithmetic levels in 2011 over the previous year. Lack of pre-primary school training and malnutrition among children are identified as important determinants of learning deficiencies (IAMR and Planning Commission 2011). The home environment with poor income and food security levels also acts as a deterrent for improving learning outcomes and also results in perpetuating social inequalities (see Galab et al. 2009; Ramachandran et al. 2003). Understanding the inter-relationships between different spaces (such as home sphere and school environments) and agents (children, parents and teachers, for instance) become critical for ensuring quality education and improving learner achievements.

Relationships between Agents[4]

The different agents influencing decisions and effectiveness of school education and their interactions play a critical role in ensuring participation, retention, and completion of schooling. Understanding these relationships is critical for harnessing positive synergies to attain the aims of RTE. Schools need to become pro-actively inclusive and inspirational. Teachers and managers need to acquire a new passion for education and develop a professional commitment to take pride in teaching, rather than viewing it as another commercial venture for income generation.

Parents and the community need to be engaged in the functioning of schools. By putting in place proper systems of reporting and monitoring, there can be an endeavour to stamp out corruption and improve accountability. Unfortunately, the education sector is overflowing with the bureaucracy, while remaining sorely deficient in a professional management capacity.

There are many benefits of decentralized management of schools, which are more evident in financial and administrative decision-making, and less so in their impact on enhancing the quality of education. For instance, SSA's Fourth Joint Review Mission seems to hesitatingly suggest that there may be lessons to be learned from the 'remarkable improvement in delivering quality results on scale in civil construction and financial management'. The report (GoI 2006b) points out that:

There was a clear central goals and standard setting coupled with capacity building and this was combined resolutely with local accountability... The same general principles can be applied for improvement of quality. However, an important caveat is that the process of improvement in quality of learning involves much greater and continuous human interaction. It is also much more context-specific requiring greater freedom to act and innovate, the need for which increases as one moves away from the state capital and into the classroom. It would also be important to integrate and converge various factors that contribute to a better learning environment and thereby the learning achievements of the child. (GoI 2006b)

While decentralization seems to have worked with construction of school buildings, it does not appear to have been equally effective when it comes to school maintenance. States have experienced shortfalls in managerial capacities to carry out the functions of decentralization thrust upon them, which has at times resulted in poor implementation as well as corruption (see for instance, Jhingran 2005). In other instances, it has created excessive bureaucracy and episodes of leakages and elite capture of public resources are noted (Vasavi 2004). Since India is characterized by sharp inequalities, feudal relations, and community power structures that are deeply prejudicial towards women and the lower castes, the assumption that decentralization will result in local democracy is often questioned. However, ironically, it is in such societies that decentralization is needed the most.

Involvement of citizens through establishing school monitoring committees, parent–teacher associations, village education committees, and so on at all the stages from the inception to monitoring and implementation stages can serve as a powerful means to check corruption and improve the quality of service delivery. Relatively newer tools such as social audits and public hearings which have been used in implementing the right to employment according to the Mahatma Gandhi National Rural Employment Guarantee Act (MGNREGS) and the right to information (RTI) can be potent and useful tools in the field of education too.

It is peculiar that we witness such conflicting attitudes and perceptions of parents in different circumstances vis-à-vis children. The economic cost concerns in the context of education versus value of children as labour has been discussed in some detail already. Yet, even among the economically weaker sections spending substantial sums of money towards additional private tuitions is also witnessed. The incidence of seeking tuitions has been increasing over the years as reported by the ASER annual surveys.

The relationship between teachers and students is critical which enables flow of knowledge and effective learning. What factors can aid these different relationships between agents such as the state, educational bureaucracy, school management, teachers, community/society, parents/guardians, and children to think cohesively for imparting quality education to all children is an issue that RTE will have to grapple with.

CONCLUDING REMARKS

Will operationalizing RTE be a panacea for India's inability to establish a system of elementary education that is free and of good quality? The high growth experienced over the years and its resultant additional resources has not succeeded in ensuring free and good quality education so far. The enhanced budgetary allocations are a reflection of

---

[4] This section draws from Shiv Kumar and Rustagi (2010).

the political will to boost education outcomes. The budget speech of the Finance Minister in 2012 promises higher allocations to SSA (22 per cent) and RMSA (29 per cent) compared to previous years.

Financial allocations are no doubt important for meeting educational needs. While these may be essential for providing infrastructure, its maintenance, and the management of schools, teachers, and training concerns can only be partially addressed through this. Some studies have found little association between financial allocations and ensuring equality of opportunities across sections of the population or states across India (Asadullah and Yalonetzky 2012).

The economic challenges faced by households and their impact on children's education has an overwhelming influence in constraining a sustained pursuit of seeking schooling. Under these circumstances, can legal rights to children translate into altering the inherent social and economic inequities, prevalent and persisting, in our society for long years? How will the rights be protected and the provisions as per the RTE Act provided? Correct and appropriate as they may be, can legal provisions and statutory mandates alone change the scenario to accommodate children of weaker sections without addressing the economic backwardness of the households to which they belong?

Until such time that all the households are protected or at a level where their basic needs of food, shelter, and clothing are secured, there may be a need to plan for providing additional support to households to send their wards to school for at least eight years of education initially. Incentives and support to improve education play a critical role but can only serve if quality education is ensured. The element of improving learning outcomes is, therefore, an extremely critical one. Returns to education are well documented, especially at the post-secondary education levels, but also for every additional year of schooling. The relevance of all this increases with effective learning from the schooling availed as earnings prospects improve in the economy with employment generation. While globalization and exposure to possibilities has established an aspirational spiral among all youth and adults increasing the demand for education, the current scenario of very poor learner outcomes together with high unemployment levels among the educated may disturb the signals for agents.

The current emphasis on target-based approaches, for example, those which are based on reducing disparities in enrolment and dropouts between gender and social groups, are unlikely to translate into desired outcomes unless an understanding of the reasons that constrain participation of children in schooling is developed from a localized perspective. For instance, what are the appropriate measures to improve the performance and participation among groups of children who have historically underachieved in the school system? In other words, more clarity is required in the social inclusion agenda and efforts to make this a shared vision are essential. Numerous issues remain unresolved amidst some that are not so contradictory or conflict-ridden, for which more debates and discussions are essential.

Finally, the areas where knowledge building is required and to which attention needs to be paid in order to move towards quality education as per RTE are: mapping exercises that consider social access to schools and schooling apart from spatial concerns; improving pre-schooling, reducing dropouts; assessing the functioning of schools, curriculum load, classroom transactions, and learning potentials; reforming teacher deployment and training; creating appropriate spaces for the coexistence of different types of schools if common schools or moving towards a uniform schooling structure is not on option at the moment; and developing a consensus on what constitutes good-quality education.

Appendix A18

Table A18.1 Percentage of Children Currently Attending an Educational Institute by State, Sector (2007–8)

State	6–14			15–17		
	Rural	Urban	Total	Rural	Urban	Total
Jammu & Kashmir	93.27	96.95	93.77	75.3	88.9	77.7
Himachal Pradesh	97.98	97.87	97.97	86.2	92.5	86.7
Punjab	88.70	84.42	87.38	57.6	70.5	62.1
Chandigarh	86.44	91.18	90.45	78.8	71.5	71.9
Uttarakhand	91.56	88.79	90.90	69.2	74.7	70.7
Haryana	89.99	91.81	90.44	61.6	72.7	64.2
Delhi	95.37	92.33	92.57	60.4	69.4	68.7
Rajasthan	83.63	91.54	85.25	56.2	69.3	59.2
Uttar Pradesh	84.59	80.66	83.91	56.0	59.3	56.7
Bihar	74.74	82.58	75.40	47.9	76.0	51.9
Sikkim	96.83	90.32	96.31	74.7	68.4	74.3
Arunachal Pradesh	82.79	95.44	85.54	74.4	94.8	79.8
Nagaland	95.19	95.07	95.16	79.7	90.0	82.8
Manipur	92.88	97.17	93.97	75.2	89.5	79.0
Mizoram	97.58	99.04	98.20	56.8	86.9	70.3
Tripura	88.38	93.45	89.05	64.2	87.4	68.4
Meghalaya	93.55	95.12	93.78	76.9	83.9	78.0
Assam	90.68	90.62	90.67	55.8	70.7	57.3
West Bengal	85.68	88.04	86.09	51.3	65.4	54.3
Jharkhand	84.25	93.50	85.57	51.2	76.4	56.7
Odisha	84.20	88.35	84.68	37.7	59.4	40.6
Chhattisgarh	89.69	90.64	89.83	60.3	67.6	61.3

(*Contd.*)

Table A18.1 (*Contd.*)

State	6–14			15–17		
	Rural	Urban	Total	Rural	Urban	Total
Madhya Pradesh	88.37	91.28	88.96	48.0	67.4	53.3
Gujarat	84.56	91.98	86.88	36.8	61.7	46.2
Daman & Diu	96.16	98.00	96.81	24.3	92.8	59.9
D & N Haveli	86.77	98.79	88.29	61.3	75.7	62.5
Maharashtra	91.10	93.91	92.17	63.1	69.1	65.3
Andhra Pradesh	88.33	94.23	89.82	50.9	70.7	56.3
Karnataka	90.19	96.68	92.01	55.0	74.2	61.2
Goa	94.21	92.06	93.19	58.5	69.6	65.0
Lakshadweep	100.00	93.69	97.00	89.4	84.0	86.4
Kerala	99.30	99.56	99.36	89.2	85.8	88.4
Tamil Nadu	97.45	97.24	97.37	61.0	74.5	67.0
Puducherry	96.28	99.43	97.99	63.9	78.5	71.7
A & N Islands	96.48	99.28	97.37	79.3	91.8	84.0
Total	86.19	90.57	87.16	55.3	68.6	58.8

Source: NSS 64th Round.

REFERENCES

Asadullah, M. Niaz and Gaston Yalonetzky (2012), 'Inequality of Educational Opportunity in India: Changes over time and across states', *World Development*, 40(6): 1151–63.

ASER (2012), *Annual Status of Education Report (Rural) 2011–Provisional*. New Delhi: Pratham—ASER Centre.

Bhaskaran, Resmi P., Dev Nathan, Nicola Phillips, and C. Upendranadh (2010), 'Home-based Child Labour in Delhi's Garment Sector: Contemporary Forms of Unfree Labour in Global Production', *Indian Journal of Labour Economics*, 53 (4): 607–24.

Census of India (2001), Primary Census Abstract, Registrar General of India, Government of India.

———. (2011), Provisional Population Totals, Paper 2, Vol. 2 of 2011, accessed from http://www.censusindia.gov.in/2011-prov-results/paper2-vol2/prov_results_paper2_inidavol2.html, last accessed in May 2012.

De, Anuradha, Reetika Khera, Meera Samson, and A.K. Shiva Kumar (2011), *PROBE Revisited—A Report on Elementary Education in India*. New Delhi: Oxford University Press.

Drèze, J. and A. Sen (2002), *India: Development and Participation*. New Delhi: Oxford University Press.

Duflo, E. (2001), 'Schooling and Labour Market Consequences of School Construction in Indonesia: Evidence from an unusual policy experiment', *American Economic Review*, 91: 795–814.

Galab, S., H. Moestue, P. Antony, A. McCoy, C. Ravi, and P. Prudhvikar Reddy (2009), 'Enhancing Child Learning in Andhra Pradesh', in P. Rustagi (ed.), *Concerns, Conflicts and Cohesions: Universalization of Elementary Education in India*. New Delhi: Oxford University Press, pp. 230–55.

Government of India [GoI] (2006a), 'Towards Faster and More Inclusive Growth—An Approach to the 11th Five Year Plan', Government of India, New Delhi. http://planningcommission.nic.in/plans/planrel/app11_16jan.pdf, last accessed in September 2012.

———. (2006b), *India Sarva Shiksha Abhiyan Fourth Joint Review Mission* (17–27 July 2006). Available at: http://ssa.nic.in/monitoring/FINAL_AIDE_MEMOIRE_26_1.pdf, last accessed in April 2009.

———. (2012), *Economic Survey 2011–12*. New Delhi: Ministry of Finance, Government of India, March.

IAMR and Planning Commission (2011), *India Human Development Report—Towards Social Inclusion*. New Delhi: Institute of Applied Manpower Research and Planning Commission, Government of India, Oxford University Press.

Jhingran, Dhir (2005), *The Learning Challenge in Primary Education*. New Delhi: APH.

Mehta, Arun C. (2011), 'Elementary Education in India: Progress towards UEE', National University of Education Planning and Administration (NUEPA) and Department of School Education and Literacy, Ministry of Human Resource Development, Government of India.

Mehrotra, Santosh K. and Enrique Delamonica (2007), *Eliminating Human Poverty: Macroeconomic and Social Policies for Equitable Growth*. London: Zed Press.

MHRD (2011), *Sarva Shiksha Abhiyan—Framework for Implementation (Based on the Right of Children to Free and Compulsory Education Act, 2009)*. New Delhi: Department of School Education and Literacy, Ministry of Human Resource and Development, Government of India, March.

Nathan, Dev, Balwant Mehta, and Ann George (2012), 'Child Labour in Cotton Growing Fields', Institute for Human Development (IHD), New Delhi (mimeo).

National Sample Survey Office [NSSO] (2010), 'Education in India: 2007–08, Participation and Expenditure', NSS 64th Round, National Sample Survey Office, Ministry of Statistics and Programme Implementation, Government of India, May.

NUEPA (2011), *Elementary Education in India—Progress towards UEE*. New Delhi: National University of Educational Planning and Administration, Flash Statistics, DISE 2009–10.

Premi, M.K and D.N. Das (2012), *Population of India 2011*. New Delhi: BR Publishing Corporation.

PROBE Team (1999), *Public Report on Basic Education in India*. New Delhi: Oxford University Press.

Psacharopoulos, G. and H.A. Patrinos (2002), 'Returns to Investment in Education: A Further Update', The World Bank, Policy Research Working Paper, No. 2881.

Ramachandran, Vimala, Kameshwari Jandhyala, and Aarti Saihjee (2003), 'Through the Life Cycle of Children—Factors that Facilitate/Impede Successful Primary Education Completion', *Economic and Political Weekly*, 38(47): 4994–5002, 22 November.

Rustagi, Preet, Sunil Kumar Mishra, and Balwant Singh Mehta (2011), 'Scheduled Tribe Children in India: Multiple Deprivations and Locational Disadvantage', IHD-UNICEF Working Paper Series on Children of India: Rights and Opportunities, No. 8, UNICEF and Institute for Human Development, New Delhi.

Sengupta, Arjun, K.P. Kannan, and G. Raveendran (2008), 'India's Common People: Who Are They, How Many Are They, How Do They Live?', *Economic and Political Weekly*, 43(11): 49–63, 15 March.

Shiva Kumar, A.K. and Preet Rustagi (2010), *Elementary Education in India: Progress, Setbacks, and Challenges*. Institute for Human Development-Oxfam India working papers series, OIWPS-III.

Tilak, Jandhyala B.G. (2009), 'Universalizing Elementary Education: A Review of Progress, Policies and Problems' in Preet Rustagi (ed.), *Concerns, Conflicts and Cohesions: Universalisation of Elementary Education in India*. New Delhi: Oxford University Press, pp. 33–71.

Vasavi, R.A. (2004), 'In the Labyrinth of the Education Bureaucracy', *Seminar*, 536: 30–2.

19

Prosecuting Corruption in India
Evidence from Karnataka

*P.G. Babu, Vikas Kumar, and Poonam Mehra**

INTRODUCTION

Government agencies, an activist judiciary, the media, and civil society armed with the Right to Information Act (RTI), 2005, are exposing corruption[1] at all levels in Indian public life in an unprecedented manner.[2] These exposures have triggered a debate on the need for a more effective national anti-corruption agency. One of the recurrent themes of this ongoing debate is that the liberalization of the Indian economy has accentuated corruption in public life. But this is contestable since liberalization has removed a whole range of goods and services from the realm of corruption. Three questions define this debate. First, whether competition in the market place reduces corruption. While one might be tempted to answer in the affirmative, the answer is not all that simple because corruption could affect the free entry of firms into a market.[3] Competition, in fact, is not necessarily an exogenous parameter in a context where institutions are weak. Second, whether there has been a secular decline in the incidence of petty, retail, or decentralized corruption, which involves bribing officials to get things like cooking gas, passports, and telephones, due to technological and institutional innovations since liberalization and whether this decline is shifting public attention to cases of grand, bulk, or centralized corruption like the 2G spectrum allocation scam.[4] Third, whether the recent increase in the incidence of corruption could be attributed to better accounting procedures and information flow in general and targeting of bulk corruption in particular rather than to an absolute

---

* We are grateful to Manavi Belgaumkar, Dharmendra Chatur, Tasneem Deo, Rajeev Kadambi, Vandana Kamat, and Sumandro C. for research assistance to A. Narayana, Romar Correa, Gopal Kadekodi, Kanagasabapathy, Sudhir Krishnaswamy, V. Santhakumar, S.L. Shetty, Gyanendra Singh, Alok Tiwari, and the participants of IDR 2012 Workshop at the Indira Gandhi Institute of Development Research for helpful comments and discussions, and to Azim Premji University for institutional support. The data used in this chapter was obtained in June 2011 from the Public Information Officer, the Karnataka Lokayukta under the Right to Information Act, 2005. The usual disclaimer applies.

[1] There is no unanimity on how to define corruption. What counts as corruption generally depends on the context (Shleifer and Vishny 1993, Bardhan 1997, and Rose-Ackerman 1997). In our context, corruption is synonymous with corruption in government, where a public official uses his/her position for private gains or is offered inducements. However, our data does not allow a distinction between bribery or inducement and extortion.

[2] For instance, the Comptroller and Auditor General (CAG) and public interest litigators exposed the spectrum allocation scam, while Karnataka's Lokayukta exposed the mining scam in Karnataka.

[3] For an analysis of this question, see Bliss and Di Tella (1997).

[4] See Bardhan (1997) for a distinction between centralized and decentralized corruption. Also, see Moody-Stuart (1994) on grand corruption and Wade (1982), who argues that high and low corruptions are structurally inter-twined.

increase in the level of corruption across the economy. The bottom line is that there is a deep disagreement over how corruption affects people and why people are concerned about corruption.

People, particularly the growing urban middle classes, are agitated that corruption is corroding the democracy and public infrastructure, while the industry is concerned that corruption is affecting growth and damaging Brand India. Industry leaders like Jamshyd Godrej, Keshub Mahindra, Deepak Parekh, and Azim Premji identified the 'strong nexus between certain corporates, bureaucrats and power-brokers' as 'one of the greatest threats to the Indian economy' and urged the government to address the problem of corruption (*Economic Times* 2011).[5] The Federation of Indian Chambers of Commerce and Industry (FICCI), one of the oldest industry associations of India, adopted a resolution asking its members to introduce self-regulatory mechanisms and set an example for politicians and bureaucrats (Kumar 2011). More recently, the newly elected president of the Confederation of Indian Industry (CII), Adi Godrej exhorted the government to institute an ombudsman 'to keep a check on governance'. But even as the political class is divided and defensive and appears to act only when pushed by others, the need for a stringent anti-corruption legislation and the institution of an independent national agency is being debated in the streets across the country. Last year the streets literally forced the Parliament to agree in principle to a national anti-corruption institution, even though it was bitterly divided on the exact design of that institution.[6]

But disagreements notwithstanding, there is a general agreement that prosecution of corruption cases has not kept pace with detection, which explains the current public obsession with speedy prosecution. Last year, public frustration with delays in prosecution found expression in widespread support for social activist and anti-corruption crusader Anna Hazare's stringent draft anti-corruption legislation and pressure on the Parliament to consider on a priority basis a bill for the institution of a national anti-corruption agency. Unfortunately, the debate on the design of anti-corruption agency has been taking place within an empirical vacuum as if the country is making the first attempt to come to terms with a new problem. There is hardly any attempt to learn from the performance of existing institutional models within the country (see the section 'Background' for a discussion) or elsewhere. The paucity of empirical evaluations of the existing anti-corruption agencies in India is exemplified by the latest Parliamentary Standing Committee Report.[7] But the best case for a national anti-corruption ombudsman is to show that the existing ombudsmen in the states are effective or, at least, their flaws are tractable. So, for instance, an assessment of the Karnataka Lokayukta,[8] constituted under the Karnataka Lokayukta Act, 1984, the best known example of a provincial ombudsman within India, could provide valuable inputs for the design of the national anti-corruption ombudsman.

This chapter examines all cases handled by Karnataka's Lokayukta between 1995 and 2011, using data obtained through a petition filed under the RTI Act, 2005. It explores the impact of institutional leadership, stability of tenures, public awareness and empowerment, and past performance of the Lokayukta on its performance measured in terms of the number of cases initiated, convictions secured, and cases against officials belonging to the highest cadres.

The rest of the discussion is organized as follows. The next section puts our main query in its perspective and provides a background to India's anti-corruption laws and agencies in general, and Karnataka's anti-corruption

---

[5] There is a large literature on the effect of corruption on economic outcomes. For instance, Mauro (1995) argued that corruption lowers investment and, by implication, economic growth. Fisman (2001) studies the impact of corruption on share prices and returns. The relationship between corruption and the shadow economy has been the subject of a number of studies (Shleifer and Vishny 1993, Johnson et al. 1997, Friedman et al. 2000, Choi and Thum 2005, Echazu and Bose 2008).

[6] The current interest in corruption is not confined to India, though. The UN Convention Against Corruption, a legally binding anti-corruption convention, was adopted in 2003 (United Nations 2003), ratified by India only recently in 2011 (*Times of India* 2011). Transparency International periodically chronicles the level of corruption across the world. The United Kingdom has adopted the Bribery Act, 2010 (The Foreign and Commonwealth Office 2011). In the aftermath of the Arab Spring that claimed a few regimes and shook a number of others, the Chinese Communist Party, too, is concerned that corruption could threaten the domestic power structure in China and jeopardize growth (*Reuters* 2012).

[7] For exceptions see Narayana et al. 2012, who discuss a few key indicators of the Karnataka Lokayukta's performance, and Stark (2011), who compares the number of cases handled by the Kerala Lokayukta across districts during 2004–9. Others have investigated corruption in the public distribution system (Livemint 2007, India Corruption Study 2010) and employment guarantee schemes (*India Today* 2012, India Corruption Study 2010). Bertrand et al. (2007) study corruption in regional transport offices in Delhi through experiments. See Wade (1982), Oldenburg (1987), and Gupta (1995) for field studies on corruption and related issues at the local level. See Visvanathan (1999) for an excellent analysis of the Lentin Report on a specific case of corruption in the public healthcare system.

[8] Lokayukta refers both to the state-level anti-corruption institution as well as the chairperson of the institution. The (proposed) national counterpart of Lokayukta is known as Lokpal. In the 1960s, L.M. Singhvi coined the word *Lokpal* to indigenize the word ombudsman and it is supposed to stand for 'Protector of the People' (Standing Committee 2011: para 3.3). Actually, *Lokpal* refers to *king* or *guardian of a world* (Bahari 2002: 727).

agency in particular. The following section introduces the data and presents our results. The final section offers concluding remarks.

BACKGROUND

The recent public attention on corruption might make it look like a post-liberalization,[9] if not a modern, ill. The problem of corruption involving state officials is, however, as old as the state itself. But the understanding of 'corruption in the government' is relatively new. As Banerjee et al. (2012: 2) point out, 'corruption in government arises out of the fact that the government operates in situations where it does not want the price mechanism to operate and ... design the bureaucrat's task accordingly, despite the fact this may lead to bribe-taking or other distortions'. A typical bureaucrat's task might then involve greater reliance on non-market mechanisms, which is why the focus of current literature on corruption has moved away from studying the incentives to be corruptible to the design of the tasks themselves. Put another way, it is the question of fighting the effects of corruption head on ex-post or redesigning a bureaucrat's job and addressing the causes of corruption ex-ante (Rose-Ackerman 1997; Acemoglu and Verdier 1998; Banerjee 1997). While in practice both are required, the focus in this chapter, however, is entirely on the former—prosecution of corruption, and, in particular, on the recent Indian debate on the need for a powerful agency for this purpose.

Let us turn now to the background of relevant Indian national and regional acts and laws, which have a bearing on prosecution of corruption cases. The Indian Penal Code (IPC), Sections 161 to 165A, makes acceptance of side payments by a public servant a punishable offence. The Parliament adopted the Prevention of Corruption Act, 1947 as it was felt that the IPC was inadequate for prosecuting corrupt officials. This Act was amended in 1964 and 1967 and ultimately replaced by the Prevention of Corruption Act, 1988. The 1960s were, in fact, witness to many anti-corruption initiatives.[10]

The Central Bureau of Investigation (CBI), which was established as the national investigative agency in 1963, derives its investigative powers through the Delhi Special Police Establishment Act, 1946. The Special Police Establishment, a division within the CBI, has the powers to investigate corruption charges involving public servants national and state government officials with the consent of the relevant administrations (CBI n.d.). A year later, the Prevention of Corruption Act, 1947 was amended. The Central Vigilance Commission (CVC) was established in the same year. CVC appoints Chief Vigilance Officers to various ministries and public sector undertakings in order to monitor any offenses or abuse of position and power by public servants. On the basis of the reports of these officers, the CBI can register cases for investigation, if the offenses fall under the Prevention of Corruption Act (CVC n.d.). The respective ministries or departments deal with purely internal irregularities. Of course, for the successful functioning of any such system, the reporting obligations of public servants (of any wrong doing of their colleagues) are extremely vital, which are codified under Section 39 of the Code of Criminal Procedure, 1973. Failure to report it is treated as an offence. To protect whistleblowers, the Parliament is deliberating the Public Interest Disclosure and Protection of Persons Making the Disclosure Bill, 2010.

Interestingly, the institution of an anti-corruption ombudsman was also first discussed by Parliament in the early 1960s and the Santhanam Committee on the Prevention of Corruption, 1964 was constituted by the Government of India. But for various reasons a suitable legislation could not be adopted. So, while India still does not have a national anti-corruption ombudsman, the idea of such an institution is not new to the country. The idea has, in fact, survived the scrutiny of the National Commission to Review the Working of the Constitution (2000), two Administrative Reforms Commissions (1966 and 2005), four Parliamentary Standing Committees (1996, 1998, 2001, and 2011), and parliamentary review of nine anti-corruption bills (1968, 1971, 1977, 1985, 1989, 1996, 1998, 2001, and 2011). In the meantime, half of the states and union territories have already constituted anti-corruption agencies under provincial legislations. Odisha was the first state to legislate on this matter (1970), while Maharashtra was the first to constitute an anti-corruption agency (1972) (Odisha Government n.d.; Standing Committee 2011: para 3.8).[11]

---

[9] Post-independence India has seen three mass mobilizations against corruption in public life. Two of these happened in the late 1970s and late 1980s, that is, before liberalization of the economy. On both these occasions the ruling party lost the following elections.

[10] A discussion on why a number of anti-corruption initiatives are clustered around the mid- and late 1960s and towards the end of each of the successive decades will require a considerable digression. But it bears noting that there seems to be a ten-year cycle of public interest in corruption. Also, see Footnote 9.

[11] To put the Indian experience relating to ombudsmen in an international perspective, note that the debates with regard to the role of an ombudsman in ensuring accountability by the government are not unique to India and have taken place in many developing countries (Hatchard 1992; Stark 2011). The ombudsman, as a modern institution, was first established in Sweden in 1809. In 1966 Guyana became the first developing country in the world to adopt the institution of an ombudsman. Over the years the institution

Karnataka, the subject of this chapter's empirical analysis, had a Vigilance Commission, which was abolished when the Lokayukta was formed. According to the rationale of the Karnataka Lokayukta Act, 1984, the Lokayukta is empowered to look 'into complaints against the administrative actions, including cases of corruption, favouritism and official indiscipline in administrative machinery (Section 1)... relatable to matters specified in List II or List III of the Seventh Schedule to the Constitution, taken by or on behalf of the Government of Karnataka or certain public authorities in the State of Karnataka (including any omission or commissions in connection with or arising out of such action) in certain cases and for matters connected therewith or ancillary thereto' (Preamble). The Act applies to both serving and retired (only for possible offences committed when in office) public servants. The Lokayukta is headed by a retired judge of the Supreme Court or a retired Chief Justice of a high court for a fixed term of five years and is assisted by at least one Upa-Lokayukta, who is a retired high court judge, Lokayukta police, and public prosecutors. The Lokayukta and Upa-Lokayukta can be removed from office only through impeachment (Karnataka Lokayukta n.d.).

The Lokayukta deals with both 'complaint involving a grievance or an allegation'. Complaints are filed through an affidavit submitted to the Lokayukta or Upa-Lokayukta. The police wing of the Lokayukta can raid the office and/or residential premises of a public servant to ascertain disproportionate assets. Alternatively, the Lokayukta police can lay a trap to catch public servants red-handed in the act of accepting a bribe. *Traps* are initiated in response to complaints, while *raids* are conducted on the basis of information collected by the Lokayukta police. Note that the Lokayukta can prima facie reject citizen complaints or treat them as merely cases of grievance that do not require criminal prosecution. After a raid or trap is conducted, further investigations are conducted. After the completion of the investigation, if a case is not abated due to the death of the accused, the Lokayukta can either close the case or recommend further action. Cases are closed by filing a B Report (closed without trial as the charges could not be established in the investigation) or a C Report (closed as further investigation not possible either for lack of leads or for other technical reasons). Otherwise a request is made to the competent authority to sanction prosecution. If the authority grants sanction, then a charge sheet is filed and the official is tried. If more than one person is involved in a case, then each person is tried separately.

---

of an ombudsman has evolved from an agency to deal with public complaints regarding injustice and maladministration meted out by government officials to one that deals with a wider range of issues of concern to the people like human rights (Canineu n.d.).

DATA AND ANALYSIS

Data on cases of corruption handled by Karnataka's Lokayukta were obtained through a petition filed under the RTI Act, 2005. The data set includes 2,614 cases between 25 July 1995 and 26 March 2011. It contains information about 355 *suo motu* raids against 357 officials and 2,259 investigations in response to complaints against 2,679 officials (including 24 officials belonging to the highest cadres, two councillors, two members of the legislative assembly, and one petty official belonging to the office of the Lokayukta) and 61 private persons (Figure 19.1).

Our data is restricted to cases of corruption filed under the Prevention of Corruption Act, 1988 but excludes grievances. Moreover, our data does not include 'government referred cases'. We have information about the year and district in which the case was filed and whether the case was initiated *suo motu* by the agency (raid) or in response to a citizen complaint (trap). In addition, it gives information about the name, designation, and department of the official or private individual involved and the stage of prosecution. In some cases, additional remarks are provided, mostly giving the source from which information about the stage was sourced. In a few cases, we also have information about interim action, mostly suspensions (61 cases), departmental inquiries (24 cases), and transfers (13 cases). But unfortunately, we do not have any information on the year of transition from one stage to another and the value of corruption and the magnitude of punishment in the case of conviction.

Four other shortcomings of the data bear mentioning. First, the Lokayukta case file suffers from massive underreporting because in many cases it is inefficient to resort to the long winding legal process, when an immediate solution is required, for example, when one needs a better ward in a public hospital or seeks resumption of electricity or water supplies. Second, activists working as rent seekers (*Deccan Herald* 2012a) or parties interested in distracting specific officials could inflate the number of citizen complaints. While anecdotal evidence suggests the existence of such agents, we do not have information to weed them out of the data or, at least, estimate their overall contribution to the Lokayukta's caseload. Third, at least some of the cases investigated by the Lokayukta relate to breakdown of ongoing relationships between officials and private parties. Once again we do not have information to weed out such cases. Fourth, we do not know whether our cases relate to centralized or retail corruption.

Within the limitations of the data, we examine a number of issues highlighted by the public debate on Lokpal. The issues examined below can be grouped into a few broad categories—institutional incentives to act against corruption,

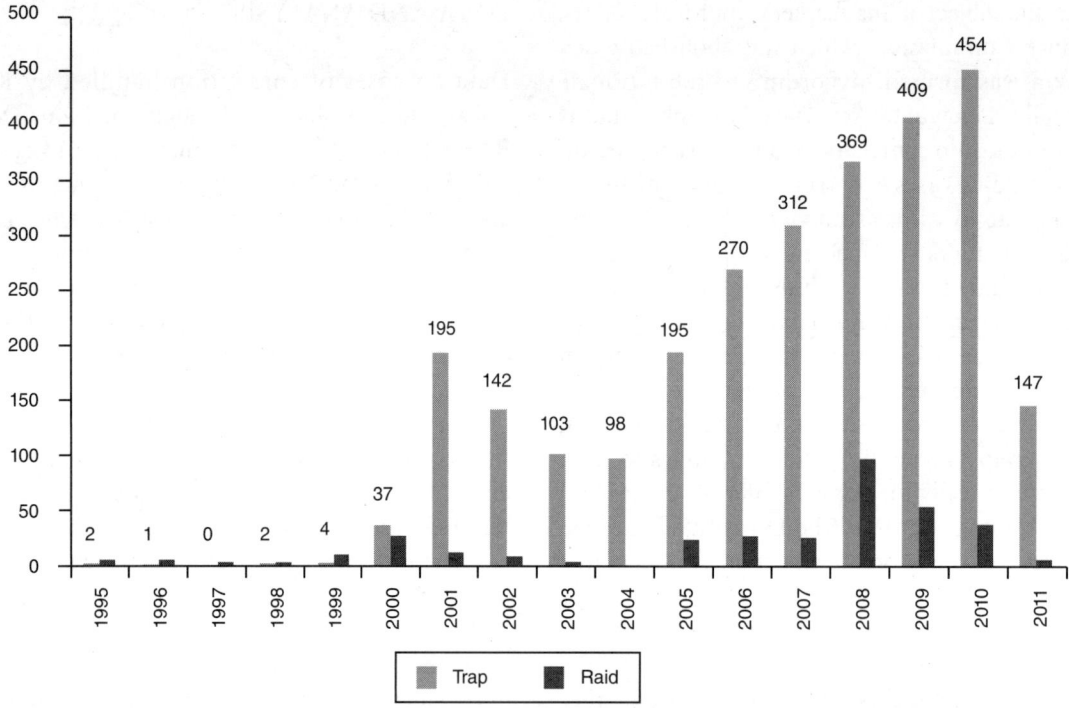

Figure 19.1 Number of Cases Initiated in Different Years

Source: Authors' own.

institutional focus and allocation of scarce prosecutorial resources (departmental, hierarchical, and geographical concentration of cases), institutional performance, and impact of the investigations and punishment on incidence of corruption.

Institutional incentives

A vocal section of civil society is demanding a stringent law to empower the national anti-corruption agency to pursue cases of corruption on its own. The Karnataka Lokayukta had that power under the Prevention of Corruption Act, 1988 to investigate cases of corruption and recently it was also provided with *suo motu* powers to initiate criminal investigation under the Karnataka Lokayukta Act. However, between 1995 and 2011, Karnataka's Lokayukta carried out only 355 *suo motu* raids, whereas it responded to over 2,259 citizen complaints. In other words, for every case of corruption initiated by the department *suo motu* it investigated more than six cases in response to citizen complaints. Moreover, the share of raid cases has been decreasing over the years, whereas as discussed next this ratio is expected to become stable over time (Figure 19.2). Past *suo motu* raids enhance public faith in the anti-corruption agency and encourage citizens to lodge complaints. As citizen complaints grow the agency gets a better idea of the loci of corruption and they can better plan raids. Moreover, growth in citizen complaints on the one hand encourages officials that there is popular faith in and support for the anti-corruption agency and on the other indirectly warns them that a lacklustre performance can invite a public outcry. This process of mutual learning should ultimately stabilize in the long run. So, the ratio of trap to raid cases should also become stable. However, in the present case, a comparison of raid and trap cases suggests that one of the most active Lokayuktas is, in fact, primarily driven by citizen complaints. This in turn suggests that the legal power to initiate action is in itself not sufficient for a pro-active anti-corruption agency. Institutional incentives for *suo motu* action seem to lie elsewhere.

Institutional Leadership

Institutional leadership of the Lokayukta is widely believed to have a significant impact on its performance.[12] The most obvious measure of performance of a Lokayukta is the number of new cases filed during his/her tenure (Table 19.1). Our data covers the terms of four different Lokayuktas

---

[12] Aiyappa (2011) highlights the reduced caseload of the Lokayukta after Period J4. But this could be due to instability arising out of the state government's inability to find a Lokayukta.

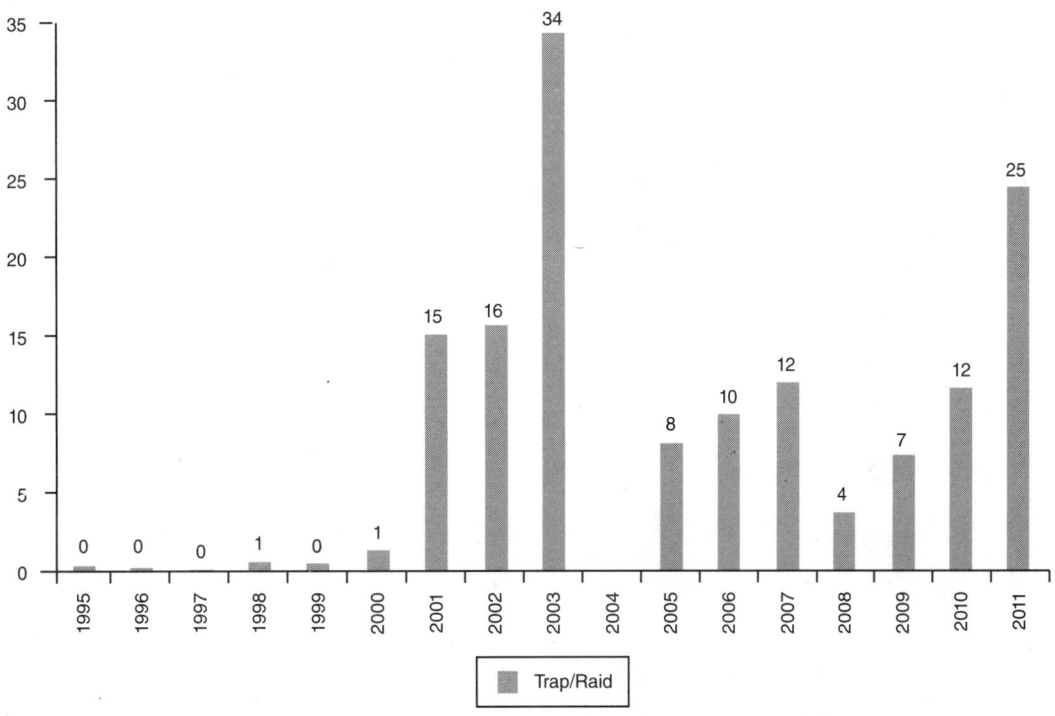

Figure 19.2 Ratio of Trap to Raid Cases Initiated in Different Years

Source: Authors' own.

Table 19.1 Tenures of Chief Ministers and Lokayuktas (25 July 1995–26 March 2011)*

Tenure Code	Lokayukta	Beginning	End	Tenure (in days)
J1	Justice Rabindranath Pyne	25 January 1991	2 June 1996	314
J2	Justice S.A. Hakeem	3 June 1996	1 July 2001	1,855
J3	Justice N. Venkatachala	2 July 2001	2 August 2006	1,858
J4	Justice Santosh Hedge	3 August 2006	2 August 2011	1,697

Chief Minister	Party	Beginning	End	Tenure (in days)
H.D. Deve Gowda	Janata Dal	11 December 1994	31 May 1996	312
J.H. Patel	Janata Dal	31 May 1996	7 October 1999	1,224
No Chief Minister (Governor in charge)	NA	8 October 1999	10 October 1999	3
S.M. Krishna	Indian National Congress	11 October 1999	28 May 2004	1692
Dharam Singh	Indian National Congress	28 May 2004	28 January 2006	610
No chief minister (Governor in charge)	NA	29 January 2006	2 February 2006	5
H.D. Kumaraswamy	Janata Dal (Secular)	3 February 2006	8 October 2007	613
President's rule (Governor in charge)	NA	9 October 2007	11 November 2007	34
B.S. Yeddyurappa	Bharatiya Janata Party	12 November 2007	19 November 2007	8
No Chief Minister (Governor in charge)	NA	20 November 2007	27 May 2008	190
No Chief Minister (Governor in charge)	NA	28 May 2008	29 May 2008	2
B.S. Yeddyurappa	Bharatiya Janata Party	30 May 2008	31 July 2011	1031

Note: * Our data correspond to the period between 25 July 1995 and 26 March 2011.

Source: Narayana et al. (2012); Onc Bangalore (n.d.).

272 INDIA DEVELOPMENT REPORT

(divided into four periods identified in Table 19.1 using codes J1 through J4) and many chief ministers. About 65 per cent of the cases in our dataset were initiated during Period J4 (2006–11) (Figure of the 19.3). Similarly, 45 per cent cases were initiated when B.S. Yeddyurappa (2007, 2008–11) was the chief minister (Figure 19.4), whose tenure

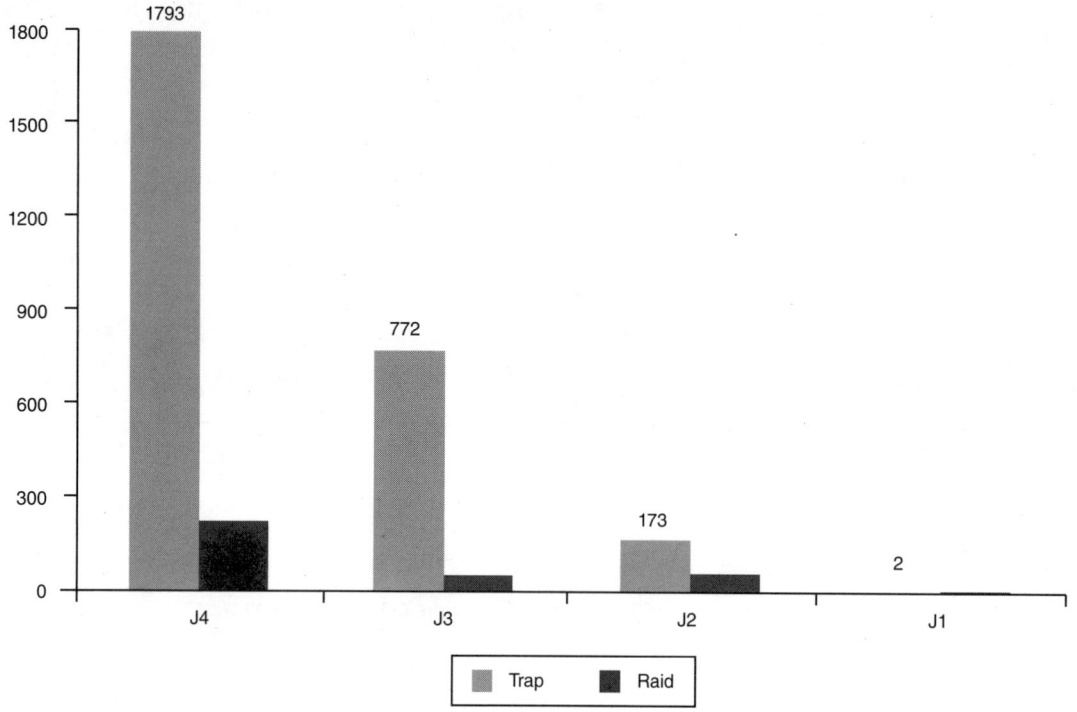

Figure 19.3 Trap and Raid Cases Initiated under Different Lokayuktas

Source: Authors' own.

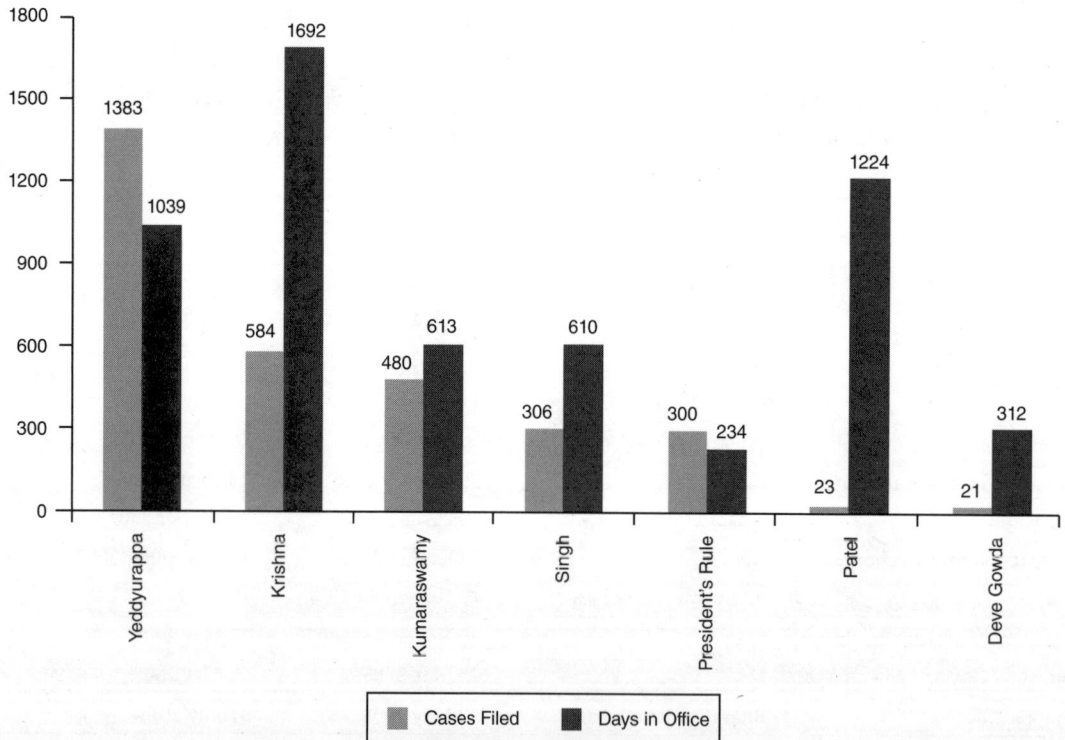

Figure 19.4 Cases Initiated under Different Chief Ministers

Source: Authors' own.

overlapped with Period J4. Even if cases initiated per day are the yardstick, more cases were initiated during Period J4 and during the tenure of Yeddyurappa (Figures 19.4 and 19.5).

Another measure of performance is the number of cases against officials belonging to the highest cadres. Two-thirds of the cases against the highest officials were initiated during Period J4 (Figure 19.6). Similarly, a third of the cases against the highest officials were initiated during President's rule, when the state was governed by the Governor because no party had a majority to form a government (Figure 19.7). It is indeed interesting that cases against a third of the highest officials ever probed by the agency began during President's rule, which accounts for just 0.64 years out of 15.68 years covered by the data. But one could argue that possibly the propensity to corruption among the officials belonging to the highest cadres differs between President's rule and chief ministers' rule. But this objection is not tenable because most of the officials belonging to the highest cadres (18 out of 24) were raided for accumulated disproportionate assets rather than being caught in acts of corruption. But even if the argument were true, it is not clear why only the officials belonging to the highest cadres should be more corruptible during President's rule. Further, if the propensity to combat corruption in the higher echelons of the bureaucracy did not differ between President's and chief ministers' rule, then officials belonging to the highest cadres should have the same probability of getting caught irrespective of who is in power because most of the officials belonging to the highest cadres were raided. But the fact that the contrary is true suggests the existence of a possible nexus between the highest bureaucrats and politicians.

Yet another yardstick of performance is the number of convictions. Period J3 stands out in this regard. Two-thirds of the cases in which convictions were secured where either initiated or concluded during Period J3 (Table 19.2). In fact, Period J3 marks the turnaround in the public visibility of the Lokayukta. The number of cases handled by Lokayukta grew manifold during this period.

While the above measures give a glimpse of how leadership affects the performance of the incumbent, an important measure of the impact of individual styles on institutional performance is provided by the ratio of trap to raid cases filed. Period J3 was marked by an excessive focus on traps at the expense of raids, which are more likely to target higher officials (Figure 19.8). Unsurprisingly, during Period J3 very few officials belonging to the highest cadres were investigated (Figure 19.6).

Departmental Spread

A mapping of the loci of corruption would help focus scarce prosecutorial resources of understaffed and underfunded Lokayuktas. A department-wise analysis of the data would in principle map both the focus of the Lokayukta's work as

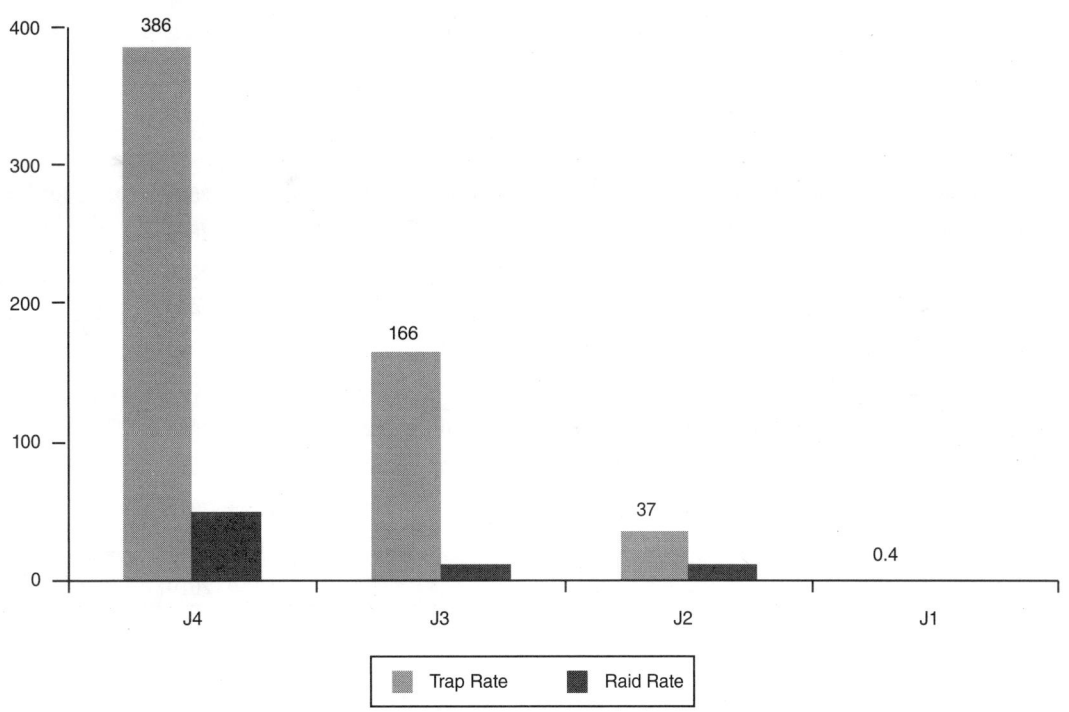

Figure 19.5 Trap and Raid Cases Initiated Per Year under Different Lokayuktas

Source: Authors' own.

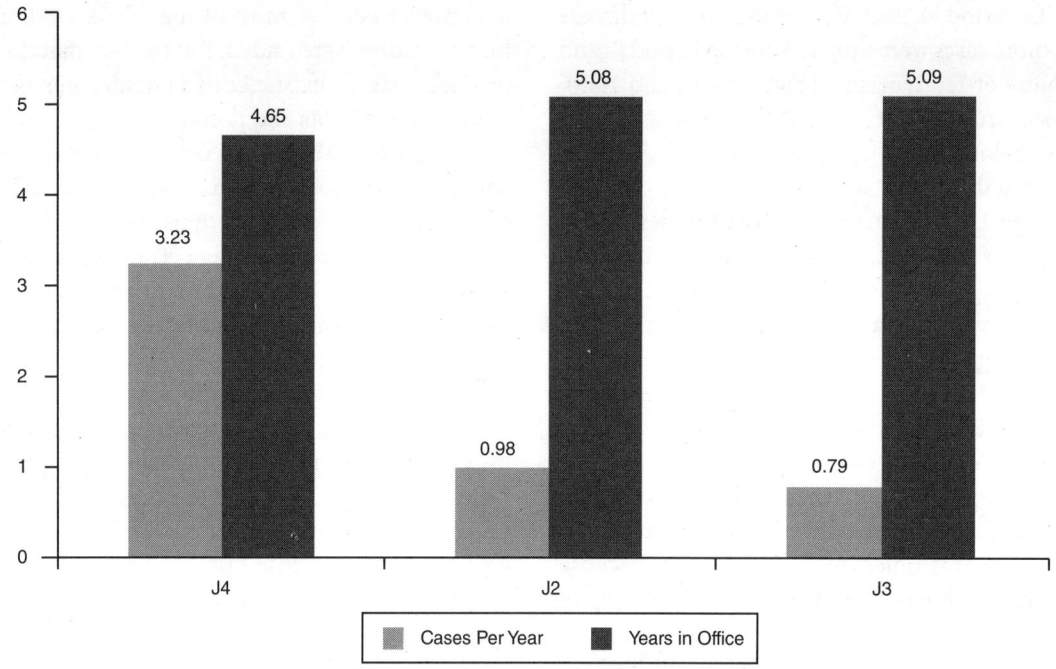

Figure 19.6 Cases against Officials of Highest Cadres under Different Lokayuktas

Source: Authors' own.

Table 19.2 Cases Resulting in Conviction

S. No.	Type	District	Department	Designation	Start	Started	End	Completion	Years for Completion of Trial
1	Trap	Mysore	NA	Petty	2000	J2	2010	J4	10
2	Trap	Mangalore	Local government	Petty	2001	J2	2005	J3	4
3	Trap	Bengaluru city	Administration	Mid-ranking official	2001	J3	NA	NA	NA
4	Trap	Bengaluru city	Social welfare	Professional	2001	J3	2007	J4	6
5	Trap	Bengaluru city	Social welfare	Higher official	2001	J3	2005	J3	4
6	Trap	Ramanagara	Administration	Mid-ranking official	2002	J3	2009	J4	7
7	Trap	Bengaluru city	Administration	Mid-ranking official	2002	J3	2006	J3	4
8	Trap	Bengaluru city	Administration	Mid-ranking official	2002	J3	2005	J3	3
9	Trap	Bengaluru city	Social welfare	Mid-ranking official	2002	J3	2005	J3	3
10	Trap	Bengaluru city	Social welfare	Mid-ranking official	2002	J3	2005	J3	3
11	Trap	Bengaluru city	Economic	Petty	2002	J3	2005	J3	3
12	Trap	Bengaluru city	Local government	Mid-ranking official	2002	J3	2005	J3	3
13	Trap	Mysore	Local government	Mid-ranking official	2007	J4	2011	J4	4
14	Trap	Mysore	Local government	Petty	2007	J4	2011	J4	4
15	Trap	Mysore	Administration	Petty	2007	J4	2011	J4	4
16	Raid	Hassan	Economic	Petty	2009	J4	2010	J4	1

Source: Authors' own tabulation.

well as the loci of corruption in the state. But actually the distribution is not determined by the Lokayukta's focus because an overwhelming majority of the cases arises out of citizen complaints. So, the above departmental mapping is more likely to correspond to the loci of corruption from the perspective of citizens. According to our data, more

PROSECUTING CORRUPTION IN INDIA 275

than 80 per cent of the cases were related to four essential functions of the government: local governance (22.67 per cent), administration—taluka/district office, police, court, tax, land, revenue (35.94 per cent), welfare (14.92 per cent), and regulation (4.42 per cent) (Figure 19.9). The rest of the cases were divided among agriculture and irrigation

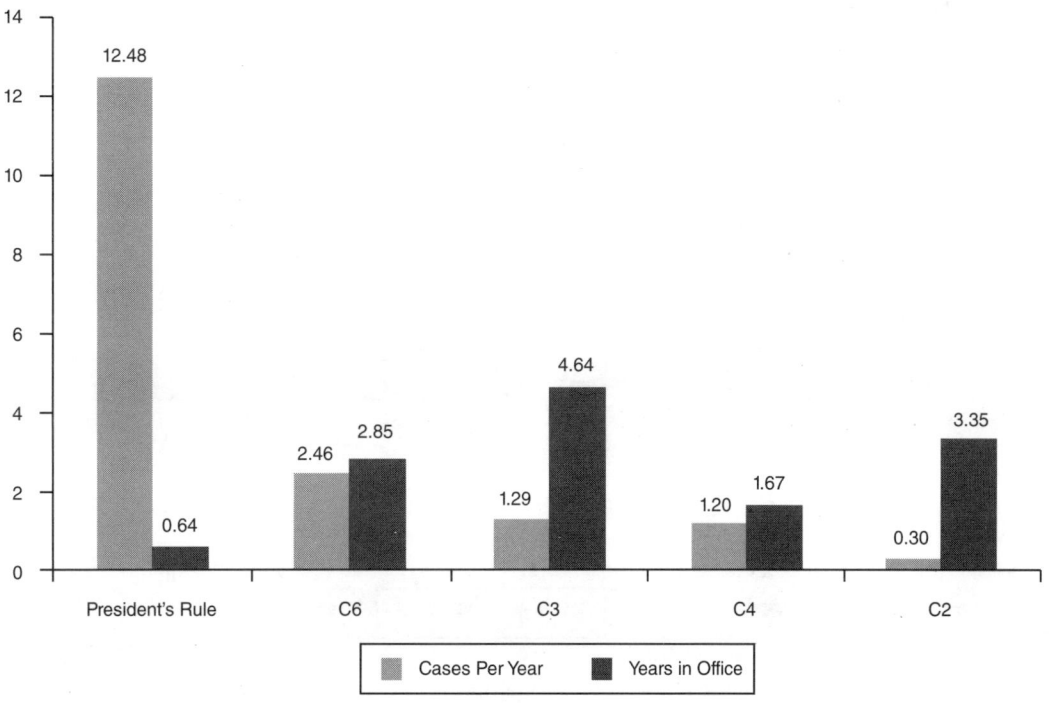

Figure 19.7 Cases against Officials of Highest Cadres under Different Chief Ministers

Source: Authors' own.

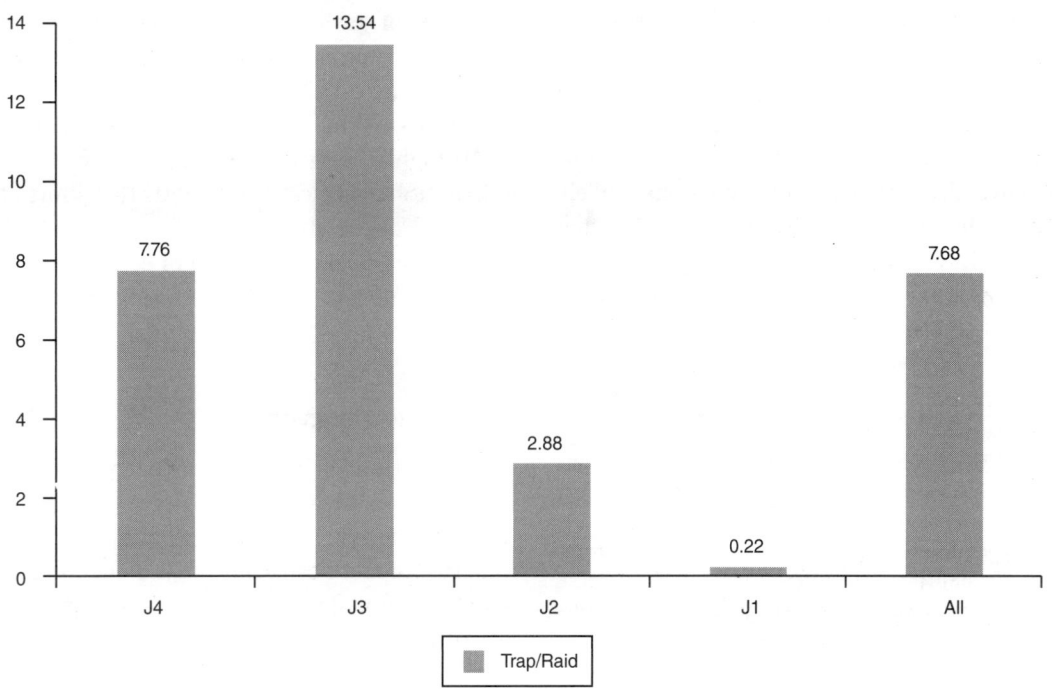

Figure 19.8 Ratio of Trap to Raid Cases Initiated under Different Lokayuktas

Source: Authors' own.

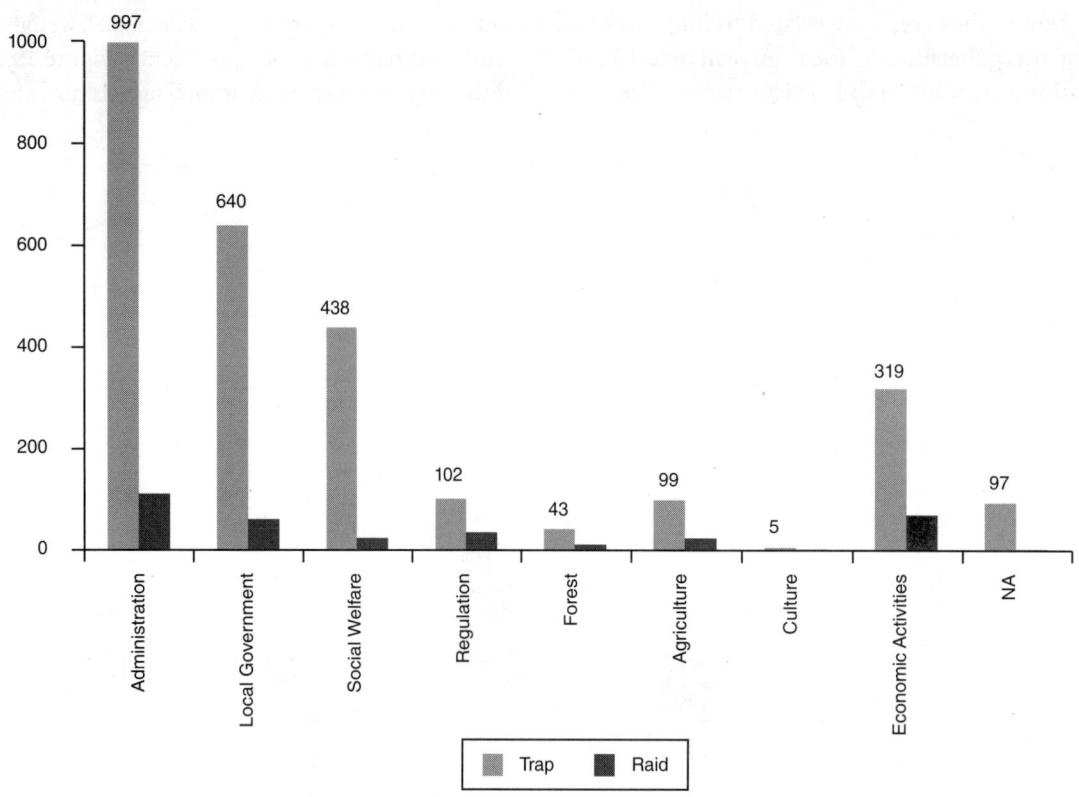

Figure 19.9 Departmental Spread of Corruption

Source: Authors' own.

(4.17 per cent), forest (1.81 per cent), and economic activities (12.66 per cent).[13] This distribution does not vary much across raid and trap cases, except that raid cases involve more officials from regulatory functions and officials from departments engaged in economic activities.

Given the growing importance of the welfare functions of the state, the overall share of essential functions is likely to increase rather than decrease. Also, it is worrying that populist and possibly self-serving governments at the centre and in states are willing to pour more resources in the leaking bucket of social welfare. More importantly, it bears noting that privatization of even all the economic activities of the state will not have a major impact on the level of corruption measured by the number of cases because a bulk of the corruption can be traced back to the essential functions of the state. So, the above distribution apart from highlighting the need to sharpen the focus of anti-corruption agencies also suggests that short of a thorough overhaul of the structure of the country's administrative systems, ex-post prosecution of corruption or withdrawal from economic activities cannot reduce the level of corruption.

Hierarchical Spread

The question of inclusion of petty officials within the jurisdiction of a national ombudsman is one of the contentious issues in the Lokpal debate. We classify the officials into four broad groups—higher officials (directors, CEOs, commissioners, registrars, members of the legislative assembly, corporators, etc.), middle-ranking officials (officers, inspectors, managers, etc.), petty officials (clerks, peons, assistants, guards, stenographers, village accountants, bill collectors, drivers, etc.), and officials from professional

---

[13] Hitherto estimates of the departmental distribution of corruption in India have relied on public perception surveys (Transparency International 2005, India Corruption Study 2010) or self-disclosure (iPaidABribe.com n.d.; Paul and Shah 1997). Data 'on the nature, number, pattern, types, location, frequency and values' of corruption collected by iPaidABribe.com suffers from a self-reporting bias. In addition, it is restricted to those who are computer literate. In contrast, the data used in this study can be divided into two parts—self-reported (trap cases) and Lokayukta-reported (raid cases). Even in trap cases the Lokayukta verifies complaints and drops bogus cases and cases in which complainants have alternative remedies.

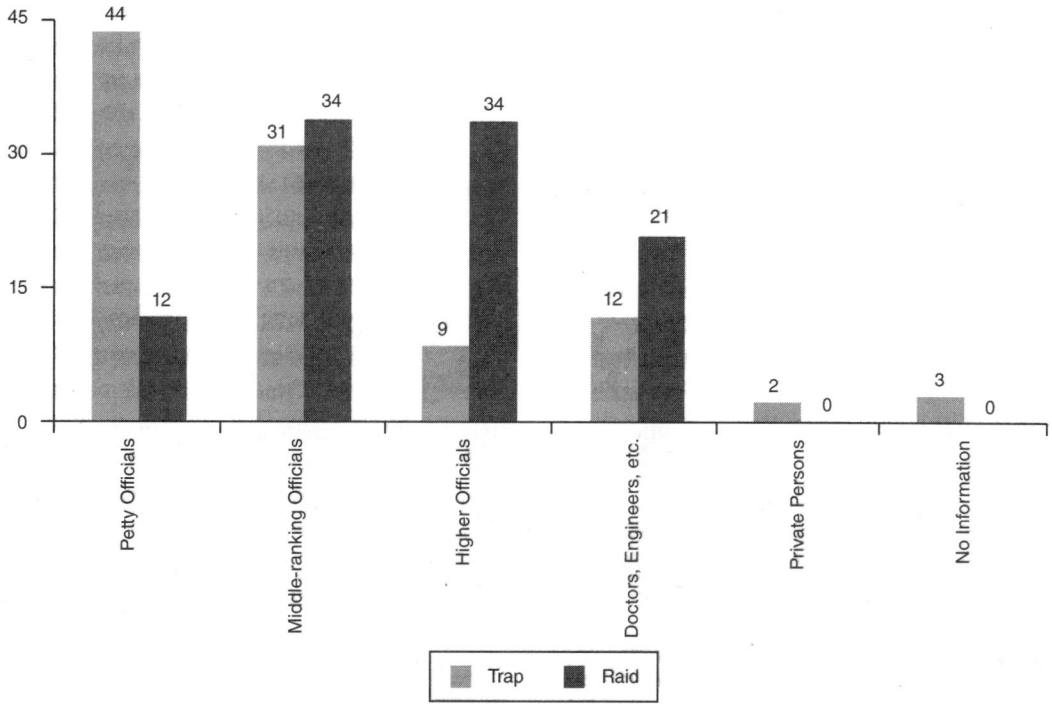

Figure 19.10 Share of Different Tiers of Bureaucracy in Corruption

Source: Authors' own.

cadres (doctors, engineers, lawyers, geologists, college lecturers, etc.).[14]

A few facts emerge from our data. First, about 40 per cent of the officials against whom the Lokayukta has proceeded against are petty officials, who are more likely to be trapped than raided, while about 10 per cent are higher officials (Figure 19.8). (The share of higher officials is less than 20 per cent even if higher officials from professional cadres are included.) Only 24 officials (0.77 per cent) belong to the highest cadre including IAS, IPS, IFS, and KAS officials and only two are/were members of the legislature (Figure 19.10). This suggests that using the same agency to deal with corruption involving all the tiers of bureaucracy and all kinds of corruption will overburden the agency with petty corruption cases and spread the prosecutorial focus thin.[15] Moreover, given that the existing agency is citizen complaint driven, in the absence of changes to its design,

petty corruption which directly affects people, would continue to account for the bulk of its workload.

Second, corruption is a group activity. While involving too many people could lead to collective action problems, it could be difficult to manipulate the system alone and thus a potentially corrupt official needs accomplices. Of the 355 raid cases, which targeted individual officials by design, only two involved more than one official. But of the 2,259 trap cases, 385 involved more than one person. The maximum number of officials trapped together in a case was eight. While one in every six trap cases involved more than one person, more than a third of the persons trapped were trapped together with others. Of the six IAS/IPS/KAS officials (MLAs) trapped, three (one) were trapped with middle-ranking or higher officials except in one case where a petty official was involved. In fact, higher officials as a whole have a greater share of those caught together with others. In other words, higher officials seem to be using lower officials as conduits for corrupt dealings. Also, 56 of the 61 private individuals were trapped with government officials, whereas in five cases they were trapped alone (most likely because the official counterpart of the private agent failed to show up

---

[14] Alternatively, the officials involved can be classified according to whether they are gazetted, a scheme followed by the National Crime Records Bureau (The NCRB 2010). A more elaborate classification is the Group A, B, C, and D classification scheme (Standing Committee 2011: para 8.1). Unfortunately, we do not have information to follow either of these alternatives.

[15] Inadvisability of treating petty and grand corruption alike and using the same agencies and legal instruments to deal with them

has been questioned for quite some time (for example, Rowat 1984, Panchu 2011).

or did not fall in the trap). This suggests that some officials rely on private individuals as accomplices.

Geographical Distribution

If economic activities and government offices are unevenly distributed across the state, then cases of corruption should also be distributed unevenly. Six districts—Bengaluru Urban, Bengaluru Rural (including Ramanagara), Belgaum, Kolar (including Chikaballapur), Mysore, and Gulbarga (including Yadgiri)—accounted for more than half of the trap and raid cases (Figure 19.11a). The first five, which include the capital of the state, ranked high among the districts of Karnataka in terms of human development and are also among the leading industrial centres of the state. However, Gulbarga is the most backward district of Karnataka (Government of Karnataka 2006: 7). The districts with the highest incidence of corruption normalized by population are: Bengaluru Rural (including Ramanagara), Bengaluru Urban, Kodagu, Hasan, Chikamagalur, and Kolar (Figure 19.11b). Barring Kodagu, all these districts are among the relatively developed districts of the state.

Processing of Cases

Of the 3,097 cases investigated by the Lokayukta between 1995 and 2011, 20 cases had to be dropped due to the death of the individual under investigation and 327 cases were dropped after the investigation did not yield sufficient evidence to proceed further. Of the rest, trials could be completed only in 78 cases, which accounts for a trial completion rate of 4 per cent, leading to a mere 16 convictions. The conviction rate of 20 (25) per cent in trap (raid) cases investigated by the Karnataka Lokayukta is much lower than the rate of convictions in criminal prosecutions in anti-corruption cases in India in recent years, which is between 34 and 40 per cent (NCRB 2007–9, Table 9.1, Col. 23).

Why has one of the most active Lokayuktas failed to secure convictions? One could argue that most of the accused were not guilty. However, it is difficult to believe that in an overwhelming majority of trap cases the charges could not be sustained in courts since in these cases officials were caught red-handed committing acts of corruption. Alternatively, given the poor image of the government and the bureaucracy, it is tempting to believe that in most cases either sanction for prosecution was not given or the agency failed to complete investigations. But the data tell a different story (Figures 19.12, 19.13, and 19.14). Figure 19.12 traces the lifecycle of the stock of cases, whereas Figures 19.13 and 19.14 show the rate of processing of cases and the average age of cases pending processing at different stages respectively.

In 80.43 (55.68) per cent of the trap (raid) cases, investigations have been completed. The average age of a trap (raid) case pending investigation is 1.05 (2.11) years. Of the cases that were investigated and found fit for filing of charges, sanction for prosecution was obtained in 94.42

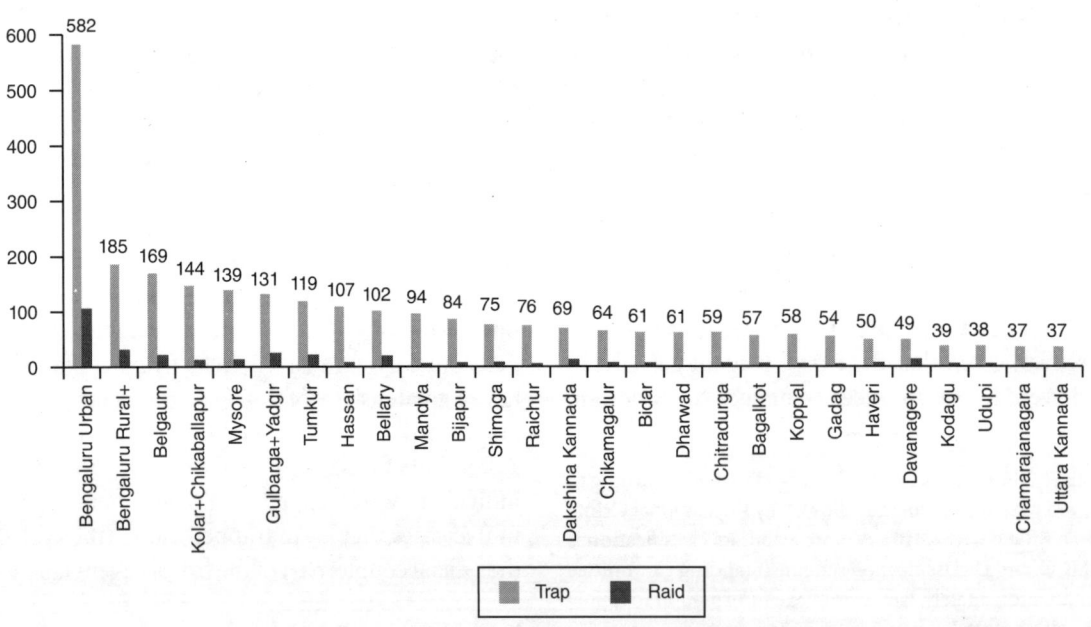

Figure 19.11a   Geographical Spread of Corruption

Source: Authors' own.

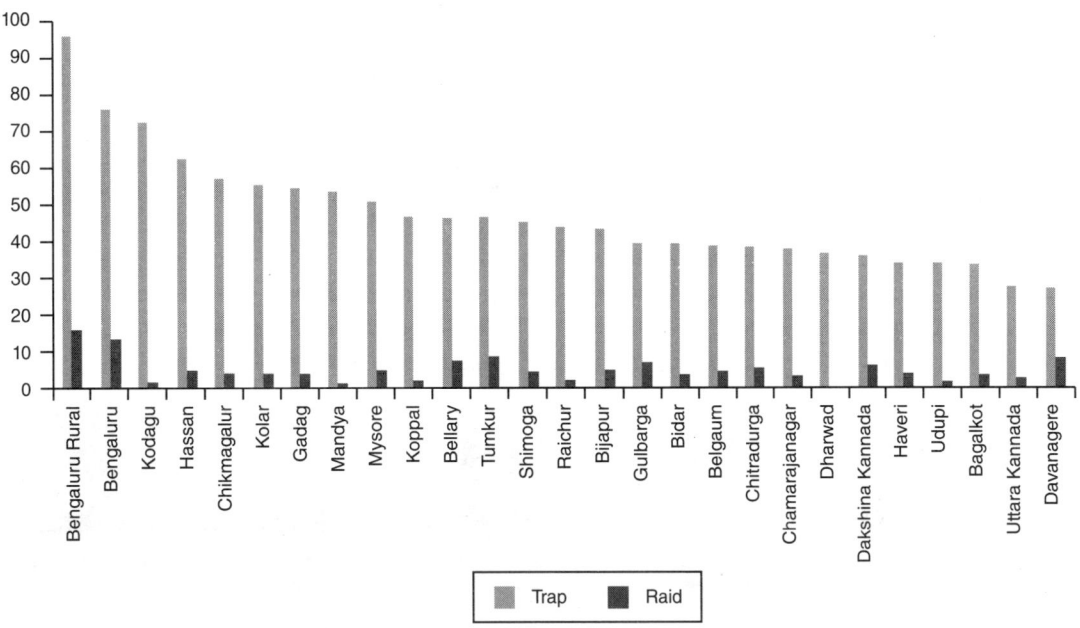

Figure 19.11b Number of Cases per Million Population

Source: Authors' own.

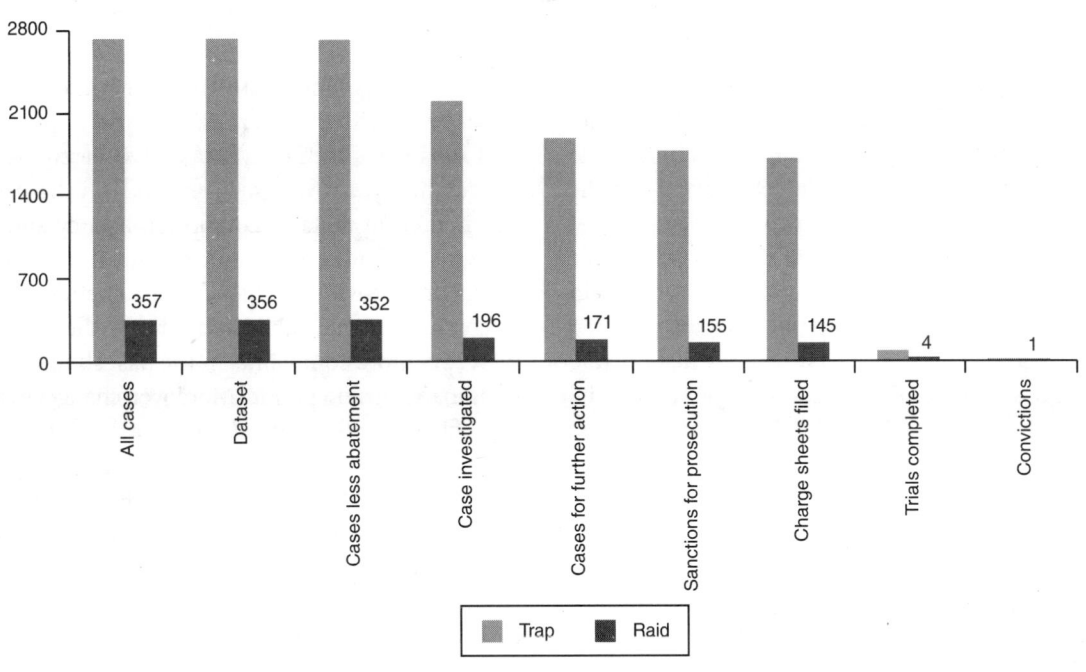

Figure 19.12 The Life Cycle of Cases

Source: Authors' own.

(90.64) per cent cases. Trap (raid) cases in which sanction is awaited are on an average 1.59 (3.19) years old. In only two cases sanction was denied. Of all the trap (raid) cases in which sanction was granted charge sheets were filed in 96.29 (93.55) per cent cases. Trap (raid) cases in which charge sheets are pending are on an average 2.53 (3.40) years old. Up until this stage the rate at which cases are processed is comparable to processing of criminal cases by other agencies. The bottleneck lies after this stage. Of the trap (raid) cases in which charge sheets have been filed, 95.68

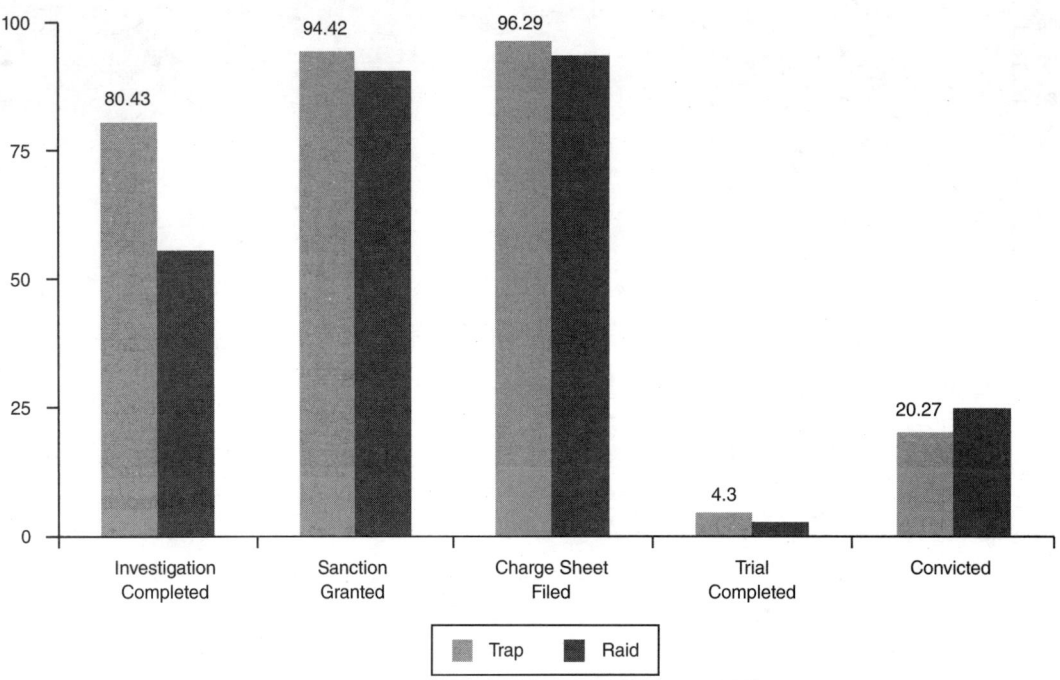

Figure 19.13 Rate of Processing of Cases (in %) at Different Stages

Source: Authors' own.

(97.24) per cent are under trial. The average age of the trap (raid) cases under trial is 5.08 (7.95) years. Further, of all the trap (raid) cases investigated and under trial only 15 (1) have resulted in convictions. The average age of cases at the time of conviction was about 4.2 years. Of these cases just one involves a higher official (Figure 19.15). In passing, note that insofar as higher officials are over-represented in raid cases, which have lower processing rates and are pending for longer durations (Figure 19.14), we can say that the rate at which a case is processed decreases with the rank of the officials.

Analysis

We do not have information on the value of bribes in case of traps and the assets of the accused in the case of raids. We also do not have information on the time spent by a case at different stages of processing and the quantum of punishment in case of convictions.[16] So, our econometric analysis is confined to an analysis of the determinants of the number of cases initiated in a district in a given year. We used a count regression model to analyse the data.

Our analysis allows us to make a few interesting claims.[17] Let us begin with the direct and indirect impacts of the past performance of the Lokayukta on its current performance. As mentioned above, *suo motu* raids in the past enhance public faith in the anti-corruption agency and encourage citizens to lodge complaints. Similarly, past citizen complaints provide the agency with a better idea of the loci of corruption and public support for the anti-corruption drive. So, more complaints in the past should lead to more raids in the current period. Moreover, changes in the stock of cases filed should potentially alter corrupt officials' estimates of the risks involved in corrupt dealings. We found that more traps (raids) in the past year have a positive impact on the number of trap (raid) cases in the current year. Cases initiated in the last year positively affect the number of cases filed in the current year, which is likely to be driven by the way bureaucratic performance is gauged through annually ratcheting up of targets. However, the stock of cases accumulated in all previous years does not significantly affect cases filed in the current year possibly because of tardy prosecution resulting in very few convictions. We also checked the cross-effects between cases of different types.

---

[16] The NCRB (2010) classifies punishment into four categories: dismissal, removal, major penalty, and minor penalty. But our data provides information only regarding dismissals.

[17] However, definitive conclusions can be drawn only after a systematic assessment of the performance of other state Lokayuktas.

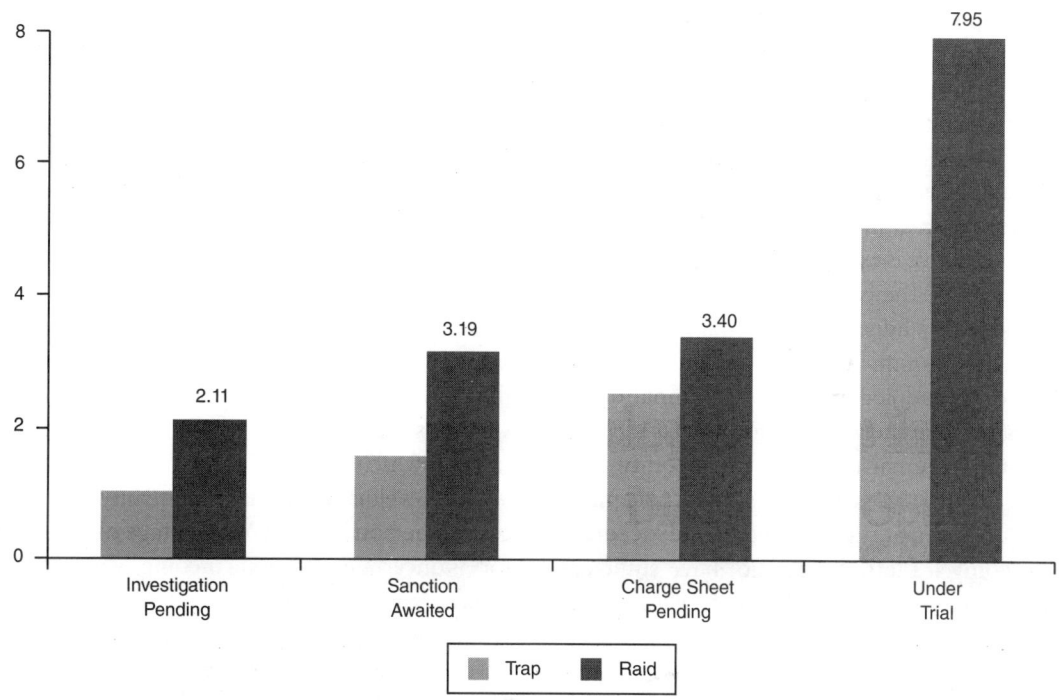

Figure 19.14 Average Age of Pending Cases (in Years) at Different Stages of Prosecution

Source: Authors' own.

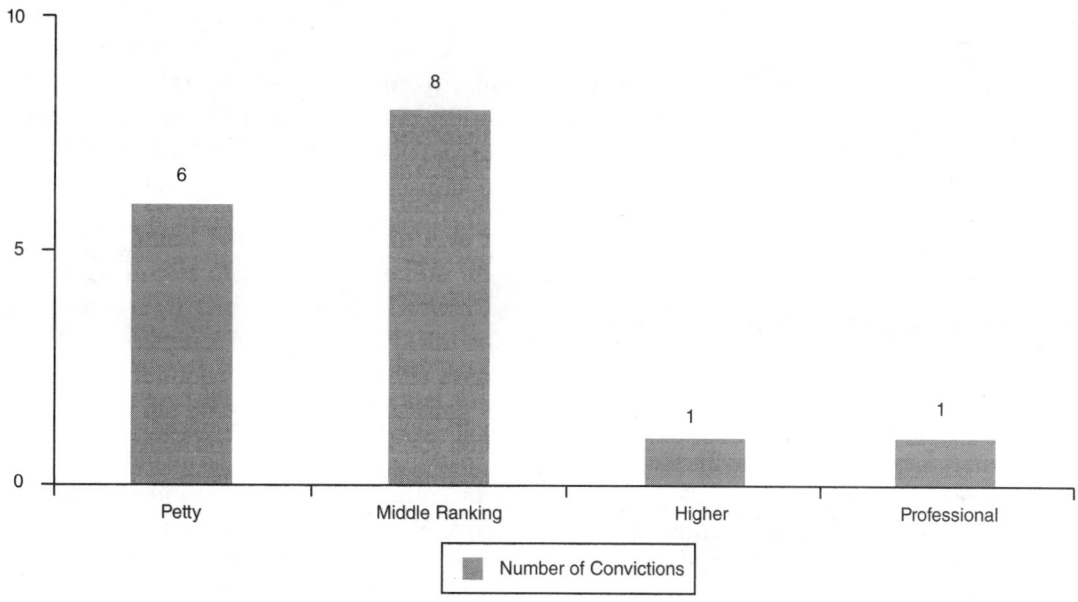

Figure 19.15 Distribution of Convictions by Designation of Officials

Source: Authors' own.

We found that more raids (traps) in the past year increase trap (raid) cases in the current year.

But more than investigations, convictions should alert potentially corrupt officials to the risk of getting caught and should, therefore, suppress the number of trap as well as raid cases. We found that the spurt in convictions in 2005, when about half of the convictions were secured, had a negative impact on the number of cases filed in later years. The small magnitude of the effect of convictions can be attributed to the fact that the actual number of convictions is minuscule as compared to the total stock of cases (less than half a per cent).

Cases initiated should also depend on the demand (official and citizen) for prosecution. Official demand in turn depends on who occupies the office of the Lokayukta, how serious the state government is about tackling corruption, and stability of tenures. The state government's seriousness depends on the party in power, the chief minister in office, and public awareness about the problem of corruption and means to tackle it legally. Institutional stability also has a role to play in this regard. A new Lokayukta may put in extra effort soon after assuming office to announce his arrival and also before leaving office to embellish his legacy. Conversely, instability (frequent changes in the institution's leadership) should lead to a lesser number of investigations because the incoming leadership needs time to settle, whereas the outgoing leadership may not have sufficient incentive to pursue cases with zeal. The stability of leadership of the agency captures the certainty within the organization and should lead to more investigations because the agency is in a position to concentrate on pursing suspected officials. However, it is also likely that potentially corruptible officials lie low when the leadership of the agency is stable. Regarding the influence of the political leadership, it bears noting that state governments may support the Lokayukta in election years, when the ruling party is seeking re-election.[18]

We compared periods in which the office of Lokayukta or chief minister was occupied by one person with periods in which there was a change of leadership so that there was more than one person in office during the period of interest. The number of cases initiated is significantly less in periods with one Lokayukta. Similarly, the effect of a stable political leadership on the number of trap and raid cases filed is negative, even though insignificant. However, more raids (but not traps) in a Vidhan Sabha election year suggest that the officials could be under pressure to *show* results around elections. But parliamentary elections, in which local issues are not important, have a negative but insignificant impact on both raid and trap cases filed.[19]

Citizens' demand for prosecution depends on their awareness and empowerment. For want of reliable measures of awareness and empowerment at the district level, we capture awareness through literacy and empowerment through female workforce participation. Citizen demand also depends on the incidence of corruption, which depends on the number of officials (captured indirectly by the size of the economy and population because we do not have year- and district-wise data), size of the economy, and quality of government (captured using infant mortality rate). But note that other things being equal, a higher level of corruption translates into poor public education and health infrastructure, which in turn will negatively affect the economy and so forth. So, the 1991 measures of these variables are used, whereas the earliest year in the dataset is 1995.

Infant mortality rate has a negative effect on the number of cases, whereas the effect of other human development indicators is uncertain. Per capita income, which can be treated as a proxy of capacity to pay, is found to be positively (negatively) related with number of raid (trap) cases. But the overall size of the economy measured by district domestic product is always negatively related with the number of cases. The size of the economy actually shares a U-shaped relationship with the level of corruption measured by the number of cases, which supports our finding that both the most and least developed districts record more cases of corruption (see the section 'Geographical Distribution'). The former provide more opportunities of extraction from industries and citizens who have a higher paying capacity for subsidized services offered by the state whereas the latter receive massive government aid that is easy to siphon off. This claim is also supported by the greater share of the industrialized districts in cases of corruption in economic and regulatory functions of the state filed by the Lokayukta.

THE WAY AHEAD

The Indian debate on a national anti-corruption ombudsman has focused extensively on remedying institutional inefficiencies at the complaint and investigation stage in the Lokpal. No matter how successful these innovations are, they will neither address the structural problems inherent in the way in which the administration works, nor tackle the core problem with a criminal justice system in India, namely, the trial stage. Our study of the performance of the Karnataka Lokayukta suggests that short of a thorough overhaul of the structure of the country's administrative system, ex-post prosecution of corruption or withdrawal from economic activities cannot reduce the level of corruption. Our analysis also suggests that the overburdened legal system, with a growing number of cases pending in understaffed

---

[18] Kunicová and Rose-Ackerman (2005) discuss the impact of the design of the electoral system on the level of corruption, whereas Chong et al. (2011) discuss the effect of exposure of corruption on electoral outcomes. Gupta (2011) discusses the relationship between electoral politics and grand corruption in India, whereas Banerjee and Pande (2007) study the relationship between ethnicity and quality of winners of elections in north India.

[19] Differences in voting behaviour in parliamentary and provincial elections is widespread in India.

and underequipped courts[20] governed by archaic laws, seems to be the real bottleneck. The system can be easily manipulated to drag a trial.[21] Any legislation built around a criminal conviction model to tackle corruption is bound to face the same environmental limits, namely, the efficacy of the criminal justice system.

So, without highly contentious legal reforms, an extremely powerful agency, which the civil society is demanding, can at best marginally improve investigation rates and filing of charges in corruption cases without securing more convictions. But the price that the civil society is asking of us for this marginal improvement[22] is heavy because an ombudsman armed with sweeping powers could disturb the precarious balance of power among different arms and tiers of the government.

In fact, as highlighted by Klitgaard (1988), red tape in bureaucracy is often a byproduct of attempts to reduce corruption. This alerts us to the importance of evaluating both the direct and indirect costs as well as benefits associated with anti-corruption mechanisms. In that vein, in this chapter we examined the problems associated with one such anti-corruption mechanism—creation of an ombudsman. It is also important to recognize the possibility that anti-corruption departments could be driven by performance targets or alternatively anti-corruption laws could be misused to target opponents (political or otherwise). In such cases where the ombudsmen or the activists themselves could make false accusations with an ulterior motive, one should worry about suitably circumscribing the powers of such agencies to minimize collateral costs. This also suggests a more cautious approach to investigation that may cause delay, may after all, be efficient (see, for instance, Wilson 1989).

One also needs to keep in mind the wider effects of control of corruption. For example, if as shown in this chapter, most cases investigated by the ombudsman are based on complaints, the officials might tend to 'please the clients' rather than perform their roles efficiently. Also, often the officials may have more information on the decision-making situations that they are involved in than any third party such as investigators. In such cases, the tendency would be to 'go by the book' or 'please the masses' and disregard the additional information available to them, which may actually lead to different 'correct' decisions.[23] For all these reasons, 'investigating and prosecuting corruption' is a lot more difficult design problem than what is commonly understood. If civil society's demands, which confound the structurally different bulk and retail corruptions requiring different anti-corruption machineries, are followed then we may end up with an ill-conceived agency with thinly spread prosecutorial resources. A careful approach to the design of an anti-corruption body would be based not only on an assessment of the performance of the Central Bureau of Investigation and the Central Vigilance Commission, different state-level Lokayuktas, and reports of various enquiry commissions that have probed cases of corruption, but also on a comparison of different models of anti-corruption agencies in other parts of the world.

---

[20] Prashant Bhushan, a senior lawyer and member of anti-corruption crusader Anna Hazare's core group, attributes delays to inadequate number of judges, prosecutors, and investigators and the low rate of conviction to inadequate coordination between investigators and prosecutors and the poor quality of charge sheets (Venkatesan 2011). But we do not have data to verify his claim. We can add to this list the insufficient administrative control of the Lokayukta on its police wing.

[21] The accused can seek a stay on investigation (at least 13 cases in our data) or interim relief from a higher court after conviction in a lower court (*Deccan Herald* 2012b). The accused can also bribe the investigator or, in the case of trap, even the complainant. Media abounds in anecdotal evidence regarding corruption within the Lokayukta. In fact, in 2000 the Lokayukta raided its own official, a first divisional assistant working with the Lokayukta department in district Tumkur. Like most of the other cases this case is yet to be concluded.

[22] Our analysis suggests that even within the existing legal and bureaucratic framework, the Karnataka Lokayukta is able to achieve very high processing rates in the pre-trial stages. So, misunderstandings regarding how the current system operates have been the cause of much of the misguided focus on the pre-trial stage. This mismatch between popular perception and reality has been under discussion for long (Palmer 1985, Alexander 1995, Quah 2003).

[23] For a rigorous analysis of these effects, see Prendergast (2000).

REFERENCES

Acemoglu, D. and T. Verdier (1998), 'Property Rights, Corruption and the Allocation of Talent: A General Equilibrium Approach', *Economic Journal*, 108: 1381–403.

Aiyappa, M. (2011), 'Complaints at Karnataka Lokayukta dwindle', *Times of India*, 23 November 23. Available at http://timesofindia.indiatimes.com/city/bangalore/Complaints-at-Karnataka-Lokayukta-dwindle/articleshow/10836823.cms, accessed on 30 March 2012.

Alexander, P.C. (1995), *The Perils of Democracy*. Mumbai: Somaiya Publications.

Bahari, H. (2002), *Hindi Sabdakosh*. Delhi: Rajpal and Sons.

Banerjee, A.V. (1997) 'A Theory of Misgovernance', *Quarterly Journal of Economics*, 112: 1289–332.

Banerjee, A.V. and R. Pande (2007), 'Parochial Politics: Ethnic Preferences and Politician Corruption', RWP07-031, KSG Faculty Research Working Paper Series.

Banerjee, A.V., R. Hanna, and S. Mullainathan (2012), 'Corruption', MIT Mimeo.

Bardhan, Pranab (1997), 'Corruption and Development: A Review of Issues', *Journal of Economic Literature*, 35: 1320–46.

Bertrand, M., S. Djankov, R. Hanna, and S. Mullainathan (2007), 'Obtaining a Driving License in India: An Experimental Approach to Studying Corruption', *Quarterly Journal of Economics*, 122: 1639–76.

Bliss, C. and R. Di Tella (1997), 'Does Competition Kill Corruption?', *Journal of Political Economy*, 105(5): 1001–23.

Canineu, M. (n.d.), 'The Role of Ombuds Agencies in Police Accountability in the Commonwealth', Commonwealth Human Rights Initiative, New Delhi.

Choi, J.P. and M. Thum (2005), 'Corruption and the Shadow Economy', *International Economic Review*, 46: 817–36.

Chong, A., L. De La O, Ana, D. Karlan, and L. Wantchekon (2011), 'Looking Beyond the Incumbent: The Effects of Exposing Corruption on Electoral Outcomes', NBER Working Paper 17679.

CBI (n.d.), 'A Brief History of CBI'. Available at: http://www.cbi.nic.in/history.php, last accessed on 2 November 2012.

CVC (n.d.), 'Frequently Asked Questions'. Available at: http://www.cvc.nic.in/faqs.htm, last accessed on 2 November 2012.

Deccan Herald (2012a), "Tainted' DGET officer goes scot-free, holds key position', 11 February. Available at http://www.deccanherald.com/content/226487/tainted-dget-officer-goes-scot.html, accessed on 4 February 2012.

———. (2012b), 'Scribe falls into Lokayukta net', 14 April, p. 4.

Echazu, L. and P. Bose (2008), 'Corruption, Centralization, and the Shadow Economy', *Southern Economic Journal*, 75(2): 524–37.

Economic Times (2011), 'Corporate leaders like Azim Premji, Deepak Parekh write to government, suggest reforms to curb graft', 11 October. Available at: http://articles.economictimes.indiatimes.com/2011-10-11/news/30266850_1_corruption-hits-deepak-parekh-lokpal-bill, last accessed on 24 March 2012.

Fisman, R. (2001), 'Estimating the Value of Political Connections', *American Economic Review*, 91: 1095–102.

Friedman, E., S. Johnson, D. Kaufmann, and P. Zoido-Lobatón (2000), 'Dodging the grabbing hand: the determinants of unofficial activity in 69 countries', *Journal of Public Economics*, 76: 459–93.

Government of Karnataka (2006), *Karnataka: Human Development Report 2005*. Planning and Statistics Department, Government of Karnataka.

Gupta, A. (1995), 'Blurred Boundaries: The Discourse of Corruption, the Culture of Politics, and the Imagined State', *American Ethnologist*, 22(2): 375–402.

———. (2011), 'The Political Economy of Liberalization in India', Thursday Colloquium, Azim Premji University, Bangalore, 11 August.

Hatchard, John (1992), 'Developing Governmental Accountability: The Role of the Ombudsman', *Third World Legal Studies* 11: Article 9. Available at: http://scholar.valpo.edu/twls/vol11/iss1/9, last accessed on 6 April 2012.

India Corruption Study (2010), *India Corruption Study 2010: Is the Scenario Changing*, New Delhi: Centre for Media Studies.

India Today (2012), 'Can't do much to prevent corruption in National Rural Employment Guarantee Scheme: Jairam', 15 April. Available at http://indiatoday.intoday.in/story/cant-do-much-to-prevent-corruption-in-nregs-jairam-ramesh/1/184610.html, last accessed on 23 April 2012.

iPaidaBribe.com (n.d.). Available at: www.IPaidaBribe.com, accessed on 30 March 2012.

Johnson, S., D. Kaufmann, and A. Shleifer (1997), 'The Unofficial Economy in Transition', *Brookings Paper on Economic Activity*, 2: 159–221.

Karnataka Lokayukta (n.d.), Available at: http://www.lokayukta.kar.nic.in., last accessed on

Klitgaard, R. (1988), *Controlling Corruption*. Berkeley and Los Angeles: University of California Press.

Kumar, R. (2011), 'Indian corruption: Time to fight back', *East Asia Forum*, 20 January. Available at: http://www.eastasiaforum.org/2011/01/20/indian-corruption-time-to-fight-back/, accessed on 24 March 2012.

Kunicová, Jana and Susan Rose-Ackerman (2005), 'Electoral Rules and Constitutional Structures as Constraints on Corruption', *British Journal of Political Science*, 35: 573–606.

Livemint (2007), 'Corruption catalogue: Public Distribution System'. Available at: http://www.livemint.com/2007/05/02160432/A348945B-1EC7-4808-8D72-E5ED35A26BE2ArtVPF.pdf, accessed on 23 April 2012.

Mauro, Paolo (1995), 'Corruption and Growth', *Quarterly Journal of Economics*, 100: 681–712.

Moody-Stuart, G. (1994), 'Grand Corruption in Third World Development', Working Paper, Transparency International, Berlin.

Narayana, A., S. Krishnaswamy, and V. Kumar (2012), 'Lokpal Bill: Lessons from the Karnataka Lokayukta's Performance', *Economic and Political Weekly*, 47: 12–16.

Odisha Government (n.d.). Available at: http://rtiorissa.gov.in/dept_home.php?id=24&oid=193&sid=2, last accessed on 6 April 2012.

Oldenburg, Philip (1987), 'Middlemen in Third-World Corruption', *World Politics*, 39: 508–35.
One Bangalore (n.d.), 'Chief Ministers'. Available at: http://www.onlinebangalore.com/gove/karg/chief/html, last accessed on 2 November 2012.
Palmer, L. (1985), *The Control of Bureaucratic Corruption: Case Studies in Asia*. New Delhi: Allied Publications.
Panchu, S. (2011), 'Lokpal: Where Do We Stand Now, and How We Got Here', *Economic and Political Weekly*, 46(41): 19–21.
Paul, S. and M. Shah (1997), 'Corruption in Public Service Delivery', in S. Guhan and S. Paul (eds), *Corruption in India: Agenda for Action*. New Delhi: Vision Books.
Prendergast, C. (2000), *Investigating Corruption*. Washington, DC: World Bank Development Research Group: Public Economics, Policy Research Working Paper No. 2500.
Prevention of Corruption Act (1988), Available at: http://lokayukta.kar.nic.in/preact.htm, last accessed on 17 April 2012.
Quah, Jon S.T. (2003), 'Combating Corruption in India, Some Lessons from Asian Experiences', in Stephn Howes, A. Lahiri, and N. Stern (eds), *State-Level Reforms in India: Towards More Effective Government*. New Delhi: MacMillan.
Reuters (2012), 'China's Wen: corruption could threaten power structure'. Available at: http://www.reuters.com/article/2012/03/26/us-china-wen-corruption-idUSBRE82P0L720120326, accessed on 30 March 2012.
Rose-Ackerman, Susan (1997), 'The Political Economy of Corruption', in Kimberly Ann Elliott (ed.) *Corruption and the Global Economy*, Chapter 2. Washington, D.C.: Institute for International Economics.
Rowat, D.C. (1984), 'The Suitability of the Ombudsman Plan for Developing Countries', *International Review of Administrative Sciences*, 50(3): 207–11.
Shleifer, A. and R.W. Vishny (1993), 'Corruption', *Quarterly Journal of Economics*, 108: 599–618.
Standing Committee (2011), *The 48th Report of the Department Related Standing Committee on Personnel, Public Grievances, Law and Justice on The Lokpal Bill, 2011* (presented to the Rajya Sabha on 9 December 2011). Available at: http://www.prsindia.org/uploads/media/Lokpal/SCR%20Lokpal%20Bill%202011.pdf, last accessed on 12 December 2011.
Stark, Joshua J.M. (2011), 'Kerala's Ombudsman: A Mismatch of Mission and Capabilities', *Governance*, 24(2): 389–92. Available at: <http://www.accountabilityindia.in/sites/default/files/the_kerala_ombudsman.pdf>, last accessed on 18 February 2011.
The Foreign and Commonwealth Office (2011), *The Bribery Act 2010*. Available at: http://www.fco.gov.uk/en/global-issues/conflict-minerals/legally-binding-process/uk-bribery-act, last accessed on 30 March 2012.
The Karnataka Lokayukta Act (1984), Available at: http://www.kar.nic.in/lokayukta/karnataka_lokayukta_act.htm, last accessed on 15 April 2012.
———. (2010), Available at: http://dpal.kar.nic.in/ao2010%5C25 of2010(E).pdf, last accessed on 21 December 2011.
The National Crime Records Bureau (2007–2009), *Crime in India*. Available at: http://ncrb.nic.in/, last accessed on 20 December 2011.
———. (2010), *Crime in India*. Available at: http://ncrb.nic.in/, last accessed on 18 October 2012.
Times of India (2011), 'India ratifies UN convention against corruption', 13 May (Available at: http://articles.timesofindia.indiatimes.com/2011-05-13/india/29539746_1_convention-fight-corruption-assets, last accessed on 30 March 2012.
Transparency International (2005), *India Corruption Study*. Available at http://www.transparency.org/regional_pages/asia_pacific/newsroom/news_archive2/india_corruption_study_2005, last accessed on 6 April 2012.
United Nations (2003), *UN Convention against Corruption*. Available at: http://www.unodc.org/unodc/en/treaties/CAC/, last accessed on 30 March 2012.
Venkatesan, V. (2011), 'Whole Bill diluted', *Frontline*, 29 January. Available at: http://www.frontline.in/stories/20120127290101200.htm, accessed on 1 October 2011.
Visvanathan, Shiv (1999), 'The Great Indian Novel: Reflections on the Lentin Report', *Economic and Political Weekly*: 34: PE 39-PE 48, (30 January–5 February).
Wade, Robert (1982), 'The system of administrative and political corruption: Canal irrigation in South India', *Journal of Development Studies*, 18: 287–328.
Wilson, J.Q. (1989), *Bureaucracy: What Government Agencies Do and Why They Do It*. New York: Basic Books.

A Statistical Profile of India's Development

A1 NATIONAL INCOME

Table A1.1 Key National Accounts Aggregates—2004–5 Series (at Constant Prices)

(Rupees, Crore)

Year	GDP at Factor Cost		Net Factor Income from Abroad	GNP at Factor Cost (2+3)		Consumption of Fixed Capital	NNP at Factor Cost (4–5)	NDP at Factor Cost (2–5)	Indirect Taxes Less Subsidies (9–2)	GDP at Market Prices (2+8)		NDP at Market Prices (7+8)		GNP at Market Prices (4+8)		NNP at Market Prices (6+8)	
1	2		3	4		5	6	7	8	9		10		11		12	
1950–1	279618	..	–941	278677	..	23272	255405	256346	14319	293937	..	270665	..	292996	..	269724	..
1951–2	286147	2.3	–588	285558	2.5	22754	262804	263393	16452	302599	2.9	279845	3.4	302010	3.1	279256	3.5
1952–3	294267	2.8	–476	293791	2.9	22249	271541	272018	16277	310544	2.6	288295	3.0	310068	2.7	287818	3.1
1953–4	312177	6.1	–394	311784	6.1	21852	289931	290325	17466	329643	6.2	307791	6.8	329250	6.2	307397	6.8
1954–5	325431	4.2	–601	324830	4.2	18845	305985	306585	20072	345503	4.8	326657	6.1	344902	4.8	326057	6.1
1955–6	333766	2.6	–224	333542	2.7	19305	314238	314462	22918	356684	3.2	337380	3.3	356460	3.4	337156	3.4
1956–7	352766	5.7	–348	352418	5.7	20226	332192	332540	23816	376582	5.6	356356	5.6	376234	5.5	356008	5.6
1957–8	348500	–1.2	–530	347970	–1.3	20977	326992	327523	26533	375033	–0.4	354056	–0.6	374503	–0.5	353525	–0.7
1958–9	374948	7.6	–729	374219	7.5	22164	352054	352784	27801	402749	7.4	380585	7.5	402020	7.3	379855	7.4
1959–60	383153	2.2	–1289	381864	2.0	22951	358913	360202	30167	413320	2.6	390369	2.6	412031	2.5	389080	2.4
1960–1	410279	7.1	–1540	408739	7.0	22978	385761	387301	25758	436037	5.5	413059	5.8	434497	5.5	411519	5.8
1961–2	423011	3.1	–2058	420953	3.0	24109	396844	398902	29259	452270	3.7	428161	3.7	450212	3.6	426103	3.5
1962–3	431960	2.1	–2366	429594	2.1	25475	404119	406485	33567	465527	2.9	440052	2.8	463161	2.9	437686	2.7
1963–4	453829	5.1	–2382	451446	5.1	26919	424527	426910	39603	493432	6.0	466513	6.0	491049	6.0	464130	6.0
1964–5	488247	7.6	–3054	485193	7.5	28867	456327	459381	41960	530207	7.5	501341	7.5	527153	7.4	498287	7.4
1965–6	470402	–3.7	–3247	467155	–3.7	30505	436650	439897	45830	516232	–2.6	485727	–3.1	512985	–2.7	482480	–3.2
1966–7	475189	1.0	–3166	472024	1.0	32679	439345	442511	40757	515946	–0.1	483268	–0.5	512781	0.0	480102	–0.5
1967–8	513860	8.1	–3895	509965	8.0	34913	475052	478947	42464	556324	7.8	521411	7.9	552429	7.7	517516	7.8
1968–9	527270	2.6	–3712	523558	2.7	36783	486775	490488	47902	575172	3.4	538390	3.3	571460	3.4	534677	3.3
1969–70	561630	6.5	–3978	557652	6.5	39218	518434	522411	51157	612787	6.5	573568	6.5	608809	6.5	569591	6.5
1970–1	589786	5.0	–4115	585672	5.0	43805	541867	545981	54603	644389	5.2	600584	4.7	640275	5.2	596470	4.7
1971–2	595741	1.0	–4039	591703	1.0	45727	545976	550015	59235	654976	1.6	609250	1.4	650938	1.7	605211	1.5
1972–3	593843	–0.3	–3705	590138	–0.3	47452	542686	546391	57509	651352	–0.6	603900	–0.9	647647	–0.5	600195	–0.8
1973–4	620872	4.6	–3374	617498	4.6	49560	567937	571311	51946	672818	3.3	623257	3.2	669444	3.4	619883	3.3
1974–5	628079	1.2	–2642	625437	1.3	52696	572741	575383	52714	680793	1.2	628097	0.8	678151	1.3	625455	0.9
1975–6	684634	9.0	–2278	682355	9.1	55576	626779	629058	58451	743085	9.1	687509	9.5	740806	9.2	685230	9.6
1976–7	693191	1.2	–2095	691096	1.3	59199	631897	633992	62252	755443	1.7	696244	1.3	753348	1.7	694149	1.3
1977–8	744972	7.5	–1749	743223	7.5	61780	681442	683191	65277	810249	7.3	748468	7.5	808500	7.3	746719	7.6
1978–9	785964	5.5	–1667	784297	5.5	64302	719996	721663	70570	856534	5.7	792233	5.8	854867	5.7	790566	5.9
1979–80	745083	–5.2	–310	744772	–5.0	67432	677340	677651	66585	811668	–5.2	744236	–6.1	811357	–5.1	743925	–5.9

(Contd.)

Table A1.1 (Contd.)

(Rupees, Crore)

Year	GDP at Factor Cost		Net Factor Income from Abroad	GNP at Factor Cost (2+3)		Consumption of Fixed Capital	NNP at Factor Cost (4-5)	NDP at Factor Cost (2-5)		Indirect Taxes Less Subsidies (9-2)	GDP at Market Prices (2+8)		NDP at Market Prices (7+8)		GNP at Market Prices (4+8)		NNP at Market Prices (6+8)	
1	2		3	4		5	6	7		8	9		10		11		12	
1980-1	798506	7.2	-2	798504	7.2	71144	727359	727362	7.3	67834	866340	6.7	795196	6.8	866338	6.8	795193	6.9
1981-2	843426	5.6	-1102	842324	5.5	74843	767481	768583	5.7	74948	918374	6.0	843531	6.1	917272	5.9	842429	5.9
1982-3	868091	2.9	-3803	864288	2.6	79154	785134	788937	2.6	82203	950294	3.5	871140	3.3	946491	3.2	867337	3.0
1983-4	936269	7.9	-4218	932051	7.8	83101	848950	853168	8.1	83291	1019560	7.3	936459	7.5	1015342	7.3	932241	7.5
1984-5	973357	4.0	-5872	967485	3.8	88877	878609	884480	3.7	85158	1058515	3.8	969638	3.5	1052643	3.7	963767	3.4
1985-6	1013866	4.2	-5867	1007999	4.2	94855	913143	919010	3.9	100267	1114133	5.3	1019277	5.1	1108266	5.3	1013410	5.2
1986-7	1057612	4.3	-6541	1051071	4.3	100613	950457	956999	4.1	109738	1167350	4.8	1066737	4.7	1160809	4.7	1060195	4.6
1987-8	1094992	3.5	-8783	1086209	3.3	107745	978464	987247	3.2	118647	1213639	4.0	1105894	3.7	1204856	3.8	1097111	3.5
1988-9	1206243	10.2	-12546	1193697	9.9	113560	1080137	1092683	10.7	124243	1330486	9.6	1216926	10.0	1317940	9.4	1204380	9.8
1989-90	1280228	6.1	-13461	1266767	6.1	120321	1146446	1159907	6.2	129387	1409615	5.9	1289294	5.9	1396154	5.9	1275833	5.9
1990-1	1347889	5.3	-16849	1331040	5.1	128735	1202305	1219154	5.1	139726	1487615	5.5	1358880	5.4	1470766	5.3	1342031	5.2
1991-2	1367171	1.4	-17630	1349541	1.4	137663	1211877	1229507	0.8	136166	1503337	1.1	1365673	0.5	1485707	1.0	1348043	0.4
1992-3	1440503	5.4	-17812	1422692	5.4	145847	1276845	1294656	5.3	145252	1585755	5.5	1439908	5.4	1567944	5.5	1422097	5.5
1993-4	1522343	5.7	-16205	1506138	5.9	152023	1354116	1370320	5.8	138748	1661091	4.8	1509068	4.8	1644886	4.9	1492864	5.0
1994-5	1619694	6.4	-16430	1603264	6.4	162292	1440972	1457402	6.4	152008	1771702	6.7	1609410	6.6	1755272	6.7	1592980	6.7
1995-6	1737740	7.3	-17672	1720069	7.3	172589	1547480	1565152	7.4	168159	1905899	7.6	1733311	7.7	1888228	7.6	1715639	7.7
1996-7	1876319	8.0	-16949	1859370	8.1	183611	1675759	1692708	8.1	173467	2049786	7.5	1866175	7.7	2032837	7.7	1849226	7.8
1997-8	1957031	4.3	-13824	1943208	4.5	198048	1745160	1758984	3.9	175767	2132798	4.0	1934751	3.7	2118975	4.2	1920927	3.9
1998-9	2087827	6.7	-14687	2073140	6.7	211888	1861252	1875939	6.6	176872	2264699	6.2	2052811	6.1	2250012	6.2	2038124	6.1
1999-2000	2246276	7.6	-16375	2229900	7.6	228651	2001250	2017625	7.6	210087	2456363	8.5	2227712	8.5	2439987	8.4	2211337	8.5
2000-1	2342774	4.3	-23800	2318974	4.0	244116	2074858	2098658	4.0	211230	2554004	4.0	2309888	3.7	2530204	3.7	2286088	3.4
2001-2	2472052	5.5	-21371	2450681	5.7	259944	2190737	2212108	5.4	208228	2680280	4.9	2420336	4.8	2658909	5.1	2398965	4.9
2002-3	2570690	4.0	-18960	2551730	4.1	273367	2278363	2297323	3.9	214323	2785013	3.9	2511646	3.8	2766053	4.0	2492686	3.9
2003-4	2777813	8.1	-20693	2757120	8.0	291027	2466093	2486786	8.2	228441	3006254	7.9	2715227	8.1	2985561	7.9	2694534	8.1
2004-5	2971464	7.0	-22375	2949089	7.0	319891	2629198	2651573	6.6	270745	3242209	7.8	2922318	7.6	3219834	7.8	2899943	7.6
2005-6	3253073	9.5	-24896	3228177	9.5	350894	2877284	2902180	9.5	290171	3543244	9.3	3192351	9.2	3518348	9.3	3167455	9.2
2006-7	3564364	9.6	-29515	3534849	9.5	385699	3149149	3178664	9.5	307125	3871489	9.3	3485789	9.2	3841974	9.2	3456274	9.1
2007-8	3896636	9.3	-17179	3879457	9.7	427630	3451829	3469008	9.1	354311	4250947	9.8	3823319	9.7	4233768	10.2	3806140	10.1
2008-9	4158676	6.7	-25384	4133292	6.5	468903	3664388	3689772	6.4	257674	4416350	3.9	3947446	3.2	4390966	3.7	3922062	3.0
2009-10	4507637	8.4	-27664	4479973	8.4	520320	3959653	3987317	8.1	272542	4780179	8.2	4259859	7.9	4752515	8.2	4232195	7.9
2010-11#	4885954	8.4	-52776	4833178	7.9	564463	4268715	4321491	8.4	350869	5236823	9.6	4672360	9.7	5184047	9.1	4619584	9.2
2011-12@	5222027	6.9	-50489	5171538	7.0	603289	4568249	4618739	6.9	405658	5627685	7.5	5024397	7.5	5577196	7.6	4973907	7.6

(Rupees, Crore)

Year	GDP at Factor Cost				Private Final Consumption Expenditure in Domestic Market (PFCE)		Government Final Consumption Expenditure (GFCE)		Gross Domestic Capital Formation (Adjusted)		Net Domestic Capital Formation (Adjusted)		Per Capita GNP at Factor Cost		Per Capita NNP at Factor Cost		Per Capita NDP at Factor Cost		Population (million)
	Public Sector	Per cent of GDP	Private Sector	Per cent of GDP													(in Rupees)***		
	13		14		15		16		17		18		19		20		21		22
1950-1	..	..	..	..	252210	..	17979	..	37952	..	14680	..	77626	..	71144	..	7141	..	359
1951-2	..	..	..	..	268241	6.4	18166	1.0	45402	19.6	22648	54.3	78235	0.8	72001	1.2	7216	1.1	365
1952-3	..	..	..	..	279065	4.0	18187	0.1	34569	-23.9	12320	-45.6	78976	0.9	72995	1.4	7312	1.3	372
1953-4	..	..	..	..	295842	6.0	18415	1.3	37494	8.5	15642	27.0	82265	4.2	76499	4.8	7660	4.8	379
1954-5	..	..	..	..	305547	3.3	18523	0.6	43625	16.4	24780	58.4	84153	2.3	79271	3.6	7943	3.7	386
1955-6	..	..	..	..	308468	1.0	19036	2.8	53301	22.2	33997	37.2	84871	0.9	79959	0.9	8002	0.7	393
1956-7	..	..	..	..	322114	4.4	20361	7.0	68397	28.3	48172	41.7	87885	3.6	82841	3.6	8293	3.6	401
1957-8	..	..	..	..	315751	-2.0	22929	12.6	61936	-9.4	40958	-15.0	85078	-3.2	79949	-3.5	8008	-3.4	409
1958-9	..	..	..	..	344737	9.2	23742	3.5	57638	-6.9	35474	-13.4	89526	5.2	84224	5.3	8440	5.4	418
1959-60	..	..	..	..	348659	1.1	24168	1.8	60617	5.2	37666	6.2	89640	0.1	84252	0.0	8455	0.2	426
1960-1	34181	8.3	376099	91.7	368492	5.7	25473	5.4	71204	17.5	48226	28.0	94180	5.1	88885	5.5	8924	5.5	434
1961-2	38248	9.0	384763	91.0	374774	1.7	27415	7.6	70461	-1.0	46353	-3.9	94809	0.7	89379	0.6	8984	0.7	444
1962-3	44642	10.3	387317	89.7	379656	1.3	33078	20.7	80465	14.2	54990	18.6	94624	-0.2	89013	-0.4	8953	-0.3	454
1963-4	49014	10.8	404815	89.2	393780	3.7	40647	22.9	86431	7.4	59512	8.2	97294	2.8	91493	2.8	9201	2.8	464
1964-5	53365	10.9	434882	89.1	417303	6.0	42464	4.5	95423	10.4	66557	11.8	102361	5.2	96271	5.2	9692	5.3	474
1965-6	58427	12.4	411975	87.6	417673	0.1	46580	9.7	105331	10.4	74826	12.4	96321	-5.9	90031	-6.5	9070	-6.4	485
1966-7	62074	13.1	413115	86.9	423101	1.3	47380	1.7	110327	4.7	77649	3.8	95358	-1.0	88757	-1.4	8940	-1.4	495
1967-8	66162	12.9	447698	87.1	447037	5.7	48658	2.7	105744	-4.2	70831	-8.8	100784	5.7	93884	5.8	9465	5.9	506
1968-9	71711	13.6	455560	86.4	458780	2.6	51211	5.2	103563	-2.1	66781	-5.7	101073	0.3	93972	0.1	9469	0.0	518
1969-70	77429	13.8	484201	86.2	475820	3.7	56050	9.4	114995	11.0	75777	13.5	105416	4.3	98003	4.3	9875	4.3	529
1970-1	84379	14.3	505407	85.7	491979	3.4	61370	9.5	114805	-0.2	71000	-6.3	108257	2.7	100160	2.2	10092	2.2	541
1971-2	89373	15.0	506368	85.0	501551	1.9	67386	9.8	124404	8.4	78678	10.8	106806	-1.3	98552	-1.6	9928	-1.6	554
1972-3	95111	16.0	498732	84.0	504911	0.7	68031	1.0	118705	-4.6	71253	-9.4	104081	-2.6	95712	-2.9	9637	-2.9	567
1973-4	104801	16.9	516071	83.1	517302	2.5	67936	-0.1	141782	19.4	92222	29.4	106465	2.3	97920	2.3	9850	2.2	580
1974-5	107183	17.1	520896	82.9	516912	-0.1	65398	-3.7	134485	-5.1	81789	-11.3	105470	-0.9	96584	-1.4	9703	-1.5	593
1975-6	116631	17.0	568003	83.0	546267	5.7	71715	9.7	120945	-10.1	65369	-20.1	112414	6.6	103259	6.9	10363	6.8	607
1976-7	128872	18.6	564319	81.4	557159	2.0	77084	7.5	143053	18.3	83855	28.3	111467	-0.8	101919	-1.3	10226	-1.3	620
1977-8	135443	18.2	609529	81.8	602591	8.2	79719	3.4	166843	16.6	105063	25.3	117228	5.2	107483	5.5	10776	5.4	634
1978-9	145322	18.5	640642	81.5	639420	6.1	85618	7.4	198541	19.0	134239	27.8	121034	3.2	111110	3.4	11137	3.3	648
1979-80	151576	20.3	593506	79.7	625078	-2.2	90975	6.3	175445	-11.6	108013	-19.5	112164	-7.3	102009	-8.2	10206	-8.4	664
1980-1	166492	20.9	632014	79.1	681341	9.0	95196	4.6	190472	8.6	119327	10.5	117600	4.8	107122	5.0	10712	5.0	679

(Contd.)

Table A1.1 (Contd.)

(Rupees, Crore)

Year	GDP at Factor Cost				Private Final Consumption Expenditure in Domestic Market (PFCE)		Government Final Consumption Expenditure (GFCE)		Gross Domestic Capital Formation (Adjusted)		Net Domestic Capital Formation (Adjusted)		Per Capita GNP at Factor Cost		Per Capita NNP at Factor Cost (in Rupees)***		Per Capita NDP at Factor Cost		Population (million)	
	Public Sector	Per cent of GDP	Private Sector	Per cent of GDP																
	13		14		15		16		17		18		19		20		21		22	
1981-2	175098	20.8	668328	79.2	709436	4.1	99203	4.2	180032	-5.5	105189	-11.8	121723	3.5	110908	3.5	11107	3.7	692	1.9
1982-3	192390	22.2	675702	77.8	715596	0.9	108747	9.6	185456	3.0	106301	1.1	122075	0.3	110895	0.0	11143	0.3	708	2.3
1983-4	204486	21.8	731783	78.2	772008	7.9	113612	4.5	198020	6.8	114919	8.1	128914	5.6	117421	5.9	11800	5.9	723	2.1
1984-5	219079	22.5	754278	77.5	791646	2.5	122059	7.4	207992	5.0	119115	3.7	130918	1.6	118892	1.3	11969	1.4	739	2.2
1985-6	238589	23.5	775277	76.5	826793	4.4	134924	10.5	224567	8.0	129712	8.9	133510	2.0	120946	1.7	12172	1.7	755	2.2
1986-7	256748	24.3	800863	75.7	849359	2.7	147610	9.4	232623	3.6	132010	1.8	136326	2.1	123276	1.9	12412	2.0	771	2.1
1987-8	273324	25.0	821668	75.0	876709	3.2	159705	8.2	263265	13.2	155520	17.8	137844	1.1	124171	0.7	12529	0.9	788	2.2
1988-9	291910	24.2	914333	75.8	935012	6.7	168458	5.5	295654	12.3	182094	17.1	148285	7.6	134179	8.1	13574	8.3	805	2.2
1989-90	316888	24.8	963340	75.2	977478	4.5	177460	5.3	319689	8.1	199368	9.5	154108	3.9	139470	3.9	14111	4.0	822	2.1
1990-1	324105	24.0	1023784	76.0	1025024	4.9	183488	3.4	379436	18.7	250701	25.7	158646	2.9	143302	2.7	14531	3.0	839	2.1
1991-2	342514	25.1	1024657	74.9	1046061	2.1	183180	-0.2	316769	-16.5	179106	-28.6	157657	-0.6	141574	-1.2	14363	-1.2	856	2.0
1992-3	351656	24.4	1088847	75.6	1068930	2.2	189503	3.5	357710	12.9	211862	18.3	163153	3.5	146427	3.4	14847	3.4	872	1.9
1993-4	366675	24.1	1155668	75.9	1116629	4.5	200751	5.9	365948	2.3	213926	1.0	168850	3.5	151807	3.7	15362	3.5	892	2.3
1994-5	394562	24.4	1225132	75.6	1168153	4.6	203529	1.4	437224	19.5	274932	28.5	176183	4.3	158349	4.3	16015	4.3	910	2.0
1995-6	429215	24.7	1308525	75.3	1237508	5.9	219412	7.8	471242	7.8	298653	8.6	185352	5.2	166754	5.3	16866	5.3	928	2.0
1996-7	443401	23.6	1432918	76.4	1333463	7.8	229594	4.6	475526	0.9	291915	-2.3	196551	6.0	177142	6.2	17893	6.1	946	1.9
1997-8	487652	24.9	1469379	75.1	1363604	2.3	255429	11.3	546285	14.9	348238	19.3	201578	2.6	181033	2.2	18247	2.0	964	1.9
1998-9	517785	24.8	1570042	75.2	1446320	6.1	286572	12.2	566930	3.8	355042	2.0	210899	4.6	189344	4.6	19084	4.6	983	2.0
1999-2000	571480	25.4	1674796	74.6	1558648	7.8	320320	11.8	666908	17.6	438257	23.4	222767	5.6	199925	5.6	20156	5.6	1001	1.8
2000-1	573221	24.5	1769553	75.5	1618072	3.8	324727	1.4	630056	-5.5	385940	-11.9	227574	2.2	203617	1.8	20595	2.2	1019	1.8
2001-2	606189	24.5	1865863	75.5	1691864	4.6	332369	2.4	658827	4.6	398883	3.4	235642	3.5	210648	3.5	21270	3.3	1040	2.1
2002-3	638405	24.8	1932285	75.2	1739821	2.8	331753	-0.2	708637	7.6	435270	9.1	241641	2.5	215754	2.4	21755	2.3	1056	1.5
2003-4	658944	23.7	2118869	76.3	1834475	5.4	340962	2.8	819925	15.7	528898	21.5	257194	6.4	230046	6.6	23198	6.6	1072	1.5
2004-5	680519	22.9	2290945	77.1	1925592	5.0	354518	4.0	1064041	29.8	744150	40.7	270807	5.3	241432	4.9	24349	5.0	1089	1.6
2005-6	717726	22.1	2535347	77.9	2089852	8.5	386007	8.9	1236927	16.2	886033	19.1	291879	7.8	260152	7.8	26240	7.8	1106	1.6
2006-7	776503	21.8	2787861	78.2	2270688	8.7	400579	3.8	1402369	13.4	1016670	14.7	315049	7.9	280673	7.9	28330	8.0	1122	1.4
2007-8	829152	21.3	3067484	78.7	2479686	9.2	438919	9.6	1656892	18.1	1229262	20.9	340901	8.2	303324	8.1	30483	7.6	1138	1.4
2008-9	918804	22.1	3239872	77.9	2656483	7.1	484459	10.4	1570333	-5.2	1101430	-10.4	358171	5.1	317538	4.7	31974	4.9	1154	1.4
2009-10	1046657	23.2	3460980	76.8	2852301	7.4	553709	14.3	1838870	17.1	1318550	19.7	382904	6.9	338432	6.6	34080	6.6	1170	1.4
2010-11#					3087047	8.2	597154	7.8	1974172	7.4	1409709	6.9	407519	6.4	359925	6.4	36438	6.9	1186	1.4
2011-12@							620497	3.9					430244	5.6	380054	5.6	38425	5.5	1202	1.3

Notes: # – Quick Estimates @ – Advance Estimates.

Source: Central Statistics Office (CSO) and Press Release dated 31 January 2012.

Table A1.2 Key National Accounts Aggregates—2004–5 Series (at Current Prices)

(Rupees, Crore)

Year	GDP at Factor Cost		Net Factor Income from Abroad	GNP at Factor Cost (2+3)	Consumption of Fixed Capital	NNP at Factor Cost (4–5)	NDP at Factor Cost (2–5)	Indirect Taxes less Subsidies	GDP at Market Prices (2+8)		NDP at Market Prices (7+8)		GNP at Market Prices (4+8)		NNP at Market Prices (6+8)	
1	2		3	4	5	6	7	8	9		10		11		12	
2010–11#	7157412	17.5	–78900	7078512	753473	6325038	6403938	516736	7674148	18.8	6920674	19.3	7595248	18.3	6841774	18.7
2011–12@	8279975	15.7	–81699	8198276	869398	7328878	7410578	632203	8912178	16.1	8042781	16.2	8830479	16.3	7961081	16.4

Table A1.2 (Continued)

Year	GDP at Factor Cost				Private Final Consumption Expenditure in Domestic Market (PFCE)		Government Final Consumption Expenditure (GFCE)		Gross Domestic Capital Formation (Adjusted)	Net Domestic Capital Formation (Adjusted)	Gross Domestic Savings#	Net Domestic Savings#	Per Capita GNP at Factor Cost	Per Capita NDP at Factor Cost	Population (million)	
	Public Sector	Per cent of GDP	Private Sector	Per cent of GDP									(in Rupees)***			
1	13	14			15		16		17	18	19	20	21	22	23	
2010–11#	1499671	21.0	5657741	79.0	4359792	17.1	910719	17.6	2692031	1938558	2481931	1728458	596839	533308	1186	1.4
2011–12@							1023829						682053	609724	1202	1.3

Notes: # – Quick Estimates; @ – Advance Estimates.

Source: Central Statistics Office (CSO) and Press Release dated 31 January 2012.

Table A1.3 Gross and Net Domestic Savings by Type of Institutions (at Current Prices)

(Rupees, Crore)

Year	GDP at Current Market Prices	NDP at Current Market Prices	Domestic Savings				Household Sector Savings		
			GDS	Consumption of Fixed Capital	NDS		Gross	Consumption of Fixed Capital	Net
1	2	3	4	5	6		7	8	9
2004–5 Series									
1950–1	10401	9870	989	9.5	531	5.1	458	4.6	681	6.5	422	2.5	259	2.6
1951–2	11054	10478	1079	9.8	576	5.2	503	4.8	634	5.7	442	1.7	192	1.8
1952–3	10850	10266	954	8.8	585	5.4	369	3.6	695	6.4	434	2.4	261	2.5
1953–4	11810	11254	943	8.0	557	4.7	386	3.4	672	5.7	401	2.3	272	2.4
1954–5	11170	10664	1105	9.9	506	4.5	599	5.6	774	6.9	338	3.9	436	4.1
1955–6	11371	10829	1422	12.5	542	4.8	880	8.1	1041	9.2	356	6.0	685	6.3
1956–7	13547	12961	1696	12.5	586	4.3	1110	8.6	1222	9.0	374	6.3	849	6.5
1957–8	13951	13297	1485	10.6	654	4.7	831	6.3	1028	7.4	404	4.5	625	4.7
1958–9	15551	14837	1450	9.3	714	4.6	736	5.0	986	6.3	428	3.6	557	3.8
1959–60	16384	15621	1803	11.0	763	4.7	1040	6.7	1267	7.7	432	5.1	835	5.3
1960–1	17942	17134	2079	11.6	808	4.5	1271	7.4	1226	6.8	428	4.4	798	4.7
1961–2	19010	18114	2211	11.6	896	4.7	1315	7.3	1237	6.5	453	4.1	784	4.3
1962–3	20429	19458	2613	12.8	971	4.8	1642	8.4	1519	7.4	467	5.1	1052	5.4
1963–4	23462	22378	2912	12.4	1085	4.6	1827	8.2	1589	6.8	522	4.5	1067	4.8
1964–5	27367	26127	3358	12.3	1240	4.5	2118	8.1	1897	6.9	565	4.9	1331	5.1
1965–6	28857	27464	4086	14.2	1393	4.8	2693	9.8	2596	9.0	598	6.9	1997	7.3
1966–7	32669	31036	4526	13.9	1633	5.0	2893	9.3	3161	9.7	688	7.6	2473	8.0
1967–8	38261	36394	4629	12.1	1867	4.9	2762	7.6	3275	8.6	791	6.5	2484	6.8
1968–9	40512	38514	4881	12.0	1999	4.9	2882	7.5	3277	8.1	850	6.0	2427	6.3
1969–70	44605	42306	6285	14.1	2299	5.2	3986	9.4	4375	9.8	1018	7.5	3357	7.9
1970–1	47638	44834	6821	14.3	2804	5.9	4017	9.0	4531	9.5	1315	2.8	3216	7.2
1971–2	50999	47921	7687	15.1	3078	6.0	4609	9.6	5229	10.3	1394	2.7	3835	8.0
1972–3	56214	52789	7952	14.1	3425	6.1	4527	8.6	5330	9.5	1495	2.7	3835	7.3
1973–4	68420	64308	11466	16.8	4112	6.0	7355	11.4	8020	11.7	1767	2.6	6254	9.7
1974–5	80770	75473	13482	16.7	5297	6.6	8186	10.8	8677	10.7	2212	2.7	6465	8.6
1975–6	86707	80444	15066	17.4	6263	7.2	8803	10.9	9790	11.3	2623	3.0	7168	8.9
1976–7	93422	86615	17582	18.8	6807	7.3	10774	12.4	11206	12.0	2890	3.1	8316	9.6
1977–8	105848	98520	20345	19.2	7328	6.9	13017	13.2	13679	12.9	3014	2.8	10665	10.8

Year														
1978-9	114647	106536	24110	21.0	8111	7.1	15999	15.0	16482	14.4	3287	2.9	13195	12.4
1979-80	125729	115842	25068	19.9	9887	7.9	15181	13.1	16338	13.0	3997	3.2	12341	10.7
1980-1	149642	138220	26590	17.8	11422	7.6	15168	11.0	18116	12.1	4510	3.0	13606	9.8
1981-2	175805	161884	30692	17.5	13921	7.9	16771	10.4	19013	10.8	5516	3.1	13497	8.3
1982-3	196644	180529	34956	17.8	16114	8.2	18842	10.4	21972	11.2	6116	3.1	15856	8.8
1983-4	229021	211052	39239	17.1	17970	7.8	21269	10.1	26955	11.8	6633	2.9	20321	9.6
1984-5	256611	235635	45786	17.8	20976	8.2	24810	10.5	32796	12.8	7582	3.0	25214	10.7
1985-6	289524	264387	53414	18.4	25137	8.7	28277	10.7	36666	12.7	8815	3.0	27852	10.5
1986-7	323949	295611	58693	18.1	28338	8.7	30355	10.3	42111	13.0	9719	3.0	32392	11.0
1987-8	368211	335019	73707	20.0	33192	9.0	40515	12.1	57304	15.6	11860	3.2	45445	13.6
1988-9	436893	398042	87492	20.0	38850	8.9	48642	12.2	67063	15.3	13359	3.1	53704	13.5
1989-90	501928	456680	106730	21.3	45248	9.0	61482	13.5	82985	16.5	14970	3.0	68015	14.9
1990-1	586212	533562	134408	22.9	52650	9.0	81758	15.3	108603	18.5	16900	2.9	91703	17.2
1991-2	673875	609248	143530	21.3	64627	9.6	78904	13.0	105632	15.7	20061	3.0	85571	14.0
1992-3	774545	700407	164621	21.3	74138	9.6	90483	12.9	127943	16.5	22011	2.8	105932	15.1
1993-4	891355	808498	192994	21.7	82856	9.3	110138	13.6	151454	17.0	25419	2.9	126035	15.6
1994-5	1045590	948842	246668	23.6	96749	9.3	149919	15.8	187142	17.9	28608	2.7	158533	16.7
1995-6	1226725	1114139	289265	23.6	112586	9.2	176679	15.9	198585	16.2	32364	2.6	166222	14.9
1996-7	1419277	1289429	318387	22.4	129848	9.1	188539	14.6	224653	15.8	35489	2.5	189165	14.7
1997-8	1572394	1425127	379790	24.2	147267	9.4	232523	16.3	284127	18.1	40784	2.6	243343	17.1
1998-9	1803378	1639637	418159	23.2	163740	9.1	254419	15.5	352114	19.5	46857	2.6	305257	18.6
1999-2000	2012198	1825726	516846	25.7	186472	9.3	330374	18.1	438851	21.8	56622	2.8	382229	20.9
2000-1	2168652	1961761	515545	23.8	206892	9.5	308653	15.7	463750	21.4	64354	3.0	399396	20.4
2001-2	2348330	2119480	585375	24.9	228850	9.7	356526	16.8	545288	23.2	72607	3.1	472682	22.3
2002-3	2530663	2284482	656229	25.9	246180	9.7	410049	17.9	564161	22.3	80986	3.2	483174	21.2
2003-4	2837900	2565746	823775	29.0	272155	9.6	551621	21.5	657587	23.2	93078	3.3	564510	22.0
2004-5	3242209	2922318	1050703	32.4	319891	9.9	730812	25.0	763685	23.6	111036	3.4	652649	22.3
2005-6	3693369	3329648	1235151	33.4	363721	9.8	871430	26.2	868988	23.5	125369	3.4	743619	22.3
2006-7	4294706	3875977	1485909	34.6	418729	9.7	1067180	27.5	994396	23.2	143895	3.4	850501	21.9
2007-8	4987090	4502394	1836332	36.8	484695	9.7	1351637	30.0	1118347	22.4	163673	3.3	954674	21.2
2008-9	5630063	5064866	1802620	32.0	565198	10.0	1237422	24.4	1330873	23.6	196670	3.5	1134203	22.4
2009-10	6457352	5799454	2182970	33.8	657897	10.2	1525073	26.3	1639038	25.4	229627	3.6	1409411	24.3
2010-11#	7674148	6920674	2481931	32.3	753473	9.8	1728458	25.0	1749311	22.8	270049	3.5	1479262	21.4
2011-12@	8912178	8042781	–	–	–	–	–	–	–	–	–	–	–	–

(Contd.)

Table A1.3 (Contd.)

(Rupees, Crore)

	Private Corporate Sector Savings						Public Sector Savings				
	Gross		Consumption of Fixed Capital		Net		Gross		Consumption of Fixed Capital		Net
	10		11		12		13		14		15
2004–2005 Series											
1950-1	93	0.9	22	0.2	71	0.7	215	2.1	87	0.8	128	1.3
1951-2	136	1.2	29	0.3	107	1.0	309	2.8	105	0.9	204	1.9
1952-3	64	0.6	36	0.3	28	0.3	195	1.8	115	1.1	80	0.8
1953-4	90	0.8	38	0.3	52	0.5	181	1.5	118	1.0	63	0.6
1954-5	118	1.1	43	0.4	75	0.7	213	1.9	124	1.1	89	0.8
1955-6	134	1.2	48	0.4	86	0.8	247	2.2	138	1.2	109	1.0
1956-7	155	1.1	57	0.4	98	0.8	318	2.4	155	1.1	163	1.3
1957-8	121	0.9	72	0.5	49	0.4	336	2.4	178	1.3	158	1.2
1958-9	140	0.9	84	0.5	56	0.4	325	2.1	202	1.3	123	0.8
1959-60	185	1.1	96	0.6	89	0.6	351	2.1	236	1.4	115	0.7
1960-1	281	1.6	114	0.6	167	1.0	572	3.2	266	1.5	306	1.8
1961-2	320	1.7	139	0.7	181	1.0	654	3.4	303	1.6	351	1.9
1962-3	344	1.7	162	0.8	182	0.9	750	3.7	342	1.7	408	2.1
1963-4	394	1.7	169	0.7	225	1.0	929	4.0	394	1.7	535	2.4
1964-5	389	1.4	203	0.7	186	0.7	1072	3.9	472	1.7	600	2.3
1965-6	405	1.4	230	0.8	175	0.6	1085	3.8	564	2.0	521	1.9
1966-7	424	1.3	269	0.8	155	0.5	941	2.9	676	2.1	265	0.9
1967-8	410	1.1	304	0.8	106	0.3	944	2.5	772	2.0	172	0.5
1968-9	439	1.1	330	0.8	109	0.3	1165	2.9	818	2.0	347	0.9
1969-70	549	1.2	360	0.8	189	0.4	1361	3.1	921	2.1	440	1.0
1970-1	672	1.4	419	0.9	253	0.6	1618	3.4	1070	2.2	548	1.2
1971-2	769	1.5	477	0.9	292	0.6	1689	3.3	1207	2.4	482	1.0
1972-3	806	1.4	545	1.0	261	0.5	1816	3.2	1385	2.5	431	0.8
1973-4	1083	1.6	648	0.9	435	0.7	2363	3.5	1697	2.5	666	1.0
1974-5	1465	1.8	875	1.1	590	0.8	3340	4.1	2209	2.7	1131	1.5
1975-6	1083	1.2	1032	1.2	51	0.1	4192	4.8	2608	3.0	1584	2.0
1976-7	1181	1.3	1060	1.1	121	0.1	5195	5.6	2857	3.1	2338	2.7
1977-8	1413	1.3	1133	1.1	280	0.3	5253	5.0	3181	3.0	2072	2.1
1978-9	1652	1.4	1255	1.1	397	0.4	5976	5.2	3569	3.1	2407	2.3
1979-80	2398	1.9	1536	1.2	862	0.7	6331	5.0	4354	3.5	1977	1.7

Year															
1980-1	2339	1.6	1851	1.2	488	0.4	6135	4.1	5061	3.4	1074	0.8			
1981-2	2560	1.5	2287	1.3	273	0.2	9120	5.2	6118	3.5	3002	1.9			
1982-3	2980	1.5	2667	1.4	313	0.2	10004	5.1	7331	3.7	2673	1.5			
1983-4	3254	1.4	2990	1.3	264	0.1	9030	3.9	8347	3.6	683	0.3			
1984-5	4040	1.6	3490	1.4	550	0.2	8950	3.5	9904	3.9	-954	-0.4			
1985-6	5426	1.9	4200	1.5	1226	0.5	11322	3.9	12123	4.2	-801	-0.3			
1986-7	5336	1.6	4869	1.5	467	0.2	11246	3.5	13750	4.2	-2504	-0.8			
1987-8	5932	1.6	5469	1.5	463	0.1	10471	2.8	15863	4.3	-5392	-1.6			
1988-9	8486	1.9	6540	1.5	1946	0.5	11943	2.7	18951	4.3	-7008	-1.8			
1989-90	11845	2.4	7769	1.5	4076	0.9	11900	2.4	22509	4.5	-10609	-2.3			
1990-1	15164	2.6	9271	1.6	5893	1.1	10641	1.8	26479	4.5	-15838	-3.0			
1991-2	20304	3.0	12033	1.8	8271	1.4	17594	2.6	32533	4.8	-14939	-2.5			
1992-3	19968	2.6	14940	1.9	5028	0.7	16709	2.2	37187	4.8	-20478	-2.9			
1993-4	29866	3.4	17570	2.0	12296	1.5	11674	1.3	39867	4.5	-28193	-3.5			
1994-5	35260	3.4	21262	2.0	13998	1.5	24266	2.3	46878	4.5	-22612	-2.4			
1995-6	59153	4.8	26826	2.2	32327	2.9	31527	2.6	53396	4.4	-21869	-2.0			
1996-7	62540	4.4	33089	2.3	29451	2.3	31194	2.2	61270	4.3	-30076	-2.3			
1997-8	66080	4.2	38551	2.5	27529	1.9	29583	1.9	67931	4.3	-38348	-2.7			
1998-9	69191	3.8	44243	2.5	24948	1.5	-3146	-0.2	72641	4.0	-75787	-4.6			
1999-2000	87234	4.3	50914	2.5	36320	2.0	-9238	-0.5	78936	3.9	-88174	-4.8			
2000-1	81062	3.7	59437	2.7	21625	1.1	-29266	-1.3	83101	3.8	-112367	-5.7			
2001-2	76906	3.3	67176	2.9	9730	0.5	-36820	-1.6	89067	3.8	-125887	-5.9			
2002-3	99217	3.9	72983	2.9	26234	1.1	-7148	-0.3	92211	3.6	-99360	-4.3			
2003-4	129816	4.6	80218	2.8	49598	1.9	36372	1.3	98859	3.5	-62487	-2.4			
2004-5	212519	6.6	99850	3.1	112669	3.9	74499	2.3	109005	3.4	-34506	-1.2			
2005-6	277208	7.5	118967	3.2	158241	4.8	88955	2.4	119385	3.2	-30430	-0.9			
2006-7	338584	7.9	143347	3.3	195237	5.0	152929	3.6	131487	3.1	21442	0.6			
2007-8	469023	9.4	175895	3.5	293128	6.5	248962	5.0	145127	2.9	103835	2.3			
2008-9	417467	7.4	205849	3.7	211618	4.2	54280	1.0	162679	2.9	-108399	-2.1			
2009-10	532136	8.2	238071	3.7	294065	5.1	11796	0.2	190199	2.9	-178403	-3.1			
2010-11#	602464	7.9	277675	3.6	324789	4.7	130155	1.7	205749	2.7	-75594	-1.1			
2011-12@	–	–	–	–	–	–	–	–	–	–	–	–			

Note: Figures in italics are as percentages to GDP at current prices except those for net savings in cols (6), (9), (12), and (15) which are as percentages to NDP at current market prices.
– Quick Estimates @ – Advance Estimates.
Source: Central Statistics Office (CSO) and Press Release dated 31 January 2012.

Table A1.4 Gross Capital Formation by Type of Institutions at 2004–5 Prices

(Rupees, Crore)

Year	Gross Capital Formation (GCF)						Finances for Gross Capital Formation (derived)	Errors and Omissions**	Gross Capital Formation Adjusted		Consumption of Fixed Capital		Net Capital Formation		Net Capital Formation Adjusted	
	Aggregate GCF		Public Sector	Private Corporate Sector	Household Sector	Valuables*										
	(3+4+5+6)								(2+8)				(2−10)		(8+11)	
1	2		3	4	5	6	7	8	9		10		11		12	
1950–1	44906	15.3	..	..	..	..	968	−6954	37952	12.9	23272	7.9	21634	8.0	14680	5.4
1951–2	43721	14.4	..	..	..	..	1262	1681	45402	15.0	22754	7.5	20967	7.5	22648	8.1
1952–3	38177	12.3	..	..	..	..	920	−3608	34569	11.1	22249	7.2	15928	5.5	12320	4.3
1953–4	36322	11.0	..	..	..	..	930	1172	37494	11.4	21852	6.6	14470	4.7	15642	5.1
1954–5	44702	12.9	..	..	..	..	1121	−1077	43625	12.6	18845	5.5	25857	7.9	24780	7.6
1955–6	52404	14.7	..	..	..	..	1461	897	53301	14.9	19305	5.4	33099	9.8	33997	10.1
1956–7	66673	17.7	..	..	..	..	2056	1725	68397	18.2	20226	5.4	46447	13.0	48172	13.5
1957–8	64707	17.3	..	..	..	..	1958	−2771	61936	16.5	20977	5.6	43730	12.4	40958	11.6
1958–9	56303	14.0	..	..	..	..	1826	1335	57638	14.3	22164	5.5	34139	9.0	35474	9.3
1959–60	66092	16.0	..	..	..	..	2034	−5475	60617	14.7	22951	5.6	43141	11.1	37666	9.6
1960–1	72888	16.7	..	..	..	..	2560	−1684	71204	16.3	22978	5.3	49910	12.1	48226	11.7
1961–2	78315	17.3	..	..	..	..	2556	−7853	70461	15.6	24109	5.3	54206	12.7	46353	10.8
1962–3	84590	18.2	..	..	..	..	3053	−4125	80465	17.3	25475	5.5	59115	13.4	54990	12.5
1963–4	94416	19.1	..	..	..	..	3352	−7985	86431	17.5	26919	5.5	67497	14.5	59512	12.8
1964–5	104783	19.8	..	..	..	..	3958	−9359	95423	18.0	28867	5.4	75916	15.1	66557	13.3
1965–6	106516	20.6	..	..	..	..	4685	−1185	105331	20.4	30505	5.9	76011	15.6	74826	15.4
1966–7	108878	21.1	..	..	..	..	5449	1450	110327	21.4	32679	6.3	76199	15.8	77649	16.1
1967–8	112930	20.3	..	..	..	..	5466	−7186	105744	19.0	34913	6.3	78017	15.0	70831	13.6
1968–9	112807	19.6	..	..	..	..	5297	−9244	103563	18.0	36783	6.4	76025	14.1	66781	12.4
1969–70	118969	19.4	..	..	..	..	6526	−3973	114995	18.8	39218	6.4	79750	13.9	75777	13.2
1970–1	116172	18.0	..	..	..	..	7215	−1367	114805	17.8	43805	6.8	72367	12.0	71000	11.8
1971–2	130450	19.9	..	..	..	..	8165	−6046	124404	19.0	45727	7.0	84724	13.9	78678	12.9
1972–3	128154	19.7	..	..	..	..	8249	−9449	118705	18.2	47452	7.3	80702	13.4	71253	11.8
1973–4	134853	20.0	..	..	..	..	11858	6929	141782	21.1	49560	7.4	85293	13.7	92222	14.8
1974–5	143814	21.1	..	..	..	..	14135	−9329	134485	19.8	52696	7.7	91118	14.5	81789	13.0
1975–6	130852	17.6	..	..	..	..	14949	−9907	120945	16.3	55576	7.5	75276	10.9	65369	9.5
1976–7	149120	19.7	..	..	..	..	16273	−6067	143053	18.9	59199	7.8	89921	12.9	83855	12.0
1977–8	169879	21.0	..	..	..	..	18880	−3036	166843	20.6	61780	7.6	108099	14.4	105063	14.0
1978–9	187597	21.9	..	..	..	..	24238	10944	198541	23.2	64302	7.5	123295	15.6	134239	16.9

Year													
1979-80	180621	22.3	:	:	25648	175445	21.6	67432	8.3	113189	15.2	108013	14.5
1980-1	179291	20.7	:	:	28684	190472	22.0	71144	8.2	108147	13.6	119327	15.0
1981-2	208992	22.8	:	:	33303	180032	19.6	74843	8.1	134149	15.9	105189	12.5
1982-3	215016	22.6	:	:	37522	185456	19.5	79154	8.3	135862	15.6	106301	12.2
1983-4	217263	21.3	:	:	41756	198020	19.4	83101	8.2	134162	14.3	114919	12.3
1984-5	234656	22.2	:	:	49078	207992	19.6	88877	8.4	145780	15.0	119115	12.3
1985-6	256490	23.0	:	:	59648	224567	20.2	94855	8.5	161635	15.9	129712	12.7
1986-7	272223	23.3	:	:	65048	232623	19.9	100613	8.6	171610	16.1	132010	12.4
1987-8	272081	22.4	:	:	80532	263265	21.7	107745	8.9	164336	14.9	155520	14.1
1988-9	308637	23.2	:	:	99796	295654	22.2	113560	8.5	195077	16.0	182094	15.0
1989-90	322370	22.9	:	:	119009	319689	22.7	120321	8.5	202049	15.7	199368	15.5
1990-1	363028	24.4	:	:	152604	379436	25.5	128735	8.7	234294	17.2	250701	18.4
1991-2	326803	21.7	:	:	146907	316769	21.1	137663	9.2	189140	13.8	179106	13.1
1992-3	376493	23.7	:	:	178437	357710	22.6	145847	9.2	230646	16.0	211862	14.7
1993-4	351032	21.1	:	:	197785	365948	22.0	152023	9.2	199010	13.2	213926	14.2
1994-5	409939	23.1	:	:	258561	437224	24.7	162292	9.2	247647	15.4	274932	17.1
1995-6	485871	25.5	:	:	310045	471242	24.7	172589	9.1	313282	18.1	298653	17.2
1996-7	442800	21.6	:	:	336125	475526	23.2	183611	9.0	259189	13.9	291915	15.6
1997-8	523635	24.6	:	:	402092	546285	25.6	198048	9.3	325587	16.8	348238	18.0
1998-9	550691	24.3	:	:	436521	566930	25.0	211888	9.4	338803	16.5	355042	17.3
1999-2000	671671	27.3	334869		538834	666908	27.2	228651	9.3	443021	19.9	438257	19.7
2000-1	626207	24.5	435729	41054	528299	630056	24.7	244116	9.6	382091	16.5	385940	16.7
2001-2	695012	25.9	485556	40414	571146	658827	24.6	259944	9.7	435068	18.0	398883	16.5
2002-3	714890	25.7	462424	45933	627743	708637	25.4	273367	9.8	441523	17.6	435270	17.3
2003-4	798715	26.6	455392	47263	762416	819925	27.3	291027	9.7	507688	18.7	528898	19.5
2004-5	1052231	32.5	240580	334869	41054	1064040	1064041	32.8	319891	9.9	732340	25.1	744150	25.5
2005-6	1223717	34.5	281995	415752	40414	1279753	1236927	34.9	350894	9.9	872823	27.3	886033	27.8
2006-7	1410754	36.4	324020	578377	45933	1531432	1402369	36.2	385699	10.0	1025055	29.4	1016670	29.2
2007-8	1653438	38.9	382431	768352	47263	1900762	1656892	39.0	427630	10.1	1225808	32.1	1229262	32.2
2008-9	1626220	36.8	429285	541902	59987	1931380	1570333	35.6	468903	10.6	1157317	29.3	1101430	27.9
2009-10	1814641	38.0	448485	595046	94524	2363670	1838870	38.5	520320	10.9	1294321	30.4	1318550	31.0
2010-11#	2015837	38.5	477165	671349	125192	2692030	1974172	37.7	564463	10.8	1451374	31.1	1409709	30.2
2011-12@	2132719			725167									

Note: Finances for Gross Capital Formation = Gross Domestic Savings + Net Foreign Capital Inflow or Outflow

\# – Quick Estimates @ – Advance Estimates

* Excluding works of art and antiques (Valuables are a new item in the 1999–2000 series)

** Errors and Omissions at current prices have been deflated by the implicit price deflators of capital formation by the CSO.

Source: Central Statistical Office (CSO).

Table A1.5 Gross Capital Formation by Type of Institutions at Current Prices

(Rupees, Crore)

Year	Aggregate (3+4+5+6)		Gross Capital Formation (GCF)					Gross Domestic Savings	Net Foreign Capital Inflow (–) Outflow (+)	Finances for Gross Capital Formation (7+8)	Errors and Omissions (9–2)
			Public Sector		Private Corporate Sector		Household Sector		Valuables		
1	2		3		4		5		6	7	8	9	10
2004–5 Series
1950–1	1133	10.9	290	2.8	225	2.2	619	5.9	0	989	–21	968	–165
1951–2	1218	11.0	334	3.0	264	2.4	620	5.6	0	1079	183	1262	44
1952–3	1014	9.3	306	2.8	86	0.8	623	5.7	0	954	–34	920	–95
1953–4	901	7.6	355	3.0	15	0.1	530	4.5	0	943	–13	930	29
1954–5	1148	10.3	498	4.5	158	1.4	492	4.4	0	1105	16	1121	–28
1955–6	1437	12.6	594	5.2	230	2.0	612	5.4	0	1422	39	1461	24
1956–7	2006	14.8	758	5.6	359	2.7	889	6.6	0	1696	360	2056	49
1957–8	2045	14.7	891	6.4	417	3.0	737	5.3	0	1485	473	1958	–87
1958–9	1784	11.5	900	5.8	261	1.7	624	4.0	0	1450	376	1826	42
1959–60	2212	13.5	1057	6.4	322	2.0	834	5.1	0	1803	231	2034	–178
1960–1	2618	14.6	1278	7.1	569	3.2	770	4.3	0	2079	481	2560	–58
1961–2	2830	14.9	1298	6.8	784	4.1	748	3.9	0	2211	345	2556	–274
1962–3	3199	15.7	1607	7.9	573	2.8	1020	5.0	0	2613	440	3053	–146
1963–4	3649	15.6	1881	8.0	922	3.9	846	3.6	0	2912	440	3352	–297
1964–5	4335	15.8	2196	8.0	956	3.5	1183	4.3	0	3358	600	3958	–377
1965–6	4736	16.4	2472	8.6	740	2.6	1524	5.3	0	4086	599	4685	–51
1966–7	5380	16.5	2424	7.4	659	2.0	2297	7.0	0	4526	923	5449	69
1967–8	5827	15.2	2553	6.7	864	2.3	2410	6.3	0	4629	837	5466	–361
1968–9	5768	14.2	2472	6.1	814	2.0	2482	6.1	0	4881	416	5297	–471
1969–70	6746	15.1	2575	5.8	715	1.6	3456	7.7	0	6285	241	6526	–220
1970–1	7297	15.3	3044	6.4	1093	2.3	3160	6.6	0	6821	394	7215	–82
1971–2	8545	16.8	3601	7.1	1270	2.5	3674	7.2	0	7687	478	8165	–380
1972–3	8891	15.8	4273	7.6	1415	2.5	3202	5.7	0	7952	297	8249	–641
1973–4	11314	16.5	5172	7.6	1733	2.5	4408	6.4	0	11466	392	11858	545
1974–5	15009	18.6	5886	7.3	2820	3.5	6303	7.8	0	13482	653	14135	–874
1975–6	16018	18.5	7848	9.1	2298	2.7	5872	6.8	0	15066	–117	14949	–1070
1976–7	16939	18.1	9172	9.8	1413	1.5	6354	6.8	0	17582	–1309	16273	–666
1977–8	19222	18.2	8901	8.4	2495	2.4	7826	7.4	0	20345	–1465	18880	–341

Year												
1978-9	22937	20.0	10738	9.4	2375	2.1	9824	8.6	0	..	24110	128	24238	1301
1979-80	26355	21.0	12878	10.2	3220	2.6	10257	8.2	0	..	25068	580	25648	-707
1980-1	27003	18.0	13727	9.2	3769	2.5	9506	6.4	0	..	26590	2094	28684	1682
1981-2	38403	21.8	19382	11.0	9623	5.5	9399	5.3	0	..	30692	2611	33303	-5100
1982-3	43356	22.0	23412	11.9	10711	5.4	9233	4.7	0	..	34956	2566	37522	-5833
1983-4	45792	20.0	24562	10.7	7569	3.3	13661	6.0	0	..	39239	2517	41756	-4037
1984-5	55269	21.5	29499	11.5	10853	4.2	14917	5.8	0	..	45786	3292	49078	-6191
1985-6	67954	23.5	34522	11.9	15304	5.3	18128	6.3	0	..	53414	6234	59648	-8306
1986-7	76008	23.5	40619	12.5	16614	5.1	18775	5.8	0	..	58693	6355	65048	-10960
1987-8	83223	22.6	39696	10.8	13043	3.5	30484	8.3	0	..	73707	6825	80532	-2691
1988-9	104160	23.8	47073	10.8	17207	3.9	39880	9.1	0	..	87492	12304	99796	-4364
1989-90	120007	23.9	54207	10.8	20813	4.1	44987	9.0	0	..	106730	12279	119009	-998
1990-1	146018	24.9	62000	10.6	25055	4.3	58963	10.1	0	..	134408	18196	152604	6586
1991-2	151563	22.5	68494	10.2	39537	5.9	43531	6.5	0	..	143530	3377	146907	-4656
1992-3	187768	24.2	73854	9.5	51338	6.6	62576	8.1	0	..	164621	13816	178437	-9331
1993-4	189737	21.3	81283	9.1	51737	5.8	56716	6.4	0	..	192994	4791	197785	8048
1994-5	242514	23.2	101530	9.7	74575	7.1	66408	6.4	0	..	246668	11893	258561	16047
1995-6	319603	26.1	105091	8.6	121646	9.9	92866	7.6	0	..	289265	20780	310045	-9558
1996-7	313055	22.1	110633	7.8	119430	8.4	82993	5.8	0	..	318387	17738	336125	23069
1997-8	385445	24.5	116367	7.4	131728	8.4	137350	8.7	0	..	379790	22302	402092	16647
1998-9	424046	23.5	130898	7.3	121379	6.7	171768	9.5	0	..	418159	18362	436521	12475
1999-2000	542682	27.0	154164	7.7	140750	7.0	232248	11.5	15519	0.8	516846	21988	538834	-3848
2000-1	525078	24.2	155299	7.2	106524	4.9	248530	11.5	14724	0.7	515545	12754	528299	3222
2001-2	602456	25.7	169269	7.2	121187	5.2	297813	12.7	14187	0.6	585375	-14229	571146	-31310
2002-3	633277	25.0	163403	6.5	145011	5.7	310906	12.3	13957	0.6	656229	-28486	627743	-5534
2003-4	742717	26.2	187730	6.6	186088	6.6	344327	12.1	24572	0.9	823775	-61359	762416	19699
2004-5	1052231	32.5	240580	7.4	334869	10.3	435729	13.4	41054	1.3	1050703	13337	1064040	11809
2005-6	1266073	35.7	293350	7.9	500675	13.6	430657	11.7	41392	1.1	1235151	44602	1279753	13680
2006-7	1540583	39.8	356556	8.3	624179	14.5	510140	11.9	49709	1.2	1485909	45523	1531432	-9151
2007-8	1896799	44.6	441923	8.9	863147	17.3	538137	10.8	53592	1.1	1836332	64430	1900762	3963
2008-9	2000103	45.3	531730	9.4	636314	11.3	759846	13.5	72213	1.3	1802620	128760	1931380	-68723
2009-10	2332380	48.8	591622	9.2	820966	12.7	803481	12.4	116312	1.8	2182970	180700	2363670	31290
2010-11	2749189	52.5	676220	8.8	928512	12.1	981620	12.8	162837	2.1	2481931	210099	2692030	-57159
2011-12	3154812													

(Contd.)

Table A1.5 (Contd.)

(Rupees, Crore)

Year	GCF Adjusted (2+10) 11	Consumption of Fixed Capital (CFC) 12	Net Capital Formation (NCF) (2–12) 13	NCF Adjusted (13+10) 14	Price Deflators GDCF (Unadjusted) 15	Price Deflators GDP at Market Prices 16
1						
2004–5 Series					(2004–5=100)	
1950–1	968	531	602	437	2.5	3.5
	9.3		6.1	4.4		
1951–2	1262	576	641	686	2.8	3.7
	11.4		6.1	6.5		
1952–3	920	585	430	335	2.7	3.5
	8.5		4.2	3.3		
1953–4	930	557	344	373	2.5	3.6
	7.9		3.1	3.3		
1954–5	1121	506	643	615	2.6	3.2
	10.0		6.0	5.8		
1955–5	1461	542	894	919	2.7	3.2
	12.8		8.3	8.5		
1956–7	2056	586	1420	1470	3.0	3.6
	15.2		11.0	11.3		
1957–8	1958	654	1391	1304	3.2	3.7
	14.0		10.5	9.8		
1958–9	1826	714	1070	1112	3.2	3.9
	11.7		7.2	7.5		
1959–50	2034	763	1449	1271	3.3	4.0
	12.4		9.3	8.1		
1960–1	2560	808	1810	1752	3.6	4.1
	14.3		10.6	10.2		
1961–2	2556	896	1935	1660	3.6	4.2
	13.4		10.7	9.2		
1962–3	3053	971	2229	2082	3.8	4.4
	14.9		11.5	10.7		
1963–4	3352	1085	2564	2267	3.9	4.8
	14.3		11.5	10.1		
1964–5	3958	1240	3095	2718	4.1	5.2
	14.5		11.8	10.4		
1965–6	4685	1393	3343	3292	4.4	5.6
	16.2		12.2	12.0		
1966–7	5449	1633	3747	3816	4.9	6.3
	16.7		12.1	12.3		
1967–8	5466	1867	3960	3599	5.2	6.9
	14.3		10.9	9.9		
1968–9	5297	1999	3769	3298	5.1	7.0
	13.1		9.8	8.6		
1969–70	6526	2299	4447	4227	5.7	7.3
	14.6		10.5	10.0		
1970–1	7215	2804	4493	4411	6.3	7.4
	15.1		10.0	9.8		
1971–2	8165	3078	5467	5087	6.6	7.8
	16.0		11.4	10.6		
1972–3	8249	3425	5465	4824	6.9	8.6
	14.7		10.4	9.1		
1973–4	11858	4112	7202	7747	8.4	10.2
	17.3		11.2	12.0		
1974–5	14135	5297	9713	8839	10.4	11.9
	17.5		12.9	11.7		
1975–6	14949	6263	9756	8686	12.2	11.7
	17.2		12.1	10.8		
1976–7	16273	6807	10132	9465	11.4	12.4
	17.4		11.7	10.9		
1977–8	18880	7328	11893	11552	11.3	13.1
	17.8		12.1	11.7		
1978–9	24238	8111	14826	16127	12.2	13.4
	21.1		13.9	15.1		
1979–80	25648	9887	16468	15761	14.6	15.5
	20.4		14.2	13.6		

Year								
1980–1	28684	19.2	11422	15581	11.3	17262	12.5	15.1	17.3
1981–2	33303	18.9	13921	24482	15.1	19382	12.0	18.4	19.1
1982–3	37522	19.1	16114	27241	15.1	21408	11.9	20.2	20.7
1983–4	41756	18.2	17970	27823	13.2	23786	11.3	21.1	22.5
1984–5	49078	19.1	20976	34293	14.6	28102	11.9	23.6	24.2
1985–6	59648	20.6	25137	42817	16.2	34511	13.1	26.5	26.0
1986–7	65048	20.1	28338	47670	16.1	36710	12.4	27.9	27.8
1987–8	80532	21.9	33192	50031	14.9	47340	14.1	30.6	30.3
1988–9	99796	22.8	38850	65309	16.4	60946	15.3	33.7	32.8
1989–90	119009	23.7	45248	74759	16.4	73761	16.2	37.2	35.6
1990–1	152604	26.0	52650	93368	17.5	99954	18.7	40.2	39.4
1991–2	146907	21.8	64627	86936	14.3	82281	13.5	46.4	44.8
1992–3	178437	23.0	74138	113630	16.2	104299	14.9	49.9	48.8
1993–4	197785	22.2	82856	106881	13.2	114929	14.2	54.1	53.7
1994–5	258561	24.7	96749	145765	15.4	161812	17.1	59.2	59.0
1995–6	310045	25.3	112586	207017	18.6	197459	17.7	65.8	64.4
1996–7	336125	23.7	129848	183208	14.2	206277	16.0	70.7	69.2
1997–8	402092	25.6	147267	238178	16.7	254825	17.9	73.6	73.7
1998–9	436521	24.2	163740	260306	15.9	272781	16.6	77.0	79.6
1999–2000	538834	26.8	186472	356210	19.5	352362	19.3	80.8	81.9
2000–1	528299	24.4	206892	318186	16.2	321407	16.4	83.9	84.9
2001–2	571146	24.3	228850	373606	17.6	342297	16.2	86.7	87.6
2002–3	627743	24.8	246180	387097	16.9	381563	16.7	88.6	90.9
2003–4	762416	26.9	272155	470562	18.3	490262	19.1	93.0	94.4
2004–5	1064041	32.8	319891	732340	25.1	744150	25.5	100.0	100.0
2005–6	1279754	34.7	363721	902352	27.1	916033	27.5	103.5	104.2
2006–7	1531433	35.7	418729	1121854	28.9	1112704	28.7	109.2	110.9
2007–8	1900762	38.1	484695	1412104	31.4	1416067	31.5	114.7	117.3
2008–9	1931380	34.3	565198	1434905	28.3	1366182	27.0	123.0	127.5
2009–10	2363670	36.6	657897	1674483	28.9	1705773	29.4	128.5	135.1
2010–11#	2692031	35.1	753473	1995716	28.8	1938558	28.0	136.4	146.5
2011–12@									158.4

Notes: # – Quick Estimates @ – Advance Estimates
* Excluding works of art and antiques (Valuables are a new item in the 1999–2000 series)
** Errors and Omissions at current prices have been deflated by the implicit price deflators of capital formation by the CSO.

Source: Central Statistics Office (CSO)

Table A1.6 Net Capital Stock by Type of Institutions and Capital–Output Ratios

(Rupees, Crore)

Year (As on March 31)	Net Capital Stock				Net Fixed Capital Stock				Inventory		
	Total (3+4)	Public Sector	Private Sector	of which: Household Sector	Total (7+8)	Public Sector	Private Sector	of which: Household Sector	Total (11+12)	Public Sector	Private Sector	of which: Household Sector
1	2	3	4	5	6	7	8	9	10	11	12	13
At 2004-5 Prices												
1981	2605754	1235331	1370423	1004803	2420794	1145979	1274816	964630	184959	89352	95607	40172
1982	2743247	1318108	1425139	1035496	2534698	1220131	1314566	993440	208549	97976	110573	42056
1983	2882991	1409245	1473746	1057800	2656584	1306554	1350031	1012841	226406	102691	123715	44959
1984	3001855	1497658	1504197	1068607	2767966	1393352	1374614	1018587	233889	104306	129583	50020
1985	3150405	1591852	1558553	1099039	2899142	1481010	1418132	1044755	251263	110842	140421	54284
1986	3315728	1685508	1630220	1137851	3037190	1568093	1469096	1076786	278539	117414	161124	61065
1987	3492607	1793149	1699459	1174788	3192866	1672829	1520037	1105529	299742	120320	179422	69259
1988	3665540	1884551	1780988	1222560	3359789	1769331	1590458	1147415	305750	115220	190530	75145
1989	3820546	1979629	1840918	1249654	3490625	1865180	1625446	1159196	329921	114449	215472	90459
1990	4022682	2068588	1954094	1324091	3676701	1948855	1727845	1231890	345981	119733	226248	92201
1991	4262863	2163959	2098903	1420564	3901819	2038973	1862846	1323104	361044	124986	236057	97460
1992	4460929	2251927	2209002	1477235	4101677	2131591	1970086	1380016	359252	120336	238916	97219
1993	4699590	2335734	2363856	1560227	4322007	2209816	2112192	1460822	377583	125919	251664	99405
1994	4904834	2420240	2484593	1629251	4531066	2291221	2239846	1531908	373767	129020	244748	97342
1995	5161259	2523759	2637500	1710982	4765963	2395483	2370480	1606714	395296	128276	267021	104268
1996	5484866	2612865	2872001	1826824	5055295	2485180	2570115	1710111	429571	127686	301885	116713
1997	5754679	2688370	3066309	1907791	5347663	2559756	2787907	1803544	407016	128614	278402	104246
1998	6094390	2758725	3335666	2029354	5670445	2625879	3044567	1913249	423945	132846	291099	116105
1999	6447090	2837039	3610051	2150595	6028367	2701689	3326677	2038425	418723	135350	283374	112169
2000	6891842	2934058	3957784	2353154	6420229	2779581	3640648	2224524	471613	154477	317136	128630
2001	7271744	3021821	4249924	2567307	6782811	2856614	3926197	2412705	488933	165206	323727	154602
2002	7705843	3116920	4588923	2803186	7220391	2941507	4278884	2652257	485452	175413	310039	150930
2003	8113468	3166236	4947233	3063538	7607968	2996149	4611819	2894626	505501	170087	335414	168912
2004	8609784	3261602	5348183	3346468	8082616	3094537	4988079	3158104	527168	167065	360103	188365
2005	9325629	3394064	5931565	3697195	8718310	3210527	5507783	3464195	607319	183537	423782	233000
2006	10162674	3564427	6598247	4001974	9477355	3359644	6117711	3750983	685319	204783	480536	250991
2007	11158662	3771783	7386879	4344316	10355166	3551576	6803590	4053200	803496	220207	583289	290116

Year													
2008	12323856	4031621	8292235	4666636	11396937	3776175	7620762	4367515	926919	255446	671473	299121	
2009	13514747	4328000	9186747	5094476	12417268	4032691	8384577	4794010	1097479	295309	802170	300466	
2010	14700599	4645250	10055349	5507538	13503037	4310486	9192551	5198184	1197562	334764	862798	309354	

At Current Prices

Year													
1981	381233	168224	213009	141378	336190	152560	183630	124900	45043	15665	25140	16478	
1982	466429	202906	263523	174450	412320	184090	228230	156246	54110	18817	30801	18204	
1983	544617	241621	302995	199816	483334	220917	262416	179874	61283	20704	35801	19942	
1984	610697	276579	334117	219969	543421	254296	289125	197217	67275	22283	39897	22752	
1985	709431	328219	381213	250891	632303	302799	329504	224975	77128	25419	46181	25917	
1986	838910	396186	442725	292151	748919	367373	381546	262539	89991	28813	55462	29612	
1987	945774	446642	499132	328669	845094	415654	429440	295165	100680	30989	63814	33504	
1988	1096266	513265	583001	383027	986587	481752	504835	345464	109679	31513	72221	37564	
1989	1257225	601677	655548	422895	1127218	567828	559390	374904	130007	33849	89136	47991	
1990	1445467	700416	745051	475888	1295073	661818	633254	421019	150394	38598	103733	54869	
1991	1661241	799572	861669	547476	1491824	755467	736356	486165	169418	44105	117012	61311	
1992	1979590	946092	1033498	651891	1794064	898711	895353	586877	185525	47380	130216	65014	
1993	2251444	1059651	1191793	736064	2035292	1004551	1030741	661893	216152	55100	152166	74171	
1994	2558501	1178773	1379728	849863	2325850	1117284	1208565	769237	232651	61489	161308	80626	
1995	2944457	1374072	1570384	953980	2679088	1306560	1372529	868016	265368	67513	190051	85965	
1996	3465230	1576816	1888414	1136990	3156594	1505114	1651480	1038686	308637	71703	230542	98304	
1997	3929493	1795077	2134416	1267858	3623379	1718791	1904588	1171695	306114	76286	222722	96162	
1998	4405445	1985920	2419525	1434204	4075274	1903823	2171450	1324234	330172	82097	240524	109970	
1999	4912608	2162705	2749902	1600042	4574887	2074887	2500000	1491170	337721	87818	243203	108872	
2000	5573495	2348754	3224741	1887781	5169558	2243012	2926546	1748869	403936	105742	298195	138912	
2001	6101181	2503144	3598037	2127805	5654170	2381319	3272850	1951473	447011	121824	325186	176332	
2002	6703508	2689132	4014376	2411809	6235353	2554591	3680762	2221306	468155	134541	333614	190503	
2003	7220873	2824189	4396683	2687542	6731516	2690817	4040699	2485206	489356	133372	355984	202336	
2004	8027105	3042007	4985098	3109668	7511410	2910477	4600933	2891209	515694	131530	384165	218459	
2005	9325629	3394064	5931565	3697195	8718310	3210527	5507783	3464195	607319	183537	423782	233000	
2006	10529765	3708043	6821722	4143789	9822493	3495119	6327374	3885662	707272	212924	494348	258127	
2007	12256314	4166344	8089970	4806495	11381055	3923696	7457359	4493287	875259	242648	632611	313208	
2008	14338731	4706109	9632622	5540229	13266787	4411927	8854860	5191606	1071944	294182	777762	348623	
2009	16958893	5450275	11508618	6575996	15592935	5084542	10508393	6197146	1365958	365733	1000225	378850	
2010	19402011	6307830	13094181	7454967	17872806	5885792	11987014	7041892	1529205	422038	1107167	413075	

(Contd.)

Table A1.6 (Contd.)

(Rupees, Crore)

	Average Capital–Output Ratio (ACOR)						Incremental Capital–Output Ratio (ICOR)	
	Net Capital Stock to Output*			Net Fixed Capital Stock to Output*			NDCF to Output	NFCF to Output
	Total	Public Sector	Private Sector	Total	Public Sector	Private Sector		
	14	15	16	17	18	19	20	21
At 2004–5 Prices								
1981	–	–	–	–	–	–		
1982	3.48	9.06	2.23	3.22	8.40	2.06	2.40	2.16
1983	3.57	8.80	2.29	3.29	8.15	2.10	2.55	2.68
1984	3.45	8.85	2.16	3.18	8.22	1.98	5.22	5.80
1985	3.48	8.81	2.16	3.20	8.19	1.97	1.79	1.97
1986	3.52	8.57	2.19	3.23	7.97	1.98	3.80	4.10
1987	3.56	8.45	2.22	3.25	7.87	1.99	3.76	3.89
1988	3.63	8.40	2.26	3.32	7.86	2.02	3.48	3.96
1989	3.43	8.26	2.11	3.13	7.77	1.87	5.14	5.23
1990	3.38	7.93	2.10	3.09	7.47	1.85	1.73	1.62
1991	3.40	8.21	2.11	3.11	7.74	1.87	2.97	2.77
1992	3.55	8.13	2.25	3.25	7.68	2.00	4.23	3.70
1993	3.54	8.28	2.25	3.25	7.84	2.01	17.30	18.44
1994	3.50	8.19	2.24	3.23	7.75	2.01	3.25	3.26
1995	3.45	7.89	2.24	3.19	7.48	2.02	2.83	2.68
1996	3.40	7.45	2.26	3.14	7.08	2.02	3.16	2.60
1997	3.32	7.46	2.22	3.07	7.10	2.00	2.77	2.59
1998	3.37	6.88	2.35	3.13	6.55	2.14	2.29	2.21
1999	3.34	6.61	2.39	3.12	6.29	2.19	5.25	4.66
2000	3.31	6.04	2.46	3.08	5.74	2.26	3.04	2.94
2001	3.37	6.23	2.53	3.15	5.89	2.33	3.09	2.62
2002	3.39	6.03	2.59	3.17	5.70	2.41	4.76	4.29
2003	3.44	5.81	2.71	3.23	5.49	2.53	3.52	3.72
2004	3.36	5.76	2.67	3.15	5.46	2.49	5.11	4.76
2005	3.38	5.82	2.71	3.17	5.52	2.52	2.79	2.43
2006	3.36	5.77	2.72	3.13	5.45	2.53	4.52	3.71
2007	3.35	5.59	2.77	3.12	5.27	2.56	3.54	2.92
2008	3.38	5.56	2.83	3.14	5.22	2.61	3.68	3.06
							4.23	3.45

Year								
2009	3.50	5.33	3.01	3.23	4.98	2.75	4.99	4.46
2010	3.54	4.99	3.11	3.25	4.64	2.85	4.43	3.50

At Currrent Prices

Year								
1981	—	—	—	—	—	—	0.83	0.74
1982	2.90	7.19	1.98	2.56	6.52	1.71	0.93	0.90
1983	3.10	7.01	2.16	2.75	6.38	1.87	1.29	1.37
1984	3.02	6.89	2.07	2.68	6.32	1.79	0.83	0.91
1985	3.08	7.09	2.09	2.75	6.53	1.80	1.24	1.30
1986	3.26	7.32	2.19	2.91	6.78	1.89	1.47	1.47
1987	3.37	7.15	2.29	3.01	6.65	1.97	1.36	1.52
1988	3.42	7.03	2.35	3.06	6.57	2.03	1.38	1.40
1989	3.29	6.87	2.24	2.96	6.47	1.93	1.04	0.97
1990	3.29	6.92	2.21	2.94	6.54	1.88	1.37	1.28
1991	3.24	7.08	2.15	2.91	6.69	1.83	1.47	1.28
1992	3.32	6.96	2.24	2.99	6.59	1.93	1.18	1.26
1993	3.36	7.01	2.29	3.04	6.65	1.98	1.29	1.29
1994	3.27	6.77	2.26	2.97	6.42	1.96	1.09	1.03
1995	3.20	6.65	2.21	2.91	6.31	1.94	1.31	1.07
1996	3.19	6.48	2.22	2.90	6.18	1.94	1.34	1.24
1997	3.15	6.86	2.17	2.89	6.56	1.92	1.24	1.19
1998	3.20	6.46	2.26	2.96	6.19	2.02	1.98	1.75
1999	3.10	6.10	2.22	2.87	5.85	2.01	1.33	1.29
2000	3.16	5.94	2.33	2.93	5.68	2.12	2.26	1.91
2001	3.27	6.04	2.47	3.03	5.76	2.24	2.59	2.32
2002	3.30	5.91	2.54	3.07	5.62	2.32	2.23	2.35
2003	3.33	5.64	2.62	3.10	5.36	2.41	2.49	2.32
2004	3.24	5.63	2.56	3.03	5.38	2.36	1.90	1.65
2005	3.27	5.63	2.62	3.06	5.36	2.43	2.47	2.03
2006	3.28	5.82	2.64	3.06	5.50	2.45	2.44	2.02
2007	3.22	5.73	2.62	3.00	5.40	2.42	2.19	1.82
2008	3.25	5.77	2.66	3.01	5.42	2.45	2.52	2.06
2009	3.30	5.57	2.76	3.05	5.21	2.53	2.13	1.91
2010	3.35	5.31	2.84	3.08	4.95	2.60	2.45	1.96

Note: * Average of beginning and year–end capital stock as ratio of the year's Net Domestic Product (NDP) at factor cost for respective sectors $ Based on increase in NDP at factor cost.

Source: CSO, National Accounts Statistics.

Table A1.7 Rank of States in Descending Order of Per Capita State Domestic Product in Real Terms

Arranged as per 2009–10 Per Capita

	Per Capita GSDP at 1980–1 Prices				Per Capita GSDP at 1999–2000 Prices						Per Capita GSDP at 2004–5 Prices				
	1981–2	Rank	1990–1	Rank	CAGR 1990–1 over 1980–1	2000–1	Rank	2008–9	Rank	CAGR 2008–9 over 2000–1	2005–6	Rank	2009–10	Rank	CAGR 2009–10 over 2005–6
Goa	3895	2	5597	2	4.1	46202	3	68001	3	4.9	93118	1	113024	1	12.7
Chandigarh						51978	1	84337	1	6.2	88385	2	104065	2	18.0
Delhi	4600	1	6146	1	3.3	42164	4	67853	4	6.1	70370	3	93760	3	16.1
Puducherry	3097	4	3416	7	1.1	37362	8	72593	2	8.7	63940	4	83410	4	21.9
Maharashtra	2695	7	3776	5	3.8	25754	8	41318	6	6.1	45658	6	64091	5	16.0
Andaman & Nicobar Islands	2759	5	2916	10	0.6	26752	7	34067	12	3.1	48105	5	61092	6	28.4
Haryana	2705	6	3784	4	3.8	26559	6	45699	5	7.0	45293	7	60993	7	–3.2
Gujarat	2280	8	2953	8	2.9	21761	12	40487	7	8.1	42088	8	55738	8	–2.2
Tamil Nadu	1743	14	2482	12	4.0	22306	10	34549	11	5.6	38791	12	52933	9	5.4
Sikkim	1757	13	3621	6	8.4	18131	16	28778	15	5.9	32965	14	52619	10	7.6
Kerala	1683	17	2076	17	2.4	22680	11	38945	8	7.0	39420	10	51541	11	4.7
Himachal Pradesh	1888	10	2483	11	3.1	24591	9	38345	9	5.7	39555	9	50993	12	–5.6
Punjab	3174	3	4216	3	3.2	28589	5	37153	10	3.3	39169	11	49153	13	2.4
Uttarakhand						16476	19	28450	16	7.1	31009	16	48819	14	14.8
Karnataka	1739	16	2376	13	3.5	19641	13	31157	13	5.9	32894	15	43507	15	11.8
Nagaland	1742	15	2184	16	2.5	16585	18	25654	18	5.6	35288	13	41693	16	8.2
Arunachal Pradesh	1850	12	2929	9	5.2	16292	23	24633	20	5.3	30990	17	41582	17	2.3
Andhra Pradesh	1673	18	2293	15	3.6	18121	15	30405	14	6.7	30868	18	41226	18	0.1
Mizoram						18610	14	23795	21	3.1	28562	20	37844	19	5.0
Meghalaya	1529	20	1808	22	1.9	16525	20	24706	19	5.2	28824	19	36623	20	4.5
Tripura	1411	25	1804	23	2.8	16574	22	23755	22	4.6	28035	21	34466	21	7.6
West Bengal	1871	11	2369	14	2.7	17820	17	26522	17	5.1	26295	22	32423	22	–0.1
Chhattisgarh						13257	27	22753	23	7.0	22829	24	31209	23	–1.3
Jammu & Kashmir	2019	9				16065	21	20321	26	3.0	25949	23	30929	24	6.7
Odisha	1371	26	1708	24	2.5	11851	30	20981	25	7.4	21393	26	29334	25	0.3
Rajasthan	1416	24	2028	18	4.1	15119	24	21898	24	4.7	22426	25	27441	26	–8.6
Manipur	1586	19	1976	19	2.5	14034	26	17937	28	3.1	21376	27	24778	27	2.9
Jharkhand						12270	29	17641	29	4.6	20249	28	23920	28	–4.5

	Per Capita GSDP at 1980–1 Prices					Per Capita GSDP at 1999–2000 Prices					Per Capita GSDP at 2004-5 Prices				
	1981–2	Rank	1990–1	Rank	CAGR 1990–1 over 1980–1	2000–1	Rank	2008–9	Rank	CAGR 2008–9 over 2000–1	2005–6	Rank	2009–10	Rank	CAGR 2009–10 over 2005–6
Assam	1485	22	1702	25	1.5	13515	25	18002	27	3.6	19453	29	23260	29	−1.3
Madhya Pradesh	1529	21	1839	20	2.1	13067	28	16986	30	3.3	18284	30	22065	30	6.3
Uttar Pradesh	1449	23	1816	21	2.5	10874	31	14370	31	3.5	15362	31	18865	31	−4.7
Bihar	1080	27	1315	26	2.2	6662	32	10702	32	6.1	9176	32	13215	32	−7.2

Arranged as per 2009–10 Per Capita

	Per Capita GSDP at 1980–1 Prices					Per Capita GSDP at 1999–2000 Prices					Per Capita GSDP at 2004-5 Prices				
	1981–2	Rank	1990–1	Rank	CAGR 1990–1 over 1980–1	2000–1	Rank	2008–9	Rank	CAGR 2008–9 over 2000–1	2005–6	Rank	2009–10	Rank	CAGR 2009–10 over 2005–6
Goa	3083	2	4665	2	4.7	40208	2	59003	3	4.9	43363	1	96139	1	10.5
Chandigarh						47757	1	77528	1	6.2	27640	2	93123	2	16.4
Delhi	4229	1	5644	1	3.3	38971	3	63355	2	6.3	28362	3	89252	3	15.4
Puducherry	2817	4	3100	8	1.1	33502	4	60232	4	7.6	17137	4	74605	4	20.2
Maharashtra	2452	6	3432	5	3.8	22387	8	35647	6	6.0	19556	6	57942	5	14.5
Haryana	2419	7	3420	6	3.9	24428	6	41950	5	7.0	79238	7	55139	6	−4.4
Andaman & Nicobar Islands	2544	5	2532	10	−0.1	23844	7	31626	11	3.6	8280	5	54975	7	26.7
Gujarat	2011	8	2235	11	1.2	18097	12	32321	9	7.5	66548	8	47640	8	−4.1
Tamil Nadu	1555	15	2200	12	3.9	19833	11	30250	12	5.4	34706	12	47186	9	3.9
Kerala	1487	18	1782	18	2.0	19976	10	34762	7	7.2	35564	10	45223	10	3.0
Punjab	2818	3	3762	3	3.3	25870	5	33265	8	3.2	40792	11	43133	11	0.7
Sikkim	1644	13	3327	7	8.1	15383	18	24733	17	6.1	29334	15	42413	12	4.7
Uttarakhand						14604	22	24934	15	6.9	16147	17	42258	13	12.8
Himachal Pradesh	1718	11	3762	4	9.1	21724	9	32937	10	5.3	80850	9	41083	14	−8.1
Nagaland	1553	16	1990	16	2.8	15481	17	17129	26	1.3	22237	13	38921	15	7.2
Karnataka	1563	14	2119	14	3.4	17419	13	27586	13	5.9	17781	14	38330	16	10.1
Arunachal Pradesh	1692	12	2695	9	5.3	15170	20	22177	20	4.9	34664	16	37394	17	1.0
Andhra Pradesh	1504	17	2069	15	3.6	16405	16	27373	14	6.6	41007	18	36800	18	−1.3
Mizoram						16774	14	21262	21	3.0	25599	21	34189	19	3.7
Tripura	1298	24	1620	23	2.5	15333	19	22493	19	4.9	19183	19	33464	20	7.2
Meghalaya	1367	22	1698	21	2.4	14928	21	22578	18	5.3	25656	20	31861	21	2.7
West Bengal	1727	10	2166	13	2.5	16452	15	24986	16	5.4	32806	22	29352	22	−1.4

(Contd.)

Table A1.7 (Contd.)

	Per Capita GSDP at 1980–1 Prices			CAGR 1990–1 over 1980–1	Arranged as per 2009–10 Per Capita					Per Capita GSDP at 2004–5 Prices			
					Per Capita GSDP at 1999–2000 Prices								
	1981–2	Rank	1990–1	Rank	CAGR 1990-1 over 1980-1	2000–1	Rank	2008–9	Rank	CAGR 2008–9 over 2000–1	2005–6	Rank	2009–10	Rank	CAGR 2009–10 over 2005–6
Jammu and Kashmir	1777	9	1764	19	-0.1	13820	23	17590	25	3.1	18451	23	26770	23	4.8
Chhattisgarh						11546	28	19883	22	7.0	34660	25	26019	24	-3.5
Rajasthan	1261	26	1804	17	4.1	13464	24	19428	23	4.7	56497	24	24124	25	-10.1
Orissa	1265	25	1537	26	2.2	10509	30	18340	24	7.2	28667	27	23640	26	-2.4
Manipur	1443	19	1756	20	2.2	12686	25	16228	28	3.1	19784	26	22275	27	1.5
Jharkhand						10660	29	15964	29	5.2	34451	28	20705	28	-6.2
Assam	1374	20	1545	25	1.3	12419	26	16293	27	3.5	25880	29	20281	29	-3.0
Madhya Pradesh	1369	21	1586	24	1.6	11750	27	14930	30	3.0	13542	30	19337	30	4.6
Uttar Pradesh	1299	23	1624	22	2.5	9714	31	12612	31	3.3	27716	31	16481	31	-6.3
Bihar	933	27	1139	27	2.2	6111	32	9867	32	6.2	23952	32	12029	32	-8.2

1999–2000 series—For the state Arunachal Pradesh, Jharkhand, Gujarat, Kerala, Manipur, Meghalaya, Mizoram, Sikkim, Tamil Nadu, and Delhi data for 2009–10 pertains to 2008–9.
1999–2000 series—For the state Goa, Jammu & Kashmir, Tripura, and A&N Islands data pertains to 2007–8, whereas for Nagaland data is for the year 2006–7.
2004–5 series—Ranked according to 2009–10 data.
2004–5 series—For the state Andaman and Nicobar Islands, Arunachal Pradesh, Goa, Gujarat, Kerala, Madhya Pradesh, Mizoram, and West Bengal data for 2010–11 pertains to 2009–10.
2004–5 series—Nagaland data available up to 2008–9 and is repeated for 2009–10 and 2010–11.

Note: '..' not relevant/not available.

Source: CSO and individual states relevant ministry department.

Table A2 PRODUCTION

Table A2.1 Production Trends in Major Agricultural Crops

(Million tonnes)

Year	Rice	Wheat	Coarse Cereals	Cereals	Pulses	Food-grains	Oil-seeds#	Cotton Lint@	Jute & Mesta*	Tobacco	Sugar cane	Tea* (Jan–Dec) Mn.kgs	Coffee*
1	2	3	4	5	6	7	8	9	10	11	12	13	14
1950–1	20.58	6.46	15.38	42.42	8.41	50.83	5.16	3.04	3.31	0.26	57.05	279.00	24.00
1951–2	21.30	6.18	16.09	43.57	8.42	51.99	5.03	3.28	4.72	0.21	61.63	291.00	24.00
1952–3	22.90	7.50	19.61	50.01	9.19	59.20	4.73	3.34	5.32	0.25	51.00	306.00	21.00
1953–4	28.21	8.02	22.97	59.20	10.62	69.82	5.37	4.13	3.77	0.27	44.41	267.00	25.00
1954–5	25.22	9.04	22.82	57.08	10.95	68.03	6.40	4.45	3.86	0.26	58.74	293.00	26.00
1955–6	27.56	8.76	19.49	55.81	11.05	66.85	5.73	4.18	5.39	0.30	60.54	308.00	35.00
1956–7	29.04	9.40	19.87	58.31	11.55	69.86	6.36	4.92	5.81	0.31	69.05	309.00	43.00
1957–8	25.53	7.99	21.23	54.75	9.56	64.31	6.35	4.96	5.33	0.24	71.16	311.00	44.00
1958–9	30.85	9.96	23.18	63.99	13.15	77.14	7.30	4.88	6.91	0.32	73.36	325.00	47.00
1959–60	31.68	10.32	22.87	64.87	11.80	76.67	6.56	3.68	5.69	0.29	77.82	326.00	50.00
1960–1	34.57	11.00	23.74	69.31	12.70	82.02	6.98	5.60	5.26	0.31	110.00	321.00	68.00
1961–2	35.66	12.07	23.22	70.95	11.76	82.71	7.28	4.85	8.24	0.34	103.97	354.00	46.00
1962–3	33.21	10.78	24.63	68.62	11.53	80.15	7.39	5.54	7.19	0.34	91.91	347.00	56.00
1963–4	37.00	9.85	23.72	70.57	10.07	80.64	7.13	5.75	7.98	0.36	104.23	346.00	69.00
1964–5	39.31	12.26	25.37	76.94	12.42	89.36	8.56	6.01	7.66	0.36	121.91	372.00	61.00
1965–6	30.59	10.40	21.42	62.41	9.94	72.35	6.40	4.85	5.78	0.29	123.99	366.00	64.00
1966–7	30.44	11.39	24.05	65.88	8.35	74.23	6.43	5.27	6.58	0.35	92.83	376.00	78.00
1967–8	37.61	16.54	28.80	82.95	12.10	95.05	8.30	5.78	7.59	0.37	95.50	385.00	71.00
1968–9	39.76	18.65	25.18	83.59	10.42	94.01	6.85	5.45	3.84	0.36	124.68	402.00	73.00
1969–70	40.43	20.09	27.29	87.81	11.69	99.50	7.73	5.56	6.79	0.34	135.02	396.00	63.00
1970–1	42.22	23.83	30.55	96.60	11.82	108.42	9.63	4.76	6.19	0.36	126.37	419.00	110.20
1971–2	43.07	26.41	24.60	94.08	11.09	105.17	9.08	6.95	6.84	0.42	113.57	435.00	68.90
1972–3	39.24	24.74	23.14	87.12	9.91	97.03	7.14	5.74	6.09	0.37	124.87	456.00	91.10
1973–4	44.05	21.78	28.83	94.66	10.01	104.67	9.39	6.31	7.68	0.46	140.81	472.00	86.40
1974–5	39.58	24.10	26.13	89.81	10.02	99.83	9.15	7.16	5.83	0.36	144.29	489.00	92.50
1975–6	48.74	28.84	30.41	107.99	13.04	121.03	10.61	5.95	5.91	0.35	140.60	487.00	84.00
1976–7	41.92	29.01	28.88	99.81	11.36	111.17	8.43	5.84	7.10	0.42	153.01	512.00	102.20
1977–8	52.67	31.75	30.02	114.44	11.97	126.41	9.66	7.24	7.15	0.49	176.97	556.00	125.10

(Contd.)

Table A2.1 (Contd.)

(Million tonnes)

Year	Rice	Wheat	Coarse Cereals	Cereals*	Pulses	Food-grains	Oil-seeds#	Cotton Lint@	Jute & Mesta*	Tobacco	Sugar cane	Tea* (Jan–Dec) Mn.kgs	Coffee*
1	2	3	4	5	6	7	8	9	10	11	12	13	14
1978-9	53.77	35.51	30.44	119.72	12.18	131.90	10.10	7.96	8.33	0.45	151.66	564.00	110.50
1979-80	42.33	31.83	26.97	101.13	8.57	109.70	8.74	7.65	7.96	0.44	128.83	544.00	149.80
1980-1	53.63	36.31	29.02	118.96	10.63	129.59	9.37	7.01	8.16	0.48	154.25	569.60	118.60
1981-2	53.25	37.45	31.09	121.79	11.51	133.30	12.08	7.88	8.37	0.52	186.36	560.40	150.00
1982-3	47.12	42.79	27.75	117.66	11.86	129.52	10.00	7.53	7.17	0.58	189.51	560.70	130.00
1983-4	60.10	45.48	33.90	139.48	12.89	152.37	12.69	6.39	7.72	0.49	174.08	581.50	105.00
1984-5	58.34	44.07	31.17	133.58	11.96	145.54	12.95	8.51	7.79	0.49	170.32	639.90	195.10
1985-6	63.83	47.05	26.20	137.08	13.36	150.44	10.83	8.73	12.65	0.44	170.65	656.20	122.30
1986-7	60.56	44.32	26.83	131.71	11.71	143.42	11.27	6.91	8.62	0.46	186.09	624.60	192.30
1987-8	56.86	46.17	26.36	129.39	10.96	140.35	12.65	6.38	6.78	0.37	196.74	674.30	123.00
1988-9	70.49	54.11	31.47	156.07	13.85	169.92	18.03	8.74	7.86	0.49	203.04	701.10	215.00
1989-90	73.57	49.85	34.76	158.18	12.86	171.04	16.92	11.42	8.29	0.55	225.57	684.10	180.00
1990-1	74.29	55.14	32.70	162.13	14.26	176.39	18.61	9.84	9.23	0.56	241.05	720.34	170.00
1991-2	74.68	55.69	25.99	156.36	12.02	168.38	18.60	9.71	10.29	0.58	254.00	754.19	208.00
1992-3	72.86	57.21	36.59	166.66	12.82	179.48	20.11	11.40	8.59	0.60	228.03	703.93	169.40
1993-4	80.30	59.84	30.81	170.95	13.31	184.26	21.50	10.74	8.42	0.56	229.66	760.83	208.00
1994-5	81.81	65.77	29.88	177.46	14.04	191.50	21.34	11.89	9.08	0.57	275.54	752.90	180.00
1995-6	76.98	62.10	29.03	168.11	12.31	180.42	22.10	12.86	8.81	0.54	281.10	756.02	223.00
1996-7	81.73	69.35	34.11	185.19	14.25	199.44	24.38	14.23	11.13	0.62	277.56	780.14	205.00
1997-8	82.54	66.35	30.40	179.29	12.97	192.26	21.32	10.85	11.02	0.64	279.54	835.60	228.30
1998-9	86.08	71.29	31.33	188.70	14.91	203.61	24.75	12.29	9.81	0.74	288.72	855.20	265.00
1999-2000	89.68	76.37	30.34	196.39	13.41	209.80	20.71	11.53	10.55	0.52	299.32	836.80	292.00
2000-1	84.98	69.68	31.08	185.74	11.07	196.81	18.44	9.52	10.56	0.34	295.96	848.40	301.00
2001-2	93.34	72.77	33.37	199.48	13.37	212.85	20.66	10.00	11.68	0.55	297.21	847.40	301.00
2002-3	71.82	65.76	26.07	163.65	11.13	174.77	14.84	8.62	11.28	0.49	287.38	846.00	275.00
2003-4	88.53	72.15	37.60	198.28	14.91	213.19	25.19	13.73	11.17	0.55	233.86	850.50	270.00
2004-5	83.13	68.64	33.46	185.23	13.13	198.36	24.35	16.43	10.27	0.55	237.09	906.84	281.90
2005-6	91.79	69.35	34.06	195.20	13.39	208.60	27.98	18.50	10.84	0.55	281.17	1000.00	300.00
2006-7	93.35	75.81	33.92	203.08	14.20	217.28	24.29	22.63	11.27	0.52	355.52	900.00	300.00

Year											
2007–8	96.69	78.57	40.76	216.02	14.76	230.78	29.76	25.88	11.21	0.49	348.19	na	na
2008–9	99.18	80.68	40.03	219.90	14.57	234.47	27.72	22.28	10.37	na	285.03	na	na
2009–10	89.09	80.80	33.55	203.45	14.66	218.11	24.88	24.02	11.82				5.98
2010–11	95.98	86.87	43.68	226.53	18.24	244.78	32.48	33.00	10.62				
2011–12A	103.41	90.23	41.91	235.54	17.02	252.56	30.06	35.20	11.57				

Decadal Growth Rates in Per Cent per Annum

Period											
1950–1 to 1959–60	4.34	4.93	2.51	3.75	3.51	3.72	4.11	3.98	4.82	2.81	6.98	1.73	11.96
1960–1 to 1969–70	1.92	9.46	1.92	3.35	–0.22	2.89	1.47	0.21	–2.60	0.91	2.29	2.21	4.16
1970–1 to 1979–80	2.58	5.02	1.56	2.98	0.12	2.72	1.53	2.85	2.90	2.43	2.59	2.99	5.98
1980–1 to 1989–90	4.03	3.29	0.43	2.97	1.27	2.83	6.10	3.50	0.91	–0.10	3.31	2.84	4.44
1990–1 to 1999–2000	2.00	3.12	–0.10	2.08	0.14	1.90	0.81	0.35	2.35	–0.86	2.75	1.99	5.79
2000–1 to 2009–10	2.39	2.15	3.41	2.34	2.67	2.49	6.50	15.56	–0.56	2.04	2.30	2.83	0.18

Notes: Decadal Growth Rates is worked out on three year moving averages. It indicates compound growth rate in the production data calculated for the specified period using the semi-log model lnY = a+bt, where t = time, Y = production and the compound growth is obtained by taking antilog of "b", deducting one from it and multiplying it with 100.

A: Third advance estimate. na: not available

* Production in million bales of 180 kgs each. @ Production in million bales of 170 kgs each. # Total of nine oilseeds out of eleven.

Source: GoI (2012), Agricultural Statistics At A Glance, Ministry of Agriculture and GoI (2012), Economic Survey 2011–12, Ministry of Finance and various earlier issues.

Table A2.2 Trends in Yields of Major Crops

(kg per hectare)

Year	Rice	Wheat	Coarse Cereals	Cereals	Pulses	Food-grains	Total # Oilseeds	Sugar-cane	Tea	Coffee	Cotton (Lint)	Jute & Mesta	Tobacco
1	2	3	4	5	6	7	8	9	10	11	12	13	14
1950–1	668	663	408	542	441	522	481	33422	na	na	88	1043	731
1951–2	714	653	414	557	448	536	430	31786	na	na	85	1074	723
1952–3	764	763	462	607	463	580	424	29495	na	na	89	1028	675
1953–4	902	750	506	678	489	640	488	31497	na	na	100	992	737
1954–5	820	803	520	664	500	631	511	36303	na	na	100	1021	737
1955–6	874	708	449	639	476	605	474	32779	na	na	88	1038	739
1956–7	900	695	473	664	495	629	509	33683	na	na	104	977	728
1957–8	790	682	495	630	424	587	502	34325	na	na	105	944	669
1958–9	930	789	519	707	541	672	561	37658	na	na	104	1130	836
1959–60	937	772	522	713	475	662	470	36414	971	448	86	1049	716
1960–1	1013	851	528	753	539	710	507	45549	na	na	125	1049	766
1961–2	1028	890	519	763	485	706	493	42349	na	na	103	1104	811
1962–3	931	793	556	733	475	680	482	40996	na	na	122	1041	842
1963–4	1033	730	540	757	416	687	481	46353	na	na	119	1130	817
1964–5	1078	913	514	817	520	757	561	46838	na	na	122	1136	876
1965–6	862	827	483	676	438	629	419	43717	na	na	104	936	778
1966–7	863	887	533	707	377	644	428	40336	na	na	114	1058	834
1967–8	1032	1103	608	840	534	783	530	40665	na	na	123	1137	871
1968–9	1076	1169	545	843	490	781	473	49236	na	na	122	855	821
1969–70	1073	1208	578	865	531	805	522	49121	na	na	122	1120	770
1970–1	1123	1307	665	949	524	872	579	48322	1182	816	106	1032	810
1971–2	1141	1380	564	936	501	858	526	47511	1221	499	151	1107	914
1972–3	1070	1271	548	886	474	813	452	50933	1271	620	127	1104	837
1973–4	1151	1172	623	918	427	827	555	51163	1311	554	142	1188	1001
1974–5	1045	1338	606	907	455	824	529	49855	1353	593	161	1068	954
1975–6	1235	1410	694	1041	533	944	627	50903	1341	488	138	1164	950
1976–7	1089	1387	689	985	494	894	512	53383	1407	544	144	1173	969
1977–8	1308	1480	710	1100	510	991	563	56160	1519	652	157	1108	979
1978–9	1328	1568	721	1136	515	1022	570	49114	1528	564	167	1186	1109
1979–80	1074	1436	652	982	385	876	516	49358	1455	749	160	1177	1031
1980–1	1336	1630	695	1142	473	1023	532	57844	1491	624	152	1130	1065
1981–2	1308	1691	733	1157	483	1032	639	58359	1461	691	166	1311	1172

Year													
1982–3	1231	1816	685	1150	519	1035	563	56441	1422	573	163	1265	1157
1983–4	1457	1843	813	1296	548	1162	679	55978	1468	453	141	1320	1120
1984–5	1417	1870	795	1285	526	1149	684	57673	1606	830	196	1242	1113
1985–6	1552	2046	664	1323	547	1175	570	59889	1641	507	197	1524	1111
1986–7	1471	1916	675	1266	506	1128	605	60444	1508	791	169	1454	1187
1987–8	1465	2002	721	1315	515	1173	629	60006	1628	508	168	1274	1155
1988–9	1689	2244	814	1493	598	1331	824	60992	1693	878	202	1540	1307
1989–90	1745	2121	922	1530	549	1349	742	65612	1652	478	252	1646	1335
1990–1	1740	2281	900	1571	578	1380	771	65395	1794	732	225	1634	1353
1991–2	1751	2394	778	1574	533	1382	719	66069	1800	746	216	1662	1369
1992–3	1744	2327	1063	1654	573	1457	797	63843	1664	582	257	1658	1425
1993–4	1888	2380	939	1701	598	1501	799	67120	1796	712	249	1713	1463
1994–5	1911	2559	929	1760	610	1546	843	71254	1767	614	257	1760	1486
1995–6	1797	2483	940	1703	552	1491	851	67787	1770	731	242	1712	1356
1996–7	1882	2679	1072	1831	635	1614	926	66496	1809	675	265	1818	1444
1997–8	1900	2485	986	1775	567	1552	816	71134	1865	746	208	1792	1394
1998–9	1921	2590	1068	1856	634	1627	944	71203	1803	877	224	1722	1451
1999–2000	1986	2778	1034	1926	635	1704	853	70935	1702	947	225	1836	1211
2000–1	1901	2708	1027	1844	544	1626	810	68577	1673	959	190	1867	1318
2001–2	2079	2762	1131	1980	607	1734	913	67370	1800	937	186	2007	1565
2002–3	1744	2610	966	1753	543	1535	691	63576	1800	839	191	1960	1506
2003–4	2077	2713	1221	1987	635	1727	1064	59380	1800	1000	307	2008	1486
2004–5	1984	2602	1153	1918	577	1652	885	64752	1800	1000	318	2019	1498
2005–6	2102	2619	1172	1968	598	1715	1004	66928	1500	1000	362	2173	1351
2006–7	2131	2708	1182	2021	612	1756	916	69022	1667	1000	421	2170	1274
2007–8	2202	2802	1431	2151	625	1860	1115	68877	1500	750	467	2101	1255
2008–9	2178	2907	1459	2284	659	1909	1006	64553	1500	750	403	2071	1456
2009–10	2125	2839	1212	na	630	1798	959	70020	1500	750	403	2349	1559
2010–11*	2240	2938	1528	na	689	1921	1159	68596	1500	750	510	2212	na
2011–12**	2207	na	1504	na	593	1757	na	68093	na	na	512	2217	na

Note: na: not available.

Data for tea and coffee is for calander year

* Fourth Advance Estimates as released on 19.07.2011.

**First Advance Estimates released on 14.09.2011.

The yield rates given above have been worked out on the basis of production & area figures taken in '000 units.

Source: Directorate of Economics and Statistics, Department of Agriculture and Cooperation.

Table A2.3 Horticulture and Livestock Production

(000 'tonnes)

	1991–2	1992–3	1993–4	1994–5	1995–6	1996–7	1997–8	1998–9	1999–2000	2000–1	2001–2
Horticulture Production											
Total	96562	107388	114616	118394	125483	128482	128611	146020	149187	143806	145785
Fruits	28632	32955	37255	38603	41507	40458	43263	44042	45496	45370	43001
Apple	1148	1148	1298	1183	1215	1308	1321	1380	1047	1227	1158
Banana	7790	10460	11901	13168	13095	12440	13340	15073	16814	14137	14210
Citrus Fruit	2822	2979	3912	3701	3798	4456	4311	4575	4651	4386	4789
Lemon	na	na	924	970	920	1048	1101	1260	1492	1377	1414
Mosambi	na	na	825	887	880	844	882	773	1017	1160	1210
Orange	na	na	1058	709	1162	1720	1472	1674	1658	1414	1660
Grapes	668	653	703	673	604	1135	969	1083	1138	1057	1184
Guava	1095	1204	1273	1388	1501	1601	1614	1801	1711	1632	1716
Litchi	244	261	313	333	365	378	455	429	433	412	356
Mango	8716	9223	10113	10993	10811	9981	10234	9782	10504	10057	10020
Papaya	805	804	1266	1373	1330	1299	1619	1582	1666	1796	2590
Pineapple	769	859	1007	1055	1071	925	937	1006	1025	1211	1182
Sapota	396	423	481	496	570	589	644	668	635	741	594
Vegetables	58532	63806	65787	67286	71594	75074	72683	87536	90831	93920	88622
Brinjal	na	na	4612	6232	6443	6586	7735	7882	8117	7652	8348
Cabbage	2771	3237	3593	3906	3862	3613	5324	5624	5909	5507	5678
Cauliflower	2998	3612	2873	3244	2474	3419	4471	4691	4718	4696	4891
Okra	1887	2738	3029	3989	4032	3040	3211	3380	3419	3352	3325
Onion	4706	3490	4006	4040	4080	4180	3620	5330	4900	4721	5252
Peas	852	1492	1528	2306	2341	2339	2422	2706	2712	3008	2038
Tomato	4243	4550	4934	5261	5442	5788	6184	8272	7427	7242	7462
Potato	18195	18479	17392	17401	18843	24216	17652	22495	25000	22243	24456
Sweet potato	1131	1216	1221	1166	1138	1102	1048	1152	1007	1007	1130
Tapioca	5833	5413	6029	5857	5443	5663	6682	5830	6014	6768	6516
Coconuts*	10080	11241	11975	13300	12952	13061	12717	126	12129	12597	12822
Cashewnut	305	349	348	322	418	430	360	460	520	450	460
Flowers	na	na	233	261	334	367	366	419	509	556	535
Plantation Crops	7498	8347	8866	9767	9630	9730	9449	11063	9278	9458	9697
Spices	1900	2280	2470	2477	2410	2805	2801	3091	3023	3023	3765
Livestock Production											
Milk 56	58	61	64	66	69	72	75	78	81	84	
Fish (000 tonnes)	4157	4365	4644	4789	4949	5348	5388	5298	5675	5656	5956
Eggs (Mn. Nos)	21983	22929	24167	25975	27198	27496	28689	29476	30447	36632	38729

Table A2.3 (Contd.)

(000 'tonnes)

	2002–3	2003–4	2004–5	2005–6	2006–7	2007–8	2008–9	2009–10	2010–11
Horticulture Production									
Total	144380	153302	166939	182816	191813	211235	214716	223089	240531
Fruits	45203	45942	50867	55356	59563	65587	68466	71516	74878
Apple	1348	1522	1739	1814	1624	2001	1985	1777.2	2891
Banana	13304	13857	16745	18888	20998	23823	26217	26470	29780
Citrus Fruit	5677	5787	5933	6139	7145	8015	8608	9638	7464
Lemon	1440	1493	1033	2159	2310	2502	2572	2629	2108
Mosambi	785	2019	2079	2139	2909	3399	3567	3882	1316
Orange	1137	1244	1236	1299	1358	1462	1634	2084	3255
Grapes	1248	1475	1565	1650	1685	1735	1878	881	1235
Guava	1793	1831	1683	1737	1831	1981	2270	2572	2462
Litchi	476	479	369	392	403	418	423	483	497
Mango	12733	11490	11830	12663	13734	13997	12750	15027	15188
Papaya	2147	1692	2535	2139	2482	2909	3629	3914	4196
Pineapple	1172	1234	1279	1263	1362	1245	1341	1387	1415
Sapota	913	921	1077	1114	1216	1258	1308	1347	1424
Vegetables	84815	88334	101246	111399	114993	128449	129077	133738	146554
Brinjal	8001	8477	8601	9365	9453	9678	10378	10563	11896
Cabbage	5392	5595	6114	5637	5584	5910	6870	7281	7949
Cauliflower	4444	4940	4515	5323	5538	5777	6532	6569	6745
Okra	1887	3631	3512	3975	4070	4179	4528	4803	5784
Onion	4210	6268	7761	9433	10847	13900	13565	12159	15118
Peas	852	1901	1945	2270	2402	2491	2916	3029	3517
Tomato	7617	8126	8825	9820	10055	10303	11149	12433	16826
Potato	23161	27926	28788	29175	28600	34658	34391	36577	42339
Sweet potato	1130	1179	1179	1066	1067	1094	1120	1095	1047
Tapioca	5426	5950	7463	7855	8232	9056	9623	8060	8076
Coconuts*	12822	12178	8829	14809	15831	14748	14748	15730	10840
Cashewnut	460	535	544	579	620	665	695	613	675
Flowers	735	580	659	654	880	868	987	1021	1031
Plantation Crops	9697	13161	9835	11263	12007	11300	11336	11928	12007
Spices	3765	5113	4001	5108	3953	4357	4145	4016	5350
Livestock Production									
Milk	86	88	93	97	103	108	112	116	122
Fish (000 tonnes)	6200	6399	6304	6572	6869	7127	7620	7914	8290
Eggs (Mn. Nos)	39823	40403	45201	56235	50663	53583	55562	60267	63024

Note: * Coconut production is in number of nuts in thousands. (1453.24 nuts = 1 ton); na: Not Available.

Source: National Horticulture Board, Ministry of Agriculture, Government of India, *Indian Horticulture Data Base—2011 and Economic Survey 2011–12*.

Table A2.4 Value of Output from Agriculture, Horticulture, and Livestock

At Constant (1999–2000) Prices

	Agriculture, Horticulture, and Livestock	Agriculture (4 to 11)	Cereals	Pulses	Oilseeds	Sugars	Fibres	Drugs and Narcotics	Condiments and Spices	Others	Horticulture (Fruits and Vegetables)	Livestock
1	2	3	4	5	6	7	8	9	10	11	12	13
1950–1	114288 (100.0)	81834 (71.6)	30342 (26.5)	11506 (10.1)	8242 (7.2)	4156 (3.6)	3856 (3.4)	2397 (2.1)	3308 (2.9)	18029 (15.8)	15269 (13.4)	32454 (28.4)
1955–6	131256 (100.0)	97145 (74.0)	38660 (29.5)	14542 (11.1)	9370 (7.1)	5103 (3.9)	5155 (3.9)	2738 (2.1)	3615 (2.8)	17963 (13.7)	14284 (10.9)	34111 (26.0)
1960–1	150683 (100.0)	112933 (74.9)	48004 (31.9)	16140 (10.7)	11082 (7.4)	6820 (4.5)	6543 (4.3)	2879 (1.9)	4164 (2.8)	17301 (11.5)	16286 (10.8)	37750 (25.1)
1965–6	142745 (100.0)	104853 (73.5)	42806 (30.0)	12736 (8.9)	10467 (7.3)	8146 (5.7)	5530 (3.9)	3137 (2.2)	4047 (2.8)	17984 (12.6)	20113 (14.1)	37893 (26.5)
1970–1	178061 (100.0)	137394 (77.2)	65096 (36.6)	15204 (8.5)	15023 (8.4)	8040 (4.5)	6066 (3.4)	3994 (2.2)	5491 (3.1)	18479 (10.4)	32064 (18.0)	40667 (22.8)
1975–6	198834 (100.0)	151065 (76.0)	73311 (36.9)	16992 (8.5)	15702 (7.9)	9220 (4.6)	6547 (3.3)	4365 (2.2)	5668 (2.9)	19261 (9.7)	36383 (18.3)	47769 (24.0)
1980–1	217185 (100.0)	158845 (73.1)	81070 (37.3)	14339 (6.6)	14469 (6.7)	9611 (4.4)	8028 (3.7)	5134 (2.4)	6877 (3.2)	19316 (8.9)	42003 (19.3)	58339 (26.9)
1985–6	256810 (100.0)	179269 (69.8)	93326 (36.3)	17202 (6.7)	16267 (6.3)	10226 (4.0)	10652 (4.1)	5703 (2.2)	8672 (3.4)	17222 (6.7)	48268 (18.8)	77540 (30.2)
1990–1	311709 (100.0)	218761 (70.2)	110632 (35.5)	19042 (6.1)	26828 (8.6)	14252 (4.6)	11244 (3.6)	6889 (2.2)	10230 (3.3)	19644 (6.3)	54299 (17.4)	92949 (29.8)
1991–2	307565 (100.0)	211309 (68.7)	107007 (34.8)	15914 (5.2)	26739 (8.7)	15184 (4.9)	11267 (3.7)	7150 (2.3)	9863 (3.2)	18184 (5.9)	53401 (17.4)	96056 (31.3)
1992–3	324203 (100.0)	223278 (68.9)	112932 (34.8)	17378 (5.4)	28753 (8.9)	13413 (4.1)	12736 (3.9)	6688 (2.1)	11408 (3.5)	19970 (6.2)	58365 (18.0)	100925 (31.1)
1993–4	334774 (100.0)	229088 (68.4)	117026 (35.0)	17918 (5.4)	29960 (8.9)	13673 (4.1)	12183 (3.6)	7489 (2.2)	12010 (3.6)	18829 (5.6)	60670 (18.1)	105686 (31.6)
1994–5	349934 (100.0)	240065 (68.6)	121714 (34.8)	18200 (5.2)	31095 (8.9)	15821 (4.5)	13542 (3.9)	7299 (2.1)	12278 (3.5)	20115 (5.7)	63620 (18.2)	109870 (31.4)
1995–6	345152 (100.0)	231521 (67.1)	114805 (33.3)	16387 (4.7)	31227 (9.0)	16018 (4.6)	14578 (4.2)	7407 (2.1)	11957 (3.5)	19141 (5.5)	67337 (19.5)	113631 (32.9)
1996–7	371946 (100.1)	254335 (68.4)	126197 (33.9)	19216 (5.2)	34597 (9.3)	16101 (4.3)	16234 (4.4)	9025 (2.4)	13325 (3.6)	19639 (5.3)	76864 (20.7)	117612 (31.6)
1997–8	362742 (100.0)	241889 (66.7)	122973 (33.9)	17432 (4.8)	30681 (8.5)	16093 (4.4)	12785 (3.5)	8841 (2.4)	13255 (3.7)	19830 (5.5)	77849 (21.5)	120853 (33.3)
1998–9	387159 (100.0)	261325 (67.5)	129346 (33.4)	20243 (5.2)	34509 (8.9)	18806 (4.9)	14383 (3.7)	9517 (2.5)	15704 (4.1)	18817 (4.9)	84982 (22.0)	125834 (32.5)

Year													
1999–2000	398044 (100.0)	268514 (67.5)	134096 (33.7)	18153 (4.6)	28625 (7.2)	24669 (6.2)	13373 (3.4)	10752 (2.7)	15447 (3.9)	23397 (5.9)	86155 (21.6)	129531 (32.5)
2000–1	387120 (100.0)	253424 (65.5)	125541 (32.4)	15669 (4.0)	26637 (6.9)	24640 (6.4)	10792 (2.8)	9950 (2.6)	15907 (4.1)	24287 (6.3)	91786 (23.7)	133696 (34.5)
2001–2	416580 (100.0)	276721 (66.4)	135004 (32.4)	18576 (4.5)	29550 (7.1)	24576 (5.9)	11527 (2.8)	10093 (2.4)	17393 (4.2)	30002 (7.2)	93809 (22.5)	139860 (33.6)
2002–3	380277 (100.0)	236627 (62.2)	110732 (29.1)	15698 (4.1)	22612 (5.9)	23591 (6.2)	10324 (2.7)	10120 (2.7)	16442 (4.3)	27109 (7.1)	94090 (24.7)	143649 (37.8)
2003–4	431612 (100.0)	284284 (65.9)	132338 (30.7)	20762 (4.8)	34841 (8.1)	19635 (4.5)	15097 (3.5)	9509 (2.2)	18644 (4.3)	33459 (7.8)	90392 (20.9)	147328 (34.1)
2004–5	430812 (100.0)	276567 (64.2)	125257 (29.1)	17868 (4.1)	33898 (7.9)	19994 (4.6)	18130 (4.2)	10985 (2.5)	19014 (4.4)	31422 (7.3)	94500 (21.9)	154245 (35.8)
2005–6	454452 (100.0)	293857 (64.7)	132879 (29.2)	18435 (4.1)	38208 (8.4)	22527 (5.0)	19502 (4.3)	11466 (2.5)	19446 (4.3)	31393 (6.9)	102594 (22.6)	160595 (35.3)
2006–7	472921 (100.0)	305857 (64.7)	137544 (29.1)	19622 (4.1)	33439 (7.1)	27832 (5.9)	23678 (5.0)	12093 (2.6)	20305 (4.3)	31343 (6.6)	107537 (22.7)	167064 (35.3)
2007–8	497887 (100.0)	324023 (65.1)	146429 (29.4)	20407 (4.1)	39481 (7.9)	27258 (5.5)	26820 (5.4)	11730 (2.4)	20519 (4.1)	31377 (6.3)	113734 (22.8)	173864 (34.9)

Note: Horticulture includes flouriculture.

Source: Central Statistical Organisation [CSO] (2009), *National Accounts Statistics*, New Delhi: Ministry of Statistics and Programme Implementation. Hereafter referred to as CSO (2009).

Table A2.4 (Contd.)

At Current Prices

	Agriculture, Horticulture, and Livestock	Agriculture (16 to 23)	Cereals	Pulses	Oilseeds	Sugars	Fibres	Drugs and Narcotics	Condiments and Spices	Others	Horticulture# (Fruits and Vegetables)	Livestock
1	14	15	16	17	18	19	20	21	22	23	24	25
1950-1	5581 (100.0)	4502 (80.7)	2013 (36.1)	333 (6.0)	442 (7.9)	184 (3.3)	227 (4.1)	150 (2.7)	157 (2.8)	996 (17.8)	406 (7.3)	1079 (19.3)
1955-6	4889 (100.0)	3830 (78.3)	1808 (37.0)	238 (4.9)	298 (6.1)	219 (4.5)	268 (5.5)	139 (2.8)	97 (2.0)	762 (15.6)	582 (11.9)	1060 (21.7)
1960-1	7455 (100.0)	5993 (80.4)	3114 (41.8)	459 (6.2)	594 (8.0)	325 (4.4)	400 (5.4)	192 (2.6)	192 (2.6)	717 (9.6)	770 (10.3)	1462 (19.6)
1965-6	10920 (100.0)	8901 (81.5)	4787 (43.8)	702 (6.4)	958 (8.8)	531 (4.9)	452 (4.1)	276 (2.5)	260 (2.4)	933 (8.5)	1399 (12.8)	2019 (18.5)
1970-1	17864 (100.0)	14600 (81.7)	7975 (44.6)	990 (5.5)	1779 (10.0)	781 (4.4)	907 (5.1)	427 (2.4)	448 (2.5)	1292 (7.2)	2715 (15.2)	3264 (18.3)
1975-6	29208 (100.0)	22957 (78.6)	12917 (44.2)	1580 (5.4)	2259 (7.7)	1488 (5.1)	1086 (3.7)	726 (2.5)	772 (2.6)	2129 (7.3)	4274 (14.6)	6251 (21.4)
1980-1	46568 (100.0)	36073 (77.5)	18393 (39.5)	3168 (6.8)	4168 (9.0)	2983 (6.4)	2021 (4.3)	1088 (2.3)	964 (2.1)	3288 (7.1)	7886 (16.9)	10494 (22.5)
1985-6	74590 (100.0)	52816 (70.8)	27805 (37.3)	4939 (6.6)	5621 (7.5)	3448 (4.6)	2842 (3.8)	1783 (2.4)	1988 (2.7)	4390 (5.9)	14474 (19.4)	21774 (29.2)
1990-1	142473 (100.0)	100766 (70.7)	47167 (33.1)	9280 (6.5)	17738 (12.5)	6899 (4.8)	5810 (4.1)	3165 (2.2)	3528 (2.5)	7180 (5.0)	23450 (16.5)	41707 (29.3)
1991-2	169581 (100.0)	119017 (70.2)	58776 (34.7)	8209 (4.8)	19995 (11.8)	7604 (4.5)	7272 (4.3)	3484 (2.1)	5152 (3.0)	8526 (5.0)	27018 (15.9)	50564 (29.8)
1992-3	186080 (100.0)	128208 (68.9)	64315 (34.6)	9588 (5.2)	19740 (10.6)	8411 (4.5)	6808 (3.7)	3590 (1.9)	5887 (3.2)	9869 (5.3)	31364 (16.9)	57873 (31.1)
1993-4	214623 (100.0)	147921 (68.9)	71910 (33.5)	12216 (5.7)	23098 (10.8)	10670 (5.0)	9535 (4.4)	4397 (2.0)	6010 (2.8)	10086 (4.7)	35723 (16.6)	66702 (31.1)
1994-5	247830 (100.0)	171977 (69.4)	82034 (33.1)	13518 (5.5)	25789 (10.4)	13048 (5.3)	13851 (5.6)	4300 (1.7)	7342 (3.0)	12094 (4.9)	40435 (16.3)	75853 (30.6)
1995-6	265922 (100.0)	180310 (67.8)	83992 (31.6)	13896 (5.2)	27641 (10.4)	13043 (4.9)	14198 (5.3)	5688 (2.1)	7906 (3.0)	13944 (5.2)	49475 (18.6)	85611 (32.2)
1996-7	312401 (100.0)	215596 (69.0)	103982 (33.3)	17091 (5.5)	33091 (10.6)	14022 (4.5)	15338 (4.9)	7000 (2.2)	9464 (3.0)	15607 (5.0)	57870 (18.5)	96806 (31.0)
1997-8	316883 (100.0)	210082 (66.3)	102639 (32.4)	15079 (4.8)	28988 (9.1)	15899 (5.0)	13038 (4.1)	8607 (2.7)	9866 (3.1)	15966 (5.0)	75309 (23.8)	106801 (33.7)

Year	Total										
1998–9	369041 (100.0)	251158 (68.1)	124114 (33.6)	19475 (5.3)	35312 (9.6)	18643 (5.1)	14536 (3.9)	9094 (2.5)	13254 (3.6)	16729 (4.5)	83367 (22.6)	117882 (31.9)
1999–2000	398044 (100.0)	268514 (67.5)	134096 (33.7)	18153 (4.6)	28625 (7.2)	24669 (6.2)	13373 (3.4)	10752 (2.7)	15447 (3.9)	23397 (5.9)	86155 (21.6)	129531 (32.5)
2000–1	390235 (100.0)	251179 (64.4)	122687 (31.4)	16995 (4.4)	25860 (6.6)	27151 (7.0)	11093 (2.8)	10949 (2.8)	13394 (3.4)	23051 (5.9)	94893 (24.3)	139057 (35.6)
2001–2	422293 (100.0)	275113 (65.1)	133744 (31.7)	20220 (4.8)	30081 (7.1)	27049 (6.4)	11144 (2.6)	10620 (2.5)	13955 (3.3)	28299 (6.7)	102959 (24.4)	147180 (34.9)
2002–3	407479 (100.0)	253350 (62.2)	116165 (28.5)	17583 (4.3)	28815 (7.1)	25270 (6.2)	11001 (2.7)	11454 (2.8)	13469 (3.3)	29593 (7.3)	106633 (26.2)	154129 (37.8)
2003–4	476748 (100.0)	313778 (65.8)	139522 (29.3)	22063 (4.6)	47723 (10.0)	22867 (4.8)	17853 (3.7)	11394 (2.4)	15686 (3.3)	36669 (7.7)	108522 (22.8)	162970 (34.2)
2004–5	495137 (100.0)	314906 (63.6)	137669 (27.8)	19843 (4.0)	46024 (9.3)	27992 (5.7)	18517 (3.7)	12868 (2.6)	15598 (3.2)	36396 (7.4)	114225 (23.1)	180231 (36.4)
2005–6	553433 (100.0)	357041 (64.5)	155830 (28.2)	24283 (4.4)	49684 (9.0)	34621 (6.3)	20320 (3.7)	14320 (2.6)	17383 (3.1)	40600 (7.3)	137894 (24.9)	196392 (35.5)
2006–7	613137 (100.0)	399153 (65.1)	173810 (28.3)	30297 (4.9)	47556 (7.8)	39558 (6.5)	26205 (4.3)	16085 (2.6)	21670 (3.5)	43971 (7.2)	145008 (23.7)	213984 (34.9)
2007–8	691650 (100.0)	451049 (65.2)	195755 (28.3)	30824 (4.5)	69155 (10.0)	39019 (5.6)	34216 (4.9)	15924 (2.3)	23278 (3.4)	42877 (6.2)	168518 (24.4)	240601 (34.8)

Note: Horticulture includes flouriculture.

Source: CSO (2009).

Table A2.5 Structural Changes in Indian Industry and Decadal Growth

Sector Group	Weight as per Index Numbers						Growth Rates Per Cent Per Annum				
	1956=100	1960=100	1970=100	1980-1=100	1993-4=100	2004-5=100	1970-1 to 1980-1	1980-1 to 1990-1	1990-1 to 1993-4	1993-4 to 2004-5	2004-5 to 2011-12
Mining and Quarrying	7.47	9.72	9.69	11.5	10.47	14.16	4.6	7.6	1.4	3.2	4.2
Manufacturing	88.85	84.91	81.08	77.1	79.36	75.53	4.7	7.7	2.4	6.6	9.0
Electricity	3.68	5.37	9.23	11.4	10.17	10.32	4.2	9.1	6.8	5.4	5.7
General Index	100	100	100	100	100	100	7.6	7.9	2.9	6.2	8.1
Use-based category											
Basic Goods	22.33	25.11	32.28	39.42	35.51	45.68	6.0	7.9	5.8	4.8	5.8
Capital Goods	4.71	11.76	15.25	16.43	9.69	8.83	5.6	11.3	-3.9	7.1	16.5
Intermediate Goods	24.59	25.88	20.95	20.51	26.44	15.69	3.5	6.3	4.9	6.8	5.5
Consumer Goods	48.37	37.25	31.52	23.65	28.36	29.81	3.4	6.5	2.2	6.8	9.3
Consumer Durables	2.21	5.68	3.41	2.55	5.12	8.46	4.6	14.8	0.7	9.8	17.9
Consumer Non-durables	46.16	31.57	28.11	21.1	23.25	21.35	3.3	5.1	2.6	5.9	4.5

Note: Growth indicates compound growth rate in index numbers of industrial production for groups and general index calculated for the specified period using the semi-log model ln Y = a+bt, where t = time, Y + index value and the compound growth is obtained by taking antilog of 'b', deducting one from it and mutiplying it with 100.

Table A2.6 Index of Industrial Production with Major Groups and Sub-groups

Major Groups	Weights	Annual Average Growth		Full Fiscal Year Averages Based On 1993–4=100															
		1993–4 to 2008–9	1980–1 to 1992–3	2008–9	2007–8	2006–7	2005–6	2004–5	2003–4	2002–3	2001–2	2000–1	1999–2000	1998–9	1997–8	1996–7	1995–6	1994–5
1	2	3	4	5	6	7	8	9	10	11	12	13	14	15	16	17	18	19
General Index	100.00	7.0	6.8	275.4 (2.8)	268.0 (8.5)	247.1 (11.6)	221.5 (8.2)	204.8 (8.4)	189.0 (7.0)	176.6 (5.7)	167.0 (2.7)	162.6 (5.0)	154.9 (6.7)	145.2 (4.1)	139.5 (6.7)	130.8 (6.1)	123.3 (13.0)	109.1 ...
Mining and Quarrying	10.47	3.9	7.0	176.0 (2.6)	171.6 (5.1)	163.2 (5.4)	154.9 (1.0)	153.4 (4.4)	146.9 (5.2)	139.6 (5.8)	131.9 (1.2)	130.3 (2.8)	126.7 (1.0)	125.4 (–0.8)	126.4 (6.9)	118.2 (–1.9)	120.5 (9.7)	109.8 (9.8)
Manufacturing	79.36	7.5	6.5	295.1 (2.8)	287.2 (9.0)	263.5 (12.5)	234.2 (9.1)	214.6 (9.2)	196.6 (7.4)	183.1 (6.0)	172.7 (2.9)	167.9 (5.3)	159.4 (7.1)	148.8 (4.4)	142.5 (6.7)	133.6 (7.3)	124.5 (14.1)	109.1 (9.1)
Electricity	10.17	5.5	8.6	223.7 (2.8)	217.7 (6.4)	204.7 (7.2)	190.9 (5.2)	181.5 (5.2)	172.6 (5.1)	164.3 (3.2)	159.2 (3.1)	154.4 (4.0)	148.5 (7.3)	138.4 (6.5)	130.0 (6.6)	122.0 (4.0)	117.3 (8.1)	108.5 (8.5)

Use-based Classification

Basic Goods	35.57	5.7	7.3	229.6 (2.5)	223.9 (6.8)	209.7 (10.6)	189.6 (6.6)	177.9 (5.5)	168.6 (5.4)	159.9 (4.9)	152.5 (2.6)	148.7 (3.8)	143.3 (5.5)	135.8 (1.6)	133.6 (6.9)	125.0 (3.0)	121.4 (10.8)	109.6 (9.6)
Capital Goods	9.26	9.8	8.8	396.8 (7.0)	370.8 (18.0)	314.2 (18.5)	265.1 (15.5)	229.6 (13.9)	201.5 (13.6)	177.4 (10.5)	160.6 (–3.0)	165.6 (1.4)	163.3 (6.9)	152.7 (12.6)	135.6 (5.8)	128.2 (11.5)	115.0 (5.3)	109.2 (9.2)
Intermediate Goods	26.51	6.6	5.2	256.6 (–2.8)	264.1 (9.0)	242.4 (12.3)	215.9 (2.3)	211.1 (6.1)	199.0 (6.4)	187.1 (3.9)	180.1 (1.6)	177.2 (4.5)	169.5 (8.8)	155.8 (6.1)	146.8 (8.0)	135.9 (8.1)	125.7 (19.4)	105.3 (5.3)
Consumer Goods	28.66	7.8	5.8	306.6 (4.4)	293.6 (6.1)	276.8 (10.2)	251.2 (11.9)	224.4 (11.7)	200.9 (7.1)	187.5 (7.1)	175.1 (6.1)	165.1 (7.9)	153.0 (5.7)	144.8 (2.2)	141.7 (5.5)	134.3 (6.2)	126.5 (12.8)	112.1 (12.1)
Consumer Durables	5.36	9.5	10.6	376.2 (–0.5)	378.0 (–1.0)	382.0 (9.8)	347.9 (14.6)	303.5 (14.4)	265.4 (11.6)	237.8 (–6.3)	253.7 (12.0)	226.5 (14.0)	198.7 (14.1)	174.1 (5.6)	164.9 (7.8)	152.9 (4.6)	146.2 (25.8)	116.2 (16.2)
Consumer Non-Durables	23.30	7.3	5.1	286.3 (4.4)	274.2 (8.6)	252.6 (10.4)	228.9 (11.0)	206.2 (10.8)	186.1 (5.8)	175.9 (12.0)	157.0 (4.0)	151.0 (6.0)	142.5 (3.2)	138.1 (1.2)	136.5 (4.8)	130.2 (6.6)	122.1 (9.8)	111.2 (11.2)

Group-wise Index Number of Industrial Production

Food Products	9.08	4.2	5.0	178.9 (–9.7)	198.2 (7.0)	185.2 (8.6)	170.6 (2.0)	167.3 (–0.4)	167.9 (–0.5)	168.7 (11.0)	152.0 (–1.6)	154.5 (10.1)	140.3 (4.2)	134.7 (0.7)	133.8 (–0.4)	134.3 (3.5)	129.8 (6.7)	121.6 (21.6)
Beverages, Tobacco and Related Products	2.38	12.6	1.4	578.5 (16.2)	498.0 (12.0)	444.5 (11.0)	400.3 (15.7)	345.9 (10.8)	312.1 (8.5)	287.6 (27.9)	224.8 (12.2)	200.4 (4.3)	192.1 (7.6)	178.5 (12.9)	158.1 (19.4)	132.4 (13.5)	116.7 (13.3)	103.0 (3.0)
Cotton Textiles	5.52	3.4	3.7	160.9 (–1.9)	164.0 (4.3)	157.3 (14.8)	137.0 (8.5)	126.3 (7.6)	117.4 (–3.1)	121.2 (–2.7)	124.5 (–2.2)	127.3 (2.9)	123.7 (6.7)	115.9 (–7.7)	125.6 (2.4)	122.7 (12.1)	109.5 (10.5)	99.1 (–0.9)
Wool, Silk, and Man-made Fibre Textiles	2.26	7.3	–0.6	281.2 (0.0)	281.2 (4.8)	268.4 (7.8)	248.9 (–0.0)	249.0 (3.5)	240.5 (6.8)	225.1 (3.0)	218.5 (4.4)	209.3 (5.8)	197.8 (11.9)	176.8 (2.8)	172.0 (18.5)	145.1 (10.5)	131.3 (14.7)	114.5 (14.5)
Jute and Other Vegetable Fibre Textiles	0.59	1.2	–0.3	108.6 (–10.0)	120.7 (33.1)	90.7 (–15.8)	107.7 (0.5)	107.2 (3.7)	103.4 (–4.2)	107.9 (8.3)	99.6 (–5.9)	105.8 (0.8)	105.0 (–0.9)	106.0 (–7.3)	114.3 (16.9)	97.8 (–4.5)	102.4 (7.7)	95.1 (–4.9)

(Contd.)

Table A2.6 (Contd.)

Full Fiscal Year Averages Based On 1993-94=100

Major Groups	Weights	Annual Average Growth		2008-9	2007-8	2006-7	2005-6	2004-5	2003-4	2002-3	2001-2	2000-1	1999-2000	1998-9	1997-8	1996-7	1995-6	1994-5
		1993-4 to 2008-9	1980-1 to 1992-3															
1	2	3	4	5	6	7	8	9	10	11	12	13	14	15	16	17	18	19
Textile Products (including Wearing Apparel)	2.54	8.3	7.4	312.5 (5.8)	295.5 (3.7)	285.0 (11.5)	255.5 (16.3)	219.6 (19.2)	184.3 (-3.2)	190.3 (14.4)	166.3 (2.4)	162.4 (4.0)	156.1 (2.0)	153.1 (-3.5)	158.7 (8.5)	146.3 (9.4)	133.7 (35.7)	98.5 (-1.5)
Wood and Wood Products, Furniture and Fixtures	2.70	2.2	6.6	115.6 (-9.6)	127.9 (40.5)	91.0 (29.1)	70.5 (-5.7)	74.8 (-8.4)	81.7 (6.8)	76.5 (-17.6)	92.8 (-11.0)	104.3 (2.9)	101.4 (-16.2)	121.0 (-5.8)	128.5 (-2.6)	131.9 (7.1)	123.2 (24.1)	99.3 (-0.7)
Paper and Paper Products and Printing, Publishing and Allied Industries	2.65	6.8	6.2	260.0 (1.8)	255.3 (2.7)	248.6 (8.7)	228.6 (-0.9)	230.7 (10.5)	208.7 (15.6)	180.5 (6.8)	169.0 (3.0)	164.0 (-9.1)	180.5 (6.3)	169.8 (16.0)	146.4 (6.9)	136.9 (9.1)	125.5 (15.6)	108.6 (8.6)
Leather and Leather and Fur Products	1.14	3.3	4.9	156.3 (-6.9)	167.8 (11.7)	150.2 (0.6)	149.3 (-4.8)	156.9 (6.7)	147.0 (-3.9)	152.9 (-3.2)	158.0 (5.3)	150.0 (10.7)	135.5 (13.8)	119.1 (8.1)	110.2 (2.2)	107.8 (9.4)	98.5 (13.7)	86.6 (-13.4)
Basic Chemicals and Chemical Products (except products of petroleum and coal)	14.00	8.3	9.0	326.3 (4.1)	313.4 (10.6)	283.4 (9.6)	258.5 (8.3)	238.6 (14.5)	208.4 (8.7)	191.8 (3.7)	185.0 (4.8)	176.6 (7.3)	164.6 (10.0)	149.7 (6.6)	140.4 (14.4)	122.7 (4.8)	117.1 (11.2)	105.3 (5.3)
Rubber, Plastic, Petroleum and Coal Products	5.73	6.2	6.6	242.6 (-1.5)	246.4 (8.9)	226.3 (12.9)	200.5 (4.3)	192.2 (2.4)	187.7 (4.5)	179.7 (5.5)	170.4 (11.1)	153.4 (11.8)	137.2 (-1.1)	138.7 (11.3)	124.6 (5.2)	118.4 (2.0)	116.1 (7.8)	107.7 (7.7)
Non-metallic Mineral Products	4.40	8.5	4.6	327.0 (1.2)	323.2 (5.7)	305.8 (12.8)	271.1 (11.0)	244.3 (1.5)	240.6 (3.7)	232.0 (5.1)	220.7 (1.1)	218.2 (-1.2)	220.8 (24.4)	177.5 (8.3)	163.9 (13.4)	144.5 (7.9)	133.9 (23.6)	108.3 (8.3)
Basic Metal and Alloy Industries	7.45	8.4	2.1	325.1 (4.0)	312.7 (12.1)	278.9 (22.9)	227.0 (15.8)	196.1 (5.4)	186.0 (9.2)	170.4 (9.2)	156.0 (4.3)	149.6 (1.8)	146.9 (5.0)	139.9 (-2.5)	143.5 (2.6)	139.8 (6.7)	131.0 (15.8)	113.1 (13.1)
Metal Products and Parts except Machinery & Equipment	2.81	3.7	5.2	165.9 (-4.0)	172.9 (-5.6)	183.2 (11.4)	164.4 (-1.1)	166.3 (-5.7)	157.3 (3.7)	151.7 (-6.4)	142.6 (-10.0)	158.5 (15.0)	137.8 (-1.2)	139.5 (17.0)	119.2 (7.9)	110.5 (9.7)	100.7 (-4.6)	105.6 (5.6)
Machinery and Equipment other than Transport Equipment	9.57	10.4	15.0	429.1 (8.8)	394.4 (10.4)	357.1 (14.2)	312.8 (12.0)	279.4 (19.8)	233.3 (15.8)	201.4 (1.6)	198.3 (1.3)	195.8 (7.3)	182.5 (17.7)	155.0 (1.5)	152.7 (5.8)	144.3 (5.0)	137.4 (18.7)	115.8 (15.8)
Transport Equipment and Parts	3.98	9.7	6.0	387.9 (2.5)	378.4 (2.9)	367.7 (15.0)	319.7 (12.7)	283.7 (4.1)	272.6 (17.0)	232.9 (14.6)	203.3 (6.8)	190.3 (-2.0)	194.1 (5.7)	183.6 (20.1)	152.9 (2.5)	149.1 (12.5)	132.5 (17.4)	112.9 (12.9)
Other Manufacturing Industries	2.56	9.5	11.5	358.9 (0.4)	357.4 (19.8)	298.4 (7.8)	276.9 (25.2)	221.2 (18.5)	186.6 (7.7)	173.3 (0.1)	173.2 (8.9)	159.1 (11.6)	142.5 (-16.0)	169.7 (1.0)	168.0 (-1.3)	170.2 (24.7)	136.5 (25.8)	108.5 (8.5)

Notes: Figures in brackets are percentage variations over the previous year.
(QE = Quick Estimate).

Source: Central Statistical Organisation (CSO), Ministry of Statistics and Programme Implementation.

Table A2.7 Index of Industrial Production with Major Groups and Sub-groups
Full Fiscal Year Averages Based On 2004–5=100

	Weight	Annual Average Growth	Index						
			2005–6	2006–7	2007–8	2008–9	2009–10	2010–11	2011–12
General Index	1000.00	8.0	108.6	122.6	141.7	145.2	152.9	165.5	170.2
			8.6	12.9	15.6	2.5	5.3	8.2	2.8
1 Mining and Quarrying	141.57	3.7	102.3	107.5	112.5	115.4	124.5	131.0	128.4
			2.3	5.1	4.7	2.6	7.9	5.2	-2.0
2 Manufacturing	755.27	9.0	110.3	126.8	150.1	153.8	161.3	175.6	180.8
			10.3	15.0	18.4	2.5	4.9	8.9	3.0
3 Electricity	103.16	5.9	105.2	112.8	120.0	123.3	130.8	138.0	149.3
			5.2	7.2	6.4	2.8	6.1	5.5	8.2
Use-based Classification									
1 Basic Goods	456.82	6.0	106.1	115.6	125.9	128.1	134.1	142.2	150.0
			6.1	9.0	8.9	1.7	4.7	6.0	5.5
2 Capital Goods	88.25	16.1	118.1	145.6	216.2	240.6	243.0	278.9	267.5
			18.1	23.3	48.5	11.3	1.0	14.8	-4.1
3 Intermediate Goods	156.86	5.4	106.6	118.8	127.5	127.6	135.3	145.3	143.9
			6.6	11.4	7.3	0.1	6.0	7.4	-1.0
4 Consumer Goods	298.08	9.4	110.7	128.6	151.2	152.6	164.3	178.3	186.1
			10.7	16.2	17.6	0.9	7.7	8.5	4.4
Durables	84.60	17.1	116.2	145.6	193.8	215.4	252.0	287.7	295.0
			16.2	25.3	33.1	11.1	17.0	14.2	2.5
Non-durables	213.47	5.4	108.6	121.9	134.3	127.7	129.5	135.0	143.0
			8.6	12.2	10.2	-4.9	1.4	4.2	5.9
Major Industry Groups of Manufacturing Sector (2–Digit Level)									
NIC Code									
15 Food Products and Beverages	72.76	7.7	113.2	131.2	147.5	135.4	133.5	142.9	164.1
			13.2	15.9	12.4	-8.2	-1.4	7.0	14.8
16 Tobacco Products	15.70	1.4	101.0	102.9	98.4	102.7	102.0	104.0	110.0
			1.0	1.9	-4.4	4.4	-0.7	2.0	5.8
17 Textiles	61.64	4.3	108.3	116.8	124.6	120.1	127.4	135.9	133.8
			8.3	7.8	6.7	-3.6	6.1	6.7	-1.5
18 Wearing Apparel, Dressing and Dyeing of Fur	27.82	4.5	114.1	137.2	149.9	134.6	137.1	142.2	131.4
			14.1	20.2	9.3	-10.2	1.9	3.7	-7.6
19 Luggage, Handbags, Saddlery, Harness & Footwear; Tanning and Dressing of Leather Products	5.82	2.7	90.9	104.0	110.0	104.4	105.8	114.3	118.4
			-9.1	14.4	5.8	-5.1	1.3	8.0	3.6

(Contd.)

Table A2.7 (Contd.)

	Weight	Annual Average Growth	Index						
			2005-6	2006-7	2007-8	2008-9	2009-10	2010-11	2011-12
20 Wood & Products of Wood and Cork Except Furniture, Articles of Straw & Plating Materials	10.51	7.0	106.8 / 6.8	126.0 / 18.0	148.0 / 17.5	155.3 / 4.9	160.1 / 3.1	156.5 / -2.2	158.5 / 1.3
21 Paper and Paper Products	9.99	4.7	106.3 / 6.3	111.0 / 4.4	112.6 / 1.4	118.0 / 4.8	121.1 / 2.6	131.4 / 8.5	137.7 / 4.8
22 Publishing, Printing & Reproduction of Recorded Media	10.78	10.3	113.7 / 13.7	122.8 / 8.0	140.2 / 14.2	142.4 / 1.6	133.8 / -6.0	148.9 / 11.3	192.9 / 29.6
23 Cork, Refined Petroleum Products & Nuclear Fuel	67.15	3.4	100.6 / 0.6	112.6 / 11.9	119.6 / 6.2	123.4 / 3.2	121.8 / -1.3	121.5 / -0.2	125.4 / 3.2
24 Chemicals & Chemical Products	100.59	3.0	101.0 / 1.0	110.4 / 9.3	118.4 / 7.2	115.0 / -2.9	120.7 / 5.0	123.1 / 2.0	122.6 / -0.4
25 Rubber & Plastics Products	20.25	9.4	112.3 / 12.3	119.6 / 6.5	135.7 / 13.5	142.6 / 5.1	167.4 / 17.4	185.2 / 10.6	185.8 / 0.3
26 Other Non-metallic Mineral Products	43.14	6.9	107.8 / 7.8	119.5 / 10.9	130.6 / 9.3	134.9 / 3.3	145.4 / 7.8	151.4 / 4.1	158.9 / 5.0
27 Basic Metals	113.35	9.9	115.5 / 15.5	132.6 / 14.8	156.3 / 17.9	159.0 / 1.7	162.4 / 2.1	176.7 / 8.8	192.0 / 8.7
28 Fabricated Metal Products, Except Machinery & Equipment	30.85	10.8	111.1 / 11.1	133.3 / 20.0	143.8 / 7.9	144.0 / 0.1	158.6 / 10.1	182.8 / 15.3	203.2 / 11.2
29 Machinery & Equipment nec	37.63	14.3	126.1 / 26.1	150.9 / 19.7	185.0 / 22.6	171.0 / -7.6	198.0 / 15.8	256.3 / 29.4	241.2 / -5.9
30 Office Accounting & Computing Machinery	3.05	7.1	145.3 / 45.3	155.5 / 7.0	164.8 / 6.0	148.8 / -9.7	154.4 / 3.8	146.3 / -5.2	150.3 / 2.7
31 Electrical Machinery & Apparatus nec	19.80	31.7	116.8 / 16.8	131.6 / 12.7	373.0 / 183.4	530.8 / 42.3	459.2 / -13.5	472.1 / 2.8	366.2 / -22.4
32 Radio, TV & Communication Equipment & Apparatus	9.89	45.6	122.7 / 22.7	312.8 / 154.9	604.2 / 93.2	726.7 / 20.3	809.1 / 11.3	911.5 / 12.7	950.1 / 4.2
33 Medical, Precision & Optical Instruments, Watches and Clocks	5.67	3.0	95.4 / -4.6	104.8 / 9.9	111.4 / 6.3	119.8 / 7.5	100.9 / -15.8	107.8 / 6.8	119.6 / 10.9
34 Motor Vehicles, Trailers & Semi-trailers	40.64	15.3	110.1 / 10.1	138.0 / 25.3	151.2 / 9.6	138.0 / -8.7	179.1 / 29.8	233.3 / 30.3	258.6 / 10.8
35 Other Transport Equipment	18.25	13.4	115.3 / 15.3	132.9 / 15.3	129.0 / -2.9	134.0 / 3.9	171.1 / 27.7	210.7 / 23.1	234.6 / 11.3
36 Furniture Manufacturing nec	29.97	5.2	116.2 / 16.2	111.7 / -3.9	132.7 / 18.8	142.5 / 7.4	152.7 / 7.2	141.2 / -7.5	138.6 / -1.8

Note: Figures in *italics* are percentage variations over the previous year.

Source: Central Statistical Organisation (CSO), Ministry of Statistics and Programme Implementation.

A3 BUDGETARY TRANSACTIONS

Table A3.1 Budgetary Position of Government of India

(Rupees, Crore)

Budget Heads	1990–1 Actuals	1991–2 Actuals	1992–3 Actuals	1993–4 Actuals	1994–5 Actuals	1995–6 Actuals	1996–7 Actuals	1997–8 Actuals	1998–9 Actuals	1999–2000 Actuals
1	2	3	4	5	6	7	8	9	10	11
(1) Revenue Receipts	54954	66030	74128	75453	91083	110130	126279	133886	149485	181482
(a) Tax Revenue (net to centre)	42978	50069	54044	53449	67454	81939	93701	95672	104652	128271
(b) Non-tax Revenue	11976	15961	20084	22004	23629	28191	32578	38214	44833	53211
(2) Capital Receipts	50344	45384	48490	66400	69655	68145	74728	98167	129856	116571
(a) Non-Debt Capital Receipts	5712	9059	8317	6143	11952	7902	7995	9230	16507	11854
of which:										
(a.1) Recovery of Loans	5712	6021	6356	6191	6345	6505	7540	8318	10633	10131
(a.2) Other Receipts	0	3038	1961	–48	5607	1397	455	912	5874	1723
of which:										
(a.2.1) Disinvestment of Equity of PSEs	0	3038	1961	–48	5078	362	380	912	5874	1724
(b) Borrowings and Other Liabilities	44632	36325	40173	60257	57703	60243	66733	88937	113349	104717
(3) Total Receipts	105298	111414	122618	141853	160738	178275	201007	232053	279341	298053
	[18.0]	(5.8)	(10.1)	(15.7)	(13.3)	(10.9)	(12.8)	(15.4)	(20.4)	(6.7)
		[16.5]	[15.8]	[15.9]	[15.4]	[14.5]	[14.2]	[14.8]	[15.5]	[14.8]
(4) Non-plan Expenditure	76198	80469	85958	98998	113361	131901	147473	172991	212548	221902
(a) On Revenue Account	60850	67234	72925	83545	93847	110839	127298	145176	176900	202309
of which:										
(a.I) Interest Payment	21471	26563	31035	36695	44049	50031	59478	65637	77882	90249
% to Total Expenditure	20.4	23.8	25.3	25.9	27.4	28.1	29.6	28.3	27.9	30.3
(a.II) Pension	2138	2416	3005	3338	3643	4277	5094	6881	10057	14286
% to Total Expenditure	2.0	2.2	2.5	2.4	2.3	2.4	2.5	3.0	3.6	4.8
(a.III) Subsidies	12158	12253	10824	11605	11854	12666	15499	18540	23593	24487
% to Total Expenditure	11.5	11.0	8.8	8.2	7.4	7.1	7.7	8.0	8.4	8.2
(b) On capital account	15348	13235	13033	15453	19514	21062	20175	27815	35648	19593
(5) Plan expenditure	29118	30961	36660	42855	47378	46374	53534	59077	66818	76182
(a) On Revenue Account	12666	15074	19777	24624	28265	29021	31635	35174	40519	46800
(b) On Capital Account	16452	15887	16883	18231	19113	17353	21899	23903	26299	29382
(6) Total Expenditure (4+5)	105316	111430	122618	141853	160739	178275	201007	232068	279366	298084
		(5.8)	(10.0)	(15.7)	(13.3)	(10.9)	(12.8)	(15.5)	(20.4)	(6.7)
(7) Revenue Deficit	18562	16261	18574	32716	31029	29730	32654	46449	67909	67596
	[3.2]	[2.4]	[2.4]	[3.7]	[3.0]	[2.4]	[2.3]	[3.0]	[3.8]	[3.4]
(8) Fiscal Deficit	44650	36325	40173	60257	57703	60243	66733	88937	113349	104717
	[7.6]	[5.4]	[5.2]	[6.8]	[5.5]	[4.9]	[4.7]	[5.7]	[6.3]	[5.2]
(9) Primary Deficit	23134	9762	9138	23562	13655	10212	7255	23300	35467	14468
	[3.9]	[1.4]	[1.2]	[2.6]	[1.3]	[0.8]	[0.5]	[1.5]	[2.0]	[0.7]

(Contd.)

Table A3.1 (Contd.)

(Rupees, Crore)

Budget Heads		2000-1 Actuals	2001-2 Actuals	2002-3 Actuals	2003-4 Actuals	2004-5 Actuals	2005-6 Actuals	2006-7 Actuals	2007-8 Actuals	2008-9 Actuals	2009-10 Actuals	2010-11 Actuals	2011-12 Budget	2011-12 Revised	2012-13 Budget
1		12	13	14	15	16	17	18	19	20	21	22	23	24	25
(1)	Revenue Receipts	192605	201306	230834	263813	305991	347077	434387	541864	540259	572811	788471	789892	766989	935685
(a)	Tax Revenue (net to centre)	136658	133532	158544	186982	224798	270264	351182	439547	443319	456536	569869	664457	642252	771071
(b)	Non-tax Revenue	55947	67774	72290	76831	81193	76813	83205	102317	96940	116275	218602	125435	124737	164614
(2)	Capital receipts	132987	161004	182414	207390	192264	158661	149000	170807	343697	451676	408857	467837	551730	555241
(a)	Non-debt Capital Receipts of which:	14171	20049	37342	84118	66467	12226	6427	43895	6705	33194	35266	55020	29751	41650
(a.1)	Recovery of Loans	12046	16403	34191	67165	62043	10645	5893	5100	6139	8613	12420	15020	14258	11650
(a.2)	Other Receipts of which:	2125	3646	3151	16953	4424	1581	534	38795	566	24581	22846	40000	15493	30000
(a.2.1)	Disinvestment of Equity of PSEs	2125	3646	3151	16953	4424	1581	534	38795	566	24581	22846	40000	15493	30000
(b)	Borrowings and Other Liabilities	118816	140955	145072	123272	125797	146435	142573	126912	336992	418482	373591	412817	521980	513590
(3)	Total Receipts	325592	362310	413248	471203	498255	505738	583387	712671	883956	1024487	1197328	1257729	1318719	1490926
		(9.2)	(11.3)	(14.1)	(14.0)	(5.7)	(1.5)	(15.4)	(22.2)	(24.0)	(15.9)	(16.9)	(5.0)	(10.1)	(13.1)
		[15.0]	[15.4]	[16.3]	[6.6]	[15.4]	[13.7]	[13.6]	[14.3]	[15.7]	[15.9]	[15.6]	[14.1]	[14.8]	[14.7]
(4)	Non-plan Expenditure	242942	261259	302708	348989	453454	476958	555945	681161	843495	721096	818299	816182	892116	969900
(a)	On Revenue Account of which:	226782	239954	268074	283502	384329	439376	514609	594433	793798	657925	726491	733558	815740	865596
(a.I)	Interest Payment	99314	107460	117804	124088	126934	132630	150272	171030	192204	213093	234022	267986	275618	319759
	% to Total Expenditure	30.5	29.6	28.4	26.3	21.7	21.5	20.7	19.3	17.2	20.8	19.5	21.3	20.9	21.4
(a.II)	Pension	14379	14436	14496	15905	18300	20256	22104	24261	32940	56149	57405	56149	56190	63183
	% to Total Expenditure	4.4	4.0	3.5	3.4	3.1	3.3	3.0	2.7	2.9	5.5	4.8	4.5	4.3	4.2
(a.III)	Subsidies	26838	31210	43533	44479	46077	47782	57685	71786	130083	142201	173420	143570	216297	190015
	% to Total Expenditure	8.2	8.6	10.5	9.4	7.9	7.7	7.9	8.1	11.6	13.9	14.5	11.4	16.4	12.7
(b)	On Capital Account	16160	21305	34634	65487	69125	37582	41336	86728	49697	63171	91808	82624	76376	104304
(5)	Plan Expenditure	82669	101194	111470	122280	132293	140638	169860	205082	275235	303391	379029	441547	426604	521025
(a)	On Revenue Account	51076	61657	71569	78638	87495	111858	142418	173572	234774	253884	314232	363604	346201	420513
(b)	On Capital Account	31593	39537	39901	43642	44798	28780	27442	31510	40461	49507	64797	77943	80404	100512
(6)	Total Expenditure (4+5)	325611	362453	414178	471269	585747	617596	725805	886243	1118730	1024487	1197328	1257729	1318720	1490925
		(9.2)	(11.3)	(14.3)	(13.8)	(24.3)	(5.4)	(17.5)	(22.1)	(26.2)	(-8.4)	(16.9)	(5.0)	(10.1)	(13.1)
(7)	Revenue Deficit	85234	100162	107879	98261	78338	92300	80222	52569	253539	338998	252252	307270	394951	350424
		[3.9]	[4.3]	[4.3]	[3.5]	[2.4]	[2.5]	[1.9]	[1.1]	[4.5]	[5.2]	[3.3]	[3.4]	[4.4]	[3.4]

(8) Fiscal Deficit	118816 [5.5]	140955 [6.0]	145072 [5.7]	123273 [4.3]	125794 [3.9]	146435 [4.0]	142573 [3.3]	126912 [2.5]	336992 [6.0]	418482 [6.5]	373591 [4.9]	412817 [4.6]	521980 [5.9]	513590 [5.1]
(9) Primary Deficit	19502 [0.9]	33495 [1.4]	27268 [1.1]	−815 [0.0]	−1140 [0.0]	13805 [0.4]	−7699 [−0.2]	−44118 [−0.9]	144788 [2.6]	205389 [3.2]	139569 [1.8]	144831 [1.6]	246362 [2.8]	193831 [1.9]

Notes: (1) Figures in round brackets are variations over the previous year in percentages.
(2) Figures in square brackets are percentages to GDP at current market prices
(3) GDP data is as per the revised series from 2004–5 and data for 2012–13 projected at Rs 10159884 crore assuming 14% growth.

Source: *Budget at a Glance and Expenditure Budget*, Ministry of Finance, Government of India.

Table A3.2 Consolidated Budgetary Position of State Governments at a Glance

(Rupees, Crore)

Year	1990–1 Accounts	1991–2 Accounts	1992–3 Accounts	1993–4 Accounts	1994–5 Accounts	1995–6 Accounts	1996–7 Accounts	1997–8 Accounts	1998–9 Accounts	1999–2000 Accounts
Total Revenue Receipts	66467	80536	91090	104997	120303	134507	150041	166820	172787	202927
% change over the year	(17.6)	(21.2)	(13.1)	(15.3)	(14.6)	(11.8)	(11.5)	(11.2)	(3.6)	(17.4)
% to GDP	11.3	12.0	11.8	11.8	11.5	11.0	10.6	10.6	9.6	10.1
Revenue Expenditure	71776	86186	96205	108868	127009	143127	166919	184312	217249	257475
% change over the year	(19.2)	(20.1)	(11.6)	(13.2)	(16.7)	(12.7)	(16.6)	(10.4)	(17.9)	(18.5)
% to GDP	12.2	12.8	12.4	12.2	12.1	11.7	11.8	11.7	12.0	12.8
Surplus(+)/Deficit(−)	−5309	−5650	−5115	−3871	−6706	−8620	−16878	−17492	−44462	−54548
% change over the year	(−22.9)	(−10.3)	(−10.4)	(−5.3)	(−51.6)	(−0.9)	(−1.9)	(−40.2)	(−44.9)	(−19.4)
% to GDP	4.2	4.0	3.9	3.2	4.1	3.5	3.0	3.7	4.7	5.1
Total Capital Receipts	24693	27238	30073	28489	43190	42805	42011	58907	85363	101925
Capital Expenditure	19312	21743	23129	24980	32138	31506	32335	39612	44169	50501
% change over the year	(−16.6)	(−12.6)	(−6.4)	(−8.0)	(−28.7)	(−2.0)	(−2.6)	(−22.5)	(−11.5)	(−14.3)
% to GDP	3.3	3.2	3.0	2.8	3.1	2.6	2.3	2.5	2.4	2.5
Surplus(+)/Deficit(−)	5381	5495	6944	3509	11052	11299	9676	19295	41194	51424
Total Receipts	91160	107773	121163	133486	163493	177312	192051	225727	258151	304852
% change over the year	(19.0)	(18.2)	(12.4)	(10.2)	(22.5)	(8.5)	(8.3)	(17.5)	(14.4)	(18.1)
% to GDP	15.6	16.0	15.6	15.0	15.6	14.5	13.5	14.4	14.3	15.2
Total Expenditure	91088	107929	119335	133849	159147	174632	199254	223924	261419	307977
% change over the year	(18.6)	(18.5)	(10.6)	(12.2)	(18.9)	(9.7)	(14.1)	(12.4)	(16.7)	(17.8)
% to GDP	15.5	16.0	15.4	15.0	15.2	14.2	14.0	14.2	14.5	15.3
Overall Surplus(+)/Deficit(−)	72	−156	1828	−363	4346	2680	−7203	1803	−3268	−3125
Fiscal Deficit	18787	18900	20891	20364	27308	30870	36561	43474	73295	90099
% to GDP	3.2	2.8	2.7	2.3	2.6	2.5	2.6	2.8	4.1	4.5
Revenue Deficit	5309	5651	5114	3872	6706	8620	16878	17492	44462	54549
% to GDP	0.9	0.8	0.7	0.4	0.6	0.7	1.2	1.1	2.5	2.7
Net RBI Credit	420	−340	176	591	48	16	898	1543	5579	1312

Table A3.2 (Contd.)

(Rupees, Crore)

	2000–1 Accounts	2001–2 Accounts	2002–3 Accounts	2003–4 Accounts	2004–5 Accounts	2005–6 Accounts	2006–7 Accounts	2007–8 Accounts	2008–9 Accounts	2009–10 Accounts	2010–11 Budget	2010–11 Revised	2011–12 Budget
Total Revenue Receipts	232509	249422	273674	309187	363512	431021	530556	623748	694657	768140	913040	968070	1121840
% change over the year	(14.6)	(7.3)	(9.7)	(13.0)	(17.6)	(18.6)	(23.1)	(17.6)	(11.4)	(10.6)	(18.9)	(26.0)	(15.9)
% to GDP	10.7	10.6	10.8	10.9	11.2	11.7	12.4	12.5	12.3	11.9	11.9	10.9	12.6
Revenue Expenditure	287825	309819	330853	372594	402670	438034	505699	580805	681985	799150	937410	993250	1102140
% change over the year	(11.8)	(7.6)	(6.8)	(12.6)	(8.1)	(8.8)	(15.4)	(14.9)	(17.4)	(17.2)	(17.3)	(24.3)	(11.0)
% to GDP	13.3	13.2	13.1	13.1	12.4	11.9	11.8	11.6	12.1	12.4	12.2	11.1	12.4
Surplus(+)/Deficit(−)	−55316	−60397	−57179	−63407	−39158	−7013	24857	42943	12672	−31020	−24370	−25180	19700
Total Capital Receipts	109705	115714	140866	205641	200148	164607	142802	141987	198634	239500	242860	236600	275080
% change over the year	(7.6)	(5.5)	(21.7)	(46.0)	(−2.7)	(−17.8)	(−13.2)	(−0.6)	(39.9)	(20.6)	(1.4)	(−1.2)	(16.3)
% to GDP	5.1	4.9	5.6	7.2	6.2	4.5	3.3	2.8	3.5	3.7	3.2	2.7	3.1
Capital Expenditure	52010	58861	79396	141709	150758	123648	151585	171520	200347	216180	237180	243100	287600
% change over the year	(3.0)	(13.2)	(34.9)	(78.5)	(6.4)	(−18.0)	(22.6)	(13.2)	(16.8)	(7.9)	(9.7)	(12.5)	(18.3)
% to GDP	2.4	2.5	3.1	5.0	4.6	3.3	3.5	3.4	3.6	3.3	3.1	2.7	3.2
Surplus(+)/Deficit(−)	57695	56853	61470	63932	49390	40959	−8783	−29533	−3713	23320	5680	−6500	−12530
Total Receipts	342214	365136	414539	514828	563660	595628	673358	765735	891292	1007630	1155900	1204670	1396920
% change over the year	(12.3)	(6.7)	(13.5)	(24.2)	(9.5)	(5.7)	(13.1)	(13.7)	(16.4)	(13.1)	(14.7)	(19.6)	(16.0)
% to GDP	15.8	15.5	16.4	18.1	17.4	16.1	15.7	15.4	15.8	15.6	15.1	13.5	15.7
Total Expenditure	339835	368680	410249	514302	553428	561682	657280	752324	882333	1015330	1174580	1236350	1389750
% change over the year	(10.3)	(8.5)	(11.3)	(25.4)	(7.6)	(1.5)	(17.0)	(14.5)	(17.3)	(15.1)	(15.7)	(21.8)	(12.4)
% to GDP	15.7	15.7	16.2	18.1	17.1	15.2	15.3	15.1	15.7	15.7	15.3	13.9	15.6
Overall Surplus(+)/Deficit(−)	2379	−3544	4290	526	10232	33946	16078	13411	8959	−7700	−18690	−31690	7180
Fiscal Deficit	87923	94260	99726	120631	107774	90084	77509	75455	134589	188820	198540	206670	197720
% to GDP	4.1	4.0	3.9	4.3	3.3	2.4	0.4	0.3	0.2	−0.1	−0.2	−0.4	0.1
Revenue Deficit	55316	60398	57179	63407	39158	7013	−24857	−42943	−12672	31020	24370	25180	−19700
% to GDP	2.6	2.6	2.3	2.2	1.2	0.2	0.0	0.0	0.0	0.0	0.0	0.0	0.0
Net RBI Credit	−1092	3451	−3100	293	−2705	2425	640	1140	−1609	190	0	2520	0

Note: GDP data is as per the revised series from 2004–5 and data for 2012–13 projected at Rs 10159884 crore assuming 14% growth.

Source: RBI (2012), *State Finances—A Study of Budgets and Previous Issues*, Mumbai.

A4 MONEY AND BANKING

Table A4.1 Money Stock Measures

(Rupees, Crore)

31st March	Currency in Circulation	Cash with Banks	Currency with the Public 4=2−3	'Other' Deposits with the RBI	Bankers' Deposits with RBI	Components of Money Supply		Reserve Money (3+4+5+6)	Money Supply (M3)
						Demand Deposits	Time Deposits		
1	2	3	4=2−3	5	6	7	8	9	11
1950–1	..	..	1405	24	59	591	331	1494	2352
1951–2	1292	43	1249	18	47	545	325	1357 (−9.2)	2137 (−9.1)
1952–3	1273	45	1228	14	47	521	357	1334 (−1.7)	2121 (−0.7)
1953–4	1330	41	1289	12	42	527	372	1385 (3.8)	2200 (3.7)
1954–5	1417	40	1377	7	48	571	424	1472 (6.3)	2379 (8.1)
1955–6	1614	43	1571	9	53	637	466	1676 (13.9)	2683 (12.8)
1956–7	1668	45	1623	8	58	711	527	1734 (3.5)	2869 (6.9)
1957–8	1720	46	1674	16	68	723	750	1804 (4.0)	3164 (10.3)
1958–9	1846	54	1792	15	68	719	950	1929 (6.9)	3476 (9.9)
1959–60	2001	70	1931	17	93	772	1163	2111 (9.4)	3883 (11.7)
1960–1	2154	56	2098	13	71	757	1095	2239 (6.1)	3964 (2.1)
1961–2	2256	54	2202	23	73	824	1198	2352 (5.0)	4247 (7.1)
1962–3	2439	60	2379	30	77	908	1243	2546 (8.2)	4560 (7.4)
1963–4	2670	64	2606	32	79	1115	1285	2781 (9.2)	5037 (10.5)
1964–5	2841	72	2769	22	99	1289	1418	2962 (6.5)	5498 (9.2)
1965–6	3112	78	3034	17	104	1478	1605	3233 (9.1)	6134 (11.6)
1966–7	3289	90	3199	41	134	1711	1867	3464 (7.1)	6817 (11.1)
1967–8	3468	92	3376	56	137	1918	2110	3662 (5.7)	7460 (9.4)
1968–9	3794	112	3682	81	194	2016	2527	4069 (11.1)	8306 (11.3)
1969–70	4160	165	3995	58	173	2483	3103	4390 (7.9)	9639 (16.0)
1970–1	4557	186	4371	60	205	2943	3646	4822 (9.8)	11020 (14.3)
1971–2	5006	205	4801	80	296	3442	4370	5382 (11.6)	12693 (15.2)
1972–3	5680	242	5438	58	295	4204	5313	6033 (12.1)	15013 (18.3)
1973–4	6595	274	6321	53	625	4826	6424	7273 (20.6)	17624 (17.4)
1974–5	6701	354	6347	75	828	5553	7574	7604 (4.6)	19549 (10.9)
1975–6	7053	348	6705	77	678	6543	9155	7808 (2.7)	22480 (15.0)
1976–7	8288	415	7873	121	1389	8030	11757	9798 (25.5)	27781 (23.6)
1977–8	9152	521	8631	70	1719	5687	18518	10941 (11.7)	32906 (18.4)

Year													
1978-9	10835	604	10231	166	3081	6895	22820	14082	(28.7)	40112	(21.9)
1979-80	12382	728	11654	391	3800	7955	27226	16573	(17.7)	47226	(17.7)
1980-1	14307	881	13426	411	4734	9587	32350	19452	(17.4)	55774	(18.1)
1981-2	15411	937	14474	168	5419	10295	37815	20998	(7.9)	62752	(12.5)
1982-3	17639	980	16659	186	5285	11690	44649	23110	(10.1)	73184	(16.6)
1983-4	20643	1040	19603	291	8060	13504	53127	28994	(25.5)	86525	(18.2)
1984-5	23875	1203	22672	595	10746	16648	63018	35216	(21.5)	102933	(19.0)
1985-6	26524	1465	25059	289	11352	18747	75299	38165	(8.4)	119394	(16.0)
1986-7	29913	1531	28382	309	14586	22825	90116	44808	(17.4)	141632	(18.6)
1987-8	35122	1563	33559	397	17970	24599	105720	53489	(19.4)	164275	(16.0)
1988-9	40119	1790	38329	694	22145	27763	126707	62958	(17.7)	193493	(17.8)
1989-90	48286	1986	46300	598	28707	34162	149890	77591	(23.2)	230950	(19.4)
1990-1	55282	2234	53048	674	31823	39170	172936	87779	(13.1)	265828	(15.1)
1991-2	63738	2640	61098	885	34882	52423	202643	99505	(13.4)	317049	(19.3)
1992-3	71326	3053	68273	1313	38140	54480	239950	110779	(11.3)	364016	(14.8)
1993-4	85396	3095	82301	2525	50751	65952	280306	138672	(25.2)	431084	(18.4)
1994-5	104681	4000	100681	3383	61218	88193	335338	169283	(22.1)	527596	(22.4)
1995-6	122569	4311	118258	3344	68544	93233	384356	194457	(14.9)	599191	(13.6)
1996-7	137217	5130	132087	3194	59574	105334	455397	199985	(2.8)	696012	(16.2)
1997-8	151056	5477	145579	3541	71806	118725	553488	226402	(13.2)	821332	(18.0)
1998-9	175846	6902	168944	3736	79703	136388	671892	259286	(14.5)	980960	(19.4)
1999-2000	197061	7979	189082	3034	80460	149681	782378	280555	(8.2)	1124174	(14.6)
2000-1	218205	8654	209550	3630	81477	166270	933771	303311	(8.1)	1313220	(16.8)
2001-2	250974	10179	240794	2850	84147	179199	1075512	337970	(11.4)	1498355	(14.1)
2002-3	282473	10892	271581	3242	83346	198757	1244379	369061	(9.2)	1717960	(14.7)
2003-4	327028	12057	314971	5119	104365	258626	1426960	436512	(18.3)	2005676	(16.7)
2004-5	368661	12347	356314	6478	113996	286998	1595887	489135	(12.1)	2245677	(12.0)
2005-6	429578	17454	412124	6869	135511	407423	1893104	571958	(16.9)	2719519	(21.1)
2006-7	504099	21244	482854	7496	197295	477604	2342113	708890	(23.9)	3310068	(21.7)
2007-8	590801	22390	568410	9054	328447	578372	2862046	928302	(31.0)	4017882	(21.4)
2008-9	691153	25703	665450	5570	291275	588688	3535105	987998	(6.4)	4794812	(19.3)
2009-10	799549	32056	767493	3839	352299	717970	4113430	1155686	(17.0)	5602731	(16.8)
2010-11	949659	35463	914197	3713	423509	717660	4863979	1376881	(19.1)	6499548	(16.0)
2011-12	1067890	41290	1026600	3060	356290	700210	5614200	1427240	(3.7)	7344070	(13.0)

(Contd.)

Table A4.1 (Contd.)

(Rupees, Crore)

31st March	Sources of Change in Money Supply (M3)							
	Net Bank Credit to Government	Net RBI Credit to Central Government	Bank Credit to Commercial Sector	Net Foreign Exchange Assets of Banking Sector	Government's Currency Liabilities to Public	Net Non-monetary Liabilities of Bkg. Sector	Net Non-monetary Liabilities of RBI	RBI's Gross Claims on Banks
1	12	13	14	15	16	17	18	19
1950-1	808	..	588	860	241	145	68	..
1951-2	..	..	..	..	..	..	..	..
1952-3	..	..	..	..	..	..	..	..
1953-4	..	..	..	..	..	..	..	..
1954-5	..	..	..	..	..	..	..	..
1955-6	1105	..	829	764	189	204	88	..
1956-7	..	..	..	..	..	..	..	..
1957-8	..	..	..	..	..	..	..	..
1958-9	..	..	..	..	..	..	..	..
1959-60	..	..	..	..	..	..	..	..
1960-1	2489	..	1503	178	206	413	250	..
1961-2	2691	..	1643	121	227	435	247	..
1962-3	2893	..	1860	79	236	507	278	..
1963-4	3135	..	2119	114	256	586	304	..
1964-5	3342	..	2369	95	275	583	340	..
1965-6	3809	..	2656	71	287	689	360	..
1966-7	4008	..	3142	149	310	792	434	..
1967-8	4254	..	3564	161	317	836	422	..
1968-9	4697	..	4072	326	341	1130	590	..
1969-70	4752	3291	5407	584	360	1464	630	..
1970-1	5455	3667	6522	551	384	1892	866	642
1971-2	6625	4249	7363	619	412	2325	1271	531
1972-3	7976	5461	8762	583	457	2765	1435	480
1973-4	8939	6092	10791	663	502	3271	1641	731
1974-5	9999	6620	12730	414	531	4125	2061	981
1975-6	10629	6331	15614	939	556	5257	2645	1315
1976-7	11804	7147	18851	2529	568	5971	3433	1404
1977-8	13727	6887	21222	4445	593	7081	3708	926
1978-9	15930	9077	25532	5338	603	7292	3735	1117

1979–80	20014	11727	31011	5343	592	9734	4558	1200
1980–1	25718	15278	36641	4730	618	11934	5360	1276
1981–2	30633	18486	43462	2768	657	14768	6522	1673
1982–3	35257	21853	51162	1828	682	15745	6074	2025
1983–4	40642	25802	60726	1646	720	17208	5311	2771
1984–5	50343	31857	70953	3134	778	22274	8737	3174
1985–6	58321	38047	82803	3872	939	26542	10707	2462
1986–7	72020	45138	94741	4815	1192	31136	13444	2760
1987–8	84370	51697	107487	5672	1380	34634	14225	4441
1988–9	96475	58200	127882	6800	1475	39139	16936	7079
1989–90	117151	72013	151704	6818	1555	46278	17536	7472
1990–1	140193	86758	171769	10581	1621	58336	27022	10007
1991–2	158263	92266	187993	21226	1704	52137	27415	5102
1992–3	176238	96523	220135	24443	1824	58624	28246	9885
1993–4	203918	96783	237774	54612	1990	67210	26037	5552
1994–5	222419	98913	292723	79032	2379	68958	29358	13470
1995–6	257778	118768	344648	82141	2503	87880	32297	21955
1996–7	288620	120702	376307	105496	2918	77330	35184	7005
1997–8	330597	133617	433310	138095	3352	84022	43282	7096
1998–9	386677	145416	495990	177853	3846	83406	60540	13262
1999–2000	441378	139829	586564	205648	4578	113994	70222	16785
2000–1	511955	146534	679218	249820	5354	133126	79345	12965
2001–2	589565	141384	759647	311035	6366	168258	101220	10748
2002–3	676523	112985	898981	393715	7071	258330	127141	7160
2003–4	742904	36920	1016151	526586	7296	287261	107585	5419
2004–5	752436	−23258	1275912	649255	7448	439374	119776	5258
2005–6	759416	5160	1688681	726194	7656	462429	122463	5795
2006–7	827626	2136	2128862	913179	8161	567761	177019	7635
2007–8	899518	−114636	2578990	1295131	9224	764980	210221	4590
2008–9	1277333	61761	3013337	1352184	10054	859652	387930	10357
2009–10	1669186	211581	3490081	1281469	11270	850602	301615	1169
2010–11	1982771	394035	4233242	1393327	12724	1124680	368274	5159
2011–12	2360780	528680	4950280	1523670	14110	1504760	597540	

Note: 1 Figures in brackets are percentage change over the year.

Source: RBI Handbook on Statistics on the Indian Economy.

Table A4.2 Selected Indicators of Scheduled Commercial Bank Operations (Year-end Outstandings)

(Rupees, Crore)

Year	Aggregate Deposits	Demand Deposits	Time Deposits	Bank Credit	C/D Ratio	Food Credit	Non-food Credit	Investments	I/D Ratio	Govt. Securities	Other Approved Securities	Cash in Hand	Balances with RBI	Borrowings from RBI
1	2	3	4	5	6	7	8	9	10	11	12	13	14	15
1950-1	882	593	290	547	62.0	.	.	.	.	.	.	35	58	12
1951-2	852 (-3.4)	566 (-4.6)	286 (-1.4)	522 (-4.6)	61.3	.	.	.	.	296	.	35	46	56
1952-3	832 (-2.3)	522 (-7.8)	310 (8.4)	529 (1.3)	63.6	.	.	.	.	303	.	32	43	19
1953-4	848 (1.9)	522 (0.0)	326 (5.2)	538 (1.7)	63.4	.	.	.	.	319	.	32	41	31
1954-5	943 (11.2)	567 (8.6)	375 (15.0)	623 (15.8)	66.1	.	.	.	.	344	.	32	46	37
1955-6	1043 (10.6)	631 (11.3)	412 (9.9)	761 (22.2)	73.0	.	.	.	.	360	.	36	49	65
1956-7	1175 (12.7)	704 (11.6)	472 (14.6)	900 (18.3)	76.6	.	.	.	.	347	.	34	54	103
1957-8	1452 (23.6)	731 (3.8)	721 (52.8)	963 (7.0)	66.3	.	.	.	.	440	.	37	68	42
1958-9	1635 (12.6)	722 (-1.2)	913 (26.6)	1014 (5.3)	62.0	.	.	.	.	613	.	43	64	62
1959-60	1902 (16.3)	781 (8.2)	1121 (22.8)	1128 (11.2)	59.3	.	.	.	.	715	.	62	91	79
1960-1	1736 (-8.7)	710 (-9.1)	1026 (-8.5)	1336 (18.4)	77.0	.	.	.	.	559	.	46	71	95
1961-2	1917 (10.4)	786 (10.7)	1131 (10.2)	1408 (5.4)	73.4	.	.	.	.	601	.	49	75	53
1962-3	2042 (6.5)	867 (10.3)	1175 (3.9)	1588 (12.8)	77.8	.	.	.	.	593	.	52	74	71
1963-4	2285 (11.9)	1071 (23.5)	1214 (3.3)	1817 (14.4)	79.5	.	.	.	.	640	.	58	89	84
1964-5	2583 (13.0)	1239 (15.7)	1344 (10.7)	2035 (12.0)	78.8	.	.	.	.	718	.	67	96	153
1965-6	2950 (14.2)	1427 (15.2)	1523 (13.3)	2287 (12.4)	77.5	.	.	.	.	811	.	73	97	74
1966-7	3425 (16.1)	1649 (15.6)	1776 (16.6)	2692 (17.7)	78.6	.	.	.	.	893	.	87	129	140
1967-8	3856 (12.6)	1845 (11.9)	2011 (13.2)	3032 (12.6)	78.6	.	.	.	.	967	.	89	132	104
1968-9	4338 (12.5)	1934 (4.8)	2404 (19.5)	3396 (12.0)	78.3	.	.	.	.	1055	.	109	166	106
1969-70	5028 (15.9)	2235 (15.6)	2793 (16.2)	3971 (16.9)	79.0	56	3915	1481	29.5	1167	314	146	176	238
1970-1	5906 (17.5)	2626 (17.5)	3280 (17.4)	4684 (18.0)	79.3	214	4469	1772	30.0	1362	410	167	197	368
1971-2	7106 (20.3)	3127 (19.1)	3979 (21.3)	5263 (12.4)	74.1	345	4918	2190	30.8	1650	539	181	267	208
1972-3	8643 (21.6)	3794 (21.3)	4849 (21.9)	6115 (16.2)	70.8	340	5775	2897	33.5	2161	736	221	279	139
1973-4	10139 (17.3)	4336 (14.3)	5803 (19.7)	7399 (21.0)	73.0	367	7032	3286	32.4	2362	924	246	610	409
1974-5	11827 (16.6)	4963 (14.5)	6865 (18.3)	8762 (18.4)	74.1	613	8149	3915	33.1	2826	1088	296	612	473
1975-6	14155 (19.7)	5817 (17.2)	8338 (21.5)	10877 (24.1)	76.8	1521	9356	4607	32.5	3283	1324	305	608	798
1976-7	17566 (24.1)	6943 (19.4)	10623 (27.4)	13173 (21.1)	75.0	2191	10982	5536	31.5	3930	1606	354	1146	967
1977-8	22211 (26.4)	4872 (-29.8)	17340 (63.2)	14939 (13.4)	67.3	1984	12955	7897	35.6	5907	1990	469	1674	331
1978-9	27016 (21.6)	5826 (19.6)	21190 (22.2)	18285 (22.4)	67.7	2210	16075	9109	33.7	6622	2488	557	2634	546
1979-80	31759 (17.6)	6643 (14.0)	25116 (18.5)	21537 (17.8)	67.8	2100	19437	10624	33.5	7444	3181	616	3634	739

Year	(1)	(2)	(3)	(4)	(5)	(6)	(7)	(8)	(9)	(10)	(11)	(12)	(13)	(14)	(15)
1980-81	37988	(19.6)	7798	(17.4)	30190	(20.2)	25371	(17.8)	66.8	1759	23612	13186	34.7	9219	3967	766	4092	589
1981-82	43733	(15.1)	8383	(7.5)	35350	(17.1)	29682	(17.0)	67.9	2127	27555	15141	34.6	10157	4984	788	4883	831
1982-83	51358	(17.4)	9984	(19.1)	41374	(17.0)	35493	(19.6)	69.1	2965	32528	18334	35.7	12078	6257	878	5208	815
1983-84	60596	(18.0)	11312	(13.3)	49284	(19.1)	41294	(16.3)	68.1	4022	37272	21246	35.1	13473	7772	928	7783	1336
1984-85	72244	(19.2)	14132	(24.9)	58113	(17.9)	48953	(18.5)	67.8	5665	43287	28138	38.9	18697	9441	1044	6884	1558
1985-86	85404	(18.2)	15612	(10.5)	69792	(20.1)	56067	(14.5)	65.6	5535	50533	30553	35.8	19045	11509	1127	11053	954
1986-87	102724	(20.3)	19227	(23.2)	83496	(19.6)	63308	(12.9)	61.6	5104	58204	38582	37.6	24847	13735	1174	14381	1293
1987-88	118045	(14.9)	20247	(5.3)	97798	(17.1)	70536	(11.4)	59.8	2190	68346	46504	39.4	30517	15987	1306	17656	1753
1988-89	140150	(18.7)	23342	(15.3)	116808	(19.4)	84719	(20.1)	60.4	769	83950	54662	39.0	35815	18847	1444	21376	3527
1989-90	166959	(19.1)	28856	(23.6)	138103	(18.2)	101453	(19.8)	60.8	2006	99446	64369	38.6	42292	22078	1649	23463	2399
1990-91	192541	(15.3)	33192	(15.0)	159349	(15.4)	116301	(14.6)	60.4	4506	111795	75065	39.0	49998	25067	1804	23861	3468
1991-92	230758	(19.8)	45088	(35.8)	185670	(16.5)	125592	(8.0)	54.4	4670	120922	90196	39.1	62727	27469	2008	34179	577
1992-93	268572	(16.4)	46461	(3.0)	222111	(19.6)	151982	(21.0)	56.6	6743	145239	105656	39.3	75945	29711	2293	28535	1619
1993-94	315132	(17.3)	56572	(21.8)	258560	(16.4)	164418	(8.2)	52.2	10907	153510	132523	42.1	101202	31321	2283	47760	1813
1994-95	386859	(22.8)	76903	(35.9)	309956	(19.9)	211560	(28.7)	54.7	12275	199286	149253	38.6	117685	31568	2972	60029	7415
1995-96	433819	(12.1)	80614	(4.8)	353205	(14.0)	254015	(20.1)	58.6	9791	244224	164782	38.0	132227	32555	3113	50667	4847
1996-97	505599	(16.5)	90610	(12.4)	414989	(17.5)	278401	(9.6)	55.1	7597	270805	190514	37.7	158890	31624	3347	49848	560
1997-98	598485	(18.4)	102513	(13.1)	495972	(19.5)	324079	(16.4)	54.1	12485	311594	218705	36.5	186957	31748	3608	57698	395
1998-99	714025	(19.3)	117423	(14.5)	596602	(20.3)	368837	(13.8)	51.7	16816	352021	254595	35.7	223217	31377	4362	63548	2894
1999-2000	813345	(13.9)	127366	(8.5)	685978	(15.0)	435958	(18.2)	53.6	25691	410267	308944	38.0	278456	30488	5330	57419	6491
2000-1	962618	(18.4)	142552	(11.9)	820066	(19.5)	511434	(17.3)	53.1	39991	471443	370159	38.5	340035	30125	5658	59544	3896
2001-2	1103360	(14.6)	153048	(7.4)	950312	(15.9)	589723	(15.3)	53.4	53978	535745	438269	39.7	411176	27093	6245	62402	3616
2002-3	1280853	(16.1)	170289	(11.3)	1110564	(16.9)	729215	(23.7)	56.9	49479	679736	547546	42.7	523417	24129	7567	58335	79
2003-4	1504416	(17.5)	225022	(32.1)	1279394	(15.2)	840785	(15.3)	55.9	35961	804824	677588	45.0	654758	22830	7898	68997	0
2004-5	1700198	(13.0)	248028	(10.2)	1452171	(13.5)	1100428	(30.9)	64.7	41121	1059308	739154	43.5	718982	20172	8472	88105	50
2005-6	2109049	(24.0)	364640	(47.0)	1744409	(20.1)	1507077	(37.0)	71.5	40691	1466386	717454	34.0	700742	16712	13046	127061	1488
2006-7	2611933	(23.8)	429731	(17.9)	2182203	(25.1)	1931189	(28.1)	73.9	46521	1884669	791516	30.3	776058	15458	16139	180222	6245
2007-8	3196939	(22.4)	524310	(22.0)	2672630	(22.5)	2361914	(22.3)	73.9	44399	2317515	971715	30.4	958661	13053	18044	257122	4000
2008-9	3834110	(19.9)	523085	(-0.2)	3311025	(23.9)	2775549	(17.5)	72.4	46211	2729338	1166410	30.4	1155786	10624	20281	238195	11728
2009-10	4492826	(17.2)	645610	(23.4)	3847216	(16.2)	3244788	(16.9)	72.2	48489	3196299	1384752	30.8	1378395	6358	25578	281390	42
2010-11	5207969	(15.9)	641705	(-0.6)	4566264	(18.7)	3942083	(21.5)	75.7	64283	3877800	1501619	28.8	1499148	4471	30346	319163	5031
2011-12	6112480	(17.4)	739700	(15.3)	5372780	(17.7)	4704790	(19.3)	77.0	79790	4625000	1744960	28.5	1742080	2880	39710	346550	6330

Note: Data in brackets are percentage change over the year. Data relate to amount outstanding as on last Friday of March up to 1984-85 and last reporting Friday of March thereafter.

Source: RBI Handbook on Statistics on the Indian Economy.

Table A4.3 Trends in Statewise Bank Deposits and Credit and Credit–Deposit Ratios (For Scheduled Commercial Banks)

(Amount in Rupees Lakh)
(C–D ratio in per cent)

A. Credit as per Sanction
All-India

Sr. No.	Name of the State	1990 Deposits	1990 Credit	1990 C–D Ratio	2000 Deposits	2000 Credit	2000 C–D Ratio	2010 Deposits	2010 Credit	2010 C–D Ratio
		2	3	4	5	6	7	8	9	10
	Northern Region	**3783818**	**1852805**	**49.0**	**19041422**	**9739486**	**51.1**	**100649707**	**74865766**	**74.4**
1	Haryana	343323	207800	60.5	1705324	722307	42.4	10917186	6913799	63.3
2	Himachal Pradesh	120970	43810	36.2	622061	147768	23.8	2688534	1135494	42.2
3	Jammu & Kashmir	154801	48410	31.3	861572	288257	33.5	3400264	1576863	42.2
4	Punjab	866825	382339	44.1	3871531	1524386	39.4	13319996	9525631	46.4
5	Rajasthan	464714	266119	57.3	2383883	1113365	46.7	10673608	9430676	71.5
6	Chandigarh	131307	88990	67.8	629387	516131	82.0	3148778	4127919	131.1
7	Delhi	1701878	815337	47.9	8967665	5427273	60.5	56501341	42155385	74.6
	North-Eastern Region	**284528**	**156136**	**54.9**	**1320854**	**370619**	**28.1**	**7694832**	**2734989**	**35.5**
8	Arunachal Pradesh	10500	3962	37.7	53745	8426	15.7	412623	113653	27.5
9	Assam	190029	111206	58.5	844415	270116	32.0	4859374	1836661	37.8
10	Manipur	8441	6259	74.1	45944	17204	37.4	269940	113526	42.1
11	Meghalaya	27901	5409	19.4	140283	22862	16.3	764267	195779	25.6
12	Mizoram	6518	2449	37.6	32136	7475	23.3	223934	119102	53.2
13	Nagaland	18056	5732	31.7	76967	11805	15.3	418779	126912	30.3
14	Tripura	23083	21119	91.5	127363	32731	25.7	745915	229357	30.7
	Eastern Region	**2634843**	**1404673**	**53.3**	**11072192**	**4100430**	**37.0**	**52726122**	**26797559**	**50.8**
15	Bihar	831687	305763	36.8	3740345	839907	22.5	10036678	2912488	29.0
16	Jharkhand							6358255	2232417	
17	Odisha	236511	212135	89.7	1274401	529269	41.5	8242456	4481961	54.4
18	Sikkim	10626	3466	32.6	46259	6982	15.1	313443	116666	37.2
19	West Bengal	1551026	881723	56.8	5977611	2718645	45.5	27613971	16995081	61.5
20	Andaman & Nicobar Isl.	4993	1586	31.8	33576	5627	16.8	161320	58946	36.5
	Central Region	**2449509**	**1153270**	**47.1**	**11356328**	**3847499**	**33.9**	**52019055**	**24588387**	**47.3**
21	Chhattisgarh							4777733	2497583	60.6
22	Madhya Pradesh	663276	438386	66.1	3088838	1516374	49.1	11818274	7161668	

23	Uttar Pradesh	1786233	714884	40.0	8267490	2331126	28.2	31226045	13512867	43.3
24	Uttarakhand							4197003	1416268	
	Western Region	**4443860**	**2900815**	**65.3**	**20556221**	**15506982**	**75.4**	**144881683**	**114595664**	**79.1**
25	Goa	132893	41802	31.5	651837	155213	23.8	2919943	772947	26.5
26	Gujarat	1023400	580777	56.7	4832709	2367981	49.0	21521713	14049803	65.3
27	Maharashtra	3281222	2276380	69.4	15018478	12974914	86.4	120199142	99685976	82.9
28	Dadra & Nagar Haveli	1358	763	56.2	16679	3135	18.8	96419	57811	60.0
29	Daman & Diu	4987	1093	21.9	36517	5740	15.7	144466	29127	20.2
	Southern Region	**3594581**	**2963494**	**82.4**	**18794952**	**12443052**	**66.2**	**98131505**	**90934567**	**92.7**
30	Andhra Pradesh	937420	753568	80.4	4635925	2977888	64.2	24926361	26208546	105.1
31	Karnataka	839437	690159	82.2	4591065	2907938	63.3	28977498	22482520	77.6
32	Kerala	655482	413602	63.1	3904494	1621489	41.5	15209669	9601091	63.1
33	Tamil Nadu	1133998	1090732	96.2	5517493	4888289	88.6	28363655	32289381	113.8
34	Lakshadweep	790	133	16.8	6272	467	7.4	42846	3122	7.3
35	Puducherry	27454	15300	55.7	139702	46981	33.6	611475	349908	57.2
	All-India Total	17191139	241700652	1406.0	82141969	46008068	56.0	456102905	334516932	73.3

(Contd.)

Table A4.3 (Contd.)

(Amount in Rupees Lakh)
(C–D ratio in per cent)

B. Credit as per Utilization*
All-India

Sr. No.	Name of the State	Deposits	1990 Credit	C-D Ratio	Deposits	2000 Credit	C-D Ratio	Deposits	2010 Credit	C-D Ratio
1		11	12	13	14	15	16	17	18	19
	Northern Region	**3783818**	**1802060**	**47.6**	**19041422**	**9438960**	**49.6**	**100649707**	**75432430**	**74.9**
1	Haryana	343323	257609	75.0	1705324	909933	53.4	10917186	8312600	76.1
2	Himachal Pradesh	120970	46420	38.4	622061	166611	26.8	2688534	1372495	51.0
3	Jammu & Kashmir	154801	51823	33.5	861572	265903	30.9	3400264	1623776	47.8
4	Punjab	866825	400556	46.2	3871531	1581875	40.9	13319996	9724277	73.0
5	Rajasthan	464714	285759	61.5	2383883	1194403	50.1	10673608	10308477	96.6
6	Chandigarh	131307	72203	55.0	629387	500162	79.5	3148778	4208921	133.7
7	Delhi	1701878	687690	40.4	8967665	4820073	53.7	56501341	39881883	70.6
	North-Eastern Region	**284528**	**199251**	**70.0**	**1320854**	**404662**	**30.6**	**7694832**	**3012267**	**39.1**
8	Arunachal Pradesh	10500	5813	55.4	53745	11975	22.3	412623	141838	34.4
9	Assam	190029	149019	78.4	844415	299402	35.5	4859374	1966381	40.5
10	Manipur	8441	6545	77.5	45944	17393	37.9	269940	121014	44.8
11	Meghalaya	27901	7066	25.3	140283	22807	16.3	764267	249731	32.7
12	Mizoram	6518	2689	41.3	32136	8355	26.0	223934	129298	57.7
13	Nagaland	18056	6812	37.7	76967	12017	15.6	418779	168298	40.2
14	Tripura	23083	21307	92.3	127363	32714	25.7	745915	235706	31.6
	Eastern Region	**2634843**	**1386527**	**52.6**	**11072192**	**4117102**	**37.2**	**52726122**	**28221876**	**53.5**
15	Bihar	831687	324759	39.0	3740345	868956	23.2	10036678	2985296	29.7
16	Jharkhand							6358255	2338019	
17	Odisha	236511	218827	92.5	1274401	545252	42.8	8242456	4791857	58.1
18	Sikkim	10626	4738	44.6	46259	7040	15.2	313443	155277	49.5
19	West Bengal	1551026	836552	53.9	5977611	2686600	44.9	27613971	17885138	64.8
20	Andaman & Nicobar Isl.	4993	1651	33.1	33576	9254	27.6	161320	66289	41.1
	Central Region	**2449509**	**1220987**	**49.8**	**11356328**	**4174173**	**36.8**	**52019055**	**26551858**	**51.0**
21	Chhattisgarh							4777733	2663570	
22	Madhya Pradesh	663276	451579	68.1	3088838	1622800	52.5	11818274	7530334	63.7

23	Uttar Pradesh	1786233	769408	43.1	8267490	2551373	30.9	31226045	14785790	47.4
24	Uttarakhand							4197003	1602165	
	Western Region	**4443860**	**2831762**	**63.7**	**20556221**	**15325358**	**74.6**	**144881683**	**108269990**	**74.7**
25	Goa	132893	43536	32.8	651837	165428	25.4	2919943	814295	27.9
26	Gujarat	1023400	647145	63.2	4832709	2584718	53.5	21521713	16184381	75.2
27	Maharashtra	3281222	2135568	65.1	15018478	12520590	83.4	120199142	91117226	75.8
28	Dadra & Nagar Haveli	1358	2647	194.9	16679	22623	135.6	96419	89530	92.9
29	Daman & Diu	4987	2866	57.5	36517	31999	87.6	144466	64557	44.7
	Southern Region	**3594581**	**2990607**	**83.2**	**18794952**	**12547813**	**66.8**	**98131505**	**93028512**	**94.8**
30	Andhra Pradesh	937420	768271	82.0	4635925	3034465	65.5	24926361	27343795	109.7
31	Karnataka	839437	709924	84.6	4591065	3005359	65.5	28977498	23304623	80.4
32	Kerala	655482	413377	63.1	3904494	1628146	41.7	15209669	9813784	64.5
33	Tamil Nadu	1133998	1081914	95.4	5517493	4825191	87.5	28363655	32200891	113.5
34	Lakshadweep	790	152	19.2	6272	571	9.1	42846	3298	7.7
35	Puducherry	27454	16969	61.8	139702	54082	38.7	611475	362119	59.2
	All-India Total	17191139	10431194	60.7	82141969	46008068	56.0	456102905	334516932	73.3

Notes: * Use of bank credit in another place from the place of sanction captures utilization of bank credit and C–D ratio as per utilization. Data for 1990, 2000, and 2010 relate to end–March.

Source: epwrfits.in.

Table A4.4 Distribution of Outstanding Credit of Scheduled Commercial Banks according to Occupation

(Rupees, Crore)

Occupation	March 2010			March 2005			March 2000		
	No. of Accounts	Credit Limit Amount	Amount Outstanding	No. of Accounts	Credit Limit Amount	Amount Outstanding	No. of Accounts	Credit Limit Amount	Amount Outstanding
I. Agriculture (Direct+Indirect)	427698	465828	390298 (11.7)	26656308	149143	124385 (10.8)	20532891	53554	45638 (9.9)
II. Industry	32541	2092561	1355232 (40.5)	3716669	714005	446825 (38.8)	5354140	271867	213779 (46.5)
1. Mining and Quarrying	255	64705	43363 (1.3)	18141	31760	15817 (1.4)	6611	6377	4852 (1.1)
2. Food Manufacturing and Processing	4530	129978	89917 (2.7)	232424	66490	31050 (2.7)	108750	22804	17624 (3.8)
3. Textiles	5323	214269	135923 (4.1)	225788	91265	52407 (4.5)	186917	38887	30586 (6.6)
4. Paper Paper Products and Printing	706	40799	28421 (0.8)	47359	15948	10615 (0.9)	45509	6033	4907 (1.1)
5. Leather and Leather Products	802	12016	7295 (0.2)	25988	6221	4148 (0.4)	19693	3607	2731 (0.6)
6. Rubber and Rubber Products	640	33886	22335 (0.7)	45811	15272	8986 (0.8)	14395	3687	2767 (0.6)
7. Chemicals and Chemical Products	1230	151625	88048 (2.6)	97054	70565	39233 (3.4)	94993	35783	26758 (5.8)
8. Basic Metals and Metal Products	2015	298467	187978 (5.6)	133686	85590	53855 (4.7)	93764	29842	24792 (5.4)
9. Engineering	3061	193141	99963 (3.0)	229269	60410	40415 (3.5)	112711	33734	25138 (5.5)
10. Vehicles Vehicle Parts and Transport equipments	760	83124	57766 (1.7)	40873	29420	18897 (1.6)	41942	11713	8056 (1.8)
11. Other Industries	7579	76890	47157 (1.4)	2313243	78474	52691 (4.6)	4546356	36708	30609 (6.7)
12. Electricity Gas and Water	82	216132	152187 (4.5)	5140	50744	36317 (3.2)	2686	11296	8574 (1.9)
13. Construction	2916	367772	261272 (7.8)	282672	76442	58376 (5.1)	63972	6616	5599 (1.2)
III. Transport Operations	9624	114785	85757 (2.6)	577543	17762	13721 (1.2)	974401	10524	8075 (1.8)
IV. Professional and Other Services	45158	423111	305375 (9.1)	1469713	80093	55266 (4.8)	1831185	18422	14653 (3.2)
V. Personal Loans	506866	806443	558895 (16.7)	32835257	347598	255982 (22.2)	14420051	61077	51639 (11.2)
(i) Loans for Purchase of Consumer Durables	9105	7686	5759 (0.2)	1510200	8057	6349 (0.6)	1187325	3426	2781 (0.6)
(ii) Loans for Housing	60378	376623	306307 (9.2)	3666450	145034	126797 (11.0)	2253390	21001	18525 (4.0)
(iii) Rest of the Personal Loans	437383	422134	246829 (7.4)	27658607	194507	122836 (10.7)	10979336	36650	30332 (6.6)
VI. Trade	68072	513732	305482 (9.1)	6091108	173357	129646 (11.2)	7072533	85882	71618 (15.6)
1. Retail Trade	63033	225781	163480 (4.9)	5591844	78494	56127 (4.9)	6595516	31197	25662 (5.6)
VII. Finance	10673	307558	243139 (7.3)	107968	91440	73277 (6.4)	70485	30166	21873 (4.8)
VIII. All Others	85847	144679	100990 (3.0)	5696228	72867	53368 (4.6)	4114711	37604	32806 (7.1)
Total Bank Credit	1186479	4868697	3345169 (100.0)	77150794	1646266	1152468 (100)	54370397	569096	460081 (100)
Of which: 1. Artisans and Village Industries			1288321	7904	6149 (0.5)	2013171	3016	2677 (0.6)
2. Other Small Scale Industries			939186	62853	47076 (4.1)	2126150	43600	35070 (7.6)

Table A4.4 (Contd.)

(Rupees, Crore)

Occupation	March 1990				December 1980				December 1975			
I. Agriculture (Direct+Indirect)	24520595	19313	16626	(15.9)	10339615	4920	3722	(15.7)	3042170	1493	1071	(10.7)
II. Industry	4125322	59762	50846	(48.7)	837313	17124	11555	(48.8)	304873	9009	5777	(57.7)
1. Mining and Quarrying	8858	982	877	(0.8)	3987	267	191	(0.8)	1985	188	132	(1.3)
2. Food Manufacturing and Processing	94534	5454	4288	(4.1)	37993	1737	955	(4.0)	18060	877	379	(3.8)
3. Textiles	87634	8611	7495	(7.2)	54963	2943	1983	(8.4)	31457	1619	1056	(10.5)
4. Paper Paper Products and Printing	36906	1860	1623	(1.6)	20952	550	417	(1.8)	10103	255	178	(1.8)
5. Leather and Leather Products	11173	1093	1004	(1.0)	5117	234	169	(0.7)	2691	91	71	(0.7)
6. Rubber and Rubber Products	11853	1002	887	(0.9)	6458	320	245	(1.0)	3330	145	104	(1.0)
7. Chemicals and Chemical Products	64825	7493	6352	(6.1)	43149	2176	1410	(6.0)	20827	933	590	(5.9)
8. Basic Metals and Metal Products	74936	6166	5398	(5.2)	45392	1962	1324	(5.6)	23462	1070	755	(7.5)
9. Engineering	88135	10613	8926	(8.6)	54149	3454	2389	(10.1)	27082	1868	1231	(12.3)
10. Vehicles Vehicle Parts and Transport equipments	25597	2667	2306	(2.2)	13991	855	550	(2.3)	8510	433	311	(3.1)
11. Other Industries	3577835	8740	7384	(7.1)	529390	1065	767	(3.2)	146478	829	547	(5.5)
12. Electricity Gas and Water	2773	1121	843	(0.8)	702	291	125	(0.5)	1650	174	106	(1.1)
13. Construction	23431	1566	1438	(1.4)	12638	230	180	(0.8)	5477	90	70	(0.7)
III. Transport Operations	1240476	4146	3286	(3.2)	378273	1324	1078	(4.6)	103758	328	259	(2.6)
IV. Personal Loans and Professional Other Services	8125421	11200	9791	(9.4)	3612241	1574	1336	(5.6)	1568584	636	496	(5.0)
1. Professional Services	1592015	1129	967	(0.9)	187091	115	93	(0.4)	45752	38	30	(0.3)
2. Other Services	1664209	2413	2126	(2.0)	701956	437	366	(1.5)	217046	204	150	(1.5)
3. Personal Loan	4869197	7,658	6698	(6.4)	2267767	937	810	(3.4)	1305786	394	317	(3.2)
(i) Loans for Purchase of Consumer Durables	420095	507	443	(0.4)	191480	43	35	(0.1)	93277	20	12	(0.1)
(ii) Loans for Housing	547114	2908	2536	(2.4)	205250	293	252	(1.1)	21839	108	93	(0.9)
(iii) Rest of the Personal Loans	3901988	4243	3719	(3.6)	1871037	601	524	(2.2)	1190670	266	211	(2.1)
V. Trade	8837621	17121	14486	(13.9)	1886767	7224	4653	(19.7)	444255	3252	1820	(18.2)
1. Retail Trade	8438399	6319	5560	(5.3)	1735156	1050	801	(3.4)	360391	385	263	(2.6)
VI. Financial Institutions	14122	2708	2234	(2.1)	8633	368	228	(1.0)	12060	315	151	(1.5)
1. Leasing/Hire Purchase and Finance Units	3801	920	771	(0.7)	..	..	..	..	..	..	..	..
2. Housing Finance Companies/Corporations	186	144	134	(0.1)	..	..	..	..	..	..	..	..
VII. Miscellaneous	6987129	7405	7042	(6.8)	3185453	1335	1100	(4.6)	1883382	670	442	(4.4)
Total Bank Credit	53850686	121654	104312	(100)	20248295	33868	23673	(100)	7359082	15703	10015	(100)
Of which: 1. Artisans and Village Industries	2151263	1061	926	(0.9)	..	..	..	..	..	..	..	..
2. Other Small Scale Industries	1606146	14098	11986	(11.5)	668570	3709	2844	(12.0)	262301	1773	1178	(11.8)

Note: .. not available. Figures in brackets are percentages to total bank credit.
Source: epwrfits.in.

A5 CAPITAL MARKET

Table A5.1 Resources Mobilization from the Primary Market

(Rupees, Crore)

Year	Total		Category-wise					Issue Type			
			Public		Right		Listed		IPOs		
	Number	Amount	Number	Amount	Number	Amount	Number	Amount	Number	Amount	
1	2	3	4	5	6	7	8	9	10	11	
1993–4	1143	24372	773	15449	370	8923	451	16508	692	7864	
1994–5	1735	27632	1342	21045	350	6588	453	11061	1239	16572	
1995–6	1738	20804	1426	14240	299	6564	368	9880	1357	10924	
1996–7	889	14277	751	11557	131	2719	167	8326	717	5950	
1997–8	114	4569	62	2862	49	1708	59	3522	52	1048	
1998–9	59	5587	32	5019	26	568	40	5182	18	405	
1999–2000	94	7817	65	6257	28	1560	42	5098	51	2719	
2000–1	151	6108	124	5379	27	729	37	3386	114	2722	
2001–2	35	7543	20	6502	15	1041	28	6341	7	1202	
2002–3	27	4070	14	3639	12	431	20	3032	6	1038	
2003–4	57	23273	35	22265	22	1007	36	19838	21	3434	
2004–5	60	28256	34	24640	26	3616	37	14507	23	13749	
2005–6	139	27382	103	23294	36	4088	60	16446	79	10936	
2006–7	124	33508	85	29796	39	3710	47	5002	77	28504	
2007–8	124	87029	92	54511	32	32518	39	44434	85	42595	
2008–9	47	16220	22	3582	25	12637	25	12637	21	2082	
2009–10	76	57555	47	49236	29	8319	34	30359	39	24696	
2010–11	91	67609	68	58105	23	9503	28	22599	53	35559	
2011–12											
Apr-11	6	2023	6	2023	0	0	0	0	6	2023	
May-11	5	4781	5	4781	0	0	1	4578	4	203	
Jun-11	7	1196	4	1141	3	55	3	55	3	141	
Jul-11	5	1447	3	1382	2	65	2	65	3	1382	
Aug-11	11	3559	8	3240	3	319	3	319	4	605	
Sep-11	13	3125	11	1476	2	1649	2	1649	9	627	
Oct-11	0	0	0	0	0	0	0	0	0	0	
Nov-11	2	1062	2	1062	0	0	0	0	0	0	
Dec-11	3	14492	3	14492	0	0	0	0	0	0	
Jan-12	4	12127	4	12127	0	0	0	0	0	0	
Feb-12	5	792	2	672	3	120	3	120	2	672	
Mar-12	9	3870	6	3702	3	168	3	168	3	251	

Table A5.1 (Contd.)

(Rupees, Crore)

Year	Instrument-wise									
	Equities				CCPS		Bonds		Others	
	At Par		At Premium							
	Number	Amount	Number	Amount	Number	Amount	Number	Amount	Number	Amount
1	12	13	14	15	16	17	18	19	20	21
1993-4	608	3808	383	9220	1	2	9	1991	142	9351
1994-5	942	5529	651	12441	7	124	0	0	135	9538
1995-6	1181	4958	480	9727	8	145	6	2086	63	3888
1996-7	697	3433	148	4412	5	75	10	5400	29	957
1997-8	64	271	33	1610	3	10	4	1550	10	1128
1998-9	20	197	20	660	3	78	10	4450	6	202
1999-2000	30	786	52	3780	0	0	10	3200	2	51
2000-1	84	818	54	2408	2	142	10	2704	1	36
2001-2	7	151	8	1121	0	0	16	5601	4	670
2002-3	6	143	11	1314	0	0	8	2600	2	13
2003-4	14	360	37	18589	0	0	6	4324	0	0
2004-5	6	420	49	23968	0	0	5	3867	0	0
2005-6	10	372	128	27000	0	0	0	0	1	10
2006-7	2	12	119	32889	0	0	2	356	1	249
2007-8	7	387	113	79352	2	5687	2	1603	0	0
2008-9	5	96	40	14176	1	448	1	1500	0	0
2009-10	1	9	71	54866	1	180	3	2500	0	0
2010-11	2	50	78	57617	1	490	10	9451	0	0
2011-12										
Apr-11	0	0	6	2023	0	0	0	0	0	0
May-11	0	5	4781	0	0	0	0	0	0	0
Jun-11	2	86	4	110	0	0	1	1000	0	0
Jul-11	1	13	4	1434	0	0	0	0	0	0
Aug-11	0	0	7	924	0	0	4	2635	0	0
Sep-11	0	0	11	2275	0	0	2	849	0	0
Oct-11	0	0	0	0	0	0	0	0	0	0
Nov-11	0	0	0	0	0	0	2	1062	0	0
Dec-11	0	0	0	0	0	0	3	14492	0	0
Jan-12	0	0	0	0	0	0	4	12127	0	0
Feb-12	1	5	4	786	0	0	0	0	0	0
Mar-12	0	0	6	419	0	0	3	3451	0	0

Note: Instrument-wise break up may not tally with the total number of issues, as for one issue there could be more than one instruments.

Source: SEBI (2012), *Handbook of Statistics on the Indian Securities Market 2010* and SEBI Bulletins.

Table A5.2 Trends in Resource Mobilization by Mutual Funds (Sector-wise)

(Rupees, Crore)

Year	Gross Mobilization					Redemption*					Net Inflow				Assets at the end of Period
	Private Sector	Public Sector	UTI	Total		Private Sector	Public Sector	UTI	Total		Private Sector	Public Sector	UTI	Total	
1	2	3	4	5		6	7	8	9		10	11	12	13	14
1993-4	1549	9527	51000	62076	(7.0)	na	na	na	na		na	na	na	na	na
1994-5	2084	2143	9500	13727	(1.3)	na	na	na	na		na	na	na	na	na
1995-6	312	296	5900	6508	(0.5)	na	na	na	na		na	na	na	na	na
1996-7	346	151	4280	4777	(0.3)	na	na	na	na		na	na	na	na	na
1997-8	1974	332	9100	11406	(0.7)	na	na	na	na		na	na	na	na	na
1998-9	7847	1671	13193	22711	(1.3)	6394	1336	15930	23660		1453	335	-2737	-949	68193
1999-2000	43726	3817	13698	61241	(3.0)	28559	4562	9150	42271		15167	-745	4548	18970	107946
2000-1	75009	5535	12413	92957	(4.3)	65160	6580	12090	83830		9849	-1045	323	9127	90586
2001-2	147798	12082	4643	164523	(7.0)	134748	10673	11927	157348		13050	1409	-7284	7175	100594
2002-3	284096	23515	7096	314707	(12.4)	272026	21954	16530	310510		12070	1561	-9434	4197	109299
2003-4	534649	31548	23992	590189	(20.8)	492105	28951	22326	543382		42544	2597	1666	46807	139616
2004-5	736463	56589	46656	839708	(25.9)	728864	59266	49378	837508		7599	-2677	-2722	2200	149600
2005-6	914703	110319	73127	1098149	(29.7)	871727	103940	69704	1045370		42977	6379	3424	52779	231862
2006-7	1599873	196340	142280	1938493	(45.1)	1520836	188719	134954	1844508		79038	7621	7326	93985	326292
2007-8	3780753	346126	337498	4464377	(89.5)	3647449	335448	327678	4310575		133304	10677	9820	153802	505152
2008-9	4292751	710472	423131	5426354	(96.4)	4326768	701092	426790	5454650		-34018	9380	-3658	-28296	417300
2009-10	7698483	1438688	881851	10019023	(155.2)	7643555	1426189	866198	9935942		54928	12499	15653	83080	613979
2010-11	6922924	1152733	783858	8859515	(115.4)	6942140	1166288	800494	8908921		-19215	-13555	-16636	-49406	592250
2011-12	5683744	1135935	522453	6819679	(76.5)	5699189	1135935	525637	6841702		-15445	6578	-3184	22024	587217
Apr-11	628601	72750	73642	774993		478539	55895	56228	590662		150062	16855	17414	184331	785374
May-11	505533	51652	51290	608476		547245	57273	52807	657325		-41712	-16855	-1517	-48850	731448
Jun-11	455425	49331	42276	547032		499350	58093	52031	609474		-43925	2472	-9755	-62442	673176
Jul-11	474051	52661	41445	568157		436453	46060	34633	517146		37598	6601	6812	51011	728187
Aug-11	392941	47172	32877	472991		399426	49242	38920	487588		-6485	-2070	-6043	-14598	696738
Sep-11	408892	45997	46256	501145		451979	54381	48959	555318		-43087	-8384	-2702	-54173	641937
Oct-11	446459	48217	35126	529802		410298	44273	33945	488516		36161	3944	1181	41287	695437
Nov-11	462998	45860	36154	545011		459630	45390	36220	541239		3368	471	-66	3772	681655
Dec-11	450141	49704	35394	535238		507432	53633	37593	598658		-57291	-3930	-2199	-63420	611402

Jan-12	462669	48136	41103	551907	444594	46259	37502	528354	18075	1877	3601	23553	659153
Feb-12	442483	44159	37790	524431	445776	42325	35059	523160	-3294	1834	2731	1271	675238
Mar-12	553551	580296	49100	660496	618467	583111	61740	744262	-64915	3763	-12641	-39718	

Notes: * Includes repurchases as well as redemption;   na: Not Available
   Figures in brackets are percentages to GDP at cuurent market prices
1. IDBI principal has now become principal MF a private ector mutual fund.
2. Erstwhile UTI has been divided into UTI mutual fund (registered with SEBI) and the specified undertaking of UTI (not registered with SEBI)
3. Above data contain information only of UTI mutual fund.
4. Net assets pertaining to funds of funds schemes is not included in the above data.

Source: Securities and Exchange Board of India.

Table A5.3 Trends in Resource Mobilization by Mutual Funds

(Rupees, Crore)

Year	UTI	Bank-sponsored MFs			Institution-Sponsored MFs	Private Sector MFs						Grand Total
		Total (4+5)	Joint Ventures Predominantly Indian	Others		Total (8 to 11)	Indian	Foreign	Joint Ventures Predominantly Indian	Joint Ventures Predominantly Foreign		(2+3+6+7)
	1	2	3	4	5	6	7	8	10	11		12
Sales : All Schemes												
1999–2000	13536	1828	na	na	2211	42164	6688			19937	15539	59739
2000–1	12413	2181	na	na	4011	74352	19901			33655	20796	92957
2001–2	4643	4242	na	na	9371	146267	33634			64237	48396	164523
2002–3	7062	11090	na	na	17535	278986	83351		124122	71513		314673
2003–4	na	46661	30995	59451	21897	521632	143050		238037	140545		590190
2004–5	na	90446	48167	89059	12800	736462	242428		337109	156925		839708
2005–6	na	137226	52512	161501	46220	914703	256752		311433	346518		1098149
2006–7	na	214013	143324	346270	124607	1599972	479754		498319	621899		1938592
2007–8	na	489594	347405	426323	194030	3780752	1369180	182305	836538	1392729		4464376
2008–9	na	773728	451533	976457	363066	4289559	1782552	257363	373772	1875872		5426353
2009–10	na	1427990	612440	942234	987155	7603878	3687355	229299	286312	3400912		10019023
2010–11	na	1554674	466091	713751	470820	6834021	3295349	302821	264996	2970855		8859515
2011–12	na	1179842			34490	5605347	2499093	263418	181574	2661262		6819679
Redemptions: All Schemes												
1999–2000	9663	1744	na	na	1864	27933	5718			11574	10641	41204
2000–1	12090	4125	na	na	3147	64467	17576			28538	18353	83829
2001–2	11927	3329	na	na	8550	133542	31181		59122	43239		157348
2002–3	7246	10536	na	na	16121	267322	79341		119648	68333		301225
2003–4	na	43183	29970	62490	19796	480402	133131		219991	127280		543381
2004–5	na	92460	43973	85562	16183	728865	237060		335607	156198		837508
2005–6	na	129535	48942	154351	44108	871727	238053		304245	329429		1045370
2006–7	na	203293	135645	335629	120381	1520838	450447		478934	591457		1844512
2007–8	na	471274	343980	429427	191851	3647450	1311006	175937	819387	1341120		4310575
2008–9	na	773407	443905	959516	357112	4324131	1806550	263674	387959	1865948		5454650
2009–10	na	1403421	611618	956778	982284	7550237	3662271	227512	293349	3367105		9935942
2010–11	na	1568396	464964	716961	487808	6852717	3307494	303621	269602	2972000		8908921
2011–12	na	1181925			37588	5622189	2521602	264844	180947	2654796		6841702

Net Sales

Year										
1999–2000	3873	84	na	na	347	14231	970	4898	8363	18535
2000–1	323	−1944	na	na	864	9885	2325	2443	5117	9128
2001–2	−7284	913	na	na	821	12725	2453	5157	5115	7175
2002–3	−184	554	na	na	1414	11664	4010	3180	4474	13448
2003–4	na	3478	na	na	2101	41230	9919	13265	18046	46809
2004–5	na	−2014	1025	−3039	−3383	7597	5368	727	1502	2200
2005–6	na	7691	4194	3497	2112	42976	18699	17089	7188	52779
2006–7	na	10720	3570	7150	4226	79134	29307	30442	19385	94080
2007–8	na	18320	7679	10641	2179	133302	58174	51609	6368	17151	153801
2008–9	na	321	3425	−3104	5954	−34572	−23998	9924	−6311	−14187	−28297
2009–10	na	24569	7628	16941	4871	53641	25084	33807	1797	−7037	83081
2010–11	na	−13722	822	−14544	−16988	−18696	−12145	−1145	−800	−4606	−49406
2011–12	na	−2083	1127	−3210	−3098	−16842	−22509	6466	−1426	627	−22023

Assets under Management

Year										
1999–2000	76547	7842	na	na	3570	25046	2331	9724	12991	113005
2000–1	58017	3333	na	na	3507	25730	3370	8620	13740	90587
2001–2	51434	3970	na	na	4234	40956	5177	15502	20277	100594
2002–3	13516	4491	na	na	5935	55522	10180	15459	29883	79464
2003–4	na	28085	na	na	6539	108625	19885	33143	51964	143249
2004–5	na	29103	6595	22508	3010	117487	30750	30885	55852	149600
2005–6	na	45119	13186	31933	5229	181514	50602	74144	56768	231862
2006–7	na	54570	16807	37763	9643	262175	80157	104779	77239	326388
2007–8	na	81229	32174	49055	14337	442942	166104	165790	31168	79880	538508
2008–9	na	81013	31127	49886	23092	389180	153432	180163	32728	22857	493285
2009–10	na	130429	46637	83792	42304	574792	235585	267481	50253	21473	747525
2010–11	na	122798	49496	73302	11195	566545	241048	254045	54679	16773	700538
2011–12	na	119677	51082	68595	5799	539316	190584	274487	57693	16552	664792

Note: na: Not Available; figures in square brackets are percentages to GDP at current market prices (New series).

Source: Association of Mutual Funds in India (AMFI), (Website: www.amfiindia.com).

Table A5.4 Trends in FII Investments

Year	Gross Purchases (Rs crore)	Gross Sales (Rs crore)	Net Investment Total (Rs crore)		Equity	Debt	Net-Investment (US $ mn)	Cumulative Net Investment (US $ mn)
1	2	3	4		5	6	7	8
1992-3	17	4	13	23.53	na	na	4	4
1993-4	5593	467	5127	8.35	na	na	1634	1638
1994-5	7631	2835	4796	37.15	na	na	1528	3167
1995-6	9694	2752	6942	28.39	na	na	2036	5202
1996-7	15554	6980	8575	44.88	na	na	2432	7635
1997-8	18695	12737	5958	68.13	na	na	1650	9285
1998-9	16116	17699	-1584	109.82	na	na	-386	8899
1999-2000	56857	46735	10122	82.20	na	na	2474	11372
2000-1	74051	64118	9933	86.59	10124	-46	2160	13531
2001-2	50071	41308	8763	82.50	8067	685	1839	15371
2002-3	47062	44372	2689	94.28	2528	162	566	15936
2003-4	144855	99091	45764	68.41	39960	5805	10005	25942
2004-5	216951	171071	45880	78.85	44123	1759	10352	36293
2005-6	346976	305509	41467	88.05	48801	-7334	9363	45657
2006-7	520506	489665	30841	94.07	25237	5607	6821	52477
2007-8	948018	881839	66179	93.02	53403	12776	16442	68919
2008-9	614579	660389	-45811	107.45	-47706	1895	-9838	58167
2009-10	846438	703780	142658	83.15			30253	89335
2010-11	992599	846161	146438	85.25			32226	121561
2011-2								
Apr-11	76732	69536	7196	90.62	7213	-17	1616	123175
May-11	77046	81322	-4276	105.55			-948	122227
Jun-11	80624	75741	4883	93.94	4572	311	1083	123310
Jul-11	77218	66566	10653	86.21	8030	2623	2399	125709
Aug-11	69590	77493	-7903	111.36			-1766	123943
Sep-11	64868	66735	-1866	102.88	-158	-1707	-342	123600
Oct-11	64411	61332	3079	95.22	1677	1401	634	124235
Nov-11	62296	65559	-3263	105.24			-586	123649

Dec-11	92020	70147	76.23	21873	23.77		4195	127844
Jan-12	76548	50220	65.61	26329	34.40	10358	15971	5087	132930
Feb-12	103634	68406	66.01	35228	33.99	25212	10016	7164	140095
Mar-12	147612	93104	63.07	54508	36.93			

Note: na: Not Available; Net Investment in US $ mn at monthly exchange rate.

Source: Securities and Exchange Board of India (SEBI), (Website: www.sebi.gov.in).

Table A5.5 Business Growth of Capital Market Segment of National Stock Exchange

Month/Year	No. of Companies Listed*	No. of Companies Permitted to Trade$	No. of Companies Available for Trading*@	Trading Days	No. of Companies/ Securities Traded	No. of Trades (million)	Traded Quantity (million)	Turnover (Rs crore)	Average Daily Turnover (Rs crore)	Average Trade Size (Rs)	Demat Securities Traded (million)	Demat Turnover (Rs crore)	Market Capitalization (Rs crore)*	% to GDP
1	2	3	4	5	6	7	8	9	10	11	12	13	14	15
(Nov–Mar)														
1994-5	135	543	678	102	na	0.3	139	1805	17	56310			363350	34.8
1995-6	422	847	1269	246	na	7	3991	67287	276	101505			401459	32.7
1996-7	550	934	1484	250	na	26	13556	294503	1176	112086			419367	29.5
1997-8	612	745	1357	244	na	38	13569	370193	1520	97054			481503	30.6
1998-9	648	609	1254	251	na	55	16533	414474	1651	75954	854	23818	491175	27.2
1999–2000	720	479	1152	254	na	98	24270	839052	3303	85244	15377	711706	1020426	50.7
2000-1	785	320	1029	251	1201	167.6	32953.6	1339510	5337	86980	30722.2	1264337	657847	30.3
2001-2	793	197	890	247	1019	175.3	27840.8	513167	2078	29270	27771.7	512866	636861	27.1
2002-3	818	107	788	251	899	240	36407	617989	2462	25776	36405	617984	537133	21.2
2003-4	909	18	787	254	804	378	71330	1099535	4329	29090	71330	1099534	1120976	39.5
2004-5	970	1	839	253	870	451	79769	1140071	4471	25283	79769	1140072	1585585	48.9
2005-6	1069	0	929	251	956	609	84449	1569556	6253	25777	84449	1569558	2813201	76.2
2006-7	1228	0	1084	249	1191	785	85546	1945285	7812	24790	85546	1945287	3367350	78.4
2007-8	1381	0	1236	251	1264	1173	149847	3551038	14148	30280	149847	3551038	4858122	97.4
2008-9	1432	0	1291	243	1327	1365	142636	2752023	11325	20161	142636	2752023	2896194	51.4
2009-10	1470	37	1359	244	1968	1682	221553	4138024	16959	24608	221553	4138024	6009173	93.1
2010-11	1574	61	1484	255	1607	1551	182452	3577412	14048	23009	182452	3577412	6702616	87.3
2011-12	1646	73	1563	249	1807	1439	161699	2810892	135816	235014	161699	2810892	6096518	68.4
Apr–11	1578	61	1488	18	1589	107	12943	228348	12686	21281	12943	228348	6753614	
May–11	1585	61	1495	22	1560	115	11586	233876	10631	21281	11586	233876	6569743	
Jun–11	1599	61	1509	22	1663	116	12230	222457	10112	19188	12230	222457	6574743	
Jul–11	1606	60	1514	21	1600	116	12259	230003	10953	19862	12259	230003	6462238	
Aug–11	1615	60	1523	21	1611	124	13311	235253	11203	19036	13311	235253	5921684	
Sep–11	1622	60	1530	21	1698	123	13230	235270	11203	19191	13230	235270	5820334	
Oct–11	1631	66	1543	19	1614	101	10121	193293	10173	19185	10121	193293	6101891	
Nov–11	1633	66	1545	20	1640	111	12380	206344	10317	18522	12380	206344	5547723	

Dec–11	1640	71	1556	21	1675	108	11512	188886	8995	17562	11512	188886	5232273
Jan–12	1641	71	1557	22	1721	131	14830	236872	10767	18050	14830	236872	5937039
Feb–12	1644	71	1560	20	1649	154	20799	327808	16390	21353	20799	327808	6233250
Mar–12	1646	73	1563	22	1807	133	16498	272482	12386	20503	16498	272482	6096518

Note: Figures in brackets are percentages to GDP at current market prices. GDP data are as per revised series from 2004–5 and as per 1999–2000 series before 2004–5.

na: not available.

Source: NSE News (various issues).

Table A5.6 Settlement Statistics of Capital Market Segment of NSE of India

1	No. of Trades (million) 2	Traded Quantity (number) 3	Number of Shares (Deliverable) 4	Per cent of Shares Delivered to Total Trade 5	Trading Value (Rs. crore) 6	Value of Shares Deliverable (Rs. crore) 7	Percentage of Delivered to Value of Shares Traded 8	Short Delivery (million) 9	Per cent of Short Delivery to Total Delivery 10	Funds Pay in (Rs crore) 11
(Nov–Mar)										
1994-5	0.3	133	69	51.74	1728	898	51.98	1	0.85	300
1995-6	6	3901	726	18.62	65742	11775	17.91	18	2.46	3258
1996-7	26	13432	1645	12.25	292314	32640	11.17	38	2.32	7212
1997-8	38	13522	2205	16.31	370010	59775	16.15	33	1.51	10827
1998-9	55	16531	2799	16.93	413573	66204	16.01	31	1.09	12175
1999-2000	96	23861	4871	20.42	803050	82607	10.29	63	1.3	27992
2000-1	161	30420	5020	16.50	1263898	106277	8.41	34	0.68	45937
2001-2	172	27470	5930	21.59	508121	71766	14.12	36	0.61	28048
2002-3	240	36541	8235	22.54	621569	87956	14.15	47	0.57	34092
2003-4	375	70453	17555	24.92	1090632	221364	20.30	101	0.58	81588
2004-5	449	78800	20228	25.67	1140969	277101	24.29	87	0.43	97241
2005-6	600	81844	22724	27.77	1516839	409353	26.99	89	0.39	131426
2006-7	786	85051	23907	28.11	1940094	544435	28.06	77	0.32	173188
2007-8	1165	148123	36797	24.84	3519919	972803	27.64	100	0.27	309543
2008-9	1364	141893	30393	21.42	2749450	611535	22.44	63	0.21	220704
2009-10	1679	220587	47482	21.53	4129213	917706	22.22	86	0.18	278387
2010-11	1549	180769	49827	27.56	3566995	979269	27.45	91	0.18	293354
2011-12										
Apr-11	107	12953	3830	29.57	230464	65874	28.58	10.9	0.28	20358
May-11	116	11868	3496	29.46	237410	68823	28.99	11.3	0.32	20526
Jun-11	116	11939	3290	27.56	220179	62575	28.42	4.3	0.13	18508
Jul-11	115	11910	3487	29.28	226774	66105	29.15	4.7	0.13	19660
Aug-11	125	13593	4002	29.44	241215	69674	28.88	4.8	0.12	22199
Sep-11	116	12540	3289	26.23	220544	58806	26.66	4.4	0.13	22570
Oct-11	106	10518	3065	29.14	202460	56906	28.11	5.2	0.17	19270
Nov-11	112	12247	3604	29.43	204909	58486	28.54	5.5	0.15	18643
Dec-11	110	11630	3253	27.97	198607	54283	27.33	3.9	0.12	18070
Jan-12	127	14416	3782	26.23	226526	60687	26.79	6.3	0.17	18502
Feb-12	152	20280	5208	25.668	320929	91699	28.57	5.3	0.1	31946
Mar-12	136	16627	4087	24.58	273871	71350	26.05	3.6	0.09	21501

Source: NSE News (various issues).

Table A5.7 Business Growth of Futures and Options Market Segment, National Stock Exchange

Month/Year	Index Futures		Stock Futures		Interest Rate Futures		Index Options		Stock Options		Total		Average Daily Turnover (Rs crore)
	Number of Contracts Traded	Turnover (Rs crore)	Number of Contracts Traded	Turnover (Rs crore)	Number of Contracts Traded	Turnover (Rs crore)	Number of Contracts Traded	Notional Turnover (Rs crore)	Number of Contracts Traded	Notional Turnover (Rs crore)	Number of Contracts Traded	Notional Turnover (Rs crore)	
1	2	3	4	5	6	7	8	9	10	11	12	13	14
2000-1	90580	2365	–	–	–	–	–	–	–	–	90580	2365	11
2001-2	1025588	21482	1957856	51516	–	–	175900	3766	1037529	25163	4196873	101926	410
2002-3	2126763	43952	10675786	286532	–	–	442241	9248	3523062	100133	16768909	439862	1752
2003-4	17192274	554463	32485160	1305949	1013	20	1732414	52823	5583071	217212	56993932	2130467	8288
2004-5	21635449	772174	47043066	1484067	0	0	3293558	121954	5045112	168858	77017185	2547053	10107
2005-6	58537886	1513791	80905493	2791721	0	0	12935116	338469	5240776	508930	157619271	5152911	19220
2006-7	81487424	2539576	104955401	3830972	0	0	25157438	791912	5283310	480995	216883573	7643455	29543
2007-8	156598579	3820667	203587952	7548563	0	0	55366038	1362111	9460631	359136	425013200	13090477	52153
2008-9	210428103	3570111	221577980	3479642	0	0	212088444	3731501	13295970	229227	657390497	11010481	45311
2009-10	178306889	3934389	145591240	5195247	0	0	341379523	8027964.2	14016270	506065	679293922	17663664.6	72392
2010-11	165023653	4356755	186041459	5495757	0	0	650638557	18365365.8	32508393	1030344	1034212062	29248221.1	115150
2011-12	146188740	3577998	158344617	4074671	0	0	864017736	22720031.6	36494371	977031	1205045464	31349731.7	125903
2011-2													
Apr-11	10271439	282303	12880705	353159	0	0	56031353	1645880.67	2356517	69958	81540014	2351300	130628
May-11	11888838	305745	13474455	336689	0	0	68034536	1892896.48	2643996	69808	96041825	2605138	118415
Jun-11	10313335	265178	12993351	322695	0	0	64833325	1784570.47	2604328	65733	90744339	2438177	110826
Jul-11	10048859	265641	12260020	349891	0	0	66268437	1867725.51	2800430	81708	91377746	2564965	122141
Aug-11	14585694	347177	13366537	333791	0	0	86141851	2209523.65	2791679	73258	116885761	2963749	141131
Sep-11	14796435	346826	13329926	326290	0	0	83122036	2085730.04	3057248	76418	114305645	2835264	135013
Oct-11	11289988	265945	11358625	279971	0	0	63950603	1621118.72	2541568	66187	89140784	2233221	117538
Nov-11	13469578	312139	13398165	305421	0	0	80542787	2027236.37	2951899	71762	110362429	2716559	135828
Dec-11	13886601	307198	12755993	279921	0	0	86880013	2108751.25	3225407	72993	116748014	2768863	131851
Jan-12	10856475	250738	13958030	350848	0	0	62424041	1542542.16	4157796	107359	91396342	2251487	102340
Feb-12	11289436	291138	15306021	451869	0	0	65316148	1777219.75	4028055	121551	95939660	2641778	132089
Mar-12	13492062	337972	13262789	384126	0	0	80472606	2156836.57	3335448	100296	110562905	2979231	135420

Note: Notional Turnover = (Strike price + Premium) * Quantity; (–) Means the period when derivative trade was not operational.

Source: NSE News (various issues).

Table A5.8 Business Growth on the WDM Segment: NSE

(Rupees, Crore)

Year	Number of Trades	Trading Value (Rs crore)	Average Daily Trading Value (Rs crore)	Average Trade Size (Rs crore)	Market Capitalization
1	2	3	4	5	6
1994-5	1021	6781	35	6.6	158181
1995-6	2991	11868	41	4.0	207783
1996-7	7804	42278	145	5.4	292772
1997-8	16821	111263	385	6.6	343191
1998-9	16092	105469	365	6.6	411470
1999-2000	46987	304216	1035	6.5	494033
2000-1	64470	428582	1483	6.6	580835
2001-2	144851	947191	3278	6.5	756794
2002-3	167778	1068701	3598	6.4	864481
2003-4	189518	1316096	4477	6.9	1215864
2004-5	124308	887294	3039	7.1	1461734
2005-6	61891	475524	1755	7.7	1567574
2006-7	19575	219106	898	11.2	1784801
2007-8	16179	282317	1138	17.5	2123346
2008-9	16129	335952	1412	20.8	2848315
2009-10	24069	563816	2359	23.4	3165929
2010-11	20383	559447	2256	27.5	3594877
2011-12	23447	633179	2649	27.0	4272736
2012-13	1700	47743	2652	28.1	4311227
2011-12					
Apr-11	1194	39752	2484	33.3	3658038
May-11	1136	36350	1731	32.0	3706540
Jun-11	1791	50823	2310	28.4	3772038
Jul-11	2012	46973	2237	23.4	3804757
Aug-11	2411	54826	2741	22.7	3888976
Sep-11	2122	50314	2516	23.7	3895599
Oct-11	1643	36282	2016	22.1	3936784
Nov-11	1567	43847	2192	28.0	3936784
Dec-11	2971	89337	4254	30.1	4048159
Jan-12	2999	75125	3577	25.1	4128774
Feb-12	1979	55793	2937	28.2	4238129
Mar-12	1622	53757	2688	33.1	4272736

Source: NSE News (various issues).

Table A5.9 Business Growth and Settlement of Capital Market Segments, Bombay Stock Exchange

Month/Year	No. of Companies/ Listed*	No. of Trading Days	No. of Trades (lakhs)	Total Shares Traded (crore)	Total Turnover (Rs crore)	Total Average Daily Turnover (Rs crore)	Market Capitalization (Rs crore)	% to GDP	Number of Shares Crore	Per cent of Total Shares Traded	Total Deliveries Value (Rs crore)	Per cent of Total Turnover
1	2	3	4	5	6	7	8	9	10	11	12	13
2011–12												
Apr-11	5069	18	327	623	69336	3852	6908090		219	35.2	17952	25.9
May-11	5078	22	336	539	59494	2704	6731869		215	39.8	15828	26.6
Jun-11	5085	22	335	571	59337	2697	6730947		216	37.9	15983	26.9
Jul-11	5096	21	337	630	59555	2836	6617273		233	36.9	16217	27.2
Aug-11	5086	21	331	563	53301	2538	6061626		224	39.7	15049	28.2
Sep-11	5092	21	334	518	54360	2589	5953887		201	38.8	14094	25.9
Oct-11	5102	19	279	374	43515	2290	6240155		152	40.7	11408	26.2
Nov-11	5105	20	295	464	43872	2194	5672255		211	45.4	11684	26.6
Dec-11	5112	21	269	407	39492	1881	5348645		170	41.9	11521	29.2
Jan-12	5115	22	352	546	52571	2390	6059347		211	38.7	13788	26.2
Feb-12	5122	20	415	683	69947	3497	6356697		240	35.2	18722	26.8
Mar-12	5133	22	333	624	62717	2851	6214941		268	42.9	19263	30.7
1993–4	3585	218	123	758	84536	388	368071	41.3	na		15861	18.8
1994–5	4702	231	196	1072	67749	293	468837	44.8	447	41.7	26641	39.3
1995–6	5603	232	171	772	50064	216	563748	46.0	268	34.7	11527	23.0
1996–7	5832	240	155	809	124190	517	505137	35.6	212	26.2	10993	8.9
1997–8	5853	244	196	859	207113	849	630221	40.1	244	28.4	22512	10.9
1998–9	5849	243	354	1293	310750	1279	619532	34.4	506	39.1	85617	27.6
1999–2000	5815	251	740	2086	686428	2735	912842	45.4	943	45.2	174740	25.3
2000–1	5869	251	1428	2585	1000032	3984	571553	26.4	867	33.5	166941	16.7
2001–2	5782	247	1277	1822	307292	1244	612224	26.1	577	31.7	59980	19.5
2002–3	5650	251	1413	2214	314073	1251	572197	22.6	699	31.6	48741	15.5
2003–4	5528	254	2028	3904	503053	1981	1201207	42.3	1332	34.1	107153	21.3
2004–5	4731	253	2374	4772	518715	2050	1698428	52.4	1875	39.3	140056	27.0
2005–6	4781	251	2639	6644	816073	3251	3022191	81.8	3007	47.6	320111	39.2
2006–7	4821	249	3462	5608	956185	3840	3545041	82.5	2297	41.1	298885	31.3
2007–8	4887	251	5303	9860	1578856	6290	5138015	103.0	3616	36.9	478034	30.3
2008–9	4929	243	5408	7396	1100074	4527	3086076	54.8	1966	26.7	230332	20.9
2009–10	4975	244	6056	11365	1378809	5651	6165619	95.5	3636	32.0	311364	22.6
2010–11	5067	255	5285	9908	1105027	4333	6839084	89.1	3769	38.0	302126	27.3
2011–12	5133	249	3944	6541	667498	2681	6214941	69.7	2560	39.1	181560	27.2

Source: BSE-Key Statistics.

Table A5.10 Working of Clearing Corporation of India Limited (CCIL)

	Outright			Repo			Forex*			CBLO**		
	Number of Trades	Average Trades	Volume	Average Volume	Number of Trades	Average Trades	Volume	Average Volume	Number of Trades	Average Trades	Volume	Average Volume	Number of Trades	Average Trades	Volume	Average Volume

	Number of Trades	Average Trades	Volume	Average Volume	Number of Trades	Average Trades	Volume	Average Volume	Number of Trades	Average Trades	Volume	Average Volume	Number of Trades	Average Trades	Volume	Average Volume
2002–3	191843	646	1076147	3623	11672	39	468229	1577	100232	1101	136102	1496	159	3	852	16
2003–4	243585	820	1575133	5303	20927	71	943189	3208	330517	1425	501342	2161	3060	10	76851	262
2004–5	160682	550	1134222	3884	24364	83	1557907	5335	466327	1976	899782	3813	29351	101	976757	3345
2005–6	125509	467	864751	3215	25673	88	1694509	5803	489649	2084	1179688	5020	67463	229	2953134	10045
2006–7	137100	562	1021536	4187	29008	99	2556501	8755	606808	2550	1776981	7466	85881	292	4732271	16096
2007–8	188843	765	1653851	6696	26612	91	3948751	13523	757074	3181	3133665	13167	113277	385	8110828	27588
2008–9	245964	1047	2160233	9192	24280	85	4094286	14266	837520	3657	3758904	16414	118941	414	8824784	30748
2009–10	316956	1332	2913890	12243	28651	101	6072829	21308	883949	3843	2988971	12996	142052	498	15541378	54531
2010–11	332540	1346	2870952	11623	27409	93	4099284	13943	1150037	4792	4191037	17463	145383	495	12259745	41700
2011–12	412266	1732	3488203	14656	29806	102	3763877	12934	1283178	5579	4642573	20185	143949	495	11155428	38335
Apr-11	14735	921	131216	8201	1922	96	288957	14448	79165	4948	337134	21071	11281	564	1123203	56160
May-11	20201	962	168386	8018	2829	113	397430	15897	102173	5109	381797	19090	12219	489	1023117	40925
Jun-11	37286	1695	301242	13693	3002	115	432893	16650	104404	4746	421159	19144	13163	506	1074134	41313
Jul-11	31155	1558	271702	13585	2481	95	293702	11296	97252	5119	342443	18023	11808	454	1066156	41006
Aug-11	40537	2027	337403	16870	2547	106	354985	14791	112083	5604	414273	20714	11262	469	939134	39131
Sep-11	30777	1539	270500	13525	2396	100	333486	13895	125709	6616	406327	21386	13348	556	1082850	45119
Oct-11	24193	1344	204016	11334	2266	99	303543	13198	107213	6307	355334	20902	11550	502	957934	41649
Nov-11	30660	1533	237619	11881	2332	97	318173	13257	123940	6886	383888	21327	10926	455	789739	32906
Dec-11	55540	2645	465586	22171	2415	93	258626	9947	115349	5767	389073	19454	10948	421	688828	26493
Jan-12	61783	2942	529194	25200	2217	89	222805	8912	105034	5528	395900	20837	11285	451	698979	27959
Feb-12	39452	2076	341994	18000	2784	121	279898	12169	101814	5091	390382	19519	11858	516	761801	33122
Mar-12	25947	1297	229346	11467	2615	105	279377	11175	109042	5452	424862	21243	14301	572	949556	37982

Notes: * Commenced operations from 12 November 2002, cash and Tom settlement is with effect from 5 February 2004.
** Commenced operation from 20 January 2003.

Source: Rakshitra, CCIL.

A6 PRICES

Table A6.1 Wholesale Price Index: Point-to-Point and Average Annual Changes

Year	Point-to-Point (Mar–Mar)				Average			
	All Commodities	Annual Change (per cent)	Food Index	Annual Change (per cent)	All Commodities	Annual Change (per cent)	Food Index	Annual Change (per cent)
Base Year August 1939=100								
1950–1					409.7	—	416.4	—
1951–2					434.6	6.1	398.3	−4.3
1952–3	385.2		365.0		380.6	−12.4	351.3	−11.8
Base Year 1952–3=100								
1953–4	100.3	0.3	98.6	0.3	101.2	1.2	100.1	0.1
1954–5	90.8	−9.5	82.9	−15.9	89.6	−11.5	82.1	−18.0
1955–6	98.1	8.0	92.8	11.9	92.5	3.2	86.3	5.1
1956–7	105.6	7.6	102.3	10.2	105.3	13.8	102.3	18.5
1957–8	105.4	−0.2	102.3	0.0	108.4	2.9	106.4	4.0
1958–9	112.4	6.6	113.8	11.2	112.9	4.2	115.2	8.3
1959–60	118.9	5.8	117.0	2.8	117.1	3.7	119.3	3.6
1960–1	127.5	7.2	117.5	0.4	124.9	6.7	120.0	0.6
1961–2	123.5	−3.1	119.1	1.4	125.1	0.2	120.1	0.1
1962–3	127.1	2.9	123.4	3.6	127.9	2.2	126.1	5.0
Base Year 1961–2=100								
1962–3	104.4	4.4	104.2	4.2	103.8	3.8	105.0	5.0
1963–4	113.3	8.5	120.2	15.4	110.2	6.2	113.9	8.5
1964–5	122.6	8.2	132.8	10.5	122.3	11.0	133.1	16.9
1965–6	136.8	11.6	149.1	12.3	131.6	7.6	145.0	8.9
1966–7	159.4	16.5	188.6	26.5	149.9	13.9	171.0	17.9
1967–8	159.7	0.2	192.9	2.3	167.3	11.6	208.0	21.6
1968–9	164.8	3.2	186.2	−3.5	165.4	−1.1	197.0	−5.3
1969–70	175.9	6.7	199.8	7.3	171.6	3.7	197.0	0.0
1970–1	181.6	3.2	201.4	0.8	181.1	5.5	204.0	3.6
1971–2	192.2	5.8	216.2	7.3	188.4	4.0	210.0	2.9

(*Contd.*)

Table A6.1 (*Contd.*)

Year	Point-to-Point (Mar-Mar)				Average			
	All Commodities	Annual Change (per cent)	Food Index	Annual Change (per cent)	All Commodities	Annual Change (per cent)	Food Index	Annual Change (per cent)
Base Year 1970-1=100								
1971–2	108.1	8.2	110.1	10.1	105.6	5.6	106.3	6.3
1972–3	121.9	12.8	128.2	16.4	116.2	10.0	123.0	15.8
1973–4	157.5	29.2	154.8	20.8	139.7	20.2	147.5	19.9
1974–5	174.6	10.9	172.9	11.7	174.9	25.2	176.6	19.7
1975–6	162.6	–6.9	145.4	–15.9	173.0	–1.1	169.3	–4.2
1976–7	182.9	12.5	172.4	18.6	176.6	2.1	165.5	–2.2
1977–8	182.9	0.0	168.1	–2.5	185.8	5.2	177.1	7.0
1978–9	189.0	3.3	164.9	–1.9	185.8	0.0	167.4	–5.5
1979–80	232.6	23.1	209.7	27.2	217.6	17.1	195.6	16.9
1980–1	269.5	15.9	245.1	16.9	257.3	18.2	239.2	22.3
1981–2	276.4	2.6	238.8	–2.6	281.3	9.3	254.8	6.5
1982–3	294.3	6.5	257.8	7.9	288.7	2.6	252.3	–1.0
Base Year 1981–2=100								
1982–3	107.1	7.1	109.0	9.0	104.9	4.9	106.8	6.8
1983–4	114.8	7.2	119.4	9.5	112.8	7.5	119.8	12.2
1984–5	121.2	5.6	122.2	2.3	120.1	6.5	125.2	4.5
1985–6	127.4	5.1	128.5	5.2	125.4	4.4	127.9	2.2
1986–7	134.2	5.3	138.6	7.8	132.7	5.8	140.9	10.2
1987–8	148.5	10.7	157.7	13.9	143.6	8.2	153.5	8.9
1988–9	156.6	5.5	164.7	4.4	154.3	7.5	166.3	8.3
1989–90	170.1	8.6	173.1	5.1	165.7	7.4	174.1	4.7
1990–1	191.7	12.7	204.0	17.9	182.7	10.3	193.6	11.2
1991–2	217.7	13.6	239.4	17.3	207.8	13.7	228.8	18.2
1992–3	233.1	7.1	256.8	7.3	228.6	10.0	253.7	10.9
1993–4	257.6	10.5	270.0	5.2	247.8	8.4	270.5	6.6
1994–5	284.9	10.6	298.9	10.7	274.7	10.9	297.2	9.9

Base Year 1993–4=100

Year								
1994–5	116.9	16.9	114.1	14.1	112.8	12.8	115.3	15.3
1995–6	122.2	4.5	120.3	5.4	121.6	7.8	122.8	6.5
1996–7	128.8	5.4	135.0	12.2	127.2	4.7	132.4	7.8
1997–8	134.4	4.3	140.3	3.9	132.8	4.3	137.8	4.1
1998–9	141.6	5.4	153.8	9.6	140.7	6.0	154.2	11.9
1999–2000	149.5	5.6	160.6	4.4	145.3	3.2	155.7	1.0
2000–1	159.1	6.4	157.8	−1.7	155.7	7.2	156.7	0.6
2001–2	161.9	1.8	162.7	3.1	161.3	3.6	163.2	4.1
2002–3	171.6	6.0	168.8	3.7	166.8	3.4	167.9	2.9
2003–4	179.8	4.8	174.9	3.6	175.9	5.5	175.2	4.3
2004–5	189.4	5.3	180.1	3.0	187.3	6.5	181.4	3.5

Base Year 2004–5=100

Year								
2005–6	105.7	4.2	103.9	5.2	105.7	4.2	103.6	3.6
2006–7	112.8	6.7	113.9	9.6	112.8	6.7	111.8	7.9
2007–8	121.5	7.7	121.6	6.7	121.5	7.7	118.1	5.6
2008–9	123.5	1.6	130.5	7.3	123.5	1.6	128.7	9.0
2009–10	136.3	10.4	154.6	18.5	136.3	10.4	147.4	14.5
2010–11	149.5	9.7	165.1	6.8	149.5	9.7	163.8	11.1
2011–12	159.8	6.9	179.1	8.5	159.8	6.9	175.6	7.2

Note: With effect from 17 October 2009 Office of the Economic Adviser discontinued dessimination of price data on a weekly basis and started giving monthly data from September. Hence in this table point-to-point basis has been worked out by using March data instead of end-March data for all the years.

Source: Office of the Economic Adviser, Ministry of Commerce and Industry, Government of India.

Table A6.2 Cost of Living Indices

(A) Consumer Price Index for Industrial Workers

Year	Annual Average					Point-to-Point			
	Total Index	Annual Change (per cent)	Food Index	Annual Change (per cent)		Total Index	Annual Change (per cent)	Food Index	Annual Change (per cent)
1	2	3	4	5		6	7	8	9
Base Year = 1949=100									
1950-1	101	na	na	na		103	na	na	na
1951-2	105	4.0	na	na		98	-4.9	na	na
1952-3	104	-1.0	na	na		104	6.1	105	na
1953-4	106	1.9	109	na		101	-2.9	101	-3.8
1954-5	99	-6.6	101	-7.3		96	-5.0	92	-8.9
1955-6	96	-3.0	92	-8.9		105	9.4	105	14.1
1956-7	107	11.5	105	14.1		111	5.7	112	6.7
1957-8	112	4.7	112	6.7		116	4.5	118	5.4
1958-9	118	5.4	118	5.4		121	4.3	125	5.9
1959-60	123	4.2	125	5.9		124	2.5	126	0.8
1960-1	124	0.8	126	0.8		126	1.6	126	0.0
1961-2	127	2.4	126	0.0		131	4.0	130	3.2
1962-3	131	3.1	131	4.0		134	2.3	135	3.8
1963-4	137	4.6	138	5.3		143	6.7	143	5.9
1964-5	157	14.6	162	17.4		159	11.2	162	13.3
1965-6	169	7.6	174	7.4		174	9.4	177	9.3
1966-7	191	13.0	198	13.8		200	14.9	210	18.6
1967-8	213	11.5	228	15.2		213	6.5	226	7.6
1968-9	212	-0.5	223	-2.2		207	-2.8	212	-6.2
Base Year 1960=100									
1968-9	174	-18.3	192	-15.8		170		183	
1969-70	177	1.7	193	0.5		179	5.3	194	6.0
1970-1	186	5.1	202	4.7		184	2.8	195	0.5
1971-2	192	3.2	205	1.5		194	5.4	205	5.1
1972-3	207	7.8	223	8.8		216	11.3	236	15.1
1973-4	250	20.8	279	25.1		275	27.3	305	29.2
1974-5	317	26.8	358	28.3		321	16.7	359	17.7
1975-6	313	-1.3	342	-4.5		286	-10.9	296	-17.5
1976-7	301	-3.8	317	-7.3		312	9.1	332	12.2
1977-8	324	7.6	345	8.8		321	2.9	336	1.2
1978-9	331	2.2	346	0.3		332	3.4	341	1.5

Year								
1979-80	360	8.8	373	7.8	373	12.3	385	12.9
1980-1	401	11.4	419	12.3	420	12.6	437	13.5
1981-2	451	12.5	476	13.6	457	8.8	475	8.7
1982-3	486	7.8	508	6.7	502	9.8	522	9.9
1983-4	547	12.6	581	14.4	558	11.2	583	11.7
Base Year 1982=100								
1983-4	111	11.0	117	17.0	114	14.0	117	17.0
1984-5	118	6.3	122	4.3	120	5.3	120	2.6
1985-6	126	6.8	128	4.9	130	8.3	132	10.0
1986-7	137	8.7	141	10.2	138	6.2	142	7.6
1987-8	149	8.8	152	7.8	153	10.9	156	9.9
1988-9	163	9.4	169	11.2	163	6.5	169	8.3
1989-90	173	6.1	177	4.7	177	8.6	178	5.3
1990-1	193	11.6	199	12.4	201	13.6	207	16.3
1991-2	219	13.5	230	15.6	229	13.9	241	16.4
1992-3	240	9.6	254	10.4	243	6.1	253	5.0
1993-4	258	7.5	272	7.1	267	9.9	281	11.1
1994-5	279	8.1	297	9.2	293	9.7	311	10.7
1995-6	313	12.2	337	13.5	319	8.9	339	9.0
1996-7	342	9.3	369	9.5	351	10.0	373	10.0
1997-8	366	7.0	388	5.1	380	8.3	401	7.5
1998-99	414	13.1	445	14.7	414	8.9	445	11.0
1999-2000	428	3.4	446	0.2	434	4.8	446	0.2
2000-1	444	3.7	453	1.6	445	2.5	446	0.0
2001-2	463	4.3	446	−1.5	468	5.2	462	3.6
2002-3	482	4.1	477	7.0	487	4.1	479	3.7
2003-4	500	3.8	495	3.8	504	3.5	494	3.1
2004-5	520	3.9	506	2.2	525	4.2	502	1.6
Base Year 2001=100								
2004-5	112	3.9	na	na	113	3.7	na	na
2005-6	117	4.3	na	na	119	5.3	na	na
2006-7	125	6.7	126	na	127	6.7	129	na
2007-8	133	6.4	136	7.9	137	7.9	141	9.3
2008-9	145	9.0	153	12.5	148	8.0	156	10.6
2009-10	163	12.4	176	15.0	170	14.9	181	16.0
2010-11	180	10.4	194	10.2	185	8.8	196	8.3
2011-12	195	8.3	na	na	201		na	

Note: na: not available.
Source: Labour Bureau.

Table A6.3 Cost of Living Index

(B) Consumer Price Index for Agricultural Labourers

July–June	Annual Average*				Point-to-Point**			
	Total Index	Annual Change (per cent)	Food Index	Annual Change (per cent)	Total Index	Annual Change (per cent)	Food Index	Annual Change (per cent)
1	2	3	4	5	6	7	8	9
Base Year 1960=100								
1964-5	143		na				na	
1965-6	153	7.0	na		156		na	
1966-7	190	24.2	na		207	32.7	na	
1967-8	206	8.4	na		191	-7.7	na	
1968-9	185	-10.2	na		186	-2.6	na	
1969-70	193	4.3	na		196	5.4	na	
1970-1	192	-0.7	206		189	-3.6	202	
1971-2	200	4.2	215	4.4	204	7.9	220	8.9
1972-3	225	12.9	246	14.4	242	18.6	266	20.9
1973-4	283	25.4	313	27.2	321	32.6	356	33.8
1974-5	368	30.3	413	31.8	375	16.8	420	18.0
1975-6	317	-13.9	345	-16.4	280	-25.3	298	-29.0
1976-7	302	-4.8	324	-6.2	319	13.9	345	15.8
1977-8	323	7.1	349	7.9	312	-2.2	334	-3.2
1978-9	317	-1.7	340	-2.6	318	1.9	340	1.8
1979-80	360	13.3	390	14.4	376	18.2	409	20.3
1980-1	409	13.9	449	15.2	429	14.1	470	14.9
1981-2	448	9.5	492	9.6	443	3.3	483	2.8
1982-3	481	7.4	527	7.2	509	14.9	559	15.7
1983-4	523	8.5	573	8.6	511	0.4	555	-0.7
1984-5	525	0.5	569	-0.7	530	3.7	570	2.7
1985-6	555	5.6	600	5.5	561	5.8	606	6.3
1986-7	578	4.2	623	3.9	588	4.8	633	4.5
1987-8	650	12.6	706	13.3	671	14.1	728	15.0
1988-9	724	11.3	791	12.0	736	9.7	802	10.2
1989-90	752	3.9	814	2.9	759	3.1	817	1.9
1990-1	830	10.4	900	10.5	876	15.4	949	16.2
1991-2	1007	21.3	1106	22.9	1068	21.9	1175	23.8

1992–3	1072	6.5	1171	5.9	1057	−1.0	1145	−2.6
1993–4	1147	7.0	1251	6.9	1189	12.5	1295	13.1
1994–5	1283	11.9	1400	11.9	1337	12.4	1455	12.4
Base Year 1986–87=100								
1995–6	239		241		247		250	
1996–7	260	8.6	264	9.4	259	4.9	258	3.2
1997–8	269	3.5	269	2.1	282	8.9	286	10.9
1998–9	299	11.1	305	13.3	301	6.7	306	7.0
1999–2000	309	3.5	314	2.8	310	3.0	310	1.3
2000–1	304	−1.7	299	−4.7	306	−1.3	299	−3.5
2001–2	311	2.2	304	1.6	314	2.6	306	2.3
2002–3	323	3.8	316	4.0	330	5.1	324	5.9
2003–4	332	3.0	326	3.0	336	1.8	329	1.5
2004–5	342	2.9	335	2.8	345	2.7	336	2.1
2005–6	358	4.7	351	4.9	370	7.2	365	8.6
2006–7	380	6.1	376	7.0	392	5.9	389	6.6
2007–8	409	7.6	406	8.2	423	7.9	422	8.5
2008–9	462	13.0	464	14.2	484	14.4	488	15.6
2009–10	530	14.7	540	16.4	547	13.0	555	13.7
2010–11	579	9.2	582	7.8	598	9.3	593	6.8

Notes: * Average based on Agricultural year i.e July–June of every year.
** June over June every year.
na: not available.
Base is revised to 1986-7 w.e.f. November 1995.
Though the base of the series is 1960 = 100, the data is available only from September 1964.

Source: Labour Bureau, Ministry of Labour & Employment, Government of India.

A7 BALANCE OF PAYMENTS

Table A7.1 Foreign Exchange Reserves (End Period)

End of	SDRs			Gold			Foreign Currency Assets			Reserve Tranche Position in IMF			Total	
	In million SDRs	Rupees crore	In millions of US Dollar		Rupees crore	In millions of US Dollar		Rupees crore	In millions of US Dollar		Rupees crore	In millions of US Dollar	Rupees crore	In millions of US Dollar
1	2	3	4		5	6		7	8		9	10	11	12
1990-1	76	200	102		6828	3496		4388	2236				11416	5834
1991-2	66	233	90		9039	3499		14578	5631				23850	9220
1992-3	13	55	18		10549	3380		20140	6434				30744	9832
1993-4	76	339	108		12794	4078		47287	15068				60420	19254
1994-5	5	23	7		13752	4370		66006	20809				79781	25186
1995-6	56	280	82		15658	4561		58446	17044				74384	21687
1996-7	1	7	2		14557	4054		80368	22367				94932	26423
1997-8	1	4	1		13394	3391		102507	25975				115905	29367
1998-9	6	34	8		12559	2960		125412	29522				138005	32490
1999-2000	3	16	4		12973	2974		152924	35058				165913	38036
2000-1	2	11	2		12711	2725		184482	39554				197204	42281
2001-2	8	50	10		14868	3047		249118	51049				264036	54106
2002-3	3	19	4		16785	3534		341476	71890		3190	672	361470	76100
2003-4	2	10	2		18216	4198		466215	107448		5688	1311	490129	112959
2004-5	3	20	5		19686	4500		593121	135571		6289	1438	619116	141514
2005-6	2	12	3		25674	5755		647327	145108		3374	756	676387	151622
2006-7	1	8	2		29573	6784		836597	191924		2044	469	868222	199179
2007-8	11	74	18		40124	10039		1196023	299230		1744	436	1237965	309723
2008-9	1	–	1		48800	9577		1230100	241426		5000	981	1283900	251985
2009-10	3297	22600	5006		81200	17986		1149700	254685		6200	1380	1259700	279057
2010-11	2882	20400	4569		102600	22972		1224900	274330		13200	2947	1361000	304818
2011-12														
April-11	2882	20700	4671		105600	23790		1251700	282037		13400	3013	1391400	313511
May-11	2882	20800	4613		109800	24391		1258800	279537		13400	2975	1402800	311516
June-11	2883	20600	4614		110300	24668		1267600	283458		13300	2975	1411900	315715
July-11	2883	20400	4609		111900	25349		1263700	286160		13100	2972	1409100	319090
Aug-11	2884	21300	4638		130300	28319		1316300	286034		13800	2991	1481800	321982
Sep-11	2884	22000	4504		140300	28667		1349000	275699		12800	2612	1524100	311482

Oct-11	2884	22400	4574	131400	26896	1378600	282087	13000	2653	1545300	316210
Nov-11	2885	23400	4476	146300	28041	1423000	272771	13500	2596	1606200	307884
Dec-11	2885	23600	4429	141800	26620	1400600	262933	14400	2706	1580400	296688
Jan-12	2885	22200	4475	132800	26728	1285900	258830	13600	2734	1454500	292766
Feb-12	2885	22000	4490	137700	28128	1275100	260544	13800	2828	1448600	295989
Mar-12											

Notes: 1. Gold was valued at Rs.84.39 per 10 grams till 16 October 1990. It has been valued close to international market price with effect from 17 October 1990.
2. Conversion of SDRs into US dollar is done at exchange rates released by the IMF.
3. With effect from 1 April 1991 the conversion of foreign currency assets into US dollar is done at week end rates for week end–data and or month–end rate for month end–data based on New York closing exchange rates. Prior to that it was done by using representative exchange rate released by the IMF.
4. Since March 1993, foreign exchange holdings are converted into rupees at rupee–US dollar market exchange rates.
5. Reserve tranche position has been reported as part of reserves since 2002–3.

Source: RBI: Monthly Bulletin (various issues).

Table A7.2 Balance of Payments 1990–1 to 2010–11

(US$ million)

Year / Item	1990–1 Cedit	1990–1 Debit	1990–1 Net	1991–2 Cedit	1991–2 Debit	1991–2 Net	1992–3 Cedit	1992–3 Debit	1992–3 Net	1993–4 Cedit	1993–4 Debit	1993–4 Net	1994–5 Cedit	1994–5 Debit	1994–5 Net
A. Current Account															
1. Merchandise	18477	27915	–9438	18266	21064	–2798	18869	24316	–5447	22683	26739	–4056	26855	35904	–9049
2. Invisibles	7464	7706	–242	9502	7882	1620	9334	7413	1921	11319	8422	2897	15554	9874	5680
a. Services	4551	3571	980	5022	3815	1207	4730	3601	1129	5264	4730	534	6135	5533	602
a.1. Travel	1456	392	1064	1977	465	1512	2098	385	1713	2222	497	1725	2365	818	1547
a.2. Transportation	983	1093	–110	939	1288	–349	982	1485	–503	1433	1765	–332	1696	1863	–167
a.3. Insurance	111	88	23	108	126	–18	158	146	12	124	196	–72	152	181	–29
a.4. G.n.i.e.	15	173	–158	17	120	–103	75	100	–25	30	153	–123	10	165	–155
a.5. Miscellaneous	1986	1825	161	1981	1816	165	1417	1485	–68	1455	2119	–664	1912	2506	–594
Soft Ware Services															
Business Services															
Financial Services															
Communication Services															
b. Transfers	2545	15	2530	4258	16	4242	4228	13	4215	5660	27	5633	8533	24	8509
b.1. Official Transfers	462	1	461	460	1	459	364	1	363	374	5	369	421	5	416
b.2. Private Transfers	2083	14	2069	3798	15	3783	3864	12	3852	5286	22	5264	8112	19	8093
c. Income	368	4120	–3752	222	4051	–3829	376	3799	–3423	395	3665	–3270	886	4317	–3431
c.1. Investment Income	368	4120	–3752	222	4051	–3829	376	3799	–3423	395	3665	–3270	886	4317	–3431
c.2. Compensation of Employees	.	.	.	.	.	.	.	.	.	.	.	.	.	.	.
Total Current Account (1+2)	25941	35621	–9680	27768	28946	–1178	28203	31729	–3526	34002	35161	–1159	42409	45778	–3369
B. Capital Account															
1. Foreign Investment (a+b)	113	10	103	151	18	133	589	32	557	4609	376	4233	5763	956	4807
a. Foreign Investment in India	113	10	103	151	18	133	589	32	557	4609	376	4233	5753	831	4922
a.1. Foreign Direct Investment in India	107	10	97	147	18	129	345	30	315	651	65	586	1351	8	1343
a.2. Foreign Portfolio Investment in India	6	0	6	4	0	4	244	2	242	3958	311	3647	4402	823	3579
b. Foreign Investment Abroad	.	.	.	.	.	.	.	.	.	0	0	0	10	125	–115
2. Loans (a+b+c)	9432	3899	5533	9419	5437	3982	8671	8260	411	9970	8158	1812	10930	7895	3035
a. External Assistance	3397	1193	2204	4367	1333	3034	3302	1446	1856	3475	1580	1895	3193	1675	1518
a.1. External Assistance by India	0	6	–6	0	5	–5	0	3	–3	0	6	–6	2	10	–8
a.2. External Assistance to India	3397	1187	2210	4367	1328	3039	3302	1443	1859	3475	1574	1901	3191	1665	1526

b. Commercial Borrowings (MT & LT)	4282	2028	2254	3152	1690	1462	1179	1545	-366	3015	2329	686	4249	3125	1124
b.1. Commercial Borrowings by India	30	24	6	19	13	6	12	20	-8	102	24	78	97	3	94
b.2. Commercial Borrowings to India	4252	2004	2248	3133	1677	1456	1167	1525	-358	2913	2305	608	4152	3122	1030
c. Short Term Credit to India	1753	678	1075	1900	2414	-514	4190	5269	-1079	3480	4249	-769	3488	3095	393
3. Banking Capital (a=b)	10106	9424	682	10961	10394	567	11998	8172	3826	11501	9237	2264	7020	7354	-334
a. Commercial Banks	7960	7056	904	9068	8930	138	10653	7723	2930	10614	8956	1658	6449	7075	-626
a.1. Assets of Commercial Banks	425	789	-364	1336	1107	229	1234	161	1073	276	1120	-844	241	1203	-962
a.2. Liabilities of Commercial Banks	7535	6267	1268	7732	7823	-91	9419	7562	1857	10338	7836	2502	6208	5872	336
a.2.a. Non-Resident Deposits of Commercial Banks	7348	5811	1537	7696	7406	290	9188	7187	2001	8851	7644	1207	5805	5633	172
b. Others	2146	2368	-222	1893	1464	429	1345	449	896	887	281	606	571	279	292
4. Rupee Debt Service	0	1193	-1193	0	1240	-1240	0	878	-878	0	1054	-1054	0	983	-983
5. Other Capital	3117	1186	1931	2808	2335	473	1359	1399	-40	2873	1234	1639	2202	225	1977
B. Capital Account	22768	15712	7056	23339	19424	3915	22617	18741	3876	28953	20059	8894	25915	17413	8502
C. Errors and Omissions	132	0	132	0	138	-138	0	0	0	800	800	0	654	0	654
D. Overall Balance	48841	51333	-2492	51107	48508	2599	50820	51410	-590	63755	55220	8535	68978	63191	5787
E. Monetary Movements	3136	644	2492	1245	3844	-2599	1623	1033	590	321	8856	-8535	0	5787	-5787
E.1. I.M.F	1858	644	1214	1245	460	785	1623	335	1288	321	133	188	0	1143	-1143
E.2. Foreign Exchange Reserves (Increase –/Decrease +) SDR Allocation	1278	0	1278	0	3384	-3384	0	698	-698	0	8723	-8723	0	4644	-4644

(Contd.)

Table A7.2 (Contd.)

(US$ million)

Year / Item	1995–6 Cedit	1995–6 Debit	1995–6 Net	1996–7 Cedit	1996–7 Debit	1996–7 Net	1997–8 Cedit	1997–8 Debit	1997–8 Net	1998–9 Cedit	1998–9 Debit	1998–9 Net	1999–2000 Cedit	1999–2000 Debit	1999–2000 Net
A. Current Account															
1. Merchandise	32310	43670	−11359	34133	48948	−14815	35680	51187	−15507	34298	47544	−13246	37542	55383	−17841
2. Invisibles	17664	12217	5447	21405	11209	10196	23244	13236	10008	25770	16562	9208	30312	17169	13143
a. Services	7344	7544	−200	7474	6748	726	9429	8110	1319	13186	11021	2165	15709	11645	4064
a.1. Travel	2712	1168	1544	2878	858	2020	2914	1437	1477	2993	1743	1250	3036	2139	897
a.2. Transportation	2011	2169	−158	1953	2394	−441	1836	2522	−686	1925	2680	−755	1707	2410	−703
a.3. Insurance	179	143	36	217	153	64	240	183	57	224	112	112	231	122	109
a.4. G.n.i.e.	13	218	−205	72	178	−106	276	160	116	597	325	272	582	270	312
a.5. Miscellaneous	2430	3847	−1417	2354	3165	−811	4163	3808	355	7447	6161	1286	10153	6704	3449
Soft Ware Services															
Business Services															
Financial Services															
Communication Services															
b. Transfers	8891	39	8852	12858	81	12777	12254	45	12209	10649	62	10587	12672	34	12638
b.1. Official Transfers	351	6	345	423	13	410	379	0	379	308	1	307	382	0	382
b.2. Private Transfers	8540	32	8507	12435	68	12367	11875	45	11830	10341	61	10280	12290	34	12256
c. Income	1430	4634	−3205	1073	4380	−3307	1561	5081	−3520	1935	5479	−3544	1931	5490	−3559
c.1. Investment Income	1430	4634	−3205	1073	4380	−3307	1561	5020	−3459	1893	5462	−3569	1783	5478	−3695
c.2. Compensation of Employees	.	.	.	.	.	.	0	61	−61	42	17	25	148	12	136
Total Current Account (1+2)	49974	55886	−5912	55538	60157	−4619	58924	64423	−5499	60068	64106	−4038	67854	72552	−4698
B. Capital Account															
1. Foreign Investment (a+b)	5644	1029	4615	7825	1861	5964	9266	3913	5353	5892	3580	2312	12240	7123	5117
a. Foreign Investment in India	5629	826	4804	7817	1663	6154	9169	3779	5390	5743	3331	2412	12121	6930	5191
a.1. Foreign Direct Investment in India	2174	30	2143	2864	22	2842	3596	34	3562	2518	38	2480	2170	3	2167
a.2. Foreign Portfolio Investment in India	3456	795	2660	4953	1641	3312	5573	3745	1828	3225	3293	−68	9951	6927	3024
b. Foreign Investment Abroad	15	203	−188	8	198	−190	97	134	−37	149	249	−100	119	193	−74
2. Loans (a+b+c)	11331	9132	2200	17720	12925	4795	17301	12502	4799	14771	10353	4418	13060	11459	1601
a. External Assistance	2933	2066	868	3056	1955	1101	2885	2000	885	2726	1927	799	3074	2183	891
a.1. External Assistance by India	0	17	−17	0	8	−8	0	22	−22	0	21	−21	0	10	−10
a.2. External Assistance to India	2933	2049	884	3056	1947	1109	2885	1978	907	2726	1906	820	3074	2173	901

b. Commercial Borrowings (MT & LT)	4261	2977	1284	7579	4723	2856	7382	3372	4010	7231	2864	4367	3207	2874	333
b.1. Commercial Borrowings by India	9	0	9	8	0	8	11	0	11	5	0	5	20	0	20
b.2. Commercial Borrowings to India	4252	2977	1275	7571	4723	2848	7371	3372	3999	7226	2864	4362	3187	2874	313
c. Short Term Credit to India	4137	4089	48	7085	6247	838	7034	7130	-96	4814	5562	-748	6779	6402	377
3. Banking Capital (a=b)	6453	5690	763	8018	5789	2229	8910	9803	-893	8898	8199	699	10659	8532	2127
a. Commercial Banks	6172	5234	938	7632	5407	2225	8164	9424	-1260	7469	7916	-447	10259	7955	2304
a.1. Assets of Commercial Banks	867	1252	-385	755	1625	-870	580	2775	-2195	1344	2741	-1397	2653	1863	790
a.2. Liabilities of Commercial Banks	5304	3982	1322	6877	3782	3095	7584	6649	935	6125	5175	950	7606	6092	1514
a.2.a. Non-Resident Deposits of Commercial Banks	4929	3824	1104	6775	3425	3350	7532	6407	1125	6001	5040	961	7405	5865	1540
b. Others	281	456	-175	386	382	4	746	379	367	1429	283	1146	400	577	-177
4. Rupee Debt Service	0	952	-952	0	727	-727	0	767	-767	0	802	-802	0	711	-711
5. Other Capital	748	3285	-2537	2629	2883	-254	3815	2463	1352	4611	2801	1810	4572	2262	2310
B. Capital Account	24176	20087	4089	36192	24185	12007	39292	29448	9844	34172	25735	8437	40531	30087	10444
C. Errors and Omissions	601	0	601	0	595	-595	166	0	166	0	177	-177	656	0	656
D. Overall Balance	74752	75974	-1222	91730	84937	6793	98382	93871	4511	94240	90018	4222	109041	102639	6402
E. Monetary Movements	2937	1715	1222	0	6793	-6793	0	4511	-4511	0	4222	-4222	0	6402	-6402
E.1. I.M.F	0	1715	-1715	0	975	-975	0	618	-618	0	393	-393	0	260	-260
E.2. Foreign Exchange Reserves (Increase –/ Decrease +)	2937	0	2937	0	5818	-5818	0	3893	-3893	0	3829	-3829	0	6142	-6142
SDR Allocation															

(Contd.)

Table A7.2 (Contd.)

(US$ million)

Year / Item	2000–1			2001–2			2002–3			2003–4			2004–5		
	Cedit	Debit	Net	Cedit	Debit	Net	Cedit	Debit	Net	Cedit	Debit	Net	Cedit	Debit	Net
A. Current Account															
1. Merchandise	45452	57912	–12460	44703	56277	–11574	53774	64464	–10690	66285	80003	–13718	85206	118908	–33702
2. Invisibles	32267	22473	9794	36737	21763	14974	41925	24890	17035	53508	25707	27801	69533	38301	31232
a. Services	16268	14576	1692	17140	13816	3324	20763	17120	3643	26868	16724	10144	43249	27823	15426
a.1. Travel	3497	2804	693	3137	3014	123	3312	3341	–29	5037	3602	1435	6666	5249	1417
a.2. Transportation	2046	3558	–1512	2161	3467	–1306	2536	3272	–736	3207	2328	879	4683	4539	144
a.3. Insurance	270	223	47	288	280	8	369	350	19	419	363	56	870	722	148
a.4. G.n.i.e.	651	319	332	518	283	235	293	228	65	240	212	28	401	411	–10
a.5. Miscellaneous	9804	7672	2132	11036	6772	4264	14253	9929	4324	17965	10219	7746	30629	16902	13727
Soft Ware Services	6341	591	5750	7556	672	6884	9600	737	8863	12800	476	12324	17700	800	16900
Business Services	.	.	.	.	.	.	.	.	.	.	.	.	5167	7318	–2151
Financial Services	.	.	.	.	.	.	.	.	.	.	.	.	512	832	–320
Communication Services	.	.	.	.	.	.	.	.	.	.	.	.	1384	738	646
b. Transfers	13317	211	13106	16218	362	15856	17640	802	16838	22736	574	22162	21691	906	20785
b.1. Official Transfers	252	0	252	458	0	458	451	0	451	554	0	554	616	356	260
b.2. Private Transfers	13065	211	12854	15760	362	15398	17189	802	16387	22182	574	21608	21075	550	20525
c. Income	2682	7686	–5004	3379	7585	–4206	3522	6968	–3446	3904	8409	–4505	4593	9572	–4979
c.1. Investment Income	2554	7218	–4664	3254	7098	–3844	3405	6949	–3544	3774	7531	–3757	4124	8219	–4095
c.2. Compensation of Employees	128	468	–340	125	487	–362	117	19	98	130	878	–748	469	1353	–884
Total Current Account (1+2)	77719	80385	–2666	81440	78040	3400	95699	89354	6345	119793	105710	14083	154739	157209	–2470
B. Capital Account															
1. Foreign Investment (a+b)	17720	11858	5862	15488	8802	6686	14001	9840	4161	32682	18938	13744	46934	33934	13000
a. Foreign Investment in India	17650	10859	6791	15389	7243	8146	13928	7913	6015	32540	16862	15678	46899	31601	15298
a.1. Foreign Direct Investment in India	4031	0	4031	6130	5	6125	5095	59	5036	4322	0	4322	6052	65	5987
a.2. Foreign Portfolio Investment in India	13619	10859	2760	9259	7238	2021	8833	7854	979	28218	16862	11356	40847	31536	9311
b. Foreign Investment Abroad	70	999	–929	99	1559	–1460	73	1927	–1854	142	2076	–1934	35	2333	–2298
2. Loans (a+b+c)	23806	18542	5264	11601	12862	–1261	11568	15418	–3850	19667	24031	–4364	30287	19378	10909
a. External Assistance	2941	2531	410	3352	2235	1117	2878	6006	–3128	3350	6208	–2858	3809	1886	1923
a.1. External Assistance by India	0	17	–17	0	87	–87	0	32	–32	24	128	–104	24	128	–104
a.2. External Assistance to India	2941	2514	427	3352	2148	1204	2878	5974	–3096	3326	6080	–2754	3785	1758	2027

b.	Commercial Borrowings (MT & LT)	9621	5318	4303	2687	4272	-1585	3514	5206	-1692	5228	8153	-2925	9084	3890	5194
b.1.	Commercial Borrowings by India	0	5	-5	3	0	3	9	0	9	3	0	3	0	232	-232
b.2.	Commercial Borrowings to India	9621	5313	4308	2684	4272	-1588	3505	5206	-1701	5225	8153	-2928	9084	3658	5426
c.	Short Term Credit to India	11244	10693	551	5562	6355	-793	5176	4206	970	11089	9670	1419	17394	13602	3792
3.	Banking Capital (a=b)	9744	11705	-1961	13870	11006	2864	18958	8533	10425	19222	13189	6033	14581	10707	3874
a.	Commercial Banks	9423	11305	-1882	13385	10725	2660	18422	8287	10135	18887	12386	6501	14304	10325	3979
a.1.	Assets of Commercial Banks	206	4380	-4174	1267	1711	-444	6089	976	5113	950	161	789	505	552	-47
a.2.	Liabilities of Commercial Banks	9217	6925	2292	12118	9014	3104	12333	7311	5022	17937	12225	5712	13799	9773	4026
a.2.a.	Non-Resident Deposits of Commercial Banks	8988	6672	2316	11435	8681	2754	10214	7236	2978	14281	10639	3642	8071	9035	-964
b.	Others	321	400	-79	485	281	204	536	246	290	335	803	-468	277	382	-105
4.	Rupee Debt Service	0	617	-617	0	519	-519	0	474	-474	0	376	-376	0	417	-417
5.	Other Capital	2856	2564	292	2298	1517	781	1841	1263	578	4314	2615	1699	6737	6081	656
B.	Capital Account	54126	45286	8840	43257	34706	8551	46368	35528	10840	75885	59149	16736	98539	70517	28022
C.	Errors and Omissions	0	305	-305	0	194	-194	0	200	-200	602	0	602	607	0	607
D.	Overall Balance	131845	125976	5868	124697	112940	11757	142067	125082	16985	196280	164859	31421	253885	227726	26159
E.	Monetary Movements	1448	7316	-5868	0	11757	-11757	0	16985	-16985	0	31421	-31421	0	26159	-26159
	E.1.I.M.F	0	26	-26	0	0	0	0	0	0	0	0	0	0	0	0
	E.2. Foreign Exchange Reserves (Increase – / Decrease +) SDR Allocation	1448	7290	-5842	0	11757	-11757	0	16985	-16985	0	31421	-31421	0	26159	-26159

(Contd.)

Table A7.2 (Contd.)

(US$ million)

Year / Item	2005-6			2007-8 (R)			2008-9 (R)			2000-10 (R)			2010-11 (PR)		
	Cedit	Debit	Net	Cedit	Debit	Net	Cedit	Debit	Net	Cedit	Debit	Net	Cedit	Debit	Net
A. Current Account															
1. Merchandise	105152	157056	−51904	166162	257629	−91467	189001	308520	−119519	182442	300644	−118203	250468	381061	−130593
2. Invisibles	89687	47685	42002	148875	73144	75731	167819	76214	91604	163430	83408	80022	198248	113600	84647
a. Services	57659	34489	23170	90342	51490	38853	105963	52047	53916	96045	60029	36016	132880	84064	48816
a.1. Travel	7853	6638	1215	11349	9258	2091	10894	9425	1469	11859	9343	2517	15275	11108	4167
a.2. Transportation	6325	8337	−2012	10014	11514	−1500	11310	12820	−1509	11178	11933	−756	14271	13880	391
a.3. Insurance	1062	1116	−54	1639	1044	595	1422	1130	292	1591	1285	306	1948	1400	549
a.4. G.n.i.e.	314	529	−215	331	376	−45	389	793	−404	441	525	−84	535	820	−285
a.5. Miscellaneous	42105	17869	24236	67010	29298	37712	81947	27879	54069	70977	36944	34033	100851	56856	43995
Soft Ware Services	23600	1338	22262	40300	3358	36942	46300	2564	43736	49705	1468	48237	55460	2194	53265
Business Services	9307	7748	1559	16772	16553	219	18602	15318	3285	11321	18049	−6728	24050	27765	−3715
Financial Services	1209	965	244	3217	3133	84	4428	2958	1469	3693	4642	−950	6508	7483	−975
Communication Services	1575	289	1286	2408	860	1548	2298	1087	1211	1228	1355	−127	1562	1152	410
b. Transfers	25620	933	24687	44261	2316	41945	47547	2749	44798	54363	2318	52045	56265	3125	53140
b.1. Official Transfers	669	475	194	753	514	239	645	413	232	727	473	254	647	631	16
b.2. Private Transfers	24951	458	24493	43508	1802	41706	46903	2336	44567	53636	1845	51791	55618	2494	53125
c. Income	6408	12263	−5855	14272	19339	−5068	14309	21419	−7110	13022	21061	−8038	9102	26412	−17309
c.1. Investment Income	6229	11491	−5262	13811	18244	−4433	13483	20109	−6626	12108	19355	−7248	7986	24384	−16398
c.2. Compensation of Employees	179	772	−593	461	1095	−635	825	1309	−484	915	1705	−791	1116	2028	−912
Total Current Account (1+2)	194839	204741	−9902	315037	330774	−15737	356820	384735	−27914	345872	384052	−38181	448716	494661	−45945
B. Capital Account															
1. Foreign Investment (a+b)	77298	61770	15528	271122	227796	43326	171660	163318	8342	198653	148291	50362	289416	249763	39652
a. Foreign Investment in India	77082	55687	21395	268408	206410	61998	170415	142531	27885	197643	132158	65485	286077	228722	57355
a.1. Foreign Direct Investment in India	8962	61	8901	34844	116	34728	41903	166	41738	37746	4637	33109	32902	7018	25884
a.2. Foreign Portfolio Investment in India	68120	55626	12494	233564	206294	27270	128512	142365	−13853	159897	127521	32376	253175	221704	31471
b. Foreign Investment Abroad	216	6083	−5867	2713	21385	−18672	1245	20787	−19542	1010	16133	−15123	3339	21042	−17703
2. Loans (a+b+c)	39479	31570	7909	82192	41539	40653	62217	53902	8314	74163	61716	12447	107726	79289	28437
a. External Assistance	3631	1929	1702	4241	2126	2114	5230	2792	2439	5897	3007	2890	7882	2941	4941
a.1. External Assistance by India	24	88	−64	23	28	−4	71	417	−347	51	422	−371	76	102	−26
a.2. External Assistance to India	3607	1841	1766	4217	2098	2119	5159	2374	2785	5846	2585	3261	7806	2840	4967

		C1	C2	C3	C4	C5	C6	C7	C8	C9	C10	C11	C12	C13	C14	C15
b.	Commercial Borrowings (MT & LT)	14343	11835	2508	30293	7684	22609	15222	7361	7861	15003	13003	2000	24113	11606	12506
b.1.	Commercial Borrowings by India	0	251	-251	1593	1624	-31	1997	783	1214	973	1505	-531	1840	1513	328
b.2.	Commercial Borrowings to India	14343	11584	2759	28700	6060	22640	13225	6578	6647	14029	11498	2531	22272	10094	12179
c.	Short Term Credit to India	21505	17806	3699	47658	31729	15930	41765	43750	-1985	53264	45706	7558	75732	64742	10990
3.	Banking Capital (a=b)	21658	20285	1373	55814	44055	11759	65207	68453	-3245	61499	59416	2083	92323	87361	4962
a.	Commercial Banks	20586	20144	442	55735	43623	12112	65094	67868	-2774	60893	58966	1927	90621	86189	4433
a.1.	Assets of Commercial Banks	772	3947	-3175	19562	12668	6894	25823	28725	-2902	17097	15259	1838	35369	38666	-3297
a.2.	Liabilities of Commercial Banks	19814	16197	3617	36173	30955	5217	39270	39142	128	43796	43707	88	55252	47523	7730
a.2.a.	Non-Resident Deposits of Commercial Banks	17835	15046	2789	29400	29222	179	37147	32858	4290	41355	38433	2922	49252	46014	3238
b.	Others	1072	141	931	79	432	-353	114	585	-471	606	449	157	1702	1172	529
4.	Rupee Debt Service	0	572	-572	0	122	-122	0	100	-100	0	97	-97	0	68	-68
5.	Other Capital	5941	4709	1232	29229	18261	10969	16685	22602	-5916	11451	24613	-13162	9890	20885	-10994
B.	Capital Account	144376	118906	25470	438357	331772	106585	315770	308375	7395	345766	294132	51634	499355	437366	61989
C.	Errors and Omissions	0	516	-516	1316	0	1316	440	0	440	0	12	-12	0	2993	-2993
D.	Overall Balance	339215	324163	15052	754710	662546	92164	673030	693109	-20080	691638	678197	13441	948071	935021	13050
E.	Monetary Movements	0	15052	-15052	0	92164	-92164	20080	0	20080	0	13441	-13441	0	13050	-13050
E.1.	I.M.F	0	0	0	0	0	0	0	0	0	0	0	0	0	0	0
E.2.	Foreign Exchange Reserves (Increase – / Decrease +) SDR Allocation	0	15052	-15052	0	92164	-92164	20080	0	20080	0	13441	-13441	0	13050	-13050

Notes: Increase (-ve)/ Decrease (+ve)
PR: Partially Revised; P: Preliminary.
Source: RBI, *Monthly Bulletin* (various issues).

Table A7.3 Invisibles in India's Balance of Payments—by Category: Receipts & Payments

Invisibles: Receipts

US$ million

	Invisibles	% to Current Account Receipts	Services	of which: Travel	Trans-portation	Insurance	G.n.i.e	Miscella-neous	of which: Software Services	Transfers	of which: Private Transfers	of which: Workers Remittances	Income
1990–1	7464	28.8	4551	1456	983	111	15	1986		2545	2083		368
1991–2	9502	34.2	5022	1977	939	108	17	1981		4258	3798		222
1992–3	9334	33.1	4730	2098	982	158	75	1417		4228	3864		376
1993–4	11319	33.3	5264	2222	1433	124	30	1455		5660	5286		395
1994–5	15554	36.7	6135	2365	1696	152	10	1912		8533	8112		886
1995–6	17664	35.3	7344	2712	2011	179	13	2430	754	8891	8540		1430
1996–7	21405	38.5	7474	2878	1953	217	72	2354		12858	12435		1073
1997–8	23244	39.4	9429	2914	1836	240	276	4163		12254	11875		1561
1998–9	25770	42.9	13186	2993	1925	224	597	7447		10649	10341		1935
1999–2000	30312	44.7	15709	3036	1707	231	582	10153	3962	12672	12290	7423	1931
2000–1	32267	41.5	16268	3497	2046	270	651	9804	6341	13317	13065	7747	2682
2001–2	36737	45.1	17140	3137	2161	288	518	11036	7556	16218	15760	6578	3379
2002–3	41925	43.8	20763	3312	2536	369	293	14253	9600	17640	17189	9914	3522
2003–4	53508	44.7	26868	5037	3207	419	240	17965	12800	22736	22182	10379	3904
2004–5	69533	44.9	43249	6666	4683	870	401	30629	17700	21691	21075	9973	4593
2005–6	89687	46.0	57659	7853	6325	1062	314	42105	23600	25620	24951	10455	6408
2006–7	114558	47.1	73780	9123	7974	1195	253	55235	31300	31470	30835	14740	9308
2007–8	148875	47.3	90342	11349	10014	1639	331	67010	40300	44261	43508	21922	14272
2008–9	167819	47.0	105963	10894	11310	1422	389	81948		47548	46903	23866	14309
2009–10	163404	47.3	95789	11859	11177	1603	440	70680		54623	53900		13022
2010–11	197583	48.9	131972	15275	14277	1949	534	99937		56509	55861		9102

Table A7.3 (Contd.)

Invisibles: Payments

US$ million

	Invisibles Pay	% to Current Account Payments	Services	of which: Travel	Transportation	Insurance	G.n.i.e	Miscellaneous	of which: Software Services	Transfers	of which: Private Transfers	of which: Workers Remittances	Income
1990–1	7706	21.6	3571	392	1093	88	173	1825		15	14		4120
1991–2	7882	27.2	3815	465	1288	126	120	1816		16	15		4051
1992–3	7413	23.4	3601	385	1485	146	100	1485		13	12		3799
1993–4	8422	24.0	4730	497	1765	196	153	2119		27	22		3665
1994–5	9874	21.6	5533	818	1863	181	165	2506		24	19		4317
1995–6	12217	21.9	7544	1168	2169	143	218	3847		38	32		4634
1996–7	11209	18.6	6748	858	2394	153	178	3165		81	68		4380
1997–8	13236	20.5	8110	1437	2522	183	160	3808		45	45		5081
1998–9	16562	25.8	11021	1743	2680	112	325	6161		62	61		5479
1999–2000	17169	23.7	11645	2139	2410	122	270	6704	138	34	34	29	5490
2000–1	22473	28.0	14576	2804	3558	223	319	7672	591	211	211	124	7686
2001–2	21763	27.9	13816	3014	3467	280	283	6772	672	362	362	292	7585
2002–3	24890	27.9	17120	3341	3272	350	228	9929	737	802	802	757	6968
2003–4	25707	24.3	16724	3602	2328	363	212	10219	476	574	574	522	8409
2004–5	38301	24.4	27823	5249	4539	722	411	16902	800	906	550	421	9572
2005–6	47685	23.3	34489	6638	8337	1116	529	17869	1338	933	458	354	12263
2006–7	62341	24.6	44311	6684	8068	642	403	28514	2267	1391	1010	823	16639
2007–8	73144	22.4	51490	9258	11514	1044	376	29298	3358	2316	1802	1585	19339
2008–9	76214	19.8	52047	9425	12820	1130	793	27879	2814	2749	2336	1928	21416
2009–10	83413	21.1	60033	9342	11934	1286	526	36945		2318	1845		21062
2010–11	111397	22.6	84308	11232	13880	1400	820	56976		3124	2493		23965

Source: RBI Bulletins.

A8 EXCHANGE RATE

Table A8.1 Exchange Rate for the Indian Rupee vis-à-vis Some Select Currencies (Indian Rupee per Currency)

(Indian Rupee per Currency, Per cent appreciation (+), depreciation (−))

Countries	Currency	(Per cent Appreciation (+) Depreciation (−))			2011–12	2010–11	2009–10	2008–9	2007–8	2006–7	2005–6	2004–5	2003–4
		2007–8 to 2011–12	2000–1 to 2007–8	1992–3 to 2000–1									
1	2	3	4	5	6	7	8	9	10	11	12	13	14
Developing Countries													
Argentina	Pesos	24.1	253.1	−41.8	11.4274	11.5754	12.5273	14.1849	12.9466	14.7763	15.0767	15.3410	16.1597
Bangladesh	Taka	7.6	47.4	−21.6	0.6224	0.6491	0.6864	0.6696	0.5859	0.6534	0.6776	0.7430	0.7868
Brazil	Reais	−17.6	10.9	62.6	28.2226	26.4058	25.3597	23.2585	21.7126	21.0144	19.0588	15.6705	15.6941
China	Yuan	−10.7	2.2	−14.4	7.4966	6.7905	6.9476	6.6975	5.3983	5.7269	5.4380	5.4287	5.5518
Colombia	Pesos	−16.6	4.9	59.2	0.0262	0.0242	0.0233	0.0219	0.0201	0.0193	0.0193	0.0177	0.0163
Hongkong	Hongkong Dollar	−4.0	13.5	−26.2	6.1618	5.8600	6.1186	5.9143	5.1628	5.8157	5.6992	5.7654	5.9055
Indonesia	Rupiah for Rs. 100	−16.7	15.1	155.0	0.5400	0.5100	0.4800	0.4500	0.4400	0.5000	0.4600	0.4900	0.5400
Israel	New Sheqalim	−6.0	9.7	−7.9	13.2358	12.2951	12.3179	12.4426	10.1666	10.4195	9.7004	10.0834	10.2961
Iran	Rials	9.3	496.8	957.9	0.0044	0.0044	0.0048	0.0048	0.0043	0.0049	0.0049	0.0051	0.0055
Kenya	Shillings	18.8	−2.1	29.6	0.5367	0.5648	0.6195	0.6378	0.6020	0.6331	0.5948	0.5676	0.6059
Korea	Won	−12.3	−9.3	−14.3	0.0431	0.0396	0.0392	0.0378	0.0431	0.0479	0.0437	0.0405	0.0388
Kuwait	Dinar	−3.1	3.5	−40.3	173.7438	160.2081	165.0189	168.4316	143.8620	156.3220	151.5909	152.8179	154.8108
Malaysia	Ringgit	−14.4	0.6	−13.7	15.6436	14.5107	13.7080	13.3863	11.9490	12.5313	11.7354	11.8240	12.0927
Mexico	Pesos	1.1	29.4	77.4	3.7856	3.6575	3.6162	3.8266	3.7042	4.1110	4.1236	3.9637	4.2427
Mynammar	Kyats	−5.5	−5.6	−37.7	8.8770	8.1940	8.6639	8.3931	7.3408	7.8830	7.5783	7.8673	7.7193
Nigeria	Naira	18.3	34.0	205.4	0.3091	0.3021	0.3170	0.3657	0.3267	0.3526	0.3396	0.3394	0.3512
Pakistan	Rupees	12.1	24.1	26.4	0.5469	0.5335	0.5719	0.6131	0.6616	0.7480	0.7414	0.7656	0.7980
Philippines	Pesos	−10.4	8.3	5.9	1.1112	1.0227	1.0050	0.9961	0.9101	0.8961	0.8139	0.8052	0.8405
Qatar	Riyals	−4.0	13.5	−42.2	13.1651	12.5170	13.0341	12.6356	11.0606	12.4311	12.1604	12.3438	12.6242
Russia	Rubles	4.3	1.1	308.9	1.6173	1.5081	1.5442	1.6861	1.6059	1.6930	1.5586	1.5705	1.5347
Saudi Arabia	Riyals	−4.0	13.6	−42.2	12.7789	12.1499	12.6517	12.2650	10.7397	12.0826	11.8169	11.9817	12.2662
Singapore	Singapore Dollar	−16.4	−3.6	−38.4	38.2050	34.1980	33.2420	31.9279	27.2703	28.9137	26.6126	26.8174	26.5658
South Africa	Rand	−19.7	10.4	45.0	6.4327	6.3326	6.0670	5.1647	5.6506	6.4244	6.9259	7.1835	6.4017
Sri Lanka	Rupees	−1.4	56.4	2.9	0.4245	0.4062	0.4124	0.4187	0.3647	0.4287	0.4375	0.4423	0.4747
Thailand	Baht	−13.7	−7.8	−5.6	1.5659	1.4644	1.4089	1.3511	1.1938	1.2247	1.0944	1.1212	1.1322
UAE	Dirhams	−4.0	13.5	−42.2	13.0486	12.4063	12.9187	12.5238	10.9627	12.3211	12.0528	12.2345	12.5125

Industrialized Countries

Country	Currency												
Australia	Australian Dollar	−28.9	−45.1	−25.4	50.0432	42.8855	40.1362	35.5707	46.3457	59.1513	33.4597	33.2255	31.9391
Canada	Canadian Dollar	−15.6	−22.1	−29.3	48.2480	44.8207	43.5204	40.7358	38.9961	39.7525	37.1031	35.1410	33.9613
Denmark	Kroner	−1.6	−27.3	−21.3	8.8378	8.0737	8.9947	8.7006	7.6468	7.7798	7.2204	7.5888	7.2409
Egypt@	Pounds	9.6	65.0	−22.9	8.2558	7.4992	8.2198	9.0505	7.3475	7.6214	7.6980	7.5595	7.0436
Japan	Yen	−24.5	17.3	−48.8	0.6062	0.5317	0.5112	0.4577	0.3526	0.3870	0.3910	0.4177	0.4065
Sweden	Kroner	−11.6	−21.0	−12.3	7.3047	6.4806	6.4540	6.4557	6.1246	6.2967	5.7616	6.2032	5.9038
Switzerland	Swiss Francs	−23.3	−22.5	−30.8	54.2842	44.9343	44.6078	41.6134	34.7538	36.5363	34.7475	36.7018	34.8506
USA	Dollar	−4.0	13.5	−42.2	47.9210	45.5620	47.4440	45.9940	40.2610	45.2495	44.2640	44.9313	45.9523
UK	Pound	1.5	−16.4	−33.9	76.5039	70.7718	75.6159	77.6422	80.8135	85.6614	79.0826	82.9049	77.8144
Euro*		−1.4	−27.3		65.9161	60.1876	67.0113	64.9633	56.9463	58.0174	53.8508	56.4764	53.8682
Belgium	Franc			−30.1									
France	Franc			−30.9									
Germany	Deutsche Mark			−30.2									
Italy	Lire			−18.0									
Netherlands	Guidars			−30.1									

(*Contd.*)

Table A3.1 (Contd.)

(Indian Rupee per Currency, Per cent appreciation (+), depreciation (–))

Countries	Currency	2002–3	2001–2	2000–1	1999–2000	1998–9	1997–8	1996–7	1995–6	1994–5	1993–4	1992–3
1	2	15	16	17	18	19	20	21	22	23	24	25
Developing Countries												
Argentina	Pesos	14.3886	38.8523	45.7084	43.3557	42.0833	37.1769	35.5186	33.4673	31.4292	31.4681	26.6057
Bangladesh	Taka	0.8360	0.8401	0.8638	0.8717	0.8850	0.8308	0.8408	0.8269	0.7803	0.7872	0.6772
Brazil	Reais	15.1325	19.7735	24.0767	23.8689	31.8292	33.8634	34.7196	35.3031	39.1494	na	na
China	Yuan	5.8483	5.7623	5.5188	5.2347	5.0807	4.4845	4.2731	4.0212	3.6714	4.8262	4.7265
Colombia	Pesos	0.0181	0.0207	0.0211	0.0234	0.0284	0.0306	0.0340	0.0350	0.0376	0.0357	0.0336
Hongkong	Hongkong Dollar	6.2067	6.1156	5.8603	5.5801	5.4298	4.7997	4.5883	4.3261	na	na	na
Indonesia	Rupiah for Rs. 100	0.5380	0.4603	0.5065	0.5771	0.4271	0.7962	1.5020	1.4706	1.4396	1.4917	1.2915
Israel	New Sheqalim	10.1067	11.0219	11.1494	10.4712	10.7340	10.5738	10.9408	11.0092	10.4087	10.9033	10.2729
Iran	Rials	0.0061	0.0210	0.0259	0.0247	0.0240	0.0212	0.0203	0.0191	0.0180	0.0189	0.0240
Kenya	Shillings	0.6171	0.6069	0.5892	0.5950	0.6660	0.6176	0.6297	0.6108	0.6235	0.4816	0.7637
Korea	Won	0.0366	0.0366	0.0391	0.0370	0.0324	0.0327	0.0340	0.0434	0.0393	0.0389	0.0335
Kuwait	Dinar	160.3546	155.4482	148.8285	142.0738	138.2576	122.2153	118.2228	112.0032	105.4957	104.7558	88.8899
Malaysia	Ringgit	12.7384	12.5510	12.0225	11.4037	10.8537	11.6454	14.1980	13.3682	12.1725	12.0456	10.3802
Mexico	Pesos	4.8020	5.1857	4.7948	4.5998	4.4165	4.6122	4.6207	4.9147	7.7052	10.0183	8.5058
Myanmar	Kyats	7.5343	7.0246	6.9312	6.8564	6.6762	5.9017	5.9233	5.8780	5.3482	5.1081	4.3172
Nigeria	Naira	0.3915	0.4247	0.4379	0.4526	1.1099	1.6976	1.6222	1.5292	1.4286	1.4260	1.3372
Pakistan	Rupees	0.8183	0.7683	0.8211	na	0.9248	0.8869	0.9462	1.0293	1.0230	1.0762	1.0377
Philippines	Pesos	0.9254	0.9263	0.9858	1.0950	1.0413	1.1239	1.3523	1.2887	1.2171	1.1321	1.0440
Qatar	Riyals	13.2984	13.1027	12.5510	11.9049	11.5556	10.2083	9.7530	9.1929	8.6258	8.6166	7.2559
Russia	Rubles	1.5333	1.6044	1.6229	1.6659	3.0225	6.3164	6.6361	na	na	na	na
Saudi Arabia	Riyals	12.9255	12.7353	12.1991	11.5712	11.2316	9.9221	9.4795	8.9365	8.3839	8.3750	7.0525
Singapore	Singapore Dollar	27.3712	26.3138	26.2953	25.5899	25.0326	23.9932	25.1511	23.7289	21.0641	19.5843	16.2014
South Africa	Rand	4.9676	5.0024	6.2406	7.0305	7.2370	7.8762	7.9170	9.0987	8.7600	9.3804	9.0462
Sri Lanka	Rupees	0.5021	0.5214	0.5705	0.6064	0.6349	0.6181	0.6331	0.6403	0.6332	0.6430	0.5868
Thailand	Baht	1.1330	1.0702	1.1007	1.1406	1.0826	1.0132	1.3925	1.3392	1.2540	1.2397	1.0396
UAE	Dirhams	13.1807	12.9867	12.4399	11.7996	11.4533	10.1221	9.6706	9.1153	8.5529	8.5438	7.1946

Industrialized Countries

Country	Currency											
Australia	Australian Dollar	27.2332	24.5242	25.4605	27.9504	26.1329	26.6049	27.9927	25.1736	23.2975	21.4904	18.9865
Canada	Canadian Dollar	31.2670	30.4655	30.3841	29.4549	27.9707	26.4924	26.0882	24.5541	22.7636	23.9404	21.4763
Denmark	Kroner	6.4496	5.6630	5.5580	6.0144	6.3500	5.4598	5.9560	6.0235	5.1095	4.7572	4.3740
Egypt@	Pounds	8.3395	10.7979	12.1250	12.7805	12.4978	10.1804	10.5960	10.1179	9.2948	9.2811	9.3450
Japan	Yen	0.3968	0.3812	0.4134	0.3885	0.3285	0.3028	0.3152	0.3470	0.3160	0.2908	0.2116
Sweden	Kroner	5.2250	4.5397	4.8370	5.1488	5.2952	4.7664	5.1786	4.7913	4.1536	3.9656	4.2416
Switzerland	Swiss Francs	32.7045	28.1828	26.9186	27.9034	29.2689	25.4335	27.3567	28.6217	23.8712	21.4164	18.6180
USA	Dollar	48.4060	47.6938	45.6855	43.3340	42.0620	37.1580	35.5010	33.4670	31.3980	31.3640	26.4110
UK	Pound	74.8163	68.2784	67.5734	69.8414	69.5458	60.9916	56.3256	52.3998	48.8361	47.1939	44.6586
Euro*		47.9158	42.1360	41.4221	44.7065							
Belgium	Franc					1.1719	1.0151	1.1106	1.1382	0.9760	0.8235	0.8193
France	Franc					7.21	6.23	6.75	6.75	5.84	5.46	4.98
Germany	Deutsche Mark					24.18	20.94	22.87	23.40	20.10	18.72	16.87
Italy	Lire					0.02	0.02	0.02	0.02	0.02	0.02	0.02
Netherlands	Guidars					21.44	18.60	20.39	20.89	17.92	16.68	14.98

Notes: * Consisting of Currencies of Belgium, France, Germany, Netherlands and Italy Euro currency came into existence with effect from January 1, 1998; in their cases per cent appreciation or depreciation worked out is for the period 1992–3 to 1998–9 and 2000–1 to 2008–9 for the purpose of comparability.

@ Data for Egypt is as at the end of the period.

The liberalized exchange rate management system (LERMS) was instituted in March 1992 in conjunction with other measures of liberalisation in the areas of trade, industry and foreign investment and the import of Gold. The ultimate convergence of the dual rates was made effective as of 1 March 1993.

Source: International Financial Statistics (various issues), International Monetary Fund.

Table A8.2 Indices of Real Effective Exchange Rate (REER) and Nominal Effective Exchange Rate (NEER) of the Indian Rupee

Year	(36-Currency Export and Trade-based Weights) (Base: 2004–5=100)						(6-Currency Trade-based Weights)				
	Trade-based Weights				Export-based Weights			Base: 2004–5=100 (April–March)		Base: 2010–11=100 (April–March)	
	REER		NEER		REER		NEER	REER		NEER	REER
	2		3		4		5	6	7	8	9
1											
2004–5	100.00		100.00		100.00		100.00	100.00	100.00	108.92	87.05
2005–6	103.10	(3.1)	102.24	(2.2)	102.74	(2.7)	102.20 (2.2)	103.04 (3.0)	105.17 (5.2)	112.20 (3.0)	91.52 (5.1)
2006–7	101.29	(–1.8)	97.63	(–4.5)	101.05	(–1.6)	98.00 (–4.1)	98.09 (–4.8)	104.30 (–0.8)	106.81 (–4.8)	90.76 (–0.8)
2007–8	108.52	(7.1)	104.75	(7.3)	108.57	(7.4)	105.61 (7.8)	104.62 (6.7)	112.76 (8.1)	113.92 (6.7)	98.13 (8.1)
2008–9	97.80	(–9.9)	93.34	(–10.9)	97.77	(–9.9)	93.99 (–11.0)	90.42 (–13.6)	102.32 (–9.3)	98.46 (–13.6)	89.05 (–9.3)
2009–10 (P)	94.73	(–3.1)	90.93	(–2.6)	95.26	(–2.6)	91.41 (–2.7)	87.07 (–3.7)	101.97 (–0.3)	94.81 (–3.7)	88.74 (–0.3)
2010–11 (P)	102.34	(8.0)	93.66	(3.0)	103.52	(8.7)	94.74 (3.6)	91.83 (5.5)	114.91 (12.7)	100.00 (5.5)	100.00 (12.7)
2011–12 (P) April	104.44	(1.0)	93.06	(0.4)	105.68	(0.6)	94.31 (0.3)	90.43 (0.2)	117.43 (1.3)	98.47 (0.2)	102.19 (1.3)
May	102.97	(–1.4)	92.00	(–1.1)	104.25	(–1.4)	93.29 (–1.1)	89.33 (–1.2)	116.46 (–0.8)	97.27 (–1.2)	101.34 (–0.8)
June	103.26	(0.3)	92.00	(0.0)	104.72	(0.5)	93.39 (0.1)	89.32 (–0.0)	116.13 (–0.3)	97.27 (0.0)	101.06 (–0.3)
July	104.39	(1.1)	92.62	(0.7)	106.15	(1.4)	94.22 (0.9)	90.34 (1.1)	117.72 (1.4)	98.37 (1.1)	102.44 (1.4)
August	102.37	(–1.9)	90.64	(–2.1)	104.34	(–1.7)	92.41 (–1.9)	88.13 (–2.4)	115.66 (–1.7)	95.97 (–2.4)	100.65 (–1.7)
September	99.40	(–2.9)	87.89	(–3.0)	101.04	(–3.2)	89.40 (–3.3)	85.08 (–3.5)	112.46 (–2.8)	92.64 (–3.5)	97.87 (–2.8)
October	96.80	(–2.6)	85.50	(–2.7)	98.37	(–2.6)	86.94 (–2.8)	82.35 (–3.2)	108.92 (–3.1)	89.67 (–3.2)	94.78 (–3.2)
November	94.48	(–2.4)	83.00	(–2.9)	95.84	(–2.6)	84.41 (–2.9)	80.00 (–2.9)	106.25 (–2.5)	87.11 (–2.9)	92.46 (–2.4)
December	91.36	(–3.3)	80.83	(–2.6)	92.82	(–3.2)	82.22 (–2.6)	78.06 (–2.4)	103.75 (–2.4)	85.01 (–2.4)	90.29 (–2.3)
January	94.57	(3.5)	83.24	(3.0)	96.05	(3.5)	84.65 (3.0)	80.49 (3.1)	106.41 (2.6)	87.64 (3.1)	92.60 (2.6)
February	98.09	(3.7)	86.34	(3.7)	99.47	(3.6)	87.67 (3.6)	83.24 (3.4)	110.40 (3.7)	90.64 (3.4)	96.08 (3.8)
March	95.89	(–2.2)	84.40	(–2.2)	97.35	(–2.1)	85.80 (–2.1)	81.60 (–2.0)	108.78 (–1.5)	88.86 (–2.0)	94.66 (–1.5)

Note: P: Provisional. The base year is changed from 1993–4 to 2004–5.

Source: RBI Bulletin.

A9 FOREIGN TRADE

Table A9.1 India's Foreign Trade

(US$ million)

Year	Exports			Imports			Trade Balance		
	Oil	Non-Oil	Total	Oil	Non-Oil	Total	Oil	Non-Oil	Total
1	2	3	4	5	6	7	8	9	10
1970-1	11	2020	2031	180	1983	2162	−169	38	−131
1971-2	14	2138	2152	260	2182	2442	−246	−44	−290
1972-3	38	2531	2569	266	2167	2433	−228	364	136
1973-4	16	3223	3238	719	3074	3793	−703	149	−554
1974-5	17	4175	4192	1457	4234	5691	−1440	−59	−1499
1975-6	22	4627	4649	1412	4652	6064	−1390	−25	−1415
1976-7	21	5708	5728	1574	4077	5652	−1554	1630	77
1977-8	18	6280	6299	1806	5205	7012	−1788	1075	−713
1978-9	17	6943	6960	2038	6241	8279	−2021	703	−1318
1979-80	23	7903	7926	4035	7256	11291	−4011	647	−3364
1980-1	32	8453	8485	6655	9212	15867	−6623	−758	−7382
1891-2	246	8458	8704	5786	9387	15173	−5540	−929	−6469
1982-3	1278	7830	9108	5816	8970	14787	−4538	−1141	−5679
1983-4	1536	7914	9449	4673	10638	15311	−3137	−2724	−5862
1984-5	1529	8349	9878	4550	9863	14412	−3020	−1514	−4534
1985-6	527	8378	8905	4078	11989	16067	−3551	−3611	−7162
1986-7	322	9423	9745	2200	13527	15727	−1878	−4104	−5982
1987-8	500	11588	12089	3118	14038	17156	−2618	−2450	−5067
1988-9	349	13622	13970	3009	16488	19497	−2660	−2867	−5527
1989-90	418	16194	16613	3768	17452	21219	−3349	−1258	−4607
1990-1	523	17623	18145	6028	18044	24073	−5505	−422	−5927
1991-2	415	17451	17865	5325	14086	19411	−4910	3365	−1545
1992-3	476	18061	18537	6100	15782	21882	−5624	2279	−3344
1993-4	398	21841	22238	5754	17553	23306	−5356	4288	−1068
1994-5	417	25914	26331	5928	22727	28654	−5511	3187	−2324
1995-6	454	31341	31795	7526	29150	36675	−7072	2192	−4880
1996-7	482	32988	33470	10036	29096	39132	−9554	3892	−5663
1997-8	353	34654	35006	8164	33321	41485	−7811	1333	−6478
1998-9	89	33129	33219	6399	35990	42389	−6309	−2861	−9170
1999-2000	39	36784	36822	12611	37059	49671	−12573	−276	−12848
2000-1	1870	42691	44560	15650	34886	50537	−13780	7804	−5976
2001-2	2119	41708	43827	14000	37413	51413	−11881	4295	−7587
2002-3	2577	50143	52719	17640	43773	61412	−15063	6370	−8693
2003-4	3568	60274	63843	20569	57580	78149	−17001	2694	−14307
2004-5	6989	76547	83536	29844	81673	111517	−22855	−5127	−27981
2005-6	11640	91451	103091	43963	105203	149166	−32323	−13752	−46075
2006-7	18635	107779	126414	56945	128790	185735	−38311	−21011	−59321
2007-8	28363	134541	162904	79645	171795	251439	−51281	−37254	−88535
2008-9	27547	157748	185295	93672	210025	303696	−66125	−52277	−118401
2009-10	28192	150559	178751	87136	201237	288373	−58944	−50678	−109621
2010-11	41404	209733	251136	105964	263805	369769	−64561	−54072	−118633
2011-12	55604	249020	304624	154906	334511	489417	−99302	−85491	−184794

Source: RBI Bulletins.

Table A9.2 Changing Scenerio in Foreign Trade

(US$ million)

Year	Gems and Jewellery	Chemicals and Products	Textile and Textile Products	Petroleum Products	Machinery and Instruments	Exports - Transport Equipment	Manufacture of Metals	Iron Ore	Iron & Steel	Electronic Goods	Top Ten Commodities/ Groups	Total Exports
1987-8	2015.1 (16.7)	791.6 (6.5)	3013.8 (24.9)	500.4 (4.1)	397.0 (3.3)	195.2 (1.6)	222.3 (1.8)	427.7 (3.5)	21.6 (0.2)	154.1 (1.3)	7738.8 (64.0)	12088.5 (100.0)
1988-9	3032.8 (21.7)	1090.5 (7.8)	3037.7 (21.7)	348.7 (2.5)	509.5 (3.6)	250.7 (1.8)	305.1 (2.2)	464.8 (3.3)	52.1 (0.4)	200.5 (1.4)	9292.4 (66.5)	13970.4 (100.0)
1989-90	3180.7 (19.1)	1553.8 (9.4)	3746.5 (22.6)	418.4 (2.5)	603.9 (3.6)	316.0 (1.9)	445.7 (2.7)	557.1 (3.4)	98.9 (0.6)	302.7 (1.8)	11223.7 (67.6)	16612.5 (100.0)
1990-1	2924.1 (16.1)	1728.0 (9.5)	4342.6 (23.9)	522.7 (2.9)	696.2 (3.8)	400.6 (2.2)	456.3 (2.5)	584.7 (3.2)	161.1 (0.9)	232.4 (1.3)	12048.7 (66.4)	18145.2 (100.0)
1991-2	2738.2 (15.3)	1868.8 (10.5)	4693.1 (26.3)	414.7 (2.3)	581.4 (3.3)	496.4 (2.8)	484.2 (2.7)	582.3 (3.3)	153.5 (0.9)	265.2 (1.5)	12277.8 (68.7)	17865.4 (100.0)
1992-3	3071.7 (16.6)	1786.1 (9.6)	5007.4 (27.0)	476.2 (2.6)	541.6 (2.9)	533.7 (2.9)	560.2 (3.0)	381.2 (2.1)	306.1 (1.7)	212.3 (1.1)	12876.5 (69.5)	18537.2 (100.0)
1993-4	3995.8 (18.0)	2377.2 (10.7)	5472.3 (24.6)	397.8 (1.8)	638.9 (2.9)	591.9 (2.7)	663.2 (3.0)	438.0 (2.0)	568.4 (2.6)	303.6 (1.4)	15447.1 (69.5)	22238.3 (100.0)
1994-5	4500.4 (17.1)	3066.8 (11.6)	7117.7 (27.0)	416.9 (1.6)	726.7 (2.8)	771.3 (2.9)	706.2 (2.7)	413.1 (1.6)	528.4 (2.0)	412.2 (1.6)	18659.7 (70.9)	26330.5 (100.0)
1995-6	5274.8 (16.6)	3597.0 (11.3)	8031.6 (25.3)	453.7 (1.4)	829.8 (2.6)	924.9 (2.9)	826.4 (2.6)	514.5 (1.6)	696.7 (2.2)	670.1 (2.1)	21819.5 (68.6)	31794.9 (100.0)
1996-7	4752.7 (14.2)	3912.8 (11.7)	8635.8 (25.8)	481.8 (1.4)	1057.1 (3.2)	968.7 (2.9)	913.5 (2.7)	480.7 (1.4)	769.8 (2.3)	783.7 (2.3)	22756.6 (68.0)	33469.7 (100.0)
1997-8	5345.5 (15.3)	4396.3 (12.6)	9050.4 (25.9)	352.8 (1.0)	1195.7 (3.4)	929.1 (2.7)	1023.2 (2.9)	476.2 (1.4)	874.7 (2.5)	759.6 (2.2)	24403.5 (69.7)	35006.4 (100.0)
1998-9	5929.3 (17.8)	4009.2 (12.1)	8866.3 (26.7)	89.4 (0.3)	1154.8 (3.5)	761.8 (2.3)	1040.0 (3.1)	384.0 (1.2)	579.1 (1.7)	502.8 (1.5)	23316.7 (70.2)	33218.7 (100.0)
1999-2000	7502.3 (20.4)	4706.5 (12.8)	9822.1 (26.7)	38.9 (0.1)	1183.2 (3.2)	810.2 (2.2)	1225.6 (3.3)	271.2 (0.7)	833.0 (2.3)	681.0 (1.8)	27074.0 (73.5)	36822.4 (100.0)
2000-1	7384.0 (16.6)	5885.9 (13.2)	11285.0 (25.3)	1869.7 (4.2)	1580.1 (3.5)	991.9 (2.2)	1577.7 (3.5)	357.6 (0.8)	1028.3 (2.3)	1051.5 (2.4)	33011.7 (74.1)	44560.3 (100.0)
2001-2	7306.3 (16.7)	6051.8 (13.8)	10206.5 (23.3)	2119.1 (4.8)	1734.1 (4.0)	1020.9 (2.3)	1604.0 (3.7)	426.4 (1.0)	898.1 (2.0)	1171.3 (2.7)	32538.5 (74.2)	43826.7 (100.0)
2002-3	9029.9 (17.1)	7455.3 (14.1)	11617.0 (22.0)	2576.5 (4.9)	2008.4 (3.8)	1333.9 (2.5)	1847.6 (3.5)	867.9 (1.6)	1856.0 (3.5)	1252.7 (2.4)	39845.2 (75.6)	52719.4 (100.0)

Year												Total
2003–4	10573.3 (16.6)	9445.9 (14.8)	12791.5 (20.0)	3568.4 (5.6)	2776.3 (4.3)	1956.0 (3.1)	2426.5 (3.8)	1125.8 (1.8)	2477.8 (3.9)	1728.3 (2.7)	48869.8 (76.5)	63842.6 (100.0)
2004–5	13761.8 (16.5)	12443.7 (14.9)	13555.3 (16.2)	6989.3 (8.4)	3719.4 (4.5)	2829.7 (3.4)	3401.5 (4.1)	3277.3 (3.9)	3921.0 (4.7)	1831.8 (2.2)	65730.8 (78.7)	83535.9 (100.0)
2005–6	15529.1 (15.1)	14769.5 (14.3)	16402.1 (15.9)	11639.6 (11.3)	5077.5 (4.9)	4323.0 (4.2)	4233.2 (4.1)	3801.1 (3.7)	3548.3 (3.4)	2173.1 (2.1)	81496.5 (79.1)	103090.5 (100.0)
2006–7	15977.0 (12.6)	17335.5 (13.7)	17373.2 (13.7)	18678.7 (14.8)	6722.8 (5.3)	4949.9 (3.9)	5081.2 (4.0)	3902.0 (3.1)	5238.6 (4.1)	2854.0 (2.3)	98112.9 (77.6)	126414.1 (100.0)
2007–8	19688.3 (12.1)	22375.2 (13.7)	20691.5 (12.7)	28377.0 (17.4)	9132.6 (5.6)	7028.2 (4.3)	7054.8 (4.3)	5814.9 (3.6)	5449.2 (3.3)	3511.7 (2.2)	129123.2 (79.2)	162983.9 (100.0)
2008–9	27705.0 (15.2)	23828.0 (13.0)	19864.7 (10.9)	26829.6 (14.7)	10953.0 (6.0)	11142.1 (6.1)	7550.8 (4.1)	4723.6 (2.6)	5822.5 (3.2)	7127.5 (3.9)	145546.7 (79.7)	182630.5 (100.0)
2009–10	29081.1 (16.3)	24410.4 (13.7)	19142.8 (10.7)	28192.0 (15.8)	9551.4 (5.3)	9791.3 (5.5)	5526.4 (3.1)	6029.8 (3.4)	3639.6 (2.0)	5624.4 (3.1)	140989.2 (78.9)	178751.4 (100.0)
2010–11	36673.8 (14.5)	31130.6 (12.3)	22391.1 (8.9)	42087.8 (16.7)	11968.8 (4.7)	18447.4 (7.3)	9491.7 (3.8)	4632.1 (1.8)	6590.3 (2.6)	8952.8 (3.5)	192366.3 (76.2)	252354.3 (100.0)

(Contd.)

Table A9.2 (Contd.)

(US$ million)

Year	Imports													
	Petroleum, Crude and Products	Electronic Goods	Gold and Silver	Machinery	Pearls & Precious Stones	Organic and Inorganic Chemicals	Iron and Steel	Transport Equipment	Fertilizers	Edible Oils	Top 10 Commodities	Total Imports/All Commodities
1987-8	3118.1 (18.2)	0.0 (0.0)	0.0 (0.0)	2016.5 (11.8)	1556.7 (9.1)	834.4 (4.9)	1017.8 (5.9)	586.1 (3.4)	391.8 (2.3)	747.2 (4.4)	10268.6 (59.9)	17155.7 (100.0)
1988-9	3009.0 (15.4)	0.0 (0.0)	0.0 (0.0)	1809.5 (9.3)	2192.8 (11.2)	1307.9 (6.7)	1335.0 (6.8)	519.8 (2.7)	644.7 (3.3)	503.9 (2.6)	11322.6 (58.1)	19497.2 (100.0)
1989-90	3767.5 (17.8)	0.0 (0.0)	0.0 (0.0)	1929.9 (9.1)	2554.6 (12.0)	1153.8 (5.4)	1352.4 (6.4)	889.3 (4.2)	1082.9 (5.1)	125.4 (0.6)	12855.8 (60.6)	21219.2 (100.0)
1990-1	6028.1 (14.3)	0.0 (0.0)	0.0 (0.0)	2100.0 (5.0)	2083.1 (4.9)	1275.6 (3.0)	1177.6 (2.8)	930.5 (2.2)	984.3 (2.3)	181.6 (0.4)	14760.8 (35.0)	42217.7 (100.0)
1991-2	5324.8 (27.4)	0.0 (0.0)	0.0 (0.0)	1457.5 (7.5)	1957.1 (10.1)	1378.7 (7.1)	798.9 (4.1)	371.2 (1.9)	954.2 (4.9)	100.5 (0.5)	12342.9 (63.6)	19410.5 (100.0)
1992-3	6100.0 (27.9)	0.0 (0.0)	0.0 (0.0)	1652.6 (7.6)	2442.1 (11.2)	1427.5 (6.5)	778.6 (3.6)	461.8 (2.1)	977.7 (4.5)	57.6 (0.3)	13897.9 (63.5)	21881.6 (100.0)
1993-4	5753.5 (24.7)	912.4 (3.9)	0.0 (0.0)	1881.9 (8.1)	2634.5 (11.3)	1370.7 (5.9)	795.0 (3.4)	1270.4 (5.5)	825.9 (3.5)	53.1 (0.2)	15497.4 (66.5)	23306.2 (100.0)
1994-5	5927.8 (20.7)	1228.1 (4.3)	712.6 (2.5)	2727.8 (9.5)	1629.7 (5.7)	2137.1 (7.5)	1163.6 (4.1)	1113.6 (3.9)	1052.4 (3.7)	198.8 (0.7)	17891.5 (62.4)	28654.4 (100.0)
1995-6	7525.8 (20.5)	1752.3 (4.8)	867.1 (2.4)	3924.4 (10.7)	2106.0 (5.7)	2565.5 (7.0)	1446.2 (3.9)	1105.1 (3.0)	1682.7 (4.6)	676.2 (1.8)	23651.3 (64.5)	36675.3 (100.0)
1996-7	10036.2 (25.6)	1423.8 (3.6)	991.5 (2.5)	3644.3 (9.3)	2925.0 (7.5)	2660.9 (6.8)	1370.6 (3.5)	1484.3 (3.8)	911.2 (2.3)	825.1 (2.1)	26272.9 (67.1)	39132.4 (100.0)
1997-8	8164.0 (19.7)	2087.8 (5.0)	3169.3 (7.6)	3621.9 (8.7)	3342.1 (8.1)	2956.1 (7.1)	1421.1 (3.4)	1051.3 (2.5)	1116.6 (2.7)	743.9 (1.8)	27674.1 (66.7)	41484.5 (100.0)
1998-9	6398.6 (15.1)	2223.0 (5.2)	5072.1 (12.0)	3044.5 (7.2)	3760.3 (8.9)	2683.7 (6.3)	1063.5 (2.5)	798.2 (1.9)	1076.4 (2.5)	1803.9 (4.3)	27924.2 (65.9)	42388.7 (100.0)
1999-2000	12611.4 (25.4)	2796.6 (5.6)	4706.1 (9.5)	2745.0 (5.5)	5436.0 (10.9)	2866.3 (5.8)	951.7 (1.9)	1136.6 (2.3)	1399.1 (2.8)	1856.8 (3.7)	36505.6 (73.5)	49670.7 (100.0)
2000-1	15650.1 (31.0)	3508.5 (6.9)	4638.0 (9.2)	2708.8 (5.4)	4807.7 (9.5)	2443.9 (4.8)	777.8 (1.5)	700.3 (1.4)	751.8 (1.5)	1308.2 (2.6)	37295.1 (73.8)	50536.5 (100.0)
2001-2	14000.3 (27.2)	3782.0 (7.4)	4582.3 (8.9)	2970.8 (5.8)	4622.6 (9.0)	2799.6 (5.4)	833.7 (1.6)	1149.4 (2.2)	679.0 (1.3)	1355.6 (2.6)	36775.3 (71.5)	51413.3 (100.0)
2002-3	17639.5 (28.7)	5599.4 (9.1)	4288.3 (7.0)	3565.6 (5.8)	6062.8 (9.9)	3025.2 (4.9)	943.7 (1.5)	1897.4 (3.1)	625.8 (1.0)	1814.2 (3.0)	45461.9 (74.0)	61412.1 (100.0)

Year											
2003–4	20569.5 (26.3)	7506.1 (9.6)	6856.4 (8.8)	4743.6 (6.1)	7128.7 (9.1)	4031.9 (5.2)	1506.1 (1.9)	3227.9 (4.1)	720.8 (0.9)	2542.5 (3.3)	58833.5 (75.3)	78149.1 (100.0)
2004–5	29844.1 (26.8)	9993.2 (9.0)	11150.0 (10.0)	6817.8 (6.1)	9422.7 (8.4)	5699.9 (5.1)	2669.7 (2.4)	4327.4 (3.9)	1377.1 (1.2)	2465.3 (2.2)	83767.2 (75.1)	111517.4 (100.0)
2005–6	43963.1 (29.5)	13241.7 (8.9)	11317.7 (7.6)	10009.8 (6.7)	9134.4 (6.1)	6984.1 (4.7)	4572.2 (3.1)	8838.5 (5.9)	2127.0 (1.4)	2024.0 (1.4)	122212.6 (75.2)	149165.7 (100.0)
2006–7	57143.6 (30.8)	15972.6 (8.6)	14646.0 (7.9)	13850.4 (7.5)	7487.5 (4.0)	7830.7 (4.2)	6424.7 (3.5)	9438.6 (5.1)	3144.1 (1.7)	2108.3 (1.1)	138046.5 (74.3)	185735.2 (100.0)
2007–8	79683.5 (31.7)	20219.8 (8.0)	17875.7 (7.1)	19870.1 (7.9)	7975.5 (3.2)	9901.5 (3.9)	8692.8 (3.5)	20121.5 (8.0)	5408.6 (2.2)	2559.9 (1.0)	192308.8 (76.4)	251562.3 (100.0)
2008–9	91291.2 (31.3)	23149.3 (7.9)	18682.6 (6.4)	20914.5 (7.2)	14439.1 (5.0)	12157.7 (4.2)	9363.7 (3.2)	13022.9 (4.5)	13577.4 (4.7)	3438.5 (1.2)	220036.9 (75.5)	291474.6 (100.0)
2009–10	87135.9 (30.2)	20952.5 (7.3)	29783.2 (10.3)	19710.6 (6.8)	16298.8 (5.7)	11926.3 (4.1)	8259.1 (2.9)	11708.4 (4.1)	6829.2 (2.4)	5600.5 (1.9)	218204.4 (75.7)	288372.9 (100.0)
2010–11	106068.3 (30.1)	21504.8 (6.1)	35693.7 (10.1)	23305.9 (6.6)	31306.2 (8.9)	14749.9 (4.2)	10278.6 (2.9)	11015.0 (3.1)	6949.4 (2.0)	6458.8 (1.8)	267330.4 (75.8)	352575.0 (100.0)

Source: RBI (2011), *Handbook of Statistics on Indian Economy*.

Table A9.3 Foreign Trade with Major Trading Partners

(US$ million)

	China		Germany		Australia		USA		Switzerland		UK	
	Export 2	Import	Export 3	Import	Export 4	Import	Export 5	Import	Export 6	Import	Export 7	Import
1987-8	15 (0.1)	119 (0.7)	817 (6.8)	1665 (9.7)	139 (1.1)	388 (2.3)	2252 (18.6)	1544 (9.0)	157 (1.3)	182 (1.1)	783 (6.5)	1410 (8.2)
1988-9	91 (0.7)	98 (0.5)	854 (6.1)	1697 (8.7)	183 (1.3)	488 (2.5)	2574 (18.4)	2237 (11.5)	188 (1.3)	194 (1.0)	796 (5.7)	1656 (8.5)
1989-90	24 (0.1)	40 (0.2)	1064 (6.4)	1674 (7.9)	201 (1.2)	539 (2.5)	2686 (16.2)	2561 (12.1)	219 (1.3)	219 (1.0)	961 (5.8)	1783 (8.4)
1990-1	18 (0.1)	31 (0.1)	1421 (7.8)	1936 (8.0)	179 (1.0)	816 (3.4)	2673 (14.7)	2923 (12.1)	224 (1.2)	268 (1.1)	1186 (6.5)	1613 (6.7)
1991-2	48 (0.3)	21 (0.1)	1270 (7.1)	1559 (8.0)	203 (1.1)	586 (3.0)	2921 (16.4)	1995 (10.3)	219 (1.2)	151 (0.8)	1138 (6.4)	1202 (6.2)
1992-1	141 (0.8)	126 (0.6)	1427 (7.7)	1657 (7.6)	223 (1.2)	838 (3.8)	3516 (19.0)	2147 (9.8)	199 (1.1)	378 (1.7)	1213 (6.5)	1417 (6.5)
1993-4	279 (1.3)	302 (1.3)	1539 (6.9)	1790 (7.7)	245 (1.1)	659 (2.8)	3999 (18.0)	2737 (11.7)	221 (1.0)	506 (2.2)	1379 (6.2)	1536 (6.6)
1994-5	254 (1.0)	761 (2.7)	1748 (6.6)	2187 (7.6)	346 (1.3)	915 (3.2)	5021 (19.1)	2906 (10.1)	247 (0.9)	824 (2.9)	1690 (6.4)	1559 (5.4)
1995-6	333 (1.0)	812 (2.2)	1977 (6.2)	3145 (8.6)	376 (1.2)	1022 (2.8)	5520 (17.4)	3861 (10.5)	282 (0.9)	1021 (2.8)	2011 (6.3)	1918 (5.2)
1996-7	615 (1.8)	757 (1.9)	1893 (5.7)	2831 (7.2)	385 (1.2)	1317 (3.4)	6555 (19.6)	3686 (9.4)	300 (0.9)	1127 (2.9)	2047 (6.1)	2135 (5.5)
1997-8	718 (2.1)	1119 (2.7)	1924 (5.5)	2529 (6.1)	438 (1.3)	1486 (3.6)	6803 (19.4)	3717 (9.0)	368 (1.0)	2641 (6.4)	2141 (6.1)	2444 (5.9)
1998-9	427 (1.3)	1097 (2.6)	1852 (5.6)	2141 (5.1)	387 (1.2)	1445 (3.4)	7200 (21.7)	3640 (8.6)	319 (1.0)	2942 (6.9)	1855 (5.6)	2621 (6.2)
1999-2000	539 (1.5)	1287 (2.6)	1738 (4.7)	1842 (3.7)	403 (1.1)	1082 (2.2)	8396 (22.8)	3564 (7.2)	354 (1.0)	2598 (5.2)	2035 (5.5)	2707 (5.4)
2000-1	831 (1.9)	1502 (3.0)	1908 (4.3)	1760 (3.5)	406 (0.9)	1063 (2.1)	9305 (20.9)	3015 (6.0)	438 (1.0)	3160 (6.3)	2299 (5.2)	3168 (6.3)
2001-2	952 (2.2)	2036 (4.0)	1788 (4.1)	2028 (3.9)	418 (1.0)	1306 (2.5)	8513 (19.4)	3150 (6.1)	409 (0.9)	2871 (5.6)	2161 (4.9)	2563 (5.0)
2002-3	1976 (3.7)	2792 (4.5)	2107 (4.0)	2405 (3.9)	504 (1.0)	1337 (2.2)	10896 (20.7)	4444 (7.2)	383 (0.7)	2330 (3.8)	2496 (4.7)	2777 (4.5)

2003–4	2955 (4.6)	4053 (5.2)	2545 (4.0)	2919 (3.7)	584 (0.9)	2649 (3.4)	11490 (18.0)	5035 (6.4)	450 (0.7)	3313 (4.2)	3023 (4.7)	3234 (4.1)
2004–5	5616 (6.7)	7098 (6.4)	2826 (3.4)	4015 (3.6)	720 (0.9)	3825 (3.4)	13766 (16.5)	7001 (6.3)	541 (0.6)	5940 (5.3)	3681 (4.4)	3566 (3.2)
2005–6	6759 (6.6)	10868 (7.3)	3586 (3.5)	6024 (4.0)	821 (0.8)	4947 (3.3)	17353 (16.8)	9455 (6.3)	480 (0.5)	6556 (4.4)	5059 (4.9)	3930 (2.6)
2006–7	8294 (6.6)	17461 (9.4)	3980 (3.1)	7546 (4.1)	925 (0.7)	7008 (3.8)	18866 (14.9)	11736 (6.3)	467 (0.4)	9124 (4.9)	5618 (4.4)	4175 (2.2)
2007–8	10871 (6.7)	27146 (10.8)	5122 (3.1)	9885 (3.9)	1152 (0.7)	7815 (3.1)	20731 (12.7)	21067 (8.4)	614 (0.4)	9758 (3.9)	6706 (4.1)	4954 (2.0)
2008–9	9354 (5.0)	32497 (10.7)	6389 (3.4)	12006 (4.0)	1439 (0.8)	11099 (3.7)	21150 (11.4)	18561 (6.1)	769 (0.4)	11870 (3.9)	6650 (3.6)	5872 (1.9)
2009–10	11618 (6.5)	30824 (10.7)	5413 (3.0)	10318 (3.6)	1385 (0.8)	12407 (4.3)	19535 (10.9)	16974 (5.9)	589 (0.3)	14698 (5.1)	6221 (3.5)	4462 (1.5)
2010–11	19396 (7.7)	40225 (11.4)	6784 (2.7)	11448 (3.2)	1723 (0.7)	10233 (2.9)	25673 (10.2)	18530 (5.3)	755 (0.3)	21730 (6.2)	7219 (2.9)	5116 (1.5)

(Contd.)

Table A9.3 (Contd.)

(US$ million)

	Singapore		UAE		Japan		Italy		Hong Kong		Total	
1	Export 8	Import	Export 9	Import	Export 10	Import	Export 11	Import	Export 12	Import	Export 13	Import
1987–8	211 (1.7)	323 (1.9)	239 (2.0)	588 (3.4)	1245 (10.3)	1640 (9.6)	384 (3.2)	395 (2.3)	344 (2.8)	93 (0.5)	12089 (100.0)	17156 (100.0)
1988–9	(1.7) (1.6)	429 (2.2)	293 (2.1)	602 (3.1)	1488 (10.6)	1817 (9.3)	373 (2.7)	347 (1.8)	565 (4.0)	121 (0.6)	13970 (100.0)	19497 (100.0)
1989–90	280 (1.7)	540 (2.5)	427 (2.6)	857 (4.0)	1639 (9.9)	1692 (8.0)	457 (2.7)	464 (2.2)	537 (3.2)	149 (0.7)	16613 (100.0)	21219 (100.0)
1990–1	379 (2.1)	796 (3.3)	439 (2.4)	1059 (4.4)	1694 (9.3)	1808 (7.5)	558 (3.1)	608 (2.5)	597 (3.3)	166 (0.7)	18145 (100.0)	24073 (100.0)
1991–2	389 (2.2)	695 (3.6)	739 (4.1)	1248 (6.4)	1652 (9.2)	1369 (7.1)	580 (3.2)	448 (2.3)	614 (3.4)	106 (0.5)	17865 (100.0)	19411 (100.0)
1992–1	589 (3.2)	632 (2.9)	814 (4.4)	1112 (5.1)	1437 (7.7)	1428 (6.5)	622 (3.4)	524 (2.4)	765 (4.1)	170 (0.8)	18537 (100.0)	21882 (100.0)
1993–4	752 (3.4)	627 (2.7)	1158 (5.2)	1003 (4.3)	1741 (7.8)	1522 (6.5)	604 (2.7)	538 (2.3)	1250 (5.6)	189 (0.8)	22238 (100.0)	23306 (100.0)
1994–5	770 (2.9)	900 (3.1)	1266 (4.8)	1533 (5.4)	2027 (7.7)	2040 (7.1)	858 (3.3)	741 (2.6)	1517 (5.8)	287 (1.0)	26331 (100.0)	28654 (100.0)
1995–6	902 (2.8)	1092 (3.0)	1428 (4.5)	1607 (4.4)	2216 (7.0)	2468 (6.7)	1014 (3.2)	1064 (2.9)	1821 (5.7)	388 (1.1)	31795 (100.0)	36675 (100.0)
1996–7	978 (2.9)	1063 (2.7)	1476 (4.4)	1736 (4.4)	2006 (6.0)	2187 (5.6)	934 (2.8)	987 (2.5)	1863 (5.6)	319 (0.8)	33470 (100.0)	39132 (100.0)
1997–8	780 (2.2)	1198 (2.9)	1692 (4.8)	1780 (4.3)	1899 (5.4)	2145 (5.2)	1115 (3.2)	922 (2.2)	1932 (5.5)	316 (0.8)	35006 (100.0)	41485 (100.0)
1998–9	518 (1.6)	1384 (3.3)	1868 (5.6)	1721 (4.1)	1652 (5.0)	2466 (5.8)	1055 (3.2)	1088 (2.6)	1881 (5.7)	449 (1.1)	33219 (100.0)	42389 (100.0)
1999–2000	673 (1.8)	1534 (3.1)	2083 (5.7)	2334 (4.7)	1685 (4.6)	2536 (5.1)	1120 (3.0)	735 (1.5)	2511 (6.8)	818 (1.6)	36822 (100.0)	49671 (100.0)
2000–1	877 (2.0)	1464 (2.9)	2598 (5.8)	659 (1.3)	1795 (4.0)	1842 (3.6)	1309 (2.9)	724 (1.4)	2641 (5.9)	852 (1.7)	44560 (100.0)	50537 (100.0)
2001–2	972 (2.2)	1304 (2.5)	2492 (5.7)	915 (1.8)	1510 (3.4)	2146 (4.2)	1207 (2.8)	705 (1.4)	2366 (5.4)	729 (1.4)	43827 (100.0)	51413 (100.0)
2002–3	1422 (2.7)	1435 (2.3)	3328 (6.3)	957 (1.6)	1864 (3.5)	1836 (3.0)	1357 (2.6)	812 (1.3)	2613 (5.0)	973 (1.6)	52719 (100.0)	61412 (100.0)

Year												Total
2003-4	2125 (3.3)	2085 (2.7)	5126 (8.0)	2060 (2.6)	1709 (2.7)	2668 (3.4)	1729 (2.7)	1071 (1.4)	3262 (5.1)	1493 (1.9)	63843 (100.0)	78149 (100.0)
2004-5	4006 (4.8)	2651 (2.4)	7348 (8.8)	4641 (4.2)	2128 (2.5)	3235 (2.9)	2286 (2.7)	1373 (1.2)	3692 (4.4)	1730 (1.6)	83536 (100.0)	111517 (100.0)
2005-6	5425 (5.3)	3354 (2.2)	8592 (8.3)	4354 (2.9)	2481 (2.4)	4061 (2.7)	2519 (2.4)	1856 (1.2)	4471 (4.3)	2207 (1.5)	103091 (100.0)	149166 (100.0)
2006-7	6069 (4.8)	5490 (3.0)	12032 (9.5)	8658 (4.7)	2863 (2.3)	4596 (2.5)	3583 (2.8)	2674 (1.4)	4681 (3.7)	2484 (1.3)	126414 (100.0)	185735 (100.0)
2007-8	7379 (4.5)	8123 (3.2)	15637 (9.6)	13483 (5.4)	3858 (2.4)	6326 (2.5)	3914 (2.4)	3907 (1.6)	6313 (3.9)	2698 (1.1)	163132 (100.0)	251654 (100.0)
2008-9	8450 (4.6)	7655 (2.5)	24477 (13.2)	23791 (7.8)	3026 (1.6)	7886 (2.6)	3825 (2.1)	4428 (1.5)	6655 (3.6)	6452 (2.1)	185295 (100.0)	303696 (100.0)
2009-10	7592 (4.2)	6455 (2.2)	23970 (13.4)	19499 (6.8)	3630 (2.0)	6734 (2.3)	3400 (1.9)	3862 (1.3)	7888 (4.4)	4734 (1.6)	178751 (100.0)	288373 (100.0)
2010-11	10631 (4.2)	6690 (1.9)	34105 (13.5)	28298 (8.0)	5212 (2.1)	8151 (2.3)	4577 (1.8)	4076 (1.2)	10359 (4.1)	8523 (2.4)	252354 (100.0)	352575 (100.0)

Note: Figures in brackets are percentages to total export/import.

The countries are selected as per the the following criteria. USA, UAE, and China are top in both import and export in 2008–9. UK,Singapore,UAR and Germany are top destination of exports in 2008–9.

Australia, and Switzerland are 2 top import destination to India in 2008–9. Japan,Italy and Hongkong are another three partners in trade where both export and imports are above $1000 million.

Source: Directorate General of Commercial Intelligence and Statistics (DGCI &S).

A10 FOREIGN INVESTMENT AND NRI DEPOSITS

Table A10.1 Foreign Investment Inflows

(US$ million)

Year	Direct Investment (I+II+III)	I. Equity (a+b+c+d+e)	a. Government (SIA/FIPB)	b. RBI	c. NRI	d. Acquisition of Shares*	e. Equity Capital of Unincorporated Bodies#	II. Reinvested Earnings+	III. Other Capital++	Portfolio Investment (a+b+c)	a. GDRs/ADRs##	b. FIIs**	c. Offshore Funds and Others	Total (A+B)
1990–1	97	0	0	0	0	0	0	0	0	6	0	0	6	103
1991–2	129	129	66	0	63	0	0	0	0	4	0	0	4	133
1992–3	315	315	222	42	51	0	0	0	0	244	240	1	3	559
1993–4	586	586	280	89	217	0	0	0	0	3567	1520	1665	382	4153
1994–5	1314	1314	701	171	442	0	0	0	0	3824	2082	1503	239	5138
1995–6	2144	2144	1249	169	715	11	0	0	0	2748	683	2009	56	4892
1996–7	2821	2821	1922	135	639	125	0	0	0	3312	1366	1926	20	6133
1997–8	3557	3557	2754	202	241	360	0	0	0	1828	645	979	204	5385
1998–9	2462	2462	1821	179	62	400	0	0	0	–61	270	–390	59	2401
1999–2000	2155	2155	1410	171	84	490	0	0	0	3026	768	2135	123	5181
2000–1	4029	2400	1456	454	67	362	61	1350	279	2760	831	1847	82	6789
2001–2	6130	4095	2221	767	35	881	191	1645	390	2021	477	1505	39	8151
2002–3	5035	2764	919	739	—	916	190	1833	438	979	600	377	2	6014
2003–4	4322	2229	928	534	—	735	32	1460	633	11377	459	10918	—	15699
2004–5	6051	3778	1062	1258	—	930	528	1904	369	9315	613	8686	16	15366
2005–6	8961	5975	1126	2233	—	2181	435	2760	226	12492	2552	9926	14	21453
2006–7	22826	16481	2156	7151	—	6278	896	5828	517	7003	3776	3225	2	29829
2007–8	34835	26864	2298	17127	—	5148	2291	7679	292	27271	6645	20328	298	62106
2008–9	41874	32066	5400	21332	—	4632	702	9032	776	–13,855	1162	–15,017	—	28019
2009–10	37745	27146	3471	18987	—	3148	1540	8668	1931	32376	3328	29048	—	70121
2010–11	32901	20304	1945	12994	—	4491	874	11939	658	31471	2049	29422	—	64372

Notes: *Relates to acquisition of shares of Indian companies by non-residents under section 6 of FEMA, 1999; #figures for equity capital of unincorporated bodies for 2011–12 are estimated based on average of previous two years; ##represents the amount raised by Indian corporate through Global Depository Receipts (GDRs) and American Depository Receipts (ADRs); and **represents inflow of funds (net) through Foreign Institutional Investors (FIIs).

Source: RBI Bulletin.

Table A10.2 NRI Deposits—Outstandings

(US$ million)

End-March	FCNR(A)	FCNR(B)	NR(E)RA	NR(NR)RD	NRO	Total
1991	10103	0	3618	0	0	13986
1992	9792	0	3025	0	0	13549
1993	10617	0	2740	621	0	15015
1994	9300	1108	3523	1754	0	16230
1995	7051	3063	4556	2486	0	17166
1996	4255	5720	3916	3542	0	17446
1997	2306	7496	4983	5604	0	20393
1998	1	8467	5637	6262	0	20369
1999	0	7835	6045	6618	0	20498
2000	0	8172	6758	6754	0	21684
2001	0	9076	7147	6849	0	23072
2002	0	9673	8449	7052	0	25174
2003	0	10199	14923	3407	0	28529
2004	0	10961	20559	1746	0	33266
2005	0	11452	21291	232	0	32975
2006	0	13064	22070	0	1148	36282
2007	0	15129	24495	0	1616	41240
2008	0	14168	26716	0	2788	43672
2009	0	13211	23570	0	4773	41554
2010	0	14258	26251	0	7381	47890
2011	0	15597	26378	0	9707	51682
2012	0	15167	30502	0	12250	57919

Notes: All figures are inclusive of interest. FCNR(A)—foreign currency non-resident (account); FCNR(B)—foreign currency non-resident (banks); NR(NR)RD—non resident (non repatriable) rupee deposits (introduced in June 2002; FCNR(A)—foreign currency non-resident (accounts) (introduced in May 2003); NR(E)RA—non resident (external) rupee accounts and NRO—non reident ordinary account.

Total for the years 1993 to 1998 includes FC(B7O)D—Foreign Currency (bank and other) Deposits and FC(O)N—Foreign Currency (ordinary) Non-repatriable Deposits.

Source: RBI Bulletins.

Table A10.3 FDI Inflows: Year-wise, Route-wise, Sector-wise Break up, and Country-wise Break up (August 1991 to November 2009)

Actual Inflows of FDI/NRI: Year-wise and Route-wise

	Rs crore					US$ million				
1	Govt's Approval (FIPB, SIA route)	RBI's Automatic Approval of Shares	Amount of Inflows on Acquisition	RBI's Various NRI Scheme	Total	Govt's Approval (FIPB, SIA route)	RBI's Automatic Approval	Amount of Inflows on Acquisition of Shares	RBI's Various NRI Scheme	Total
	2	3	4	5	6	7	8	9	10	11
2000	63368	16975	20581	3488	104411	1474	395	479	81	2429
2001	96386	32411	29622	2293	160711	2142	720	658	51	3571
2002	69580	39030	52623	111	161344	1450	813	1096	2	3361
2003	42956	23400	29284	–	95639	934	509	637	–	2079
2004	48517	54221	45076	–	147814	1055	1179	980	–	3213
2005	49728	68687	74292	–	192707	1136	1558	1661	–	4355
2006	69683	321758	112131	–	503572	1534	7121	750	–	11120
2007	107873	361001	186075	–	654950	2586	8889	4447	–	15921
2008	135588	1004681	256986	–	1595295	3209	23651	10234	–	37094
2009	229717	919849	160233	–	1309799	4680	19056	3308	–	27044
2010	115966	655519	188664	–	960149	2542	14354	4,111	–	21007
2011	134782	878222	206619	–	1273623	2933	19053	5,590	–	27576
2012 (Jan–Feb)	14531	135066	62018	–	211615	291	2685	1,239	–	4215
Total as on 29-2-2012	1178620	4510877	1676244	5890	7371631	25965	99981	36,903	134	162983

Source: www.Dipp.nic.in (SIA Newsletter).

A11 POPULATION

Table A11.1 State-wise Population 1951–2001

(in Millions)

State/UTs	2011	Decadal Growth (%) (2001–2011)	2001	Decadal Growth (%) (1991–2001)	1991	Decadal Growth (%) (1981–91)	1981	Decadal Growth (%) (1971–81)	1971	Decadal Growth (%) (1961–71)	1961	Decadal Growth (%) (1951–61)	1951	Decadal Growth (%) (1941–51)
1	2	3	4	5	6	7	8	9	10	11	12	13	14	15
India	1210.19	17.6	1028.74	21.5	846.39	23.9	683.33	24.7	548.16	24.8	439.23	21.6	361.09	13.3
Andhra Pradesh	84.67	11.1	76.21	14.6	66.51	24.2	53.55	23.1	43.50	20.9	35.98	15.6	31.12	14.0
Arunachal Pradesh	1.38	25.7	1.10	27.2	0.87	36.9	0.63	35.0	0.47	38.9	0.34	..	..	..
Assam	31.17	16.9	26.66	18.9	22.41	24.2	18.04	23.4	14.63	35.0	10.84	35.0	8.03	19.9
Bihar	103.80	25.1	83.00	28.6	64.53	-7.7	69.92	24.1	56.35	21.3	46.45	19.8	38.78	10.3
Goa	1.46	8.0	1.35	15.4	1.17	16.2	1.01	26.7	0.80	34.7	0.59	7.9	0.55	1.1
Gujarat	60.38	19.2	50.67	22.7	41.31	21.2	34.09	27.7	26.70	29.4	20.63	26.9	16.26	18.7
Haryana	25.35	19.9	21.15	28.5	16.46	27.4	12.92	28.8	10.04	32.2	7.59	33.8	5.67	7.6
Himachal Pradesh	6.86	12.8	6.08	17.6	5.17	20.8	4.28	23.7	3.46	23.0	2.81	17.9	2.39	5.4
Jammu and Kashmir	12.55	23.7	10.14	29.9	7.80	30.3	5.99	29.7	4.62	29.7	3.56	9.4	3.25	10.4
Karnataka	61.13	15.7	52.85	17.5	44.98	21.1	37.14	26.7	29.30	24.2	23.59	21.6	19.40	19.4
Kerala	33.39	4.9	31.84	9.4	29.10	14.3	25.45	19.2	21.35	26.3	16.90	24.8	13.55	22.8
Madhya Pradesh	72.60	20.3	60.35	24.3	48.57	-8.0	52.79	26.7	41.65	28.7	32.37	24.2	26.07	8.7
Maharashtra	112.37	16.0	96.88	22.7	78.94	25.7	62.78	24.5	50.41	27.5	39.55	23.6	32.00	19.3
Manipur	2.72	18.9	2.29	24.9	1.84	29.3	1.42	32.4	1.07	37.6	0.78	34.9	0.58	12.9
Meghalaya	2.96	27.8	2.32	30.7	1.78	32.9	1.34	32.0	1.01	31.6	0.77	26.9	0.61	9.0
Mizoram	1.09	22.6	0.89	28.8	0.69	39.7	0.49	48.8	0.33	24.8	0.27	35.7	0.20	28.1
Nagaland	1.98	-0.5	1.99	64.5	1.21	56.1	0.78	50.2	0.52	39.8	0.37	73.2	0.21	12.1
Odisha	41.95	14.0	36.81	16.3	31.66	20.1	26.37	20.2	21.95	25.0	17.55	19.8	14.65	6.4
Punjab	27.70	13.7	24.36	20.1	20.28	20.8	16.79	23.9	13.55	21.7	11.14	21.5	9.16	-4.6
Rajasthan	68.62	21.4	56.51	28.4	44.01	28.4	34.26	33.0	25.77	27.8	20.16	26.2	15.97	15.2
Sikkim	0.61	12.4	0.54	33.3	0.41	28.5	0.32	50.5	0.21	29.6	0.16	17.4	0.14	13.1
Tamil Nadu	72.14	15.6	62.41	11.7	55.86	15.4	48.41	17.5	41.20	22.3	33.69	11.8	30.12	14.7
Tripura	3.67	14.7	3.20	16.0	2.76	34.2	2.06	31.7	1.56	36.6	1.14	78.7	0.64	24.6
Uttar Pradesh	199.58	20.1	166.20	25.9	132.00	19.1	110.86	25.5	88.34	19.8	73.76	16.7	63.22	11.8
West Bengal	91.35	13.9	80.18	16.5	68.80	26.1	54.58	23.2	44.31	26.9	34.93	32.8	26.30	13.2
Uttrakhand	10.11	19.1	8.49	19.3	7.11	..	..	..	..	..	..	..	..	..

(Contd.)

Table A11.1 (Contd.)

(in Millions)

State/UTs	2011	Decadal Growth (%) (2001–2011)	2001	Decadal Growth (%) (1991–2001)	1991	Decadal Growth (%) (1981–91)	1981	Decadal Growth (%) (1971–81)	1971	Decadal Growth (%) (1961–71)	1961	Decadal Growth (%) (1951–61)	1951	Decadal Growth (%) (1941–51)
1	2	3	4	5	6	7	8	9	10	11	12	13	14	15
Jharkhand	32.97	22.3	26.95	23.4	21.84	..	..	..	..	..	..	..	..	..
Chhattisgarh	25.54	22.6	20.83	18.3	17.62	..	..	..	..	..	..	..	..	..
Union Territories														
Andaman & Nicobar	0.38	5.6	0.36	26.7	0.28	48.7	0.19	64.3	0.12	−82.0	0.64	106.5	0.31	−8.8
Chandigarh	1.06	17.2	0.90	40.3	0.64	42.0	0.45	75.9	0.26	114.2	0.12	−50.0	0.24	4.3
Dadra & Nagar Haveli	0.34	55.9	0.22	59.4	0.14	32.7	0.10	40.5	0.07	27.6	0.06	38.1	0.04	5.0
Daman and Diu	0.24	53.8	0.16	54.9	0.10	29.1	0.08	25.4	0.06	70.3	0.04	−24.5	0.05	14.0
Delhi	16.75	21.0	13.85	47.0	9.42	51.5	6.22	55.2	4.01	50.7	2.66	52.5	1.74	90.0
Lakshadweep	0.06	6.7	0.06	17.3	0.05	30.0	0.04	25.0	0.03	33.3	0.02	14.3	0.02	16.7
Puducherry	1.24	27.7	0.97	20.5	0.81	33.8	0.60	28.0	0.47	27.9	0.37	16.4	0.32	11.2

Source: Census of India 2011, *Primary Census Abstract* and Census of India 1991 *Final Population Totals: Paper 1 of 1992, Vol. II.*

Table A11.2 State-wise Rural and Urban Population of India: 1951–2001

(in Million)

State/UTs	2011 Rural	2011 Urban		2001 Rural	2001 Urban		1991 Rural	1991 Urban		1981 Rural	1981 Urban	
India	833.1	377.1	(31.2)	742.6	286.1	(27.8)	628.69	217.61	(25.7)	523.87	159.46	(23.3)
Andhra Pradesh	56.3	28.4	(33.5)	55.4	20.8	(27.3)	48.62	17.89	(26.9)	41.06	12.49	(23.3)
Arunachal Pradesh	1.1	0.3	(22.6)	0.9	0.2	(20.8)	0.75	0.11	(12.8)	0.59	0.04	(6.5)
Assam	26.8	4.4	(14.1)	23.2	3.4	(12.9)	19.93	2.49	(11.1)	16.26	1.78	(9.9)
Bihar	92.1	11.7	(11.3)	74.3	8.7	(10.5)	75.02	11.35	(17.6)	61.20	8.72	(12.5)
Goa	0.6	0.9	(62.1)	0.7	0.7	(49.7)	0.69	0.48	(41.0)	0.69	0.32	(32.1)
Gujarat	34.7	25.7	(42.6)	31.7	18.9	(37.4)	27.06	14.25	(34.5)	23.48	10.60	(31.1)
Haryana	16.5	8.8	(34.8)	15.0	6.1	(28.9)	12.41	4.06	(24.6)	10.10	2.83	(21.9)
Himachal Pradesh	6.2	0.7	(10.0)	5.5	0.6	(9.8)	4.72	0.45	(8.7)	3.96	0.33	(7.6)
Jammu and Kashmir	9.1	3.4	(27.2)	7.6	2.5	(24.8)	5.88	1.84	(23.6)	4.73	1.26	(21.0)
Karnataka	37.6	23.6	(38.6)	34.9	18.0	(34.0)	31.07	13.91	(30.9)	26.41	10.73	(28.9)
Kerala	17.5	15.9	(47.7)	23.6	8.3	(26.0)	21.42	7.68	(26.4)	20.68	4.77	(18.7)
Madhya Pradesh	52.5	20.1	(27.6)	44.4	16.0	(26.5)	50.84	15.34	(31.6)	41.59	10.59	(20.1)
Maharashtra	61.5	50.8	(45.2)	55.8	41.1	(42.4)	48.40	30.54	(38.7)	40.79	21.99	(35.0)
Manipur	1.9	0.8	(30.2)	1.7	0.6	(25.1)	1.33	0.51	(27.5)	1.05	0.38	(26.4)
Meghalaya	2.4	0.6	(20.1)	1.9	0.5	(19.6)	1.45	0.33	(18.6)	1.09	0.24	(18.0)
Mizoram	0.5	0.6	(51.5)	0.4	0.4	(49.6)	0.37	0.32	(46.1)	0.37	0.12	(24.7)
Nagaland	1.4	0.6	(29.0)	1.6	0.3	(17.2)	1.00	0.21	(17.2)	0.66	0.12	(15.5)
Odisha	35.0	7.0	(16.7)	31.3	5.5	(15.0)	27.43	4.24	(13.4)	23.26	3.11	(11.8)
Punjab	17.3	10.4	(37.5)	16.1	8.3	(33.9)	14.29	5.99	(29.5)	12.14	4.65	(27.7)
Rajasthan	51.5	17.1	(24.9)	43.3	13.2	(23.4)	33.94	10.07	(22.9)	27.05	7.21	(21.0)
Sikkim	0.5	0.2	(25.0)	0.5	0.1	(11.1)	0.37	0.04	(9.1)	0.27	0.05	(16.1)
Tamil Nadu	37.2	35.0	(48.4)	34.9	27.5	(44.0)	36.78	19.08	(34.2)	32.46	15.95	(33.0)
Tripura	2.7	1.0	(26.2)	2.7	0.5	(17.1)	2.34	0.42	(15.3)	1.83	0.23	(11.0)
Uttar Pradesh	155.1	44.5	(22.3)	131.7	34.5	(20.8)	111.51	27.61	(20.9)	90.96	19.90	(17.9)
West Bengal	62.2	29.1	(31.9)	57.7	22.4	(28.0)	49.37	18.71	(27.2)	40.13	14.45	(26.5)
Uttarakhand	7.0	3.1	(30.6)	6.3	2.2	(25.7)	..	..		..	..	
Jharkhand	25.0	7.9	(24.1)	21.0	6.0	(22.2)	..	..		..	..	
Chhattisgarh	19.6	5.9	(23.2)	16.6	4.2	(20.1)	..	..		..	..	

(Contd.)

Table A11.2 (Contd.)

(in Million)

State/UTs	2011 Rural	2011 Urban		2001 Rural	2001 Urban		1991 Rural	1991 Urban		1981 Rural	1981 Urban	
Union Territories												
Andaman & Nicobar	0.2	0.1	(35.8)	0.2	0.1	(32.6)	0.21	0.08	(26.7)	0.14	0.05	(23.8)
Chandigarh	0.0	1.0	(97.3)	0.1	0.8	(89.7)	0.07	0.58	(89.7)	0.03	0.42	(93.6)
Dadra & Nagar Haveli	0.2	0.2	(46.6)	0.2	0.1	(22.9)	0.13	0.01	(8.7)	0.10	0.01	(6.7)
Daman and Diu	0.1	0.2	(75.3)	0.1	0.1	(36.3)	0.05	0.05	(47.1)	0.05	0.03	(36.7)
Delhi	0.4	16.3	(97.5)	0.9	12.9	(93.2)	0.92	8.47	(89.9)	0.45	5.77	(92.7)
Lakshadweep	0.0	0.1	(78.1)	0.0	0.0	(44.2)	0.02	0.03	(55.8)	0.02	0.02	(47.5)
Puducherry	0.4	0.9	(68.3)	0.3	0.6	(66.6)	0.30	0.52	(64.0)	0.29	0.32	(52.3)

(in Million)

State/UTs	1971 Rural	1971 Urban		1961 Rural	1961 Urban		1951 Rural	1951 Urban	
India	439.05	109.11	(19.9)	360.30	78.94	(18.0)	298.64	62.44	(17.3)
Andhra Pradesh	35.10	8.40	(19.3)	29.71	6.28	(17.4)	25.69	5.42	(17.4)
Arunachal Pradesh	0.45	0.02	(3.6)	0.34	..		..	..	
Assam	13.34	1.29	(8.8)	10.06	0.78	(7.2)	7.68	0.35	(4.3)
Bihar	50.72	5.63	(10.0)	42.53	3.91	(8.4)	36.16	2.63	(6.8)
Goa	0.59	0.20	(25.5)	0.50	0.09	(14.7)	0.48	0.07	(13.0)
Gujarat	19.20	7.50	(28.1)	15.32	5.32	(25.8)	11.84	4.43	(27.2)
Haryana	8.26	1.77	(17.7)	6.28	1.31	(17.2)	4.71	0.97	(17.1)
Himachal Pradesh	3.22	0.24	(7.0)	2.63	0.18	(6.3)	2.23	0.15	(6.5)
Jammu and Kashmir	3.76	0.86	(18.6)	2.97	0.59	(16.7)	2.80	0.46	(14.0)
Karnataka	22.18	7.12	(24.3)	18.32	5.27	(22.3)	14.95	4.45	(23.0)
Kerala	17.81	3.47	(16.2)	14.35	2.55	(15.1)	11.72	1.83	(13.5)
Madhya Pradesh	34.87	6.79	(16.3)	27.75	4.63	(14.3)	22.94	3.13	(12.0)
Maharashtra	34.70	15.71	(31.2)	28.39	11.16	(28.2)	22.80	9.20	(28.8)
Manipur	0.93	0.14	(13.1)	0.71	0.07	(8.7)	0.58	0.03	(4.8)
Meghalaya	0.87	0.15	(14.5)	0.65	0.12	(15.2)	0.55	0.06	(9.9)

Mizoram	0.30	0.04	(11.4)	0.25	0.01	(5.3)	0.19	0.01	(3.6)
Nagaland	0.47	0.05	(9.9)	0.35	0.02	(5.1)	0.21	0.00	(0.9)
Odisha	20.10	1.85	(8.4)	16.44	1.11	(6.3)	14.05	0.59	(4.1)
Punjab	10.34	3.22	(23.7)	8.57	2.57	(23.1)	7.17	1.99	(21.7)
Rajasthan	21.22	4.54	(17.6)	16.87	3.28	(16.3)	13.02	2.96	(18.5)
Sikkim	0.19	0.02	(9.5)	0.16	0.07	(43.2)	0.14	0.03	(21.7)
Tamil Nadu	28.73	12.47	(30.3)	24.70	8.99	(26.7)	22.79	7.33	(24.4)
Tripura	1.39	0.16	(10.4)	1.04	0.10	(9.0)	0.60	0.04	(6.8)
Uttar Pradesh	75.95	12.39	(14.0)	64.28	9.48	(12.9)	54.59	8.63	(13.6)
West Bengal	33.35	10.97	(24.7)	26.39	8.54	(24.5)	20.02	6.28	(23.9)
Uttarakhand	:	:		:	:		:	:	
Jharkhand	:	:		:	:		:	:	
Chhattisgarh	:	:		:	:		:	:	
Union Territories									
Andaman & Nicobar	0.09	0.03	(22.6)	0.05	0.01	(2.2)	0.02	0.01	(2.6)
Chandigarh	0.02	0.23	(90.7)	0.02	0.10	(82.5)	0.02	0.00	(0.0)
Dadra & Nagar Haveli	0.07	0.00	(0.0)	0.06	0.00	(0.0)	0.04	0.00	(0.0)
Daman and Diu	0.04	0.02	(38.1)	0.02	0.01	(35.1)	0.03	0.02	(36.7)
Delhi	0.42	3.66	(91.5)	0.30	2.36	(88.7)	0.31	1.44	(82.4)
Lakshadweep	0.03	0.00	(0.0)	0.02	0.00	(0.0)	0.02	0.00	(0.0)
Puducherry	0.27	0.20	(42.3)	0.28	0.09	(24.4)	0.32	0.00	(0.0)

Note: Figures within brackets represents urban share in total population in percentages.

Source: Census of India 2011, *Provisional Population Totals*, Part 1 of 2001 and Census of India 1991, *Final Population Totals, Paper-1 of 1992, Vol-II.*

Table A11.3 State-wise Sex Ratio (females per 1000 males)

State/UTs	1901	1911	1921	1931	1941	1951	1961	1971	1981	1991	2001	2011
1	2	3	4	5	6	7	8	9	10	11	12	13
India	972	964	955	950	945	946	941	930	934	927	933	940
Andhra Pradesh	985	992	993	987	980	986	981	977	975	972	978	992
Arunachal Pradesh	na	na	na	na	na	na	894	861	862	859	893	919
Assam	919	915	896	874	875	868	869	896	910	923	935	954
Bihar	1061	1051	1020	995	1002	1000	1005	957	948	907	919	916
Goa	1091	1108	1120	1088	1084	1128	1066	981	975	967	961	968
Gujarat	954	946	944	945	941	952	940	934	942	934	920	918
Haryana	867	835	844	844	869	871	868	867	870	865	861	877
Himachal Pradesh	884	889	890	897	890	912	938	958	973	976	968	974
Jammu and Kashmir	882	876	870	865	869	873	878	878	892	896	892	883
Karnataka	983	981	969	965	960	966	959	957	963	960	965	968
Kerala	1004	1008	1011	1022	1027	1028	1022	1016	1032	1036	1058	1084
Madhya Pradesh	972	967	949	947	946	945	932	920	921	912	919	930
Maharashtra	978	966	950	947	949	941	936	930	937	934	922	925
Manipur	1037	1029	1041	1065	1055	1036	1015	980	971	958	978	987
Meghalaya	1036	1013	1000	971	966	949	937	942	954	955	972	985
Mizoram	1113	1120	1109	1102	1069	1041	1009	946	919	921	935	976
Nagaland	973	993	992	997	1021	999	933	871	863	886	900	931
Odisha	1037	1056	1086	1067	1053	1022	1001	988	981	971	972	978
Punjab	832	780	799	815	836	844	854	865	879	882	876	893
Rajasthan	905	908	896	907	906	921	908	911	919	910	921	926
Sikkim	916	951	970	967	920	907	904	863	835	878	875	888
Tamil Nadu	1044	1042	1029	1027	1012	1007	992	978	977	974	987	995
Tripura	874	885	885	885	886	904	932	943	946	945	948	961
Uttar Pradesh	938	916	908	903	907	908	907	876	882	876	898	908
West Bengal	945	925	905	890	852	865	878	891	911	917	934	947
Uttrakhand	918	907	916	913	907	940	947	940	936	936	962	963
Jharkhand	1032	1021	1002	989	978	961	960	945	940	922	941	947
Chhattisgarh	1046	1039	1041	1043	1032	1024	1008	998	996	985	989	991

Union Territories

Andaman & Nicobar	318	352	303	495	574	625	617	644	760	818	846	881
Chandigarh	771	720	743	751	763	781	652	749	769	790	777	817
Dadra & Nagar Haveli	960	967	940	911	925	946	963	1007	974	952	812	777
Daman and Diu	995	1040	1143	1088	1080	1125	1169	1099	1062	969	1034	6200
Delhi	862	793	733	722	715	768	785	801	808	827	821	866
Lakshadweep	1063	987	1027	994	1018	1043	1020	978	975	943	948	939
Puducherry	na	1058	1053	na	na	1030	1013	989	985	979	1001	1039

Note: Excludes Mao–Maram, Paomata and Purul sub–divisions of Senapati district of Manipur.

Source: Census of India 2011, *Provisional Population Totals*, Part 1 of 2011.

Table A11.4 State-wise Literacy Rate: 1951 to 2001

(In Percentage of Population)

State/Uts	2011			2001			1991			1981			1971			1961			1951		
	Persons	Male	Female	Persons	Male	Female	Persons	Male	Female	Persons	Male	Female	Persons	Male	Female	Persons	Male	Female	Persons	Male	Female
1	2	3	4	5	6	7	8	9	10	11	12	13	14	15	16	17	18	19	20	21	22
India	74.0	82.1	65.5	64.8	75.3	53.7	52.2	64.1	39.3	43.6	56.4	29.8	34.5	39.5	18.7	28.3	34.40	12.9	18.3	24.9	7.9
Male–female gap	(16.7)			(21.6)			(24.8)			(26.6)			(24.0)			(25.1)			(18.3)		
Andhra Pradesh	67.7	75.6	59.7	60.5	70.3	50.4	44.1	55.1	32.7	35.7	46.8	24.2	24.6	33.1	15.8	21.2	30.20	12.0	13.2	19.7	6.5
Arunachal Pradesh	67.0	73.7	59.6	54.3	63.8	43.5	41.6	51.5	29.7	25.5	35.1	14.0	11.3	17.8	3.7	47.9	na	na	na	na	na
Assam	73.2	78.8	67.3	63.3	71.3	54.6	52.9	61.9	43.0	na	na	na	28.7	na	na	33.0	37.30	16.0	18.3	27.4	7.9
Bihar	63.8	73.4	53.3	47.0	59.7	33.1	38.5	52.5	22.9	32.0	46.6	16.5	19.9	30.6	8.7	21.8	29.80	6.9	12.2	20.5	3.8
Goa	87.4	92.8	81.8	82.0	88.4	75.4	75.5	83.6	67.1	64.7	76.0	55.2	na	54.3	35.1	36.2	na	na	23.0	na	na
Gujarat	79.3	87.2	70.7	69.1	79.7	57.8	61.3	73.1	48.6	52.2	65.1	38.5	35.8	46.1	24.8	30.5	41.10	19.1	23.1	32.3	13.5
Haryana	76.6	85.4	66.8	67.9	78.5	55.7	55.9	69.1	40.5	43.9	58.5	26.9	26.9	37.2	14.9	24.1	na	na	na	na	na
Himachal Pradesh	83.8	90.8	76.6	76.5	85.3	67.4	63.9	75.4	52.1	51.2	64.3	37.7	32.0	43.1	20.2	24.9	27.20	6.2	7.7	12.6	2.4
Jammu and Kashmir	68.7	78.3	58.0	55.5	66.6	43.0	na	na	na	32.7	44.2	19.6	18.6	na	na	13.0	17.00	4.3	na	na	na
Karnataka	75.6	82.9	68.1	66.6	76.1	56.9	56.0	67.3	44.3	46.2	58.7	33.2	31.5	48.6	27.8	29.8	36.10	14.2	19.3	29.1	9.2
Kerala	93.9	96.0	92.0	90.9	94.2	87.7	89.8	93.6	86.2	81.6	87.7	75.7	60.4	74.0	64.5	55.1	55.00	38.9	40.7	50.2	31.5
Madhya Pradesh	70.6	80.5	60.0	63.7	76.1	50.3	44.2	58.4	28.9	34.2	48.4	19.0	22.1	32.7	10.9	20.5	27.00	6.7	9.8	16.2	3.2
Maharashtra	82.9	89.8	75.5	76.9	86.0	67.0	64.9	76.6	52.3	55.8	69.7	41.0	39.2	51.0	26.4	35.1	42.00	16.8	20.9	31.4	9.7
Manipur	79.9	86.5	73.2	70.5	80.3	60.5	59.9	71.6	47.6	49.6	64.1	34.6	32.9	46.0	19.5	36.0	45.10	15.9	11.4	20.8	2.4
Meghalaya	75.5	77.2	73.8	62.6	65.4	59.6	49.1	53.1	44.9	42.0	46.6	37.2	29.5	34.1	24.6	na	na	na	na	na	na
Mizoram	91.6	93.7	89.4	88.8	90.7	86.7	82.3	85.6	78.6	74.3	79.4	68.6	na	60.5	46.7	na	na	na	na	na	na
Nagaland	80.1	83.3	76.7	66.6	71.2	61.5	61.6	67.6	54.8	50.2	58.5	40.3	27.4	35.0	18.7	20.4	24.00	11.3	10.4	15.0	5.7
Odisha	73.5	82.4	64.4	63.1	75.3	50.5	49.1	63.1	34.7	41.0	56.5	25.1	26.2	38.3	13.9	25.2	34.70	8.6	15.8	27.3	4.5
Punjab	76.7	81.5	71.3	69.7	75.2	63.4	58.5	65.7	50.4	48.1	55.5	39.6	33.7	40.4	25.9	31.5	33.00	14.1	15.2	21.0	8.5
Rajasthan	67.1	80.5	52.7	60.4	75.7	43.9	38.6	55.0	20.4	30.1	44.8	14.0	19.1	28.7	8.5	18.1	23.70	5.8	8.9	14.4	3.0
Sikkim	82.2	87.3	76.4	68.8	76.0	60.4	56.9	65.7	46.7	41.6	53.0	27.4	17.7	na	na	14.2	19.60	4.3	7.3	12.8	1.3
Tamil Nadu	80.3	86.8	73.9	73.5	82.4	64.4	62.7	73.8	51.3	54.4	68.1	40.4	39.5	51.8	26.9	36.4	44.50	18.2	20.8	31.7	10.0
Tripura	87.8	92.2	83.2	73.2	81.0	64.9	60.4	70.6	49.7	50.1	61.5	38.0	31.0	40.2	21.2	24.3	29.60	10.2	15.5	22.3	8.0
Uttar Pradesh	69.7	79.2	59.3	56.3	68.8	42.2	41.6	55.7	25.3	33.3	47.4	17.2	21.7	31.5	10.6	20.7	27.30	7.0	10.8	17.4	3.6
West Bengal	77.1	82.7	71.2	68.6	77.0	59.6	57.7	67.8	46.6	48.6	59.9	36.1	33.2	42.8	22.4	34.5	40.10	17.0	24.0	34.2	12.2
Uttarakhand	79.6	88.3	70.7	71.6	83.3	59.6	na	na	na	na	na	na	na	na	na	na	na	na	na	na	na
Jharkhand	67.6	78.5	56.2	53.6	67.3	38.9	na	na	na	na	na	na	na	na	na	na	na	na	na	na	na
Chhattisgarh	71.0	81.5	60.6	64.7	77.4	51.9	na	na	na	na	na	na	na	na	na	na	na	na	na	na	na

Union Territories

Andaman & Nicobar	86.3	90.1	81.8	81.3	86.3	75.2	73.0	79.0	65.5	63.2	70.3	53.2	43.6	na	na	40.1	42.40	19.4	25.8	34.2	12.3
Chandigarh	86.4	90.5	81.4	81.9	86.1	76.5	77.8	82.0	72.3	74.8	78.9	69.3	61.6	na	na	55.1	na	na	na	na	na
Dadra & Nagar Haveli	77.7	86.5	65.9	57.6	71.2	40.2	40.7	53.6	27.0	32.7	44.7	20.4	15.0	na	na	11.6	14.70	4.1	4.0	na	na
Daman and Diu	87.1	91.5	79.6	78.2	86.8	65.6	71.2	82.7	59.4	59.9	74.5	46.5	44.8	na	na	34.9	na	na	22.9	na	na
Delhi	86.3	91.0	80.9	81.7	87.3	74.7	75.3	82.0	67.0	71.9	79.3	62.6	56.6	na	na	62.0	60.80	42.5	38.4	43.0	32.3
Lakshadweep	92.3	96.1	88.3	86.7	92.5	80.5	81.8	90.2	72.9	68.4	81.2	55.3	43.7	na	na	27.2	35.80	11.0	15.2	25.6	5.3
Puducherry	86.6	92.1	81.2	81.2	88.6	73.9	74.7	83.7	65.6	65.1	77.1	53.0	46.0	na	na	43.7	50.40	24.6	na	na	na

Note: Excludes Mao–Maram, Paomata and Purul sub–divisions of Senapati district of Manipur.

Source: Census of India 2011, *Provisional Population Tables* and *Economic Survey 2009–10* for the year 1981 Economic Survey: 1991–92.

Table A11.5 State-wise Infant Mortality Rate: 1961, 1981, 1991, 2001, and 2010

(Number per thousand)

State/UTs	2010			2001			1991			1981			1961		
	Persons	Male	Female	Persons	Male	Female	Persons	Male	Female	Persons	Male	Female	Persons	Male	Female
1	2	3	4	5	6	7	8	9	10	11	12	13	14	15	16
India	47	46	49	71	na	na	77	79	74	115	122	108	115	122	108
Andhra Pradesh	46	44	47	66	na	na	55	67	51	91	100	82	91	100	82
Arunachal Pradesh	31	31	32	44	na	na	91	111	103	126	141	111	126	141	111
Assam	58	56	60	78	na	na	92	96	87	—	—	—	—	—	—
Bihar	48	46	50	67	na	na	75	62	89	94	95	94	94	95	94
Goa	10	6	15	36	na	na	51	56	48	90	87	93	57	60	56
Gujarat	44	41	47	64	na	na	78	74	82	115	120	110	84	81	84
Haryana	48	46	49	69	na	na	52	57	54	126	132	119	94	87	119
Himachal Pradesh	40	35	47	64	na	na	82	84	81	143	160	126	92	101	89
Jammu and Kashmir	43	41	45	45	na	na	na	na	na	108	115	99	78	78	78
Karnataka	38	37	39	58	na	na	74	81	53	81	87	74	77	74	79
Kerala	13	13	14	16	na	na	42	45	41	54	61	48	52	55	48
Madhya Pradesh	62	62	63	97	na	na	133	131	136	150	158	140	150	158	140
Maharashtra	28	27	29	49	na	na	74	72	76	119	131	106	92	96	89
Manipur	14	11	16	25	na	na	28	29	27	32	31	33	32	31	33
Meghalaya	55	55	56	52	na	na	80	79	82	79	81	76	79	81	76
Mizoram	37	36	39	23	na	na	53	51	56	83	94	70	69	73	65
Nagaland	23	19	28	na	na	na	51	51	52	68	76	58	68	76	58
Odisha	61	60	61	98	na	na	125	129	111	163	172	153	115	119	111
Punjab	34	33	35	54	na	na	74	81	53	127	138	114	77	74	79
Rajasthan	55	52	57	83	na	na	87	94	79	141	146	135	114	114	114
Sikkim	30	28	32	52	na	na	60	58	62	127	135	118	96	105	87
Tamil Nadu	24	23	24	53	na	na	54	55	51	104	114	93	86	89	82
Tripura	27	25	29	49	na	na	82	81	84	130	143	116	111	106	116
Uttar Pradesh	61	58	63	85	na	na	99	98	104	130	131	128	130	131	128
West Bengal	31	29	32	53	na	na	62	75	51	95	103	57	95	103	57
Chhattisgarh	51	48	54	na	na	na	na	na	na	na	na	na	na	na	na
Jharkhand	42	41	44	na	na	na	na	na	na	na	na	na	na	na	na
Uttarakhand	38	37	39	na	na	na	na	na	na	na	na	na	na	na	na

Union Territories

Andaman & Nicobar	25	24	27	30	na	na	69	71	61	95	114	76	77	78	66
Chandigarh	22	20	25	32	na	na	48	50	47	118	141	96	53	53	53
Dadra & Nagar Haveli	38	36	40	61	na	na	81	84	73	117	149	82	98	102	93
Daman and Diu	23	22	23	na	na	na	56	61	50	90	87	93	57	60	56
Delhi	30	29	31	51	na	na	54	55	51	100	108	92	67	66	70
Lakshadweep	25	21	29	30	na	na	91	100	78	132	170	88	118	124	88
Puducherry	22	22	22	21	na	na	34	32	35	84	100	68	73	77	68

Note: na: Not applicable or not relevant.

Source: *SRS Bulletin* December 2011; *Economic Survey 2009–10*, and *2002–3*; and *National Human Development Report 2001*, Planning Commission.

Table A11.6 Number of Child Population in the Age Group 0–6 Years by Sex

State/UTs	Number Child Population in the Age Group 0–6 Years by Sex							Proportion of Children to Total Population						Sex Ratio	
	2001			2011				2001			2011			2001	2011
	Persons	Male	Female	Persons	Male	Female		Persons	Male	Female	Persons	Male	Female		
1	2	3	4	5	6	7		8	9	10	11	12	13	14	15
India	163837395	85008267	78829128	158789287	82952135	75837152		15.93	15.97	15.88	13.12	13.30	12.93	927	914
Andhra Pradesh	10171857	5187321	4984536	8642686	4448330	4194356		13.35	13.46	13.23	10.21	10.46	9.95	961	943
Arunachal Pradesh	205871	104833	101038	202759	103430	99329		18.75	18.08	19.50	14.66	14.36	15.00	964	960
Assam	4498075	2289116	2208959	4511307	2305088	2206219		16.87	16.62	17.15	14.47	14.45	14.50	965	957
Bihar	16806063	8652705	8153358	18582229	9615280	8966949		20.25	20.01	20.51	17.90	17.75	18.07	942	933
Goa	145968	75338	70630	139495	72669	66826		10.83	10.96	10.69	9.57	9.81	9.32	938	920
Gujarat	7532404	4000148	3532256	7494176	3974286	3519890		14.87	15.16	14.54	12.41	12.62	12.18	883	886
Haryana	3335537	1833655	1501882	3297724	1802047	1495677		15.77	16.14	15.36	13.01	13.34	12.62	819	830
Himachal Pradesh	793137	418426	374711	763864	400681	363183		13.05	13.55	12.53	11.14	11.53	10.74	896	906
Jammu and Kashmir	1485803	765394	720409	2008642	1080662	927980		14.65	14.28	15.06	16.01	16.21	15.77	941	859
Karnataka	7182100	3690958	3491142	6855801	3527844	3327957		13.59	13.72	13.45	11.21	11.36	11.07	946	943
Kerala	3793146	1935027	1858119	3322247	1695935	1626312		11.91	12.51	11.35	9.95	10.59	9.36	960	959
Madhya Pradesh	10782214	5579847	5202367	10548295	5516957	5031338		17.87	17.75	18.00	14.53	14.67	14.38	932	912
Maharashtra	13671126	7146432	6524694	12848375	6822262	6026113		14.11	14.18	14.04	11.43	11.69	11.16	913	883
Manipur	326366	166746	159620	353237	182684	170553		14.23	14.35	14.10	12.98	13.34	12.61	957	934
Meghalaya	467979	237215	230764	555822	282189	273633		20.18	20.17	20.19	18.75	18.91	18.60	973	970
Mizoram	143734	73176	70558	165536	83965	81571		16.18	15.94	16.43	15.17	15.20	15.14	964	971
Nagaland	289678	147524	142154	285981	147111	138870		14.56	14.09	15.08	14.44	14.34	14.54	964	944
Odisha	5358810	2744552	2614258	5035650	2603208	2432442		14.56	14.71	14.41	12.00	12.28	11.73	953	934
Punjab	3171829	1763801	1408028	2941570	1593262	1348308		13.02	13.58	12.38	10.62	10.89	10.32	798	846
Rajasthan	10651002	5579616	5071386	10504916	5580212	4924704		18.85	18.97	18.72	15.31	15.67	14.92	909	883
Sikkim	78195	39842	38353	61077	31418	29659		14.46	13.81	15.20	10.05	9.77	10.37	963	944
Tamil Nadu	7235160	3725616	3509544	6894821	3542351	3352470		11.59	11.86	11.32	9.56	9.80	9.32	942	946
Tripura	436446	222002	214444	444055	227354	216701		13.64	13.52	13.77	12.10	12.15	12.04	966	953
Uttar Pradesh	31624628	16509033	15115595	29728235	15653175	14075060		19.03	18.85	19.22	14.90	14.97	14.82	916	899
West Bengal	11414222	5824180	5590042	10112599	5187264	4925335		14.24	14.05	14.44	11.07	11.05	11.09	960	950
Uttarakhand	1360032	712949	647083	1328844	704769	624075		16.02	16.48	15.54	13.14	13.67	12.58	908	886
Jharkhand	4956827	2522036	2434791	5237582	2695921	2541661		18.40	18.16	18.64	15.89	15.92	15.85	965	943
Chhattisgarh	3554916	1800413	1754503	3584028	1824987	1759041		17.06	17.19	16.94	11.18	10.89	11.54	975	964

Union Territories

Andaman & Nicobar	44781	22885	21896	39497	20094	19403	12.57	11.86	13.42	10.40	9.93	10.92	957	966
Chandigarh	115613	62664	52949	117953	63187	54766	12.84	12.36	13.45	11.18	10.89	11.54	845	867
Dadra & Nagar Haveli	40199	20308	19891	49196	25575	23621	18.23	16.69	20.13	14.35	13.24	15.78	979	924
Daman and Diu	20578	10685	9893	25880	13556	12324	13.01	11.55	15.06	10.65	9.03	13.28	926	909
Delhi	2016849	1079618	937231	1970510	1055735	914775	14.56	14.19	15.01	11.76	11.76	11.76	868	866
Lakshadweep	9091	4641	4450	7088	3715	3373	14.99	14.91	15.08	11.00	11.22	10.77	959	908
Puducherry	117159	59565	57594	127610	64932	62678	12.02	12.23	11.82	10.25	10.64	9.89	967	965

Note: Excludes Mao–Maram, Paomata and Purul sub-divisions of Senapati district of Manipur.

Source: Census of India 2011, *Provisional Population Tables* and *Economic Survey 2009–10*, for the year 1981 *Economic Survey 1991–92*.

A12. SOCIAL SECTOR

Table A12.1 Human Development Index for India by State 1981, 1991, and 2001

State/UTs	HDI 1981									HDI 1991									HDI 2001		
	Rural		Urban		Combined		Gender Disparity Index		Rural		Urabn		Combined		Gender Disparity Index		Combined	
	Value	Rank	Value	Rank	Value	Rank	Value	Rank	Value	Rank	Value	Rank	Value	Rank	Value	Rank	Value	Rank
1	2	3	4	5	6	7	8	9	10	11	12	13	14	15	16	17	18	19
India	0.263		0.442		0.302		0.620		0.340		0.511		0.381		0.676		0.472	
Andhra Pradesh	0.262	25	0.425	23	0.298	23	0.744	10	0.344	23	0.473	29	0.377	23	0.801	23	0.416	10
Arunachal Pradesh	0.228	28	0.419	24	0.242	31	0.537	28	0.300	28	0.572	15	0.328	29	0.776	28	*	
Assam	0.261	26	0.380	28	0.272	26	0.462	32	0.326	26	0.555	19	0.348	26	0.575	30	0.386	14
Bihar	0.220	30	0.378	29	0.237	32	0.471	30	0.286	30	0.460	31	0.308	32	0.469	32	0.367	15
Goa	0.422	5	0.517	10	0.445	5	0.785	2	0.534	3	0.658	3	0.575	4	0.775	13	*	
Gujarat	0.315	14	0.458	18	0.360	14	0.723	6	0.380	18	0.532	23	0.431	17	0.714	22	0.479	6
Haryana	0.332	13	0.465	17	0.360	15	0.536	24	0.409	15	0.562	17	0.443	16	0.714	17	0.509	5
Himachal Pradesh	0.374	10	0.600	1	0.398	10	0.783	4	0.442	12	0.700	1	0.469	13	0.858	4	*	
Jammu and Kashmir	0.301	17	0.468	16	0.337	19	0.584	19	0.364	22	0.575	14	0.402	21	0.740	25	*	
Karnataka	0.295	18	0.489	14	0.346	16	0.707	20	0.367	21	0.523	24	0.412	19	0.753	11	0.478	7
Kerala	0.491	1	0.544	6	0.500	2	0.872	1	0.576	1	0.628	9	0.591	3	0.825	2	0.638	1
Madhya Pradesh	0.209	32	0.395	26	0.245	30	0.664	25	0.282	32	0.491	28	0.328	30	0.662	28	0.394	12
Maharashtra	0.306	15	0.489	15	0.363	13	0.740	15	0.403	16	0.548	21	0.452	15	0.793	15	0.523	4
Manipur	0.440	2	0.553	5	0.461	4	0.802	3	0.503	7	0.618	12	0.536	9	0.815	3	*	
Meghalaya	0.293	20	0.442	21	0.317	21	0.799	12	0.332	24	0.624	10	0.365	24	0.807	12	*	
Mizoram	0.381	9	0.558	4	0.411	8	0.502	18	0.464	10	0.648	5	0.548	7	0.770	6	*	
Nagaland	0.295	19	0.519	8	0.328	20	0.783	16	0.442	13	0.633	7	0.486	11	0.729	21	*	
Orissa	0.252	27	0.368	31	0.267	27	0.547	27	0.328	25	0.469	30	0.345	28	0.639	27	0.404	11
Punjab	0.386	8	0.494	13	0.411	9	0.688	14	0.447	11	0.566	16	0.475	12	0.710	19	0.537	2
Rajasthan	0.216	31	0.386	27	0.256	28	0.650	17	0.298	29	0.492	27	0.347	27	0.692	16	0.424	9
Sikkim	0.302	16	0.515	11	0.342	18	0.643	23	0.398	17	0.618	11	0.425	18	0.647	20	*	
Tamil Nadu	0.289	21	0.445	19	0.343	17	0.710	9	0.421	14	0.560	18	0.466	14	0.813	9	0.531	3
Tripura	0.264	23	0.498	12	0.287	24	0.422	31	0.368	20	0.551	20	0.389	22	0.531	29	*	
Uttar Pradesh	0.227	29	0.398	25	0.255	29	0.447	29	0.284	31	0.444	32	0.314	31	0.520	31	0.388	13
West bengal	0.264	24	0.427	22	0.305	22	0.556	26	0.370	19	0.511	26	0.404	20	0.631	26	0.472	8

Andaman & Nicobar	0.335	12	0.575	2	0.394	11	0.645	21	0.528	5	0.653	4	0.574	5	0.857	1	*
Chandigarh	0.437	4	0.565	3	0.550	1	0.719	7	0.501	8	0.694	2	0.674	1	0.764	7	*
Dadra & Nagar Haveli	0.269	22	0.268	32	0.276	25	0.888	11	0.310	27	0.519	25	0.361	25	0.832	14	*
Daman and Diu	0.409	6	0.518	9	0.438	6	0.760	5	0.492	9	0.629	8	0.544	8	0.714	8	*
Delhi	0.439	3	0.531	7	0.495	3	0.595	22	0.530	4	0.635	6	0.624	2	0.690	10	*
Lakshadweep	0.395	7	0.371	30	0.434	7	0.688	8	0.520	6	0.545	22	0.532	10	0.680	24	*
Pondicherry	0.338	11	0.443	20	0.386	12	0.753	13	0.556	2	0.591	13	0.571	6	0.783	5	*

Note: * Not available for the year 2001.

The HDI is a composite of variables capturing attainments in three dimensions of human development viz. economic, educational, and health.

This has been worked out by a combination of measures: per capita monthly expenditures adjusted for inequality; a combination of litracy rate and intensity of formal education, and a combination of life expectancy at age 1 and infant mortality rate.

For details see the technical note in the source for the estimation methodology.

Source: Planning Commission (2002): *National Human Development Report, 2001*, March.

Table A12.2 Number and Per cent of Population below Poverty Line and Poverty Line (in Rs)

State	Rural 1973–4			Urban 1973–4			Combined 1973–4		Rural 1983–4			Urban 1983–4			Combined 1983–4	
	No. of Persons (Lakh)	% of Persons	Poverty Line (Rs)	No. of Persons (Lakh)	% of Persons	Poverty Line (Rs)	No. of Persons (Lakh)	% of Persons	No. of Persons (Lakh)	% of Persons	Poverty Line (Rs)	No. of Persons (Lakh)	% of Persons	Poverty Line (Rs)	No. of Persons (Lakh)	% of Persons
Andhra Pradesh	178.21	48.41	41.71	47.48	50.61	53.96	225.69	48.86	114.34	26.53	72.66	50.24	36.30	106.43	164.58	28.91
Arunachal Pradesh	2.57	52.67	49.82	0.09	36.92	50.26	2.66	51.93	2.70	42.60	98.32	0.12	21.73	97.51	2.82	40.88
Assam	76.37	52.67	49.82	5.46	36.92	50.26	81.83	51.21	73.43	42.60	98.32	4.26	21.73	97.51	77.69	40.47
Bihar	336.52	62.99	57.68	34.05	52.96	61.27	370.57	61.91	417.70	64.37	97.48	44.35	47.33	111.80	462.05	62.22
Goa	3.16	46.85	50.47	1.00	37.69	59.48	4.16	44.26	1.16	14.81	88.24	1.07	27.00	126.47	2.23	18.90
Gujarat	94.61	46.35	47.10	43.81	52.57	62.17	138.42	48.15	72.88	29.80	83.29	45.04	39.14	123.22	117.92	32.79
Haryana	30.08	34.23	49.95	8.24	40.18	52.42	38.32	35.36	22.03	20.56	88.57	7.57	24.15	103.48	29.60	21.37
Himachal Pradesh	9.38	27.42	49.95	0.35	13.17	51.93	9.73	26.39	7.07	17.00	88.57	0.34	9.43	102.26	7.41	16.40
Jammu & Kashmir	18.41	45.51	46.59	2.07	21.32	37.17	20.48	40.83	13.11	26.04	91.75	2.49	17.76	99.62	15.60	24.24
Karnataka	128.40	55.14	47.24	42.27	52.53	58.22	170.67	54.47	100.50	36.33	83.31	49.31	42.82	120.19	149.81	38.24
Kerala	111.36	59.19	51.68	24.16	62.74	62.78	135.52	59.79	81.62	39.03	99.35	25.15	45.68	122.64	106.77	40.42
Madhya Pradesh	231.21	62.66	50.20	45.09	57.65	63.02	276.30	61.78	215.48	48.90	83.59	62.49	53.06	122.82	277.97	49.78
Maharashtra	210.84	57.71	50.47	76.58	43.87	59.48	287.42	53.24	193.75	45.23	88.24	97.14	40.26	126.47	290.89	43.44
Manipur	5.11	52.67	49.82	0.75	36.92	50.26	5.86	49.96	4.76	42.60	98.32	0.89	21.73	97.51	5.65	37.02
Meghalaya	4.88	52.67	49.82	0.64	36.92	50.26	5.52	50.20	5.04	42.60	98.32	0.57	21.73	97.51	5.62	38.81
Mizoram	1.62	52.67	49.82	0.20	36.92	50.26	1.82	50.32	1.58	42.60	98.32	0.37	21.73	97.51	1.96	36.00
Nagaland	2.65	52.67	49.82	0.25	36.92	50.26	2.90	50.81	3.19	42.60	98.32	0.31	21.73	97.51	3.50	39.25
Orissa	142.24	67.28	46.87	12.23	55.62	59.34	154.47	66.18	164.65	67.53	106.28	16.66	49.15	124.81	181.31	65.29
Punjab	30.47	28.21	49.95	10.02	27.96	51.93	40.49	28.15	16.79	13.20	88.57	11.85	23.79	101.03	28.64	16.18
Rajasthan	101.41	44.76	50.96	27.10	52.13	59.99	128.51	46.14	96.77	33.50	80.24	30.06	37.94	113.55	126.83	34.46
Sikkim	1.09	52.67	49.82	0.10	36.92	50.26	1.19	50.86	1.24	42.60	98.32	0.10	21.73	97.51	1.35	39.71
Tamil Nadu	172.60	57.43	45.09	66.92	49.40	51.54	239.52	54.94	181.61	53.99	96.15	78.46	46.96	120.30	260.07	51.66
Tripura	7.88	52.67	49.82	0.66	36.92	50.26	8.54	51.00	8.35	42.60	98.32	0.60	21.73	97.51	8.95	40.03
Uttar Pradesh	449.99	56.53	48.92	85.74	60.09	57.37	535.73	57.07	448.03	46.45	83.85	108.71	49.82	110.23	556.74	47.07
West Bengal	257.96	73.16	54.49	41.34	34.67	54.81	299.30	63.43	268.60	63.05	105.55	50.09	32.32	105.91	318.69	54.85
All India	2612.90	56.44	49.63	600.46	49.01	56.64	3213.36	54.88	2519.57	45.65	89.50	709.40	40.79	115.65	3228.97	44.48

Table A12.2 (Contd.)

State	Rural			Urban			Combined		
				1993–4					
	No. of Persons (Lakh)	% of Persons	Poverty Line (Rs)	No. of Persons (Lakh)	% of Persons	Poverty Line (Rs)	No. of Persons (Lakh)	% of Persons	
Andhra Pradesh	74.49	15.92	163.02	74.47	38.33	278.14	153.97	22.19
Arunachal Pradesh	3.62	45.01	232.05	0.11	7.73	212.42	3.73	39.35
Assam	94.33	45.01	232.05	2.03	7.73	212.42	96.36	40.86
Bihar	450.86	58.21	212.16	42.49	34.50	238.49	493.35	54.96
Goa	0.38	5.34	194.94	1.53	27.03	328.56	1.91	14.92
Gujarat	62.16	22.18	202.11	43.02	27.89	297.22	105.19	24.21
Haryana	36.56	28.02	233.79	7.31	16.38	258.23	43.88	25.05
Himachal Pradesh	15.40	30.34	233.79	0.46	9.18	253.61	15.86	28.44
Jammu & Kashmir	19.05	30.34	233.79	1.86	9.18	253.61	20.92	25.17
Karnataka	95.99	29.88	186.63	60.46	40.14	302.89	156.46	33.16
Kerala	55.95	25.76	243.84	20.46	24.55	280.54	76.41	25.43
Madhya Pradesh	216.19	40.64	193.10	82.33	48.38	317.16	298.52	42.52
Maharashtra	193.33	37.93	194.94	111.90	35.15	328.56	305.22	36.86
Manipur	6.33	45.01	232.05	0.47	7.73	212.42	6.80	33.78
Meghalaya	7.09	45.01	232.05	0.29	7.73	212.42	7.38	37.92
Mizoram	1.64	45.01	232.05	0.30	7.73	212.42	1.94	25.66
Nagaland	4.85	45.01	232.05	0.20	7.73	212.42	5.05	37.92
Orissa	140.90	49.72	194.03	19.70	41.64	298.22	160.60	48.56
Punjab	17.76	11.95	233.79	7.35	11.35	253.61	25.11	11.77
Rajasthan	94.68	26.46	215.89	33.82	30.49	280.85	128.50	27.41
Sikkim	1.81	45.01	232.05	0.03	7.73	212.42	1.84	41.43
Tamil Nadu	121.70	32.48	196.53	80.40	39.77	296.63	202.10	35.03
Tripura	11.41	45.01	232.05	0.38	7.73	212.42	11.79	39.01
Uttar Pradesh	496.17	42.28	213.01	108.28	35.39	258.65	604.46	40.85
West Bengal	209.90	40.80	220.74	44.66	22.41	247.53	254.56	35.66
All India	2440.31	37.27	205.84	763.37	32.36	281.35	3203.67	35.97

(Contd.)

Table A12.2 (Contd.)

State	Rural 1999–2000 (30-day Recall Period)			Urban			Combined			Rural 2004-5 (Based on MRP Consumption)			Urban			Combined	
	No. of Persons (Lakh)	% of Persons	Poverty Line (Rs)	No. of Persons (Lakh)	% of Persons	Poverty Line (Rs)	No. of Persons (Lakh)	% of Persons	No. of Persons (Lakh)	% of Persons	Poverty Line (Rs)	No. of Persons (Lakh)	% of Persons	Poverty Line (Rs)	No. of Persons (Lakh)	% of Persons
Andhra Pradesh	58.13	11.05	262.94	60.88	26.63	457.40	119.01	15.77	43.21	7.50	292.95	45.50	20.70	542.89	88.71	11.10
Arunachal Pradesh	3.80	40.04	365.43	0.18	7.47	343.99	3.98	33.47	1.47	17.00	387.64	0.07	2.40	378.84	1.54	13.40
Assam	92.17	40.04	365.43	2.38	7.47	343.99	94.55	36.09	41.46	17.00	387.64	0.93	2.40	378.84	42.39	15.00
Bihar	376.51	44.30	333.07	49.13	32.91	379.78	425.64	42.60	262.92	32.90	354.36	27.09	28.90	435.00	290.01	32.50
Goa	0.11	1.35	318.63	0.59	7.52	539.71	0.70	4.40	54.72	31.20	322.41	16.39	34.70	560.00	71.11	32.00
Gujarat	39.80	13.17	318.94	28.09	15.59	474.41	67.89	14.07	0.13	1.90	362.25	1.62	20.90	665.90	1.74	12.00
Haryana	11.94	8.27	362.81	5.39	9.99	420.20	17.34	8.74	46.25	13.90	353.93	21.18	10.10	541.16	67.43	12.50
Himachal Pradesh	4.84	7.94	367.45	0.29	4.63	420.20	5.12	7.63	14.57	9.20	414.76	7.99	11.30	504.49	22.56	9.90
Jammu & Kashmir	2.97	3.97	367.45	0.49	1.98	420.20	3.46	3.48	4.10	7.20	394.28	0.17	2.60	504.49	4.27	6.70
Karnataka	59.91	17.38	309.59	44.49	25.25	511.44	104.40	20.04	2.20	2.70	391.26	2.34	8.50	553.77	4.54	4.20
Kerala	20.97	9.38	374.79	20.07	20.27	477.06	41.04	12.72	89.76	40.20	366.56	10.63	16.30	451.24	100.39	34.80
Madhya Pradesh	217.32	37.06	311.34	81.22	38.44	481.65	298.54	37.43	43.33	12.00	324.17	53.28	27.20	599.66	96.60	17.40
Maharashtra	125.12	23.72	318.63	102.87	26.81	539.71	227.99	25.02	23.59	9.60	430.12	13.92	16.40	559.39	37.51	11.40
Manipur	6.53	40.04	365.43	0.66	7.47	343.99	7.19	28.54	141.99	29.80	327.78	66.97	39.30	570.15	210.97	32.40
Meghalaya	7.89	40.04	365.43	0.34	7.47	343.99	8.23	33.87	128.43	22.20	362.25	131.40	29.00	665.90	259.83	25.20
Mizoram	1.40	40.04	365.43	0.45	7.47	343.99	1.85	19.47	2.86	17.00	387.64	0.14	2.40	378.84	3.00	13.20
Nagaland	5.21	40.04	365.43	0.28	7.47	343.99	5.49	32.67	3.32	17.00	387.64	0.12	2.40	378.84	3.43	14.10
Orissa	143.69	48.01	323.92	25.40	42.83	473.12	169.09	47.15	0.78	17.00	387.64	0.11	2.40	378.84	0.89	9.50
Punjab	10.20	6.35	362.68	4.29	5.75	388.15	14.49	6.16	2.94	17.00	387.64	0.09	2.40	378.84	3.03	14.50
Rajasthan	55.06	13.74	344.03	26.78	19.85	465.92	81.83	15.28	129.29	39.80	325.79	24.30	40.30	528.49	153.59	39.90
Sikkim	2.00	40.04	365.43	0.04	7.47	343.99	2.05	36.55	9.78	5.90	410.38	3.52	3.80	466.16	13.30	5.20
Tamil Nadu	80.51	20.55	307.64	49.97	22.11	475.60	130.48	21.12	66.69	14.30	374.57	40.50	28.10	559.63	107.18	17.50
Tripura	12.53	40.04	365.43	0.49	7.47	343.99	13.02	34.44	0.85	17.00	387.64	0.02	2.40	378.84	0.87	15.20
Uttar Pradesh	412.01	31.22	336.88	117.88	30.89	416.29	529.89	31.15	56.51	16.90	351.86	58.59	18.80	547.42	115.10	17.80
West Bengal	180.11	31.85	350.17	33.38	14.86	409.22	213.49	27.02	4.70	17.00	387.64	0.14	2.40	378.84	4.85	14.40
All India	1932.43	27.09	327.56	670.07	23.62	454.11	2602.50	26.10	357.68	25.30	365.84	100.47	26.30	483.26	458.15	25.50

Table A12.2 (Contd.)

2004–5 (Based on URP Consumption)

State	Rural			Urban			Combined		
	No. of Persons (Lakh)	% of Persons	Poverty Line (Rs)	No. of Persons (Lakh)	% of Persons	Poverty Line (Rs)	No. of Persons (Lakh)	% of Persons
Andhra Pradesh	64.70	11.20	292.95	61.40	28.00	542.89	126.10	15.80
Arunachal Pradesh	1.94	22.30	387.64	0.09	3.30	378.84	2.03	17.60
Assam	54.50	22.30	387.64	1.28	3.30	378.84	55.77	19.70
Bihar	336.72	42.10	354.36	32.42	34.60	435.00	369.15	41.40
Goa	71.50	40.80	322.41	19.47	41.20	560.00	90.96	40.90
Gujarat	0.36	5.40	362.25	1.64	21.30	665.90	2.01	13.80
Haryana	63.49	19.10	353.93	27.19	13.00	541.16	90.69	16.80
Himachal Pradesh	21.49	13.60	414.76	10.60	15.10	504.49	32.10	14.00
Jammu & Kashmir	6.14	10.70	394.28	0.22	3.40	504.49	6.36	10.00
Karnataka	3.66	4.60	391.26	2.19	7.90	553.77	5.85	5.40
Kerala	103.19	46.30	366.56	13.20	20.20	451.24	116.39	40.30
Madhya Pradesh	75.05	20.80	324.17	63.83	32.60	599.66	138.89	25.00
Maharashtra	32.43	13.20	430.12	17.17	20.20	559.39	49.60	15.00
Manipur	175.65	36.90	327.78	74.03	42.10	570.15	249.68	38.30
Meghalaya	171.13	29.60	362.25	146.25	32.20	665.90	317.38	30.70
Mizoram	3.76	22.30	387.64	0.20	3.30	378.84	3.95	17.30
Nagaland	4.36	22.30	387.64	0.16	3.30	378.84	4.52	18.50
Odisha	1.02	22.30	387.64	0.16	3.30	378.84	1.18	12.60
Punjab	3.87	22.30	387.64	0.12	3.30	378.84	3.99	19.00
Rajasthan	151.75	46.80	325.79	26.74	44.30	528.49	178.49	46.40
Sikkim	15.12	9.10	410.38	6.50	7.10	466.16	21.63	8.40
Tamil Nadu	87.38	18.70	374.57	47.51	32.90	559.63	134.89	22.10
Tripura	1.12	22.30	387.64	0.02	3.30	378.84	1.14	20.10
Uttar Pradesh	76.50	22.80	351.86	69.13	22.20	547.42	145.62	22.50
West Bengal	6.18	22.30	387.64	0.20	3.30	378.84	6.38	18.90
All India	473.00	33.40	365.84	117.03	30.60	483.26	590.03	32.80

Source: Planning Commission.

Table A12.3 Poverty Line and Number of Poor in Rural and Urban Areas across States, 1993–4, 2004–5, and 2009–10, New Method

States	Poverty Line (in Rupees)						Number of Poor (in Lakhs)					
	Rural			Urban			Rural			Urban		
	1993–4	2004–5	2009–10	1993–4	2004–5	2009–10	1993–4	2004–5	2009–10	1993–4	2004–5	2009–10
Andhra Pradesh	244.1	433.4	693.8	282.0	563.2	926.4	240.2	180.0	127.9	68.4	55.0	48.7
Arunachal Pradesh	285.1	547.1	773.3	297.1	618.5	925.2	4.8	3.2	2.7	0.3	0.6	0.8
Assam	266.3	478.0	691.7	306.8	600.0	871.0	115.1	89.4	105.3	7.3	8.3	11.2
Bihar	236.1	433.4	655.6	266.9	526.2	775.3	367.1	451.0	498.7	32.3	42.8	44.8
Chhattisgarh	229.1	398.9	617.3	283.5	513.7	806.7	96.8	97.8	108.3	10.8	13.7	13.6
Delhi	315.4	541.4	747.8	320.3	642.5	1040.3	1.6	1.1	0.3	15	18.3	22.9
Goa	316.2	608.8	931.0	306.0	671.2	1025.4	1.8	1.8	0.6	0.8	1.7	0.6
Gujarat	279.4	501.6	725.9	320.7	659.2	951.4	120.8	128.5	91.6	43.2	42.9	44.6
Haryana	294.1	529.4	791.6	312.1	626.4	975.4	52.2	38.8	30.4	10.8	15.9	19.6
Himachal Pradesh	272.7	520.4	708.0	316.0	605.7	888.3	18.6	14.3	5.6	0.7	0.3	0.9
Jammu & Kashmir	289.1	522.3	722.9	281.1	602.9	845.4	20.4	11.6	7.3	1.4	2.9	4.2
Jharkhand	227.7	404.8	616.3	304.1	531.4	831.2	122.2	116.2	102.2	21.3	16	24.0
Karnataka	266.9	417.8	629.4	294.8	588.1	908.0	181.8	134.7	97.4	51.5	51.8	44.9
Kerala	286.5	537.3	775.3	289.2	584.7	830.7	73.6	42.2	21.6	19.9	19.8	18.0
Madhya Pradesh	232.5	408.4	631.9	274.5	532.3	771.7	175.8	254.4	216.9	41.8	61.3	44.9
Maharashtra	268.6	484.9	743.7	329.0	631.9	961.1	302.3	277.8	179.8	96.5	114.6	90.9
Manipur	322.3	578.1	871.0	366.3	641.1	955.0	9.1	6.7	8.8	4.1	2.3	3.7
Meghalaya	284.1	503.3	689.9	393.4	745.7	989.8	6	2.9	3.5	0.9	1.2	1.4
Mizoram	316.5	639.3	850.0	355.7	699.8	939.3	0.6	1.1	1.6	0.2	0.4	0.6
Nagaland	381.7	687.3	1016.8	409.6	782.9	1147.6	2.2	1.5	2.8	0.6	0.2	1.4
Odisha	224.2	407.8	567.1	279.3	497.3	736.0	178.5	198.8	135.5	16.3	22.8	17.7
Puducherry	220.3	385.5	641.0	264.3	506.2	777.7	0.8	0.8	0.0	1.9	0.7	0.1
Punjab	286.9	543.5	830.0	342.3	642.5	960.8	30.2	36.7	25.1	17.6	16.9	18.4
Rajasthan	271.9	478.0	755.0	300.5	568.2	846.0	146.0	166.4	133.8	33.2	43.5	33.2
Sikkim	266.6	531.5	728.9	362.2	741.7	1035.2	1.3	1.5	0.7	0.1	0.2	0.1
Tamil Nadu	252.6	441.7	639.0	288.2	559.8	800.8	191.1	134.4	78.3	68.1	59.7	43.5
Tripura	275.8	450.5	663.4	316.6	555.8	782.7	8.7	11.9	5.4	1.2	1.5	0.9
Uttar Pradesh	244.3	435.1	663.7	281.3	532.1	799.9	571.7	600.5	600.6	112.3	130.1	137.3
Uttaranchal	249.5	486.2	719.5	306.7	602.4	898.6	18.5	23.1	10.3	2.4	6.6	7.5
West Bengal	235.5	445.4	643.2	295.2	572.5	830.6	218.6	227.5	177.8	62.2	60.8	62.5

Andaman & Nicobar Island	252.6	441.7	639.0	288.2	559.8	800.8	0.1	0.1	0.01	0.02	0.01	0.004
Chandigarh	342.3	642.5	960.8	342.3	642.5	960.8	0.2	0.2	0.03	0.8	0.9	0.92
Dadra & Nagar Haveli	268.6	484.9	743.7	329.0	631.9	961.1	1.0	1.11	1.02	0.05	0.14	0.25
Daman & Diu	316.2	608.8	931.0	306.0	671.2	1025.4	0.1	0.02	0.22	0.08	0.13	0.54
Lakshadweep	286.5	537.3	775.3	289.2	584.7	830.7	0.01	0.001	0.03	0.05	0.04	0.01
All India	–	446.7	672.8	–	578.8	859.6	3279.7	3258.1	2782.1	744.2	814.1	764.7

Note and Source: Number of poor for 1993–4 are estimated based on head count ratio population computed from the estimates of number of poor as per the earlier method of the Planning Commission and obtained from, http://www.indiastat.com/table/economy/8/incidenceofpoverty/221/8107/data.aspx. Head count ration for 31 states and union territories is from the *Report of the Expert Group to Review the Methodology for Estimation of Poverty*, Planning Commission, New Delhi (Chairperson: Late Professor Suresh D. Tendulkar), 2009. For the remaining five union territories of Andaman & Nicobar Islands, Chandigarh, Dadra & Nagar Haveli, Daman & Diu, and Lakshadweep we used incidence provided by C. Ravi through a personal communication. The population of undivided states of Bihar, Madhya Pradesh, and Uttar Pradesh was divided based on their share as per the National Sample Survey region unit level data of 1993–4, which is an overestimate for Uttaranchal because the relevant region had one district (Bareily) which is not part of the new state. For updates of 2004–5 and for 2009–10 we used *Press Note on Poverty Estimates, 2009–10*, Planning Commission, New Delhi, 2012. These estimates have been computed by Durgesh C. Pathak and Srijit Mishra, authors of Chapter 15, of this volume.

Table A12.4 Head Count Ratio and Share of Poor for Rural and Urban Areas across States, 1993–4 to 2009–10, New Method

States	Head Count Ratio (per cent)									Share of Poor (per cent)								
	Rural			Urban			Combined			Rural			Urban			Combined		
	1993–4	2004–5	2009–10	1993–4	2004–5	2009–10	1993–4	2004–5	2009–10	1993–4	2004–5	2009–10	1993–4	2004–5	2009–10	1993–4	2004–5	2009–10
Andhra Pradesh	48.1	32.3	22.8	35.2	23.4	17.7	44.6	29.6	21.1	7.3	5.5	4.6	9.2	6.8	6.4	7.7	5.8	5.0
Arunachal Pradesh	60.0	33.6	26.2	22.6	23.5	24.9	54.5	31.4	25.9	0.1	0.1	0.1	0.0	0.1	0.1	0.1	0.1	0.1
Assam	54.9	36.4	39.9	27.7	21.8	26.1	51.8	34.4	37.9	3.5	2.7	3.8	1.0	1.0	1.5	3.0	2.4	3.3
Bihar	62.3	55.7	55.3	44.7	43.7	39.4	60.5	54.4	53.5	11.2	13.8	17.9	4.3	5.3	5.9	9.9	12.1	15.3
Chhattisgarh	55.9	55.1	56.1	28.1	28.4	23.8	50.9	49.4	48.7	3.0	3.0	3.9	1.5	1.7	1.8	2.7	2.7	3.4
Delhi	16.2	15.6	7.7	15.7	12.9	14.4	15.7	13.0	14.2	0.0	0.0	0.0	2.0	2.2	3.0	0.4	0.5	0.7
Goa	25.5	28.1	11.5	14.6	22.2	6.9	20.8	24.9	8.7	0.1	0.1	0.0	0.1	0.2	0.1	0.1	0.1	0.0
Gujarat	43.1	39.1	26.7	28.0	20.1	17.9	37.8	31.6	23.0	3.7	3.9	3.3	5.8	5.3	5.8	4.1	4.2	3.8
Haryana	40.0	24.8	18.6	24.2	22.4	23.0	35.9	24.1	20.1	1.6	1.2	1.1	1.5	2.0	2.6	1.6	1.3	1.4
Himachal Pradesh	36.7	25.0	9.1	13.6	4.6	12.6	34.6	22.9	9.5	0.6	0.4	0.2	0.1	0.0	0.1	0.5	0.4	0.2
Jammu & Kashmir	32.5	14.1	8.1	6.9	10.4	12.8	26.3	13.1	9.4	0.6	0.4	0.3	0.2	0.4	0.5	0.5	0.4	0.3
Jharkhand	65.9	51.6	41.6	41.8	23.8	31.1	60.7	45.3	39.1	3.7	3.6	3.7	2.9	2.0	3.1	3.6	3.2	3.6
Karnataka	56.6	37.5	26.1	34.2	25.9	19.6	49.5	33.3	23.6	5.5	4.1	3.5	6.9	6.4	5.9	5.8	4.6	4.0
Kerala	33.9	20.2	12.0	23.9	18.4	12.1	31.3	19.6	12.0	2.2	1.3	0.8	2.7	2.4	2.4	2.3	1.5	1.1
Madhya Pradesh	49.0	53.6	42.0	31.8	35.1	22.9	44.6	48.6	36.7	5.4	7.8	7.8	5.6	7.5	5.9	5.4	7.8	7.4
Maharashtra	59.3	47.9	29.5	30.3	25.6	18.3	47.8	38.2	24.5	9.2	8.5	6.5	13.0	14.1	11.9	9.9	9.6	7.6
Manipur	64.4	39.3	47.4	67.2	34.5	46.4	65.1	37.9	47.1	0.3	0.2	0.3	0.6	0.3	0.5	0.3	0.2	0.4
Meghalaya	38.0	14.0	15.3	23.0	24.7	24.1	35.2	16.0	17.1	0.2	0.1	0.1	0.1	0.1	0.2	0.2	0.1	0.1
Mizoram	16.6	23.0	31.1	6.3	7.9	11.5	11.8	15.4	21.1	0.0	0.0	0.1	0.0	0.0	0.1	0.0	0.0	0.1
Nagaland	20.1	10.0	19.3	21.8	4.3	25.0	20.4	8.8	20.9	0.1	0.0	0.1	0.1	0.0	0.2	0.1	0.0	0.1
Odisha	63.0	60.8	39.2	34.5	37.6	25.9	59.1	57.2	37.0	5.4	6.1	4.9	2.2	2.8	2.3	4.8	5.4	4.3
Puducherry	28.1	22.9	0.2	32.4	9.9	1.6	30.9	14.2	1.2	0.0	0.0	0.0	0.3	0.1	0.0	0.1	0.0	0.0
Punjab	20.3	22.1	14.6	27.2	18.7	18.1	22.4	20.9	15.9	0.9	1.1	0.9	2.4	2.1	2.4	1.2	1.3	1.2
Rajasthan	40.8	35.8	26.4	29.9	29.7	19.9	38.3	34.4	24.8	4.5	5.1	4.8	4.5	5.3	4.3	4.5	5.2	4.7
Sikkim	33.0	31.8	15.5	20.4	25.9	5.0	31.8	30.9	13.1	0.0	0.0	0.0	0.0	0.0	0.0	0.0	0.0	0.0
Tamil Nadu	51.0	37.5	21.2	33.7	19.7	12.8	44.6	29.4	17.1	5.8	4.1	2.8	9.2	7.3	5.7	6.4	4.8	3.4
Tripura	34.3	44.5	19.8	25.4	22.5	10.0	32.9	40.0	17.4	0.3	0.4	0.2	0.2	0.2	0.1	0.2	0.3	0.2
Uttar Pradesh	50.9	42.7	39.4	38.3	34.1	31.7	48.4	40.9	37.7	17.4	18.4	21.6	15.1	16.0	18.0	17.0	17.9	20.8
Uttaranchal	36.7	35.1	14.9	18.7	26.2	25.2	32.0	32.7	18.0	0.6	0.7	0.4	0.3	0.8	1.0	0.5	0.7	0.5
West Bengal	42.5	38.2	28.8	31.2	24.4	22.0	39.4	34.2	26.7	6.7	7.0	6.4	8.4	7.5	8.2	7.0	7.1	6.8

Andaman & Nicobar Island	4.8	4.1	0.4	2.0	0.8	0.3	4.1	3.0	0.4	0.0	0.0	0.0	0.0
Chandigarh	32.6	34.7	10.3	12.4	10.1	9.2	14.1	11.6	9.2	0.0	0.1	0.1	0.0
Dadra & Nagar Haveli	71.9	63.6	55.9	34.7	17.8	17.7	68.3	49.3	39.1	0.0	0.0	0.0	0.0
Daman & Diu	20.1	2.6	34.2	14.6	14.4	33.0	17.3	8.8	33.3	0.0	0.0	0.1	0.0
Lakshadweep	3.6	0.4	22.2	16.4	10.5	1.7	11.1	6.4	6.8	0.0	0.0	0.0	0.0
All India	50.1	42.0	33.8	31.5	25.5	20.9	45.2	37.2	29.8	100.0	100.0	100.0	100.0

Note and Source: As in Table A12.3. Head count ratio of 1993–4 at all-India level does not match with Planning Commission estimates because ours includes the five smaller union territories of Andaman & Nicobar Islands, Chandigarh, Dadra & Nagar Haveli, Daman & Diu, and Lakshadweep and also because of the rounding off. These estimates have been computed by the authors (Durgesh C. Pathak and Srijit Mishra) of Chapter 15, of this volume.

Table A12.5 Education Statistics

Year	Number of Educational Institutions					Enrolment by Stages in School				Drop-out Rates of All Student			Pupil Teacher Ratio		
	Primary	Upper Primary	High/Hr. Sec./Inter/Pre. Jr. Colleges	Colleges for General Education	Colleges for Professional Education	Universities/Deemed Univ., etc.	Primary	Middle/Upper Primary	High/Hr. Sec./Inter/Pre. Jr. Colleges	I-V	I-VIII	I-X	Primary	Middle/Upper Primary	High/Hr. Sec./Inter/Pre. Jr. Colleges
1950-1	209671	13596	7416	370	208	27	19.2	3.1	1.5				24	20	21
1955-6	278135	21730	10838	466	218	31	24.6	4.8	2.6						
1960-1	330399	49663	17329	967	852	45	35.0	6.7	3.4	64.9	78.3		36	31	25
1965-6	391064	75798	27614	1536	770	64	50.5	10.5	5.7						
1970-1	408378	90621	37051	2285	992	82	57.0	13.3	7.6	67	77.9		39	32	25
1975-6	454270	106571	43054	3667	3276	101	65.6	16.0	8.9						
1980-1	494503	118555	51573	3421	3542	110	73.8	20.7	11.0	58.7	72.7	82.5	38	33	27
1985-6	528872	134846	65837	4067	1533	126	87.4	27.1	16.5						
1990-1	560935	151456	79796	4862	886	184	97.4	34.0	19.1	42.6	60.9	71.3	43	37	31
1991-2	566744	155926	82576	5058	950	196	100.9	35.6	20.4						
1992-3	571248	158498	84608	5334	989	207	99.6	34.1	20.5	45	61.1	72.9			
1993-4	570455	162804	89226	5639	1125	213	97.0	34.1	20.7						
1994-5	586810	168772	94946	6089	1230	219	105.1	36.4	22.1						
1995-6	593410	174145	99274	6569	1354	226	107.1	37.5	22.9	42.1	58.8	69.6	43	37	32
1996-7	603646	180293	103241	6759	1770	228	108.2	38.1	24.0	40.2	56.5	70.0			
1997-8	619222	185961	107140	7199	2075	229	110.3	39.5	25.4	39.2	56.1	69.3			
1998-9	628994	193093	112050	7494	2113	237	111.7	40.4	26.7	41.5	56.3	66.7			
1999-2000	641695	198004	116820	7782	2124	244	113.6	41.3	28.0	40.3	55.1	67.0			
2000-1	638738	206269	126047	7929	2223	254	113.8	42.8	27.6	40.7	53.7	68.6	43	38.0	32.0
2001-2	664041	219626	133492	8737	2409	272	113.9	44.8	30.5	39	54.6	66.0	43	34.0	34.0
2002-3	651382	245274	137207	9166	2610	304	122.4	46.9	33.2	34.9	52.8	62.6	42	34.0	33.0
2003-4	712239	262286	145962	9427	2751	304	128.3	48.7	35.0	31.5	52.3	62.7	45	35.0	33.0
2004-5	767520	274731	152049	10377	3201	407	130.8	51.2	37.1	29	50.8	61.9	46	35.0	33.0
2005-6	771082	288199	154032	11549	4991	350	132.1	52.2	38.4	25.7	48.8	61.6	46	34.0	33.0
2006-7	784852	305584	169568	11458	7024	368	133.7	54.5	22.8						

Source: Department of Education.

Table A12.6 Indian Health Statistics

Year	Central Sector Expenditure on Health (Rs crore)			Allopathic Medicine			Ayush (Indian System of Medicine)							
	Family Welfare	Central Sector Health	ISM&H/ AYUSH	Number of Medical College	Number of Admission	Total Ayush Hospital			No. of Beds/ Hospitals	No. of Dispensaries AYUSH Practitioners			
						Number	No. Per Crore Population	No. of Beds		Dispensaries	No. Per Crore Population	Practitioners	No. Per Crore Population
1991–2	na	na	na	146	12199	2723	315	37826	13.9	20879	2417	562016	6506
1992–3	1000	291	11	146	11241	2777	315	38661	13.9	21120	2396	568486	6448
1993–4	1270	462	21	146	10400	2807	312	42043	15.0	21221	2359	573226	6373
1994–5	1430	552	26	152	12249	2845	310	42831	15.1	21496	2343	581703	6341
1995–6	1581	646	24	165	7039	2848	304	48484	17.0	20904	2235	586998	6275
1996–7	1535	792	23	165	3568	2856	300	51328	18.0	19464	2041	591510	6203
1997–8	1822	706	33	165	3949	2930	302	52088	17.8	19762	2033	602036	6194
1998–9	2343	818	50	147	11733	3045	308	55421	18.2	20075	2027	609404	6154
1999–2000	3100	930	49	147	10104	3880	385	74611	19.2	20707	2053	681124	6753
2000–1	3090	1095	79	189	18168	3943	383	69476	17.6	20627	2005	688802	6696
2001–2	3614	1290	82	na	na	3909	374	69049	17.7	20239	1936	691470	6613
2002–3	3917	1360	90	na	na	3224	304	70336	21.8	20974	1974	695024	6542
2003–4	4409	1326	134	na	na	3136	291	63816	20.3	21246	1969	699883	6486
2004–5	4862	1772	199	229	24690	3158	288	64869	20.5	21138	1929	706586	6449
2005–6	5673	2254	291	242	26449	3340	300	66125	19.8	21476	1928	713684	6405
2006–7	7487	1982	317	262	28928	3360	297	68155	20.3	21769	1925	725568	6415
2007–8	10380	2100	488	266	30290	na	na	na	na	na	na	na	na
2008–9	11930	3650	534	289	32815	na	na	na	na	na	na	na	na
2009–10	11930	3650	na	na	na	na	na	na	na	na	na	na	na

Source: National Health Profile 2010, Ministry of Health, and Family Welfare.

A13 EMPLOYMENT

Table A13.1 Total Population, Workers, and Non-workers as Per Population Censuses

(Number in Million)

Year	Total Population			Workers			Non-workers		
	Persons	Males	Females	Persons	Males	Females	Persons	Males	Females
(1)	(3)	(4)	(5)	(6)	(7)	(8)	(9)	(10)	(11)
2001	1028.6 (100.0)	532.2 (100.0)	496.4 (100.0)	402.2 (39.1)	275.0 (51.7)	127.2 (25.6)	626.4 (60.9)	257.1 (48.3)	369.2 (74.4)
1991	846.3 (100.0)	439.2 (100.0)	407.1 (100.0)	306.0 (36.2)	218.6 (49.8)	87.4 (21.5)	510.1 (60.3)	205.0 (46.7)	305.2 (75.0)
1981	683.3 (100.0)	353.3 (100.0)	330.0 (100.0)	244.6 (35.8)	181.0 (51.2)	63.6 (19.3)	420.7 (61.6)	162.9 (46.1)	257.8 (78.1)
1971	548.2 (100.0)	284.0 (100.0)	264.1 (100.0)	180.7 (33.0)	144.4 (50.8)	36.3 (13.7)	367.5 (67.0)	134.8 (47.5)	232.7 (88.1)
1961	439.2 (100.0)	226.3 (100.0)	212.9 (100.0)	188.4 (42.9)	129.0 (57.0)	59.4 (27.9)	249.9 (56.9)	96.8 (42.8)	153.1 (71.9)
1951	361.1 (100.0)	185.6 (100.0)	175.5 (100.0)	139.5 (38.6)	99.1 (53.4)	40.4 (23.0)	217.4 (60.2)	84.2 (45.4)	133.1 (75.8)
1941	318.7 (100.0)	163.8 (100.0)	154.8 (100.0)	na	na	na	na	na	na
1931	279.0 (100.0)	143.1 (100.0)	135.9 (100.0)	120.6 (43.2)	83.0 (58.0)	37.6 (27.7)	157.9 (56.6)	59.5 (41.6)	98.5 (72.5)
1921	251.3 (100.0)	128.6 (100.0)	122.8 (100.0)	117.9 (46.9)	77.8 (60.5)	40.1 (32.7)	133.4 (53.1)	50.7 (39.4)	82.7 (67.3)
1911	252.1 (100.0)	128.4 (100.0)	123.7 (100.0)	121.4 (48.1)	79.6 (62.0)	41.8 (33.8)	131.1 (52.0)	49.0 (38.2)	82.1 (66.4)
1901	238.4 (100.0)	120.9 (100.0)	117.5 (100.0)	111.4 (46.7)	74.1 (61.3)	37.3 (31.7)	127.6 (53.5)	47.1 (39.0)	80.5 (68.5)

Note: Figures in brackets are percentages to respective totals.
The 1981 data include interpolated data for Assam and 1991 figures include projected data for Jammu & Kashmir.
The 2001 data include estimated total for Kachch district, Morvi, Maliya-Miyana, and Wankaner talukas of Rajkot district, Jodiya taluka of Jamnagar district of Gujarat State, and entire Kinnaur district of HP where census was not conducted due to natural calamities.

Source: Census document: 2001 and 1961.
(In the 1961 census document a note on the working force estimates 1901–61 by BR Kalra is available).

Table A13.2 Number of Persons Employed per 1000 Persons according to Usual Status and Current Weekly Status Approaches Worker Population Ratios (WPRs) also called Work Force Participation Rates (WFPRs)

Round No.	Survey Period Month	Year	WPRs: Male									WPRs: Female								
			Usual Status				Current Weekly Status		Current Daily Status		ps		Usual Status All (ps+ss)		Current Weekly Status		Current Daily Status	
			ps		All (ps+ss)															
			Rural	Urban	Rural	Urabn	Rural	Urban	Rural	Urban	Rural	Urban	Rural	Urabn	Rural	Urban	Rural	Urban
1	2	3	4	5	6	7	8	9	10	11	12	13	14	15	16	17	18	19
27	Oct–Sep	1972–3	na	na	565	533	549	521			na	na	330	143	287	131		
32	Jul–Jun	1977–8	537	497	552	508	519	490			248	123	331	156	232	125		
38	Jan–Dec	1983	528	500	547	512	511	492	482	473	248	120	340	151	227	118	198	106
43	Jul–Jun	1987–88	517	496	539	506	504	492	501	477	245	118	323	152	220	119	207	110
45	Jul–Jun	1989–90	537	501	548	512	528	503			252	124	319	146	230	121		
46	Jul–Jun	1990–91	542	508	553	513	535	506			242	123	292	143	230	124		
47	Jul–Dec	1991	538	511	546	516	534	509			244	120	294	132	238	117		
48	Jan–Dec	1992	541	502	556	507	536	501			250	125	313	146	244	122		
49	Jan–Jun	1993	532	506	545	509	527	504			243	113	311	130	232	109		
50	Jul–Jun	1993–94	538	513	553	521	531	511	504	496	234	121	328	155	267	139	219	120
51	Jul–Jun	1994–95	547	514	560	519	541	511			237	112	317	136	241	117		
52	Jul–Jun	1995–96	542	522	551	525	538	520			234	107	295	124	233	109		
53	Jan–Dec	1997	541	516	550	521	535	513			222	111	291	131	222	114		
54	Jan–Jun	1998	530	506	539	509	524	504			207	99	263	114	202	99		
55	Jul–Jun	1999–2000	522	513	531	518	510	509	478	490	231	117	299	139	253	128	204	111
56	Jul–Jun	2000–1	532	525	544	531	525	519			221	116	287	140	217	117		
57	Jul–Jun	2001–2	531	547	546	553	523	542			241	110	314	139	241	111		
58	Jul–Dec	2002	537	530	546	534	529	523			214	118	281	140	219	118		
59	Jan–Dec	2003	536	535	547	541	525	528			235	119	311	146	236	121		
60	Jan–Jun	2004	527	531	542	540	511	525	471	504	228	121	315	150	245	136	190	118
61	Jul–Jun	2004–5	535	541	546	549	524	534	488	519	242	135	327	166	275	152	216	133
62	Jul–Jun	2005–6	537	534	549	540	524	529	491	513	224	121	310	143	257	132	203	118
64	Jul–Jun	2007–8	538	550	548	554	525	545	490	529	216	118	289	138	237	129	187	113
66	Jul–Jun	2009–10	537	539	547	543	531	536	501	522	202	119	261	138	223	130	182	117

Notes: (i) Dark lines represent regular Quinquennial Surveys; others are thin sample surveys.
(ii) Worker population rations (WPRs) represent the ratio of worker population in total population in the respective categories.

Source: NSS 66th Round (Jul–Jun 2009–10): Employment and Unemployment Situation in India and earlier NSS Report.

Table A13.3 Per 1000 Distribution of the Usually Employed by Status of Employment for All, i.e., Principal and Subsidiary Status Workers

Round No.	Survey Month	Period Year	WPRs: Male						WPRs: Female					
			Self-employed	Rural Regular Wage/Salaried	Casual Labour	Self-employed	Urban Regular Wage/Salaried	Casual Labour	Self-employed	Rural Regular Wage/Salaried	Casual Labour	Self-employed	Urban Regular Wage/Salaried	Casual Labour
1	2	3	4	5	6	7	8	9	10	11	12	13	14	15
27	Oct–Sep	1972–3	659	121	220	392	507	101	645	41	314	484	279	237
32	Jul–Jun	1977–8	628	106	266	404	464	132	321	28	351	495	249	256
38	Jan–Dec	1983	605	103	292	409	437	154	619	28	353	458	258	284
43	Jul–Jun	1987–88	586	100	314	417	437	146	608	37	355	471	275	254
45	Jul–Jun	1989–90	597	98	305	423	413	164	609	28	363	486	292	222
46	Jul–Jun	1990–91	557	128	315	407	442	151	586	38	376	490	259	251
47	Jul–Dec	1991	595	92	313	489	399	172	568	31	401	470	280	250
48	Jan–Dec	1992	608	83	309	412	394	193	591	32	377	425	288	287
49	Jan–Jun	1993	591	79	330	389	395	216	585	23	392	407	262	331
50	Jul–Jun	1993–94	577	85	338	417	420	163	586	27	387	458	284	258
51	Jul–Jun	1994–95	604	68	328	404	431	165	570	22	408	426	301	273
52	Jul–Jun	1995–96	590	77	333	410	425	165	564	24	412	400	332	268
53	Jan–Dec	1997	594	73	333	400	415	185	570	21	409	397	313	290
54	Jan–Jun	1998	553	70	377	425	395	181	534	25	442	384	327	288
55	Jul–Jun	1999–2000	550	88	362	415	407	168	573	31	396	453	333	214
56	Jul–Jun	2000–1	589	95	316	414	411	175	593	32	375	444	315	241
57	Jul–Jun	2001–2	580	81	339	430	415	154	589	29	382	441	298	261
58	Jul–Dec	2002	569	88	344	443	407	150	558	36	406	459	308	233
59	Jan–Dec	2003	578	87	335	429	415	156	616	33	351	454	339	207
60	Jan–Jun	2004	572	93	335	441	406	153	615	38	347	446	362	192
61	Jul–Jun	2004–5	581	90	329	448	406	146	637	37	326	477	356	167
62	Jul–Jun	2005–6	567	100	333	427	420	157	622	39	339	438	356	167
64	Jul–Jun	2007–8	554	91	355	427	420	154	583	41	376	423	379	199
66	Jul–Jun	2009–10	535	85	380	411	419	170	557	44	399	411	393	196

Notes: (i) Dark lines represent regular Quinquennial Surveys; others are thin sample surveys.
(ii) Worker population rations (WPRs) represent the ratio of worker population in total population in the respective categories.

Source: NSS 66th Round (Jul–Jun 2009–10): Employment and Unemployment Situation in India and earlier NSS Reports.

Table A13.4 Unemployment Rate (Number of Persons Unemployed Per 1000 Persons in the Labour Force)

Round No.	Survey Month	Period Year	Male Rural				Male Urban				Female Rural				Female Urban			
			Usual Status	Usual Adjusted Status	Current Weekly Status	Current Daily Status	Usual Status	Usual Adjusted Status	Current Weekly Status	Current Daily Status	Usual Status	Usual Adjusted Status	Current Weekly Status	Current Daily Status	Usual Status	Usual Adjusted Status	Current Weekly Status	Current Daily Status
1	2	3	4	5	6	7	8	9	10	11	12	13	14	15	16	17	18	19
27	Oct–Sep	1972–3	—	12	30	38	—	48	60	80	—	5	55	112	—	60	90	137
32	Jul–Jun	1977–8	22	13	36	71	65	54	71	94	55	20	41	92	178	124	109	145
38	Jan–Dec	1983	21	14	37	75	59	51	67	92	14	7	43	90	69	49	75	110
43	Jul–Jun	1987–88	28	18	42	46	61	52	66	88	35	24	44	67	85	62	92	120
45	Jul–Jun	1989–90	16	13	26	—	44	39	45	—	8	6	21	—	39	27	40	—
46	Jul–Jun	1990–91	13	—	—	—	45	—	—	—	4	—	—	—	54	—	—	—
47	Jul–Dec	1991	20	16	22	—	43	39	45	—	18	7	12	—	56	51	50	—
48	Jan–Dec	1992	16	—	—	—	46	—	—	—	12	—	—	—	67	—	—	—
49	Jan–Jun	1993	16	—	—	—	38	—	—	—	10	—	—	—	43	—	—	—
50	Jul–Jun	1993–94	20 (11)	14 (8)	31 (17)	56 (30)	45 (24)	41 (22)	52 (28)	67 (36)	14 (3)	8 (3)	30 (8)	56 (13)	83 (11)	61 (10)	79 (12)	104 (14)
51	Jul–Jun	1994–95	12 (7)	10 (6)	18 (10)	—	37 (20)	34 (18)	39 (21)	—	5 (1)	4 (1)	12 (3)	—	41 (5)	34 (5)	40 (5)	—
52	Jul–Jun	1995–96	15 (8)	13 (7)	18 (10)	—	40 (22)	38 (21)	41 (22)	—	8 (2)	7 (2)	9 (2)	—	36 (4)	31 (4)	35 (4)	—
53	Jan–Dec	1997	16 (9)	12 (7)	20 (11)	—	37 (21)	39 (21)	43 (23)	—	9 (2)	7 (2)	18 (4)	—	51 (6)	44 (6)	58 (7)	—
54	Jan–Jun	1998	24 (13)	21 (11)	29 (15)	—	53 (28)	51 (27)	54 (29)	—	20 (4)	15 (4)	27 (6)	—	81 (9)	68 (8)	78 (8)	—
55	Jul–Jun	1999–2000	21 (11)	17 (9)	39 (21)	72 (37)	48 (26)	45 (24)	56 (30)	73 (38)	15 (4)	10 (3)	37 (10)	70 (15)	71 (9)	57 (8)	73 (10)	94 (12)
56	Jul–Jun	2000–1	16 (9)	14 (8)	23 (12)	—	42 (23)	39 (22)	48 (26)	—	6 (1)	4 (1)	18 (4)	—	38 (5)	29 (4)	39 (5)	—
57	Jul–Jun	2001–2	14 (7)	11 (6)	26 (14)	—	42 (24)	39 (22)	46 (26)	—	20 (5)	14 (5)	26 (7)	—	49 (6)	38 (5)	48 (6)	—
58	Jul–Dec	2002	18 (10)	15 (8)	28 (15)	—	47 (26)	45 (25)	55 (31)	—	10 (2)	6 (2)	16 (4)	—	61 (8)	47 (7)	57 (7)	—

(Contd.)

Table A13.4 (Contd.)

Round No	Survey Month	Period Year	Male								Female							
			Rural				Urban				Rural				Urban			
			Usual Status	Usual Adjusted Status	Current Weekly Status	Current Daily Status	Usual Status	Usual Adjusted Status	Current Weekly Status	Current Daily Status	Usual Status	Usual Adjusted Status	Current Weekly Status	Current Daily Status	Usual Status	Usual Adjusted Status	Current Weekly Status	Current Daily Status
1	2	3	4	5	6	7	8	9	10	11	12	13	14	15	16	17	18	19
59	Jan–Dec	2003	19 (10)	15 (9)	28 (15)	–	43 (24)	40 (23)	51 (28)	–	10 (2)	6 (2)	16 (4)	–	44 (5)	35 (5)	49 (6)	–
60	Jan–Jun	2004	24 (13)	18 (10)	47 (25)	90 (47)	46 (25)	40 (22)	57 (32)	81 (45)	22 (5)	13 (4)	45 (12)	93 (19)	89 (12)	67 (11)	90 (14)	117 (16)
61	July–Jun	2004–5	21 (12)	16 (9)	38 (21)	80 (42)	44 (25)	38 (22)	52 (30)	75 (42)	31 (8)	18 (6)	42 (12)	87 (21)	91 (14)	69 (12)	90 (15)	116 (18)
62	July–Jun	2005–6	25 (14)	20 (11)	43 (24)	83 (44)	48 (27)	45 (25)	58 (32)	79 (44)	22 (5)	12 (4)	33 (9)	75 (16)	79 (10)	63 (10)	77 (11)	101 (13)
64	July–Jun	2007–8	23 (13)	19 (11)	41 (22)	85 (45)	40 (23)	38 (22)	47 (27)	69 (39)	19 (4)	11 (3)	35 (9)	81 (17)	66 (8)	52 (8)	65 (9)	65 (12)
66	July–Jun	2009–10	19 (11)	16 (9)	32 (17)	64 (35)	30 (17)	28 (16)	36 (20)	51 (28)	24 (5)	16 (4)	37 (8)	80 (16)	70 (9)	57 (8)	72 (10)	91 (12)

Notes: (i) Dark lines represent regular quinquennial surveys; others are thin sample surveys.
(ii) Worker population ratios (WPRs) represent the ratio of worker population in total population in the respective categories.
(iii) Figures in brackets indicate the proportion of unemployed per 1000 persons (person–day).

Source: NSS 66th Round Report and earlier NSS Reports.

Table A13.5 State-wise Sectoral Distribution of Usual (Principal + Subsidiary) Status Workers: 1983 to 2009–10

(%)

State	Year	Agriculture			Non-agriculture			of which: Manufacturing		
		Rural	Urban	Total	Rural	Urban	Total	Rural	Urban	Total
1	2	3	4	5	6	7	8	9	10	11
Andhra Pradesh	2009–10	68.7	53.0	54.8	31.3	47.0	45.2	8.7	22.7	11.7
	2004–5	71.8	10.0	na	28.2	90.0	na	8.6	19.5	na
	1999–2000	78.8	9.6	65.5	21.2	90.4	34.5	6.2	22.0	9.2
	1993–4	79.2	16.5	67.1	20.8	83.5	32.9	7.6	22.0	10.1
	1983	80.1	15.7	69.3	19.9	84.3	30.7	7.9	25.0	10.7
Assam	2009–10	70.5	2.7	64.2	29.5	97.3	35.8	3.5	9.3	4.0
	2004–5	74.3	4.8	na	25.7	95.2	na	3.1	9.8	na
	1999–2000	67.6	5.9	60.2	32.4	94.1	39.8	5.4	12.9	6.3
	1993–4	78.9	3.0	70.5	21.1	97.0	29.5	5.5	13.8	6.4
	1983	79.3	7.4	72.3	20.7	92.6	27.7	4.4	16.2	5.6
Bihar	2009–10	66.9	14.6	61.9	33.1	85.4	38.1	5.2	11.7	5.8
	2004–5	77.9	20.5	na	22.1	79.5	na	5.7	11.6	na
	1999–2000	80.6	11.1	73.1	19.4	88.9	26.9	6.4	21.2	8.0
	1993–4	84.2	11.9	76.6	15.8	88.1	23.4	4.1	21.5	6.0
	1983	83.5	14.3	76.5	16.5	85.7	23.5	6.3	24.8	8.1
Gujarat	2009–10	78.3	5.2	53.4	21.7	94.8	46.6	5.8	29.7	13.9
	2004–5	77.3	6.2	na	22.7	93.8	na	7.8	37.2	na
	1999–2000	80.0	9.8	59.7	20.0	90.2	40.3	7.0	27.3	12.8
	1993–4	78.8	8.0	58.9	21.2	92.0	41.1	9.5	34.8	16.6
	1983	85.0	18.0	68.7	15.0	82.0	31.3	5.7	35.0	12.9
Haryana	2009–10	59.8	5.3	44.4	40.2	94.7	55.6	9.3	30.8	15.4
	2004–5	64.1	11.2	na	35.9	88.8	na	8.9	26.6	na
	1999–2000	68.4	10.6	53.0	31.6	89.4	47.0	8.3	23.9	12.5
	1993–4	71.7	11.6	56.9	28.3	88.4	43.1	4.8	28.3	10.6
	1983	77.1	16.0	64.1	22.9	84.0	35.9	6.4	26.1	10.6
Himachal Pradesh	2009–10	62.9	8.6	59.7	37.1	91.4	40.3	3.6	12.4	4.1
	2004–5	69.6	8.5	na	30.4	91.5	na	4.9	14.0	na
	1999–2000	73.8	10.4	69.6	26.2	89.6	30.4	4.7	9.5	5.0
	1993–4	79.6	17.8	75.9	20.4	82.2	24.1	3.6	4.6	3.7
	1983	87.0	12.4	82.8	13.0	87.6	17.2	3.4	12.0	3.9
Jammu and Kashmir	2009–10	59.7	11.1	50.1	40.3	88.9	49.9	7.5	20.3	10.1
	2004–5	63.9	14.1	na	36.1	85.9	na	9.8	22.7	na
	1999–2000	73.7	12.8	62.9	26.3	87.2	37.1	5.6	10.5	6.5
	1993–4	75.1	13.8	63.9	24.9	86.2	36.1	4.2	12.9	5.8
	1983	79.7	16.1	68.9	20.3	83.9	31.1	4.7	28.7	8.8
Karnataka	2009–10	75.6	9.5	55.8	24.4	90.5	44.2	5.9	20.7	10.4
	2004–5	81.0	8.2	na	19.0	91.8	na	6.2	21.7	na
	1999–2000	84.4	19.9	69.6	15.6	80.1	30.4	6.0	28.9	11.3
	1993–4	81.9	16.6	65.7	18.1	83.4	34.3	6.7	26.9	11.7
	1999–0	82.1	10.9	62.5	17.9	89.1	37.5	5.9	27.1	11.8
Kerala	2009–10	35.7	11.0	29.5	64.3	89.0	70.5	11.7	16.8	13.0
	2004–5	42.0	15.7	na	58.0	84.3	na	13.7	16.6	na
	1999–2000	48.5	9.6	38.7	51.5	90.4	61.3	14.3	23.5	16.6
	1993–4	56.0	25.4	48.1	44.0	74.6	51.9	13.5	21.4	15.5
	1983	92.8	27.7	56.3	37.2	72.3	43.7	14.7	22.5	16.1
Madhya Pradesh	2009–10	82.4	9.8	68.8	17.6	90.2	31.2	3.4	18.2	6.1
	2004–5	82.5	12.1	na	17.5	87.9	na	5.0	20.1	na
	1999–2000	87.2	15.5	73.9	12.8	84.5	26.1	4.2	21.7	7.4
	1993–4	89.9	16.4	77.7	10.1	83.6	22.3	3.5	20.5	6.3
	1983	90.3	15.4	79.5	9.7	84.6	20.5	3.9	25.9	7.1

(Contd.)

Table A13.5 (*Contd.*)

State	Year	Agriculture			(%) Non-agriculture			*of which*: Manufacturing		
		Rural	Urban	Total	Rural	Urban	Total	Rural	Urban	Total
1	2	3	4	5	6	7	8	9	10	11
Maharashtra	2009–10	79.2	4.7	52.4	20.8	95.3	47.6	4.7	22.5	11.1
	2004–5	80.0	6.8	na	20.0	93.2	na	5.6	24.2	na
	1999–2000	82.7	5.7	56.4	17.3	94.3	43.6	5.2	28.1	13.1
	1993–4	82.6	9.2	59.4	17.4	90.8	40.6	5.3	27.5	12.3
	1983	85.8	12.6	66.2	14.2	87.4	33.8	5.0	31.7	12.1
Odisha	2009–10	67.6	10.3	60.8	32.4	89.7	39.2	7.5	18.7	8.9
	2004–5	69.0	13.9	na	31.0	86.1	na	11.1	14.0	na
	1999–2000	78.5	13.3	71.0	21.5	86.7	29.0	8.5	21.7	10.0
	1993–4	81.0	15.8	73.8	19.0	84.2	26.2	6.8	19.9	8.2
	1983	79.2	16.2	73.3	20.8	83.8	26.7	8.7	24.0	10.1
Punjab	2009–10	61.8	8.3	44.2	38.2	91.7	55.8	7.4	23.8	12.8
	2004–5	66.9	5.9	na	33.1	94.1	na	7.4	26.5	na
	1999–2000	72.5	8.9	53.4	27.5	91.1	46.6	7.8	26.8	13.5
	1993–4	74.5	9.2	56.4	25.5	90.8	43.6	5.9	28.5	12.2
	1983	82.5	14.0	66.8	17.5	86.0	33.2	6.4	30.1	11.8
Rajasthan	2009–10	63.3	7.0	52.8	36.7	93.0	47.2	3.7	17.9	6.3
	2004–5	72.9	13.9	na	27.1	86.1	na	5.8	22.8	na
	1999–2000	77.6	13.1	65.9	22.4	86.9	34.1	4.9	24.3	8.4
	1993–4	79.8	16.3	69.2	20.2	83.7	30.8	4.6	21.7	7.4
	1983	86.7	27.3	77.6	13.3	72.7	22.4	4.3	23.0	7.2
Tamil Nadu	2009–10	53.9	13.6	44.6	46.1	86.4	55.4	2.4	26.6	17.1
	2004–5	65.4	8.3	na	34.6	91.7	na	14.0	30.9	na
	1999–2000	68.3	9.0	46.8	31.7	91.0	53.2	14.4	33.4	21.3
	1993–4	70.2	11.9	52.5	29.8	88.1	47.5	13.6	32.2	19.3
	1983	74.3	15.4	58.9	25.7	84.6	41.1	11.4	34.8	17.5
Uttar Pradesh	2009–10	66.9	9.1	56.1	33.1	90.9	43.9	7.3	25.1	10.7
	2004–5	72.8	10.5	na	27.2	89.5	na	8.9	28.4	na
	1999–2000	76.1	9.4	63.6	23.9	90.6	36.4	8.6	29.2	12.5
	1993–4	80.0	15.0	69.0	20.0	85.0	31.0	7.1	27.1	10.5
	1983	82.0	12.2	71.7	18.0	87.8	28.3	7.4	29.2	10.6
West Bengal	2009–10	56.2	3.6	43.8	43.8	96.4	56.2	16.6	26.7	19.0
	2004–5	62.7	2.8	na	37.3	97.2	na	13.5	27.6	na
	1999–2000	63.0	3.0	46.1	37.0	97.0	53.9	17.7	31.1	21.4
	1993–4	63.6	5.7	48.1	36.4	94.3	51.9	17.0	31.8	21.0
	1983	73.6	4.8	56.4	26.4	95.2	43.6	11.2	36.4	17.5

Note: na: not available.

Source: NSSO; Employment and Unemployment Situation in India.

A14 HOUSEHOLD INDEBTEDNESS

Table A14.1 Household Indebtedness in India: A Profile

1. Amount of Debt by Occupational Categories of Households (Rs crore)

Year	Rural Households			Urban Households			All Households (4+7)
	Cultivator	Non-cultivator	All	Self-employed	Others	All	
1	2	3	4	5	6	7	8
2002	81709	29759	111468	24341	40977	65327	176795
1991	17668	4543	22211	6306	8805	15232	37443
1981	5737	456	6193	1406	1617	3023	9216
1971	3374	474	3848	na	na	na	na

2. Proportion of Households Reporting Debt

Year	Rural Households			Urban Households		
	Cultivator	Non-cultivator	All	Self-employed	Others	All
1	2	3	4	5	6	7
2002	29.7	21.8	26.5	17.9	17.8	17.8
1991	34.6	26.8	32.0	28.5	25.9	26.9
1981	21.7	12.0	19.4	16.6	17.4	17.2
1971	44.4	33.3	41.3	na	na	na

3. Percentage Share of Outstanding Debt according to Credit Agency: Rural and Urban

		Rural					Urban		
		2002	1991	1981	1971	1961	1951	2002	1991	1981
A.	Institutional	57.1	56.6	61.2	29.2	17.3	7.2	75.1	64.3	59.9
	Government	2.3	5.7	4.0	6.7	6.6	3.7	7.6	9.3	14.6
	Co-op Scty/Banks	27.3	18.6	28.6	20.1	10.4	3.5	20.5	14.2	17.5
	Commercial Banks	24.5	29.0	28.0	2.2	0.3	0.0	29.7	17.7	22.5
	Insurance	0.3	0.5	0.3	0.1	0.0	0.0	3.5	1.4	2.1
	Provident Fund	0.3	0.9	0.3	0.1	0.0	0.0	2.0	3.3	3.2
	Other institutions	2.4	1.9	0.0	0.0	0.0	0.0	11.9	18.5	0.0
B.	Non-institutional	42.9	39.6	38.8	70.8	82.7	92.8	24.9	32.0	40.1
	Landlords	1.0	4.0	4.0	8.6	1.1	3.5	0.2	0.8	1.0
	Agrl. Moneylenders	10.0	6.3	8.6	23.1	47.0	25.2	0.9	1.2	3.6
	Proff. Moneylenders	19.6	9.4	8.3	13.8	13.8	46.4	13.2	7.9	8.9
	Traders	2.6	6.7	3.4	8.7	7.5	5.1	1.0	5.8	4.8
	Relatives/Friends	7.1	6.7	9.0	13.8	5.8	11.5	7.6	10.4	15.2
	Others	2.6	9.9	5.5	2.8	7.5	1.1	1.9	5.9	6.6
C.	Not Specified	0.0	3.8	0.0	0.0	0.0	0.0	0.0	3.6	0.0

(Contd.)

Table A14.1 (Contd.)

4. Cash Debt of Households Classified by Purpose of Loan (per cent)

		Rural Households								
		Cultivators			Non-cultivators			All Households		
		2002	1991	1981	2002	1991	1981	2002	1991	1981
1.	Farm Business									
	Capital Expenditure	34.3	14.4	45.3	6.3	2.4	8.4	26.8	12.0	42.4
	Current Expenditure	18.2	3.2	18.5	3.0	0.7	5.9	14.2	2.7	17.6
2.	Non-farm Business									
	Capital Expenditure	7.4	4.7	6.3	14.2	9.8	18.8	9.2	5.8	7.2
	Current Expenditure	2.0	1.5	1.5	4.8	3.8	4.5	2.8	2.0	1.7
3.	Households									
	Capital Expenditure in Residential Bldg	27.7	5.1	20.0	55.0	11.8	51.0	35.0	6.5	22.4
	Current Expenditure	na	0.5	na	na	0.4	na	na	0.5	na
4.	Productive Purposes (1+2+3)*	89.6	28.9	91.6	83.3	28.5	88.6	88.0	29.0	91.3
		(61.9)	(23.8)	(71.6)	(28.3)	(16.7)	(37.6)	(53.0)	(22.5)	(68.9)
5.	Other Purposes	10.4	45.4	8.1	16.4	57.6	11.4	12.0	48.0	8.5
	Repayment of Debt	1.5	na	0.8	1.3	na	1.5	1.4	na	0.8
	Expend. on Litigation	0.3	na	0.1	0.2	na	0.0	0.3	na	0.2
	Fin. Investment Expe.	0.6	na	1.0	1.0	na	0.5	0.7	na	0.9
	Other purposes	8.0	na	6.2	13.9	na	9.4	9.6	na	6.6
6.	Unspecified	0.0	25.2	0.3	0.3	13.5	0.0	0.1	22.8	0.2

		Urban Households								
		Self-employed			Others			All Households		
		2002	1991	1981	2002	1991	1981	2002	1991	1981
1.	Farm Business									
	Capital Expenditure	7.3	5.7	7.2	0.9	0.3	4.3	3.3	2.5	5.6
	Current Expenditure	4.4	0.2	8.1	0.4	0.1	1.1	1.9	0.1	4.4
2.	Non-farm Business									
	Capital Expenditure	36.1	21.1	41.6	4.8	3.3	7.3	16.5	10.8	23.2
	Current Expenditure	7.5	8.1	15.0	0.7	1.0	2.5	3.2	4.0	8.3
3.	Households									
	Capital Expenditure in Residential Bldg	32.8	28.7	13.1	72.1	44.6	54.3	57.5	37.9	35.0
	Current Expenditure	na	0.1	na	na	2.5	na	na	1.5	na
4.	Productive Purposes (1+2+3)*	88.1	63.9	85.0	78.9	51.8	69.5	82.4	56.8	76.5
		(55.3)	(35.1)	(71.9)	(6.8)	(4.7)	(15.2)	(24.9)	(17.4)	(41.5)
5.	Other Purposes	11.9	33.9	14.7	21.1	46.6	30.4	17.6	41.4	23.2
6.	Unspecified	0.0	2.2	0.3	0.1	1.4	0.2	0.0	1.8	0.2

5. Amount of Cash Borrowing and Repayments by Occupational Category of Households

Year		Round	Amount of Borrowings in Rs Cr			Amount of Repayment in Rs Cr			Share of Cultivator HHs (%)		Per cent of Repayments to Borrowings	
			Cultivator	Non-cultivator	All HHs	Cultivator	Non-cultivator	All HHs	Total Borrowings	Total Repayment	All HHs	Cultivator
2002-3	Rural	59	39294	15825	55119	17729	7154	24883	71.3	71.3	45.1	45.1
1991-92		48	10636	2862	13498	4070	1133	5203	78.8	78.3	38.5	38.3
1981-82		37	3757	427	4185	1899	193	2091	89.8	90.9	50.0	50.5
1971-2		26	1155	190	1345	1009	146	1155	85.9	87.4	85.9	87.4
			Self-employed	Others	All HHs (incl. n.r.)	Self-employed	Others	All HHs (incl. n.r.)	Share of Self-employed (%)		Per cent of Repayments to Borrowings	
									Total Borrowings	Total Repayment	All HHs	Self-employed
2002-3	Urban	26	12215	21965	34181	6679	11768	18447	35.7	36.2	54.0	54.7
1991-92		37	2815	5098	7918	1513	3027	4540	35.7	33.3	57.3	53.7
1981-82		48	830	1156	1986	536	653	1189	41.8	45.1	59.9	64.6

Note: * Figures in brackets relate to those given by NSSO for productive purposes (1+2). na : Details are not available. n.r.: Not reported.

Source: NSSO (2005), *Household Indebtedness in India as on 30-6-2002*, AIDIS Report No. 501(59/18.2/2), December.
NSSO (2006), *Household Borrowing and Repayments in India during 1.7.2002 to 30.6.2003*, AIDIS Report. No. 502(59/18.2/3), January.

A15 ECONOMIC CENSUS

Table A15.1 Trends in Employment in Agricultural (Excluding Crop Production and Plantation) and Non-agricultural Enterprises 1980–2005

Total Employment in Thousands

		Fifth Economic Census 2005			Fourth Economic Census 1998			Third Economic Census 1990			Second Economic Census 1980		
		Rural	Urban	Combined	Rural	Urban	Combined	Rural	Urban	Combined	Rural	Urban	Combined
	All-India	50185	48782	98968	39901	43399	83299	33296	38780	72076	24474	29194	53668
1	Andhra Pradesh	5718	3152	8871	4635	2877	7512	4082	2652	6734	2658	2054	4712
2	Arunachal Pradesh	64	43	107	52	28	81	62	31	93	32	13	44
3	Assam	1792	943	2735	1551	644	2195	1120	570	1689	Census not conducted		
4	Bihar	1383	893	2276	1775	1654	3429	1743	1710	3454	1532	1245	2777
5	Chattisgarh	1014	597	1610				Included in Madhya Pradesh					
6	Goa	120	125	246	98	118	216	98	121	219	136	116	252
7	Gujarat	2569	3245	5814	2351	2929	5280	2022	2704	4726	1528	2124	3652
8	Haryana	1074	1138	2212	595	964	1559	524	829	1353	370	604	974
9	Himachal Pradesh	462	205	667	387	189	577	312	156	469	236	108	344
10	Jammu and Kashmir	364	387	752	217	256	474	Census not conducted			247	242	489
11	Jharkhand	580	589	1169				Included in Bihar					
12	Karnataka	3320	2659	5978	2757	2496	5253	2588	2495	5083	2003	1863	3866
13	Kerala	3684	1876	5559	2760	1089	3849	1889	1400	3289	1603	849	2452
14	Madhya Pradesh	1868	2352	4220	2441	2815	5256	2363	2522	4886	1601	1689	3290
15	Maharashtra	4625	7201	11827	3688	6756	10445	2847	6113	8960	2145	4605	6750
16	Manipur	121	114	235	97	104	201	77	80	157	46	59	105
17	Meghalaya	137	107	245	97	87	184	85	85	170	49	59	109
18	Mizoram	32	69	101	23	54	77	21	51	72	18	27	46
19	Nagaland	73	111	184	64	111	175	50	80	130	39	36	75
20	Odisha	2572	1004	3575	2158	937	3095	1716	896	2612	1250	699	1949
21	Punjab	1059	1628	2688	743	1357	2100	580	1190	1770	415	921	1336
22	Rajasthan	2271	1969	4240	1793	1749	3542	1318	1520	2838	1138	1179	2317
23	Sikkim	41	28	69	27	21	48	28	19	47	15	15	31
24	Tamil Nadu	5188	4678	9867	3583	3608	7191	2882	3354	6236	2305	2841	5146
25	Tripura	249	130	379	168	101	268	132	89	220	83	52	134
26	Uttar Pradesh	4196	4344	8540	3232	4248	7480	2949	3959	6909	2621	3122	5743
27	Uttranchal	396	353	749				Included in Uttar Pradesh					
28	West Bengal	4921	4397	9318	4374	4397	8771	3636	3811	7448	2242	3101	5343

Table A15.1 (Contd.)

Chandigarh	13	239	252	6	212	218	8	195	203	4	117	121
Delhi	73	4007	4080	86	3415	3501	73	2012	2085	96	1375	1471
Pondicherry	64	129	193	49	132	182	30	90	120	26	55	81
A & N Islands	28	36	64	37	25	63	31	21	52	21	17	38
D & N Haveli	47	18	65	28	5	33	12	3	14	5	2	7
Daman and Diu	57	10	68	21	11	32	11	10	21	Included in Goa		
Lakshadweep	7	5	12	5	11	16	6	10	16	8	6	14

Annual Growth Rate—Employment (per cent)

		1998–2005			1990–8			1980–90	
		Rural	Urban	Combined	Rural	Urban	Combined	Rural	Urban	Combined
	All-India	(3.33)	(1.68)	(2.49)	(2.15)	(1.34)	(1.71)	(2.88)	(2.81)	(2.84)
1	Andhra Pradesh	(3.05)	(1.32)	(2.40)	(1.60)	(1.02)	(1.38)	(4.38)	(2.59)	(3.64)
2	Arunachal Pradesh	(3.07)	(6.02)	(4.17)	(–2.13)	(–1.23)	(–1.82)	(6.97)	(9.65)	(7.80)
3	Assam	(2.08)	(5.61)	(3.19)	(4.15)	(1.54)	(3.32)	Not available		
4	Bihar	(1.79)	(–1.77)	(0.27)	(–0.95)	(–0.42)	(–0.68)	(1.30)	(3.23)	(2.20)
5	Chattisgarh	(3.82)	(1.19)	(2.78)	Not available			Not available		
6	Goa	(2.99)	(0.88)	(1.87)	(0.04)	(–0.34)	(–0.17)	Not available		
7	Gujarat	(1.27)	(1.48)	(1.39)	(1.90)	(1.01)	(1.40)	(2.84)	(2.44)	(2.61)
8	Haryana	(8.80)	(2.40)	(5.12)	(1.60)	(1.90)	(1.79)	(3.56)	(3.21)	(3.34)
9	Himachal Pradesh	(2.54)	(1.13)	(2.09)	(2.73)	(2.43)	(2.63)	(2.85)	(3.73)	(3.13)
10	Jammu and Kashmir	(7.65)	(6.08)	(6.82)	Not available			Not available		
11	Jharkhand	(0.66)	(–1.21)	(–0.32)	Not available					
12	Karnataka	(2.69)	(0.91)	(1.86)	(0.79)	(0.01)	(0.41)	(2.60)	(2.96)	(2.77)
13	Kerala	(4.21)	(8.08)	(5.39)	(4.85)	(–3.09)	(1.99)	(1.66)	(5.13)	(2.98)
14	Madhya Pradesh	(1.69)	(0.54)	(1.04)	(0.41)	(1.38)	(0.92)	(3.97)	(4.09)	(4.03)
15	Maharashtra	(3.29)	(0.91)	(1.79)	(3.29)	(1.26)	(1.93)	(2.87)	(2.87)	(2.87)
16	Manipur	(3.24)	(1.28)	(2.25)	(2.85)	(3.32)	(3.09)	(5.26)	(3.16)	(4.13)
17	Meghalaya	(5.05)	(3.02)	(4.12)	(1.76)	(0.26)	(1.03)	(5.55)	(3.71)	(4.58)
18	Mizoram	(4.96)	(3.45)	(3.91)	(1.15)	(0.74)	(0.86)	(1.27)	(6.51)	(4.67)

(Contd.)

Table A15.1 (Contd.)

Annual Growth Rate—Employment (per cent)

		1998–2005			1990–8			1980–90		
		Rural	Urban	Combined	Rural	Urban	Combined	Rural	Urban	Combined
19	Nagaland	(1.95)	(0.02)	(0.75)	(3.27)	(4.08)	(3.78)	(2.44)	(8.46)	(5.70)
20	Odisha	(2.54)	(0.99)	(2.08)	(2.90)	(0.56)	(2.14)	(3.22)	(2.51)	(2.97)
21	Punjab	(5.19)	(2.64)	(3.59)	(3.15)	(1.65)	(2.16)	(3.40)	(2.60)	(2.85)
22	Rajasthan	(3.44)	(1.71)	(2.60)	(3.92)	(1.77)	(2.81)	(1.48)	(2.57)	(2.05)
23	Sikkim	(6.41)	(4.32)	(5.52)	(–0.81)	(1.33)	(0.08)	(6.36)	(2.22)	(4.48)
24	Tamil Nadu	(5.43)	(3.78)	(4.62)	(2.76)	(0.91)	(1.80)	(2.26)	(1.68)	(1.94)
25	Tripura	(5.84)	(3.71)	(5.07)	(3.05)	(1.60)	(2.48)	(4.80)	(5.50)	(5.07)
26	Uttar Pradesh	(4.98)	(1.40)	(3.03)	(1.76)	(0.88)	(1.27)	(1.19)	(2.40)	(1.87)
27	Uttranchal	(7.06)	(2.04)	(4.45)	Not available			Not available		
28	West Bengal	(1.70)	(–0.00)	(0.87)	(2.34)	(1.80)	(2.07)	(4.95)	(2.09)	(3.38)
	Chandigarh	(12.11)	(1.71)	(2.07)	(–4.30)	(1.07)	(0.89)	(6.94)	(5.25)	(5.31)
	Delhi	(–2.26)	(2.31)	(2.21)	(2.12)	(6.84)	(6.70)	(–2.81)	(3.88)	(3.55)
	Pondicherry	(3.83)	(–0.37)	(0.88)	(6.21)	(5.00)	(5.31)	(1.66)	(4.93)	(3.99)
	A & N Islands	(–3.90)	(5.15)	(0.35)	(2.25)	(2.26)	(2.25)	(4.02)	(2.39)	(3.33)
	D & N Haveli	(7.56)	(22.03)	(10.33)	(11.82)	(5.85)	(10.81)	(8.28)	(3.86)	(7.23)
	Daman and Diu	(15.32)	(–0.06)	(11.49)	(9.01)	(0.60)	(5.50)	Not available		
	Lakshadweep	(3.53)	(–9.60)	(–4.00)	(–2.17)	(0.91)	(–0.20)	(–2.99)	(5.89)	(1.40)

Notes: (I) Annual growth rate for All-India between 1990 and 2005 is worked out after excluding Jammu and Kashmir as Economic Census for 1990 was not conducted.
(ii) Annual growth rate for Bihar, Madhya Pradesh and Uttar Pradesh for 1990 to 2005 are worked out after including Jharkhand, Chattisgarh and Uttranchal, respectively.
(iii) Similarly growth rate between 1980–90 and 1990–98 for all-India excludes Assam and Jammu and Kashmir as Economic Census of Assam was not conduted in 1980 and that of J&K in 1990.

Source: GoI (2006), Press note dated June 12 on Fifth Economic Census 2005 and earlier Economic Census Reports.

Table A15.2 Trends in Number of Agricultural (Excluding Crop Production and Plantation) and Non-agricultural Enterprises

Number of Enterprises in Thousands

		Fifth Economic Census 2005			Fourth Economic Census 1998			Third Economic Census 1990			Second Economic Census 1980		
		Rural	Urban	Combined	Rural	Urban	Combined	Rural	Urban	Combined	Rural	Urban	Combined
	All-India	25809	16314	42124	17707	12641	30349	14722	10280	25002	11141	7220	18362
1	Andhra Pradesh	2896	1128	4023	2007	895	2903	1737	749	2487	1152	462	1614
2	Arunachal Pradesh	19	10	29	15	6	21	16	5	21	9	2	11
3	Assam	633	293	926	404	189	593	353	143	495	Census not conducted		
4	Bihar	872	418	1290	872	571	1443	783	445	1228	713	331	1045
5	Chattisgarh	454	202	656	Included in Madhya Pradesh								
6	Goa	43	38	81	38	34	72	34	27	61	32	21	53
7	Gujarat	1343	1075	2419	1084	830	1915	842	656	1498	699	490	1188
8	Haryana	453	375	828	237	295	533	209	248	457	159	161	320
9	Himachal Pradesh	219	52	272	182	44	225	148	35	183	115	24	139
10	Jammu and Kashmir	185	139	324	111	105	216	Census not conducted			125	71	197
11	Jharkhand	294	197	491	Included in Bihar								
12	Karnataka	1598	902	2500	1152	760	1912	1033	661	1694	883	492	1375
13	Kerala	2117	731	2848	1241	324	1565	827	402	1229	659	213	872
14	Madhya Pradesh	953	826	1778	1207	917	2124	1154	720	1873	867	474	1341
15	Maharashtra	2262	2113	4375	1613	1621	3234	1308	1315	2624	965	874	1839
16	Manipur	58	46	104	43	37	80	34	27	61	19	16	35
17	Meghalaya	56	28	85	36	20	56	32	18	50	21	12	33
18	Mizoram	18	29	47	10	15	25	10	13	23	8	6	13
19	Nagaland	21	17	38	14	16	30	13	11	24	9	7	16
20	Odisha	1425	367	1791	1157	293	1450	853	240	1094	629	174	804
21	Punjab	497	576	1072	303	415	717	254	345	599	202	261	463
22	Rajasthan	1210	746	1957	911	620	1531	689	481	1169	606	357	964
23	Sikkim	14	6	19	8	5	13	7	3	11	5	3	8
24	Tamil Nadu	2737	1710	4447	1408	1106	2514	1167	944	2111	981	787	1767
25	Tripura	136	52	188	70	34	104	61	25	85	39	14	54
26	Uttar Pradesh	2194	1822	4016	1479	1564	3043	1291	1342	2633	1151	1015	2166
27	Uttranchal	200	128	329	Included in Uttar Pradesh								
28	West Bengal	2831	1455	4286	2044	1191	3234	1818	932	2750	1044	659	1704

(Contd.)

Table A15.2 (*Contd.*)

Number of Enterprises in Thousands

	Fifth Economic Census 2005			Fourth Economic Census 1998			Third Economic Census 1990			Second Economic Census 1980		
	Rural	Urban	Combined	Rural	Urban	Combined	Rural	Urban	Combined	Rural	Urban	Combined
Chandigarh	8	58	66	3	37	40	5	29	33	1	15	16
Delhi	28	726	754	30	656	686	23	432	455	28	262	290
Pondicherry	17	33	50	13	29	43	10	21	31	10	13	23
A & N Islands	6	7	12	9	5	14	8	3	12	5	2	7
D & N Haveli	5	4	9	3	1	4	2	1	3	1	0	2
Daman and Diu	7	4	11	3	3	6	2	3	5	Included in Goa		
Lakshadweep	2	1	3	2	3	5	2	3	5	3	1	5

Annual Growth Rate-Number of Enterprises (per cent)

		1998–2005			1990–8			1980–90		
		Rural	Urban	Combined	Rural	Urban	Combined	Rural	Urban	Combined
	All-India	**(5.53)**	**(3.71)**	**(4.80)**	**(2.27)**	**(2.50)**	**(2.36)**	**(2.83)**	**(3.60)**	**(3.14)**
1	Andhra Pradesh	(5.37)	(3.35)	(4.78)	(1.82)	(2.25)	(1.95)	(4.19)	(4.96)	(4.42)
2	Arunachal Pradesh	(3.65)	(7.08)	(4.74)	(-1.14)	(2.96)	(-0.07)	(5.72)	(10.25)	(6.61)
3	Assam	(6.62)	(6.46)	(6.57)	(1.72)	(3.58)	(2.28)	Not available	Not available	Not available
4	Bihar	(4.50)	(6.46)	(3.07)	(1.35)	(3.15)	(2.03)	(0.94)	(3.00)	(1.63)
5	Chattisgarh	(3.24)	(2.64)	(3.06)	Not available	Not available	Not available	Not available	Not available	Not available
6	Goa	(1.75)	(1.75)	(1.75)	(1.46)	(2.85)	(2.09)	(1.88)	(2.96)	(2.34)
7	Gujarat	(3.11)	(3.77)	(3.40)	(3.22)	(2.99)	(3.12)	(2.78)	(4.43)	(3.64)
8	Haryana	(9.68)	(3.46)	(6.50)	(1.62)	(2.19)	(1.93)	(2.49)	(4.00)	(2.76)
9	Himachal Pradesh	(2.73)	(2.60)	(2.71)	(2.63)	(2.70)	(2.64)	Not available	Not available	Not available
10	Jammu and Kashmir	(7.64)	(4.06)	(5.99)	Not available	Not available	Not available	Not available	Not available	Not available
11	Jharkhand	(3.44)	(2.41)	(3.02)	Not available	Not available	Not available	Not available	Not available	Not available
12	Karnataka	(4.78)	(2.49)	(3.91)	(1.37)	(1.76)	(1.52)	(1.59)	(2.98)	(2.11)
13	Kerala	(7.93)	(12.33)	(8.93)	(5.21)	(-2.66)	(3.07)	(2.29)	(6.56)	(3.49)
14	Madhya Pradesh	(1.74)	(1.40)	(1.58)	(0.57)	(3.07)	(1.58)	(2.90)	(4.27)	(3.40)
15	Maharashtra	(4.95)	(3.86)	(4.41)	(2.65)	(2.65)	(2.65)	(3.09)	(4.17)	(3.61)
16	Manipur	(4.46)	(2.92)	(3.76)	(3.05)	(3.97)	(3.47)	(6.01)	(5.62)	(5.84)
17	Meghalaya	(6.48)	(5.05)	(5.98)	(1.54)	(1.56)	(1.55)	(4.44)	(4.43)	(4.24)

18	Mizoram	(8.40)	(10.39)	(9.60)	(0.91)	(0.98)	(0.95)	(2.23)	(8.77)	(5.53)
19	Nagaland	(6.05)	(1.22)	(3.64)	(1.02)	(4.51)	(2.75)	(3.91)	(4.64)	(4.24)
20	Odisha	(3.02)	(3.26)	(3.07)	(3.88)	(2.51)	(3.59)	(3.09)	(3.25)	(3.13)
21	Punjab	(7.34)	(4.80)	(5.91)	(2.19)	(2.33)	(2.27)	(2.35)	(2.81)	(2.61)
22	Rajasthan	(4.15)	(2.69)	(3.57)	(3.55)	(3.24)	(3.42)	(1.28)	(3.01)	(1.95)
23	Sikkim	(8.39)	(1.16)	(5.83)	(0.74)	(5.89)	(2.54)	(3.40)	(1.08)	(2.62)
24	Tamil Nadu	(9.96)	(6.43)	(8.49)	(2.38)	(2.00)	(2.21)	(1.75)	(1.84)	(1.79)
25	Tripura	(9.85)	(6.37)	(8.79)	(1.87)	(4.05)	(2.53)	(4.41)	(5.72)	(4.77)
26	Uttar Pradesh	(7.07)	(3.14)	(5.14)	(1.71)	(1.93)	(1.83)	(1.15)	(2.83)	(1.97)
27	Uttranchal	(7.72)	(4.16)	(6.21)	Not available			Not available		
28	West Bengal	(4.77)	(2.90)	(4.10)	(1.48)	(3.11)	(2.05)	(5.70)	(3.52)	(4.90)
	Chandigarh	(15.57)	(6.67)	(7.46)	(−6.01)	(3.22)	(2.25)	(15.16)	(6.92)	(7.72)
	Delhi	(−0.91)	(1.45)	(1.36)	(3.07)	(5.38)	(5.27)	(−1.84)	(5.12)	(4.60)
	Pondicherry	(3.37)	(1.67)	(2.22)	(3.99)	(4.47)	(4.32)	(−0.31)	(4.99)	(2.94)
	A & N Islands	(−6.16)	(−4.92)	(−1.36)	(0.82)	(3.86)	(1.78)	(4.70)	(5.08)	(4.81)
	D & N Haveli	(8.65)	(20.98)	(12.31)	(3.69)	(4.82)	(3.94)	(4.14)	(2.29)	(3.71)
	Daman and Diu	(13.64)	(1.39)	(7.85)	(2.49)	(0.66)	(1.42)	Not available		
	Lakshadweep	(1.80)	(−11.31)	(−5.02)	(−1.30)	(0.94)	(0.02)	(−4.73)	(5.77)	(−0.25)

Source: Economic Census.

A16 INTERNATIONAL COMPARISON

Table A16.1 Human Development Characteristics of Some Selected Countries

Countries	HDI Rank	Human Development Index		Life Expectancy at Birth (years)					Adult Literacy Rate (% aged 15 & above) Person	Gross Enrolment Ratio in Education (%)			GDP Per Capita (PPP US$)	Gender Inequality Index		Total Population (millions)		Total Fertility Rate (birth per woman)		
				Person	Male		Female			Primary	Secondary	Tertiary		Rank	Value					
		2000	2011	2011	2009	2011	2009	2011	2005–10	2001–10	2001–10	2001–10	2009	2011	2011	1990	2011	1990–5	2005–10	2010–15
1	2	3	4	5	6		7		8	9	10	11	12	13	14	15	16	17	18	19
Australia	2	0.906	0.929	81.9	79.0		84.0		99.0	106.4	132.7	82.3	39539	18	0.136	17.1	22.6	1.9	1.8	2
Canada	6	0.879	0.908	81.0	79.0		84.0		99.0	98.4	102.2	62.3	37808	20	0.140	27.7	34.3	1.7	1.6	1.7
Netherlands	3	0.882	0.9100	80.7	79.0		83.0		99.0	106.9	120.8	61.6	40676	2	0.052	15.0	16.7	1.6	1.7	1.8
France	20	0.846	0.884	81.5	78.0		85.0		99.0	108.7	113.0	55.3	33674	10	0.106	56.8	63.1	1.7	1.9	2
Japan	12	0.868	0.901	83.4	80.0		86.0		99.0	102.3	101.0	58.6	32418	14	0.123	123.2	126.5	1.5	1.3	1.4
United States	4	0.897	0.910	78.5	76.0		81.0		99.0	98.2	93.6	85.8	45989	47	0.299	254.9	313.1	2.0	2.1	2.1
Spain	23	0.839	0.878	81.4	79.0		85.0		97.7	107.2	120.8	73.4	32150	13	0.117	38.8	46.5	1.3	1.4	1.5
Italy	24	0.825	0.874	81.9	79.0		84.0		98.9	103.3	100.5	67.2	32430	15	0.124	57.0	60.8	1.3	1.4	1.5
New Zealand	5	0.878	0.908	80.7	78.0		82.0		99.0	101.2	126.3	83.5	37808	32	0.195	3.4	4.4	2.1	2.0	2.1
UK	28	0.833	0.863	80.2	78.0		82.0		99.0	106.4	99.0	59.0	35155	34	0.209	57.2	62.4	1.8	1.8	1.9
Germany	9	0.864	0.905	80.4	77.0		83.0		99.0	103.6	101.7	–	36838	7	0.085	79.4	82.2	1.3	1.3	1.5
Singapore	26	0.801	0.866	81.1	79.0		84.0		94.7	–	–	–	50633	8	0.086	3.0	5.2	1.8	1.3	1.4
Hong Kong	13	0.824	0.898	82.8	80.0		86.0		99.0	104.0	82.1	58.6	43229	–	–	5.7	7.1	1.3	1.0	1.1
Korea Rep	15	0.830	0.897	80.6	77.0		84.0		99.0	104.3	97.2	100.0	27100	11	0.111	43.0	48.4	1.7	1.2	1.4
Kuwait	63	0.754	0.760	74.8	76.0		80.0		93.9	94.8	89.9	18.9	–	37	0.229	2.1	2.8	3.2	2.2	2.3
UAR	30	0.753	0.846	76.5	77.0		79.0		90.0	105.4	95.2	30.4	57744	38	0.234	1.9	7.9	3.9	1.9	1.7
Chile	44	0.749	0.805	79.1	76.0		82.0		98.6	106.4	90.4	54.8	14311	68	0.374	13.2	17.3	2.6	1.9	1.8
Argentina	45	0.749	0.797	75.9	72.0		79.0		97.7	116.7	85.9	69.4	14538	67	0.372	32.5	40.8	2.9	2.3	2.2
Mexico	57	0.718	0.770	77.0	73.0		78.0		93.4	116.6	90.2	27.9	14258	79	0.448	83.4	114.8	3.2	2.2	2.2
Saudi Arabia	56	0.726	0.770	73.9	73.0		74.0		86.1	98.9	96.8	32.8	23480	135	0.646	16.3	28.1	5.4	3.2	2.6
Malaysia	61	0.705	0.761	74.2	72.0		77.0		92.5	94.6	68.7	36.5	14012	43	0.286	18.1	28.9	3.5	2.6	2.6
Russia	66	0.691	0.755	68.8	63.0		75.0		99.6	96.8	84.8	77.2	18932	59	0.338	148.1	142.8	1.5	1.4	1.5
Brazil	84	0.665	0.718	73.5	69.0		76.0		90.0	127.5	100.8	34.4	10367	80	0.449	149.6	198.7	2.6	1.9	1.8
Colombia	87	0.652	0.710	73.7	70.0		77.0		93.2	120.2	94.6	37.0	8959	91	0.482	33.2	46.9	3.0	2.5	2.3
Turkey	92	0.634	0.699	74.0	70.0		75.0		90.8	99.3	82.0	38.4	13668	77	0.443	56.1	73.6	2.9	2.1	2

Country															
Thailand	103	0.626	0.682	74.1	66.0	72.0	93.5	91.1	77.0	45.0	7995	69	0.382	56.7	69.5	2.1	1.8	1.5
China	101	0.588	0.687	73.5	72.0	75.0	94.0	112.7	78.2	24.5	6828	35	0.209	1142.1	1347.6	2.0	1.8	1.6
Jamaica	79	0.680	0.727	73.1	69.0	75.0	86.4	93.3	91.2	24.2	7633	81	0.450	2.4	2.8	2.8	2.4	2.3
Sri Lanka	97	0.633	0.691	74.9	71.0	78.0	90.6	96.9	87.0	–	4772	74	0.419	17.3	21.0	2.5	2.3	2.2
Phillippines	112	0.602	0.644	68.7	70.0	74.0	95.4	110.1	82.5	28.7	3542	75	0.427	62.4	94.9	4.1	3.1	3.1
Indonesia	124	0.543	0.617	69.4	69.0	73.0	92.2	120.8	79.5	23.5	4199	100	0.505	177.4	242.3	2.9	2.2	2.1
Egypt	113	0.585	0.644	73.2	69.0	72.0	66.4	101.1	67.2	28.5	5673		0.577	57.8	82.5	3.9	2.9	2.6
South Africa	123	0.616	0.619	52.8	50.0	53.0	88.7	101.2	93.9	–	10278	94	0.490	36.7	50.5	3.3	2.6	2.4
India	134	0.461	0.547	65.4	63.0	66.0	62.8	116.9	60.0	13.5	3296	129	0.617	862.2	1241.5	3.9	2.8	2.5
Mynamar	149	0.380	0.483	65.2	60.0	64.0	92.0	115.8	53.1	10.7	–	96	0.492	40.8	48.3	3.1	2.3	1.9
Pakistan	145	0.436	0.504	65.4	67.0	67.0	55.5	85.1	33.1	5.2	2609	115	0.573	115.8	176.7	5.7	4.0	3.2
Nepal	157	0.398	0.458	68.8	66.0	68.0	59.1	114.9	43.5	5.6	1155	113	0.558	19.1	30.5	4.9	2.9	2.6
Bangladesh	146	0.422	0.500	68.9	66.0	68.0	55.9	95.1	42.3	7.9	1416	112	0.550	115.6	150.5	4.0	2.4	2.2

Source: Human Development Report 2011.